30|10|19

THE ROUGH GUIDE TO
SRI LANKA

Written by
Gavin Thomas

This sixth edition up
Sally McLaren a

**ROUGH
GUIDES**

Contents

Introduction to
Sri Lanka

Sri Lanka has seduced travellers for centuries. Marco Polo called it the finest island of its size in the world, while successive waves of Indian, Arab and European traders and adventurers flocked to its palm-fringed shores, attracted by reports of rare spices, precious stones and magnificent elephants. Poised just above the Equator amid the balmy waters of the Indian Ocean, the island has inspired a sense of romance even in those who have never visited the place. Fancifully minded geographers, poring over maps of the island, likened its outline to a teardrop falling from the tip of India or to the shape of a pearl (the more practical Dutch compared it to a leg of ham), while even the name given to the island by early Arab traders, Serendib, gave rise to the English word "serendipity" – an unexpected discovery leading to a happy end.

Marco Polo's bold claim still holds true. Sri Lanka packs an extraordinary variety of attractions into its modest physical dimensions. Idyllic **beaches** fringe the coast, while the interior boasts a compelling variety of landscapes ranging from wildlife-rich lowland **jungles**, home to extensive populations of elephants, leopards and rare endemic bird species, to the misty heights of the **hill country**, swathed in immaculately manicured tea plantations. There are plenty of man-made attractions too. Sri Lanka boasts more than two thousand years of recorded history, and the remarkable achievements of the early Sinhalese civilization can still be seen in the sequence of **ruined cities** and great religious monuments that litter the northern plains.

The glories of this early Buddhist civilization continue to provide a symbol of national pride, while Sri Lanka's historic role as the world's oldest stronghold of Theravada **Buddhism** lends it a unique cultural identity which permeates life at every level. There's more to Sri Lanka than just Buddhists, however. The island's geographical position at one of the most important staging posts of Indian Ocean trade laid it open to a uniquely wide range of influences, as generations of Arab, Malay, Portuguese,

FACT FILE

- Lying a few degrees north of the Equator, Sri Lanka is slightly smaller than **Ireland** and a little larger than the US state of **West Virginia**.
- Sri Lanka achieved **independence** from Britain in 1948, and did away with its colonial name, Ceylon, in 1972. The country has had a functioning **democracy** since independence, and in 1960 elected the world's first female prime minister.
- Sri Lanka's **population** of 22.5 million is a mosaic of different ethnic and religious groups, the two largest being the mainly Buddhist Sinhalese (75 percent), and the predominantly Hindu Tamils (15 percent); there are also considerable numbers of Christians and Muslims. Sinhala, Tamil and English are all officially recognized **languages**.
- Sri Lankans enjoy a healthy **life expectancy** of 77 years and a **literacy rate** of almost 93 percent, but also have one of the world's highest suicide rates.
- **Cricket** is a countrywide obsession, although the official national sport is actually **volleyball**.
- The country's main **export** is clothing, followed by tea; coconuts, cinnamon and precious gems are also important. Revenues from tourism are vital to the national economy, while remittances from the hundreds of thousands of Sri Lankans working overseas (mainly in the Gulf) are also significant.

Dutch and British settlers subtly transformed its culture, architecture and cuisine, while the long-established **Tamil** population in the north have established a vibrant Hindu culture that owes more to India than to the Sinhalese south.

It was, for a while, this very diversity that threatened to tear the country apart. For almost three decades Sri Lanka was the site of one of Asia's most pernicious **civil wars**, as the Sri Lankan Army and the LTTE, or Tamil Tigers, battled it out in the island's north and east, until the final victory of government forces in 2009. The decade of postwar peace since then hasn't always been easy, but the island is now looking once again to the future with a fresh sense of optimism and energy.

Where to go

All visits to Sri Lanka currently begin at the international airport just outside **Colombo**, the island's capital and far and away its largest city – a sprawling metropolis whose contrasting districts offer an absorbing introduction to Sri Lanka's myriad cultures and multilayered history. Many visitors head straight for one of the **west coast**'s beaches, whose innumerable resort hotels still power the country's tourist industry. Destinations include the package-holiday resorts of **Negombo** and **Beruwala**, the more stylish **Bentota**, and the old hippy hangout of **Hikkaduwa**. More unspoilt countryside can be found north of Colombo at the **Kalpitiya peninsula** and in the vast **Wilpattu National Park** nearby, home to leopards, elephants and sloth bears.

Beyond Hikkaduwa, the **south coast** is significantly less developed. Gateway to the region is the marvellous old Dutch city of **Galle**, Sri Lanka's finest colonial town, beyond which lies a string of fine beaches including the ever-expanding villages of **Unawatuna** and **Mirissa** along with quieter stretches of coast at **Weligama** and **Tangalla**, as well as the lively provincial capital of **Matara**, boasting further Dutch remains. East of here, **Tissamaharama** serves as a convenient base for the outstanding **Yala** and **Bundala** national parks, and for the fascinating temple town of **Kataragama**.

ASIAN ELEPHANT, MINNERIYA NATIONAL PARK

SRI LANKAN BUDDHISM

Buddhism runs deep in Sri Lanka. The island was one of the first places to convert to the religion, in 247 BC, and has remained unswervingly faithful in the two thousand years since. As such, Sri Lanka is often claimed to be the world's oldest Buddhist country, and Buddhism continues to permeate the practical life and spiritual beliefs of the majority of the island's Sinhalese population. Buddhist temples can be found everywhere, often decorated with superb shrines, statues and murals, while the sight of Sri Lanka's orange-robed monks is one of the island's enduring visual images. Buddhist places of **pilgrimage** – the Temple of the Tooth at Kandy, the revered "footprint" of the Buddha at Adam's Peak, and the Sri Maha Bodhi at Anuradhapura – also play a vital role in sustaining the faith, while the national calendar is punctuated with **religious holidays** and festivals ranging from the monthly full-moon poya days through to more elaborate annual celebrations, often taking the form of enormous processions (peraheras), during which locals parade through the streets, often accompanied by elaborately costumed elephants. For more on Buddhism, turn to our Contexts chapter (see page 427).

Inland from Colombo rise the verdant highlands of the **hill country**, enveloped in the tea plantations (first introduced by the British) which still play a vital role in the island's economy. The symbolic heart of the region is **Kandy**, Sri Lanka's second city and the cultural capital of the Sinhalese, its colourful traditions embodied by the famous Temple of the Tooth and the magnificent Esala Perahera, Sri Lanka's most colourful festival. South of here, close to the highest point of the island, lies the old British town of **Nuwara Eliya**, centre of the country's tea industry and a convenient base for visits to the spectacular Horton Plains National Park. A string of towns and villages – including **Ella** and **Haputale** – along the southern edge of the hill country offer an appealing mixture of magnificent views, wonderful walks and olde-worlde British colonial charm. Close to the hill country's southwestern edge, the soaring summit of **Adam's Peak** is another of the island's major pilgrimage sites, while the gem-mining centre of **Ratnapura** to the south serves as a starting point for visits to the elephant-rich **Uda Walawe National Park** and the rare tropical rainforest of **Sinharaja**.

North of Kandy, the hill country tumbles down into the arid plains of the northern dry zone. This area, known as the **Cultural Triangle**, was the location of Sri Lanka's first great civilization, and its extraordinary scatter of ruined palaces, temples and dagobas still gives a compelling sense of this glorious past. Foremost among these are the fascinating ruined cities of **Anuradhapura** and **Polonnaruwa**, the marvellous cave temples of **Dambulla**, the hilltop shrines and dagobas of **Mihintale** and the extraordinary rock citadel of **Sigiriya**.

The two main gateways to **the east** are the cities of **Trincomalee** and **Batticaloa**, each boasting a clutch of colonial remains backed by bays and lagoons. Elsewhere, the east's huge swathe of coastline remains largely undeveloped. A cluster of upmarket new resort hotels dot the seafront at **Passekudah**, north of Batticaloa, although most visitors prefer the more laidback beachside charms of sleepy **Nilaveli** and **Uppuveli**, just north of Trincomalee, or the chilled-out surfing centre of **Arugam Bay**, at the southern end of the coast. Further afield, **the north** remains relatively untouristed, although increasing

numbers of visitors are making the journey to the absorbing city of **Jaffna**, while a side trip to remote **Mannar**, closer to India than Colombo, is another enticing possibility.

When to go

Sri Lanka's climate is rather complicated for such a small country, due to the fact that the island is affected by **two separate monsoons** – though this also means that there is usually good weather somewhere on the island, at most times of the year. It's worth bearing in mind, however, that the basic pattern described below can vary significantly from year to year, and that global warming has disrupted these already complex weather patterns.

The basic rainfall pattern is as follows. The main **southwest ("yala") monsoon** brings rain to the west and southwest coasts and hill country from April or May to September (wettest from April to June). The less severe **northeast ("maha") monsoon** hits the east coast from November to March (wettest from November to December); there's also a **inter-monsoonal period** of unsettled weather preceding the Maha monsoon in October and November during which heavy rainfall and thunderstorms can occur anywhere across the island. In practical terms, this means that the **best time to visit** the west and south coasts and hill country is from December to March, while the best weather on the east coast is from April or May to September.

Sri Lanka's position close to the Equator means that temperatures remain fairly constant year-round. Coastal and lowland areas enjoy average daytime temperatures of around 26–30°C (often climbing up well into the 30°Cs during the hottest part of the day). Temperatures decrease with altitude, reducing to a temperate 18–22°C in Kandy, and a pleasantly mild 14–17°C in Nuwara Eliya and the highest parts of the island – nights in the hills can be quite chilly, with temperatures sometimes falling close to freezing. Humidity is high everywhere, rising to a sweltering ninety percent at times in the southwest, and averaging sixty to eighty percent across the rest of the island.

AVERAGE MONTHLY TEMPERATURES AND RAINFALL

	Jan	Feb	Mar	Apr	May	Jun	Jul	Aug	Sep	Oct	Nov	Dec
COLOMBO												
Max/min (°C)	31/22	31/23	32/24	32/25	31/26	30/26	30/25	30/25	30/25	30/24	30/23	30/23
Max/min (°F)	88/72	88/73	89/75	89/76	88/78	87/78	86/77	86/77	86/75	86/74	87/73
Rainfall (mm)	62	69	130	253	382	186	125	114	236	369	310	168
NUWARA ELIYA												
Max/min (°C)	20/9	21/9	22/10	23/11	21/13	19/13	18/13	19/13	19/12	20/12	20/11	19/11
Max/min (°F)	68/49	70/49	72/50	73/52	70/55	66/56	65/55	66/55	67/54	68/53	68/53	67/52
Rainfall (mm)	107	75	71	151	178	176	174	159	176	228	215	194
TRINCOMALEE												
Max/min (°C)	28/24	29/24	31/25	33/26	34/26	35/26	34/26	34/25	34/25	32/25	29/24	28/24
Max/min (°F)	82/76	85/76	88/77	91/78	94/79	95/79	94/78	94/78	94/77	89/76	85/76	83/76
Rainfall (mm)	132	100	54	50	52	26	70	89	104	217	334	341

Author picks

Our much-travelled authors have visited every corner of Sri Lanka in order to uncover the very best the island has to offer. Here are some of their personal highlights.

Classic journeys Ride the hill-country train (see page 198) through tea plantations to Badulla or drive the A9 (see page 379) north to Jaffna.

Multi-faith island Make a pilgrimage to one of Sri Lanka's myriad religious destinations, including Adam's Peak (see page 252), the church of Madhu (see page 379), or the spiritual melting-pot of Kataragama (see page 192), held sacred by Buddhists, Hindus and Muslims alike.

Colonial Ceylon Step back in time amid the colonial streetscapes of Galle (see page 138), Colombo Fort (see page 69) or at the old British tea-town of Nuwara Eliya (see page 241).

Once more unto the beach Escape the crowds at the unspoiled southern beaches of Talalla (see page 174) or Kalametiya (see page 182).

Wildlife on land and at sea Experience Sri Lanka's wonderful range of fauna with highlights including whales at Mirissa (see page 169), turtles at Rekawa (see page 181), dolphins at Kalpitiya (see page 109), birds in Sinharaja (see page 273), elephants at Minneriya (see page 309) and leopards at Yala (see page 190).

Boutique bliss Crash out in style at one of the island's boutique hotels, ranging from modern beachside villas like *Rock Villa* in Bentota (see page 123) to atmospheric colonial-era lodgings like *Ferncliff* in Nuwara Eliya (see page 245).

Flavours of Sri Lanka Dive into a hopper, unpack a *lamprais*, crunch some chilli crab or feast on a classic rice and curry (see page 38) – *Nuga Gama* (see page 91) in Colombo is a great place to get your taste buds oriented.

Rugged rambling Take a walk on the wild side through the spectacular hill country at Adam's Peak (see page 252), Horton Plains (see page 250) or the Knuckles Range (see page 236) – Sri Lanka at its most scenically dramatic.

Our author recommendations don't end here. We've flagged up our favourite places – a perfectly sited hotel, an atmospheric café, a special restaurant – throughout the Guide, highlighted with the ★ symbol.

NUWARA ELIYA

YALA NATIONAL PARK

25

things not to miss

It's not possible to see everything that Sri Lanka has to offer in one trip – and we don't suggest you try. What follows, in no particular order, is a selective taste of the country's highlights, including astonishing religious and historic sites, unforgettable wildlife, scenery and beaches, and vibrant festivals. All highlights have a page reference to take you straight into the Guide, where you can find out more; the coloured numbers refer to chapters in the Guide section.

1 CRICKET
See page 48

Join the crowds of cricket-crazy spectators for a Test match in Colombo or Kandy.

2 ADAM'S PEAK
See page 252

One of Sri Lanka's foremost pilgrimage sites, this summit bears the revered impression of the Buddha's footprint, and offers one of the island's most magical views.

3 BIG BUDDHAS
See page 434

The Buddha's superhuman attributes are captured in the statues dotting the island, from the ancient figures of Aukana, Sasseruwa and Polonnaruwa's Gal Vihara to the contemporary colossi at Dambulla and Wehurukannala.

4 GALLE
See page 138

Sri Lanka's most perfectly preserved colonial townscape, with sedate streets of personable Dutch-era villas enclosed by a chain of imposing ramparts.

5 YALA NATIONAL PARK
See page 190

The most popular national park, home to elephants and the island's largest population of leopards.

6 WORLD'S END
See page 251
Marking the point at which the hill country's southern escarpment plunges sheer for almost 1km to the plains below, these dramatic cliffs offer one of the finest views in the hill country.

7 RICE AND CURRY
See page 38
Eat your way through this classic Sri Lankan feast, with its mouthwatering selection of dishes and flavours.

8 BIRDS
See page 442
Sri Lanka is one of Asia's classic birdwatching destinations, with species ranging from bee-eaters and blue magpies to colourful kingfishers and majestic hornbills.

9 KATARAGAMA
See page 192
Join the crowds thronging to the nightly temple ceremonies at this pilgrimage town, held sacred by Buddhists, Hindus and Muslims alike.

10 ANURADHAPURA
See page 326
This vast, mysterious ruined city bears witness to the great Sinhalese civilization that flourished here for some two thousand years.

11 BAWA HOTELS
See pages 37 and 122
With their blend of modern chic and superb natural settings, the hotels of architect Geoffrey Bawa exemplify contemporary Sri Lankan style.

12 SIGIRIYA
See page 300
Climb the towering rock outcrop of Sigiriya, home to the fascinating remains of one of the island's former capitals, complete with ancient graffiti and elaborate water gardens.

13 ELLA
See page 263
One of the island's most popular destinations, with marvellous views and walks among the surrounding tea plantations and hills.

14 THE PETTAH
See page 71
Colombo's colourful, chaotic bazaar district offers an exhilarating slice of Asian life.

15 WHALE- AND DOLPHIN-WATCHING
See pages 109, 169 and 355
Take to the waves in search of blue and sperm whales, or pods of spinner dolphins.

11

12

16 POLONNARUWA
See page 311
Quite simply the island's finest collection of ancient Sinhalese art and architecture.

17 BENTOTA
See page 119
The unspoiled southern end of Bentota beach is home to a fine selection of luxury beachside hotels.

18 KANDY ESALA PERAHERA
See page 210
One of Asia's most spectacular festivals, with huge processions of magnificently caparisoned elephants, ear-splitting troupes of Kandyan drummers and assorted dancers and acrobats.

19 SINHARAJA
See page 273
Unique region of pristine rainforest, home to towering trees, opulent orchids and rare endemic birds, lizards and amphibians.

20 AYURVEDA
See page 116
Sri Lanka's ancient system of healthcare uses herbal medicines and traditional techniques to promote holistic well-being.

18

19

20

21 ARUGAM BAY
See page 365
This remote east coast village has great sand and surf, lots of local wildlife and an appealingly chilled-out atmosphere.

22 KANDYAN DANCING AND DRUMMING
See page 229
Traditional Sinhalese culture at its most exuberant, with brilliantly costumed dancers performing stylized dances to an accompaniment of explosively energetic drumming.

23 DAMBULLA
See page 292
These five magical cave temples are a treasure box of Sri Lankan Buddhist art, sumptuously decorated with a fascinating array of statues, shrines and the country's finest collection of murals.

24 MIRISSA
See page 167
Laidback beachside village with a fine stretch of sand and world-class whale-watching.

25 KANDY
See page 207
Beautifully situated amid the central highlands, this historic city remains the island's most important repository of traditional Sinhalese culture, exemplified by the great Esala Perahera festival and the Temple of the Tooth.

Itineraries

Sri Lanka is one of the biggest little countries in the world. The island's modest size means that it's possible to get a good taste of what's on offer in just a couple of weeks, although, equally, attractions are crammed together so densely that you could easily spend a year in the place and still not see everything.

THE GRAND TOUR

Two weeks suffice to see Sri Lanka's headline attractions, while an extra week would allow you to add on the places listed in the itineraries below.

❶ **Kandy** Start in Kandy, cultural capital of Sri Lanka and a marvellous showcase of Sinhalese religious art, architecture and dance. See page 207

❷ **Dambulla** Drive north to the cave temples at Dambulla, crammed with Buddhist statues and decorated with Sri Lanka's finest murals. See page 292

❸ **Sigiriya** The nearby rock citadel at Sigiriya is perhaps Sri Lanka's single most dramatic attraction: the remains of a fifth-century palace perched on the summit of the vertiginous Lion Rock. See page 300

❹ **Polonnaruwa** Another short drive leads to the marvellous ruined city of Polonnaruwa, home to some of medieval Sri Lanka's finest art and architecture, including the giant Buddha statues of the Gal Vihara. See page 311

❺ **Horton Plains National Park** Return to Kandy and then continue to Nuwara Eliya for a trip to Horton Plains National Park, a marvellously rugged stretch of unspoiled hill country culminating in the spectacular view at World's End. See page 250

❻ **Ella** Continue to lively little Ella village, set in a dramatic location amid tea plantations on the edge of the hill country. See page 263

❼ **Yala National Park** Drive south to Yala National Park, home to one of the world's densest populations of leopards, and much more besides. See page 190

❽ **Mirissa** Spend some time on the beach and go on a whale-watching trip at the village of Mirissa. See page 167

❾ **Galle** Continue around the coast to the city of Galle and its time-warped old Dutch Fort – colonial Sri Lanka at its most perfectly preserved. See page 138

❿ **Colombo** Finish with a day or two in the nation's energetic capital. See page 64

WILDLIFE AND NATURE

The following itinerary, which picks up on some of the best natural attractions not covered in the Grand Tour, could be done in a week, at a push, and could thus be combined with other attractions en route during a fortnight's visit to the island.

❶ **The Knuckles Range** Hike from Kandy into the rugged Knuckles Range, one of the island's most beautiful and biodiverse areas. See page 236

❷ Nuwara Eliya Head south to this venerable old colonial town in the heart of the hill country, with spectacular walks in the surrounding countryside. See page 241

❸ Horton Plains National Park Sri Lanka's most scenically stunning national park: a misty mix of moorland and cloudforest, home to rare indigenous flora and fauna. See page 250

❹ Haputale Dramatically perched on the edge of the southern hill country and with fine hiking through the surrounding tea plantations, particularly the walk down from nearby Lipton's Seat. See page 257

❺ Bundala National Park One of Sri Lanka's premier birdwatching destinations, spread out around a stunning string of coastal lagoons. See page 184

❻ Rekawa Watch majestic marine turtles haul themselves ashore to lay their eggs on beautiful Rekawa beach. See page 181

❼ Uda Walawe National Park Superb elephant-watching opportunities, either in the wild or at the attached Elephant Transit Home. See page 276

❽ Sinharaja Stunning area of unspoiled rainforest, home to an internationally significant array of rare endemic flora and fauna. See page 273

BUDDHISM AND BEACHES

A slightly offbeat two-week alternative to the Grand Tour, featuring fewer mainstream destinations and mixing religion, culture and wildlife.

❶ Kalpitiya Superb dolphin-watching, kitesurfing and some of the island's finest eco-lodges on beautiful Alankuda beach. See page 107

❷ Wilpattu National Park Enormous and very peaceful park famous for its leopards and elephants. See page 111

❸ Anuradhapura The greatest city in Sri Lankan history, packed with monuments from over a thousand years of the island's past. See page 326

❹ Mihintale The birthplace of Buddhism in Sri Lanka, with a cluster of absorbing monuments clinging to a jungle-covered hillside. See page 339

❺ Polonnaruwa Medieval Sri Lankan art and architecture at its finest, from the flamboyant Vatadage to the brooding statues of the Gal Vihara. See page 311

❻ Batticaloa Vibrant but little-visited east coast town, famous for its "singing fish" and with a fine beach and lagoon. See page 360

❼ Arugam Bay This quirky village is one of the most appealing places to hang out for a few days around the coast. See page 365

❽ Kataragama Vibrant multi-faith pilgrimage town, a holy place for Buddhists, Hindus and Muslims. See page 192

❾ Adam's Peak The strenuous climb to the top of Adam's Peak is the island's ultimate pilgrimage, rewarded by a glimpse of the Buddha's own footprint at the summit. See page 252

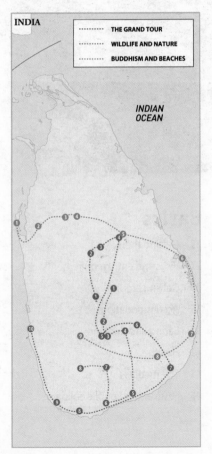

INDIA

THE GRAND TOUR

WILDLIFE AND NATURE

BUDDHISM AND BEACHES

INDIAN OCEAN

HAPUTALE

Basics

Getting there

Unless you arrive on a cruise ship, the only way to get to Sri Lanka is to fly into Bandaranaike International Airport (BMI) at Katunayake, just north of Colombo – at least pending the unlikely resumption of direct flights to Mattala Rajapakse airport at Hambantota (see below) or international ferries between Sri Lanka and India (see page 26). Air fares remain fairly constant year-round, although the further ahead you book your flight, the better chance you have of getting a good deal.

Flights from the UK and Ireland

The only nonstop scheduled flights **from the UK** to Sri Lanka are with SriLankan Airlines (**W** srilankan.com) from London Heathrow; flying time to Colombo is around eleven hours. Emirates (**W** emirates.com), Qatar Airways (**W** qatarairways. com), Etihad (**W** etihadairways.com) and Oman Air (**W** omanair.com) all offer one-stop flights from Heathrow via their home cities in the Gulf (and are generally much more comfortable than SriLankan flights), while Jet Airways (**W** jetairways.com) operates one-stop flights via Mumbai. There are also more circuitous routings via various points in Southeast Asia, including Singapore (**W** singaporeair. com), Kuala Lumpur (**W** malaysiaairlines.com) and Bangkok (**W** thaiairways.com).

Travelling **from Ireland**, you can either make your way to Heathrow and pick up an onward connection there, or fly from Dublin via one of the three Gulf cities that have direct connections with Colombo, currently Dubai (Emirates), Abu Dhabi (Etihad) and Doha (Qatar Airways). Scheduled **fares** from London to Colombo start at around £500 return year-round.

Flights from the US and Canada

It's a long journey from North America to Sri Lanka. The flight from North America to Sri Lanka takes around twenty hours minimum, necessitating at least one change of plane. **From the east coast**, the most straightforward option is to fly to London and then pick up one of the onward connections described above. There are also numerous one-stop routes via the Gulf from New York (Emirates, **W** emirates.com; Etihad, **W** etihad. com; Qatar, **W** qatarairways.com), Boston (Emirates, Qatar), and Washington and Toronto (both Emirates and Etihad).

Travelling **from the west coast**, the most direct routes go via east or Southeast Asia, stopping in Hong Kong, Kuala Lumpur, Singapore, Bangkok, Shanghai or Guangzhou, all of which have nonstop connections on to Colombo. There are also one-stop services to Colombo via the Gulf from Los Angeles (Emirates, Etihad, Qatar), San Francisco (Emirates) and Seattle (Emirates). Other USA cities with one-stop **connections** to Sri Lanka via the Gulf include Chicago (Emirates, Etihad, Qatar), Atlanta (Qatar), Dallas (Emirates, Etihad), and Orlando and Fort Lauderdale (both Emirates).

Fares to Colombo start at around $900 from New York, $1000 from Los Angeles, and Can$1400 from Toronto and Vancouver.

Flights from Australia and New Zealand

The only nonstop flight between **Australia** and Sri Lanka is the service from Melbourne with SriLankan Airlines (**W** srilankan.com). Otherwise, the most direct routings to Colombo are via Singapore, Kuala Lumpur and Bangkok. There are also a few one-stop options **from New Zealand** via Melbourne, Singapore, Bangkok and Kuala Lumpur. The most regular services are with Qantas (**W** qantas.com)

HOW DO YOU SOLVE A PROBLEM LIKE MRIA?

A few miles outside the southern town of Hambantota, the gleaming **Mattala Rajapaksa International Airport (MRIA)** is the most conspicuous of all the various vanity projects created during the rule of former president Mahinda Rajapakse. Opened in 2013 at a cost of $210m, MRIA was meant both to provide Sri Lanka with a second international airport and to serve as the major engine driving economic development of Rajapakse's impoverished home town and surrounding region. In the event it has proved an unmitigated disaster. The few airlines that decided to fly into MRIA rapidly withdrew their services due to lack of demand, and even the national flag carrier SriLankan Airlines cancelled its last remaining flights to the airport the day after Rajapakse's election defeat in January 2015. The airport's only scheduled flight at present is a solitary service from Dubai (with FlyDubai, **W** flydubai.com, via Colombo), and according to latest rumours the hangars are now being used to store not planes, but paddy.

SRI LANKA BY BOAT

The **ferry service** that formerly connected Talaimannar in northern Sri Lanka and Rameswaram in southern India was suspended at the outbreak of the civil war in 1983. Rumours that ferries would be restarted did the rounds constantly following the 2002 ceasefire, although in the end it wasn't until 2011 that services finally resumed, sailing between Colombo and Tuticorin. Sadly, after the long wait, the new ferry company lasted just six months before collapsing due to commercial difficulties. Rumours of the ferry's revival continue to surface regularly (most recently in 2017, when the state government of Tamil Nadu attempted to initiate talks on the subject), although judging by past events, it might be quite some time before this particular ship leaves harbour – if it ever does.

Pending the revival of the ferry, short of hitching a ride on a commercial vessel, the only way to get to Sri Lanka by boat is to take one of the increasing number of **cruises** which now visit the island, docking at Colombo, Galle and Hambantota.

and their budget subsidiary Jetstar (Ⓦ jetstar.com), who operate flights to Singapore (from Sydney, Melbourne, Perth and Brisbane) and to Bangkok (from Sydney and Melbourne), from where there are direct connections to Colombo. Fares from Sydney to Colombo with most carriers generally start at around Aus$800, and from Auckland at around NZ$1300.

Flights from the rest of Asia

Sri Lanka isn't normally considered part of the overland Asian trail, although the island is well connected with other countries in **South and Southeast Asia**. There are regular nonstop flights with SriLankan Airlines (Ⓦ srilankan.com) to various places in India, including Delhi, Mumbai (Bombay), Chennai (Madras), Bangalore, Thiruvananthapuram (Trivandrum), Kochi and Tiruchirappali; to Malé (Maldives) and the Seychelles with SriLankan; Bangkok with SriLankan and Thai Airways (Ⓦ thai-airways.com); Kuala Lumpur with SriLankan Airlines and Malaysia Airlines (Ⓦ malaysiaairlines.com); Singapore with SriLankan and Singapore Airlines (Ⓦ singaporeair.com); Tokyo with SriLankan; Hong Kong with SriLankan and Cathay Pacific (Ⓦ cathaypacific.com); and Beijing, Shanghai and Guangzhou with SriLankan. There are also direct connections to many places in **the Gulf**, including frequent services to Dubai (Emirates, Ⓦ emirates.com), Abu Dhabi (Etihad, Ⓦ etihad.com), Qatar (Qatar Airways, Ⓦ qatarairways.com) and Muscat (Oman Air, Ⓦ omanair.com)

Organized tours

Organized guided tours of the island – either with your own car and driver, or as part of a larger tour group – can be arranged through numerous companies both in Sri Lanka and abroad. Tours obviously take virtually all the hassle out of travelling. The downside is that they tend to be much of a muchness and you might also end up in a large group.

Almost all the leading international Sri Lankan tour operators are based in the **UK**; travellers from North America and Australasia shouldn't have any problems booking tours through these companies, although you might have to organize your own flights. Setting up a tour with a **Colombo-based operator** is a very viable alternative to arranging one at home, although they may well not work out any cheaper than their overseas rivals.

TOUR OPERATORS IN THE UK

Ampersand Travel ☎ 020 7819 9770 (UK), ☎ 1 312 281 2543 (US), Ⓦ ampersandtravel.com. Wide selection of upmarket cultural, nature and activity holidays.

CaroLanka ☎ 01822 810230, Ⓦ carolanka.co.uk. Small Sri Lankan specialist offering two general fifteen-day tours, plus customized itineraries.

Insider Tours ☎ 07964 375994, Ⓦ insider-tours.com. Sri Lanka specialist offering customized, ethical tours in conjunction with local organizations.

On the Go Tours ☎ 020 7371 1113, Ⓦ onthegotours.com. Mainstream but inexpensive eight- to fifteen-day group tours.

Red Dot Tours ☎ 0870 231 7892, Ⓦ reddottours.com. Leading Sri Lankan specialists offering holidays based around wildlife, adventure, culture, cricket, golf and more, along with wedding and honeymoon packages. They also offer cheap flights and represent an outstanding selection of properties around the island in most price ranges.

Tell Tale Travel ☎ 020 7060 4571 (UK), ☎ 1 866 211 5972 (US), Ⓦ telltaletravel.co.uk. A range of private tours aiming to take you off the beaten track, including itineraries in the east, and photographic tours.

Tikalanka ☎ 020 3137 6763, Ⓦ tikalanka.com. Tailor-made tours by a small Sri Lanka and Maldives specialist.

TransIndus ☎ 020 8566 3739 (UK), ☎ 1 866 615 1815 (US), ⓦ transindus.co.uk. Leading South Asia specialist offering nine-to sixteen-day, islandwide tours plus customized trips.

Wildlife Worldwide ☎ 01962 302 086, ⓦ wildlifeworldwide. com. Wildlife-oriented trips, including whale- and dolphin-watching tours.

TOUR OPERATORS IN SRI LANKA

Ayu in the Wild ☎ 077 248 1100, ⓦ ayuinthewild.com. Bespoke holidays designed to get you under the skin of the island, with special tours including Sri Lanka with kids and unusual "slow travel" experiences.

Boutique Sri Lanka ☎ 011 269 9213, ⓦ boutiquesrilanka. com. Huge portfolio of mid- and top-range properties, including a vast selection of villas, plus itineraries customized to suit your interests, from beaches or Ayurveda to nature, surfing and adventure.

Destination Sri Lanka ☎ 077 784 0001, ⓦ dsltours. com. Reliably excellent, very competitively priced customized islandwide tours by Nimal de Silva, one of Sri Lanka's most professional and personable driver-guides, and his team.

Eco Team ☎ 070 222 8222, ⓦ srilankaecotourism.com. Specialist eco-tourism and activity-holiday operator, offering a vast range of water- and land-based activities at locations islandwide – anything from surfing and caving to photography tours and "nature weddings".

Firefly ☎ 077 353 2933 (Sri Lanka), ☎ 020 3290 4969 (UK), ⓦ fireflysrilanka.com. Sri Lanka's only tour agency devoted exclusively to family travel, run by leading local expert (and long-term Galle resident) Emma Boyle and offering tailor-made family tours island-wide. Also rents out essential equipment for families travelling with small children.

Jetwing Eco Holidays ☎ 011 238 1201, ⓦ jetwingeco.com. Sri Lanka's leading eco-tourism operator, offering a vast range of wildlife and adventure activities including birdwatching, leopard-spotting, whale-watching, trekking, cycling, whitewater rafting and much more. Nature activities are led by an expert team of guides, including some of Sri Lanka's top naturalists.

Jetwing Travels ☎ 011 462 7739, ⓦ jetwingtravels.com. Travel division of Sri Lanka's largest hotel group, with a range of islandwide tours including trekking, cycling and Ayurveda tours.

Soul Riders Tours ☎ 077 734 9878, ⓦ soulriderstours.com. Specializes in tours on Royal Enfield motorbikes from their bases in Galle and Kandy, as well as Enfield rentals.

Sri Lanka Driver Tours ☎ 011 228 3708, ⓦ srilankadrivertours.com. Family-run business, with honest, reliable drivers and a small selection of two- to ten-day tours – or create your own.

Sri Lanka in Style ☎ 011 239 6666, ⓦ srilankainstyle.com. Luxurious tours with unusual and insightful itineraries (including golf, yoga and family) either customized or off the peg and accommodation in some of Sri Lanka's most magical villas and boutique hotels.

Visas and entry requirements

Citizens of all countries apart from the Maldives, Singapore and the Seychelles require a visa to visit Sri Lanka. Visas can still be obtained on arrival, although it's much easier (and significantly cheaper) to apply in advance at ⓦ eta.gov.lk for an online visa (also known as an "ETA", or Electronic Travel Authorization).

The visa is valid for thirty days and for two entries and currently costs $30 if bought online ($20 for citizens of SAARC countries) or $40 if bought on arrival. It's also possible to get a ninety-day tourist visa either in person or by post from your nearest embassy or consulate. You can also buy a thirty-day business visa online ($40, or $50 on arrival; $30 for SAARC nationals). For all visas your passport must be valid for six months after the date of your arrival.

The thirty-day tourist visa can be extended to three (or even six) months at the Immigration Service Centre (Mon–Fri 8.30am–1.30pm; T1962, ⓦ immigration.gov.lk) at the Department of Immigration, Sri Subhithipura Road, Battaramula, Colombo. You can extend your visa as soon as you get to Sri Lanka; the thirty days included in your original visa is included in the three months. You'll need to bring one passport photo. Fees for three-month visa extensions can be checked at ⓦ www.immigration.gov.lk; they're currently $54 for UK nationals, $16 for citizens of the Republic of Ireland, $30 for Australians, $34.50 for New Zealanders, $50 for Canadians, $100 for US citizens and $44 for South Africans. Conditions for extensions are an onward ticket and proof of sufficient funds, calculated at $15 a day, although a credit card will probably suffice. Expect the whole procedure to take an hour or two. Foreign embassies and consulates are virtually all based in Colombo (see page 95).

SRI LANKAN EMBASSIES AND CONSULATES

Australia and New Zealand ⓦ srilanka.embassy.gov.au.
Canada ⓦ www.canadainternational.gc.ca/sri_lanka.
South Africa ⓦ dirco.gov.za/colombo.
UK and Ireland ⓦ gov.uk/world/sri-lanka.
US ⓦ lk.usembassy.gov.

SRI LANKA IN THE FAST LANE

Sri Lanka's nineteenth-century highway infrastructure received a long-overdue upgrade in late 2011 with the opening of the country's first proper motorway, the **E01 Southern Expressway** from Colombo to Galle (subsequently extended from Galle to Matara in 2014, and with a further extension to Hambantota currently underway), while 2013 saw the opening of the country's second motorway, the **E03 Colombo–Katunayake Expressway**, linking the capital with the international airport. A third expressway, the **E02 Outer Circular Expressway** (serving as a Colombo ring-road and linking directly to the E01 – but not the E03) followed in 2014, and is also now being extended. The **E04 Central Expressway** from Colombo to Kandy is due to open in 2020, while there are also plans for an **E06 Ruwanpura Expressway**, connecting Colombo to Ratnapura and Pelmadulla.

The 350km network will, when finished, transform travel around many parts of the island. The Southern Expressway has already reduced the three-hour-plus slog from Colombo to Galle into a pleasant hour's drive and made the whole of the southwest and south coasts accessible as never before. Similarly, the Central Expressway to Kandy is also likely to cut current **journey times** by about two-thirds and significantly reduce onward travel times to other places in the hill country – making many of the travel times given in this book obsolete in the process.

Getting around

Getting around Sri Lanka is very much a tale of two halves. The construction of the island's ever-expanding expressway network (see above) has given Sri Lanka its biggest infrastructure upgrade since colonial times and speeded up access to some parts of the country immeasurably. Equally, recent railway improvements mean that major inter-city expresses are now both swift and comfortable. Away from the expressways and major train lines, however, getting around many parts of the island can still be a frustratingly time-consuming process.

Buses are the standard (and often the fastest) means of transport, with services reaching even the remotest corners of the island. **Trains** offer a more relaxed means of getting about and will get you to many parts of the country – eventually. If you don't want to put up with the vagaries of public transport, hiring a **car and driver** can prove a reasonably affordable and extremely convenient way of seeing the island in relative comfort. If you're really in a rush, domestic **flights** operated by Cinnamon Air and Helitours offer speedy connections between Colombo and other parts of the island.

Details of getting around by **bike** and specialist cycle tours are covered in the "Sports and outdoor activities" section (see page 48).

By bus

Buses are the staple mode of transport in Sri Lanka, and any town of even the remotest consequence will be served by fairly regular connections. Buses come in a variety of forms. The basic distinction is between government or SLTB (Sri Lanka Transport Board) buses and private services.

SLTB buses

Almost all **SLTB buses** are rattling old TATA vehicles, usually painted red. These are often the oldest and slowest vehicles on the road, but can be slightly more comfortable than private buses in that the conductor won't feel the same compulsion to squeeze as many passengers on board, or the driver to thrash the vehicle flat out in order to get to the next stop ahead of competing vehicles (accidents caused by rival bus drivers racing one another are not unknown).

Private buses

Private buses come in different forms. At their most basic, they're essentially the same as SLTB buses, consisting of large, arthritic old rust buckets that stop everywhere; the only difference is that private buses will usually be painted white and emblazoned with the stickers of whichever company runs them. Some private companies operate slightly faster services, large buses known variously as "semi-express", "express" or "intercity", which (in theory at least) make fewer stops en route.

At the top end of the scale, **private minibuses** – often described as "express" and/or "luxury" services (although the description should be taken with a large pinch of salt) – offer the fastest way of getting around. These are smaller vehicles with air-conditioning and tinted, curtained windows; luggage usually ends up in the space next to the driver (since there's nowhere else for it to go), although some conductors might make you put it on the seat next to you, and then charge you an extra fare. In theory, express minibuses only make limited stops at major bus stations en route, although in practice it's up to the driver and/or conductor as to where they stop and for how long, and how many people they're willing to cram in.

Fares, timetables and stops

Bus **fares**, on both private and SLTB services, are extremely low. For journeys on non-express buses, count on around Rs.60–70 per hour's travel, rising to around Rs.100–120 on express minibuses (more if travelling along an expressway – the Colombo to Galle bus costs around Rs.400). Note that on the latter you may have to pay the full fare for the entire route served by the bus, irrespective of where you get off. If you do want to get off before the end of the journey, let the driver/conductor know when you board.

Exact timings for buses are difficult to pin down. Longer-distance services operate (in theory, at least) according to set **timetables**; shorter-distance services tend to simply leave when full. Note that on all routes there tend to be considerably more buses **early in the day**, and that most services tail off over the course of the afternoon. The details given in the "Arrival and departure" sections in the Guide are an estimate of the total number of buses daily (both private and government). Given **journey times** represent what you might expect on a good run, without excessive stops to pick up passengers, roadworks or traffic jams en route, although all timings are extremely elastic, and don't be surprised if some journeys end up taking considerably longer. On longer trips expect the driver to make at least one stop of around twenty minutes at a café en route, especially around lunchtime. Seat **reservations** are almost unheard of except on Colombo–Jaffna services (see page 391).

Finding the bus you want can sometimes be tricky. Most buses display their destination in both Sinhala and English, although it's useful to get an idea of the Sinhala characters you're looking for (see page 454). All bus stations have one or more information booths (often unsigned wire-mesh kiosks) where staff can point you in the right direction, as well as providing the latest timetable information. If you arrive at a larger terminal by

---

> ### QUICKER BY TRAIN OR BUS?
> As a rule of thumb, **buses are generally faster than trains**, especially once you've factored in the possibility of trains running behind schedule; hill-country services from Kandy to Badulla, in particular, are grindingly slow (although very scenic). Exceptions to the bus-faster-than-train rule include the journey between **Colombo and Kandy**, where express trains are notably quicker than buses (although this will change when the new expressway opens), and services on the new line up to **Jaffna**, where trains also generally beat the bus. For specific timings, check the train timetables (see page 32) and the "Arrival and departure" sections for individual destinations in the Guide.

---

tuktuk, it's a good idea to enlist the help of your driver in locating the right bus.

Express services generally only halt at bus terminals or other recognized **stops**. Other types of services will usually stop wherever there's a passenger to be picked up – just stand by the roadside and stick an arm out (although it's best to find an official bus stop if possible – a bus icon on a blue square). If you're flagging down a bus by the roadside, one final hazard is in getting on. Drivers often don't stop completely, instead slowing down just enough to allow you to jump aboard. Keep your wits about you, especially if you're weighed down with heavy luggage, and be prepared to move fast when the bus pulls in.

By train

Originally built by the British during the nineteenth century, Sri Lanka's **train** network has seen massive changes over the past decade, transforming from a charmingly antiquated but not particularly useful relic of a bygone era to a comfortable and, on some routes, refreshingly fast way of getting around. The lines to Jaffna and Mannar, closed for decades, were reopened in 2014 and 2015 respectively, while islandwide track improvements and the addition of modern rolling stock (including smart new a/c carriages on intercity lines) have brought the entire system into the twentieth century – although many of the old rust-red-coloured colonial carriages remain in use, and trains on the gorgeous hill-country line are as grindingly slow as ever.

OBSERVATION CARS AND TOURIST CARRIAGES

Some intercity services on the hill-country route from Colombo to Kandy and Badulla carry a special carriage, the so-called **observation car**, usually at the back of the train and with large panoramic windows offering 360-degree views and seating in rather battered armchair-style seats. All seats are reservable, and get snapped up quickly, especially on the popular Colombo to Kandy run. The fare between Colombo and Kandy is currently Rs.800 one way. Rajadhani Express (☎ 011 574 7000, ⓦ rajadhani.lk) also run special **tourist carriages** which are attached to a few of the main hill-country and south coast express trains, although their services were suspended at the time of writing and the carriages themselves, although comfortable, have small windows and limited views.

Timings for journeys on some routes vary massively between express services (making only a few stops), standard intercity services, which make more stops, and slow services (such as night mail trains), which halt at practically every station en route. Latest railway **timetables** can be checked at ⓦ railway.gov.lk and at ⓦ slr.malindaprasad.com. Check out the excellent ⓦ seat61.com for more detailed coverage of Sri Lanka's railways and latest developments.

The train network

The network comprises three principal lines. The **coast line** runs along the west coast from Puttalam in the north, heading south via Negombo, Colombo, Kalutara, Bentota, Beruwala, Aluthgama,

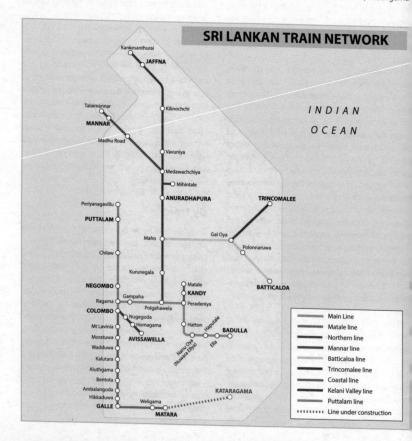

SRI LANKAN TRAIN NETWORK

INDIAN OCEAN

Kankesanthurai
JAFFNA
Talaimannar · Kilinochchi
MANNAR
Madhu Road
Vavuniya
Medawachchiya
Mihintale
ANURADHAPURA · TRINCOMALEE
Periyanagavillu
PUTTALAM
Maho · Gal Oya
Chilaw · Polonnaruwa
Kurunegala
NEGOMBO · Matale
Ragama · Gampaha · KANDY
COLOMBO · Polgahawela · Peradeniya
Nugegoda
Mt Lavinia · Homagama
Moratuwa · Hatton · Haputale · BADULLA
Wadduwa · AVISSAWELLA · Ella
Kalutara · Nanu Oya (Nuwara Eliya)
Aluthgama
Bentota
Ambalangoda · KATARAGAMA
Hikkaduwa · Weligama
GALLE · MATARA

Legend	
———	Main Line
———	Matale line
———	Northern line
———	Mannar line
———	Batticaloa line
———	Trincomalee line
———	Coastal line
———	Kelani Valley line
———	Puttalam line
•••••••	Line under construction

Ambalangoda, Hikkaduwa and Galle to Weligama and Matara (with an extension as far as Kataragama now largely complete). The **hill-country line** runs from Colombo to Kandy then on to Hatton (for Adam's Peak), Nanu Oya (for Nuwara Eliya), Haputale, Bandarawela, Ella and Badulla. The **northern line** runs from Colombo through Kurunegala to Anuradhapura and Vavuniya before terminating at Jaffna. Three additional branches run off this line: the first to Polonnaruwa and Batticaloa, the second to Trincomalee, and the third to Madhu Road, Mannar and Talaimannar.

Trains comprise three classes, though most services consist exclusively of **second- and third-class** carriages. There's not actually a huge amount of difference between the two: second-class seats have a bit more padding and there are fans in the carriages. Both second- and third-class seats can be reserved on some trains – the major benefit of pre-booking a seat is that no standing passengers are allowed in reserved carriages, so they don't get overcrowded. In unreserved carriages, the main advantage of second-class is that, being slightly more expensive, it tends also to be a bit less packed.

First class covers various different types of seating. These are available only on selected trains and must *always* be reserved in advance. The most common type of first-class seating is in conventional a/c carriages on intercity trains. On the hill-country and northern lines there are also first-class seats in blue Chinese-built trains with smart modern a/c carriages, although you can't open the windows and are rather shut off from the outside world. Some people prefer second or third class, which have open windows and are therefore much more atmospheric and breezier, and also better for photography. First class also includes the **observation car** on hill-country trains (see page 30); and (rather grotty) sleeping berths on overnight services.

The island's compact size means that, unlike in neighbouring India, there are relatively few **overnight trains**. These comprise first-class sleeping berths and second- and third-class "sleeperettes" (actually just reclining seats), plus ordinary seats.

Fares and booking

Despite recent price increases, **fares** are still extremely cheap. You can travel all the way from Colombo to Jaffna in third class, for example, for just Rs.335, while even a first-class berth on the same route costs a relatively modest Rs.1100.

Many trains now have seats in all three classes which can be **booked in advance**. Reservations can be made in person at major stations up to thirty days before travel. You can also book by phone if you have a Mobitel/Etisalat account (call ☎365). Sri Lankan Railways don't offer a web-booking service but it's possible to **reserve tickets online** through a number of private operators – ⓦ visitsrilankatours.co.uk are the best.

The bad news is that on many services, reserved seating (particularly in first class, where available), tends to **sell out** as soon as it goes on sale, and even lower classes may be booked solid – meaning that it definitely pays to book more than a month in advance using an online service. The good news (sort of) is that virtually all trains have at least some second- and third-class **unreserved carriages**. Tickets for these are sold only on the day of departure, sometimes not until an hour before departure, and there's no limit on the number of tickets sold, meaning you're guaranteed to get a ticket – if you're told a train has "sold out" it just means all the reserved seats have gone). It also, of course, means that carriages can sometimes get packed solid.

By plane

Domestic air services provide a superfast alternative to long journeys by road or rail and are memorable in their own right, with frequently beautiful views of the island from above. The main operator is **Cinnamon Air** (ⓦ cinnamonair.com), which has regular scheduled flights out of Katunayake international airport and from Water's Edge (on the southern side of Colombo) to Koggala, Dickwella, Weerawila (near Tissamaharama), Kandy, Castlereagh (near Adam's Peak), Sigiriya, Batticaloa and Trincomalee. Fares aren't particularly cheap (a one-way flight from Colombo to Trincomalee, for example, cost $262 at the time of research), although the flights are wonderfully scenic, and on many routes you'll either take off from and/or land on water, which adds an extra pinch of fun.

Much cheaper flights are offered by **Helitours** (ⓦ www.helitours.lk), who fly out of Colombo's Ratmalana airport (just north of Mount Lavinia) to Trincomalee and Jaffna, with a one-way ticket to Trincomalee, for example, costing just Rs.9250 (around $60). Helitours is a commercial offshoot of the Sri Lankan Air Force, using government planes piloted by services personnel, and generally gets good reviews. It's worth noting though that their fleet still appears to include two Chinese-made Xian MA60 planes, an aircraft which has been the subject of numerous international safety concerns. Helitours

TRAIN TIMETABLES OF MAJOR INTERCITY SERVICES

The following were correct at the time of research though are likely to change (perhaps significantly) during the lifetime of this guide. Times from Colombo given below are from Fort Station. All trains run daily unless otherwise indicated. Always check the latest times before travelling.

TRAINS IN THE SOUTH

In addition to the following, there are a considerable number of slow commuter trains running stretches of the line between Colombo and Galle; the following timetable lists express services only.

Colombo	06.55	08.35	10.30	14.25	15.50	16.46*	17.30	18.05*	19.30
Kalutara South	07.59	09.34	11.28	15.20	16.33	17.42	18.22	19.05	20.40
Aluthgama	08.20	09.54	11.50	15.35	16.48	17.57	18.40	19.31	21.20
Ambalangoda	08.48	10.19	12.12	16.08	17.09	18.18	19.19	19.54	22.10
Hikkaduwa	09.00	10.30	12.23	16.19	17.20	18.29	19.39	20.06	22.33
Galle	09.35	11.05	13.00	16.45	17.40	18.45	20.10	20.28	22.58
Weligama	10.18	11.36	13.32	17.28	18.07	19.20	–	21.17	
Matara	10.42	11.50	13.47	17.48	18.20	19.35	–	21.38	–

*Mon–Fri only

Matara	–	05.00†	06.05	06.12‡	–	09.40	13.25	14.10
Weligama	–	05.14	06.19	06.30	–	09.55	13.51	14.33
Galle	05.00*	06.00	06.55	07.25	09.00*	10.55	14.45	15.35
Hikkaduwa	05.29	06.18	07.10	07.39	09.43	11.14	15.06	15.55
Ambalangoda	05.49	06.29	07.21	07.52	10.08	11.26	15.18	16.08
Aluthgama	06.28	06.51	07.42	08.15	11.10	11.49	15.42	16.35
Kalutara South	06.48	07.10	07.58	08.35	11.53	12.15	16.05	17.02
Colombo	07.48	08.17	08.43	09.32	13.03	13.15	17.14	18.05

* Mon–Sat only; † Mon–Fri only; ‡ daily except Sat

COLOMBO–KANDY EXPRESS TRAINS

Colombo	05.55	07.00	08.30	10.35	12.40	15.35	16.35*	17.20†	17.45
Kandy	08.42	09.31	11.03	14.00	16.04	18.06	19.42	19.58	20.55

*Sat & Sun only; †Fri & Sun only

Kandy	05.00*	06.15	06.45	10.40	12.50	15.00	15.30†	16.05	16.55†
Colombo	08.13	08.52	10.11	14.05	15.27	17.36	18.50	18.57	19.30

*Sun only; †Sat & Sun only

TRAINS IN THE HILL COUNTRY

Colombo	–	05.55	08.30	09.45	12.40	20.00
Kandy	03.30	08.47	11.10	–	17.00	–
Peradeniya	03.47	08.57	11.19	12.31	–	23.06
Hatton	07.20	11.14	13.28	14.30	19.53	01.38

continued using one of these for its Jaffna flights in 2015 even after its Certificate of Airworthiness had expired, requiring passengers to sign an indemnity form before boarding the plane. If you still want to fly with Helitours, you can (hopefully) book online using their somewhat temperamental website or in person either at their offices in Colombo (Sir Chittampalam A. Gardiner Mawatha, Fort) or Jaffna (266 Stanley Road). Alternatively, try calling ☎011 3 144 244 or ☎011 3 144 944, or emailing ✉ helitourstickets@slaf.gov.lk.

By car

As Sri Lankans say, in order to **drive** around the island you'll need three things: "good horn, good brakes, good luck". Although roads are generally in reasonable condition, the myriad hazards they present – crowds of pedestrians, erratic cyclists, crazed bus drivers and suicidal dogs, to name just a few – plus the very idiosyncratic set of road rules followed by Sri Lankan drivers, makes driving a challenge in many parts of the island.

Nanu Oya	09.30	12.45	15.01	15.55	–	03.11
Haputale	12.05	14.17	16.32	17.27	–	04.57
Bandarawela	12.50	14.45	16.59	17.54	–	05.33
Ella	13.26	15.15	17.28	18.28	–	06.06
Badulla	14.30	16.06	18.22	19.17	–	07.10

Badulla	–	05.45	08.30	11.00	13.35	17.50
Ella	–	06.40	09.24	11.56	14.37	18.53
Bandarawela	–	07.15	09.57	12.29	15.22	19.29
Haputale	–	07.45	10.25	12.57	16.07	20.10
Nanu Oya	–	09.25	12.02	14.35	18.42	22.08
Hatton	07.10	10.39	13.20	16.02	20.28	23.41
Kandy	10.30	12.50	16.05	–	23.38	–
Peradeniya	10.56	13.00	16.16	18.15	–	02.07
Colombo	14.03	15.27	18.57	21.10	–	05.17

TRAINS IN THE EAST

Colombo	06.05	19.00	21.30
Polonnaruwa	12.32	01.39	–
Valaichchenai	14.00	03.05	–
Batticaloa	14.45	03.55	–
Trincomalee	–	–	05.30

Trincomalee	–	–	19.00
Batticaloa	06.10	20.15	–
Valaichchenai	07.00	21.03	–
Polonnaruwa	08.27	22.28	–
Colombo	15.15	04.53	03.30

TRAINS IN THE NORTH

Colombo Fort	05.45	06.35	08.50	11.50	19.00	20.30
Kurunegala	–	08.29	11.18	13.30	21.21	22.27
Anuradhapura	09.17	10.45	14.35	15.35	00.10	00.55
Vavuniya	10.06	11.47	–	16.25	–	02.13
Jaffna	11.51	14.37	–	18.15	–	05.10
Mannar	–	–	17.03	–	02.45	–
Talaimannar	–	–	17.33	–	03.16	–

Talaimannar	–	–	07.37	–	–	21.40
Mannar	–	–	08.08	–	–	22.13
Jaffna	06.10	09.35	–	13.45	19.00	–
Vavuniya	08.07	12.28	–	15.36	21.53	–
Anuradhapura	09.02	13.50	10.50	16.32	23.10	01.10
Kurunegala	11.10	16.28	13.56	–	01.47	03.46
Colombo Fort	12.55	18.32	16.05	20.00	04.05	06.03

Reliable **car hire companies** include Malkey (malkey.lk) and Casons Rent-A-Car (casons.lk), both of which have a good range of cars at competitive rates, with or without driver.

Self-driving

If you're determined to drive yourself, you'll need to bring an **international driving permit** with you from home and then acquire an additional permit to drive in Sri Lanka. To acquire this you'll need to visit the Automobile Association of Ceylon, 3rd floor, 40 Sir M.M. Markar Mawatha, Colombo, just a few metres from the *Ramada* hotel (011 755 5557; office open Mon–Fri 8am–4pm). Permits cost Rs.3636, are valid for up to twelve months and are issued on the spot.

It's also worth equipping yourself with a good **map or atlas** (such as the *Arjuna's Road Atlas*) – or some smartphone or tablet equivalent. In terms of driving rules, you'd do well to remember that, in Sri Lanka, might is right: drivers of larger vehicles (buses especially), will expect you to get out of the way if they're travelling faster than you. In addition, many drivers overtake freely on blind corners or in other dangerous places. Expect to confront other vehicles driving at speed on the wrong side of the road on a fairly regular basis.

Car and driver

Given the hassle of getting around by public transport, virtually all visitors opt to tour Sri Lanka by hiring a **car and driver**, which offers unlimited flexibility and can be less expensive than you might expect. Some drivers will get you from A to B but nothing more; others are Sri Lanka Tourist Board-accredited "chauffeur-guides", government-trained and holding a tourist board licence, who can double up as **guides** at all the main tourist sights and field any questions you might have about the country.

The main problem with drivers is that many of them work on **commission**, which they receive from some, but not all, hotels, plus assorted restaurants, shops, spice gardens, jewellers and so on. This means that you and your driver's opinions might not always coincide as to where you want to stay and what you want to do – some drivers will always want to head for wherever they get the best kickbacks (and you'll also pay over the odds at these places, since the hoteliers, restaurateurs or shopkeepers have to recoup the commission they're paying the driver). If you find you're spending more time stressing out about dealing with your driver than enjoying your holiday, find another one – there are plenty of decent drivers out there.

Cars and drivers can be hired through virtually every tour companies and travel agents around the island, while many hotels and guesthouses can also fix you up with a vehicle. To make sure you get a good driver, it pays to go with a **reputable company** (such as DSL Tours or Sri Lanka Driver Tours – see page 27) which pays its drivers a decent wage so they don't have to rely on commission to make ends meet. Make sure your driver speaks at least some English and emphasize from the outset where you do and don't want to go. Some drivers impose on their clients' good nature to the point of having meals with them and insisting on acting as guides and interpreters throughout the tour, even if they're not qualified to do so. If this is what you want, fine; if not, don't be afraid to make it clear that you expect to be left alone when not in the car.

Prices depend more on quality than size of transport – a posh air-conditioned car will cost more than a non-air-conditioned minivan. Rate start from around $40 per day for the smalle cars, plus the driver's fees and living allowance Most top-end hotels provide meals and accom modation for drivers either for free or for a sma additional charge. If you're staying in budge or mid-range places, you'll have to pay for you driver's room and food – as ever, it's best to try t establish a daily allowance for this at the outse of your trip to avoid misunderstandings an arguments later. Your driver will probably als expect a tip of $5–10 per day, depending on how highly trained they are. You'll also probably hav to pay for **fuel** – now pretty expensive in Sri Lank – which can add significantly to the overall cost. I addition, some companies only offer a decidedl mean 100km per day **free mileage**, which doesn go far on the island's twisty roads, so you may we have to stump up for some excess mileage as we Alternatively, you could always just hire vehicle **by the day** as you go round the island. The actu vehicle-hire cost may be a bit higher, but yo won't have to worry about having to house an feed your driver.

By rickshaw

The lines of motorized **rickshaws** that ply th streets of every city, town and village are one Sri Lanka's most characteristic sights. Known b various names – tuktuks, three-wheelers, trishaw or (rather more optimistically) "taxis" – rickshaws ar the go-to option for short journeys and can als be useful for tours and excursions and even, at pinch, for long journeys if you get stranded or car be bothered to wait around for a bus, althoug they're not particularly comfortable, and you can see much either.

Except in Colombo (see page 104), Sri Lanka rickshaws are unmetered; the **fare** will be whateve you can negotiate with the driver. *Never set o* without agreeing the fare beforehand. The majorit of Sri Lanka's tuktuk drivers are reasonably hones and you may be offered a decent fare without eve having to bargain; a small minority, however, ar complete crooks who will take you for whateve they can get. Given the wildly varying degree of probity you'll encounter, it's often difficult t know exactly where you stand. A basic fare Rs.40–50 per kilometre (which is what metere taxis in Colombo currently charge) serves as useful general rule of thumb, though unless yo have ironclad bargaining powers you'll probabl pay more than this, especially in big cities an heavily touristed areas. Also bear in mind that the longer the journey, the lower the per-kilometre rate should be. In addition, the sheer number of rickshaws in most tourist centres means that you usually have the upper hand in bargaining – if you can't agree a reasonable fare, there'll always be another driver keen to take your custom.

Finally, beware of rickshaw drivers who claim to have **no change** – this can even apply when trying to pay, say, for a Rs.70 fare with a Rs.100 note, with the driver claiming (perhaps truthfully) to have only Rs.10 or Rs.20 change, and hoping that you'll settle for a few rupees less. If you don't have change, check that the driver does before you set off. If you make the position clear from the outset, you're guaranteed that your driver will go through the hassle of getting change for you rather than risk losing your fare.

Accommodation

Sri Lanka has an excellent range of accommodation in all price brackets, from basic beachside shacks to elegant colonial mansions and sumptuous five-star resorts – indeed staying in one of the country's burgeoning number of luxury hotels and villas can be one of the principal pleasures of a visit to the island, if you can afford it.

Types of accommodation

Travellers on a budget will spend most of their time in **guesthouses**, usually family-run places either in or attached to the home of the owners. Some of the nicer guesthouses can be real homes from home, with good food and sociable hosts. Rooms at most places of these type of places cost in the region of $12–25.

Hotels come in all shapes, sizes and prices, from functional concrete boxes to luxurious establishments that are virtual tourist attractions in their own right. Some of the finest hotels (particularly in the hill country) are located in old colonial buildings, offering a wonderful taste of the lifestyle and ambience of yesteryear, while the island also boasts a number of stunning modern hotels, including many designed by Sri Lanka's great twentieth-century architect **Geoffrey Bawa** (see boxes pages 37 and 122). The coastal areas are also home to innumerable **resort hotels**, the majority of which – with a few honourable exceptions – are fairly bland, populated largely by European package tourists on full-board programmes and offering a diet of horrible buffet food and plenty of organized fun.

Sri Lanka is gradually waking up to its massive **eco-tourism** potential, and now boasts a few good eco-oriented hotels and lodges (see page 51). You can also stay in bungalows or camp within most of the island's national parks (see page 50). The national parks are the only places in Sri Lanka with official **campsites**. Elsewhere camping is not a recognized activity, and pitching your tent unofficially in rural areas or on the beach is likely to lead to problems with local landowners and villagers.

Sri Lanka also boasts a huge (and continually increasing) number of **villas** and boutique hotels, many set in old colonial villas or old tea estate bungalows (see pages 148 and 241) and offering stylish and luxurious accommodation, although they don't come cheap. There's a great selection **online** at numerous websites including Boutique Sri Lanka (Ⓦ boutiquesrilanka. com), Eden Villas (Ⓦ villasinsrilanka.com), Red Dot Tours (Ⓦ reddottours.com) and Sri Lanka in Style (Ⓦ srilankainstyle.com).

There's also a growing number of **hostels** across the country (including several in Colombo, plus others in Kandy, Galle, Unawatuna, Arugam Bay and elsewhere) offering relatively inexpensive dormitory accommodation.

Finding a room, touts and commission

There's heaps of accommodation in Sri Lanka, although despite the ever-increasing number of places to stay the growth in tourist numbers means that demand frequently outstrips supply, and it's not unknown for entire towns to fill up

---

ACCOMMODATION PRICES

The accommodation **prices** quoted in this guide are based on the cost of the least expensive double room in **high season** (roughly Dec–April in most parts of the island except on the east coast, where it's May–July). Outside these periods rates often fall considerably. All taxes and service charges have been included in the prices quoted. For more details, see "Room rates" (see page 37).

TEN MEMORABLE PLACES TO STAY

Amanwella Tangalla. See page 179
Bar Reef Resort Kalpitiya. See page 109
Club Villa Bentota. See page 123
Galle Face Hotel Colombo. See page 87
Helga's Folly Kandy. See page 224
Heritance Kandalama Dambulla. See page 297
Heritance Tea Factory Nuwara Eliya. See page 246
Jetwing Vil Uyana Sigiriya. See page 306
The Kandy House Kandy. See page 226
The Sun House Galle. See page 149

during major holidays or festivals. Most places are now bookable **online** through major portals like Ⓦ booking.com, although note that many more upmarket places now offer a "best price" guarantee when booking directly through their own website, so compare rates before you commit. You may also pay less when booking directly at smaller places, while booking direct (although less convenient) also ensures that all the money you spend stays in Sri Lanka, where it belongs, rather than having parts of it diverted into the coffers of a few international online behemoths.

If you don't have a reservation, be aware that Sri Lanka has its fair share of accommodation **touts** (or, more often, rickshaw drivers doubling as touts) who make money by demanding – often extortionate – **commission** from guesthouse owners. A few places are happy to pay to have customers brought to them, but the vast majority are not – and what makes it worse is that some touts expect to paid off even if they had no influence on your choice. One way of avoiding hassle both for you and your hosts is to ring ahead to your preferred guesthouse; many places will pick you up for free from the local bus or train station if given advance warning. If arriving by tuktuk and your driver asks if you have a booking, you might prefer to say you have (even if you haven't), which should help discourage him from trying to rinse commission out of the place you're going to.

Facilities and services

What you'll need from your room depends on where you are in the island. A fan or a/c is essential in the hot and humid lowlands, but redundant in the high hill country. Equally, hot water is a must-have in, say, lofty Nuwara Eliya, but a luxury you can possibly do without on the beach. And in a few places, like Kandy, you'll probably want a fan *and* hot water (although a/c isn't really needed unless you really suffer in the heat). Virtually all accommodation in Sri Lanka comes with **private bathroom** (we've mentioned any exceptions in the relevant listings).

In **lowland areas**, you should also always get a **fan** (usually a ceiling fan; floor-standing fans are much less common, and much less effective) – don't stay anywhere without one, unless you're happy to sleep in a puddle of sweat. It's also worth checking that the fan works properly (both that it runs at a decent speed and doesn't make a horrible noise). In lowland areas, room size and ceiling height are both important in determining how hot somewhere will be – rooms with low ceilings can become unbearably stuffy. In some areas (notably Arugam Bay) many places are built with their roofs raised slightly above the top of the walls, so that cool air can circulate freely through the gap (although, equally, it provides free access to insects). The majority of places now provide **hot water** (although in the humid lowlands, cold-water showers are no particular hardship). **Mosquito nets** are provided in many but not all places – it's well worth carrying your own. Smarter places will also usually have **air conditioning**.

Hot water usually comes as standard in the cooler **hill country**, though you're unlikely to get (or need) a fan anywhere higher than Kandy. In the highest parts of the island, particularly Nuwara Eliya, you'll often need some form of **heating** and/or a good supply of **blankets**. Few hill-country establishments provide mosquito nets, which isn't generally a problem since mozzies shouldn't be able to survive at these altitudes, though in practice you might be unlucky enough to have an unusually hardy specimen buzzing in your ear anywhere in the island.

There are a few other things worth bearing in mind when choosing a room. Check how many lights there are and whether they work (some rooms can be decidedly gloomy), and if you're staying in a family guesthouse, keep an eye out for loud children, dogs or television sets in the vicinity of your room; and make sure you get a room away from any noisy nearby roads.

Finally, remember that most Sri Lankans go to bed early. If you're staying at a small guesthouse and you go out for dinner and a few beers, it's not uncommon to find yourself locked out if you return any time after 9pm. Let your hosts know when to expect you back.

Room rates

Room rates in lower-end places reflect Sri Lanka's **bargaining culture** – exact rates are often somewhat notional, as owners will vary prices to reflect the season, levels of demand and how rich they think you look. It's always worth bargaining, even in more upmarket places, especially if you're planning to stay a few nights, or if business looks slow. If you're travelling on your own, you'll have to work harder to get a decent price since many establishments don't have **single rooms or rates** (and where they exist, they're still usually two-thirds to three-quarters of the price of a double). Try to establish what the price of a double would be, and bargain from there.

Prices in most coastal areas are also subject to **seasonal variations**. The most pronounced seasonal variation is along the west coast, where rates at almost all places rise (usually by between 25 and 40 percent) from December 1 through to mid- or late April. Some places along the south coast also put up their prices during this period. East coast places tend to raise rates by a similar level from around May through to July. Rates in particular towns also rise if there's a big festival or other event going on locally – as during the Esala Perahera at Kandy – or over important holidays, as during the Sinhalese New Year in Nuwara Eliya, when accommodation prices can double or treble.

Room rates at mid- and top-end places are often quoted in **dollars** for convenience, but are payable in rupees only (a few places along the west coast quote prices in euros, again usually payable in rupees only). Make sure you clarify whether any **additional taxes** will be added to the bill or are already included in the quoted price (the so-called "nett" rate). Many places add a ten percent "service charge" while there are also several other government taxes which may or may not be figured into the quoted price, but which can potentially add up to 27 percent to the total bill – a nasty surprise when you come to check out, especially since these taxes will most likely also have been added to your food and drink bill. Cheaper hotels and guesthouses tend to quote nett rates; upmarket places are more likely to quote rates excluding taxes and service charge, although there's no hard and fast rule.

GEOFFREY BAWA HOTELS
Avani Bentota Bentota. See page 123
Avani Kalutara Resort and Spa Kalutara. See page 113
The Blue Water Wadduwa. See page 115
Club Villa Bentota. See page 123
Heritance Ahungalla Ahungalla. See page 125
Heritance Ayurveda Maha Gedara Beruwala. See page 117
Heritance Kandalama Dambulla. See page 297
Jetwing Beach Negombo. See page 102
Jetwing Lighthouse Galle. See page 149
Lunuganga Bentota. See page 123
Paradise Road The Villa Bentota. See page 123

Eating and drinking

Sri Lanka boasts a fascinatingly idiosyncratic culinary heritage, the result of a unique fusion of local traditions and produce with recipes and spices brought to the island over the centuries by Indians, Arabs, Malays, Portuguese, Dutch and British.

The staple dish is **rice and curry**, at its finest a miniature banquet whose contrasting flavours – coconut milk, chillies, curry leaves, cinnamon, garlic and "Maldive fish" (an intensely flavoured pinch of sun-dried tuna) – bear witness to Sri Lanka's status as one of the original spice islands. There are plenty of other unique specialities to explore and enjoy – hoppers, string hoppers, *kottu rotty*, *lamprais* and *pittu* – as well as plentiful **seafood**.

Sri Lankan cuisine can be decidedly fiery – sometimes on a par with Thai, and far hotter than most Indian cooking. You'll often be asked how hot you want your food; "medium" usually gets you something that's neither bland nor requires the use of a fire extinguisher. If you do overheat during a meal, remember that water only adds to the pain of a burnt palate; a mouthful of plain rice, bread or beer is much more effective.

Sri Lankans say that you can't properly enjoy the flavours and textures of food unless you **eat with your fingers**, although tourists are always provided with cutlery by default. As elsewhere in Asia, you're meant to eat with your right hand, although this taboo isn't strictly observed – if you'd really prefer to eat with your left hand, you're unlikely to turn heads.

Costs are generally reasonable though no longer the bargain they once were. You can get a filling rice and curry meal for a couple of dollars at a local café, while main courses at most guest-houses or cheaper restaurants usually cost around $3–6, although prices in more upmarket places, in Colombo especially, are now approaching European or North American levels. Note that many places add a ten percent service charge to the bill, while more upmarket restaurants may add additional govern-ment taxes of varying amounts (10–15 percent) on top of that.

Be aware that the typical vagaries of Sri Lankan **spelling** mean that popular dishes can appear on menus in a bewildering number of forms: *idlis* can become *ittlys*, *vadais* turn into *wadais*, *kottu rotty* transforms into *kotturoti* and *lamprais* changes to *lumprice*. You'll also be regaled with plenty of unintentionally humorous offerings such as "cattle fish", "sweat and sour" or Adolf Hitler's favourite dish, "nazi goreng".

Where to eat

Where you'll eat in Sri Lanka will depend very much on where you are. Some of the island's larger cities, including Kandy, Trincomalee and Jaffna, remain a bit of a culinary desert, although Colombo, Galle, Negombo, Unawatuna, Mirissa and Ella have a burgeoning number of **independent restaurants** and plenty of choice. Away from the major tourist centres, however, good restaurants are few and far between, and you'll probably end up eating at your **guesthouse**, which at most places means rice and curry, plus a limited selection of simple fried rice and noodle dishes.

Sri Lankans themselves either eat at home or patronize the island's innumerable scruffy little **local cafés**, often confusingly signed as "hotels", which serve up filling meals for a dollar or two: rough-and-ready portions of rice and curry, plus maybe hoppers or *kottu rotty*. **Lunch packets** are also popular and, at less than a couple of dollars, the cheapest way to fill up in Sri Lanka. Sold at local cafés and street stalls in larger towns between around 11am and 2pm, these contain a filling portion of simple rice and curry wrapped in a banana leaf or newspaper (or, increasingly, packed in a styrofoam box).

Rice and curry

Served up in just about every café and restaurant across the land, **rice and curry** is the island's ubiquitous signature dish – somewhere in style between the food of South India and Southeast Asia (although bearing virtually zero resemblance to the classic curries of North India). Rice and curry can take many forms. At its simplest it can be just a single plate, with a mound of rice topped with a few dollops of veg curry and/or dhal, a hunk of chicken or fish and a spoonful of *sambol* (see below). More sophisticated versions comprise a large bowl of rice accompanied by around five to eight (sometimes more) side dishes – a kind of miniature banquet said to have been inspired by Indonesian *nasi padang*, which was transformed by the Dutch into the classic *rijsttafel*, or "rice table", and introduced to Sri Lanka sometime in the eighteenth century.

As in Southeast Asia, coconut and chilli provide the foundations for Sri Lankan cooking. Typical curry sauces (known as *kiri hodhi*, or "milk gravy") are made from coconut milk infused with chillies and various other spices usually including curry leaves, cinnamon, ginger, garlic and turmeric. A choice of either chicken or fish curry plus a serving of dhal comes as standard, with a varied range of **vegetable dishes** which might include curried pineapple, potato, aubergine (*brinjal*), sweet potato and okra (lady's fingers). Other commonly encountered local vegetables include curried jackfruit, so-called "drumsticks" (*murunga* – a bit like okra), "long beans" and kankun (also spelt kangkung), or "water spinach", usually stir-fried with other ingredients or on its own. You might also be served ash plantain (*alu kesel*), snake gourd (*patolah*), bitter gourd (*karawila*) and breadfruit (*del*), along with many more outlandish and unpronounceable types of regional produce. Another common accompaniment is **mallung**: shredded green vegetables, lightly stir-fried with spices and grated coconut.

Rice and curry is usually served with a helping of **sambol**, designed to be mixed into your food to give it a bit of extra kick. *Sambols* come in various forms, the most common being *pol sambol* (coconut *sambol*), an often eye-watering lethal combination of chilli powder, chopped onions, salt, grated coconut and Maldive fish. Treat it with caution. You might also come across the slightly less overpowering *lunu miris*, consisting of chilli powder, onions, Maldive fish and salt; and the more gentle, sweet-and-sour *seeni sambol* ("sugar sambol").

Funnily enough, the **rice** itself is often fairly uninspiring – don't expect to find the delicately

VEGETARIAN FOOD IN SRI LANKA

Surprisingly for such a Buddhist country, **vegetarian** food as a concept hasn't really caught on in Sri Lanka. That said, a large proportion of the nation's cooking is meat-free: vegetable curries, vegetable *rottys*, hoppers and string hoppers – not to mention the bewildering variety of fruit on offer. Colombo's numerous pure veg South Indian restaurants are a delight, while if you eat fish and seafood, you'll have no problems finding a meal, especially around the coast.

piced pilaus and birianis of North India. Sri Lanka produces many types of rice, but the stuff served in estaurants is usually fairly low-grade, although you nay occasionally come across the nutritious and distinctively flavoured red and yellow rice (a bit like rown rice in taste and texture) that are grown in ertain parts of the island.

Other Sri Lankan specialities

ri Lanka's tastiest snack, the engagingly named **hopper** (*appa*) is a small, bowl-shaped pancake raditionally made from a batter containing coconut nilk and palm toddy (see page 42), and is usually aten either at breakfast or, most commonly, dinner. Hoppers are cooked in a small wok-like dish, meaning that most of the mix collects in the bottom, making them soft and doughy at the ase, and thin and crispy around the edges. Various ngredients can be poured into the hopper. An egg ried in the middle produces an egg hopper, while weet ingredients like yoghurt or honey are also ometimes added. Alternatively, plain hoppers can e eaten as an accompaniment to curry. Not to be onfused with the hopper are **string hoppers** (*idi ppa*), tangled little nests of steamed rice vermicelli oodles, often eaten with a dash of dhal or curry for reakfast.

Another rice substitute is **pittu**, a mixture of lour and grated coconut, steamed in a cylindrical amboo mould – it looks a bit like coarse couscous. Derived from the Dutch *lomprijst*, **lamprais** is nother local speciality: a serving of rice baked in a lantain leaf along with accompaniments such as chunk of chicken or a boiled egg, plus some veg nd pickle.

Muslim restaurants are the place to go for **rotty** or *roti*), a fine, doughy pancake – watching these eing made is half the fun, as the chef teases small alls of dough into huge sheets of almost trans-arent thinness. A dollop of curried meat, veg or otato is then plonked in the middle and the *rotty* folded up around it; the final shape depends n the whim of the chef – some prefer crepe-like quares, others opt for samosa-style triangles,

some a spring roll. *Pol* (coconut) *rotty*, served with *lunu miris*, is a popular breakfast snack. *Rottys* can also be chopped up and stir-fried with meat and vegetables, a dish known as **kottu rotty**. You'll know when *kottu rotty* is being made because of the noise – the ingredients are usually simulta-neously fried and chopped on a hotplate using a large pair of meat cleavers, producing a noisy drumming sound – part musical performance, part advertisement.

Devilled dishes are also popular. These are usually prepared with a thick, spicy sauce plus big chunks of onion and chilli, though the end product often isn't as hot as you might fear (unless you eat all the chillies). Devilled chicken, pork, fish and beef are all common – the last is generally considered the classic devilled dish and is traditionally eaten during drinking binges. Another local staple is the **buriani**. This has little in common with the traditional, saffron-scented North Indian biriani, being simply a mound of rice with a hunk of chicken, a bowl of curry sauce and a boiled egg, but it makes a good lunchtime filler and is usually less fiery than a basic plate of rice and curry.

Seafood

Not surprisingly, **seafood** plays a major part in the Sri Lankan diet, with fish often taking the place of meat. Common fish include tuna, seer (a firm-bodied white fish), mullet and the delicious melt-in-the-mouth butterfish, as well as pomfret, bonito and shark. You'll also find lobster, plentiful crab, prawns and cuttlefish (calamari). The Negombo lagoon, just north of Colombo, is a particularly prized source of seafood, including gargantuan jumbo prawns the size of a well-fed crab.

Seafood is usually a good bet if you're trying to avoid highly spiced food. Fish is generally prepared in a fairly simple manner, usually fried (sometimes in breadcrumbs) or grilled and served with a twist of lemon or in a mild garlic sauce. You will, however, find some fiery fish curries, while chillied seafood dishes are also fairly common – chilli crab is particu-larly popular.

South Indian food

Sri Lanka boasts a good selection of "pure vegetarian" **South Indian restaurants** (vegetarian here meaning no meat, fish, eggs or alcohol); they're most common in Colombo, although they can be found islandwide wherever there's a significant Tamil population. These cheerfully no-nonsense places cater to a local clientele and serve up a delicious range of South Indian-style dishes at giveaway prices. The standard dish is the **dosa**, a crispy rice pancake served in various forms: either plain, with ghee (clarified butter), onion or, most commonly, as a masala dosa, folded up around a filling of curried potato. You'll also find **uttapam**, another (thicker) type of rice pancake that's usually eaten with some kind of curry, and **idlis**, steamed rice cakes served with curry sauces or chutneys.

Short eats

Another classic Tamil savoury which has entered the Sri Lanka mainstream is the **vadai** (or *wadai*), a spicy doughnut made of deep-fried lentils – no train or bus journey is complete without the sound of hawkers marching up and down the carriage or vehicle shouting "Vadai-vadai-vadai!". Platefuls of *vadais*, *rottys* and bread rolls are often served up in cafés under the name of **short eats** – you help yourself and are charged for what you eat, though be aware that these plates are passed around and their contents indiscriminately prodded by all and sundry, so they're not particularly hygienic.

Other cuisines

There are plenty of **Chinese restaurants** around the island, although the predominantly Cantonese-style dishes are usually spiced up for Sri Lankan tastes. As usual, Colombo has easily the best range of such places. **Indonesian dishes** introduced by the Dutch are also sometimes served in tourist restaurants – most commonly *nasi goreng* (fried rice with meat or seafood, topped with a fried egg) and *gado gado* (salad and cold boiled eggs in a peanut sauce), although these rarely taste much like the Indonesian originals.

Other cuisines are restricted to Colombo. **Thai** food has made some limited inroads, while **Japanese** cuisine is also modestly popular. Colombo is also where you'll find almost all of Sri Lanka's surprisingly small number of decent **North Indian** restaurants, along with lots of excellent **European** places. Smarter hotels all over the island make some

attempt to produce European cuisine, though with wildly varying results.

Desserts and sweets

The classic Sri Lankan dessert is **curd** (yoghurt made from buffalo milk) served with honey or **kitul** (a sweet syrup from the kitul palm). When boiled and left to set hard, kitul becomes **jaggery**, an all-purpose Sri Lanka sweet or sweetener. Another characteristic dessert is **wattalappam**, an egg pudding of Malay origins which tastes faintly like crème caramel but with a sweeter and less slippery texture. **Kiribath** is a dessert of rice cakes cooked in milk and served with jaggery – it's also traditionally made for weddings, and is often the first solid food fed to babies. A South Indian dessert you might come across is **faluda**, a colourful cocktail of milk, syrup, jelly, ice cream and ice served in a tall glass like an Indian knickerbocker glory. **Ice cream** is usually factory made and safe to eat; the most widely available brand is Elephant House.

Fruits

Sri Lanka has a bewildering variety of **fruits**, from the familiar to the less so, including several classic Southeast Asian fruits introduced from Indonesia by the Dutch. The months given in brackets below refer to the periods when each is in season (where no months are specified, the fruit is available year-round). Familiar fruits include pineapple, mangoes (April–June & Nov–Dec), avocados (April–June) and coconuts, as well as a wide variety of **bananas**, from small sweet yellow specimens to enormous red giants. **Papaya** (pawpaw), a distinctively sweet and pulpy fruit, crops up regularly in fruit salads, but the king of Sri Lankan fruits is undoubtedly the **jackfruit** (April–June & Sept–Oct), the world's largest – a huge, elongated dark-green monster, rather like an enormous marrow in shape, whose fibrous flesh can either be eaten raw or cooked in curries. **Durian** (July–Sept) is another outsized specimen, a large green beast with a spiky outer shell. It's very much an acquired taste: though the flesh smells rather like blocked drains, it's widely considered a great delicacy and has a bit of a reputation as an aphrodisiac. The strangest-looking fruit, however, is the **rambutan** (July–Sept), a delicious, lychee-like fruit enclosed in a bright-red skin covered in tentacles. Another prized Sri Lankan delicacy is the **mangosteen** (July–Sept), which looks a little like a purple tomato, with a rather hard shell-like skin that softens as the fruit ripens. The delicate and delicious flesh tastes a bit like a grape with a slight citrus tang. Equally distinctive is the **wood apple**, a round, apple-sized fruit covered in an indestructible greyish bark, inside which is a red pulpy flesh, rather bitter-tasting and full of seeds. It's sometimes served with honey poured over it. You might also come across **custard apples**, greenish, apple-sized fruits with knobbly exteriors (they look a bit like artichokes) and smooth, sweet white flesh; and **guavas**, smooth, round yellow-green fruits, usually smaller than an apple and with slightly sour-tasting flesh around a central core of seeds. Other exotic fruits you might encounter include soursop, lovi-lovi, sapodilla, rose apple, and beli fruit (not to be confused with nelli fruit, a kind of Sri Lankan gooseberry). Finally, look out for the tiny **gulsambilla** (Aug–Oct), Sri Lanka's strangest fruit – like a large, furry green seed` enclosing a tiny, tartly flavoured kernel.

Drink

It's best to avoid tap water in Sri Lanka (see page 42). **Bottled water** is available everywhere, sourced from various places in the hill country and retailed under a baffling range of names. Check that the seal hasn't been broken.

Soft drinks

International brands of **soft drinks** – Pepsi, Coca-Cola, Sprite – are widely available and cheap, but it's much more fun (and better for the Sri Lankan economy) to explore the glorious range of outlandish soft drinks produced locally by Olé, Lion and Elephant. These include old-fashioned favourites like cream soda and ginger beer, and unique local brands like Portello (which tastes a bit like Vimto) and the ultra-sweet, lollipop-flavoured Necta. **Ginger beer** is particularly common, and very refreshing – the Elephant brand uses natural ginger, which is meant to be good for the stomach and digestion.

Coconut water (*thambili*) is widely available, with streetside vendors standing ready with a machete to lop the head off a fresh coconut at your command. The slightly sour-tasting liquid isn't to everyone's taste, although it's guaranteed safe, having been locked up in the heart of the coconut and is also claimed to be an excellent hangover cure thanks to its mix of glucose and potassium – which also makes it good to drink if you're suffering from diarrhoea.

Tea and coffee

Despite the fame of Sri Lanka's **tea**, most of the stuff served up is usually fairly bland – and you won't find the marvellous masala teas of India. British-style tea with milk is often called "milk tea" (ask for milk and sugar separately if you want to add your own or you might end up with a cupful of super-sweet bilge). "Bed tea" is just ordinary tea brought to your room first thing in the morning. For more on the island's tea, see Contexts (page 445).

Coffee has always taken a backseat to tea in Sri Lanka – at least since the island's original coffee plantations were wiped out during the 1870s (see page 445). Nescafé is sometimes available, although most is made from locally raised and roasted beans grown in people's back gardens or allotments – which accounts for the distinctive taste of most island coffee, with its thin, rather bitter taste and faint aroma of pond water (not to mention the big layer of silt found at the bottom of every cup). Things are slowly changing. Proper barista-style espresso, latte and cappuccino is increasingly available, while international-quality roasts and blends are now being produced by the trailblazing **Hansa Coffee company** (W srilank-acoffee.com), the first premium coffee to come out of the island for 150 years. Based in Nuwara Eliya, Hansa's *arabica* and *robusta* blends are now served in increasing numbers of places around the island.

Alcoholic drinks

Sri Lanka has a strong drinking culture – beer was introduced by foreign captives during the Kandyan period, and the islanders have never looked back. The island's two staple forms of alcohol are lager and arrack. **Lager** is usually sold in large (625ml) bottles, or sometimes in smaller cans; draught beer is still relatively uncommon. The staple national tipple is the ubiquitous Lion Lager, an uninspiring if perfectly drinkable brew which now has a virtual islandwide monopoly. Carlsberg (brewed under licence in Sri Lanka by the Lion Brewery) can also be found in some places, while in the hill country (particularly Kandy) you might come across the locally brewed beer Anchor – soft, creamy and a bit bland. Lion also brews a very dense stout, Lion Stout, which is virtually a meal in itself, as well as Lion Strong (eight percent ABV), beloved by local alcoholics. As you'd expect, lager is relatively expensive in Sri Lankan terms, ranging from around Rs.180 in a liquor shop to Rs.400–500 or more in most bars and restaurants. Imported beers, on the rare occasions you can find them, come with a hefty mark-up.

Two more distinctively local types of booze come from the versatile coconut. **Toddy**, tapped from the flower of the coconut, is non-alcoholic when fresh but ferments into a beverage faintly reminiscent of cider – it's sold informally in villages around the country, though unless you're travelling with a Sinhala-speaker it's difficult to track down. When fermented and refined, toddy produces **arrack** (33 percent proof), Sri Lanka's national beverage for the strong-livered. Arrack is either drunk neat, mixed with Coke or lemonade or used in tourist-oriented bars and restaurants as a base for cocktails. It's available in various grades and is usually a darkish brown, though there are also clear brands like White Diamond and White Label; the smoother, double-distilled arrack tastes faintly like rum. Imported **spirits** are widely available, but are predictably expensive. There are also locally produced versions of most spirits, including rather rough whisky, brandy, rum and vodka, as well as various brands of quite palatable lemon gin.

Where to drink

Most **restaurants** and some **guesthouses** serve alcohol (if only beer), although there are numerous places that don't, and in some towns (such as Jaffna and Trinco) finding a drink can be hard work. You won't find any alcohol in local cafes, either. There are a few decent **bars** (and the occasional English-style **pub**) in Colombo, Negombo, Unawatuna and a few tourist resorts, but most local bars are gloomy and rather seedy places, and very much a male preserve. Alcohol is available only from the rather disreputable-looking **liquor shops** which can be found in just about every town in the island – usually a small kiosk, piled high with bottles of beer and arrack and protected by stout security bars. Archaic Sri Lankan laws officially prohibit **women** from buying alcohol – foreign women don't usually encounter any problems, although it's worth being aware of, particularly if you're of South Asian descent and might be mistaken for a local. In addition, you're technically not allowed to buy alcohol on full-moon (poya) days and some other public holidays, including National Day, while the sale of alcohol is also often banned during major election periods – although tourist hotels often discreetly serve foreign visitors.

Health

Sri Lanka is less challenging from a health point of view than many other tropical countries: standards of hygiene are reasonable, medical care is of a decent standard and even malaria has now been completely eliminated. Nevertheless, the island does play host to the usual gamut of tropical diseases, and it's important to make sure you protect yourself against serious illness.

You should start **planning** the health aspect of your trip well in advance of departure, especially if you're having vaccines for things like rabies or Japanese encephalitis, which need to be administered over the course of a month. It's also crucial to have adequate medical insurance (see page 58). Ensure that you're up to date with the following standard **vaccinations**: diptheria, tetanus and hepatitis A. Other jabs you might consider are tuberculosis, meningitis and typhoid.

The best way to avoid falling ill is to look after yourself. Eat properly, make sure you get enough sleep and don't try to cram too much strenuous activity into your holiday, especially in the first few days before you've acclimatized to the sun, water and food, and while you're probably still suffering jetlag. Luckily, standards of medical care in Sri Lanka are good. Most **doctors** speak English and a significant number have trained in Europe, North America or Australia. All large towns have a hospital, and you'll also find **private medical clinics** in Colombo. If you pay for treatment, remember to get receipts so that you can claim on your insurance policy. All larger towns have well-appointed **pharmacies** (signed by a red cross on a white circle) and can usually produce an English-speaking pharmacist. If you're stuck, any reputable hotel or guesthouse should be able to put you in touch with a local English-speaking doctor.

There is more on **Ayurveda**, Sri Lanka's remarkable home-grown system of holistic medical care, in our Beruwala account (see page 116).

Water and food

Avoid drinking **tap water** in Sri Lanka. Although it's generally chlorinated and safe to drink, the unfamiliar micro-organisms it contains (compared with what you're used to at home) can easily precipitate a stomach upset. Also avoid ice, unless you're sure that it's been made with boiled or purified water. Mineral water is widely available, although always check that the seal hasn't been broken – it's not unknown for bottles to be refilled with tap water. Whatever precautions you take, however, you're still likely to come into contact with local water at various points – your eating

tensils will be washed in it, and it will probably
e used without your knowledge in things like
uit juices – so it's not worth getting paranoid
bout.

Though Sri Lankan standards of **food hygiene**
re reasonable, it still pays to be careful, and the
'd travellers' adage usually applies: if you can't
ook, boil or peel something, don't eat it (although
you can't peel something, you can always wash
thoroughly in purified water). Avoid salads
nd anything which looks like it has been sitting
ncovered for a while; short eats (see page 40)
re particularly likely to be old and to have been
oked by many fingers. The busier the establish-
ent, the less probability that the food's been
tting around all day. Obviously you'll need to
se your discretion: the buffet at a five-star hotel
as more chance of being OK than a local café's
ureen of curry, which has been keeping the flies
t since dawn. Finally, remember that refrigerators
op working during power cuts (although these
re now increasingly rare), so unless you're eating
t a place with its own generator, avoid any food,
ncluding meat and ice cream, that might have
een unfrozen and then refrozen.

Diarrhoea, dysentery and giardiasis

iarrhoea remains the most common complaint
mong tourists visiting Sri Lanka. It can have many
auses, including serious diseases like typhoid or
holera, but in the vast majority of cases diarrhoea is
result of contaminated food or drink and will pass
aturally in a few days. Such diarrhoea is also often
ccompanied by cramps, nausea and vomiting, and
ever in more severe cases. You should seek medical
dvice if it continues for more than five days or if
here is blood mixed up in the faeces, in which case
ou could be suffering from giardiasis or amoebic
ysentery. With **giardiasis** you may suffer stomach
ramps, nausea and a bloated stomach. In **amoebic
ysentery**, diarrhoea is severe, with bloody stools
nd fever. If any of the above symptoms apply, see
doctor.

Treatment

ne of the biggest problems with diarrhoea is
ehydration; it's vital you keep topped up with
uids – aim for about four litres every 24 hours.
you're having more than five bouts of diarrhoea
day or are unable to eat, take **oral rehydration
alts** to replace lost salt and minerals. These can be
ought ready-prepared in sachets from pharmacies

and camping shops; alternatively, you can make
your own by mixing eight teaspoons of sugar and
half a teaspoon of salt in a litre of purified water.
Coconut water is a good alternative, especially if
you add a pinch of salt; flat cola or lemonade with
a pinch of salt also work. **Children** with diarrhoea
dehydrate much more quickly than adults, and it's
even more vital to keep them hydrated. If you have
to go on a long journey where you won't have
access to a toilet, you can temporarily bung yourself
up with a blocking drug like lomotil or loperamide,
though these simply suppress symptoms and have
no curative value. While recovering, stick to bland
foods (rice and yoghurt are traditionally recommended, and bananas help replace lost potassium)
and get plenty of rest – this is not the moment to go
rushing up Adam's Peak.

Malaria and dengue fever

Sri Lanka was officially declared **free of malaria** by
the WHO in 2016 after over three years without a
single incidence of the disease being reported – a
remarkable achievement. There's no guarantee, of
course, that the disease won't reappear, although
your doctor is unlikely to recommend you take
anti-malarials at present.

The mosquito-borne disease **dengue fever**, by
contrast, remains a genuine concern. Dengue is
particularly common in Colombo and along the
west coast, with regular outbreaks following the
southwest monsoon in October/November (one
particular violent epidemic in the first half of 2017
saw 80,000 cases reported, with 215 deaths). There
are four subtypes of dengue fever, so unfortunately
it's possible to catch it more than once. The disease
is typically characterized by the sudden onset of
high fever accompanied by chills, headache, a skin
rash and muscle or joint pains (usually affecting the
limbs and back, hence dengue fever's nickname
"break-bone fever"). The fever usually lasts three
to seven days, while post-viral weakness, lethargy
and sometimes depression can persist for anything
up to several weeks. A rare but potentially fatal
complication is **dengue haemorrhagic fever**
(DHF), which is almost entirely confined to children
under fifteen who have previously been infected
with dengue fever.

There is no **vaccine** for dengue fever, which
makes avoiding getting bitten in the first place all
the more important, although unfortunately the
mosquitoes that transmit dengue bite during the
day, making them harder to guard against than
malarial mosquitoes.

Japanese encephalitis

A third mosquito-borne disease is **Japanese encephalitis** (JE), a virus transmitted by mosquitoes which bite at night. It's particularly associated with **rural areas**, as the virus lives in wading birds, pigs and flooded rice fields. JE is most prevalent following periods of heavy rainfall resulting in large areas of stagnant water.

JE is an extremely dangerous disease, with mortality rates of up to forty percent (though tourists are only rarely affected). As with dengue fever, you won't contract JE if you don't get bitten. **Symptoms** include drowsiness, sensitivity to light and confusion. An effective vaccine exists for JE (three shots administered over 28 days), though the standard advice is that it's only worth considering if you're travelling in high-risk areas during the monsoon for a period of over a month, and especially if you'll be spending a lot of time in the country and/or camping out a lot.

Sun

The potential health risks associated with the **sun** are easily underestimated – especially since a desire to soak up the rays is often a major reason to come to Sri Lanka in the first place. Always apply sunscreen and protect your eyes with proper sunglasses. If you do get sunburnt, take plenty of warm (not cold) showers, apply calamine lotion or aloe vera gel, and drink lots of water.

A common but minor irritant is **prickly heat**, usually afflicting newly arrived visitors. It's caused by excessive perspiration trapped under the skin, producing an itchy rash. Keep cool (a/c is good), shower frequently, use talcum powder on the affected skin and wear loose (ideally cotton) clothing. At its worst, prolonged exposure to the sun and dehydration can lead to **heatstroke**, a serious and potentially life-threatening condition. Symptoms are a lack of sweat, high temperature, severe headaches, lack of coordination and confusion. If untreated, heatstroke can lead to potentially fatal convulsions and delirium. If you're suffering from heatstroke, get out of the sun, get into a tepid shower and drink plenty of water.

Hepatitis

Hepatitis is an inflammation of the liver. The disease exists in various forms, though with a shared range of symptoms, typically jaundiced skin, yellowing of the whites of the eyes and a general range of flu-like symptoms. **Hepatitis A** and **hepatitis E** are spread by contaminated food and water. If you become infected, there's little you can do except rest unfortunately, it can take a couple of weeks or more to shake off the effects. The much more serious **hepatitis B** can result in long-term liver damage and liver cancer. Like the HIV virus, it's spread via infected blood or body fluids, most commonly through sex or needle sharing. **Hepatitis C and D** are similar.

You can (and should) be **vaccinated** against hepatitis A. The hepatitis B vaccine is usually only recommended to those at especially high risk, such as healthcare workers.

Rabies

Rabies, an **animal disease** transmitted to humans by bites, scratches or licking is usually associated with dogs, but can also be transmitted by cats, monkeys, bats or any other warm-blooded animal. Once symptoms have developed the disease fatal. You are at risk if you suffer a bite that draws blood or breaks the skin, or if you are licked by an infected animal on an open wound. Bites to the face, neck and fingertips are particularly dangerous.

Fortunately, a safe and effective **vaccine** exists (three shots over 28 days), usually only recommended in Sri Lanka for long-stay visitors or those likely to be in close contact with animals. Regardless of whether you've been vaccinated or not, if you're bitten or scratched (or licked on an open wound) by an animal, clean the wound thoroughly with disinfectant as soon as possible. Iodine is ideal, but alcohol or even soap and water are better than nothing. If you've already been vaccinated, you need two booster shots three days apart. If you haven't been vaccinated, you will need to take a course of injections over the following 28 days.

Other diseases and health risks

Typhoid is a gut infection caused by contaminated water or food, and which leads to a high fever and diarrhoea. Oral and injected vaccines are available and usually recommended. A vaccination against **meningitis** is also available. This cerebral virus transmitted by airborne bacteria, can be fatal. Symptoms include a severe headache, fever, a stiff neck and a stomach rash. If you think you have it, seek medical attention immediately. Sri Lanka has experienced occasional outbreaks of **cholera** although this typically occurs in epidemics in areas of poor sanitation, and almost never affects tourists.

Initial symptoms of **tetanus** ("lockjaw") can be discomfort in swallowing and stiffness in the jaw and neck, followed by convulsions – potentially fatal. Vaccinations are typically given to children in developed countries, although "booster" vaccinations are sometime recommended for travellers to Asia. **Typhus** is spread by the bites of ticks, lice and mites. Symptoms include fever, headache and muscle pains, followed after a few days by a rash, while the bite itself often develops into a painful sore. A shot of antibiotics will shift it.

Sri Lanka has relatively few reported **HIV** and **AIDS** cases, although the obvious warnings and precautions apply.

Animals and insects

Leeches are common after rain in Sinharaja, Adam's Peak and elsewhere in the hills. They're difficult to avoid, attaching themselves to your shoes and climbing up your leg until they find flesh, and are quite capable of burrowing through a pair of socks. Once latched on, leeches will suck your blood until sated, after which they drop off of their own accord – painless but unpleasant. You can make leeches drop off harmlessly with the end of a lighted cigarette or the flame from a lighter, or by putting salt on them. Don't pull them off, however, or bits of leech might break off and become embedded in your flesh, increasing the e (or kill it) risk of the bite becoming infected.

Sri Lanka boasts five species of **poisonous snake**, all relatively common – avoid wandering through heavy undergrowth in bare feet and flip-flops. Any form of bite should be treated as quickly as possible. If bitten, you should ideally lie down in a safe place while medical help is summoned, remaining as still as possible to slow the spread of venon and removing any shoes/jewellery/watches near the bite (but do not apply a tourniquet). Try to note the appearance of the snake if at all possible in order to identify it so that the correct anti-venom can be administered.

MEDICAL RESOURCES

Canadian Society for International Health ☎ 613 241 9885, ⓦ csih.org. Extensive list of travel health centres.

CDC ☎ 1800 232 4636, ⓦ cdc.gov/travel. Official US government travel health site.

Hospital for Tropical Diseases Travel Clinic UK ⓦ www.thehtd.org/travelclinic.aspx.

International Society for Travel Medicine US ☎ 1404 373 8282, ⓦ istm.org. Has a full list of travel health clinics.

MASTA (Medical Advisory Service for Travellers Abroad) UK ⓦ masta-travel-health.com.

Tropical Medical Bureau Ireland ☎ 01 271 5200, ⓦ tmb.ie.

The Travel Doctor – TMVC ⓦ traveldoctor.com.au. Lists travel clinics in Australia, New Zealand and South Africa.

The media

Sri Lanka has an extensive English-language media, including a multitude of newspapers and radio stations. Numerous journalists were threatened, abducted or even murdered throughout the Rajapakse era, and although the situation has eased under president Maithripala Sirisena, government control of sections of the media remains an ongoing fact of island life.

Newspapers, magazines

Sri Lanka's **English-language newspapers** include three dailies – The Island (ⓦ island.lk), the Daily Mirror (ⓦ dailymirror.lk) and the Daily News (ⓦ dailynews.lk) – and three Sunday papers, the Sunday Observer (ⓦ sundayobserver.lk), the Sunday Times (ⓦ sundaytimes.lk) and the Sunday Leader (ⓦ thesundayleader.lk). The last of these was particularly known for its outspoken criticism of the Rajapakse government, which led to the killing of its editor Lasantha Wickramatunga in 2009, and it remains the most outspoken and interesting of all the island's papers. The Daily News and Sunday Observer, by contrast, are both owned by the government and tend to toe the party line of whoever is currently in power.

There are also several good, independent **online** resources for Sri Lankan news. The Colombo Telegraph (ⓦ colombotelegraph.com), run by a group of expatriate journalists, and the "citizens journalism" website ⓦ groundviews.org are both particularly good, while ⓦ theacademic.org has comprehensive links to Sri Lanka-related news stories across the web.

There are also a fair number of English-language **magazines** available. The long-running Explore Sri Lanka has decent, tourist-oriented articles about all aspects of the island, while the business-focused Lanka Monthly Digest (ⓦ lmd.lk) also sometimes runs interesting general features on the island. Hi!! magazine (ⓦ hi.lk) – Sri Lanka's answer to Hello! – is essential reading for anyone seeking an insight into the Colombo cocktail-party circuit.

Radio

There are a surprising number of **English-language radio stations** in Sri Lanka, although reception can be hit and miss outside Colombo. Most stations churn out a predictable diet of mainstream Western pop, sometimes presented by hilariously cheesy DJs. The main broadcasters include TNL Rocks (99.2 and 101.8 FM; Ⓦtnlrocks.com), Sun FM (98.7 FM; Ⓦsunfm.lk), Yes FM (100.8 FM; Ⓦyesfmonline.com), Lite FM (87.6 FM; Ⓦlite87.com), E FM (88.3 FM; Ⓦfacebook.com/efm.lk), and Gold FM (93.0 FM; Ⓦgoldfm.lk), which dishes up retro-pop and easy listening. One **Sinhala-language station** that you might end up hearing a lot of (especially if you're travelling around by bus) is Shree FM (100.0 FM; Ⓦfacebook.com/shreefmlk), beloved of bus drivers all over the island and offering a toe-curling diet of Sinhala pop interspersed by terrible adverts. For a more interesting selection of local music, try Sirasa FM (106.5 FM; Ⓦsirasa.com.

Television

You're not likely to spend much time watching **Sri Lankan television**. There are three state-run channels – Channel Eye (English), Rupavahini (Sinhala) and Nethra (Tamil), plus various local satellite TV channels which offer a small selection of English-language programming – though this is a fairly deadly mixture of shopping programmes, children's shows, pop music, soaps and the occasional duff film. Rooms in most top-end (and some mid-range) hotels have **satellite TV**, usually offering international news programmes from the BBC and/or CNN along with various channels from the India-based Star TV, including movies and sports.

Festivals and public holidays

It's sometimes claimed that Sri Lanka has more festivals than any other country in the world, and with four major religions on the island and no fewer than 25 public holidays, things can seem to grind to a halt with disconcerting frequency.

Virtually all the festivals are religious in nature and follow the **lunar calendar**, with every full moon signalling the start of a new month (an extra month is added every two or three years to keep the solar and lunar calendars in alignment). As a result, most festival **dates** vary somewhat from year t year, apart from a couple (such as Thai Pongol ar Sinhalese New Year). Muslim festivals also follow lunar calendar but without the corrective month which are inserted into the Buddhist lunar calenda meaning that the dates of these festivals gradual move backwards at the rate of about eleven day per year, completing one annual cycle roughly eve 32 years.

Buddhist festivals revolve around the days of th full moon – or **poya days** – which are official publ holidays and have special religious significance (th Buddha urged his disciples to undertake specif spiritual practices on each poya day, and accordir to traditional belief he himself was born, attaine enlightenment and died on the poya day in th lunar month of Vesak). On poya days, Sri Lanka Buddhists traditionally make offerings at their loc temple and perform other religious observance while the less pious mark the occasion with rioto behaviour and widespread drunkenness. There a usually twelve poya days each year, but due to th lack of synchronicity between lunar and Gregoria calendars some years have thirteen, with th thirteenth being known as an *adhi* ("extra") poy and named after the normal poya day before whic it falls (2018, for instance, had an Adhi Poson fall th May, while 2015 had an Adhi Esala).

The island's most important Buddhist festivals a traditionally celebrated with enormous **perahera** or parades, with scores of fabulously accoutre elephants accompanied by drummers and dance People often travel on poya days, so transpc and accommodation tend to be busy; there's als (in theory) a ban on the sale of alcohol, althoug tourist hotels and guesthouses will sometim serve you. The sale of alcohol is also forbidden ov Sinhalese/Tamil New Year and during some oth festivals (including Vesak and National Day), wi many shops closing for a number of days durir these periods.

Sri Lanka's main **Hindu festivals** rival the island Buddhist celebrations in colour – in addition the ones listed below, there are numerous oth local temple festivals, particularly in the north. S Lanka's **Muslim festivals** are more modest affai generally involving only the Muslim communi itself, with special prayers at the mosque. Th three main celebrations (all of which are publ holidays) are Milad un-Nabi (20 Nov, 2018; 10 Nc 2019; 29 Oct 2020; 19 Oct, 2021), celebrating th Prophet's birthday; Id ul-Fitr (June 5, 2019; 24 Ma 2020; 13 May, 2012), marking the end of Ramada and Id ul-Allah (12 Aug, 2019; 31 July, 2020;

July, 2021), marking the beginning of pilgrimages to Mecca.

A festival calendar

Public holidays in the list below are marked "(P)".

JANUARY

Duruthu Poya (P) Marks the first of the Buddha's three legendary visits to Sri Lanka, and celebrated with a spectacular perahera (parade) at the Raja Maha Vihara in the Colombo suburb of Kelaniya. The Duruthu Poya also marks the beginning of the three-month pilgrimage season to Adam's Peak.

Thai Pongol (Jan 14/15) (P) Hindu festival honouring the sun god Surya, Indra (the bringer of rains) and the cow (in no particular order). It's marked by ceremonies at Hindu temples, after which the first grains of the new paddy harvest are ceremonially cooked in milk in a special pot – the direction in which the liquid spills when it boils over is thought to indicate good or bad luck in the coming year.

Galle Literary Festival (late-Jan). Eminent local and international wordsmiths and culture vultures descend on Galle (see page 143).

FEBRUARY

Navam Poya (P) Commemorates the Buddha's announcement, at the age of 80, of his own impending death, celebrated with a major perahera at the Gangaramaya temple in Colombo. Although this dates only from 1979, it has become one of the island's biggest festivals, featuring a procession of some fifty elephants.

Independence Day (National Day) (Feb 4) (P) Celebrates Sri Lanka's independence on February 4, 1948, with parades, dances and games.

Maha Sivarathri (Feb/March) (P) Hindu festival dedicated to Shiva, during which devotees perform a one-day fast and an all-night vigil.

MARCH

Medin Poya (P) Marks the Buddha's first visit to his father's palace following his enlightenment.

Good Friday (March/April) (P) An Easter Passion play is performed on the island of Duwa, near Negombo.

APRIL

Bak Poya (P) Celebrates the Buddha's second visit to Sri Lanka.

Sinhalese and Tamil New Year (P) Coinciding with the start of the southwest monsoon and the end of the harvest season, the Buddhist and Hindu New Year is a family festival during which presents are exchanged and the traditional *kiribath* (rice cooked with milk and cut into diamond shapes) is prepared. Businesses close, rituals are performed, new clothes are worn and horoscopes are cast. April 13 is New Year's Eve; April 14 is New Year's Day.

MAY

Labour Day (May 1) (P) The traditional May Day bank holiday.

Vesak Poya (P) The most important of the Buddhist poyas, this is a threefold celebration commemorating the Buddha's birth, enlightenment and death, all of which are traditionally thought to have happened on the day of the Vesak Poya. In addition, the last of the Buddha's three alleged visits to Sri Lanka is claimed to have been on a Vesak Poya day. Lamps are lit in front of houses, and *pandals* (platforms decorated with scenes from the life of the Buddha) are erected throughout the country. Buses and cars are decorated with streamers, and free food (from rice and curry to Vesak sweetmeats) is distributed in roadside booths. Meanwhile, devout Buddhists visit temples, meditate and fast. The day after the Vesak Poya is also a public holiday. The sale of alcohol, meat and fish in public restaurants is prohibited for a six-day period around the poya day, though hotels and guesthouses may be able to circumvent this when serving their own guests. Vesak also marks the end of the Adam's Peak pilgrimage season.

JUNE

Poson Poya (P) Second only in importance to Vesak, Poson Poya commemorates the introduction of Buddhism to Sri Lanka by Mahinda (see page 339), marked by mass pilgrimages to Anuradhapura, while thousands of white-robed pilgrims climb to the summit of Mihintale.

JULY

Esala Poya (P) Celebrates the Buddha's first sermon and the arrival of the Tooth Relic in Sri Lanka. The lunar month of Esala is the season of festivals, most notably the great Esala Perahera in Kandy (see page 210), Sri Lanka's most extravagant festival. There are also festivals at Kataragama (see page 193), Dondra and Bellanwila (a southern Colombo suburb) and a big seven-day celebration at Unawatuna, during which thousands descend on the village and beach.

Kataragama Festival Festival at Kataragama during which Hindu devotees fire-walk and indulge in various forms of ritual self-mutilation, piercing their skin with hooks and weights, and driving skewers through their cheeks and tongues.

Vel (July/Aug) Colombo's most important Hindu festival, dedicated to Skanda/Kataragama and featuring two exuberant processions during which the god's chariot and *vel* (spear) are carried across the city from the Pettah to temples in Wellawatta and Bambalapitiya.

AUGUST

Nikini Poya (P) Marks the retreat of the Bhikkhus following the Buddha's death, commemorated by a period of fasting and of retreat for the monastic communities.

SEPTEMBER

Binara Poya (P) Commemorates the Buddha's journey to heaven to preach to his mother and other deities.

Dussehra (Sept/Oct) Also known as Durga Puja, this Hindu festival honours Durga and also commemorates the day of Rama's victory over Rawana.

OCTOBER

Vap Poya (P) Marks the Buddha's return to earth and the end of the Buddhist period of fasting.
Deepavali (late Oct/early Nov) (P) The Hindu Festival of Lights (equivalent to North India's Diwali), commemorating the return from exile of Rama, hero of the Ramayana (holy scripture), with the lighting of lamps in Tamil households (symbolic of the triumph of good over evil) and the wearing of new clothes.

NOVEMBER

Il Poya (P) Commemorates the Buddha's ordination of sixty disciples.

DECEMBER

Unduvap Poya (P) Celebrates the arrival of the bo tree sapling in Anuradhapura, brought by Ashoka's daughter, Sangamitta.
Christmas (25 Dec) (P)

Sport and outdoor activities

Sri Lanka's unspoiled environment and variety of landscapes offer all sorts of possibilities for outdoor and activity holidays. Water-based activities like diving and surfing are well covered, while there are plenty of other ways to get active, ranging from mountain biking and trekking to ballooning and yoga. As for spectator sports, if you're lucky enough to coincide with a match, a trip to watch Sri Lanka's cricket team in action is well worth the effort.

Cricket

Of all the legacies of the British colonial period, the game of **cricket** is probably held dearest by the average Sri Lankan. As in India and Pakistan, the game is undoubtedly king in the Sri Lankan sporting pantheon, with kids playing it on any patch of spare ground, improvising balls, bats and wickets out of rolled-up bits of cloth and discarded sticks.

Although the national team is a relative newcomer to international cricket – they were only accorded full Test status in 1982 – they've more than held their own since then. It's in the **one-day game**, however, that Sri Lanka has really taken the

world by storm, capped by their triumph in the 1996 World Cup, when their fearsomely talented batting line-up – led by elegant left-hander Aravinda da Silva and the explosive Sanath Jayasuriya – blasted their way to the title (a feat almost repeated by their successors at the 2007 and 2011 World Cups, where Sri Lanka ended runners-up). More recent success came with victory in the 2014 ICC World Twenty20 championship.

Modern Sri Lankan cricket has produced three of the game's unquestioned all-time greats. Arguably the world's most lethal spin bowler ever, **Muttiah Muralitharan** (or "Murali", as he's popularly known) retired in 2010 after capturing an astonishing 800 wickets in Test cricket, a record which is unlikely to be broken for many years, if ever. Only slightly less jaw-dropping have been the achievements of batsmen **Mahela Jayawardene** and **Kumar Sangakkara**, both of whom retired in from international cricket 2015. Jayawardene finished as the eighth highest-ever run-scorer in Test cricket, and the fourth-highest in ODI games, while Sangakkara ended his career at number five in the list of all-time Test match top scorers (at a staggering average of almost 60), and with only Indian great Sachin Tendulkar having garnered more ODI runs. More recently, in 2017, **Rangana Herath** became the most successful left-arm spinner in test-match history.

Watching a match

The island's principal Test-match **venues** are the Sinhalese Sports Club in Colombo (see page 81) Pallekele International Cricket Stadium in Kandy and the cricket ground in Galle. One-day and Twenty20 internationals are mainly held at Kandy, Galle, the Premadasa Stadium in Colombo, and the modern cricket stadiums in Dambulla and Hambantota Tickets for matches are available from the relevant venues. Note also that many of the tour operators we list (see page 27), Red Dot Tours in particular offer cricketing tours to Sri Lanka.

Surfing, kitesurfing and other watersports

Many of the waves that crash against the Sri Lankan coast have travelled all the way from Antarctica, and not surprisingly there are several excellent **surfing** spots. The outstanding destination is Arugam Bay on the east coast, the one place in Sri Lanka with an international reputation among surfheads. Other leading surf spots include the south coast village of Midigama, nearby Medawatta and Madiha (both on the edge of Matara), and Hikkaduwa. Boards are available to rent at all these places. Various places in Arugam Bay and Hikkaduwa arrange surfing trips around the coast. The surfing season runs from April to October at Arugam Bay, and from November to April at Hikkaduwa and at surf spots along the south coast.

North of Colombo, the Kalpitiya peninsula has emerged over the past few years as a major **kitesurfing** destination, with excellent wind conditions almost all year and a mix of sea and more sheltered lagoon kiting areas. Sri Lanka's **water-sports** capital is Bentota, whose lagoon provides the perfect venue for all sorts of activities, including jet-skiing, speedboating, waterskiing, inner-tubing, banana-boating and **windsurfing**, which is particularly good here. **Wakeboarding** is also beginning to take off – Hikkaduwa is the main centre. The island's premier **whitewater rafting** destination is Kitulgala, while some of the operators listed on page 27 can also arrange **kayaking** and **canoeing**.

Diving and snorkelling

Sri Lanka isn't usually thought of as one of Asia's premier **diving** destinations, and although you probably wouldn't come here specifically to dive, there are enough underwater attractions to make a few days' diving a worthwhile part of a visit – Ⓦ divesrilanka.com offers a handy overview of what's available. Sri Lanka is also a good and cheap place to learn to dive, with schools in Negombo, Bentota, Beruwala, Hikkaduwa, Unawatuna, Weligama, Uppuveli, Nilaveli, Batticaloa and Trincomalee – see the relevant Guide accounts for details. Diving **packages** and **courses** are good value compared to most other places in the world. A three-day Open-Water PADI course goes for around $400–4560, and two-tank dives for around $70–90, depending on the location of the dive.

The **west coast** has a well-developed network of schools and dive sites. Marine life is plentiful, while there are also some fine (and often technically challenging) underwater cave and rock complexes, and a string of wrecks. Diving on the **east coast** is also increasingly popular following the opening up of new sites and some superb wrecks, including that of the *Hermes*, near Batticaloa, a 270m-long aircraft carrier sunk during World War II and lying at a depth of 60m.

The diving **season** on the west coast runs roughly from November to April, and on the east coast from May to October; many operators have offices on both coasts, shuttling between them on a seasonal basis.

There's not a lot of really good **snorkelling** around Sri Lanka: little coral survives close to the shore, although this lack is compensated by the abundant shoals of tropical fish that frequent the coast. The island's better snorkelling spots include the beaches at Polhena (near Matara), Pigeon Island (off Trincomalee) and Uppuveli and, if you don't mind the boats whizzing around your ears, the Coral Sanctuary at Hikkaduwa.

Trekking

Sri Lanka's huge **trekking** potential remains largely unexploited. The hill country, in particular, offers the perfect hiking terrain – spectacular scenery, marvellous views and a pleasantly temperate climate. A few of the tour operators we've listed (see page 27) offer **walking tours**. Alternatively, there are good **local guides**, including Sumane Bandara Illangantilake and Ravi Desappriya in Kandy (see page 224) and a several others in Nuwara Eliya (see page 245). For jungle trekking the rainforest of Sinharaja is the place to go, while shorter guided walks are often organized from eco-lodges and eco-oriented hotels, some of which have resident guides to lead guests.

Cycling

So long as you avoid the hazardous main highways, **cycling** around Sri Lanka can be a real pleasure –the island's modest dimensions and scenic diversity make it great for touring, especially the hill country, with its cooler climate, relative lack of traffic and exhilarating switchback roads. The major caveat is **safety**: as a cyclist you are extremely vulnerable. Bus and truck drivers consider cyclists a waste of valuable tarmac, and as far as they're concerned you don't really have any right to be on the road at all: be prepared to get out of the way quickly.

Bikes are available for **hire** in most tourist towns (alternatively, just ask at your guesthouse – they'll probably have or know someone who has a spare bike knocking around). In some places it's also possible to hire good-quality mountain bikes. **Costs** vary wildly, but will rarely be more than a few dollars a day, often much less.

A number of the operators we've listed (see page 27) offer cycling or mountain-biking **tours**, usually including a mixture of on- and off-roading and with a backup vehicle in support. Other good options include Ride Lanka (Ⓦ ridelanka.com), and Action Lanka (Ⓦ actionlanka.com).

Yoga and meditation

Yoga isn't nearly as well established in Sri Lanka as it is in India, although some of the island's Ayurvedic centres offer classes as part of their treatment plans, and it's sometimes possible to enrol for them without taking an Ayurveda course. Otherwise, your options are pretty limited. Serious students of yoga might consider signing up for a stay at Ulpotha (W ulpotha.com), a wonderful rural retreat in the Cultural Triangle near Embogama (not far from the Sasseruwa and Aukana Buddhas) which attracts leading international yoga teachers; courses usually last two weeks and cost $2940 per person inclusive of accommodation, meals and tuition. Cheaper courses are also offered at *Villa de Zoysa*, in Boosa, near Galle (W yoga-srilanka.com) and at *Talalla Retreat* (see page 175) on the south coast, and at the Kandy Samadhi Centre (see page 226). **Meditation** courses are mainly concentrated around Kandy (see box, page 226).

Other activities

There are currently two **balloon** operators in Sri Lanka, Lanka Ballooning (W srilankaballoon.com) and Sun Rise Ballooning (W srilankaballooning.com), both offering daily flights (weather permitting) from Nov–April, taking off from the *Kandalama Hotel* near Dambulla and offering bird's-eye views of local forests and plains. Flights last about an hour and cost around $210 per person.

Horseriding day-trips (around $150) can be arranged through Premadasa Riding School (W premadasa.lk/recreation.htm) at various locations around the island, including Bentota, Tissa, Ella, Nuwara Eliya and Kandy. Mai Globe (W maiglobe-travels.com) also run thirteen-day horseriding tours.

Sri Lanka has three gorgeous **golf courses**, at Colombo (see page 95), near Kandy (see page 230) and in Nuwara Eliya (see page 248); a number of operators (see page 27) offer specialist golfing tours.

National parks, reserves and eco-tourism

Nature conservation has a long and illustrious history in Sri Lanka. The island's first wildlife reserve is said to have been established by King Devan-ampiya Tissa in the third century BC, while many of the national parks and reserves that make up today's well-developed network date back to colonial times and earlier.

Administered by the **Department of Wildlife Conservation** (W dwc.gov.lk), these protected areas cover almost fifteen percent of the island's land area and encompass a wide variety of terrains, from the high-altitude grasslands of Horton Plains National Park to the coastal wetlands of Bundala. Almost all harbour a rich selection of wildlife and birds, and several are also of outstanding scenic beauty.

Sri Lanka's 26 **national parks** include two marine parks at Hikkaduwa and Nilaveli (Pigeon Island). The most touristed are Yala, Uda Walawe, Horton Plains, Bundala, Minneriya and Kaudulla. A number of parks lie in areas that were affected by the civil war, and several were closed for long periods during the fighting, including Maduru Oya, Gal Oya, Wilpattu and Kumana (formerly Yala East), although all have now reopened.

There are numerous other protected areas dotted across the island that are run under government supervision. These are categorized variously as **nature reserves**, **strict nature reserves** (entry prohibited) and **sanctuaries**. In general these places possess important botanical significance but lack the wildlife found in the national parks, as at (to name just one example) the unique, World Heritage-listed Sinharaja Forest Reserve, Sri Lanka's largest pocket of undisturbed tropical rainforest.

Visiting national parks

All national parks keep the same **opening hours**: daily from 6.30am to 6.30pm. Other than in Horton Plains, where you're allowed to walk, you'll have to hire a jeep (or boat) to take you around. There are usually jeeps (plus drivers) for hire at park entrances, although it's generally easier to hire one at the place you're staying to take you to and from the park, as well as driving you around it. Count on around $25 for half a day's jeep (and driver) hire, or $45 for a full day.

All vehicles are allocated an obligatory "tracker", who rides with you and acts as a **guide**. Some are very good, but standards do vary considerably and unfortunately many trackers speak only rudimentary English. One way of insuring yourself against the chance of getting a dud tracker is to go with a good jeep **driver** – the best are expert wildlife trackers and spotters in their own right, and may also carry binoculars and wildlife identification books. Note at except at designated spots, you're supposed to stay in your vehicle at all times; in Yala, you're also obliged to keep the hood on your jeep up. Visitors re also banned from taking any disposable plastic r polythene bags or packaging into parks.

The basic **entrance charge** per person ranges om between $12 at the less popular parks up to 15 at Yala, Uda Walawe and Horton Plains (locals, by ontrast, pay entrance fees of as little as $0.25). This asic charge is significantly inflated by the various **dditional charges** which are levied, including a ervice charge" (Rs.1200/vehicle), which covers the ervices of your tracker, a "vehicle charge" (Rs.250/ ehicle); plus tax on everything at fifteen percent he exact entrance cost per person thus becomes ghtly cheaper the more people you share a ehicle with). Children aged 6–12 pay half price; nder-6s get in free. The bottom line is that, once ou've factored in the cost of transport as well, you're oking at something like **$70–90** for two people for half-day visit to a national park – it definitely pays get a group together to share transport, which arply reduces the per person costs.

It's also possible **to stay** in many national parks, ost of which are equipped with simple but dequate **bungalows** for visitors. You can book ese online at ⓦdwc.gov.lk, although the best es tend to get snapped up very quickly. The hefty arges levied on foreigners are a further disincen-ve: count on around $150/night for two people, lus you'll also have to pay two days' entrance fees lus transport costs, with a final bill roughly equiva-nt to what you'd pay in a five-star Colombo hotel.

Given all this, most people prefer to take the much ore enjoyable (and not hugely more expensive) ption of travelling with one of the growing number f companies running upmarket **tented safaris** in arks around the country. Mahoora (ⓦmahoora. is currently the biggest, running trips to most f the main national parks, as well as Sinharaja and e Knuckles. Other outfits include: Kulu Safaris ⓦkulusafaris.com) and Big Game Camps and odges (ⓦsrilankabiggamesafaris.com), both of hom operate in Yala, Uda Walawe and Wilpattu; eopard Safaris (ⓦleopardsafaris.com) and Leopard ails (ⓦleopardtrails.com), both of whom operate Yala and Wilpattu; and Aliya Safari (ⓦaliyasafari. om; Yala only).

co-tourism

i Lanka is one of the world's most biodiverse islands, nd **eco-tourism** is beginning to play an increasingly ajor role in the island's tourism industry. The island

has some splendid eco-lodges and eco-oriented hotels (see page 51); the best general eco-tourism tour operator is Jetwing Eco Holidays (☎011 238 1201, ⓦjetwingeco.com). For more on the island's wildlife, see Contexts (page 440).

Birdwatching is well established, and even if you've never previously looked at a feathered creature in your life, the island's outstanding range of colourful birdlife can prove surprisingly fasci-nating. A number of companies run specialist tours (see page 27), while bird-spotting usually forms a significant part of trips to the island's national parks – although you'll see unusual birds pretty much everywhere you go, even in the middle of Colombo.

Elephants can be seen in virtually every national park in the country as well as at the Pinnewala Elephant Orphanage, the nearby Millennium Elephant Foundation and Elephant Freedom Project, and at the Elephant Transit Home attached to Uda Walawe National Park. For **leopards**, the place to head for is Yala National Park (with Wilpattu another possibility), while **whale-watching** trips start from Mirissa, just down the coast, and from Uppuveli on the east coast. There's also superb **dolphin-watching** at Kalpitiya (plus the chance of seeing more whales). Sri Lanka is also an important nesting site for **sea turtles**; turtle watches are run nightly at the villages of Kosgoda and Rekawa.

Cultural values and etiquette

Sri Lanka is the most Westernized country in South Asia – superficially at least – and this, combined with the widespread use of English and the huge tourist industry, can often lure visitors into mistaking the island for something

---

FIVE TOP ECO-LODGES AND HOTELS

Gal Oya Lodge Gal Oya. See page 365
Jetwing Vil Uyana Sigiriya. See page 306
Kumbuk River Buttala. See page 373
Palagama Beach Kalpitiya. See page 109
Tree Tops Jungle Lodge Buttala. See page 373

more familiar than it actually is. **Scratch the surface, however, and examples of cultural difference can be found everywhere.**

Behaving yourself

They are all very rich, and for a thing that costs one shilling they willingly give five. Also they are never quiet, going here and there very quickly, and doing nothing. Very many are afraid of them, for suddenly they grow very angry, their faces become red, and they strike any one who is near with the closed hand.

From The Village in the Jungle, by Leonard Woolf

Sri Lankans place great emphasis on politeness and **manners**, as exemplified by the fabulously courteous staff at top-end hotels – raising your voice in a dispute is usually counterproductive and makes you look foolish and ill-bred. They are also very proud of their country – "Sri Lanka good?" is one of the questions most commonly asked of visitors – and tend to take a simple and unquestioning pride in their national achievements and (especially) their cricket team.

A few Western concepts have yet to make their way to the island. Nudity and toplessness are not permitted on any Sri Lankan beaches. And overt physical displays of affection in public are also frowned upon – Sri Lankan couples hide behind enormous umbrellas in the quiet corners of parks and botanical gardens.

You should eat and shake hands with people using your **right hand**. Men shouldn't offer to shake a Sri Lankan woman's hand unless she offers it herself. For advice on money and bargaining, see "Costs" (page 55).

Temple etiquette

All visitors to Buddhist and Hindu temples should be appropriately dressed. In **Buddhist temples** this means taking off shoes and headgear and covering your shoulders and legs. Beachwear is not appropriate and can cause offence. In large temples, the exact point at which you should take off shoes and hats is sometimes ambiguous; if in doubt, follow the locals. Finally, note that walking barefoot around temples can sometimes be more of a challenge than you might imagine when the tropical sun has heated the stone underfoot to oven-like temperatures – no one will mind if you keep your socks on.

You should never have yourself photographed (take a selfie) posing with a Buddha image – that with your back to the image – and, needless to sa you should always behave appropriately towar(such images. Three French tourists were give suspended jail sentences in 2012 for taking pictur of themselves kissing a Buddha statue in a temp Two other traditional Buddhist observances that a only loosely followed in Sri Lanka: the rule abo not pointing your feet at a Buddha image is n as widely followed as in, say, Thailand, though yo occasionally see people sitting in front of Buddh with their legs neatly tucked under them. Equal the traditional Buddhist rule that you should or walk around stupas in a clockwise direction is n widely observed.

The same shoe and dress rules apply in **Hindc temples**, with a couple of twists. In som non-Hindus aren't permitted to enter the inn(shrine; in others, men are required to take off th(shirts before entering, and women are sometim(barred entirely.

In some temples (Buddhist and Hindu) you w be shown around by one of the resident mon(or priests and expected to make a donation. other places, unofficial "guides" will sometim(materialize and insist on showing you round for a consideration. Try not to feel pressured in accepting the services of unofficial guides unle you want them.

Buddhism and blasphemy

Certain elements of the Sri Lanka population a becoming increasingly touchy about perceive **insults to Buddhism** and Buddhist iconograpI In 2014 British tourist Naomi Coleman (a practisin Buddhist, ironically) was detained on arrival an subsequently deported for sporting a Buddha tatt(on her arm, while another British visitor was deni(entry in 2013 for having a similar tattoo. If in dou cover up.

Be aware too that any use of a Buddha image what might be deemed an insulting context (ev(as a picture on a t-shirt, for example) may lead trouble, with incidents ranging from the arrest 2010 of two Muslim businessman for producir Buddha key-rings through to the riots whi(followed screenings of rapper Akon's "Sexy Chic video, featuring a raunchy pool party in which Buddha statue can be seen (but only if you look ve hard) in the background. Akon was subsequent denied entry to Sri Lanka, and a planned conce cancelled.

Shopping

Sri Lankan craftsmanship has a long and vibrant history, and a visit to any museum will turn up objects testifying to the skill of the island's earlier artisans, who have for centuries been producing exquisitely manufactured objects in a wide variety of media, ranging from lacework and ola-leaf manuscripts to carvings in ivory and wood and elaborate metalwork and batiks.

The quality of local craftsmanship declined following the mass influx of package tourists in the 1970s and 1980s, as local artisans began increasingly to churn out stereotypical cut-price crafts and souvenirs. Fortunately, standards have experienced something of a revival over recent years. You'll still find plenty of tourist tat – sloppily painted wooden elephants, cheesy *kolam* masks, ugly batiks and so on – but there's also a growing selection of more original and upmarket crafts available. These often show the influence of the island's leading contemporary **designers** such as batik artist Ena de Silva and Barbara Sansoni, founder of Barefoot (see page 94), whose vibrantly coloured textiles have become almost the trademark signature of modern Sri Lankan style. The superb **website** ⓦ craftrevival.org (follow the Sri Lanka link under the "InCH" tab) has copious information on all the island's traditional arts and crafts.

All larger shops have fixed, marked **prices**, though if you're making a major purchase or buying several items, a polite request for a "special price" or "small discount" might knock a few rupees off, especially for gems or jewellery. The smaller and more informal the outlet, the more scope for bargaining there's likely to be – if you're, say, buying a sarong from an itinerant hawker on the beach, you can haggle to your heart's content.

Finally, there are a couple of things you shouldn't buy. Remember that buying **coral** or **shells** (or any other marine product) contributes directly to the destruction of the island's fragile ocean environment; it's also illegal, and you're likely to end up paying a heavy fine if you try to take coral out of the country. Note that it's also illegal to export **antiques** (classified as anything over fifty years old) without a licence (see page 57).

Handicrafts

The most characteristic Sri Lankan souvenirs are brightly painted **masks**, originally designed to be worn during *kolam* dances or exorcism ceremonies (see page 127) and now found for sale wherever there are tourists. Masks vary in size from the tiny to the huge; most popular are those depicting the pop-eyed Gara Yaka or the bird demon Gurulu Raksha, though there are an increasing number of other designs available. Some masks are artificially but attractively aged to resemble antiques – a lot easier on the eye than the lurid colours in which many are painted. The centre of mask production is Ambalangoda, where there are a number of large shops selling a wide range of designs, some of heirloom quality.

Second in popularity are **elephant carvings**. These range from garish little wooden creatures painted in bright polka-dot patterns to the elegant stone carvings sold at places like Paradise Road in Colombo. **Batik**, an art introduced by the Dutch from Indonesia, is also widespread. Batik designs are often stereotypical (the Sigiriya Damsels and naff beach scenes are ubiquitous), though a few places such as Jayamali Batiks in Kandy (see page 228) produce more unusual and interesting work.

A number of other traditional crafts continue around the island with a little help from the tourist trade. **Metalwork** has long been produced in the Kandy area, and intricately embossed metal objects such as dishes, trays, candlesticks and other objects can be found in all the island's handicraft emporia, though they're rather fussy for most foreign tastes. **Leatherwork** can also be good, and you'll find a range of hats, bags, boots and footrests (the shops at Pinnewala Elephant Orphanage have a particularly good selection). **Lacquerware**, a speciality of the Matale area, can also sometimes be found, along with Kandyan-style **drums** and, occasionally, **carrom boards** (see page 54). **Wooden models** of tuktuks and other vehicles (most commonly found in Negombo) are another local speciality and make good souvenirs or children's toys, while you'll probably also see example of the ingenious local **puzzle boxes** – impossible to open until you've been shown how.

Religious items

Wood or stone **Buddha carvings** of varying standards are common. For something a bit more unusual, consider the brightly coloured **posters** or strip-pictures of Buddhist and Hindu deities which adorn tuktuks and buses across Sri Lanka and are sold by pavement hawkers and stationers' shops in larger towns and make a cheap and characterful souvenir. A visit to Kataragama or a trawl along St

Anthony's Mawatha in Colombo (see page 76) will uncover an entertaining assortment of other **religious kitsch**, from bleeding Catholic saints to illuminated Ganesh clocks.

Tea and spices

Most top-quality **Ceylon tea** is exported, but there's still plenty on sale that is likely to satisfy all but the most dedicated tea fancier. The best (and cheapest) place to buy tea is in a local supermarket; Cargills supermarkets islandwide usually have a good selection. The main local retailers are Dilmah (W dilmahtea.com) and Mlesna (W mlesnateas.com), whose teas can also be found in most supermarkets and who also run a number of dedicated tea shops in Colombo, Kandy and elsewhere, although these concentrate on more touristy offerings including boxed tea sets, flavoured teas and the like. For a real taste of Sri Lanka, look for unblended ("single estate") high-grown teas – for sale at source in tea factories (and sometimes in supermarkets and at specialist tea shops) and a far cry from the heavily mixed and homogenized teabags that pass muster in Europe and the US. You'll also find a wide range of flavoured teas made with a huge variety of ingredients, from standard offerings like lemon, orange, mint and vanilla to the more unusual banana, rum, kiwi fruit or pineapple.

Sri Lanka's **spice gardens**, mostly concentrated around Kandy and Matale, pull in loads of visitors on organized tours and sell packets of spices, often at outrageously inflated prices. You'll find identical stuff in local shops and supermarkets at a fraction of the price.

Gems and jewellery

Sri Lanka has been famous for its **precious stones** since antiquity, and gems and jewellery remain important to the national economy even today. This is nowhere more obvious than at the gem-mining centre of **Ratnapura**. All foreign visitors to the town will be offered stones to bu but unless you're an expert gemologist there's chance that you'll end up with an expensive piec of coloured glass. Ratnapura apart, you'll find **gem and jewellery shops** all over the island – th major concentrations are in Negombo, Galle an Colombo. These include large chains, such a Zam Gems (W zamgems.com) and Sifani (W sifan com), and smaller local outfits. If you are going t buy, it's worth doing some homework before yo arrive so you can compare prices with those bac home. You can get gems tested for authenticity i Colombo (see page 93).

For silver and, especially, **gold** jewellery, try Se Street in Colombo's Pettah district, which is line with shops. These see few tourists, so prices a reasonable, although the flouncy designs on offe aren't to everyone's taste.

Clothes

Sri Lanka is a bit of a disappointment when it come to **clothes**, and doesn't boast the gorgeous fabric and nimble-fingered tailors of, say, India and Thailan That said, the island is a major garment-manufac turing centre for overseas companies, and there a lots of good-quality Western-style clothes knockin around at bargain prices, as well as some good loc label. In Colombo, places to try include Odel (se page 94) and Cotton Collection (see page 94 Colourful but flimsy beachwear is flogged by shop and hawkers at all the major west-coast resorts – it cheap and cheerful, but don't expect it to last muc longer than your holiday. Most Sri Lankan wome now dress Western-style in skirts and blouse but you can still find a few shops in Colombo an elsewhere selling beautiful saris and *shalwar kamee* (pyjama suits).

CARROM

A kind of hybrid of pool, marbles and draughts (checkers), **carrom** is played throughout Sri Lanka. The game's origins are obscure: some say that it was invented by the maharajas of India, although many Indians claim that it was actually introduced by the British, while Burma, Egypt and Ethiopia are also touted as possible sources.

The game is played using a square wooden board with a pocket at each corner; the aim is to flick all your pieces (which are very similar to draughtsmen) into one of the pockets, using the heavier "striker" piece. Carrom can be played by either four or (more usually) two people. If you get hooked, you may consider a carrom board as an unusual, if bulky, souvenir.

Travelling with children

Sri Lankans love children, and travelling with kids more or less guarantees you a warm welcome wherever you go. Locals will always do whatever they can to help or entertain – there's certainly no need to worry about disapproving stares if your baby starts crying or your toddler starts monkeying around, even in quite posh establishments. Dedicated family-focused holidays can be arranged through some local and international tour operators such as Firefly (see page 27), who also rents out equipment for families travelling with young children.

All the same, travelling with **babies** may prove stressful. Powdered milk is fairly widely available, but disposable nappies and baby food are more difficult to find, while things like baby-sitting services, nursery day-care, changing facilities, high chairs and microwaves for sterilizing bottles are also the exception rather than the rule; car seats will also probably have to be brought from home. Breast-feeding in public, however discreet, is also not something that Sri Lankan women usually do, while prams are virtually useless, since there are few decent pavements to push them on. The heat, and the associated dangers of dehydration, are another concern, not to mention the risks of mosquito-borne diseases such as dengue fever.

Older children will get a lot out of a visit to the island. Sri Lanka's **beaches** are likely to provide the main attraction, with endless swathes of golden sand to muck around on and warm waters to splash about in – though you should always check local swimming conditions carefully and guard carefully against the very real possibility of sunburn and dehydration. Beaches apart, there are plenty of **wildlife** attractions. The Millennium Elephant Foundation (see page 206) offers the chance to interact with these majestic beasts, while the Elephant Orphanage at Pinnewala is another guaranteed child-pleaser. There are further elephant-spotting opportunities around Kandy, while a visit to any of the **national parks** is also likely to stimulate budding zoologists; Yala, where there's a good chance of sighting crocodiles, peacocks, flamingos and other wildlife, is a particularly good choice, as is Uda Walawe, where you'll find another elephant orphanage. **Activity sports**, such as banana-boating or kayaking at Bentota, may also

appeal, while the island's varied forms of **transport** – whether a tuktuk ride, a train trip through the hill country or a boat cruise along one of the island's rivers or lagoons – should also keep little ones entertained. Energetic kids with a head for heights might also enjoy the challenge of clambering up **Sigiriya** and its rickety iron staircases. And if you've exhausted all the preceding possibilities, you can always go **shopping**. There are plenty of fun handicrafts to be had, with gruesome masks, painted elephants and wooden toys aplenty – and if you're in Colombo, don't leave without bagging a cuddly colourful stuffed-toy animal from Barefoot (see page 94).

Costs

Rampant inflation and rising standards over recent years mean that Sri Lanka is no longer the bargain it once was, and the island now ranks as one of Asia's more expensive destinations, although it's still possible to travel on a backpacker-sized budget – just. Stay in cheap guesthouses, eat meals in local cafés and travel exclusively by public transport and you could probably get by on $20 (£13) per person per day, travelling as a couple or larger group. Check into one of the island's top hotels or villas, however, and then add in the cost of touring with your own car and driver, and two people could easily end up spending $400 (£550) a day, or more.

If you're **on a budget**, Sri Lanka can still be fairly inexpensive – you can travel by bus from one end of the island to the other for around $20, get a filling meal at local cafés for a couple of dollars, and find an OK double room for $15–20 per night. Taking a tour or renting a vehicle will obviously bump costs up considerably – a car and driver normally goes for around $55–70 (£35–45) a day. Entrance fees for archeological sites and national parks can also strain tight budgets – a day-ticket to Sigiriya, for example, currently costs $30, while the cost of visiting the country's national parks works out at somewhere around $70–90 per couple per day once you've factored in entrance fees and transport.

Note that some hotels and restaurants levy a ten percent **service charge**, while various **government taxes** also apply, although no two places seem to calculate them the same way: some places include all taxes in the quoted price (the so-called "nett" rate), others charge one or more taxes separately.

These taxes include VAT at fifteen percent, a two percent "Nation-Building Tax" and a one percent Tourist Development Tax. It's always worth checking beforehand what is and isn't included – the extra 25–28 percent added at, say, a top hotel can add a nasty twist to the bill if you're not expecting it.

Tourist prices

Another thing to bear in mind is that many places on the island apply official **tourist prices**. At all national parks and reserves, and at government-run archeological sites, the authorities operate a two-tier price system whereby foreigners pay a significantly higher entrance fee than locals, sometimes almost a hundred times more than Sri Lankan nationals. At the national parks, for example, locals pay an entrance fee of around 25 cents, while overseas visitors pay around $25 once various taxes and additional charges have been taken into account. A similar situation obtains at the sites of the Cultural Triangle – at Anuradhapura, for instance, foreigners pay $25, while locals pay nothing. This makes visiting many of Sri Lanka's biggest sights a pricier prospect than in other parts of the subcontinent, a fact of life that many visitors grumble about – although the most vociferous critics are local Sri Lankan hoteliers, drivers and others involved in the tourist trade, who have seen their businesses suffer as many visitors vote with their feet and stay on the beach.

Bargaining

As a tourist, you're likely to pay slightly over the odds for a range of things, from rickshaw rides to market groceries. It's worth remembering, however, that many prices in Sri Lanka are inherently fluid – there's often no such thing as a "correct price", only a "best price". Many hoteliers, for instance, chop and change their rates according to demand, while the price of anything from a tuktuk ride to an elephant carving might depend on anything from the time of day to the weather or the mood of the seller. Given this, it's always worth **bargaining**. The key to effective bargaining here (as throughout Asia) is to retain a sense of humour and proportion. There is nothing more ridiculous – or more damaging for local perceptions of foreign visitors – than the sight of a Western tourist arguing bitterly over the final few rupees of a budget room or a small item of shopping.

On the other hand, it's also important not to be outrageously **overcharged**. Visitors who lack a sense of local prices and pay whatever they're asked contribute to local inflation, pushing up prices both for other tourists and (more importantly) for locals.

Tipping

Tipping is a way of life in Sri Lanka – visitors will generally be expected to offer some kind of remuneration for most services, even on top of agreed fees, and the whole business of what to give and to whom can be a bit of a minefield. Many **hotels and restaurants** add a ten percent service charge to the bill, although it's worth bearing in mind that the staff who have served you won't necessarily see any of this money themselves. If a service charge hasn't been added, a tip won't necessarily be expected, although it is of course always appreciated. If you tour the island by car, your **driver** will expect a tip of around $5–10 per day, depending on his level of expertise, though you shouldn't feel obliged to give anything unless you're genuinely pleased with the service you've received (and if you're *not* happy, it's well worth explaining why). If touring a site with an official **guide**, you should always agree a fee in advance; additional tips should only be offered if you're particularly pleased with the service. When visiting **temples**, you'll probably be shown around by a resident monk or priest; it's polite to offer them something at the end of the tour – some will take this money themselves (despite the fact that Buddhist monks aren't meant to handle money); others will prefer you to place it directly in a donation box. Whatever happens, a dollar or two should suffice. Occasionally, unofficial "guides" will materialize to show you around temples – and will of course expect a tip for their troubles. Again, a dollar or two is almost certainly sufficient. Anyone else who assists you will probably welcome some kind of gratuity, though of course it's impossible to generalize and visitors will have to make (sometimes tricky) decisions about whether to offer money or not.

Travel essentials

Climate

Reflecting Sri Lanka's position close to the equator, average **temperatures** remain fairly constant year round. The main factors shaping local weather are altitude and the two **monsoons**. There is more on the island's climate in the Introduction (see page 10).

TRAVEL ADVISORIES

For current information on the security situation in Sri Lanka, check the sites listed below.

Australian Department of Foreign Affairs Ⓦ dfat.gov.au.
British Foreign & Commonwealth Office Ⓦ gov.uk/foreign-travel-advice.
Canadian Department of Foreign Affairs Ⓦ international.gc.ca.
Irish Department of Foreign Affairs Ⓦ dfa.ie.
New Zealand Ministry of Foreign Affairs Ⓦ mfat.govt.nz.
South African Department of Foreign Affairs Ⓦ www.dfa.gov.za.
US State Department Ⓦ state.gov.
South African Department of Foreign Affairs Ⓦ dirco.gov.za.

Crime and safety

Sri Lanka is a remarkably safe place to travel in, and violent crime against foreigners is virtually unheard of. **Petty theft** is less common than in many other parts of Asia (and rarer than in most European and American cities), though you should still take sensible care of your belongings. Pickpockets sometimes work in crowded areas, while thefts from hotel rooms are occasionally reported. Many hotels and guesthouses ask guests to deposit valuables in their safe, and it's sensible to do so when you can. **Muggings** are rare, though single travellers (especially women) should avoid dark beaches late at night – Negombo and Hikkaduwa have particularly bad reputations. In addition, make sure you keep a separate record of all your bank card details (along with the phone numbers needed in case of their loss) and passport information; it's worth taking a photocopy of the pages from your passport that contain your personal details.

If you do have anything stolen, you'll need to report it to the **police** – there's little chance that they will be able to recover it for you, but you'll need a report for your insurance claim. Given the fact that you might not find any English-speaking policemen on duty (even at so-called "tourist police" stations), you might try to get someone from your guesthouse to come along as an interpreter. The process of reporting a crime is usually a laborious affair, with much checking of papers and filling in of forms.

Sri Lanka used to be awash with **con artists** and **petty scams** of all sorts – particularly common around the lake in Kandy, in Galle Fort and, especially, in Colombo's Galle Face Green. Mercifully these lowlife have now largely disappeared – although it's still worth being on your guard if a plausible stranger approaches offering to ship you a parcel of free tea or to take you to a special "elephant festival" which has suddenly materialized somewhere in the neighbourhood.

Customs regulations

Entering Sri Lanka you are allowed to bring in 1.5 litres of spirits and two bottles of wine. You're not allowed to bring cartons of duty-free cigarettes into the country, although it's unlikely you'll be stopped at customs and searched. If you are caught "smuggling", your cartons will be confiscated and you'll be fined Rs.6000. There are no duty-free cigarettes on sale at the airport on arrival, either.

Leaving Sri Lanka you are permitted to export up to 10kg of tea duty-free. In theory, you're not allowed to take out more than Rs.250 in cash, though this is rarely checked. If you want to export **antiques** – defined as anything more than fifty years old – you will need authorization from the Archeological Department (Sir Marcus Fernando Mawatha, Cinnamon Gardens; ☏ 011 269 2840) depending on exactly what it is you want to export. The export of any coral, shells or other protected marine products is prohibited; taking out flora, fauna or animal parts is also forbidden.

Dangers

No **LTTE attacks** have been reported since the end of the civil war in 2009. **Landmines** and UXO (see page 376) pose a slight risk in remote areas of the north and east but are being steadily cleared. **Wildlife** doesn't normally pose a threat – although the death in 2017 of British journalist Paul McClean as a result of a crocodile attack in Arugam Bay was a tragic reminder of the potential risks posed by native fauna. An altogether more prosaic but much more serious source of danger in Sri Lanka is **traffic**. As a pedestrian you're at the very bottom of the food chain in the dog-eat-dog world of Sri Lankan road use – some bus drivers are particularly psychotic.

After road accidents, **drowning** is the second most common cause of accidental death among tourists in Sri Lanka. Currents can be strong and beaches may shelve off into deep waters with unexpected steepness – and there are no lifeguards to come and pull you out if you get into trouble. Always ask local advice before venturing into the water anywhere that is not obviously a recognized swimming spot. The only warning signs of dangerous swimming conditions are the red flags posted on the beaches outside major resort hotels. Sensible precautions include always keeping within your depth and making sure that someone on the shore knows that you're in the water. Never swim under the influence of alcohol – newspaper stories of locals washed out to sea after too many bottles of arrack are a regular occurrence.

Electricity

Sri Lanka's electricity runs at 230–240V, 50 cycles AC. Round three-pin **sockets** are the norm, though you'll also sometimes find square three-pin sockets, especially in more upmarket hotels; adaptors are cheap and widely available. Power cuts, once frequent, are now much less common, while most top-end places have their own generators.

Emergencies

For police assistance, call ☎118 or 119; for an ambulance ☎110. Note, however, that reliable emergency services are largely restricted to the major cities. If you have a medical emergency out in the countryside it may be better to try to get yourself to the nearest hospital (or find the nearest doctor) rather than waiting for an ambulance to arrive.

Insurance

It's essential to take out **insurance** before travelling to cover against theft, loss and illness or injury. A typical travel insurance policy usually provides cover for loss of baggage, tickets and – up to a certain limit – cash or cheques, as well as cancellation or early curtailment of your journey. Most of them exclude

so-called dangerous sports unless an extra premium is paid: in Sri Lanka this can mean scuba diving, whitewater rafting, kitesurfing and trekking. Many policies can be chopped and changed to exclude coverage you don't need – for example, sickness and accident benefits can often be excluded or included at will. When securing baggage cover, make sure that the per-article limit – typically under £500 – will cover your most valuable possession. If you need to make a claim, you should keep receipts for medicines and medical treatment, and in the event that you have anything stolen obtain an official statement from the police.

Internet

Virtually every guesthouse and hotel in the country has **wi-fi**, as do many restaurants and cafés, although connections are sometimes erratic. In addition, all Sri Lanka's telecom providers (see page 60) offer various **mobile broadband packages** covering almost the whole of the island. The rise of wi-fi and mobile services means that there are now very few **internet cafés** – details are given throughout the Guide, where they exist. Costs are usually between Rs.60 and Rs.120/hr.

Laundry

Most guesthouses and hotels offer a **laundry** service. Washing usually takes 24 hours and costs around Rs.75–100 for a shirt or blouse and Rs.100 or more for a pair of trousers or a light dress. There are no public coin-operated launderettes anywhere on the island.

LGBT+ travellers

There is little understanding of LGBT+ issues in Sri Lanka – LGBT+ people are generally stigmatized and homosexuality is technically **illegal** (although no one has been arrested since 1950), so discretion

---

ROUGH GUIDES TRAVEL INSURANCE

Rough Guides has teamed up with WorldNomads.com to offer great travel insurance deals. Policies are available to residents of over 150 countries, with cover for a wide range of adventure sports, 24hr emergency assistance, high levels of medical and evacuation cover and a stream of travel safety information. Roughguides.com users can take advantage of their policies online 24/7, from anywhere in the world – even if you're already travelling. And since plans often change when you're on the road, you can extend your policy and even claim online. Roughguides.com users who buy travel insurance with WorldNomads.com can also leave a positive footprint and donate to a community development project. For more information, go to ⓦ roughguides.com/travel-insurance.

is advised, and the whole scene remains rather secretive. The website Ⓦ equal-ground.org is a good first port of call for information, while Ⓦ utopia-asia.com/tipssri.htm has further links as well as listings of LGBT+-friendly accommodation and general travel information.

Mail

Postal services from Sri Lanka (Ⓦ slpost.gov.lk) are fairly reliable, at least if you stick to airmail, which takes three to four days to reach the UK and US. Surface mail is about half to one-third the cost of airmail but is horribly slow and offers lots of potential for things to get lost or damaged in transit. A postcard to the UK, Australasia or North America costs Rs.35, airmail letters from Rs.75–85. An airmail parcel to the UK costs around $17 for up to 0.5kg; rates to North America are similar and to Australia slightly cheaper. If you want to send a parcel home from Sri Lanka, you must take the contents unwrapped to the post office so that they can be inspected before wrapping (all larger post offices have counters selling glue, string and wrapping paper).

Another option is **EMS Speed** Post (Ⓦ slpost.gov.lk/services/ems), slightly faster (and more expensive) than airmail – a 0.5kg package to the UK costs around $20 (slightly more to North America, slightly less to Australia). Alternatively, a number of reputable international **couriers** have offices in Colombo (see page 95).

Maps

There are several good **maps** of Sri Lanka. The best and most detailed is the *Reise Know-How Sri Lanka Map* (1:500,000); it's also printed on indestructible waterproof paper so it won't disintegrate in the tropics and can even be used as an emergency monsoon shelter, at a pinch. If you need real detail, note that the entire island is covered by a series of 92 1:50,000 maps – detailed, but somewhat dated – available (only) from the **Survey Department** on Kirulla Rd, Havelock Town (Mon–Fri 10am–3.30pm); you'll need to show your passport to get in.

Money

The Sri Lankan **currency** is the rupee (abbreviated variously as R, R/ or R/-, and, as in this book, as Rs.). Coins come in denominations of Rs.1, 2, 5 and 10; notes come in denominations of Rs.20, 50, 100, 200, 500, 1000, 2000 and 5000. Try to avoid accepting particularly dirty, torn or disreputable-looking notes, and break big notes and stock up on change whenever you can – don't expect to be able to pay for a Rs.50 cup of tea with a Rs.5000 note.

At the time of writing, the **exchange rate** was around Rs.155 to $1, Rs.190 to €1, and Rs.220 to £1; you can check current exchange rates at Ⓦ xe.com (they also have a handy smartphone app which is super-useful for converting prices on the spot). Top-end hotels always give their prices either in **US dollars** or (occasionally) in euros, though you'll be expected to pay in rupees, with the bill converted at the current bank exchange rate. Many other tourist services are also often priced in dollars – anything from entrance tickets at archeological sites to tours, balloon trips or diving courses – though, again, payment will be expected in rupees.

Sri Lanka is well supplied with **banks**. The six main chains (most larger towns will have a branch of at least three or four of these) are the Bank of Ceylon, HNB (Hatton National Bank), Sampath Bank, Commercial Bank, People's Bank and Seylan Bank. All are open Monday to Friday from 8 or 9am in the morning until 2 or 3pm in the afternoon, and all shut at weekends. Exchange rates for foreign currency or when making withdrawals by credit or debit card are fairly uniform across the various banks; you may get fractionally better rates if you shop around, but you won't make any dramatic savings. If you need to change money **outside banking hours**, head to the nearest top-end hotel – most change cash, though at rates that are up to ten percent poorer than bank rates. Failing this, you could try at local guesthouses or shops – the more tourist-oriented the place you're in the better your chances, though you'll probably have to accept poor rates. All towns of any consequence have at least one bank **ATM** that accepts foreign debit and credit cards; ATMs at the Commercial, HNB, Sampath and Seylan banks accept both Visa and MasterCard; those at the People's Bank accept Visa only; only a few Bank of Ceylon ATMs accept foreign cards. You'll be charged a fee of around Rs.400 for ATM withdrawals on top of whatever charges your home bank may levy, although at the time of writing withdrawals from HNB ATMs were free.

You might also want to carry some **cash** with you for emergencies. US dollars, euros, pounds sterling and Australian dollars are all widely recognized and easily changed. New Zealand or Canadian dollars might occasionally cause problems, but are generally accepted in most banks. It's becoming increasingly difficult to find anywhere accepting or cashing **travellers' cheques**.

Opening hours

Most businesses, including banks and government offices, work a standard **five-day working week** from Monday to Friday 9/9.30am to 5/5.30pm. Major post offices generally operate longer hours (typically 7am–9pm), and stay open on Saturdays as well. Some museums shut on Fridays, while Hindu temples stay shut for most of the day until around 4pm to 5pm, when they open for the evening puja. Buddhist temples, by contrast, generally stay open from dawn until dusk, or later.

Phones

Phoning home from Sri Lanka is straightforward and relatively inexpensive, although if you're planning a long trip and are likely to be making a lot of calls, using your own **mobile** is easily the most cost-effective option. Ask your service provider whether your handset will work abroad and what the call costs are. Most UK, Australian and New Zealand mobiles use GSM, which works well in Sri Lanka, but US mobiles (apart from tri-band phones) won't work.

Some mobile providers have reciprocal arrangements with Sri Lankan operators and offer reasonably affordable rates using your existing SIM card – check tariffs before you travel. It's far cheaper, however, to **replace the SIM card** in your phone with a new SIM from a Sri Lankan company (assuming your phone isn't locked). This will give you a Sri Lankan phone number and you will be charged domestic rates – as low as Rs.15 per minute for international calls, and Rs.2 for local calls. The most convenient place to get a Sri Lankan SIM is **on arrival** at the airport, which has sales outlets for all the island's mobile operators. All sell tourist packages including a SIM and varying amounts of mobile data, plus texts and local and international calls for around $10 or less. SIM cards can also be picked up for just a few dollars (you'll need to show your passport when buying) from any of the island's myriad phone shops, which also sell chargers and adaptors for Sri Lankan sockets, and cards with which you can top up your airtime (or look for any shop displaying the relevant sticker). The **main operators** are Dialog (W dialog.lk), Mobitel (W mobitel.lk), Etisalat (W etisalat.lk), Airtel (W airtel.lk) and Hutch (W hutch.lk); Dialog and Mobitel are generally reckoned to have the best coverage. You can get a mobile signal pretty much everywhere on the island apart from a few remote rural locations, including some areas around Sinharaja.

Without a mobile, the easiest way to make a call is to go to one of the island's **communications bureaux**, little offices offering phone, fax and photocopying services (look out for signs advertising IDD calls), although these are becoming increasingly scarce now that pretty much everyone on the island has a mobile. You can often make calls from your **hotel room** in more upmarket places, although rates are usually sky-high. There are virtually no **payphones** anywhere.

To **call home from Sri Lanka**, dial the international access code (T 00), then the country code (UK T 44; US and Canada T 1; Ireland T 353; Australia T 61; New Zealand T 64; South Africa T 27), then the area code and subscriber number. Note that the initial zero is omitted from the area code when dialling the UK, Ireland, Australia and New Zealand from abroad.

To **call Sri Lanka from abroad**, dial your international access code then the country code for Sri Lanka (T 94), then the area code, minus the initial zero, then the subscriber number.

Photography

Most Sri Lankans love having their **photo taken** – though it's obviously polite to ask. A few of the island's more photogenic inhabitants might expect to be paid to be photographed, particularly stilt fishermen (when you can find them) and (occasionally) tea pickers in the highlands. You're not allowed to pose for photographs with Buddha images (standing with your back to the image), and photography is also generally not permitted inside the inner shrines of Hindu temples. In addition, note that flash photography can damage old murals; if you're asked not to take flash photos, don't. And do not under any circumstances photograph military or police installations or secure areas.

Time

Sri Lanka is five hours and thirty minutes ahead of **GMT**; there is no daylight-saving time/summer time in place, so clocks stay the same year round.

Tourist information

Considering the importance of tourism to the national economy, there are surprisingly few sources of official **tourist information** in Sri Lanka itself and no overseas tourist offices. For detailed information about specific areas, the best sources are the independent tour operators (see page 27) and staff at hotels and guesthouses.

The free monthly *Travel Lanka*, available from the tourist office in Colombo (see page 86), contains listings of accommodation, shops, services and transport in the capital and across the island. *Time Out Sri Lanka* (Ⓦtimeout.com/sri-lanka), widely available in Colombo, is also worth a look.

Online, the Sri Lanka Tourist Board's site (Ⓦsrilanka. travel) is a reasonable source of information. Yamu (Ⓦyamu.lk) has superb coverage of Colombo, plus patchy information on the rest of the country. You might also like to have a browse through Ari Withanage's Sri Lanka pages at Ⓦwithanage.tripod.com and the eclectic Lanka Library (Ⓦlankalibrary.com), which has loads of background on sites, culture, history and cuisine.

Travellers with disabilities

Awareness of the needs of **disabled people** remains extremely low in Sri Lanka, and there's virtually no provision for disabled travellers. Few hotels, restaurants or tourist sites are wheelchair-accessible, although there are plenty of one-storey guesthouses that might be usable – though more by accident than design. Public transport is enough of a challenge for able-bodied passengers, and completely useless for wheelchair users, so you'll need your own vehicle and a driver who is sympathetic to your needs – and even then the lack of specially adapted vehicles can make getting in and out difficult.

Pavements – where they exist – are generally uneven, full of potholes and protected by high kerbs, while the anarchic traffic presents obvious dangers to those with only limited mobility.

Weddings

Sri Lanka is one of the world's leading honeymoon destinations, and many couples go a step further and actually get married on the island – beach **weddings** are particularly popular. Arranging the ceremony independently and dealing with the attendant paperwork and bureaucracy can be difficult, however, and it's much easier to leave the details to a specialist operator. Most large hotels and a number of tour operators (see page 27) can arrange the whole wedding for you, including (if you fancy) extras like Kandyan drummers and dancers, plus optional elephants and a chorus of local girls.

Women travellers

Sexual harassment and assault are unfortunate realities of daily life in Sri Lanka – in one 2017 survey, for example, a staggering ninety percent of Sri Lankan women reported having experienced sexual harassment on public transport. Serious assaults are infrequent, although it's worth being aware of the potential for problems and the fact that unwanted and/or aggressive attention can happen not just on the street and in other public places, but even in situations where safety would normally be taken for granted, such as in hotels or when dealing with officials. It makes sense, obviously, to avoid walking alone at night in lonely places or wearing swimwear away from the beach. You should also be aware that there have been reports in recent years of foreign women having their drinks spiked in popular resort areas, as well as hotel staff trying to enter the rooms of female guests or calling them in the middle of the night.

Colombo and the west coast

JAMI UL-AFTAR MOSQUE

1

Colombo and the west coast

Sri Lanka's west coast is the island's front door and – via the international airport at Katunayake, just outside Colombo – the point of arrival for virtually all visitors to the country. This is Sri Lanka at its most developed and populous: the busiest, brashest and most Westernized part of the country, home to the capital city and the principal coastal resorts, which have now all but fused into an unbroken ribbon of development which meanders along the seaboard for over a hundred kilometres.

Situated about two-thirds of the way down the west coast, Sri Lanka's sprawling capital, **Colombo**, is one of Asia's most underrated cities, now booming in the wake of the civil war and offering a fascinating microcosm of contemporary Sri Lanka, from traditional Buddhist temples and bazaars through to soaring skyscrapers and slick bars. North of Colombo is the busy resort of **Negombo**, whose proximity to the airport makes it a popular first or last stop on many itineraries, while further up the coast the idyllic **Kalpitiya peninsula** has superb dolphin-watching and kitesurfing, and also offers a good base for visits to the vast, wildlife-rich **Wilpattu National Park**.

South of the capital is where you'll find the island's main beach resorts. The principal areas – **Kalutara**, **Beruwala** and **Bentota** – are home to endless oversize hotels catering to vacationing Europeans on two-week packages. Pockets of serenity remain, even so, along with some characterful hotels and guesthouses, while further south lies the upbeat, downmarket town of **Hikkaduwa**, Sri Lanka's original hippy hangout and still a popular with cash-strapped backpackers, who flock here for cheap sun, sand and surf.

Colombo

Sri Lanka's dynamic capital, **COLOMBO**, seems totally out of proportion with the rest of the country. The one real metropolis in a still largely agricultural island, Colombo utterly dominates the nation's economic, political and cultural life, while ongoing mega-developments in the wake of the civil war are now giving parts of the city a flavour more reminiscent of Singapore than South Asia.

Stretching for over 30km along the island's western seaboard in a seemingly formless urban straggle, the city's sprawling layout and lack of star attractions mean that it often ranks relatively low on many visitors' bucket lists. There's plenty to enjoy, however, especially if you're interested in getting behind the tourist clichés and finding out what makes contemporary Sri Lanka tick – it's definitely a place that grows on you the longer you stay, and worth a day out of even the shortest itinerary. The city musters few specific sights, but offers plenty of atmosphere and quirky character: a heady admixture of Asian anarchy, colonial charm and modern chic. Shiny high-rises rub shoulders with tumbledown local cafés and shops, while serene Buddhist shrines and colonial churches stand next to the garishly multicoloured towers of Hindu temples – all evidence of the rich stew of races and religions that have gone into the making of this surprisingly cosmopolitan city.

Brief history

In the context of Sri Lanka's almost 2500 years of recorded history, Colombo is a relative upstart. Situated on the delta of the island's fourth-longest river, the Kelani

SEEMA MALAKA TEMPLE

Highlights

Fort Explore the beautifully restored and revitalized streets of Colombo's historic colonial centre. See page 69

The Pettah Colombo's absorbing bazaar district, stuffed full of every conceivable type of merchandise, from mobile phones to Ayurvedic herbs. See page 71

Gangaramaya and Seema Malaka Step out of the urban melee of Colombo into the serene enclosures of these two contrasting Buddhist temples. See page 79

Kalpitiya peninsula Breezy Kalpitiya boasts superb dolphin-watching, beautiful beaches and lagoons, colonial remains, eco-lodges and

some of Asia's finest kitesurfing. See page 107

⑤ Wilpattu National Park One of the island's finest national parks, home to significant populations of leopards, elephants and sloth bears. See page 111

⑥ Bentota With an idyllic sandy beach and a string of elegant small-scale hotels, the southern end of Bentota offers an oasis of style and tranquillity among the brash west-coast package resorts. See page 119

⑦ Hikkaduwa Popular backpacker hangout, with good surfing, snorkelling and diving, and one of the liveliest beach scenes anywhere on the coast. See page 128

HIGHLIGHTS ARE MARKED ON THE MAP ON PAGE 66

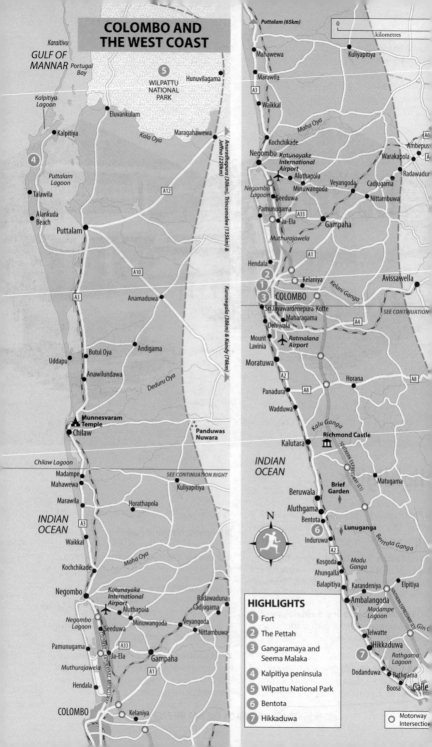

COLOMBO AND THE WEST COAST

GULF OF MANNAR

Karaitivu
Portugal Bay
Kalpitiya Lagoon
Eluvankulam
Kalpitiya
Maragahawewa
④ Puttalam Lagoon
Talawila
Alankuda Beach
Puttalam

Hunuvilagama
⑤ WILPATTU NATIONAL PARK

Kala Oya
A12

Anuradhapura (30km), Trincomalee (135km) & Jaffna (230km)
Kurunegala (38km) & Kandy (76km)

A10
Anamaduwa

A3
Butul Oya
Andigama
Uddapu
Anawilundawa
Deduru Oya

▲ Munnesvaram Temple
Chilaw

Pandu was Nuwara

Chilaw Lagoon
SEE CONTINUATION RIGHT

Madampe
Mahawewa
Kuliyapitiya
Marawila
Horathapola
INDIAN OCEAN
A3
Waikkal
Maha Oya
Kochchikade
Radawaduna
Cadjugama
Negombo
Katunayake International Airport
Aluthapola
Veyangoda
Minuwangoda
Nittambuwa
Negombo Lagoon
Seeduwa
A33
Pamunugama
Ja-Ela
Gampaha
Muthurajawela
A1
Hendala
COLOMBO
Kelaniya

N

Puttalam (65km)
0 kilometres

Mahawewa
Kuliyapitiya
Marawila
A3
Waikkal
Maha Oya
Kochchikade
Ambepus...
Negombo
Katunayake International Airport
Warakapola
A
Aluthapola
Veyangoda
Cadjugama
Radawadur...
Minuwangoda
Nittambuwa
Negombo Lagoon
Seeduwa
Gampaha
Pamunugama
A33
Ja-Ela
Muthurajawela
A1
Hendala
②
Kelaniya
Avissawella
①
COLOMBO
③ Sri Jayawardenepura-Kotte
Kelani Ganga
SEE CONTINUATION
Maharagama
Dehiwala
A4
Mount Lavinia
✈ Ratmalana Airport
Moratuwa
A2
Horana
A8
Panadura
A8
Wadduwa
Kalu Ganga
Kalutara
🏛 Richmond Castle
INDIAN OCEAN
Matugama
Beruwala
Brief Garden
Aluthgama
Bentota
⑥
Lunuganga
Induruwa
A2
Bentota Ganga
Kosgoda
Madu Ganga
Ahungalla
Balapitiya
Karandeniya
Elpitiya
Ambalangoda
Madampe Lagoon
Telwatte
⑦ Hikkaduwa
Rathgama Lagoon
Dodanduwa
Rathgama
Boosa
Galle

HIGHLIGHTS

① Fort
② The Pettah
③ Gangaramaya and Seema Malaka
④ Kalpitiya peninsula
⑤ Wilpattu National Park
⑥ Bentota
⑦ Hikkaduwa

○ Motorway Intersection

Ganga, the Colombo area had been long settled by Muslim traders, who established a flourishing trading settlement here from the eighth century onwards, but only rose to nationwide prominence at the start of the colonial period. The Sinhalese called the port Kolamba, which the poetically inclined Portuguese believed was derived from the Sinhalese word for mango trees (*kola* meaning "leaves", and *amba* meaning "mango"), although it's more likely that *kolamba* was an old Sinhala word meaning "port" or "ferry".

The colonial period

The first significant settlement in the area was 13km northeast of the modern city centre at **Kelaniya** (see page 83), site of a famous Buddhist shrine which had developed by the thirteenth century into a major town; the nearby settlement of **Kotte** (see page 407), 11km southeast of the modern city, served as the capital of the island's main Sinhalese lowland kingdom from the fourteenth to the sixteenth centuries. Despite the proximity of both Kelaniya and Kotte, however, Colombo remained a relatively insignificant fishing and trading port until the arrival of the **Portuguese** in 1518. The Portuguese constructed the fort that subsequently formed the nucleus of modern Colombo and, in 1597, attacked and destroyed both Kotte and Kelaniya. Portuguese control of Colombo only lasted until 1656, however, when they were ousted by the **Dutch** after a seven-month siege. The Dutch remained in control for almost 150 years, rebuilding the fort, reclaiming land from the swampy delta using the system of canals that survives to this day, and creating spacious new tree-lined suburbs.

In 1796, Colombo fell to the **British**, following Dutch capitulation to the French in the Napoleonic Wars. The city was made capital of Ceylon, while new road and rail links with Kandy further enhanced Colombo's burgeoning prosperity. With the construction of a new harbour at the end of the nineteenth century, the city overtook Galle as the island's main port, becoming one of the great entrepôts of Asia and acquiring the sobriquet of the "Charing Cross of the East" thanks to its location at the crossroads of Indian Ocean trade.

Independence and civil war

Colombo retained its importance following **independence**, and has continued to expand at an exponential rate ever since, though not without sometimes disastrous side effects. Growing islandwide Sinhalese–Tamil tensions erupted with tragic results in mid-1983, during the month subsequently christened **Black July**, when Sinhalese mobs, with the apparent connivance and encouragement of the police and army, went on the rampage throughout the city, murdering perhaps as many as two thousand innocent Tamils and reducing significant portions of the Pettah to ruins – a watershed in Sinhalese–Tamil relations which led shortly afterwards to fully fledged **civil war**. During the civil war itself, the city was repeatedly targeted by LTTE suicide bombers, most notably in 1996, when the massive truck-bombing of the Central Bank killed almost a hundred people and succeeded, along with other attacks, in reducing the historic Fort district to a heavily militarized ghost town.

Despite its traumatic recent past, Colombo's irrepressible commercial and cultural life continues apace, exemplified by the restoration and revitalization of Fort and by the string of ambitious new developments mushrooming across the city, most notably the monumental new Port City project (see page 77) and the string of huge new developments around Slave Island and Galle Face Green. And for all its problems, Colombo remains a fascinating melting pot of the island's Sinhalese, Tamil, Muslim, Burgher and expatriate communities, who combine to give the place a uniquely forward-thinking and outward-looking character quite unlike anywhere else in the island.

1

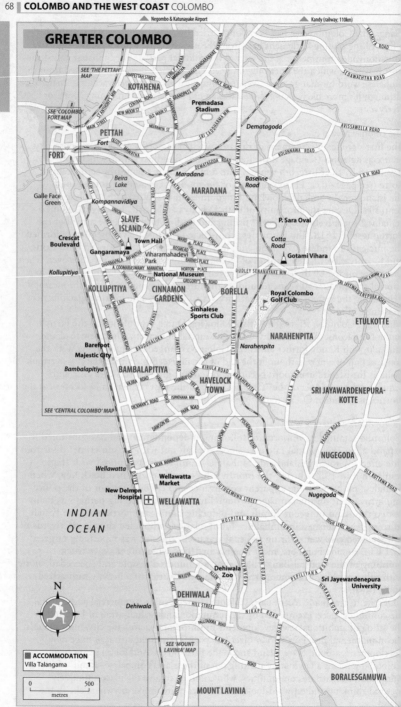

GREATER COLOMBO

▲ Negombo & Katunayake Airport   ▲ Kandy (railway; 110km)

SEE 'THE PETTAH' MAP

KOTAHENA

SEE 'COLOMBO FORT MAP

PETTAH

FORT

Fort

Beira Lake

Galle Face Green

Kompannavidiya

SLAVE ISLAND

Crescat Boulevard

Gangaramaya

Town Hall

Kollupitiya

Viharamahadevi Park

National Museum

KOLLUPITIYA

CINNAMON GARDENS

Sinhalese Sports Club

Barefoot Majestic City

Bambalapitiya

BAMBALAPITIYA

HAVELOCK TOWN

SEE 'CENTRAL COLOMBO' MAP

Maradana

MARADANA

Dematagoda

Baseline Road

P. Sara Oval

Cotta Road

Gotami Vihara

BORELLA

Royal Colombo Golf Club

NARAHENPITA

Narahenpita

ETULKOTTE

SRI JAYAWARDENEPURA-KOTTE

Wellawatta

New Delmon Hospital

Wellawatta Market

WELLAWATTA

INDIAN

OCEAN

Nugegoda

NUGEGODA

Quarry Road

Dehiwala Zoo

DEHIWALA

Dehiwala

Sri Jayewardenepura University

Sri Jayewardenepura University

BORALESGAMUWA

SEE 'MOUNT LAVINIA' MAP

MOUNT LAVINIA

N

■ ACCOMMODATION
Villa Talangama   1

0   500
metres

▼ Galle (113km)   ▼ Galle (113km)

Fort

Fort district lies at the heart of old Colombo, occupying as its name suggests the site of the city's (now-vanished) Portuguese defences. Under the British, the area developed into the centrepiece of the colonial capital, adorned with handsome Neoclassical buildings and boasting all the necessities of expatriate life in the tropics, right down to the inevitable clocktower and statue of Queen Victoria. Following independence, Fort retained its position as Colombo's administrative and financial hub until the onset of the civil war, when repeated LTTE attacks all but killed off the life of the district. By the end of the war Fort had fallen into an apparently terminal decline, its old colonial buildings largely derelict and its central streets carved up into a perplexing maze of security checkpoints and wire-mesh fences – or just placed off limits completely. Fort, it appeared, was history.

The decade since has confounded all expectations as Fort has become the focus of one of Asia's most spectacular recent **urban regeneration** projects, with checkpoints dismantled, streets reopened and many of the old colonial buildings meticulously renovated. Now restored to something approaching its former splendour (albeit still looking a bit grubby and battered in places), this is Colombo's most enjoyable neighbourhood, with plenty of old-world atmosphere, a smattering of low-key sights and some excellent places to eat and drink.

The clocktower-lighthouse

More or less at the centre of the district is the quaint **clocktower-lighthouse**. The clocktower was originally constructed in 1857, apparently at the behest of the punctilious wife of Governor Henry Ward as a result of her exasperation with oriental standards of timekeeping. A beacon was subsequently built on top of the clocktower ten years later, serving as the city's main lighthouse for a century until the surrounding buildings blocked out its beam from the sea (a new lighthouse now stands on the seafront just to the west).

Economic History Museum of Sri Lanka

Chatham St • Mon–Sat 9am–5pm • Free

One of the most impressive of all Fort's recently renovated buildings is the imposing **Central Point Building**, originally the National Mutual Building and the tallest structure in Colombo when it first opened in 1911. The building's lower two floors now host the modest **Economic History Museum of Sri Lanka**, a rather grand name for a low-key museum devoted to the history of currency in Sri Lanka and elsewhere. Objects on display include antique money and shiny modern commemorative coins, although it's the building itself which is the real star of the show, particularly the central atrium, with its magnificent circular staircase spiralling up to the topmost floor.

Janadhipathi Mawatha

Beyond the clocktower, the elegant northern section of **Janadhipathi Mawatha** (or Queen's Street, as it was known in colonial times) was for many years off limits due to the presence of the beautiful, tree-screened **President's House** (Janadhipathi Mandiraya), official residence of the Sri Lankan president. Built in the late eighteenth century as the private house of the last Dutch governor, Johan Gerard van Angelbeek, this sprawling white edifice was subsequently used as the residence of the British governor until independence, being known variously as the King's or Queen's House according to the monarch of the day. A statue stands outside of Governor Edward Barnes – all road distances in Sri Lanka are measured from here.

On the opposite side of the street is the even larger and considerably more florid colonial edifice (built in 1895) which formerly served as the city's **General Post Office**, also recently restored, its grandiose facade decorated with paired Ionic columns on the lower floor, and Corinthian above.

1

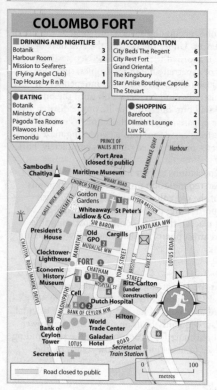

COLOMBO FORT

■ **DRINKING AND NIGHTLIFE**
Botanik	3
Harbour Room	2
Mission to Seafarers (Flying Angel Club)	1
Tap House by R n R	4

■ **ACCOMMODATION**
City Beds The Regent	6
City Rest Fort	4
Grand Oriental	1
The Kingsbury	5
Star Anise Boutique Capsule	2
The Steuart	3

● **EATING**
Botanik	2
Ministry of Crab	4
Pagoda Tea Rooms	1
Pilawoos Hotel	3
Semondu	4

● **SHOPPING**
Barefoot	2
Dilmah t Lounge	1
Luv SL	2

Road closed to public

0   100
metres

Follow the road as it turns right into Sir Baron Jayatilaka Mawatha (formerly Prince St). On your left is a beautifully restored, vaguely French-looking building from 1907 which originally housed the Colombo branch of **Whiteaway, Laidlaw & Co.**, one of the British's empire's leading department stores. Nicknamed "Right away and paid for" (no goods were sold on credit), the chain was founded by Scottish entrepreneur Robert Laidlaw in Calcutta in 1882 and subsequently expanded across India and many other parts of Asia, with branches in Ceylon, Burma, Malaya and China.

Turning right again at the junction with York Street brings you to the old home of another colonial-era retail giant, **Cargills**. Founded in 1844 as a warehouse and import business, the original store's expansive red-brick facade is still one of Fort's most instantly recognizable landmarks, although the interior is largely empty bar a small supermarket and a deeply incongruous branch of Kentucky Fried Chicken.

The port

North from Cargills, York Street becomes increasingly down-at-heel – although the planned opening of a new *Langham* hotel in the block by the junction with Sir Baron Jayatilaka Mawatha is likely to change all that, and perhaps even rescue the beautiful colonial arcade that flanks the west side of the street from its layers of dirt and neglect.

At the end of the street, Colombo's **port** is hidden behind high walls and strictly off limits. Until the early twentieth century, the island's main port was Galle, but Colombo's improved road and rail links with the rest of the country and Sri Lanka's strategic location on Indian Ocean sea routes between Europe, Asia and Australasia encouraged the British to invest in a major overhaul of the city's rather unsatisfactory harbour, during which they constructed three new breakwaters (the largest, built in 1885, is over a kilometre long).

Opposite the main entrance to the port stands the venerable **Grand Oriental Hotel**. Sadly little of the establishment's former colonial splendour remains, although there are marvellous port views from its *Harbour Room* restaurant-bar (see page 92).

St Peter's Church

Church St • Daily 7am–5pm • Free

The port area west of the *Grand Oriental Hotel* remains out of bounds, though you can duck through the security barrier to visit **St Peter's Church**, next door to the hotel, hidden away between later and much larger buildings. Occupying an old Dutch governor's residence of 1680, this was converted to serve as the British garrison church in 1821 and seems hardly to have changed since, with a time-warped interior stuffed full of old wooden benches and assorted wall memorials to British notables who expired in the city.

Southern Fort

Southern Fort is dominated by a cluster of upmarket **hotels**, the slender, cylindrical **Bank of Ceylon Tower** and the soaring twin towers of the gleaming **World Trade Center**. Opposite the World Trade Center sits the contrastingly low-rise **Dutch Hospital**. Dating (probably) from the seventeenth century, the complex comprises a neat cluster of ochre buildings arranged around a pair of courtyards, now home to an excellent selection of restaurants, cafés, bars and shops.

Tucked away in the corner of the Fort Police Station car park just west of the Dutch Hospital is a small and easily missed orange **prison cell**. This is where the last king of Kandy, **Sri Wickrama Rajasinha** (see page 212) is said to have been imprisoned before being sent into exile in India in 1815, although the so-called "cell" might actually not have been built until much later, or might simply have been the guard chamber for the British barracks which formerly stood here.

Sambodhi Chaitiya

Chaitiya Rd · No fixed hours · Free

West of the Dutch Hospital, **Chaitiya Road** (Marine Drive) sweeps north along the oceanfront, passing Fort's modern lighthouse en route to the **Sambodhi Chaitiya**, a huge dagoba on stilts, built in 1956 to mark the 2500th anniversary of the Buddha's death. Looking a bit like a gigantic lava lamp, this thoroughly peculiar structure is quite the oddest thing in Colombo. Some 260 steps climb up to the top, offering sweeping views of Fort, with the huge white President's House sulking in the trees below. It's also possible to go inside the hollow dagoba itself, painted with scenes from the Buddha's life and the history of the religion in the island.

Maritime Museum

Chaitiya Rd · Daily 10am–7pm · Free

The city's modest **Maritime Museum**, a few steps beyond the Sambodhi Chaitiya, has some rather tenuous exhibits featuring large (and largely conjectural) models of the ships on which various significant personages – Prince Vijaya, Fa-Hsien, Ibn Battuta – arrived on the island, plus later colonial vessels, along with miscellaneous bits of maritime bric-a-brac including an enormous sling once used to load elephants onto ships. You're now close to the main entrance to the port and the *Grand Oriental Hotel*, though roadblocks block further progress.

The Pettah

East of Fort, the helter-skelter bazaar district of the **Pettah** is unlike anywhere else in the island, with narrow, crowd-choked streets, merchandise piled high in tiny shops and on the pavements, and a kind of manic energy and crush more reminiscent of the big Indian cities than anything remotely Sri Lankan. Exploring can be a slow process, made additionally perilous by the porters who charge through the crowds pulling or carrying huge loads and threatening the heads and limbs of unwary tourists (except on Sundays, when most shops close and things are much more peaceful).

Shops in the Pettah are arranged in the traditional **bazaar layout**, with different streets devoted to a different goods: Front Street, for example, is full of bags and shoes; 1st Cross Street is devoted to hardware and electrical goods; 2nd and 3rd Cross Streets and Keyzer Street are stuffed with colourful fabrics, and so on. The wares on display are fairly mundane – unless you're a big fan of Taiwanese household appliances or fake Barbie dolls – although traces of older and more colourful trades survive in places.

The district is infamous in Sri Lankan history as the epicentre of the Black July massacres of 1983 (see page 415) and still retains a strongly **Tamil** (the name Pettah derives from the Tamil word *pettai*, meaning village) and, especially, **Muslim** flavour, as

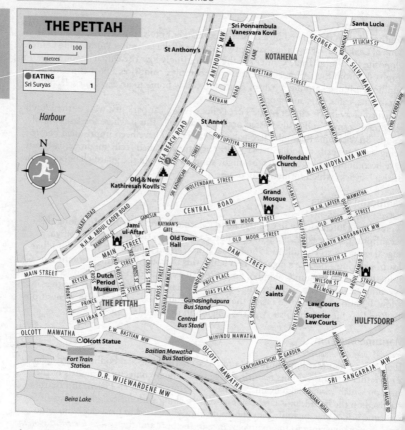

shown by its many pure veg and Muslim restaurants, quaint mosques, Hindu temples and colonial churches (many Sri Lankan Tamils are Christian rather than Hindu).

Dutch Period Museum

Prince St • Tues–Sat 9am–5pm • Rs.500

A couple of blocks north of Fort station, the **Dutch Period Museum** (closed for renovations at the time of research) occupies the old Dutch town hall, a fine colonnaded building of 1780. The mildly interesting displays on the Dutch colonial era feature the usual old coins, Kandyan and Dutch artefacts, military junk and dusty European furniture, plus a couple of miserable-looking waxworks of colonists dressed in full velvet and lace despite the sweltering heat. The main attraction, however, is the wonderfully atmospheric mansion itself, whose groaning wooden floors and staircases, great pitched roof and idyllic garden offer a beguiling glimpse into the lifestyle enjoyed by the eighteenth century's more upwardly mobile settlers.

Main Street and Jami ul-Aftar

Cutting through the heart of the Pettah, the district's principal thoroughfare **Main Street** is usually a solidly heaving bedlam of vehicles and pedestrians, with porters weaving through the throng pushing carts piled high with every conceivable type of merchandise. On the far side of the road is Colombo's most eye-catching mosque, the **Jami ul-Aftar** (not open to non-Muslims), a gloriously kitsch red-and-white

1

HENRY STEEL OLCOTT: AMERICAN BUDDHIST

On the south side of the Pettah, in front of Fort Railway Station on Olcott Mawatha, stands a statue of **Henry Steel Olcott** (1842–1907), perhaps the most influential foreigner in the modern history of Sri Lanka. Olcott was an American Buddhist and co-founder (with Madame Blavatsky, the celebrated Russian clairvoyant and spiritualist) of the Theosophical Society, a quasi-religious movement which set about promoting Asian philosophy in the West and reviving oriental spiritual traditions in the East to protect them from the attacks of European missionary Christianity. The society's utopian (if rather vague) objectives comprised a mixture of the scientific, the social, the spiritual and the downright bizarre: the mystical Madame Blavatsky, fount of the society's more arcane tenets, believed that she had the ability to levitate, render herself invisible and communicate with the souls of the dead, as well as asserting that the Theosophical Society was run according to orders received from a group of "masters" – disembodied tutelary spirits who were believed to reside in Tibet.

In 1880, Blavatsky and Olcott arrived in Ceylon, formally embracing Buddhism and establishing the **Buddhist Theosophical Society**, which became one of the principal driving forces behind the remarkable worldwide spread of Buddhism during the twentieth century. Olcott spent many of his later years touring the island, organizing Buddhist schools and petitioning the British colonial authorities to respect Sri Lanka's religious traditions, though his most visible legacy is the multicoloured Buddhist flag (see page 430) which he helped design, and which now decorates temples across the island and, indeed, worldwide.

construction of 1909 which rises gaudily above the cluttered shops of Main Street like a heavily iced cake.

The Old Town Hall and around

East of the Jami ul-Aftar (and a memorably malodorous fish market) is the intersection known as **Kayman's Gate** – the name probably refers to the crocodiles (or caimans) that were once kept in the canals surrounding Slave Island (see page 77) and in the Fort moat to deter slaves from attempting to escape. Kayman's Gate is dominated by the fancifully Moorish-style **Old Town Hall** of 1873. The wrought-iron market **pavilion** to one side still houses various marooned pieces of industrial and municipal hardware including a steamroller, old street signs and a former van of the Colombo Public Library. The caretaker may offer to unlock it for you, although you can see most of the stuff through the railings. The doors into the town hall itself are usually left open, allowing you to walk up the fine Burma teak staircase to the old council chambers, whose austere wooden fittings and stalled fans exude a positively *Marie Celeste*-like atmosphere.

The fruit and veg sellers who line the western side of the town hall building make this one of the most photogenic (and most crowded) sections of the Pettah, while just behind lies another half-submerged remnant of colonial times in the form of an elaborate wrought-iron **market building**, now occupied by a miscellany of shops. Just behind here, **4th Cross Street** is usually full of colourful lorries loading and unloading. Great sacks of chillies clutter the pavements, while merchants sit behind huge ledgers and piles of spices inside the picturesque little office-warehouses that line the street.

Sea Street

On the northern edge of the Pettah, **Gabo's Lane** is home to a few easily missed shops (on the south side of the lane) selling Ayurvedic ingredients: outlandish-looking sacks and pallets sit outside shops stuffed with bark, twigs and other strange pieces of vegetable matter. North of here the crowds begin to thin out as you head up **Sea Street**, lined by a long string of small jewellers' shops.

Sea Street's middle section is dominated by the colourful **New Kathiresan** and **Old Kathiresan kovils**, whose three gateways fill one side of the street with a great clumpy mass of Hindu statuary. The temples are dedicated to the war god Skanda and are the

1

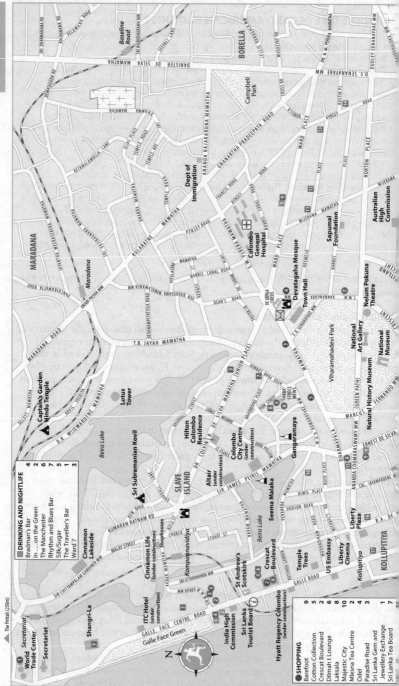

■ DRINKING AND NIGHTLIFE

Bradman's Bar	4
In . . . on the Green	2
The Manchester	6
Rhythm and Blues Bar	7
Silk/Sugar	5
The Traveller's Bar	1
Ward 7	3

● SHOPPING

Barefoot	9
Cotton Collection	5
Crescat Boulevard	2
Dilmah t Lounge	6
Laksala	8
Majestic City	10
Mlesna Tea Centre	4
Odel	2
Paradise Road	3
Sri Lanka Gem and Jewellery Exchange	7
Sri Lanka Tea Board	1

CENTRAL COLOMBO

■ ACCOMMODATION	
Backpack Lanka	16
Cinnamon Grand	6
Cinnamon Red	15
Clock Inn	23
Colombo Court	22
Colombo Haven	17
Colpetty House	20
Comfort@15	19
Drift BnB	21
Galle Face Hotel	4
Greenlands Hotel	25
Havelock Place Bungalow	28
Highbury	27
Jetwing Colombo Seven	9
Lake Lodge	10
Maniumpathy	14
Moss BNB Colombo	24
Paradise Road Tintagel	11
Ramada	3
Hotel Renuka & Renuka City Hotel	18
Shangri-La	1
Hotel Sunshine	26
Taj Samudra	2
Uga Residence	8
Unique Towers	7
Wayfarers Inn	12
YWCA International Guest House	5
Zylan	13

● EATING			
Agra	12	Gallery Café	14
Alhambra	1	Green Cabin	15
Amaravathi	10	Greenlands	17
Barefoot Café	16	The Lagoon	3
Bavarian German Restaurant	2	The Mango Tree	8
		Monsoon	6
Café Francais	5	Noodles	3
Chinese Dragon Café	18	Nuga Gama	3
Chutneys	3	Palmyrah	11
Crescat Boulevard	4	Siam House	19
Cricket Club Café	9	Upali's	7
Hotel de Pilawoos	13		

1

starting point for the annual Vel Festival (see page 47); they're usually shut during the day, but become a hive of activity towards dusk, when bare-chested, luxuriantly bearded priests conduct evening puja amid the hypnotic noise of drumming and dense swirls of smoke.

Kotahena

The suburb of **Kotahena**, northeast of the Pettah, is one of Colombo's more priestly suburbs, home to numerous colonial churches and small but brightly coloured Hindu temples. Walking north along St Anthony's Mawatha, you'll pass a string of colourful shops selling Hindu and Christian religious paraphernalia before reaching **St Anthony's Church**, where people of all faiths come to pay homage to a statue of St Anthony which is said to work miracles in solving family problems.

Santa Lucia Cathedral

St Lucia's St • No fixed hours • Free

Perhaps the most imposing church in Sri Lanka, the grand cathedral of **Santa Lucia** was built between 1873 and 1910, sports a stately grey classical facade inspired by St Peter's in Rome and seats some six thousand people – though not since the pope conducted a service here in 1994 has it been even half-full. Inside, numerous statues include an unusual dark-skinned Madonna known as Our Lady of Kotahena. Two further Neoclassical buildings – a Benedictine monastery and a convent – sit by the cathedral, creating an unexpectedly impressive architectural ensemble in this out-of-the-way corner of the city.

Wolfendahl Church

Entrance off Vivekananda Hill • Tues–Thurs & Sat 8.30am–4pm, Fri 8.30am–1.30pm (hang around if the church is shut and the caretaker will probably appear to open it for you) • Donation

Sitting unobtrusively in a quiet side street at the southern edge of Kotahena, the Dutch Reformed **Wolfendahl** (or **Wolvendaal**) **Church** of 1749 is Colombo's oldest church and one of Sri Lanka's most interesting colonial relics – although looking sadly dilapidated nowadays. Its rather severe Neoclassical exterior conceals an attractive period-piece interior complete with old tiled floor, simple stained glass, wicker seating and wooden pews, organ and pulpit. Numerous finely carved eighteenth-century floor tablets in the south transept commemorate assorted Dutch officials, including various governors whose remains were moved here from Fort in 1813.

Hulftsdorp

Various religious edifices dot the suburb of **Hulftsdorp**, named after Dutch general Gerard Hulft, who was killed in 1656 during the siege of the Portuguese fort in Colombo. These include a number of small, fanciful-looking mosques – the largest (but plainest) is the **Grand Mosque** on New Moor Street, the most important in the city, which hides shyly behind latticed orange walls. The large and striking modern building with the hat-shaped roof you can see from here is the **Superior Law Courts** (the original Neoclassical courts stand stolidly next door, two dumpy little buildings with dour Doric facades). Opposite the law courts rises the soaring spire of the pale grey Gothic Revival church of **All Saints**.

Galle Face Green

The breezy oceanfront expanse of **Galle Face Green** is one of Colombo's best-loved public spaces – even if the grass covering it tends to die off at regular intervals, meaning that it's often not so much green as a rather dusty brown. Bounded to the south by the

1

COLOMBO INTERNATIONAL FINANCE CITY

The view from Galle Face Green will soon be changed forever thanks to the huge new **Colombo International Finance City** (or "Colombo Port City" as it was previously known, and is still often called). Launched in late 2014, this ambitious scheme will construct an entire new state-of-the-art business district on 575 acres of reclaimed land between Colombo harbour and the Green, complete with offices, hotels, malls and a major new financial centre. The project is being funded by the Chinese state-owned China Communications Construction Co. (CCCC) at a cost of $1.4 billion.

Like the island's other Chinese-funded mega-developments (such as the Hambantota Port) the scheme was personally associated with ex-president **Mahinda Rajapakse** and attracted widespread criticism, being seen as a vanity project whose principal raison d'être was to provide a way for the Rajapakse clan to extort further bribes from anyone and everyone involved. Environmentalists suggested that reclaiming such a large area of land would have dire ecological consequences, while rival politicians claimed the agreement constituted a direct breach of Sri Lankan sovereignty – CCCC will keep roughly half the reclaimed land on a 99-year-lease, plus 50 acres in perpetuity, creating a kind of miniature Sri Lankan Hong Kong almost in the heart of the island's capital.

Work was temporarily halted following the election of president **Maithripala Sirisena**, but is now proceeding apace. No buildings have yet appeared (and the entire project will likely take many more years to complete), although you can already see the vast swathe of reclaimed land stretching northwest of Galle Face Green – the best views are from the overpriced *Sky Bar* on the rooftop of the *Kingsbury* hotel. A couple of strategically placed displays on the Green show the new district as it may one day look: a gleaming fantasy of slick skyscrapers, marinas and malls which will change the heart of the city beyond all recognition.

sprawling facade of the *Galle Face Hotel*, the Green was created by Sir Henry Ward, governor from 1855 to 1860, who is commemorated by an easily missed memorial plaque halfway along the promenade in which the Green is "recommended to his successors in the interest of the Ladies and Children of Colombo".

Prized and preserved by generations of city dwellers (even the railway line south, which elsewhere runs straight down the coast, was rerouted inland to avoid it), the inland side of the Green has been irrevocably transformed over the past few years thanks to the construction of the two huge high-rise towers of the vast new *Shangri-La* complex, while work continues on the similarly gargantuan new ITC One Colombo development next door – and with encroaching land reclamation from the adjacent Port City (see page 77) promising to change the Green still further in the future. Still, the salty stroll along the Green's seafront promenade remains one of the city's most enjoyable walks, with the waves crashing a few feet below and views along the breezy coast and out to sea, where gargantuan container ships line up waiting to enter the harbour. Late in the day is the best time to visit, when half the city seems to come here to gossip, fly kites and eat the crunchy *isso wade* (prawn patties) served up by the line of hawkers stretched out along the front.

The Fort end of the Green is bounded by the ponderous Neoclassical **Secretariat**, now dwarfed by the **World Trade Center** towers rising behind it. Statues of independent Sri Lanka's first four prime ministers stand in front, centred on a purposefully moustachioed D.S. Senanayake, the first post-independence prime minister, who died in 1952 from injuries sustained when he fell from his horse on the Green.

Slave Island

Immediately east of Galle Face Green is the area known as **Slave Island** (although it's not actually an island), encircled on three sides by **Beira Lake**, whose various sections are connected by stagnant, pea-green canals. The name dates back to its Dutch-era title, **Kaffir Veldt**, from the African slaves (Kaffirs) who worked in the city – at one

THE LOTUS TOWER

Rising imperiously on the east side of Beira Lake is the incongruous silhouette of the gargantuan new **Lotus Tower**, a kind of Sri Lankan version of Toronto's CN Tower and – at a height of 350m – easily the tallest structure in South Asia (and slightly taller than the Eiffel Tower, for that matter). Dominating the city skyline for miles around, the tower is one of Colombo's biggest and weirdest structures, its bulging summit formed in the shape of a lotus bud and shaded in an unholy clash of garish purples and sickly greens. Construction (costing over $100m) was funded by Chinese loans, and indeed the thing wouldn't look out of place in, say, Shanghai or Guangzhou, although in the context of Colombo's largely low-rise cityscapes it looks about as plausible as a panda at a bishops' convention.

Not quite open at the time of writing, the summit will contain a revolving restaurant, observation deck and assorted telecommunications facilities, with further amenities in the six-storey, lotus-shaped base. The tower also serves as the island's most visible monument to the Rajapakse era: a piece of blaring Buddhist symbolism built (it's said) on misappropriated land and funded by foreign cash – a fitting tribute to the pseudo-religious hypocrisy and shameless graft of the old regime.

time there were as many as four thousand of them here. After a failed insurrection in the seventeenth century, the Dutch insisted that all slaves were quartered overnight in the Kaffir Veldt, and stocked the surrounding waterways with crocodiles in order to discourage attempts at escape.

The winds of change are now transforming Slave Island more dramatically than any other part of the city. Approaching from Galle Face Green along Justice Akbar Mawatha, the vast concrete skeletons of the new Cinnamon Life and ITC One Colombo mega-developments now fill the view, while the north side of Beira Lake is being similarly transformed by the new Colombo City Centre mall and, especially, by the lopsided 240m-high **Altair skyscraper**, already popularly known as the Leaning Tower of Colombo – although it looks more like a supersized ladder propped up against a very large wall.

All of these promise to provide the district with a string of futuristic new landmarks more reminiscent of Dubai than downtown Colombo. The heart of Slave Island, however, remains largely unchanged: a capsule of ramshackle and slightly raffish old-school city life, particularly along Rifle and Malay streets, dotted with scruffy little cafés and assorted churches, mosques and temples, including several built during the colonial era for soldiers from Malaya and India serving in the British army who were garrisoned on the island. Look out too for the colourful cluster of colonial **shop-houses** at the eastern end of Akbar Mawatha, now increasingly derelict and seemingly held together only by the creeping vegetation that festoons their facades.

Sri Subramanian Kovil

Kew Rd • Usually closed except during morning and evening pujas (around 8–9am & 5–6pm) • Rs.200

Constructed for Indian troops stationed here during the colonial era, the **Sri Subramanian Kovil** is one of Colombo's most imposing Hindu temples. The entrance, just off Kumaran Ratnam Road, is marked by a towering gopuram, a great mountain of kitsch masonry flanked with incongruously Victorian-looking miniature clocktowers. The temple is dedicated to the god Subramanian (or Kataragama, as he is known to the Sinhalese; see page 192), whose peacock symbol you will see at various places inside. The interior follows the standard pattern of Sri Lankan Hindu temples, with an inner shrine constructed from solid stone enclosed within a shed-like ambulatory, and an eclectic array of images including conventional Hindu gods alongside curious little statues of the Buddha, dressed up like a Hindu deity in robes and garlands.

1

GREEN PATH ART GALLERY

Stretching west from the National Art Gallery, Ananda Coomaraswamy Mawatha (still sometimes referred to by its colonial name of Green Path) serves as an enjoyable impromptu **open-air art gallery**, with local students and other part-time painters hanging their canvases from the railings along the side of the road. All artworks on display are for sale, often at very affordable prices, and the quality is generally high. It's busiest at weekends, although there are sometimes a few paintings on display during the week as well.

Seema Malaka
Sir James Peiris Mw • Daily 7am–11pm • Rs.300

South of the Sri Subramanian Kovil, the breezy southern arm of Beira Lake attracts pelicans, egrets and cormorants and provides an attractive setting for the striking **Seema Malaka** temple. Designed by Sri Lanka's foremost twentieth-century architect, Geoffrey Bawa (see page 122), this unusual shrine is used for inaugurations of monks from the nearby Gangaramaya temple – though it was actually paid for by a Colombo Muslim who, having fallen out with his co-religionists, decided to revenge himself by endowing a Buddhist shrine.

Set on three linked platforms rising out of the lake, Seema Malaka's novel structure was inspired by the design of Sri Lankan forest monasteries such as those at Anuradhapura and Ritigala – although sadly, in a staggeringly brainless act of architectural vandalism, the southern platform has recently been extended, utterly destroying the original symmetry and scale of the design and making the whole thing look tragically lopsided. The central pavilion is still beautiful though, an intricately latticed wooden pavilion surrounded by a row of delicate Thai Buddhas and roofed with lustrous blue tiles.

Gangaramaya
Just off Sir James Peiris Mw • Daily 5am–10pm • Rs.300

Just east of the Seema Malaka lies the **Gangaramaya** temple, established during Sri Lanka's nineteenth-century Buddhist revival and now one of Colombo's most important shrines and the focus of the major **Navam Perahera** festival (see page 47). The temple itself is probably the most bizarrely eclectic in the country, home to a strange hotchpotch of objects from Sri Lanka and abroad, with statues of Thai Buddhas, Chinese bodhisattvas and Hindu deities donated by well-wishers scattered randomly here and there.

The heart of the temple comprises a serene, and relatively traditional, group of buildings clustered around a central courtyard with a small dagoba at its centre and a venerable old **bo tree** growing out of a raised platform draped in prayer flags. Across the courtyard lies the principal **image house**, its base supported by dwarfs (symbols of prosperity) in various contorted poses. Inside, the entire building is occupied by an eye-popping *tableau vivant*, centred on a gargantuan orange seated Buddha flanked by elephant tusks and surrounded by dozens of other larger-than-life Buddhas and devotees bearing garlands – thoroughly kitsch, but undeniably impressive. Next to the bo tree stands the beautiful old **library**, housed in a richly decorated wooden pavilion, its upper floor (reached via the bo tree terrace) home to a quirky assortment of Buddhist artefacts and curios.

Just off the courtyard, the temple's entertaining **museum** fills two large rooms with an astonishing treasure-trove of weird and wonderful bric-a-brac. The overall effect is rather like a vast Buddhist car-boot sale, with objects of great delicacy and value alongside pieces of pure kitsch ranging in size from the "world's smallest Buddha statue" (properly visible only through a magnifying glass) to a stuffed elephant.

1

Cinnamon Gardens

South of Slave Island stretches the much more upmarket suburb of **Cinnamon Gardens**, named for the plantations which flourished here during the nineteenth century. The capital's most sought-after residential area, Cinnamon Gardens' leafy streets preserve an aura of haughty Victorian privilege – along with their colonial street names. Many are lined with elite colleges and rambling old mansions (most now occupied by foreign embassies and government offices) concealed behind dauntingly high walls, particularly in the very exclusive rectangle of streets between Ward Place and Gregory's Road.

Viharamahadevi Park and around

Park daily 6am–6pm • Free

Hugging the northern edge of Cinnamon Gardens lies Colombo's principal open space **Viharamahadevi Park**, a haven of tropical greenery originally Victoria Park but renamed with characteristic patriotic thoroughness in the 1950s after the famous mother of King Dutugemunu (see page 190).

Facing the north side of the park is Colombo's **Town Hall** (1927) – a functional white Neoclassical structure looking something like a cross between the US Capitol and a municipal waterworks. A large photogenic **gilded Buddha** sits opposite, while immediately to the north lies lively De Soysa Circus (aka Lipton Circus) flanked by the eye-catching **Devatagaha Mosque**, a big white Moorish-looking structure that adds a quaint touch of architectural whimsy to the otherwise functional junction.

Natural History Museum

Horton Place • Mon–Thurs, Sat & Sun 9am–5pm • Rs.400 (or combined ticket with National Museum Rs.1200 if purchased before 2pm)

The lacklustre **Natural History Museum** fills three gloomy and labyrinthine floors with exhibits ranging from stuffed leopards and pickled snakes to dated, didactic and thoroughly uninteresting presentations on the island's ecology and economy. Recent renovations have smartened the place up, but not by much, while the vast quantity of stuffed animals posed in moth-eaten pomp is enough to turn a conservationist's hair grey.

National Art Gallery

Ananda Coomaraswamy Mw • Daily 9am–4pm • Free

Sri Lanka's **National Art Gallery** comprises a single large room full of twentieth-century paintings by Sri Lankan artists (along with assorted portraits of island notables) in various quasi-European styles. Unfortunately there are no labels to identify painters, titles, dates or anything else, making the whole experience rather unedifying, although it's possible to pick out a couple of rather Matisse-like canvases by George Keyt (1901–93), Sri Lanka's foremost twentieth-century painter (by the entrance on your right at the time of writing).

On the east side of the gallery rises the dramatic outline of the huge **Nelum Pokuna Theatre** (ⓦlotuspond.lk), its distinctive flower-shaped exterior inspired by the famous lotus pond (*nelum pokuna*) at Polonnaruwa (see page 311).

The National Museum

Sir Marcus Fernando Mw • Daily 9am–5pm • Rs.1000 (or Rs.1200 for a combined ticket with the Natural History Museum if purchased before 2pm) • The free "Sri Lanka Museums" app provides a detailed audioguide to various exhibits

Immediately south of Viharamahadevi Park in an elegant white Neoclassical building of 1877, Colombo's **National Museum** houses an extensive and absorbing collection of Sri Lankan artefacts from prehistoric times to the colonial era – allow at least a couple of hours to really explore the collection.

The **entrance lobby** is dominated by a famous eighth-century limestone Buddha from Anuradhapura – a classic seated image in the meditation posture whose simplicity, serenity, lack of decoration and very human features embodies much that is most characteristic of Sri Lankan art. Off to the right, **room 1** has displays on Sri Lankan prehistory, including an interesting "canoe" grave, an impressive burial urn and a life-sized diorama showing a hairy bunch of cavemen skinning a lizard.

The downstairs galleries

The museum really gets going in **room 2**, devoted to the Anuradhapura period and housing a spectacular array of stone and bronze statues alongside other artefacts, including a curious pair of "boddhisattva sandals" and a couple of intricately etched sheets of gilded metal from the Jetvanarama monastery, inscribed with Mahayana texts. Past here, **room 3** (Polonnaruwa period) has further outstanding bronzes, including figures of Shiva and Parvati showing the growing influence of Hinduism on Sri Lankan cultural during the period.

Room 4 (Transitional period) is more diverse, with assorted Chinese ceramics alongside beautifully crafted household utensils, decorative items and, highlight of the room, a stunning silver sword made for Bhuvanekabahu I of Gampola, with jewel-encrusted dragon's head handle. **Room 5** (Kandyan era) hold a further treasure-trove of luxury domestic items showing the incredibly intricate levels of craftsmanship, in a variety of materials, which were achieved by the kingdom's artisans. Most impressive, however, is the glittering **regalia and throne** of the kings of Kandy – one of the museum's highlights – which was surrendered to the British during the handover of power in 1815 and kept in Windsor Castle until being returned by George V in 1934.

Exiting room 5 brings you to a small **veranda** which is home to a display of "urinal stones" – sumptuously decorated carvings on which monks would formerly have relieved themselves in order to demonstrate their contempt for worldly riches. Beyond here lies the large **room 6** ("Stone Antiquities Gallery"), home to an impressive selection of eroded pillars, friezes and statues salvaged from archeological sites across the island. Most come from Anuradhapura and Polonnaruwa, including a sequence of pillar inscriptions used to record administrative decrees and grants of land.

The upstairs galleries

A well-hidden staircase at the back of room 6 leads upstairs to **room 7**, containing copies of frescoes from Sigiriya, the Tivanka-patamaghara in Polonnaruwa and elsewhere along with a fine collection of Orientalist watercolours by the Irish artist Andrew Nicholl (1804–86), who spent four years in Sri Lanka from 1846 to 1850. **Rooms 8–11** feature extensive collections of textiles, ceramics and coins, followed by an impressively vast array of island arts and crafts (**room 12**), assorted armaments (**room 13**) and – one of the museum's highlights – an eye-popping selection of outlandish traditional masks (**room 14**), including some magnificent over-sized creations which no one could ever possibly wear. Things dribble to a conclusion in **room 15**, with dusty displays of traditional agricultural implements plus assorted life-size waxwork dioramas showing scenes from traditional village life.

Independence Avenue and around

South of the National Museum at the end of Independence Avenue lies the bombastic **Independence Commemoration Hall**, an overblown stone replica of the wooden Audience Hall at Kandy. Continuing south brings you to the **Independence Arcade** complex, a cool white colonial landmark of 1882 occupying the former Colombo Asylum, reopened after extensive government-sponsored renovations in 2014. The complex is spread over two buildings: the Entrance Wing, with cute little cupola and clock, and the H-shaped Main Wing, both now home to an upmarket array of restaurants, cafés and boutiques.

A short walk to the east is the **Sinhalese Sports Club**, whose engagingly old-fashioned stadium, complete with antiquated scoreboard, serves as one of Colombo's two Test-match cricket venues.

1

Southern Colombo

South of Galle Face Green, southern Colombo's principal thoroughfare – the fumey **Galle Road** – arrows due south towards Mount Lavinia and beyond. The first stretch of the road has a decidedly military atmosphere, with the heavily fortified compounds of the US and Indian embassies and **Temple Trees**, the prime minister's official residence, all but hidden behind sandbagged gun emplacements and high walls topped by army watchtowers. Brief architectural relief is provided by the quaint neo-Gothic **St Andrew's Scotskirk** of 1842, just north of Temple Trees.

Continuing south, Colombo's everyday commercial life resumes as Galle Road passes through **Kollupitiya**. Many of the buildings here are functionally nondescript, with lots of the reflective glassy facades favoured by modern Sri Lankan developers, though the occasional dog-eared little café, colourful sign or curious shop survives among the bland modern office blocks.

Geoffrey Bawa's house

No.11, 33rd Lane · Mon–Sat 30min tours at 10am, 2pm & 3.30pm; Sun at 10am only (tours should be pre-booked on ☎ 011 433 7335 or via ✉ admin@gbtrust.net) · Rs.1000 · ⊕ geoffreybawa.com

Hidden away in a tiny lane off Bagatelle Road is one of Colombo's buried treasures, No.11, 33rd Lane, the former Colombo residence of architect **Geoffrey Bawa** (see page 122). The house comprises what were originally four tiny bungalows, which Bawa gradually acquired between 1959 and 1968 and then set about dramatically remodelling, knocking the four buildings together and constructing a magical little labyrinth of rooms, courtyards, lightwells, verandas and passageways. The resulting home feels far larger than the modest space it actually occupies, and is festooned with colourful artworks and artefacts – a kind of architectural sketchbook in miniature of many of the themes that can be seen in Bawa's other work around the island.

Bambalapitiya and Wellawatta

Further south along the Galle Road, the workaday suburb of **Bambalapitiya** provides an enjoyable and anarchic mix of the old and new, ranging from the large Majestic Plaza shopping mall to little lopsided shops selling household items or packets of spices, while a series of South Indian and Muslim cafés brighten the main drag with their fanciful signs.

The Galle Road becomes progressively more ramshackle and down-at-heel as it continues south into the suburb of **Wellawatta**, popularly known as "Little Jaffna" thanks to its large Tamil population. This is one of the most characterful suburbs in southern Colombo, an interesting area full of colourful local cafés and picturesque (in a grubby kind of way) shops selling saris, "fancy goods" and all sorts of other paraphernalia.

Dehiwala Zoo

Dharmapala Mw · Daily 8.30am–6pm · Rs.2500, children Rs.1250 · ⊕ nationalzoo.gov.lk · Catch any bus running along Duplication Rd/ Galle Rd to Dehiwala, and then either walk or take a tuktuk

Some 10km south of Fort in the suburb of Dehiwala, **Dehiwala Zoo** is home to a good range of global wildlife, although be aware that major concerns have been raised about the way in which its wildlife is housed and treated, particularly the small enclosures in which its big cats are housed and the infamous "elephant dance" (still staged daily at 4.30pm).

Sri Lankan species here include cute sloth bears, porcupines, jungle- and fishing-cats, myriad birds and a number of leopards, part of the zoo's collection of **big cats**, which also includes lions and tigers. The zoo's large assortment of **monkeys** includes examples of all the native primates, and there's also a wide array of other mammals, from African giraffes to Australian giant red kangaroos – and a cage full of rabbits.

Mount Lavinia

The leafy beachside suburb of **Mount Lavinia**, 11km south of Colombo Fort, is bounded by the small headland (the so-called "Mount") that is one of the few punctuating features on the coastline near the capital. This area supposedly takes its name from a certain Lavinia, the lady friend of British Governor Sir Thomas Maitland, who established a residence here in 1806. Maitland's residence was subsequently expanded by successive governors before being turned into the **Mount Lavinia Hotel**, now one of the most venerable colonial landmarks in Sri Lanka and the main reason most foreign visitors come here.

A handy bolthole if you want to escape the bustle of central Colombo for a day or two, Mount Lavinia is also home to Colombo's closest half-decent **beach**, and on Sunday afternoons half the city seems to come here to splash around in the water, play cricket and smooch under umbrellas (and if you don't fancy the public beach, note that non-guests can use both pool and private beach at the *Mount Lavinia Hotel* for $7). The proximity of the city means that the water is borderline for swimming, although the sands are now looking cleaner than they have for years following recent clean-ups, and the whole area preserves a certain raffish charm, especially at night, with the lights of the towers in central Colombo twinkling away to the north, and the more modest illuminations of the *Mount Lavinia Hotel* framing the beach to the south.

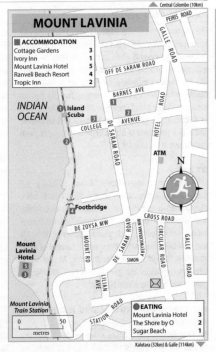

Kelaniya Raja Maha Vihara

Catch any bus to Kelaniya from Olcott Mw, outside Bastian Mawatha bus station

Ten kilometres east of Fort lies Colombo's most important Buddhist shrine, the **Kelaniya Raja Maha Vihara** – the Buddha himself is said to have taught at this spot on the last of his three visits to the island. Various temples have stood on the site; the present structure dates from the eighteenth and nineteenth centuries. A fairly modest dagoba (in the unusual "heap of paddy" shape, with sloping shoulders) marks the exact spot where the Buddha is said to have preached, though it's upstaged by the elaborate **image house** next door. Made from unusual dark orange-coloured stone, the exterior is richly decorated, with ornate doorways and pillars, plus entertaining friezes of galloping elephants and pop-eyed dwarfs around the base. Inside, the shrine's walls are covered in myriad paintings, including numerous strip panels in quasi-Kandyan style and some striking modern murals showing the Buddha's three legendary visits to Sri Lanka, including a memorable depiction of an incandescent Buddha floating in mid-air above a crowd of cowering demons.

The temple is also the focus of the extravagant two-day **Duruthu Perahera** celebrations every January.

ARRIVAL AND DEPARTURE

The opening of the various **expressways** around the city has made getting in and out of Colombo by road much quicker than previously when approaching from the north and south – and the new Kandy expressway (see page 28) will likewise massively speed up access to the hill country when open. Leaving Colombo, the city has (as you'd expect) the island's best transport connections, lying as it does at the centre of the national **rail network**, and with a vast range of **buses** departing to pretty much everywhere in the country.

BY AIR

Sri Lanka's main international airport (officially the Bandaranaike International Airport; ☎011 226 4444; ⓦairport.lk) is at Katunayake, 30km north of Colombo and 10km from Negombo. The arrivals terminal houses various bank kiosks, which change money at identical and generally competitive rates, plus a handful of ATMs accepting foreign Visa and MasterCards. All the major telecoms companies also have outlets here, making it a good place to pick up a local SIM card.

FROM THE AIRPORT TO COLOMBO, NEGOMBO AND ELSEWHERE

By taxi Taxis can be booked either at the airport taxi counter next to the tourist information desk, or the second counter outside (turn left as you leave the building). Fares are currently around Rs.2800 into Colombo (45min–1hr 15min; make sure your driver travels via expressway rather than the much slower old coastal road – assuming you don't mind paying the Rs.300 expressway toll), Rs.1600 to Negombo (20min), Rs.7500 to Kandy (3hr) and Rs.9500 to Galle (2hr). The various travel agents here also offer very cheap island-wide tours with car and driver, although these places don't have the best reputation and you're better off sorting something out in Negombo or Colombo.

By bus and tuktuk Airport buses (#187) run hourly (5am–10pm) from opposite the exit to the Central Bus Stand in Colombo (50min–1hr 15min). There are no direct buses to Negombo. If you want to reach Negombo by bus, turn right out of the terminal building and walk 250m to the airport entrance, where you'll find a tuktuk stand. From here you can catch a tuktuk to Averiwatte Bus Station (Rs.100) from where there are buses (every 30min; 45min) to Negombo. Alternatively, a tuktuk all the way to Negombo from the airport (25min) costs around Rs.800 (slightly more at night).

INTERNAL FLIGHTS

Cinnamon Air (ⓦcinnamonair.com) domestic flights leave from the international airport and from Waters Edge, in the south of the city, with scheduled services to Trincomalee (50min) via Sigiriya (35min), Batticaloa

(50min), Kandy (25min), and Castlereagh, near Adam's Peak (30min) as well as south to Hambantota (2hr) via Koggala (35min) and Dickwella (1hr). Services run daily year-round on all routes; sample fares (one way) are $176 to Kandy, $229 to Sigiriya, and $262 to Trincomalee.

Helitours (Sri Chittampalam Gardiner Mw, Slave Island, opposite the Inland Revenue Department, ☎011 314 4944, ⓦhelitours.lk) operate domestic flights three times a week from Ratmalana airport, south of Mount Lavinia, to Jaffna and Trincomalee (one way Rs.14,500/Rs.9250 respectively, although be aware of this airline's questionable safety practices (see page 31).

BY TRAIN

Colombo is the hub of the Sri Lankan rail system, with direct services to many places in the country (see page 32). Long-distance services arrive at and depart from **Colombo Fort Station** (which is actually in the Pettah not Fort), conveniently close to the cluster of top-end hotels in Fort and around Galle Face Green, but some way from the city's southern areas. A metered tuktuk from Fort Station to Kollupitiya/Bambalapitiya will cost between Rs.125 and Rs.250 depending on how far down the Galle Rd you're going, and there are fairly regular suburban trains from here south via Kollupitiya and Bambalapitiya to Mount Lavinia. Leaving Colombo you can buy tickets from the Intercity Reservation Office (daily 5am–10pm) on the left of the entrance. For information, try the helpful enquiries window (no. 7), inside the entrance arch on the right.

Destinations Anuradhapura (6 daily; 4–5hr); Batticaloa (2 daily; 8hr 30min); Ella (4 daily; 9hr); Galle (9 daily; 2hr 30min); Hatton (4 daily; 5hr 30min) Jaffna (4 daily; 7hr) Kandy (9 daily; 2hr 30min–3hr); Mannar (2 daily; 8hr 30min); Matara (7 daily; 3hr 30min); Nanu Oya (for Nuwara Eliya; 4 daily; 6hr 30min); Trincomalee (1 daily; 8hr).

BY BUS

BUS STATIONS

There are two main bus stations, lying side by side about 500m to the east of Fort station in Pettah. Almost all private buses use the packed and fumey **Bastian Mawatha** terminal, while government-run SLTB buses use the much more pleasant and orderly **Central Bus Stand** (information on ☎011 232 8081). There's a third bus station, **Gunasinghapura Bus Stand** (also known as Saunders Place Bus Stand), a little north of the Central Bus Stand, although increasingly few services leave from here and it's generally more pleasant and/or convenient to catch a service from one of the other terminals. **Arriving in Colombo**, note that private buses generally set passengers down in one of the streets surrounding Bastian

Mawatha terminal, rather than in the bus station itself. Information on major bus routes can found on the useful routemaster.lk website.

RESERVATIONS

Advance booking is still largely unheard of on most routes, although it's possible to reserve seats on a selected handful of private buses **online** at ⓦbusbooking.lk (Rs.120 booking fee).

TO THE AIRPORT/NEGOMBO

There are various options for catching a bus to the **airport** – but make sure you catch a service which travels along the expressway rather than along the much slower old coastal road. The easiest option to catch express airport bus #E3-187 from the Central Bus Stand (runs 5am–7pm; every 20min; 45min–1hr 15min). There are also private airport buses from Bastian Mawatha bus stand. There's also a range of services to **Negombo**, with the fastest and most painless option being bus #E3-240 (every 20min; 50min–1hr 15min) from the Central Bus Stand.

TO GALLE/MATARA AND THE SOUTH COAST

Travelling to **Galle**, **Matara** and other destinations along the **south coast**, you've got a choice between taking either one of the laboriously slow services down the old coastal road, which depart from the Central Bus Stand and Bastian Mawatha in the Pettah, or making your way out to **Maharagama**, around 10km southeast of the city centre, and catching a bus down the **Southern Expressway**. Expressway services are vastly quicker, and generally justify the hassle of getting out to Maharagama (see page 28), although, of course if time's not an issue you might decide to just catch one of the slower coast road buses. Even if you can't find a direct expressway bus to where you want to go (for instance **Mirissa**, **Weligama** or **Unawatuna**), it's generally quicker to take an expressway bus to either Matara or Galle and then catch an onward bus or tuktuk from there. The (roughly) 30–45min journey to Maharagama costs around Rs.500 in a metered tuktuk; alternatively, catch bus #112 (every 30min; 45min) from along the Galle Rd, or bus #138 from the road outside Bastian Mawatha bus station.

Destinations: Galle (every 30min; 3hr; or via expressway: every 15–30min; 1hr 15min); Hambantota (every 30min; 6hr; or via expressway every 90min; 4hr); Matara (every 15min; 4hr; or via expressway: every 15min; 2hr); Tangalla (hourly; 5hr; or via expressway: hourly; 3hr 30min); Tissamaharama (hourly; 7hr).

TO JAFFNA

For information about buses to Jaffna, see chapter 6 (page 376).

THE REST OF THE ISLAND

The opening of the new **expressway to Kandy** (due for 2020) will slash travel times to the hill country by at least 1hr 30min when open – for the time being, when heading to hill country destinations like **Nuwara Eliya**, **Ella** and **Haputale**, it's more enjoyable, and usually just as fast, to take the train.

Destinations: Aluthgama (every 15min; 1hr 30min); Ambalangoda (every 15min; 2hr); Anuradhapura (every 30min; 5hr 30min); Arugam Bay/Pottuvil (2 daily; 8hr); Batticaloa (hourly; 8hr); Dambulla (every 20min; 4hr); Habarana (hourly; 5hr); Hikkaduwa (every 15min; 2hr 15min); Kalpitiya (hourly; 4hr 30min); Kalutara (every 15min; 1hr); Kandy (every 15min; 3hr); Nuwara Eliya (every 30min; 5hr); Polonnaruwa (every 30min; 6hr); Trincomalee (every 30min; 7hr).

BY CAR

Car with driver Cars for airport or other short tours/transfers can be hired (expensively) through the travel desks at any of the major hotels or (more cheaply) through a local car-hire agent – reliable options include Malkey Rent-A-Car and Casons (see page 34) – or travel agent (try one of the little travel agents under the arches of the Galle Face Court Building on the corner of Galle Rd and Sir M.M. Markar Mw at the southern end of Galle Face Green). Count on around $20–25 for a trip to the airport, or $75 for transfers or day-tours to Galle and Kandy. For longer tours it's better to arrange something before you arrive with one of the larger tour operators listed in Basics (see page 27).

GETTING AROUND

By tuktuk The city has a superabundance of tuktuks – although nowadays taxis are often only a little more expensive. Many tuktuks are now metered, with a flag fare of Rs.60 plus Rs.40/km, providing a very inexpensive way of getting around. Unfortunately, a lot of drivers refuse to use them (or claim they're "broken"), while others take foreigners on ridiculously circuitous routes to bump up the fare. There are also many instances of meters being tampered with to record significantly higher fares – some people prefer just to agree a price in advance. If you still want to take a tuktuk rather than a taxi, the best option is to book via the PickMe app, which will deliver a reputable metered tuktuk to you, usually within about 5–10 minutes. It also shows your route and gives an estimated fare.

By taxi There are plenty of taxis in Colombo – often only slightly more expensive than a tuktuk, and a lot more comfortable. These can be booked via the PickMe app, and also via Uber (you might prefer to use the former,

1

given Uber's controversial employee record). You're given a range of options in terms of the vehicle you want with fares starting at around Rs.140 flag fare plus Rs.40/km. If you prefer to book by phone there are numerous radio-cab services – Kangaroo Cab (☎011 2 588 588, ⌨2588588. com) is the biggest and best.

By bus Endless lines of buses chunter along Colombo's major thoroughfares, though given the difficulty of working out routes, they're of little use to the casual visitor (and if you've got luggage, forget it). The only time you might consider a bus is to get up and down the Galle Rd in the southern half of the city between Kollupitiya and

Mount Lavinia. Buses tear up and down between Galle Fac Green and the southern suburbs literally every few second (although southbound buses and other traffic is diverte slightly inland along Duplication Rd on its way throug Kollupitiya); stops are marked by blue signs.

By suburban train Suburban trains are a useful way c reaching the southern part of the city, although they ca get packed at rush hours (roughly Mon–Fri 7.30–9.30am 4.30–6.30pm). Trains run roughly every 30min–1hr fron Fort Railway Station, calling at Kollupitiya, Bambalapitiya Wellawatta, Dehiwala and Mount Lavinia. The journe from Fort to Mount Lavinia takes around 30min.

INFORMATION AND TOURS

Tourist information The city's tourist office (open daily 7am–9pm; ☎011 242 6800, ⌨srilanka.travel) is just south of the Galle Face Hotel at 80 Galle Rd, Kollupitiya. Staff can assist with general queries and also dish out copies of the free monthly tourist guide, Travel Lanka. For listings of forthcoming events, see ⌨yamu.lk, ⌨timeout. com/sri-lanka or ⌨event.lk.

Colombo City Tours ☎011 281 4700, ⌨colombocitytours.com. City bus tours ($20–30) aboard an open-top double-decker red London-style bus.

Tours last around 3hr with three itineraries including tw daytime excursions and weekend tours by night.

Colombo City Walks ☎077 301 7091 ⌨colombocitywalks.lk. Insightful half-day walks (fron around $40) in Colombo with four contrasting itinerarie including Fort, foodie tours, and a "dodgy bar" tour, plu kayaking trips to Muthurajawela (see page 98). Walk are arranged on demand, but usually leave daily at 9am 9.30am and 3.30pm.

ACCOMMODATION

Colombo has wide range of big **top-end hotels** and also plenty of smaller and more characterful boutique hotels and guesthouses. **Cheaper rooms** are, however, extremely hard to come by (unless you don't mind being miles out in the suburbs), although there's a decent selection of dorm beds available. It pays to **book in advance**, especially if you're planning on staying at one of the smaller guesthouses.

FORT

City Beds The Regent 20 Regent Building, Sir Chittampalam A. Gardiner Mw ☎011 239 3420, ⌨citybedssrilanka.com; map p.70. Shoebox hotel on the edge of Fort with fifteen comfy, brightly painted a/c rooms – those upstairs ($5 extra) are a little bigger than those below. There's also a handy mini-kitchen with free tea, coffee and fridge, while tiptop soundproofing keeps nearby traffic noise at bay. $55

City Rest Fort 46 Hospital St ☎011 233 9340, ⌨facebook.com/cityrestfort; map p.70. Fourteen well-equipped (albeit mainly windowless) four-bed dorms, all a/c, with individual locker, reading light and plug socket for each bed, plus good bathroom facilities (with hot water). There are also four comfy and attractively decorated en-suite rooms with TV and fridge (although again, most lack windows). Nice, although overpriced at current rates. B&B: dorms $22, doubles $85

Grand Oriental York St ☎011 232 0320 ⌨grandoriental.com; map p.70. No longer nearly a grand as its name suggests, this famous old establishmer has lost most of its colonial character and is now lookin decidedly past its best. Reduced circumstances apart, it still a decent option. Rooms are comfortable enough, dated, the location right in the thick of the Fort action excellent, and there are superb port views from the fourth floor restaurant-cum-bar (see page 92) and from som deluxe rooms. A bit pricey at published rates, althoug often discounted online. $93

The Kingsbury 48 Janadhipathi Mw ☎011 242 1221 ⌨thekingsburyhotel.com; map p.70. In a prim seafront location, this is one of Colombo's older upmarke hotels, comprehensively modernized a few years back bu still offering a dash of old-world style and chic coloni touches – and often at slightly lower rates than the city other five-stars. Rooms are well equipped and offer fin city views (or sea views from suites) and facilities includ a big pool, upmarket Chinese and seafood restaurants ar the cool (but pricey) Sky Lounge bar. $188

Star Anise Boutique Capsule 15 Mudalige Mu ☎011 245 1777, ⌨thestaranise.com; map p.70. No actually a capsule hotel but a very superior hostel – ar probably a better option than the nearby City Rest Fort (se above). Beds in the a/c dorms all come with their own pul down blinds for total privacy, plus charger, light and unde bed locker, and there's also a lounge, kitchen and laundry room. B&B: singles $20, doubles $35

The Steuart 45 Hospital St ☎011 557 5575, ⓦcitrusleisure.com/steuart; map p.70. Bang in the heart of Fort, this pleasant three-star is one of the city's better bargains. The Scottish-baronial theme – complete with mock-tartan carpets – is a bit cheesy, admittedly, but the public areas (including a nice bar) are attractively kitted out with plenty of dark leather chairs and soothing wood finishes, and rooms are attractively spacious and very comfortable, if a bit plain. Online discounts can often make rates among the lowest in the area. $90

GALLE FACE GREEN

★ **Galle Face Hotel** Galle Face Green ☎011 254 1010, ⓦgallefacehotel.com; map p.74. Colombo's most famous hotel and, following recent renovations, once again one of the most memorable places to stay in town. The salty oceanfront setting can't be beaten and the whole place still boasts heaps of old-world charm – particularly the gorgeous sea-facing veranda, the ultimate venue for a romantic sundowner. Choose between a room in the older (but now comprehensively updated) Classic Wing or one in the newer and slightly less characterful Regency Wing, all kitted out in neocolonial style and combining modern comforts with traditional decor. There's also a trio of restaurants, a small pool and an attractive spa. $200

Ramada 30 Sir M.M. Markar Mw ☎011 242 2001, ⓦramadacolombo.com; map p.74. Tucked away in a quiet side street just off the bottom of Galle Face Green, this low-key hotel doesn't have the style of its near neighbours but offers an excellent location and larger-than-average, albeit rather dated) rooms at relatively inexpensive rates. Facilities include a gym, bar, swimming pool and the good Alhambra Indian restaurant (see page 90). $124

Shangri-La 1 Galle Face ☎011 788 8288, ⓦshangrila. com; map p.74. The arrival of this deluxe hotel chain in Colombo is just one sign of the city's rapidly rising international profile. Occupying a huge new complex on the inland side of Galle Face Green (with the two soaring apartment towers and vast mall still under construction at the time of writing), the hotel has almost 550 rooms offering state-of-the-art five-star comforts (and great views from higher floors), multiple eating outlets, plus pool and spa. B&B $274

Taj Samudra 25 Galle Face Centre Rd ☎011 244 6622, ⓦtajhotels.com; map p.74. Set in lush grounds spanning the eastern side of Galle Face Green, this is still one of the nicer places to stay in Colombo (despite being increasingly overshadowed by the new mega-hotels springing up alongside). Rooms (some sea-facing) are attractively furnished, if a tad small, while facilities include a health club and pool, plus a good selection of places to eat and drink. B&B $215

SLAVE ISLAND

Uga Residence 20 Park St ☎011 567 3000, ⓦugaescapes.com; map p.74. One of Colombo's ultimate boutique addresses, occupying the lovely 200-year-old villa which was formerly the birthplace and childhood home of president J.R. Jayawardene. Set around a picture-perfect sunken courtyard garden and elongated pool, the whole place offers a luxurious mix of colonial ambience and contemporary style, both in public areas and in the eleven beautifully outfitted suites. Facilities include a gym, library, bar and the upscale *Rare* restaurant. B&B $300

Unique Towers 30 Hyde Park Corner ☎011 230 2022, ⓦuniquetowers.lk; map p.74. A good option for families or larger groups, with very spacious, well-equipped and competitively priced one- to four-bed apartments with private kitchen and lounge. Not much character, but you get a lot of square-metre for your money. $130

YWCA International Guest House 393 Colvin R. de Silva Mw (Union Place) ☎011 232 4181, ⓦywcacolombo.com; map p.74. Atmospheric old Dutch colonial mansion with antique furniture scattered around the veranda and plenty of olde-worlde charm. The nine rooms (four with a/c and hot water) are simple but clean, if you don't mind the general air of mustiness, though road noise can intrude at the front. B&B: Rs.4700, a/c Rs.6750

CINNAMON GARDENS

Cinnamon Red 59 Ananda Coomaraswamy Mw ☎011 214 5145, ⓦcinnamonhotels.com; map p.74. Hip high-rise hotel, with reception on floor 7 and rooms up to level 25 – all are spacious, furnished with funky red decor and smart TVs and have brilliant city views through big picture windows. There's also a rooftop bar and skinny infinity pool, plus gym and restaurant. $136

Jetwing Colombo Seven 57 Ward Place ☎011 255 0200, ⓦjetwinghotels.com; map p.74. The first Colombo property of Sri Lanka's leading hotel chain, this smooth new hotel is one of the most stylish in the city, with crisp white rooms (and great views from higher floors), a fine spa, bright restaurant and the stunning rooftop *Ward 7* bar and pool (see page 93). B&B $165

Maniumpathy 129 Kynsey Rd ☎011 269 6988, ⓦmanorhouseconcepts.com; map p.74. Eight-room boutique hotel in a stunning 150-year-old villa set around a gorgeous verandah and idyllic walled garden (with small pool). Rooms are lovingly decorated with antique furnishings and roll-top baths and the whole place brims with period character – more atmospheric (and slightly cheaper) than the similar *Uga Residence*, although the location isn't as good. B&B $250

★ **Paradise Road Tintagel** 65 Rosmead Place ☎011 460 2121, ⓦparadiseroadhotels.com; map p.74. Superb boutique hotel set in a stunning colonial mansion which was formerly the family home of the Bandaranaike

1

family (see page 413); S.W.R.D. Bandaranaike was shot on the veranda here in 1959. The mansion has now been lavishly restored and given a cool contemporary makeover, with ten spacious and beautiful suites in muted colours, a picture-perfect little infinity pool and chi-chi little in-house restaurant. B&B $280

Wayfarers Inn 77 Rosmead Place (no sign) ☎011 269 3936; map p. 74. Set in a quiet residential area, this attractive colonial-style guesthouse has a range of comfortable fan and a/c doubles with satellite TV, hot water and fridge, plus a lovely garden to laze in. B&B: $40, a/c $50

Zylan 115 Rosmead Place ☎011 686 883, ⓦzylan. lk; map p. 74. Smooth boutique hotel in a beautifully designed modern house on exclusive Rosmead Place, with eight rooms of widely varying standards and prices (some on the small side) arranged around a bright and airy central lounge. There's also a good Japanese restaurant in-house, plus a tiny pool (more like an ambitious puddle really) up on the roof. $100

KOLLUPITIYA

Backpack Lanka 247 R.A de Mel Mw (Duplication Rd) ☎011 438 8889 or ☎077 030 0900, ⓦbackpacklanka. com; map p. 74. Functional hostel offering some of Colombo's cheapest beds in a trio of a/c four-bed mixed dorms plus a few double rooms. All are poky, windowless and rather uninviting, with a single shabby shared bathroom, although it's difficult to complain given the price and very central (albeit grubby) location. B&B: dorms Rs.1700, doubles Rs.3700

Cinnamon Grand 77 Galle Rd ☎011 243 7437, ⓦcinnamonhotels.com; map p. 74. One of Colombo's glitziest five-star, with swanky public areas and a big array of facilities including a medium-sized pool, the halcyon Angsana Spa (see page 95) and an outstanding selection of restaurants. Rooms are comfortable and well equipped if a tad bland; those higher up the building have great views over downtown Colombo. $230

★ **Clock Inn** 457 Galle Rd ☎011 250 0588, ⓦclockinn. lk; map p. 74. Smart and very professionally run hotel-cum-hostel in an excellent downtown location. The neat, well-furnished and very cosy a/c rooms are comfortable and sensibly priced, and there are also seven well-equipped four- and six-person dorms, with individual lockers and plugs for each bed and spacious bathrooms with hot water. B&B: dorms $12, doubles $50

Colombo Court 32 Alfred House Ave ☎011 464 5333, ⓦcolombocourthotel.com; map p. 74. Asia's first-ever carbon-neutral city hotel, this elegant little boutique establishment boasts impressive eco-credentials, and plenty of style too. Rooms are attractively designed with lots of dark wood, cool white walls, and strategic splashes of colour, while the surprisingly extensive facilities include

a Balinese spa, a pretty walled garden with pool and jacuzzi, cute library, rooftop and poolside café and bar, plus the upmarket Scarlet Room restaurant. $122

Colombo Haven 263/6 Galle Rd (at the very end of the small lane behind the Carnival Ice Cream Parlour) ☎011 230 1672, ⓦcolombohaven.com; map p. 74. Welcoming guesthouse with four cosy doubles (all with a/c, hot water and fridge) of varying sizes and prices. The fancy showers, with disco lights and built-in radio, are a sight to behold. B&B $60

Colpetty House 2/6 Charles Ave ☎071 703 3333, ⓦcolpettyhouse.com; map p. 74. Peaceful and homely eight-room guesthouse in the depths of an exclusive, but very central, Kollupitiya residential area. Rooms (all a/c, two with shared bathroom) are spacious and attractively furnished. B&B: $45, en suites $60

Comfort@15 15 Sellamuttu Ave ☎011 760 7600, ⓦcomfortat15.lk; map p. 74. In an airy old colonial-era building with spacious white rooms equipped with cable TV, kettle, fridge and safe, plus a nice little restaurant (breakfast only). A few rooms have partial sea views although they're hardly worth the $10 surcharge. $55

Drift BnB 646 Galle Rd ☎011 250 5536, ⓦfacebook. com/driftbnb; map p. 74. Bright and airy building with a range of attractive and unusually spacious a/c rooms and two very pleasant a/c dorms, one mixed (six-bed), the other for women only (four-bed). All dorm beds come with lockers and individual bedside plug sockets and reading lights, plus quality mattresses, and there's also a pleasant communal lounge. Dorms Rs.2400, B&B doubles Rs.850

★ **Lake Lodge** 20 Alwis Terrace ☎011 232 6443, ⓦtaruvillas.com; map p. 74. Smooth, modern boutique guesthouse by leading Sri Lankan designer Taru, with stylish rooms in a central but very peaceful location (equally convenient for Kollupitiya, Cinnamon Gardens and Slave Island). The best option in town in this price range. B&B $136

Hotel Renuka & Renuka City Hotel 328 Galle Rd ☎011 257 3598, ⓦrenukahotel.com; map p. 74. Smart mid-range hotel in two adjoining buildings (each, confusingly, with a different name), offering modern a/c rooms with satellite TV and minibar – though get a room away from the noisy Galle Rd. Facilities include a small pool, gym, and the good in-house Palmyrah restaurant (see page 91). $89

BAMBALAPITIYA

Greenlands Hotel 3A Shrubbery Gardens, off Galle Rd ☎011 258 5592, ✉greenlandshotel@gmail.com; map p. 74. Located above the popular Greenlands vegetarian restaurant (see page 92) and offering simple and old-fashioned but reasonably well-maintained a/c rooms (but wafer-thin mattresses), at rock-bottom prices. An extra Rs.650 gets you hot water and a TV. Rs.3000, a/c Rs.3700

Moss BNB Colombo 160/2 Bauddhaloka Mw ☎ 011 255 3929, ✉ mosscolombo@gmail.com; map p. 74. Intimate little fifteen-room guesthouse-cum-mini hotel tucked down an alley off Bauddhaloka Mw. The cool, white rooms are surprisingly stylish for the price, and there's a neat little lounge and friendly and efficient service. B&B $60

Hotel Sunshine 5A Shrubbery Gardens ☎ 011 401 7676, ⓦ hotelsunshine.lk; map p. 74. Functional modern hotel with spacious tiled rooms and small bathrooms (all with hot water) – looking a bit worn in places, although the non-a/c rooms are standout value at current rates. Rs.2500, a/c Rs.5500

HAVELOCK TOWN

Havelock Place Bungalow 6 Havelock Place (turn down the side road by the Laugfs petrol station) ☎ 011 258 5191, ⓦ havelockbungalow.com; map p. 74. Idyllic little boutique bolthole set in a pair of intimate colonial villas which combine old-fashioned charm with all modern amenities. There's also a small pool, a beautiful garden and a peaceful garden café – only the slightly out-of-the-way location detracts. B&B $75

Highbury 14/1 Skelton Rd ☎ 077 436 6273; map p. 74. In a time-warped old 1850s colonial villa beautifully refurbished inside with bright, airy rooms and suites arranged around a spacious central lounge. Often gets booked solid, in which case you might end up in one of the three rooms in the newer building opposite. $65

MOUNT LAVINIA

Cottage Gardens 42–48 College Ave ☎ 011 271 9692, ⓦ cottagegardenbungalows.com; map p.83. Five large and attractively furnished detached a/c cottages (each sleeping two) with kitchenette, dotted around a peaceful and very private walled garden. $35

Ivory Inn 21 De Saram Rd ☎ 011 271 5006, ✉ ivoryinn@hotmail.com; map p.83. One of Mount Lavinia's best cheapies, with spotless, nicely furnished

rooms with private balcony (plus optional a/c and hot water) in an attractive modern red-brick building in a quiet location. Rs.3500, a/c Rs.4200

Mount Lavinia Hotel 100 Hotel Rd ☎ 011 271 1711, ⓦ mountlaviniahotel.com; map p.83. Famous old landmark which retains engaging touches of colonial style, despite comprehensive modernization, and enjoys a superb location atop its little oceanfront promontory – although the whole place often gets rammed with wedding parties and events and isn't the most relaxing spot in town. Rooms are modern and fairly characterless, though with all the usual five-star mod cons; most have sea views. There's also a biggish pool, a serene spa, and a huge stretch of idyllic private beach if you want to escape from the hoi polloi. B&B $160

Ranveli Beach Resort 56/9 De Saram Rd ☎ 011 271 7385; map p.83. Dated but cosy little hotel, arranged around a small pool and sociable restaurant enclosed in an intimate little walled garden. The neat, clean, tiled rooms are a bit past their best but are well maintained and come with optional a/c ($5 extra), hot water and cable TV, and you're just metres from the beach. B&B $40

★ **Tropic Inn** 30 College Ave ☎ 011 273 8653, ⓦ tropicinn.com; map p.83. Pleasant and very peaceful small hotel, with attractive wood and wrought-iron decor. Rooms (all with hot water and a/c) are cool, clean, modern and nicely furnished. Also has a couple of good-value four-bed male and female non-a/c "dorms" – actually just a normal room with four (non-bunk) beds. Dorms $12, doubles $36

THE OUTSKIRTS

Villa Talangama Hokandara ☎ 011 274 4675, ⓦ villatalangama.com; map p.68. Attractive three-room contemporary-colonial-style villa is set in a tranquil location on the eastern edge of the city, a 30min drive (15km) from the centre, complete with its own pool and garden overlooking the birdlife-rich Talangama wetlands. B&B $173

EATING

Colombo is far and away the best place to eat in Sri Lanka – the city boasts pretty much the full range of Asian and European cuisines, including an excellent selection of **Sri Lankan**, **Chinese** and **Indian** (both north and south) restaurants – although rapidly rising prices mean that more upmarket places now cost not far off what you'll pay back home. **Lunch packets** are sold by pavement stalls and cafés all over the city – a decent-sized helping of simple rice and curry costs around Rs.200. For comprehensive restaurant listings and reviews see ⓦ yamu.lk.

FORT AND PETTAH

Botanik Rooftop of the Fairway Hotel, 7 Hospital Street ☎ 076 644 5888 ⓦ botanik.lk; map p.70. One

of Colombo's coolest new restaurants, on top of the *Fairway Hotel*, with a kind of rooftop-garden ambience (hence the name), a grand, vaguely Spanish-looking tiled bar and superb views over Fort from its terrace. The menu, designed by Michelin-starred Sri Lankan chef Rishi Naleendra, features a short but very sweet selection of international dishes (mains Rs.1200–3100), many with an Asian slant – think buffalo curd parfait or poached chicken salad with satay sauce and wombok. Or just come for a drink (see page 92). Tues & Sun 5.30pm–midnight, Wed & Thurs noon–3pm & 5.30pm–midnight, Fri noon–3pm & 5.30pm–1am, Sat 5.30pm–1am.

★ **Ministry of Crab** Dutch Hospital, Fort ☎ 011 234 2722, ⓦ ministryofcrab.com; map p.70. Regularly

1

voted one of the top 50 restaurants in Asia over recent years, the *Ministry's* unrepentantly crab-centric menu showcases this famous Sri Lankan crustacean in an array of culinary styles, ranging from the ever-popular chilli crab through to a variety of Asian-influenced styles (mains from around Rs.4000). Wildly popular, and reservations almost always needed. Daily 5–11pm.

Pagoda Tea Rooms 105 Chatham St, Fort ☎011 232 5252; map p.70. Classic Colombo café, established in 1884 and now sporting a neatly refurbished interior behind its old colonial facade – keen Duranies might recognize it as the spot where Simon Le Bon upended a table in the *Hungry like the Wolf* video. Good place for cheap chow, with a short menu (mains Rs.300–400) of *lamprais*, rice and curry and fried rice dishes, plus bakery items from the counter at the front – although not much in the way of breakfast. Daily 7.30am–5.30pm.

Pilawoos Hotel Chatham St, Fort ☎011 239 9980; map p.70. Fort offshoot of the famous *Hotel de Pilawoos* (see page 91), serving up a similar range of food including the legendary cheese kottu. Daily 6am–10pm.

Semondu Dutch Hospital, Fort ☎011 244 1590, ⓦ semondu.com; map p.70. Owned by SriLankan Airlines, this place is in danger of giving airline catering a good name, with a well-prepared international menu (pasta, curries, steaks and plenty of seafood) served up in one of Colombo's most attractive dining rooms. Mains Rs.1250–2000. Daily 11am–10pm (last orders).

Sri Suryas 255 Sea St, Pettah ☎011 242 4789; map p.72. A great spot for lunch while exploring the Pettah, this pleasant a/c restaurant serves up excellent subcontinental chow at bargain prices, majoring in South Indian thalis and dosas but with a good selection of North Indian classics too. Mains Rs.300-600. Daily 7.30am–10.45pm.

AROUND GALLE FACE GREEN

Alhambra Ramada hotel, 30 Sir M.M. Markar Mw ☎011 242 2001, ⓦ ramadacolombo.com; map p.74. Long-running North Indian restaurant (despite the Moorish name), with a range of solidly prepared and reasonably priced standards including Mughlai dishes, biryanis and tandooris, plus plenty of vegetarian options. Mains Rs.900–1500. Daily noon–2.30pm & 7–11pm.

Bavarian German Restaurant 11 Galle Face Court 2, Galle Rd ☎011 242 1577, ⓦ facebook.com/TheBavarianSL; map p.74. A rustic interior full of chunky wooden furniture provides a suitably Bavarian setting for hearty (albeit pricey) Central European dishes like beef stroganoff, pork schnitzel and chicken kiev, plus a few seafood, pasta and vegetarian options. Mains around Rs.2500. Daily noon–3pm & 6–11pm.

SLAVE ISLAND

Café Francais 48 Park St ☎011 450 2602, ⓦ cafefrancaisbypourcel.com; map p.74. Lively bistro-style French restaurant supervised by Michelin-starred brothers Jacques and Laurent Pourcel. Choose between the casual café and bar out front for snacks, tapas and drinks, or the more elegant European-style dining room around the back, serving classic French and Mediterranean dishes from a regularly changing menu. Mains from around Rs.1300. Daily 10am–1am.

★ **Monsoon** 50/2 Park Street Mews ☎011 230 2449, ⓦ monsooncolombo.com; map p. 74. At the heart of the buzzing Park Street Mews drinking and dining enclave, this superb restaurant brings an authentic taste of Southeast Asia to inner-city Colombo, served up in a spacious warehouse-style dining area which wouldn't look out of place in London or New York, and soundtracked by the energetic clatter of wok-wielding chefs in the open kitchen. Food features a wide range of shamelessly moreish, brilliantly authentic dishes from Malaysia, Indonesia, Thailand, Singapore and Vietnam featuring all sorts of regional classics: *nasi lemak, pad thai, nyonya laksa* and *pho bo,* to name just a few – all delivered to your table the moment they're ready, adding a dash of street-food spontaneity to proceedings. Mains Rs.1200–1800. Tues & Sun 6–10.30pm, Wed & Thurs noon–3pm & 6–11pm, Fri noon – 3pm & 6–11pm, Sat 6–11pm.

CINNAMON GARDENS

Agra Sri Lanka Foundation Mw ☎011 472 3333, ⓦ agracolombo.lk; map p. 74. Attractive Indian restaurant with one of the prettiest interiors in the city and a fine selection of classic North Indian and Mughlai cuisine, including plenty of kebabs, tandoori dishes and a good spread of reasonably priced vegetarian options. Attached to the enjoyable *Manchester* pub (see page 92). Mains Rs.1250–2000. Daily 11.30am–11.30pm.

The Mango Tree 82 Dharmapala Mw ☎011 587 9790, ⓦ themangotree.net; map p. 74. Reliable North Indian restaurant dishing up a range of well-prepared meat, seafood and vegetarian dishes with the emphasis on tandooris, tikkas, kebabs and hearty Punjabi-style cuisine. Mains Rs.1000–1500. Daily 11am–11pm.

★ **Upali's** 65 C.W.W. Kannangara Mw ☎011 269 5812, ⓦ upalis.com; map p. 74. One of the best places for Sri Lankan food in Colombo, serving up brilliantly authentic, sensibly priced island cuisine in a simple modern licensed restaurant – and usually rammed with locals as a result. Traditional Sinhalese cooking is the order of the day, with a distinct dash of feisty Jaffna flavours (try the signature Jaffna crab curry). Choose from all sorts of dishes including mutton, cashew (*kadju*), jackfruit, fish-head and white potato curries, spicy *rasam* soups, plus hoppers, string hoppers, *pittu* and *kottu rotty,* all served in raditional clay pots. Mains Rs.550–900. Daily 11.30am–10.30pm.

KOLLUPITIYA

Amaravathi 2 Mile Post Ave ☎011 438 8255; map p. 74. Popular a/c restaurant serving up inexpensive and tasty veg and non-veg dishes from a mainly Indian menu (both north and south) plus a few Sri Lankan offerings including good *kottu rotty*. Unlicensed. Mains Rs.900–1250. Daily 11.30am–3.30pm & 6.30–11pm.

★ **Barefoot Café** Barefoot, 706 Galle Rd ☎011 255 3075, ⊛barefootceylon.com; map p. 74. Set in the beautiful courtyard at the back of Colombo's most personable shop (see p.94), with a short but excellently prepared selection of international café-style fare (mains Rs.750–1200), plus tempting daily lunch specials, full-English breakfasts and moreish desserts and cakes. The live jazz sessions (most Sun 1–4pm) are a city institution. Mon–Sat 10am–7pm, Sun 11am–6pm.

★ **Chutneys** Cinnamon Grand, 77 Galle Rd ☎011 249 7372, ⊛cinnamonhotels.com; map p. 74. The most original restaurant in Colombo, showcasing the lesser-known culinary byways – particularly the street food – of southern India, with a tempting assortment of dishes from Kerala, Tamil Nadu, Andhra Pradesh and Karnataka. There's a good range of meat dishes, plus a superb vegetarian selection, all prepared with hearty infusions of chilli, tamarind and coconut milk, served with feisty chutneys and backed up by a range of traditional street drinks ranging from tamarind juice to *panna* (sweet and sour raw mango). Surprisingly inexpensive, too. Veg/non-veg mains Rs.570/Rs.1000–1500. Daily noon–2.30pm & 7–11pm.

Crescat Boulevard Galle Rd; map p. 74. The food court in the basement of Colombo's smartest shopping mall teems with fast-food outlets dishing up everything from Mongolian to Sri Lankan, Indian, Chinese and Malaysian cuisine, plus pizza and ice cream. Unlicensed. Daily 10am–10pm.

Cricket Club Café 12 Ernest de Silva Mw (Flower Rd) ☎011 257 4394, ⊛thecricketclubcafeceylon.com; map p. 74. Old Colombo favourite, recently relocated from its long-time home in a lovely old colonial bungalow to more cramped and less appealing premises on Flower Rd. Not as nice as before, admittedly, but still a fun place to eat, with cricketing memorabilia ranged around the walls and an unpretentious bistro-style menu featuring burgers and salads (from around Rs.900) plus more elaborate international mains (from around Rs.1300), all named after famous men in white (Ganguly's grill, Freddie's fillet o' fish, and so on). Mon–Fri 11am–11pm, Sat & Sun 9am–11pm.

Hotel de Pilawoos 417 Galle Rd ☎011 257 4795, ⊛pilawoos.lk; map p. 74. Famous local café dishing up big portions of no-nonsense grub at respectable prices

(mains around Rs.550). It's best known for its *kottu rotty* (the cheese version has a dedicated following, best eaten, it's said, after a few beers and washed down with an iced milo) and there are also plenty of burianis and burgers on the extensive menu, plus good fresh juices. Unlicensed. Daily 6am–4.30am.

Gallery Café 2 Alfred House Rd ☎011 258 2162, ⊛paradiseroad.lk; map p. 74. Colombo's most stylish café, occupying a beautiful villa which formerly housed the offices of architect Geoffrey Bawa. The outer courtyard hosts temporary exhibitions, while the inner courtyard is home to the café itself, with open-air seating and a big menu of reasonably prepared international mains (around Rs.1700–2300) – anything from butter chicken to fish 'n' chips. There's also a huge range of diet-busting puddings, plus a good wine and cocktail list. Daily 10am–midnight.

Green Cabin 453 Galle Rd ☎011 258 8811; map p. 74. Cheap and cheerful local place on Galle Rd serving up above-average rice and curry, *lamprais* and other Sri Lankan offerings, plus *kottu rotty*, hoppers and string hoppers in the evening. Mains Rs.275–500. Unlicensed. Daily 11.30am–3pm & 6.30–11pm.

The Lagoon Cinnamon Grand, 77 Galle Rd ☎011 249 7371, ⊛cinnamonhotels.com; map p. 74. Colombo's best seafood, served up in a bright glass-sided restaurant permeated with salty marine smells. Choose what you want from the superb display of fish and seafood (including prawns the size of small lobsters), and have it prepared in any one of over 25 different cooking styles, from Sri Lankan and Indian to Chinese, Thai and Continental. Buffet on Sun at lunchtime (Rs.2735). Mains around Rs.1500. Daily noon–2.30pm & 6pm–midnight.

Noodles Cinnamon Grand, 77 Galle Rd ☎011 249 7361, ⊛cinnamonhotels.com; map p. 74. This cool, noodle-centric pan-Asian restaurant dips its toes into various oriental cuisines, with a particular emphasis on Vietnamese and Japanese dishes, as well as offerings from Thailand, Singapore and China, all well prepared and very reasonably priced (mains Rs.850–1000). Daily noon–3pm & 6.30–11.30pm.

Nuga Gama Cinnamon Grand, 77 Galle Rd ☎011 249 7468; map p. 74. Looking disconcertingly like a real Sri Lankan jungle village in the heart of Colombo, *Nuga Gama*'s rustic thatched huts, dotted beneath the branches of an enormous banyan tree, offer an enjoyably offbeat setting for a evening meal in the city. The nightly set buffet (Rs.2850) is also a great place to introduce yourself to island cuisine, with a terrific array of classic local dishes, authentically prepared, laid out in seemingly endless lines of claypot bowls. Daily 7–11pm.

Palmyrah Hotel Renuka, 328 Galle Rd ☎011 257 3598, ⊛renukahotel.com; map p. 74. This unpretentious basement restaurant is one of Colombo's better places for Sri Lankan cuisine, with tasty (if rather pricey) curries, hoppers, *pittu* and *kottu rotty*, plus rich Jaffna-style meat and fish curries and a few Indian dishes. Mains Rs.1000–1500. Daily noon–2.30pm & 7–10.30pm.

BAMBALAPITIYA

Chinese Dragon Café 11 Milagiriya Ave, off Galle Rd ☎ 011 780 8080, ⓦ chinesedragoncafe.com; map p. 74. Long-running Chinese restaurant, tucked away in a rambling old mansion off Galle Rd. The extensive and affordable menu (mains around Rs.700) includes a decent range of Chinese standards prepared with the usual dash of Sri Lankan spice, plus local favourites like chilli crab and devilled chicken. Daily 11am–3pm & 6–11pm.

★ **Greenlands** 3A Shrubbery Gardens, off Galle Rd; map p. 74. A Colombo institution, hidden away in an old colonial house, this sedate South Indian vegetarian restaurant offers a big range of excellent, dirt-cheap food (with all mains under Rs.250) including *vadais* (masala, *ulundu*, curd), dosas (paper, ghee, onion) and other goodies including *idlis*, *pooris* and *bonda* (a kind of bhaji). Unlicensed. Daily 8am–10pm.

Siam House 17 Melbourne Ave ☎ 011 259 5944, ⓦ siamhouse.lk; map p. 74. Convivial Thai with smooth modern decor and a big menu featuring all the usual favourites – red and green curries, spicy salads and soups, *pad thai* – served in big portions. Mains from around Rs.110. Daily 11am–11.30pm.

MOUNT LAVINIA

Mount Lavinia Hotel 100 Hotel Rd ☎ 011 271 1711 ⓦ mountlaviniahotel.com; map p.83. There's a range of eating options at this landmark hotel. The *Governor's Restaurant* does a vast and better-than-average buffet spread (lunch $12, or $20 on Sun, dinner $19), though the number of guests can mean it's a bit like eating in the middle of a rush hour. Alternatively, the attractive and much more sedate *Seafood Cove* on the hotel's private beach offers a range of freshly caught fish (around Rs.1200–1800), cooked to suit. Governor's Restaurant daily 11am–11pm; Seafood Cove daily noon–3pm & 7–10.30pm.

The Shore by O College Ave ☎ 011 272 6638 ⓦ facebook.com/TheShoreByO; map p.83. Usually the most kicking place on the beach, with a cool open-air bar downstairs (often hosting live music events and beach parties at weekends) and a glassed-in a/c restaurant upstairs, serving a decent selection of international mains (Rs.800–1200), including plenty of seafood. Mon & Tues 5–11pm, Wed–Sun 11am–11pm.

Sugar Beach (formerly La Voile Blanche) 43/10 Beach Rd ☎ 011 703 5135; map p.83. Right on the beach this cool all-white restaurant has a rather Mediterranean feel in both looks and food, with a selection of inventive European and seafood mains menu (Rs.900–1500), plus a few Sri Lankan and Middle Eastern dishes – anything from beetroot-marinaded smoked salmon to seafood *shakshouka* – all backed up by a great selection of juices and cocktails. Daily 9am–midnight.

DRINKING AND NIGHTLIFE

Colombo tends to go to sleep at around 10pm, and **nightlife** remains fairly conspicuous by its general absence. There's a reasonable spread of places to **drink**, although nightclubs are few and far between, and tend to come and go on an annual basis. Forthcoming events are listed at ⓦ yamu.lk, ⓦ timeout.com/sri-lanka and ⓦ event.lk.

Botanik Fairway Hotel, 7 Hospital Street, Fort ☎ 076 644 5888; map p.70. This cool modern restaurant (see page 89) is also a great place for a drink, offering a peerless perch overlooking central Fort and with plenty of good, reasonably priced drinks (including excellent Asian-style cocktails and a decent wine selection) from the impressive island bar. There's also quality live music or DJ nightly except Tues. Tues & Sun 5.30pm–midnight, Wed & Thurs noon–midnight, Fri noon–1am, Sat 5.30pm–1am.

Bradman's Bar Cricket Club Café, 12 Ernest de Silva Mw (Flower Rd) ☎ 011 257 4394, ⓦ thecricketclubcafeceylon.com; map p. 74. Cosy little pub-style bar tucked away at the back of the popular *Cricket Club Café* (see page 91) with nonstop cricket on the overhead TVs – although drinks are pricey. Daily 11am–11pm.

Harbour Room Fourth floor, Grand Oriental Hotel, York St, Fort ⓦ grandoriental.com/habour-room.html; map p.70. Grab a beer from the bar of this lacklustre restaurant and head out to the tiny attached terrace for stunning views over the port below – particularly spectacular after dark. Daily 10am–11.30pm.

In … on the Green Galle Face Hotel (entrance outside, on the Galle Rd opposite The Bavarian restaurant), Kollupitiya; map p. 74. Decent stab at a traditional English pub with a reasonable if pricey selection of local tipples and respectable pub food. Happy hour 5.30–7.30pm. Thurs–Sun 4pm–midnight.

The Manchester Sri Lanka Foundation Mw (entered via Agra restaurant), Cinnamon Gardens ☎ 077 854 5824, ⓦ facebook.com/themanchestercolombo; map p. 74. Cosy pub overlooking the Royal College Rugby Ground with British pub food, reasonably priced beer (including a good selection of imported brands), single malt whiskies and decent bar food. Also hosts weekly pen-mic (Tues 8pm) and quiz nights (Wed 8pm), plus egular live music (Thurs–Sat). Daily noon–midnight.

ission to Seafarers (Flying Angel Club) 26 Church t, Fort; map p.70. In an old colonial building next to t Peter's Church, this place is actually a kind of low-key ocial club for visiting sailors docking at the adjacent port, lthough they don't seem to mind stray tourists dropping n for a cheap drink in the quiet and homely little bar. Daily –9pm.

hythm and Blues Bar 19/1 Daisy Villa Ave, R.A. e Mel Mw (Duplication Rd), Bambalapitiya ⓦbitly. om/rhythmandbluescolombo1; map p. 74. Relaxed nd completely unpretentious bar-cum-live music venue ith a mix of live bands and DJs playing Wed–Sat. Daily pm–2am.

ilk/Sugar Maitland Crescent, Cinnamon Gardens ⓣ011 268 2122, ⓦsugarcolombo.com; map p. 74. In he city's old colonial Gymkhana Club, the chic Silk lounge ar is popular with dolled-up locals and comes with proper ancefloor and music 'til late. Or head for the equally cool ugar rooftop restaurant and bar next door, which also has ve music some nights. Silk: Weds–Sat 9pm–4am (2am n Weds); Sugar daily 8am–11pm.

Tap House by R n R Dutch Hospital complex, Fort ⓣ077 377 3844, ⓦfacebook.com/TaphouseByRnr; map p.70. Conveniently central place for a cheapish beer (mugs and pitchers). There's plenty of seating in the functional interior, although it's much nicer to sit in the courtyard of the old Dutch Hospital outside – a popular spot with Colombo's bright young things after dark. Daily 11am–midnight.

★ **The Traveller's Bar** Galle Face Hotel, Galle Face Green; map p. 74. Upmarket colonial-style bar in Colombo's most historic hotel. The interior is plastered with a fascinating photo gallery of the many famous people who have stayed at the *Galle Face*, although it's even nicer to sit on the breezy veranda outside, with the Indian Ocean breaking just beyond. Daily 10.30am–11.30pm.

Ward 7 Jetwing Seven hotel, 57 Ward Place, Cinnamon Gardens ⓣ011 255 0200; map p. 74. On the rooftop of the *Jetwing Seven* hotel, this svelte bar boasts probably the best view in the southern city (only the observation deck of the Lotus Tower gets you higher), with vast vistas across a sea of lights. Decent and reasonably priced drinks list too, and the pocket-sized infinity pool looks good enough to drink too. Daily 10am–1.30am.

ENTERTAINMENT

olombo's only modern **cinema** is the Majestic ineplex, on the fourth floor of the Majestic City mall see page 94), which has four screens showing he latest Hollywood and Bollywood blockbusters ⓦceylontheatres.lk; tickets Rs.650). The landmark nodern Nelum Pokuna (ⓦlotuspond.lk) is the ity's largest theatre, but stages virtually nothing of nterest.

Barefoot Gallery 704 Galle Rd, Kollupitiya ⓣ011 50 5559, ⓦbarefootceylon.com/gallery. Next to the xcellent *Barefoot Café* (see page 91), this intimate ttle gallery hosts a roster of excellent, regularly hanging exhibitions by local and international artists nd photographers, along with a lively programme of

concerts, talks and other events. Mon–Sat 10am–7pm, Sun 11am–6pm.

Lionel Wendt Art Centre 18 Guildford Crescent, Cinnamon Gardens ⓣ011 269 5794, ⓦlionelwendt. org. This long-running theatre-cum-arts centre hosts a varied programme of dance, music and drama, along with regularly changing exhibitions, mainly photographic.

Sapumal Foundation 32/4 Barnes Place, Cinnamon Gardens ⓣ011 269 5731, ⓦartsrilanka.org/ sapumalfoundation. Lovely gallery, housed in the time-warped old bungalow which was formerly home to the artist Harry Pieris, showcasing an outstanding collection of Sri Lankan art from the 1940s onwards. Thurs–Sun 10am–1pm.

SHOPPING

olombo has a good range of shops, and a day trawling hrough its handicrafts emporia and chic boutiques can be n enjoyable way to end a visit and offload surplus rupees. When buying handicrafts, remember that the export of **ntiques** (classified as any object more than fifty years ld) is prohibited without a licence (see page 57).

GEMS AND JEWELLERY

here are gem and jewellery shops all over the city, articularly along **Sea Street** in the Pettah and on Levels and 5 of the World Trade Center in Fort at the so-called **ri Lanka Gem and Jewellery Exchange**, which is also ome to a useful **gem-testing laboratory** (Mon–Fri

10am–5.45pm ⓣ011 239 1132; tucked away at the back of level 4) run by the National Gem and Jewellery Authority (NGJA; ⓦngja.gov.lk). Staff here can tell you whether a stone is what it's claimed to be and if it's natural, but they don't offer valuations. Tests are carried out on the spot and are free (you can buy a basic certificate of authenticity for Rs.522, or a more detailed one for Rs.1555); it takes about 30min for them to analyse a gem for the basic certificate, assuming they're not already busy. The obvious drawback is that it will be difficult to get something tested without buying it first, although you might be able to persuade Colombo jewellers to send a representative with you and the gem(s) before you part with your cash.

1

SHOPPING MALLS

Crescat Boulevard Galle Rd, Kollupitiya, next to the Cinnamon Grand hotel; map p. 74. Sri Lanka's ritziest mall (not saying much, admittedly) is home to branches of the Vijitha Yapa bookshop, Mlesna and Dilmah tea shops, LuvSL, a Keells supermarket, and a good food court (see page 91). Daily 10am–7.30pm.

Majestic City Galle Rd, Bambalapitiya; map p. 74. The city's flagship shopping centre until the opening of Crescat, MC now looks very dated but retains a loyal following among Colombo's teenage mall rats. Lots of shoe and clothes shops (including branches of Odel and Cotton Collection), a big Cargills supermarket (with smart attached off-licence) and Colombo's best cinema. Daily 9am–9pm.

Odel 5 Alexandra Place, just off De Soysa Circus (Lipton Circus), Cinnamon Gardens ☎011 462 5800, ⓦodel. lk; map p. 74. Colombo's top fashionista address, this chic emporium stocks a wide range of stylish clothes from Odel's own designers and other labels alongside homeware, perfumes, food, tea, stationery, bags and books (see page 95), with a range of food outlets and cafés attached. The store is currently being developed into a fully fledged mall, which will hopefully ease current levels of manic overcrowding. There are other branches across the city (selling clothes only) including Majestic City (see above), on Galle Rd in Mount Lavinia and elsewhere. Daily 10am–9pm.

CLOTHES

Cotton Collection Dharmapala Mw, Cinnamon Gardens ☎011 237 2098, ⓦcottoncollection.lk; map p. 74. Popular local chain selling colourful cotton garments from a range of local and international labels. There are smaller branches at 26 Ernest de Silva Mw (Flower Rd), Cinnamon Gardens and at Majestic City (see above). Mon–Sat 10am–7pm.

HANDICRAFTS AND SOUVENIRS

Barefoot 706 Galle Rd, Kollupitiya ☎011 258 9305, ⓦbarefootceylon.com; map p.70. Founded in the early 1970s by leading local artist and designer Barbara Sansoni, Barefoot is Colombo's most famous, and most enjoyable, shop – a little haven of colourful arts and crafts crammed into a disorienting warren of undersized rooms. It's best known for its vibrantly coloured handwoven cotton fabrics, which more or less single-handedly established the template for modern Sri Lankan textile design (widely imitated, although never quite equalled). You can either buy them on their own or made into all sorts of objects including clothes, tablecloths, fabric-covered stationery, marvellous soft toys (grown-ups will love them too), and much more besides. There's also an excellent little bookshop (see page 95) and a beautiful courtyard café

(see page 91). Interesting temporary exhibitions are also held here (see page 93), while a local weaver can often be seen at work in the courtyard at the back. There's a second, smaller branch in the Dutch Hospital in Fort. Mon–Sat 10am–7pm, Sun 11am–6pm.

Laksala 215 Bauddhaloka Mw, Cinnamon Gardens ☎011 258 0579, ⓦlaksala.gov.lk; map p. 74. There are three branches of the government-run nationwide craft emporium in Colombo. The time-warped old flagship store in Fort (60 York St) is currently undergoing renovations and has only one room open. In the meantime, the big, bright new flagship store on Bauddhaloka Mw is the place to go, piled high with masses of touristy souvenirs (wooden elephants, ugly metalware and so on) plus a new range of more contemporary crafts in funky modern design including colourful toys, clothes, toiletries and assorted bric-a-brac. There's a third (smaller) branch attached to the National Museum. Daily 9am–9pm.

Luv SL Dutch Hospital, Fort ☎011 244 8873, ⓦodel.lk/ luvsl; map p.70. Offshoot of the Odel chain (see above), stocking a fun range of accessories, clothes and unusual souvenirs. There's another branch at Crescat Boulevard (see page 94). Daily 11am–10pm.

Paradise Road 213 Dharmapala Mw, Cinnamon Gardens ☎011 268 6043, ⓦparadiseroad.lk; map p. 74. Set in a lovely, chintzy colonial villa, this is one of the top names in Colombo chic, stocking a range of superior household items alongside miscellaneous bric-a-brac and souvenirs – their signature Sinhala and Tamil alphabet designs, which appear on many products, are particularly fun. There's also a nice little café upstairs. Daily 10am–7pm.

TEA

If you're shopping for tea, note that all the city's large supermarkets also stock a good selection of local leaves, often at significantly lower prices than the places below.

Dilmah t Lounge Chatham St, Fort ☎011 244 7168, ⓦdilmaht-lounge.com; map p.70. This place functions mainly as a café, but also has a great selection of Dilmah-branded teas for sale including single-estate, white and silver-tip teas, attractively packaged. There's a second branch at Independence Arcade (see map p.000). Daily 8am–10pm.

Mlesna Tea Centre Crescat Boulevard, Kollupitiya ⓦmlesnateas.com; map p.74. Fancy packs of souvenir teas and other tea-making paraphernalia – nice for a present or chintzy souvenir, although relatively pricey. Mon–Sat 10am–7pm, Sun 10am–6pm.

Sri Lanka Tea Board Galle Rd, Kollupitiya ☎011 25 3652, ⓦwww.pureceylontea.com; map p.74. Good selection of islandwide leaves including single-estate tea and highly prized (and highly expensive) silver tips white teas. Mon–Sat 9am–7pm.

BOOKSHOPS

Barefoot 706 Galle Rd, Kollupitiya ☎011 258 9305, ⓦbarefootceylon.com; map p.74. The best bookshop in the country, with a good selection of English-language fiction (including a comprehensive array of titles by Sri Lankan authors), plus lots of gorgeous coffee-table books and volumes on Sri Lankan art, culture and history. Mon–Sat 10am–7pm, Sun 11am–6pm.

Odel 5 Alexandra Place, just off De Soysa Circus (Lipton Circus), Cinnamon Gardens ☎011 462 5800, ⓦodel.lk; map p.74. Excellent outlet in the city's flashest department store, with a good range of Sri Lanka-related fiction and nonfiction, and lots of glossy coffee-table tomes. Daily 10am–9pm.

Vijitha Yapa Unity Plaza (next door to Majestic City), ⓦvijithayapa.com; map p.74. The biggest branch of the island's main bookshop chain, with a good range of books on Sri Lanka, plus a middling selection of English-language novels. There's another large branch in Crescat Boulevard (see map p.74) and a smaller one on Thurston Rd (map p.74). Daily 10pm–6pm.

SPORT

Cricket Most Test matches are played at the Sinhalese Sports Club (SSC), centrally located on Maitland Place in Cinnamon Gardens, although matches are sometimes held at the P. Sara Oval (aka the "Colombo Oval"), east of the centre in Borella, and at the Premadasa Stadium in Dematagoda. The Premadasa is the main venue for one-day and T20 matches (while one-dayers are also sometimes held at the SSC). Tickets are available direct from the stadia.

Diving Island Scuba (☎077 315 8245, ⓦdivelanka.com) is one of the island's top-rated dive operators, offering packages and customized tours on both east and west coasts.

Golf The beautiful Royal Colombo Golf Club is a short drive east of the city centre at 223 Model Farm Rd, Borella (☎011 269 5431, ⓦrcgcsl.com). Green fees are $70/85 per day (weekdays/weekends).

Swimming Many of the big hotels allow non-guests to use their pools for a fee, usually around Rs.1500 per day (sometimes a bit more at weekends), including the *Hilton*, *Cinnamon Lakeside* and *Cinnamon Grand*. A cheaper option is the pool at the *Ramada* (Rs.700), although the nicest option is the idyllic pool and private beach at the *Mount Lavinia Hotel*, costing a relatively modest $7.

DIRECTORY

Ayurveda There's a surprising lack of Ayurveda facilities in Colombo, although some of the city's spas (see below) offer Ayurveda treatments.

Banks and exchange There's at least one bank on virtually every city block across Colombo; all change cash and almost all now have 24hr ATMs, many of which accept foreign Visa and MasterCards.

Couriers DHL, 307 Galle Rd, Kollupitiya ☎011 462 1014 and 148 Vauxhall St ☎011 230 4304; Fedex, 340 Galle Rd, Kollupitiya (just south of the *Renuka Hotel*) ☎011 452 2222.

Embassies and consulates Australia, 21 Gregory's Rd (R.G. Senanayake Mw), Cinnamon Gardens ☎011 246 3200, ⓦsrilanka.embassy.gov.au; Canada, 33A, 5th Lane, Kollupitiya ☎011 522 6232; India, 36–38 Galle Rd, Kollupitiya ☎011 232 7587, ⓦhcicolombo.org; UK, 389 Bauddhaloka Mw, Cinnamon Gardens ☎011 539 0639, ⓦgov.uk/world/sri-lanka; USA, 210 Galle Rd, Kollupitiya ☎011 249 8500, ⓦlk.usembassy.gov.

Hospitals and health clinics If you need an English-speaking doctor, first ask at your hotel or guesthouse (or at the nearest large hotel). For more serious problems, head to one of the city's reputable private hospitals. These include Lanka Hospitals (formerly the Apollo Hospital), 578 Elvitigala Mw, Narahenpita ☎011 543 0000, ⓦlankahospitals.com; and Durdans Hospital, 3 Alfred Place, Kollupitiya ☎011 214 0000, ⓦdurdans.com.

Internet access All hotels (and many restaurants and bars) have wi-fi, although rising rents and falling demand mean that there are virtually no reliable internet cafés left in central Colombo (although there are a few places out in the suburbs).

Left luggage There's a left-luggage office (signed "cloak room"; daily 5.30am–8.30pm) at Fort Railway Station, outside the station to the left of the entrance.

Pharmacies Union Chemists (7am–11pm; open 365 days a year; ☎011 269 2532), close by at the eastern end of Union Place. There are also pharmacies in larger branches of Cargills Food City (including the one in the basement of Majestic City) and in Keells supermarket in Crescat Boulevard.

Spas There are good spas at the *Galle Face, Shangri-La, Cinnamon Lakeside* and *Mount Lavinia* hotels. Right in the city centre, the tranquil Angsana City Club and Spa, Crescat City (next to the *Cinnamon Grand* hotel; ☎011 242 4245, ⓦangsanaspa.com), offers a range of massages, facials, manicures and pedicures, and has treatment rooms for couples, steam bath and sauna, as well as a gym, café and a large rooftop infinity swimming pool, which you can use if you have a treatment. Treatments start from $60 for 30min, or $75 for 45min.

Supermarkets The main chain is Cargills Food City, which has branches at York St, Fort, in the basement of Majestic City and at many other locations around Colombo. Keells (daily 9am–9.30pm), in the basement of Crescat Boulevard, is also good.

1

Negombo and around

Sprawling **NEGOMBO** is of interest mainly thanks to its proximity to the international airport, just 10km down the road – many visitors stagger off long-haul flights straight into one of the beach hotels here, or stay as a last stop before flying home. Negombo's **beach** is very wide in places if rather shabby compared to the more pristine resorts further south; the surrounding resort area, though, is often one of the liveliest places around the coast for those in search of cheap beer and late nights. A couple of kilometres south of the beach, **Negombo Town** offers an interesting introduction to coastal Sri Lankan life, with a lively fish market, a dash of olde-worlde colonial charm and hundreds of colourful boats. There are also a number of low-key attractions scattered around Negombo, including the fine wetlands of **Muthurajawela** and the eye-catching **Angurukaramulla temple**.

Brief history

Negombo was one of the first towns in Sri Lanka to be taken by the Portuguese, who converted many of the local Karavas (see page 97), and the area remains a stronghold of **Christian Sri Lanka**, as borne out by the imposing churches and florid wayside Catholic shrines scattered about the town and its environs – hence the town's popular nickname of "Little Rome". The Dutch transformed Negombo into an important commercial centre, building a canal (and a fort to guard it) on which spices – particularly the valuable

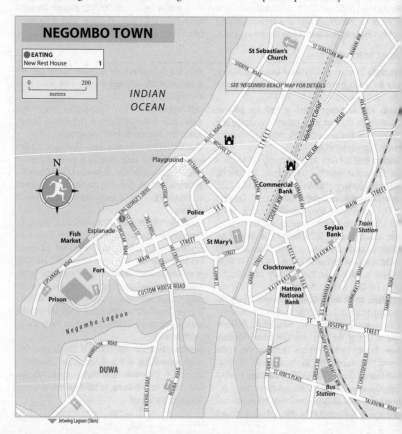

1

THE KARAVAS

The people of Negombo are **Karavas**, Tamil and Sinhalese fishermen who converted en masse to Catholicism during the mid-sixteenth century under the influence of Portuguese missionaries, taking Portuguese surnames and becoming the first of Sri Lanka's innumerable de Silvas, de Soysas and Pereras. They're also famous for their unusual fishing boats, known as **oruwas**, distinctive catamarans (a word derived from the Tamil *ketti-maran*) fashioned from a hollowed-out trunk attached to a massive sail. Hundreds of these small vessels remain in use even today, and make an unforgettable sight when the fleet returns to shore.

innamon which grew profusely in the surrounding jungles – were transported from he interior to the coast prior to being shipped abroad. Nowadays much of the town's conomy revolves around tourism, although fishing also remains vitally important, with he sea providing plentiful supplies of tuna, shark and seer, while the Negombo lagoon, backing the town, is the source of some of the island's finest prawns, crabs and lobster.

The fort and fish market

The heart of the old town is situated on the tip of a peninsula enclosing the top of he Negombo lagoon. Close to the western end of the peninsula lie the very modest emains of the old Dutch **fort**, mostly demolished by the British to make way for the rison that still stands behind the gateway. There's little to see beyond a weed-covered rchway emblazoned with the date 1678 and a very short section of ramparts topped vith a miniature clocktower added by the British.

Just north of here sits the town's time-warped rest house (see page 103) and more nodern **fish market**, with endless lines of fish laid out to dry on the sand (and even bigger flocks of crows attracted by the smell). The market is busiest early in the norning, but keeps going right on into the afternoon. There's a second, smaller fish narket on the beach in the tourist part of town, incidentally, reachable from Porutota Road down the small lane opposite *Sunny's Restaurant*.

The lagoon and around

South of the fort, the narrow channel leading into the **Negombo lagoon** stretches alongside Custom House Road, with myriad multicoloured fibreglass boats tied up under huge tropical trees. A couple of hundred metres down the road, a bridge crosses o the diminutive island of **Duwa**, offering photogenic views of long lines of colourful vooden boats tied up along the mouth of the lagoon. Duwa is also the venue for a big Passion play, staged here every Easter.

It's also well worth making time for a **boat trip** (see page 98) on the extensive lagoon tself, still fringed with dense clumps of mangroves and alive with birds, monitor lizards, nonkeys and the occasional crocodile – not to mention the many fishermen dredging the lepths for the prized jumbo prawns and other seafood which is harvested here.

St Mary's

Main St • No set hours • Free

Towering aristocratically above the low-rise streets of the old town centre, **St Mary's** is one of the finest of Negombo's many churches: a grandiose custard-yellow Neoclassical edifice, constructed over fifty years from 1874 onwards. The interior is decorated with dozens of colourful statues of po-faced saints and tableaux showing the Stations of the Cross – the importance ascribed to religious images in both Catholicism and Hinduism vas doubtless a useful factor in persuading the local Karavas to switch allegiance from one faith to the other.

BOAT TRIPS AND DIVING IN NEGOMBO

Taking a **boat trip** is a great way to get a feel for Negombo's beautifully watery landscapes. Reputable local operators include **Sarath Boat Tours** (☎071 721 3484, ⓦsarathboattours. com), who run tours combining the Dutch canal and Maha Oya river (2hr; $30), and longer trips (3hr 30min; $50) heading down the Dutch canal, over the lagoon and on to the Muthurajawela wetlands (see below); and **Captain Fernando Boat Tours** (☎077 606 1770, ⓦcaptainfernando.com), who run morning and sunset boat tours of the lagoon (2hr; Rs.3000). **Local fishermen** also hang out on the beach touting for custom and offer trips out to sea in a traditional *oruwa* catamaran (see page 97). The current starting price is usually Rs.5000, although you might be able to bargain this down to Rs.3000 or even lower for an hour's trip for two people; check that life jackets are provided.

DIVING AND WATERSPORTS

Diving trips and courses can be arranged during the diving season (Nov–March) through Negombo Diving Centre (*Port Beach Restaurant*, 285 Lewis Place ☎077 020 0192, ⓦnegombodiving.com) and Sri Lanka Diving Tours (158 Porutota Rd ☎077 068 6860, ⓦsrilanka-divingtours.com). There's currently no reliable place in Negombo to arrange **watersports** unless you head out to the well-equipped centre at the *Jetwing Lagoon* hotel (see page 102)

Main Street and the Dutch Canal

The stretch of the old town's principal thoroughfare, **Main Street**, west of St Mary's is attractively old-fashioned, lined with a string of lawyers' offices interspersed with fine old colonial-era verandaed mansions and chintzy villas decorated with elaborately carved *mal lali* eaves, shutters and wooden balconies.

East of St Mary's stretches the town's main commercial area, bounded on its west side by the old **Dutch canal** (known here as Hamilton Canal), once the major conduit for Dutch trade in the area, which arrows north, continuing all the way to the town of Puttalam. It's possible to walk along the **towpaths** which line both sides of the canal here for a few hundred metres, weaving between the fishermen who often come here to repair their nets, and then continue north as far as St Sebastian Mawatha, after which the paths become impossibly overgrown. To get a proper feel for the canal, though, you'll need to take a boat trip along it (see above), offering glimpses of toddy tappers, monitor lizards and myriad birds along the way.

Muthurajawela

20km south of Negombo (and a similar distance north of Colombo) • Boat trips daily 7am–4pm • Rs.1300/person including guide • Boats can be reserved by calling ☎011 403 0150 (office hours) or ☎077 704 3447; you can also explore the wetlands by kayak on tours arranged by Colombo City Walks (see page 86) • Transport from Muthurajawela costs around Rs.2500 by tuktuk or Rs.5000 by car and can be arranged through most guesthouses and travel agents; alternatively, catch a train to Ja-Ela, on the main Colombo–Negombo line, and then a tuktuk to the visitor centre (3km) and turn west off the main Colombo highway down Bopitiya Rd (signposted to the *Villa Palma* hotel)

At the southern end of the Negombo lagoon and close to the southern edge of the airport, **Muthurajawela** comprises a considerable area of saltwater wetland which attracts a rich variety of water-loving **birds**, including various species of colourful kingfisher, assorted herons, egrets, moorhen, duck, painted stork and many others, as well as crocodiles, macaque monkeys and a large population of water monitors. The small Muthurajawela **visitor centre** is the starting point for rewarding two-hour boat trips through the wetlands; it's best to ring in advance to make sure there's a boat available when you arrive, especially on Sundays, when lots of locals visit. Trips take you up along the idyllic old Dutch canal before reaching the Negombo lagoon itself, which you'll skirt while exploring the surrounding wetlands and mangroves.

1

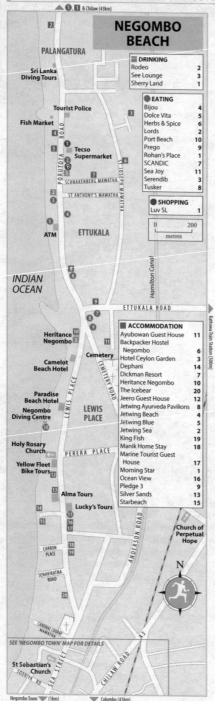

NEGOMBO BEACH

PALANGATURA

Sri Lanka Diving Tours

Tourist Police

Fish Market

Tecso Supermarket

PORUOTA ROAD

SCHNAKENBERG MAWATHA

ST ANTHONY'S MAWATHA

ETTUKALA

ATM

INDIAN OCEAN

ETTUKALA ROAD

Heritance Negombo

Camelot Beach Hotel

Paradise Beach Hotel

Negombo Diving Centre

Cemetery

CEMETERY ROAD

LEWIS PLACE

Holy Rosary Church

PERERA PLACE

Yellow Fleet Bike Tours

Alma Tours

Lucky's Tours

CARRON PLACE

SENAVIRATNA ROAD

ANDERSON ROAD

Church of Perpetual Hope

N

CARDINAL COORAY MAWATHA

SEE 'NEGOMBO TOWN' MAP FOR DETAILS

St Sebastian's Church

SOORIYA RD

SEA STREET

CHILLAW ROAD

A3

Negombo Town (1km)   Colombo (41km)

Kattuwa Train Station (500m)

Hamilton Canal

DRINKING
Rodeo	2
See Lounge	3
Sherry Land	1

EATING
Bijou	4
Dolce Vita	5
Herbs & Spice	6
Lords	2
Port Beach	10
Prego	9
Rohan's Place	1
SCANDIC	7
Sea Joy	11
Serendib	3
Tusker	8

SHOPPING
| Luv SL | 1 |

0 — 200
metres

ACCOMMODATION
Ayubowan Guest House	11
Backpacker Hostel Negombo	6
Hotel Ceylon Garden	3
Dephani	14
Dickman Resort	7
Heritance Negombo	10
The Icebear	20
Jeero Guest House	12
Jetwing Ayurveda Pavilions	8
Jetwing Beach	4
Jetwing Blue	5
Jetwing Sea	2
King Fish	19
Manik Home Stay	18
Marine Tourist Guest House	17
Morning Star	1
Ocean View	16
Pledge 3	9
Silver Sands	13
Starbeach	15

Angurukaramulla Temple

4km east of Negombo • Donation • Tuktuk drivers in Negombo offer a combined tour (lasting 2hr–2hr 30min) c the temple and Negombo Town for around Rs.1500

A short drive inland from Negombo, the eye-catching **Angurukaramulla Temple** serves as a rare beacon of Buddhism in an overwhelmingly Christian area. The temple is best known for its huge Buddha statue, built in 1980 and showing the maste seated in the *samadhi* (meditation) pose. There are also various garish Buddhist tableaux vivants, along wit a ramshackle subsidiary building fille with portraits or statues of all the major Sinhalese kings, topped with an unusual modern vatadage (circula shrine).

ARRIVAL AND DEPARTURE
NEGOMBO AND AROUN

The **bus** and **train** stations are close to one another the town centre, some way from most of Negomb accommodation. A tuktuk from either station Lewis Place/Porutota Rd shouldn't cost more tha around Rs.200, but you might have to bargain har drivers here are used to taking advantage of new arrived tourists. A tuktuk all the way to the **airpo** costs around Rs.800 (a bit more at night); the trip taxi currently costs around Rs.1500, or Rs.2000 f pick-up. There are no buses direct to the airport – th nearest you can get is Averiwatte, from where it's a Rs.800 ride by tuktuk

By bus Services leave from the modern bus static in the town centre. Heading to Colombo, be sure catch a bus via the Expressway – significantly quick and more comfortable than buses along old coast road. For the Pinnewala Elephant Orphanage take Kandy bus to Karandupana, just past Kegalle, an then follow the route described in chapter 3 (se page 206). To reach the Cultural Triangle, take bus to Kurunegala, from where there are regul onward services to Dambulla and Anuradhapur Heading towards the south coast, there are tw superfast services to Matara (at 7am and 3pm) alon the Expressway. For Galle, it's quickest to travel v Colombo.

Destinations Averiwatte (every 20min; 40min Colombo (every 15min; 1hr 15min, or 50min–1 15min via the Expressway); Kalpitiya (3–4 dail 3hr); Kandy (hourly, including one a/c bus at 7.30am 3hr 30min); Kurunegala (every 30min; 1hr 30min Matara (2 daily; 2hr 30min).

TOUR GUIDES IN NEGOMBO

All the larger hotels and various tour operators along the main road can arrange day-tours or transfers to Kandy, Colombo, Pinnewala Elephant Orphanage or pretty much anywhere else you fancy (count on around $65 to Kandy, $35 to Colombo) as well as longer tours islandwide. There are also a number of reputable independent SLTB-registered **guides** in town, including the excellent and extremely professional Mark Thamel at the *Ocean View* guesthouse (see page 102), who can customize tours to suit, either with himself or other reliable local SLTB registered guides; expect to pay around $110 per day for a couple, including guesthouse accommodation). Other local guides include: Terry at the *Jeero Guest House* (see page 101); Lakshman Bolonghe (a.k.a. "Lucky"; 146 Lewis Place ☎077 357 8487, ✉lucky_tour55@hotmail. com; Sri Shannon Tours (☎077 754 3824, ⊛srishannontours.com) and PL Tours & Travels in Palangatura (☎077 163 5021, ⊛travel-srilanka.eu).

By train Services between Negombo and Colombo are frustratingly slow. There are plans to upgrade the line, but at present it's easier and quicker to catch a bus. Most Colombo and Chilaw services (around 10 daily) also stop at Kattuwa station, which is closer to the central beach area than Negombo station. If you want to reach Kandy by train without travelling via Colombo, head to Veyangoda about 35km inland (around 45min and Rs.2000 by tuktuk; also served by infrequent buses), and pick up the train from there.

Destinations Chilaw (7–12 daily; 1hr 15min); Colombo (10–14 daily; 1hr–1hr 20min).

By car All Negombo's guesthouses should be able to arrange taxis for onward travel, and there are various companies offering vehicle rental (see page 105).

ACCOMMODATION

There's heaps of **accommodation** in Negombo. Most of the **budget** places are in Lewis Place, at the southern end of the beach area; more **upmarket** options are concentrated to the north along (or just off) Porutota Rd in the suburbs of Ettukala and Palangatura. There's also a growing number of places along St Joseph's Mw, a pleasantly peaceful alternative to the beach a few hundred metres inland.

LEWIS PLACE

Ayubowan Guest House 47/55 School Lane ☎031 223 8673, ⊛ayubowanguesthouse.com; map p.100. Tucked away on a quiet back street, this UK-owned guesthouse has just four homely a/c rooms in a very peaceful villa set in a gorgeous little garden with a small pool. B&B $65

Dephani 189/15 Lewis Place ☎031 223 8225, ⊛dephanibeach.com; map p.100. Long-running local stalwart, still popular thanks to its lovely beachfront setting behind a pretty little garden, although rooms (all a/c) are very dated and rather expensive for what you get, and you'll pay $6 extra for an upstairs room with beach view. $26

Heritance Negombo 175 Lewis Place ☎031 7431 431, ⊛heritancehotels.com; map p.100. Built on the site of the old *Brown's Beach Hotel*, Negombo's newest five-tar landmark rears high above the street on a huge stone plinth, adding a touch of welcome drama to the town's largely humdrum architecture. The enormous beachfront gardens, with vast pool meandering between palm trees, are another plus, and there's also a spa and a nice seaview bar (see page 104). Downsides include the sheer size of the place, while rooms – undersized, oddly arranged and decorated in mournful shades of industrial beige – are disappointing. An OK choice, but if you're looking for a big resort at this price you'll be better off heading to *Jetwing Beach*. $230

★ **The Icebear** 95 Lewis Place ☎031 223 3862, ⊛icebearhotel.com; map p.100. Idyllic Swiss-owned beachfront place, full of character, with ten artily furnished rooms (all with a/c and hot water) of various sizes and prices scattered around a gorgeously lush garden. €48

Jeero Guest House 239 Lewis Place ☎031 223 4210 or ☎077 6161 619; map p.100. Small family guesthouse with four spacious and comfortably furnished modern tiled rooms at very competitive rates. All have hot water, while two come with sea views and one with a/c. Rs.3000, a/c Rs.3800

King Fish 78/C Lewis Place ☎072 282 1547, ⊛kingfishguest.com; map p.100. One of Negombo's best bargains at present, offering simple but neat fan rooms with modern bathrooms, plus a few with hot water and a/c. Rs.1500, a/c Rs.3000

Manik Home Stay 90 Lewis Place ☎077 514 0761, ✉jgshehanperera@yahoo.com; map p.100. One of the best, and cheapest, budget options in town, with just three simple but neat and spacious rooms (one with a/c) set around a peaceful little courtyard garden. Rs.2500, a/c Rs.4500

1

Marine Tourist Guest House 118 Lewis Place ☎ 071 564 1827, ⓦ marine-negombo.com; map p.100. Neat and cheap modern guesthouse with large and good-value modern a/c rooms plus four-bed a/c mixed and female dorms and a nice lounge area at the back. Dorms Rs.1000pp, doubles Rs.3500

Ocean View 122 Lewis Place ☎ 031 223 8689 or ☎ 077 785 6085, ⓦ oceanview-negombo.com; map p.100. Owned by excellent local guide Mark Thamel (see page 101), this cheery and very professionally run guesthouse offers a range of neat and trim fan and a/c rooms (the latter with balcony, hot water, TV, fridge and smart bathrooms) either fronting the small garden downstairs or on the breezy balcony above. Rs.3500, a/c Rs.5000

★ **Silver Sands** 229 Lewis Place ☎ 031 222 2880, ⓦ silversandsnegombo.com; map p.100. Negombo's most appealing budget option, set in attractive white arcaded buildings running down to the beach. Rooms (some with pricey a/c) are old and fairly basic but well maintained, with private balconies and unusual but effective hooped mosquito nets. Rs.2500, a/c Rs.4900

Starbeach 83/3 Lewis Place ☎ 031 222 2606, ⓦ starbeachhotelnegombo.com; map p.100. Long-running guest-house recently given an attractive upgrade and now offering smart modern a/c rooms behind an attractive beachfront garden, although as usual you'll pay around Rs1200 extra for a view of the sea. B&B: Rs.4200

ETTUKALA AND PALANGATURA

Backpacker Hostel Negombo 60 St Joseph's Mw ☎ 077 266 1000; map p.100. Above-average hostel with accommodation in reasonably sized four-bed a/c dorms, each with its own hot-water bathroom, while beds come with individual sockets and quality mattresses. B&B Rs.1100pp

Hotel Ceylon Garden 112A St Joseph Mw ☎ 077 637 6230, ⓦ hotelceylongarden.com; map p.100. This intimate upmarket guesthouse is the only place in Negombo to make full use of the town's beautiful – if neglected – old Dutch canal, with attractive gardens running down to the water and a lovely canalside terrace, plus good-sized pool. Rooms (of varying standards and prices) are unusually spacious, while the location just off peaceful St Joseph's Mw should also appeal. B&B $45

★ **Dickman Resort** 26/7 Porutota Rd (take the road towards the St Lachlan Hotel opposite the Reef Beach Hotel, past Villa Lanka and then take the first left, opposite Gomez Place) ☎ 031 227 3421, ⓦ dickmanresort.com; map p.100. Supremely idyllic boutique hotel buried deep in the lanes off Porutota Rd. The nine rooms are superbly spacious and comfortable, while the public areas are pure Bali-chic, arranged around a little courtyard saltwater pool and a gorgeous patio restaurant area, the whole place decorated in vivid clashing blues, reds and yellows. B&B: €120

Jetwing Ayurveda Pavilions Porutota Rd ☎ 031 227 6719, ⓦ jetwinghotels.com; map p.100. Luxurious little Ayurveda retreat with twelve gorgeous miniature villas, each with its own private garden and open-air bathroom. The focus here is on Ayurveda, with four doctors, ten-odd masseurs and assistants plus a sitar-playing music therapist on hand to balance your doshas. Rates are on full-board basis and include all treatments. $330

Jetwing Beach Porutota Rd ☎ 031 227 3500, ⓦ jetwinghotels.com; map p.100. Negombo's swankiest and most stylish resort hotel, set at the quiet northern end of the beach in attractively landscaped grounds. Rooms are superbly designed, with lots of dark wood, white linen and glass-walled bathrooms, while facilities include a heavenly spa and a picture-perfect palm-studded pool. B&B $215

Jetwing Blue Porutota Rd ☎ 031 493 3595, ⓦ jetwinghotels.com; map p.100. Sprawling five-star with facilities (and prices) similar to those at the adjacent Jetwing Beach hotel – stylishly chic rooms, cool interiors, a superb swathe of beautifully tended beach, plus a good-sized pool and attractive spa. B&B $220

Jetwing Sea Porutota Rd, Palangatura ☎ 031 493 3413, ⓦ jetwinghotels.com; map p.100. At the quiet northern end of the beach, this is another old Jetwing package resort which has now reinvented itself as a rather chic contemporary hotel, with airy white interiors and well-equipped modern rooms. The beach here is large and very peaceful, best enjoyed from the attractively rustic Lellama seafood restaurant. B&B $200

★ **Morning Star** 55/1 Palangathura, Kochchikade (down the road opposite Rohan's Place) ☎ 031 227 4371, ⓦ morningstarsrilanka.com; map p.100. This gorgeous guesthouse somehow adds up to far more than the sum of its modest parts, arranged around an idyllic little walled garden which provides a peaceful haven from the streets outside. Accommodation is in painted-brick a/c cabanas with miniature sit-outs, and there's also a small pool and restaurant serving up Western and Sri Lankan breakfasts. $55

Pledge 3 3 Ettukala Rd ☎ 031 222 4005, ⓦ hotelpledge3.com; map p.100. This funky boutique-style hotel offers a rare dash of urban sophistication in dusty Negombo. Rooms come with bright, minimalist loft-style decor, huge artworks and all mod cons, while facilities include a decent-sized saltwater pool and a swish little garden restaurant. $100

AROUND NEGOMBO

Jetwing Lagoon Pamunugama Rd, Thalahena ☎ 031 223 3777, ⓦ jetwinghotels.com. Spa-resort in a lovely setting between the sea and Negombo lagoon around km southwest of Negombo town, with low-slung, white-painted, red-roofed buildings arranged around an immensely long pool. Rooms are well equipped and come with sweeping lagoon views – and there's a good watersports centre in house if you want to get out on the wet stuff yourself. $160

★ **The Wallawwa** Kotugoda, a 15min drive from the airport ☎077 363 8381, ⊛thewallawwa.com. Stylish "country house" hotel in a converted old *walauwa* (manor house). The elegantly designed rooms come with rain showers, four-poster beds and widescreen TVs, and there's also a spa, top-quality restaurant and picture-perfect pool – all at a surprisingly affordable price. $160

EATING

Negombo has one of Sri Lanka's better selections of places to eat – although, disappointingly, most are strung out along the main road, rather than on the beach itself. The town's proximity to the Negombo lagoon, source of some of the island's finest prawns and crabs, also makes it a good place for **seafood**. Some restaurants close down during the sleeper months from May to October.

NEGOMBO TOWN

New Rest House 14 Circular Rd ☎031 222 2299; map p.96. This time-warped rest house in a fine old Dutch colonial mansion has gone downhill somewhat since Queen Elizabeth stayed here in 1958 but remains a tremendously atmospheric place for a meal or drink. Locals come for the big rice and curry spreads (from a paltry Rs.280), and there are also plenty of other Sri Lankan mains (around Rs.500) plus Western and local breakfasts. Daily 6am–11pm.

NEGOMBO BEACH

★ **Bijou** 44 Porutota Rd ☎031 227 4710; map p.100. Homely Swiss-managed place offering a tempting menu of excellent Central European dishes such as pepper steak, Wiener schnitzel and fondues (order in advance), plus a range of perfectly prepared seafood. Mains Rs.1200–1600. Daily 8.30am–11pm.

Dolce Vita 27 Porutota Rd ☎031 227 4968; map p.100. Cosy little coffee shop with seating either in the homely interior or in the peaceful beachside garden at the back. Drinks include great coffee and Sri Lankan tea, and they also serve up good breakfasts, sandwiches, crêpes and home-made cake and ice-cream along with pizza (from their own pizza oven), pasta and other international mains (around Rs.1200) – although some of the dishes can be a bit hit-or-miss. Tues–Sun 8.30am–10.30pm.

Herbs & Spice Jetwing Ayurveda Pavilions, Porutota Rd ☎031 227 6719; map p.100. Something a bit different here, with an exclusively vegetarian and vegan menu, quite reasonably priced (mains Rs.500–750) and featuring all sorts of innovative offerings – coconut *rotty* stuffed with banana blossom, beetroot and mango salad, manioc pitta with coconut milk and chilli *sambol* and so on. No alcohol. Daily 7am–10pm.

★ **Lords** 80b Porutota Rd ☎077 285 3190, ⊛lordsrestaurant.net; map p.100. Buzzing restaurant and bar complex serving up a great range of well-presented international fare with a strong Asian flavour (mains around Rs.1500) – anything from Thai green curry and *nasi goreng* through to mushroom, cashew and raisin curry. There's also a good vegetarian selection and an extensive vegan menu. Live music nightly. Daily 3.30–11.30pm.

Port Beach 285 Lewis Place ☎077 020 0192; map p.100. One of Negombo's coolest after-dark chill-out spots, with a breezy seafront setting, plenty of creaky wooden decking and a decent menu featuring all the usual seafood mains (around Rs.1100) plus a superior rice and curry (Rs.750–850), if you don't mind the disappointingly miserly portion sizes. Bar stays open until 11pm. Daily 11am–9.30pm.

Prego 2 Porutota Rd ☎031 222 5655; map p.100. Cool, modern Italian restaurant specializing in delicious thin-crust Neapolitan-style pizza (Rs.1000–1600), along with home-made pasta and assorted meat and seafood mains (from Rs.1500) and classic Italian deserts, plus a good selection of Italian and Australian wines, which aren't too exorbitantly priced. Daily 10.30am–10.30pm.

★ **Rohan's Place** Porutota Rd, Kochchikade ☎077 599 2527; map p.100. If you've just landed in Sri Lanka and want a real taste of the island, this unprepossessing little establishment is hard to beat. Pride of place goes to the excellent rice and curry spreads (Rs.750), with big portions and intense flavours with an authentically spicy kick. They also do the usual seafood and devilled dishes (around Rs.1000), plus Western and Sri Lankan breakfasts. Daily 7am–1pm.

SCANDIC 45/1A Ettukala ☎075 421 5161; map p.100. In a colonial-style house just off the main drag this enjoyable restaurant boasts a homely atmosphere, very jolly service and above-average cooking, attractively presented, including good rice and curries (Rs.650–950) plus assorted other meat and seafood mains (Rs.900–1100). Daily 5–10pm.

Sea Joy 122/1 Lewis Place ☎031 222 1659; map p.100. Homespun little restaurant offering an enjoyable slice of old-style Negombo, with prices to match. The above-average rice and curry (Rs.400) is an absolute bargain, and there are also plenty of slightly pricier seafood and other dishes (around Rs.800). A good spot for breakfast, too. Outside seating in the pleasant garden round the side is nicer than in the slightly stuffy interior. Daily 7am–10pm.

1

Serendib 35a Porutota Rd (immediately south of Rodeo) ☏031 227 9129, ⊚serendibnegombo.com; map p.100. Large and usually lively restaurant with seating either indoors or in the spacious (if not particularly attractive) garden at the back. The menu features all the usual suspects – rice and curries, devilled dishes, pizza, pasta and a surfeit of seafood – reasonably prepared and served in generous portions. Mains Rs.1300–1650. Daily 8am–1am.

Tusker 83 Ettukala Rd ☏031 222 6999, ⊚bit.ly/ TuskerNegombo; map p.100. Attractive European-run restaurant in a pleasant pavilion-style structure open to the breezes but screened from the main road. Food comprises the usual range of Sri Lankan and seafood dishes (mains Rs.1300–1800) – no culinary surprises, but nicely prepared and attractively presented. Daily 11am–11pm.

DRINKING

During the season, Negombo is usually the liveliest of the west-coast resorts, with most action concentrated along the northern end of the strip around the *Rodeo* bar and *Sherry Land* – about as rowdy as Sri Lanka gets, which isn't very.

Rodeo Porutota Rd; map p.100. A large streetside cactus announces this small, vaguely Wild West themed bar, which is usually the liveliest drinking spot in town despite the complete lack of space and uncomfortable bench seats. Daily 11am–1am.

See Lounge Heritance Negombo hotel, 175 Lewis Place ☏031 7431 431; map p.100. A classier alternative to Negombo's typical drinking dives, this upstairs bar in the town's new landmark hotel offers a sedate and upmarket haven for a quiet tipple, with fine sea views through its floor-to-ceiling window. Pricey, but not too extortionate given the setting. Daily 10am–midnight.

Sherry Land 74 Porutota Rd ☏031 487 4901, ⊚sherrylandnegombo.com; map p.100. Larger and usually a bit more laidback than *Rodeo*, with seating either at the bar or in the small garden, and a decent drinks list including lots of cocktails, plus local and imported spirits and beers including rum, tequila, Corona beer, Red Bull and – yes – sherry. Reasonable food also available. Daily 11am–11.30pm.

SHOPPING

There are heaps of **handicraft shops** (and lots of places selling tea, too) all along the main road – the best selection is along Porutota Rd around the *Jetwing Blue* hotel. There are also loads of **mini-supermarkets** for daily essentials with tongue-in-cheek names including Sainsbury's and Carrefour, although the old Tesco Express has now been renamed Tecso (presumably under legal duress), while the long-running ASDA has closed.

Luv SL 12 Porutota Rd ☏031 227 7443, ⊚odel.lk/luvsl; map p.100. Negombo branch of the funky nationwide chain full of cute collectibles and cool clothing including fun T-shirts, colourful swimwear and billowy dresses. Daily 10am–8pm.

DIRECTORY

Ayurveda Ayurveda treatments are available at the beautiful *Jetwing Ayurveda Pavilions*, as well as at the *Jetwing Beach*, *Jetwing Blue* and *Jetwing Sea* hotels.

Banks and exchange There's a handy HNB ATM next to the *Topaz Beach Hotel* on Porutota Rd in the beach area, and a Seylan ATM slightly further south, as well as numerous banks with ATMs accepting foreign cards in Negombo

---

TOURING BY TUKTUK

If you've had enough of being touted by tuktuk drivers, how about driving one yourself? A number of tour agents in Negombo now offer **tuktuks for rent**, offering a fun and flexible, if not terribly speedy, way of travelling around the island. You'll need to bring an international driving licence with you and then collect a local permit from the AA in Colombo (see page 33); these cost Rs.3650 and are issued on the spot (your tuktuk rental agency might be able to do this for you for a fee). If you only have your own country driving licence you'll need to personally visit the Department of Motor Traffic in Werahera, near Mount Lavinia in Colombo, to get a permit (Rs.1000).

Operators in Negombo include **Alma Tours** (see page 105), who pioneered the self-drive tuktuk market and who have a fleet of twenty vehicles at unbeatable rates (just €10/ day). Pick & Go (see page 105) are another reputable, although more expensive, option. If you do decide to drive your own tuktuk, make sure you know exactly what insurance (if any) is provided, who pays for any damage, and what will happen in the event of a breakdown.

own. Plenty of shopkeepers along the main beach road change money.

Bike, motorbike and car rental Alma Tours (217 Lewis Place; ☎031 487 3624, ✉almatours65@yahoo.com), Yellow Fleet Bike Tours (☎077 776 5919) and Pick & Go (☎077 646 4346, ⓦpickandgotravels.com) have a range of scooters and larger motorbikes for rent for around $10–15/day. Alma Tours and Pick & Go also rent out mountain

bikes (Rs.500/day), self-drive cars and minivans (€30–40/day) and even tuktuks (see page 104).

Internet Sunrise Internet Café between *Lords and Sherry Land* (daily 8.30am–1pm & 3–9pm; Rs.330/hr) has a handful of machines.

Swimming pools Non-guests can use the pools at the *Paradise Beach Hotel, Camelot Beach Hotel* and the *Jetwing Beach* and *Jetwing Blue* hotels. All charge Rs.1000 (rising to Rs.1500 on Sat & Sun at the two Jetwing hotels).

North of Negombo

North of Negombo, the coastline becomes increasingly rocky and wild, with narrow beaches and crashing waves that make swimming impossible for most of the year. Much of the area remains largely undeveloped, although there is a cluster of appealing places to stay just north of Negombo in peaceful **Waikkal**. Heading further north brings you to the bustling fishing town of **Chilaw** and the interesting **Munnesvaram Temple**, one of Sri Lanka's most important Hindu shrines.

Waikkal

Twelve kilometres north of Negombo, the small village of **WAIKKAL** (or Waikkala, as it's often spelled) is a major **tile-making** centre, thanks to the good clay found hereabouts, and the area is dotted with quaint tile factories. These sport tall chimneys attached to barn-like buildings with sloping sides and huge roofs, and great mounds of freshly baked tiles stacked up beneath. The village also has a several good **places to stay** (see page 107).

Marawila to Madampe

Twenty kilometres north of Negombo, the strongly Catholic village of **MARAWILA** has several large churches and produces good **batiks** – a trade introduced by the Dutch from Indonesia. The Eric Suriyasena and Buddhi Keerthisena showrooms on the main road are both good places to hunt for local creations.

Beyond Marawila, the beautiful coastal road runs north through an endless succession of fishing villages, past toppling palms, Christian shrines and cemeteries, palm shacks and prawn hatcheries. A few kilometres north of Marawila is **MAHAWEWA**, also renowned for its batiks. There are various tiny "factories" dotted around the village, should you want to buy, or you can just watch how the cloth is made.

A few kilometres further north the small town of **MADAMPE** is home to the handsome **Tanniyan-valla Bahu temple**, right next to the main road. Fronting the road, the main courtyard is notable for its unusual statue of a rearing, riderless horse – said to commemorate a former traveller who once rode past the temple without paying his respects and was thrown to the ground by his mount as a result – whereupon the chastened rider vowed to erect a statue to atone for his insolence. A most plausible (if less colourful) explanation is that the horse belonged to a certain King Tanniawalaba, after whom the temple is named, and a statue of whom stands nearby, usually garlanded with flowers.

1

RAMA, SHIVA AND MUNNESVARAM

According to legend, **Munnesvaram Temple** was established by none other than **Rama** himself, after he defeated and killed Rawana, as related in the Ramayana. Following the final battle with Rawana, Rama was returning to India in his air chariot (the *Dandu Monara*, or "Wooden Peacock" – often claimed to be the earliest flying machine in world literature – whose stylized image formerly adorned the tailfins of all Air Lanka planes) when he was overcome by a sudden sense of guilt at the bloodshed occasioned by his war. Seeing a temple below, he descended and began to pray, whereupon Shiva and Parvati appeared and ordered him to enshrine lingams (symbolic of Shiva's creative powers) in three new temples: at **Koneswaram** in Trincomalee, **Thirukketheeswaram** in Mannar, and at **Munnesvaram**.

The belief that these three temples were thus established by Rama – an incarnation of the great Hindu god Vishnu – lends each an additional aura of sanctity, though the fact that they were created to enshrine a trio of lingams serves as a subtle piece of propaganda asserting the superiority of Shiva over his greatest rival in the Hindu pantheon. The paradox is that, despite Sri Lanka's close association with Vishnu in his incarnation as Rama, almost all the island's Hindu temples are dedicated to Shiva, or to deities closely related to him, and hardly any to Vishnu himself.

Chilaw and around

Some 32km north of Negombo lies the town of **CHILAW** (pronounced, Portuguese-style, "Chilao"), home to a big fish market and dominated by the eye-catching, orange-pink **St Mary's Cathedral** – testimony to the town's large Catholic population.

Munnesvaram Temple
4km east of Chilaw • No set hours • Donation

Just inland from Chilaw, the **Munnesvaram Temple** is one of the five most important Shiva temples on the island and an important pilgrimage centre. Its origins are popularly claimed to date back to the mythical era of the Ramayana, though the original temple was destroyed by the Portuguese, and the present building dates from the British era.

Munnesvaram follows the usual plan of Sri Lankan Hindu temples, with a solidly built inner shrine of stone enclosed within a larger, barn-like wooden structure, its stout outer walls painted in the traditional alternating red and white stripes. The darkly impressive **inner shrine** (*cella*) is very Indian in style; a large gilded *kodithambam* (a ceremonial pillar carried in procession during the temple festival, and a standard element of all Sri Lankan Hindu temples) stands in front of the entrance door. The **outer building** is a fine old wooden structure, slightly adulterated by bits of modern bathroom-style tiling. To the left of the entrance are various chariots used to carry images and other paraphernalia during temple festivities; more festival chariots can be found at the rear of the inner shrine, including a peacock (for Skanda), a Garuda (Vishnu) and a lion (Parvati), while the huge main chariot used in the festival is usually parked in the courtyard outside.

Uddapu

Just under 20km north of Chilaw a turn-off from the village of Butul Oya (between the 96km and 97km post) leads to **UDDAPU** (or Uddapuwa), a small and impoverished Tamil village of sandy streets and palm-thatch fishermen's shacks which provides an unlikely home for the dramatic **Draupadi Amman Temple**, whose massive gopuram towers majestically over the surrounding low-rise houses. The village is also home to a sizeable Muslim minority, with a mosque (and church, tending to local Tamil Christians) standing in the lee of the temple – the mixture of local Tamil women in colourful saris and Muslims in flowing white robes lends Uddapu a decidedly exotic appeal, quite unlike other villages hereabouts.

The temple is also the focus of a remarkable eighteen-day Hindu festival (held late July/early August; see ⓦudappu.org) culminating in the **Tee Mithi** ceremony, during which the entire male population of the village walk barefoot over a bed of red-hot coals.

ARRIVAL AND DEPARTURE

NORTH OF NEGOMBO

By bus Buses run every 30min or so to Chilaw from Colombo (2hr 15min–2hr 45min) and Negombo (1hr 30min), all passing via Waikkal (about 20–30min further on from Negombo). In Waikkal buses will drop you on the main road, from where you'll need to catch a tuktuk for the onward journey (1.5–2km) to the various accommodation options listed below.

By train There are around eight daily services from from Colombo to Chilaw (2hr 30min–3hr 30min) and Waikkal (1hr 30min–1hr 45min) via Negombo.

ACCOMMODATION

WAIKKAL

★ **Ging Oya Lodge** Kammala North (signed turn on right just before you reach the turn-off for the Club Dolphin hotel) ☏ 031 227 7822, ⓦ gingoya.com. Very peaceful retreat on a little peninsula surrounded on three sides by the Ging Oya river and screened from neighbouring houses by a swathe of jungle. Accommodation is in individual a/c chalets in the rambling, tree-studded grounds, all well equipped and furnished in attractive colonial style with open-air bathrooms. It's a 10min walk to the beach, or you can paddle there in a similar time in one of the guesthouse's free kayaks. There's also a neat little bar and good-sized pool. Excellent value. B&B €57

Ranweli Holiday Village ☏ 031 227 7359, ⓦ ranweli. com. Idyllic eco-friendly resort squeezed in between the ocean and the lagoon, with rustic but stylish a/c rooms set in low red-brick buildings connected by covered walkways. Activities include yoga and Ayurveda courses, boat trips on the lagoon, bike trips and birdwatching with the hotel's excellent naturalist, and there's also a big pool overlooking the beach. B&B $180

Rico's Shadow Kammala North ☏ 031 227 8932, ⓦ rico-shadow.com. Attractive, flag-festooned boutique guesthouse with 25 or so very comfortable rooms (all with a/c and hot water), spread over four villa-style buildings each in its own garden. They also have their own neat little pavilion restaurant 50m down the road, and guests get free use of the pool at the nearby *Villa Suriya* hotel. B&B €50

Villa Suriyagaha About 200m from Ranweli Resort ☏ 031 227 9309, ⓦ villa-suriyagaha.com. Soothing little British-owned place with four spacious and well-equipped doubles set in attractive gardens, and with a surprisingly large pool. B&B $65

MARAWILA TO MADAMPE

Horathapola Wadumunnegedara, 8km northeast of Marawila (35km northeast of Negombo; 1hr drive from airport) ☏ 071 533 8230, ⓦ horathapola.com. This lovely old 1900s plantation bungalow on a fifty-acre working organic coconut estate is an idyllic (albeit pricey) place to shift the jetlag. The five a/c rooms (plus separate lodge) are attractively decorated with antique wooden furniture, and there's a saltwater pool and jacuzzi, plus bullock cart rides through the huge gardens. Half board $345

CHILAW AND AROUND

The Mudhouse Around 30km northeast of Chilaw near the town of Anamaduwa ☏ 077 301 6191, ⓦ themudhouse.lk. Gorgeously rustic eco-retreat set within two hectares of jungle beside a lotus-strewn lake, with accommodation in simple but comfortable huts made entirely of natural local materials. Rates include local excursions and activities. Full board $340

Kalpitiya peninsula

North of Chilaw (and about 8km before reaching the town of Puttalam), a road branches off west, threading its way across the beautiful, windswept **Kalpitiya peninsula**, fringed with unspoilt beaches and bounded on opposite sides by the sea and the Puttalam lagoon. Almost untouched as recently as five years ago, the peninsula has now seen tourism explode big time. Much of this is due to Kalpitiya's status as one of Asia's premier **kitesurfing** destinations (see page 110) thanks to the unusually

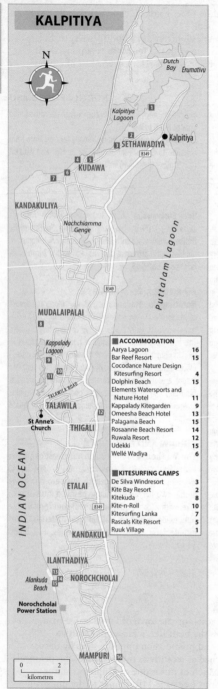

KALPITIYA

N

Dutch Bay Erumativu

Kalpitiya Lagoon

Kalpitiya

SETHAWADIYA

B349

KUDAWA

KANDAKULIYA

Nachchiamma Genge

Puttalam Lagoon

B349

MUDALAIPALAI

Kappalady Lagoon

TALAWILA ROAD

TALAWILA

St Anne's Church

THIGALI

INDIAN OCEAN

ETALAI

B349

KANDAKULI

ILANTHADIYA

NOROCHCHOLAI

Alankuda Beach

Norochcholai Power Station

MAMPURI

0   2
kilometres

Puttalam (18km) & Wilpattu National Park (66km) ▼

■ **ACCOMMODATION**
Aarya Lagoon	16
Bar Reef Resort	15
Cocodance Nature Design Kitesurfing Resort	4
Dolphin Beach	15
Elements Watersports and Nature Hotel	11
Kappalady Kitegarden	9
Omeesha Beach Hotel	13
Palagama Beach	15
Rosaanne Beach Resort	14
Ruwala Resort	12
Udekki	15
Wellé Wadiya	6

■ **KITESURFING CAMPS**
De Silva Windresort	3
Kite Bay Resort	2
Kitekuda	8
Kite-n-Roll	10
Kitesurfing Lanka	7
Rascals Kite Resort	5
Ruuk Village	1

strong and steady winds, funnelled through the Palk Strait between Sri Lanka and India, which blow around the peninsula. It's also Sri Lanka's prime **dolphin-watching** destination (see page 109), with the occasional whale thrown in for good measure too. Add in miles of unspoiled beach, lazy lagoons, pristine coastline and a handful of historic monuments and other cultural attractions and the area's massive appeal becomes self-evident, while Wilpattu National Park is also within easy striking distance, as is Anuradhapura, at a pinch.

As you head north across the peninsula, the main road skirts the southern edge of the **Puttalam Lagoon**, lined with saltpans and with views across the water to an impressive line of wind turbines opposite. After about 25km you'll pass the turn-off to **Alankuda Beach**, home to the peninsula's most alluring cluster of accommodation options, followed, around 10km further on, by the side road to the important Catholic shrine at the nineteenth-century church of **St Anne**, almost on the seafront at the village of **Talawila**, site of an important festival in March and again in July/August.

From here it's just under 20km to **KALPITIYA TOWN**, close to the northernmost tip of the peninsula: a watery, end-of-the-world sort of place, home to the modest ruins of an old **Dutch fort** and the rustic little Dutch-era **St Peter's Kirk**.

ARRIVAL AND DEPARTURE
KALPITIYA PENINSULA

Regular public transport is limited to **bus** services (roughly every hour) along the main road between the town of Puttalam and Kalpitiya Town. If you're coming without your own transport it's best to contact your accommodation in advance for details of the best way of getting there as places to stay are widely scattered around the peninsula, often in rather remote and difficult-to-find locations.

ACCOMMODATION

There are plenty of places to stay around Kalpitiya. Rates are generally on the high side, but fall

DOLPHIN- AND WHALE-WATCHING IN KALPITIYA

Over the past decade, Kalpitiya has established itself as one of Asia's best places to spot **dolphins** – on a good morning you might see literally hundreds of these beautiful creatures (mainly spinner dolphins, but also bottlenose, Risso's and humpback) coasting through the waves in every direction as far as the eye can see, occasionally launching themselves clean out of the water and spinning acrobatically through the air. The majority of dolphins follow the so-called "dolphin line" running parallel to the peninsula's west coast, inside the protecting corals of the Bar Reef which lies around 5km offshore.

The **best time** to spot dolphins is from November to March/April, outside the monsoon season, when the sea is relatively calm – sightings during this season are pretty much guaranteed, and you might even be lucky enough to spot **whales** (usually sperm, occasionally blue) while out at sea. Pretty much every guesthouse, hotel and kite camp in Kalpitiya can arrange tours. These usually leave at sunrise, last two to three hours and generally cost around $40 per person. A few places also offer dedicated (and slightly more expensive) whale-watching trips, usually heading further out to sea, beyond the reef, in search of these mighty mammals.

significantly in some places from April to November. Most accommodation is clustered in three areas: around **Kalpitiya Lagoon** at the northern end of the peninsula; around **Kappalady Lagoon**, about halfway up the peninsula; and near the southern end of the peninsula around **Alankuda Beach**. The last is home to a wonderful quartet of linked eco-resorts – the *Bar Reef Resort*, *Palagama*, *Udekki* and *Dolphin Beach* (walankuda.com) – far and away the nicest places to stay hereabouts.

SOUTHERN KALPITIYA AND ALANKUDA BEACH

Aarya Lagoon Mampuri ☏031 720 1201, ⓦaaryaresorts.com; map p.108. Small resort hotel in a very breezy location on Puttalam Lagoon. The seven large rooms all have big windows offering fine lagoon views, plus fancy bathrooms and lots of mod cons. There's also a nice infinity pool, plus restaurant and the aptly named *Breeze Bar*, although the attached minigolf course and children's play area adds an incongruous bucket-and-spade touch. B&B $157

★ **Bar Reef Resort** Alankuda Beach ☏077 721 9218, ⓦbarreefresort.com; map p.108. Alankuda's original eco-retreat, arranged around a picture-perfect infinity pool pointing towards the sea and surrounded by a trio of rustic thatched *ambalamas* and tables made out of old boats. Accommodation is in seven cabanas (sleeping up to four), with faux-mud-brick ochre walls and thatched roofs, or two stunning villas (sleeping up to eight people), resembling a pair of glamorous Indonesian longhouses. Rustic eco-chic at its very best. B&B $150

Dolphin Beach Alankuda Beach ☏032 738 8050, ⓦdolphinbeach.lk; map p.108. A bit different from the other Alankuda resorts, with accommodation in well-equipped and very comfortable Rajasthani-style a/c tents,

with attractive cushioned sit-outs in front. Meals are served in the breezy thatched dining pavilion, and there's a lovely chill-out zone in the circular beachfront *ambalama* plus a fine infinity pool. B&B $177

Omeesha Beach Hotel Ilanthadiya ☏072 999 4850, ⓦomeeshabeach-kalpitiya.com; map p.108. Spread around a long sandy garden running down to the beach, with ten non-a/c cabanas each within its own little palm-thatch-walled garden. – nice, but expensive for what you get. B&B $50

★ **Palagama Beach** Alankuda Beach ☏077 781 8970, ⓦpalagamabeach.com; map p.108. This is next door to *Bar Reef Resort*, and shares many of the same features, including a sea-facing infinity pool surrounded by *ambalamas* and accommodation scattered around lush grounds and along the beachfront. Accommodation is in a string of quaint wooden cabanas – ingeniously designed (by owner and architect Cecil Balmond) in a range of styles using local woods, palm-thatch and other local materials. There's also more conventional lodging in a pair of homely two-room villas, plus a small spa. B&B $205

Rosaanne Beach Resort Norochcholai ☏072 251 3224 ⓦroshannebeach.lk; map p.108. Appealingly low-key option, and reasonably priced (at least by Kalpitiya standards), with just six chic, attractively furnished cabanas arranged around a lovely sandy garden just 200m from the beach. B&B $94

Udekki Alankuda Beach ☏077 744 6135, ⓦudekki.com; map p.108. The funkiest of the Alankuda resorts, arranged around a wonderful "jungle" courtyard stuffed with all manner of trees and a cute little H-shaped pool. Accommodation is in a trio of whitewashed a/c villas decorated with eclectic bric-a-brac and artworks along with recycled windows, doors and cast-iron bathtubs. $160

1

KITESURFING AND WATERSPORTS IN KALPITIYA

Kalpitiya's main **kitesurfing** season is during the southwest monsoon from May to September when average wind speeds reach 20–30 knots; there's a second season (with slightly less powerful and reliable winds) during the northeast monsoon from December to March. The most popular **places** for kiting are the Kalpitiya and Kappalady lagoons, which have both shallow areas suitable for beginners and deeper waters for those with more experience. There are also good downwinder rides out at sea.

In addition to kitesurfing, a range of other watersports including **snorkelling**, **kayaking**, **deep-sea fishing** and **stand-up paddleboarding** can be organized at many places. There's particularly good **diving** at Bar Reef, just offshore from Alankuda Beach, which is home to some of Sri Lanka's most pristine and biodiverse coral gardens, with more than 150 types of coral and almost 300 species of tropical fish.

KITESURFING CAMPS IN KALPITIYA

All the accommodation places listed (see page 108) can arrange kiting, and often other watersports as well. There's also a burgeoning number of dedicated **kitesurfing camps**, usually offering simple cabana accommodation at relatively low (by Kalpitiya standards) prices, with equipment hire and lessons also available. Board-plus-kite rental generally starts from around €60/day, while one-on-one lessons starts from around €50/hr. Many places offer various packages combining bed, meals, board-hire and tuition. Recommended places include:

De Silva Windresort Sethawadiya ☎077 704 7817, ⓦsurfschool-srilanka.com; map p.108. Right on Kalpitiya Lagoon, with attractive (if rather pricey) cabanas and more basic rooms. Half board €70

Kite Bay Resort Sethawadiya ☎076 540 4707; map p.108. Popular and well-run new camp, and about as cheap as it gets in Kalpitiya, with basic cabanas and slightly fancier rooms. €20

Kitekuda Kappalady ☎072 223 2952, ⓦsrilankakiteschool.com; map p.108. Upscale, attractive and predictably expensive modern rooms on the lagoon. Full board €150

Kite-n-Roll Kappalady ☎072 112 9551, ⓦkite-n-roll.com; map p.108. Simple but refreshingly inexpensive rooms close to Kappalady Lagoon. €25

Kitesurfing Lanka Kudawa ☎077 368 6235, ⓦkitesurfinglanka.com; map p.108. Rustic bungalows and rather expensive tents close to the beach – although a couple of kilometres from the lagoon. The very well set-up attached shop provides equipment rental, repairs and lessons. Full board: doubles €98, tents €70

Rascals Kite Resort Kudawa ☎071 658 3857, ⓦrascalskiteresort.com; map p.108. Spacious, good-looking rooms and cabanas, plus local "surfaris" and exhilarating downwinders. Full board €100

Ruuk Village Thoradiya ☎072 505 6177, ⓦruukvillage.com; map p.108. On Kalpitiya Lagoon and within walking distance of Kalpitiya Town, with attractively rustic thatched cabanas complete with coconut-tree showers and 24hr solar power. B&B €46

CENTRAL KALPITIYA

Elements Watersports and Nature Hotel Kappalady ☎077 737 7387, ⓦelements-resort.com; map p.108. Five chic and spacious bungalows in a superb position between the ocean and Kappalady Lagoon, with a gorgeous saltwater infinity pool and plenty of outdoor activities including dolphin-trips, snorkelling, bike rides and birdwatching. Half board €140

Kappalady Kitegarden Kappalady ☎072 231 3129, ⓦkappaladykitegarden.com; map p.108. A tree-shaded plot by the Kappalady Lagoon with nine rooms at very competitive rates, including a few with shared bathroom, plus more expensive ones with a/c and hot water. Full board: €50; en suite €70, a/c €90

Ruwala Resort Thigali ☎032 329 9299, ⓦruwalaresort.com; map p.108. Stylish little eco-retreat set in nine acres of mangrove-fringed coconut garden next to Puttalam Lagoon. Accommodation comprises mix of lagoonside chalets plus a couple of others tucked away amid the mangroves, and there's also a long infinity pool and all sorts of outdoor activities including horseriding, diving and mangrove tours. B&B $180

NORTHERN KALPITIYA

Cocodance Nature Design Kitesurfing Resort Kudawa ☎077 114 5304, ⓦcocodance.lk; map p.108. Appealingly rustic place with cute bamboo-and-stone chalets set behind pretty little cushioned verandas. The wide range of activities includes birdwatching, boat trips and cookery classes, plus the usual kitesurfing and dolphin-watching options. B&B $50

Wellé **Wadiya** Kudawa ☎077 011 2929, ⓦwellewadiya.com; map p.108. Smart little two-storey

hotel on a nice stretch of beach, with bright and airy rooms, above-average food and all the usual activities

Wilpattu National Park

Daily 6am–6pm • $15 per person, plus the usual additional charges and taxes (see page 50).

Occupying a vast swathe of land stretching all the way up to the border of the Northern Province, **Wilpattu National Park** is the largest in Sri Lanka, and was the most popular until the onset of the civil war, when its position straddling the frontline between Sinhalese and Tamil areas led to the widespread destruction of local infrastructure and poaching of wildlife. Fully reopened only in 2009, Wilpattu has now largely recaptured its former glory, with a range and density of wildlife eclipsed only by Yala. The park is best known for its leopards and sloth bears – after Yala, Wilpattu is probably the best place to go scouting for both of these elusive species – while there are also elephants, spotted deer and sambar, water buffalo, mongooses, crocodiles and many types of bird. The lack of visitors and the size of the area open to tourists (around eight times larger than that at Yala, for instance) means that it's also supremely peaceful compared to many other parks.

An unusual feature of Wilpattu's topography are its numerous **villus**. These look like lakes (indeed the park's name derives from *villu-pattu*, "Land of Lakes"), though they're actually just depressions filled with rainwater which expand and contract with the seasons, attracting a range of water birds and wildlife.

ARRIVAL AND INFORMATION
WILPATTU NATIONAL PARK

Visiting the park The main entrance at Hunuvilagama, about 40km west of Anuradhapura and 25km northeast of Puttalam, near the turn off to the Kalpitiya peninsula. There's a second entrance at Eluvankulam, on the west side of the park off the Puttalam–Mannar road.

Public transport Reaching Wilpattu by public transport is tricky but possible. Regular (every 30min–1hr) buses between Puttalam and Anuradhapura will drop you off at the village of Maragahawewa on the main road, from where you can catch a tuktuk for the 5–10km journey

to the guesthouses around Horuvila and the nearby park entrance. Buses also run from Puttalam (every 30min; 90min) and Kalpitiya to Eluvankulam, stopping close to *Wilpattu House* (see page 111), or you can hire a boat to cross directly from Kalpitiya to Eluvankulam (around Rs.4000), or vice versa – check with *Wilpattu House*.

Tours Tours can be arranged locally or through many guesthouses and hotels in Kalpitiya and Anuradhapura; jeeps can be hired for tours of the park (Rs.6000 for 5hr) at the entrance.

ACCOMMODATION

If you fancy a real night in the wild, a number of operators – Kulu Safaris, Leopard Safaris, Leopard Trails, Big Game Camps and Mahoora (see page 50) – all operate (pricey) tented **safari camps** within the park.

LLT Safari and Tourist Inn Horuvila ☎025 325 3838, ⓦlltsafariwilpattu.com. Simple but comfy guesthouse a five-minute drive from the park, offering six clean and comfortable a/c rooms with mismatched furniture, plus a pleasant open-air restaurant, garden and in-house safari operation. **Rs.4000**

Thimbiriwewa Eco Resort Horuvila ☎077 977 8000. Green little place with a handful of rustic chalets with furniture made entirely from local recycled timber; all come with a/c and solar-powered hot water in the open-air bathrooms. **Rs.4500**

Wilpattu Corridor Horuvila ☎077 376 7113, ⓦwilpattutreehouse.com. Three well-appointed a/c

"tree houses" (more like high-rise cabanas, really) and a modern a/c room close to the Horuvila entrance to the park. B&B **$90**

Wilpattu House Eluvankulam ☎078 834 9007, ⓦwilpattuhouse.com. Accessible by public transport from both Mannar and Puttalam, this makes a great stop-off on the fascinating but little-travelled coastal route between Negombo and Mannar/Jaffna (see box, page 379). Set in a very quiet rural location on an old coconut plantation, the guesthouse offers simple homestay-style accommodation in a pair of small doubles and a standalone three-person cabin, while the very clued-up owners can also arrange onward transport to Mannar using either tuktuk (Rs.5000) or van (Rs.8000), as well as Wilpattu safaris and free early-morning birdwatching walks and jungle-river swims. No wi-fi, and you'll need to bring any beer/other provisions apart from basics with you. **Rs.2500**

South of Colombo

The coast south of Colombo is home to Sri Lanka's biggest concentration of resort hotels, catering particularly to a German and, increasingly, Eastern European clientele. This is the best-established package-holiday area on the island, and some parts, notably the main stretches of beach at **Kalutara**, **Beruwala** and **Bentota**, have largely sold out to the tourist dollar – if you're looking for unspoiled beaches and a taste of local life, these aren't the places to find them. Away from the big resort areas, pockets of interest can still be found, particularly at the bustling town of **Aluthgama**, backing the Bentota lagoon, and **Ambalangoda**, the main centre for the production of the island's eye-catching masks. Further south lies the old resort of **Hikkaduwa**, still one of the liveliest places along the coast, with good surfing, snorkelling and diving.

Heading **south out of Colombo**, the heaving Galle Road passes through a seemingly endless succession of ragtag suburbs before finally shaking itself clear of the capital, though even then a more or less continuous ribbon of development straggles all the way down the coast – according to Michael Ondaatje in his celebrated portrait of Sri Lanka, *Running in the Family*, it was said that a chicken could walk along the roofs of the houses between Galle and Colombo without once touching the ground. The endless seaside buildings mean that although the road and rail line run close to the coast for most of the way, you don't see that much of the sea, beaches or actual resorts from either.

Kalutara and around

Just over 40km from Colombo, bustling **KALUTARA** is the first town you reach travelling south that retains a recognizably separate identity from the capital. It's one of the west coast's largest settlements, but the long stretch of beach north of town remains reasonably unspoiled, dotted with a string of upmarket hotels. Sitting next to the broad estuary of the Kalu Ganga, or "Black River", from which it takes its name, Kalutara was formerly an important spice-trading centre, controlled at various times by the Portuguese, Dutch and British. Nowadays, it's more famous as the source of the island's finest **mangosteens** (in season June–Sept).

Gangatilaka Vihara

Kalutara announces its presence via the immense white dagoba of the **Gangatilaka Vihara**, immediately south of the long bridge across the Kalu Ganga. Built in the 1960 on the site of the former Portuguese fort, the dagoba has the distinction of being the largest entirely hollow stupa in the island. You can go inside the cavernously echoing interior, whose walls are ringed by a strip of 75 murals depicting various scenes from the Buddha's life; windows above the murals offer fine views of the Kalu Ganga and out to sea. Outside, the line of donation boxes flanking the roadside are fed with huge quantities of small change by local motorists, who stop here to say a prayer and offer a few coins in the hope of a safe journey.

The remainder of the temple buildings are situated in a compound on the other side of the road, featuring the usual bo tree enclosures and Buddha shrines. It's a lively complex, and a good place to watch the daily rituals of Sri Lankan Buddhism: the

---

WEST COAST DIVING AND SWIMMING LESSONS

The best season for **diving** and **swimming** on the west coast is roughly November to mid-April; at other times, heavy breakers and dangerous undertows mean that it can be risky to go in beyond chest height. For more about swimming and other marine hazards, see Basics (see page 57).

uddha images here are "fed" three times a day (rather like the package tourists at the earby resorts); devotees place food in boxes in front of the images, as well as offering owers, lighting coconut-oil lamps, tying prayers written on scraps of cloth to one of he bo trees (sometimes with coins wrapped up inside them) or pouring water into the onduits which run down to water the bo trees' roots.

ichmond Castle

latota, a few kilometres inland along the lagoon-side road immediately south of the Gangatilaka temple • Daily 9am–4pm • Rs.500

striking hybrid of Indian and British architectural styles, the imperious **Richmond astle** was built at the end of the nineteenth century by wealthy landowner and spice-rower Don Arthur de Silva Wijesinghe Siriwardena. It now serves as an educational entre for underprivileged local children. Sitting proud atop a hill at the centre of a 2-acre estate, the two-storey mansion is constructed on a lavish scale – two entire hiploads of teak from Burma were used during its construction, some of which can be een in the 99 doors and 34 window frames and in the finely carved wooden pillars in he main hall.

Wadduwa

alutara's **beach** extends north of the bridge all the way to the village of **WADDUWA**, ome 8km distant, where it's backed by a sprinkling of medium-sized resort hotels. he coast is edged with a fine – if in places rather narrow – strand of golden sand, and emains surprisingly unspoiled and quiet given the proximity of Colombo, although (as long much of the west coast) the sea can be rough at times, and most people swim in heir hotel pools.

ARRIVAL AND DEPARTURE
KALUTARA AND AROUND

y bus The bus stand is a few minutes' walk south of the angatilaka Vihara on Main St.

estinations Aluthgama (every 15min; 30min); mbalangoda (every 15min; 1hr); Colombo (every 15min; hr); Galle (every 15min; 1hr 45min); Hikkaduwa (every

15min; 1hr 15min).

By train The train station, Kalutara South, is 100m west of the bus stand; see the timetable (see page 32) for details of services.

ACCOMMODATION AND EATING

ost **accommodation** in Kalutara straggles up the each north of the lagoon, spreading from Kalutara itself Wadduwa. Distances are given from the bridge across e Kalu Ganga at the north end of town. There are also one two places to stay on the peninsula just south of town alapuwa), including the large, new *Anantara* hotel, plus number of rather dismal **budget guesthouses** in the npoverished fishing village of Keselwatta just north of the each, although if funds are tight it's really much better to ess on south to Aluthgama or Hikkaduwa. You'll most xely eat in your hotel, although there are a few simple **staurants** on the road leading to the *Avani Kalutara* esort and also flanking Abrew Rd, close to the entrance of e *Tangerine Beach Hotel*.

ALUTARA

nantara Kalutara Resort 1.5km south of Kalutara 034 222 0022, kalutara.anantara.com. This new sort, next to the *Avani*, is in a fabulous beachfront cation with sea and lagoon views, and a lush tropical arden. The rooms are spacious and tastefully decorated

with local textiles. The villas have their own private plunge pools, plus there are two outdoor pools, a yoga pavilion, a spa and water sports centre. B&B $335

★ **Avani Kalutara Resort and Spa** 1.5km south of Kalutara 034 429 7700, bit.ly/2Gry0mT. Stylish, Geoffrey Bawa-designed resort hotel in a breezy location on a narrow spit of land between the ocean and the Kalutara lagoon, with fine views over the town to one side and the ocean to the other. Rooms are elegantly furnished in minimalist style and there's a nice pool and activities including watersports on the adjacent lagoon, yoga classes and an attractive spa. B&B $195

Mermaid Hotel & Club 4.5km north of Kalutara 034 720 0478, mermaidhotelnclub.com. Well-run three-star resort attractively set in a palm grove with comfortable, wood-furnished rooms in identical two-floor blocks either side of a pool; the smarter deluxe rooms are metres from the beach. There's also a spa and gym, plus volleyball and squash courts next door. All-inclusive rates are just $20 extra. Half board $190

1

Kalutara & Colombo

0   1
kilometre

Beruwala Train Station

Kachimalai Mosque

BERUWALA, ALUTHGAMA, BENTOTA AND INDURUWA

BERUWALA

Barberyn Lighthouse

A2

Moragalla

INDIAN OCEAN

Tourist Police

Kande Vihara

B157

ALUTHGAMA

Paradise Island

Aluthgama Train Station

SEE INSET BELOW

Bentota Ganga

Wanawasa Raja Mahaviharaya

Bentota Beach Hotel

National Holiday Resort

Bentota Train Station

ELPITIYA ROAD

DEDDUWA JUNCTION

BENTOTA VILLAGE

Galapata Vihara

Dedduwa Lake

Lunuganga

A2

● DIVING AND WATERSPORTS

Malubanna	3
Sunshine Water Sports Center	2
Ypsylon Diving School	1

● EATING

Cinnamon Bey	1
Diya Sisila	6
Golden Grill Restaurant	4
Hilda's Coffee Bar	2
Malli's	5
Pier 88	7
Riverdale Restaurant	3

■ ACCOMMODATION

Amal Villa	19
Avani Bentota	10
Chami Villa	12
Cinnamon Bey	2
Club Villa	15
Eden Resort & Spa	6
Ganga Garden	26
Hemadan	28
Long Beach Cottage	22
Lunuganga	20
Nisala Arana	9
Pandanus Beach Resort & Spa	24
Panorama	1
Paradise Road The Villa	14
Riverbank Bentota	27
Rock Villa	16
Sagarika Beach Hotel	4
Saman Villas	21
Shangri Lanka Villa	17
Sri Lancashire Guesthouse	8
Susantha's	11
Vivanta by Taj	13
Waterside Bentota	7
Wunderbar Beach Hotel	18

■ AYURVEDA RESORTS

Amba Boutique Hotel	29
Ayurveda Shunyata Villa	23
Barberyn Reef Ayurveda Resort	3
Heritance Ayurveda Maha Gedara	5
Sign of Life	25

Induruwa Train Station

INDURUWA

A2

Commercial Bank

HNB Bank

Aluthgama Bus Stand

Aluthgama Train Station

B157

RIVER AVENUE

WELITOTARA ROAD

Aluthgama Wood Carvers

Bentota Ganga

Market

Nebula Supermarket

0   200
metres

N

Royal Palms 3km north of Kalutara ☏ 034 222 8113, ✆ tangerinehotels.com. Upmarket resort hotel, with other grand public areas sporting eye-catching, quasi-Indian touches, plush but bland rooms, and an enormous, serpentine pool set amid spacious grounds. Guests can also use the Ayurveda centre in the sister *Tangerine Beach Hotel* next door. B&B $165

Tangerine Beach Hotel 3km north of Kalutara ☏ 034 223 7982, ✆ tangerinehotels.com. Above-average resort hotel, the stereotypical design enlivened by quirky statues, fancy wooden doors and other whimsical touches. Rooms (some with sea views) are cheerfully furnished, and there's a big pool and spacious grounds, plus Ayurveda spa. B&B $210

WADDUWA

The Blue Water 11km north of Kalutara ☏ 038 223 5067, ✆ bluewatersrilanka.com. This large Geoffrey Bawa-designed five-star resort manages to combine size and understated style with classically simple buildings set behind a vast, imaginatively landscaped pool. The attractive rooms have all mod cons plus sea-facing balconies or terraces, and there's also a lovely little spa. B&B $195

Reef Villa & Spa 9km north of Kalutara ☏ 038 228 4442, ✆ reefvilla.com. A sumptuous mix of colonial charm and modern luxury set in a lush three-acre garden with pool and spa. Accommodation is in seven huge, high-ceilinged suites, beautifully furnished in updated Raj-era style complete with antique canopied beds and Indian ceiling punkah fans. Spectacular – and spectacularly expensive. The good (but rather pricey) restaurant is open to non-guests. B&B $550

Beruwala

BERUWALA is Sri Lanka's resort destination par excellence, perfect if you're looking for an undemanding tropical holiday with hot sun, bland food and characterless accommodation. Big resort hotels stand shoulder to shoulder along the main section of the broad and still attractive **beach** – Beruwala's so-called "Golden Mile" – often separated by stout fences and security guards from contact with the ordinary life of Sri Lanka outside. The slim stretch of beach at Moragalla, beyond the *Cinnamon Bey* hotel on Beruwala's northern shores, is more intimate, however, with a handful of budget guesthouses and cafés scattered along the waterfront (protected here by an offshore reef) and in the village behind.

Beruwala's seafront has undergone a major redevelopment over the last few years, and judging by the ongoing construction work, more hotels are set to open in the near future. Beach and resorts aside, the area (including neighbouring Bentota) has also developed into Sri Lanka's main centre for **Ayurvedic treatments** (see page 116); most of the larger hotels offer massages and herbal or steam baths, and there are also a number of specialist resorts (see page 117).

Kachimalai Mosque

North of the resorts, scruffy Beruwala town is where Sri Lanka's first recorded Muslim settlement was established, during the eighth century. Standing on a headland overlooking the harbour at the northern end of town, the **Kachimalai Mosque** is believed to be the oldest on the island, and said to mark the site of this first Arab landing. Containing the shrine of a tenth-century Muslim saint, it's an important pilgrimage site at the end of Ramadan.

Barberyn Lighthouse

No fixed hours • Rs.200 • Most resorts (or local boatmen) can organize the 10min boat ride to the island; Malubanna (see page 120) offers sunset tour from their base in Aluthgama

Less than 100m from Beruwala town, the slender white British-built **Barberyn Lighthouse** stands on its own jungly little island, home to huge colonies of crows that flock here noisily at sunset. You can climb the winding interior staircase to the top of the lighthouse for a look at the old colonial machinery and for spectacular 360-degree views.

AYURVEDA: THE SCIENCE OF LIFE

Ayurveda – from the Sanskrit, meaning "the science of life" – is an ancient system of healthcare which is widely practised in India and Sri Lanka. Its roots reach back deep into Indian history – descriptions of a basic kind of Ayurvedic medical theory are found as long ago as the second millennium BC, in the sacred proto-Hindu texts known as the Vedas.

Unlike allopathic Western medicines, which aim to determine what's making you ill, then destroy it, Ayurveda is a holistic system which regards illness as the result of a derangement in a person's basic make-up. The Ayurvedic system holds that all bodies are composed of varied combinations of five basic **elements** – ether, air, fire, water and earth – and that each body is governed by three **doshas**, or life forces: **pitta** (fire and water); **kapha** (water and earth); and **vata** (air and ether). Illness is seen as an imbalance in the proportions of these life forces, and specific diseases are considered symptoms of more fundamental problems. Ayurvedic treatments aim to rectify such imbalances, and Ayurveda doctors will typically examine the whole of a patient's lifestyle, habits, diets and emotional proclivities in order to find the roots of a disease – treatment often consists of establishing a more balanced lifestyle as much as administering specific therapies.

With the developed world's increasing suspicion of Western medicine and pharmaceuticals, Ayurveda is gaining a **growing following** among non-Sri Lankans – it's particularly popular with Germans, thousands of whom visit the island every year specifically to take Ayurvedic cures. Genuine courses of Ayurveda treatment need to last at least a week or two to have any effect, and treatment plans are usually customized by a local Ayurveda doctor to suit the needs of individual patients. Programmes usually consist of a range of herbal treatments and various types of baths and massages prescribed in combination with cleansing and revitalization techniques including yoga, meditation, special diets (usually vegetarian) and abstention from alcohol. Some of the more serious Ayurveda resorts and clinics offer the **panchakarma**, or "five-fold treatment", comprising the five basic therapies of traditional Ayurveda: therapeutic vomiting; purging; enema; blood-letting; and the nasal administration of medicines – a rather stomach-turning catalogue which offers the serious devotee the physical equivalent of a thorough spring-cleaning. A few places offer other yet more weird and wonderful traditional therapies such as treatments with leeches and fire ("moxibustion").

Although a sizeable number of people visit Sri Lankan Ayurvedic centres for the serious treatment of chronic diseases, the majority of treatments offered here are essentially cosmetic, so-called "soft" Ayurveda – **herbal** and **steam baths**, and various forms of **massage** are the overwhelming staples, promoted by virtually every larger resort hotel along the west coast. These are glorified beauty and de-stress treatments rather than genuine medicinal therapies, and whether there's anything truly Ayurvedic about many of them is a moot point, but they're enjoyable enough, if you take them for what they are and don't confuse them with genuine Ayurveda.

ARRIVAL AND DEPARTURE

By bus The nearest bus station is in Aluthgama, 2–4km south of most of the resorts and served by regular buses (every 15–20min) running between Colombo and Galle/Matara. Alternatively, you could jump off the bus between Beruwala town and Aluthgama on the main road close to the resorts, though it's difficult to know exactly where to get off – it's easier to catch a tuktuk from one of the stations.

By train The nearest train station is in Beruwala town, though it's served only by irregular, slow services. It's easier to go to Aluthgama and catch a tuktuk from there. See the timetable in Basics (p30) for full details.

ACCOMMODATION

Cinnamon Bey ☎034 229 7000, ⓦcinnamonhotels.com; map p.114. Huge, well-run resort set in twelve grassy acres beside a narrow strip of beach with two pools (one for deluxe rooms and suites), a string of restaurants, and a nice spa and gym. Rooms are fresh and contemporary, well furnished and adorned with Arabian style geometric wall tiles. B&B $287

Eden Resort and Spa ☎034 227 6075, ⓦbrownshotels.com/eden; map p.114. Glitzy five-star resort that doubles as a spa and health club. The huge list of treatments includes Ayurveda, herbal baths, reflexology

AYURVEDA AND HEALTH RESORTS ON THE WEST COAST

Amba Boutique Hotel Balapitiya ☎091 225 4500, ⓦambaboutiquehotel.com; map p.114. This six-room Ayurveda hotel, set slightly back from the beach, offers a soft introduction to Ayurveda via three experiences that differ in intensity – "Pure", "Spirit" and "Sceptic" – without any strict rules (alcohol is permitted). The cement-and-timber design is refreshingly minimal and there's a saltwater pool and modern treatment centre. Rates are for single occupancy (a second adult sharing the room costs €90 more), including treatments. €154

★ **Ayurveda Shunyata Villa** Induruwa ☎034 227 1944, ⓦayurveda-shunyata-villa.de; map p.114. Idyllic little Ayurveda retreat in serene, modern beachfront premises. Rooms have a simple but sophisticated decor, with white walls and rock-crystal jacuzzi bathrooms. There's also a nice little pool, while Ayurveda treatments are administered in the beautiful garden. Minimum stay 2–3-weeks Dec–March; minimum 1 week the rest of the year. Book well ahead. One-week full-board package €750

Barberyn Reef Ayurveda Resort Beruwala ☎034 227 6036, ⓦbarberyn.com; map p.114. The oldest of Beruwala's Ayurveda resorts, and still one of the best, with immaculate rooms set amid tranquil, frangipani-shaded grounds. Room rates include vegetarian Ayurvedic meals, free yoga and meditation classes, and airport transfers. Treatments cost €80 per person per day on top of the room rate and there's a minimum stay of one week. Full board €160

Heritance Ayurveda Maha Gedara Beruwala ☎034 555 5000, ⓦheritancehotels.com; map p.114. This long-running, rather Andalucian-looking establishment is a great choice if you're travelling with someone who doesn't want to take any Ayurveda treatments (although alcohol is restricted and the Ayurvedic diet can be bland); it has bright rooms, an attractive treatment centre and a big pool, plus daily yoga and meditation. There's a minimum stay of three days, and the option of a light treatment package with two therapies or longer *panchakarma* packages (minimum one week). Non-Ayurveda guests pay €85 less. Full board €340

Sign of Life Bentota ☎034 227 0312, ⓦsign-of-life-resort; map p.114. Next to *Saman Villas*, this homely little Ayurveda resort offers good-value courses that include accommodation (in bright white a/c rooms), Ayurvedic meals and free yoga classes. Minimum 12-day stay, and rates include all meals, treatments, yoga and meditation sessions. €130

massages and yoga lessons, and there's also a vast pool and spacious grounds, although for all the place's rather brash luxury (and meaty price tag) its public areas have all the style of a second-rate shopping mall. B&B €257

Panorama ☎034 227 7091, ⓦfacebook.com/PanoramaBeachHotel; map p.114. The cheapest accommodation hereabouts, set just back from the much narrower stretch of beach north of the main resorts. The nine rooms are clean but uninspiring, and four have partial sea views. Rs.4500

Sagarika Beach Hotel ☎077 742 4376, ⓦsagarikabeachhotel.webs.com; map p.114. Friendly, family-run hotel set back from Beruwala's Golden Mile in a shady garden with pool. The cosy, chintzy rooms have a/c, verandas or balconies, and there are also two (non-a/c) apartments. B&B: doubles €95, apartments €170

EATING

Cinnamon Bey ☎034 229 7000, ⓦcinnamonhotels. com; map p.114. This sprawling hotel boasts a great variety of restaurants and cuisines, ranging from DIY barbecue on hot coals at *Rock Salt* (daily 10.30am–5pm) to fine dining at *Fire* (daily 12.30–3pm & 7–10.30pm) – including grills and *teppenyaki* – and rooftop *MEZZ2* (daily 7.30–10.30pm), where you can feast on meze platters, grilled vegetables and charcoal-grilled meats, or sip cocktails and puff shisha beneath the stars.

Hilda's Coffee Bar ☎034 227 6311, ⓦhildascoffeebar. com; map p.114. The best of the few low-key restaurants standing side by side along Moragalla beach. The kitchen dishes up seafood, fried rice, noodles and sandwiches (mains Rs.600–1200), plus proper coffee and cocktails. There are also two spotless whitewashed one-bedroom apartments upstairs with huge sea-view balconies. Daily 7am–8.30pm.

Riverdale Restaurant ☎034 227 6116, ⓦriverdaleresortslanka.com; map p.114. Although its roadside location is uninspiring, this inexpensive restaurant serves up a wide à la carte menu (most mains Rs.450–1100) ranging from reasonably priced rice and curry through to fillet steak and chicken cordon bleu, plus pasta and pizza. It also has a small separate bar and coffee shop. Daily 7am–10pm.

DIRECTORY

Banks The larger hotels all change money at lousy rates; if you want a bank, an ATM or a post office, you'll have to go down the road to Aluthgama or up to Beruwala town.

Swimming Non-guests can use the pool at the *Ede* *Resort and Spa* for Rs.1000.

Aluthgama

Dividing Beruwala from Bentota, the lively little town of **ALUTHGAMA** offers a welcome dose of everyday life amid the big resorts and remains refreshingly unaffected by the local package-tourist industry. The main street is a colourful succession of trades: a fish market straggles part way up its west side, with all sorts of seafood lined up on benches supervised by machete-wielding fishmongers, while at the south end of the road local ladies flog great piles of lurid factory-made cloth. A photogenic vegetable market is held just south of here, past the Nebula supermarket – Mondays a● particularly lively.

Aluthgama's other attraction is its good and relatively cheap selection of **guesthouses** these places aren't actually on the beach, but slightly behind it across the beautiful lagoon at the mouth of the Bentota River – in many ways just as attractive a location as the oceanfront, especially at night, when the lights of the northern Bentota resorts twinkle prettily in the darkness across the waters. If you want the beach, it's a ten-minute walk, or a quick tuktuk ride, to the nearest section of sand at Bentota.

Kande Vihara

About 2km inland from Aluthgama (head north along the main road towards Beruwala, then turn right, opposite the road to the Club Bentota jetty, just before the bridge over the narrow Kaluwamodera Ganga) • No fixed hours • Donation

A short walk or tuktuk ride inland from Aluthgama town, the pretty hilltop **Kande Vihara** temple is home to one of Sri Lanka's **tallest Buddha statues**, completed in 2007. Seated in the *bhumisparsha* mudra ("earth witness" pose), the colossus looms impassively over the pretty white buildings of the temple below, where you'll also find an ornate eighteenth-century image house, a relic chamber with some well-preserved Kandyan-era murals, and the temple's resident elephant.

Brief Garden

Daily 8am–5pm • Rs.1000 • ☎ 077 350 9290, ⊕ briefgarden.com

About 6km inland from Aluthgama, the idyllic **Brief Garden** comprises the former house and estate of the writer and artist **Bevis Bawa**, elder brother of the architect Geoffrey Bawa; the name alludes to Bawa's father, who purchased the land with the money raised from a successful legal brief. Bevis Bawa began landscaping the five-acre gardens in 1929 and continued to work on them almost up until his death in 1992, creating a series of terraces which tumble luxuriantly down the hillside below the house – Bevis's work here served as an important inspiration to brother Geoffrey in encouraging him to embark on a career in architecture and landscape design. The gardens are nice for a stroll, but the main attraction is the **house**, a low-slung orange building stuffed with quirky artworks, some by Bawa himself, plus several pieces (including two entertaining aluminium sculptures and a big mural of Sri Lankan scenes) by the Australian artist Donald Friend, who came for a brief visit in the early 1950s and ended up staying five and a half years. Other exhibits include a fascinating collection of photographs of the imposing Bawa himself (he was 6'7'' tall), both as a young man serving as a major in the British Army and as one of Sri Lanka's leading social luminaries, posing with house guests such as Laurence Olivier and Vivien Leigh.

ARRIVAL AND DEPARTURE

Aluthgama is the area's major transport hub, with **train and bus stations** close to one another towards the northern

end of the town centre. Count on Rs.250–350 for a tuktuk ● places in Bentota and Rs.300–450 to Beruwala beach.

y bus Buses head north and south along the Galle Rd very 10–15min.

estinations Ambalangoda (every 15min; 30min); olombo (every 15min; 1hr 30min); Galle (every 15min;

1hr 30min); Hikkaduwa (every 15min; 45min); Kalutara (every 15min; 30min).

By train For details of train services, see the timetable (see page 32).

ACCOMMODATION

anga Garden Off Galle Rd, behind the Sinharaja akery ☎ 034 227 1770, ⍟ ganga-garden.com; map ».114. UK/Sinhalese-owned lagoon-side guesthouse. Rooms (all with a/c and hot water) are scrupulously maintained, while the communal veranda and gardens are great for idle lounging. B&B **Rs.7000**

Hemadan 25 River Ave ☎ 034 227 5320, ⍟ hotelhemadan.com; map p.114. Welcoming and well-run guesthouse overlooking the lagoon with a pleasantly soporific atmosphere. The airy, high-ceilinged rooms are unusually spacious and attractively furnished

(best on the upper floors, and with river views), and there's also good food in the pleasant terrace restaurant. Free boat transfers are offered to the beach opposite. Wi-fi costs a little extra. B&B **Rs.6900**

Riverbank Bentota 168/2 Welipenna Rd, 400m beyond the Nebula Supermarket ☎ 034 227 0022; map p.114. Attractive modern guesthouse beside the Bentota River with a handful of spotless, well-furnished rooms (the best on the upper floor), all with TV, a/c and river views. There's also a pool, big breakfasts and boats to the beach. B&B **Rs.7000**

EATING

Hemadan, Malubanna and *Tropical Anushka River Inn* on River Ave all serve decent **food** – alternatively, you're just a short walk (or tuktuk ride) from a handful of good restaurants in neighbouring Bentota (see page 119).

Pier 88 Welipenna Rd, behind the Nebula Supermarket ☎ 034 227 5607, ⍟ nebula88.com/pier-88-restaurant;

map p.114. Set in a vine-draped pavilion right beside the river and serving up a decent and reasonably priced range of European dishes, curries and fried rice (Rs.600–1150). Also has a well-stocked bar. Daily 8am–10pm.

SHOPPING

Various scruffy shops at the southern end of the main road through Aluthgama stock a surprisingly good selection of **handicrafts**, principally *kolam* masks and woodcarvings; it's also worth checking out the well-stocked Aluthgama

Wood Carvers shop, on River Ave just south of the *Hemadan* guesthouse. For provisions, stock up at the Nebula supermarket.

DIRECTORY

Banks There are several banks north of the bus station with ATMs accepting foreign cards.

Bentota and around

South of Aluthgama, upwardly mobile **BENTOTA** is home to a further clutch of package resorts, plus an outstanding selection of more upmarket places. The **beach** divides into two areas. At the **north** end, facing Aluthgama, lies **Paradise Island** (as it's popularly known), a narrow spit of land beautifully sandwiched between the choppy breakers of the Indian Ocean and the calm waters of the Bentota lagoon, though sadly few of the hotels really live up to the setting. Backing Paradise Island, the tranquil **Bentota Ganga** provides the setting for Sri Lanka's biggest range of watersports (see page 120), along with interesting boat trips up the river. The **southern end** of Bentota beach (south of Bentota train station) comprises a wide stretch of sand backed by dense thickets of corkscrew palms – one of the most attractive beaches on the island, although somewhat spoilt by the piles of litter that get dumped here. This is also where you'll find one of Sri Lanka's finest clusters of top-end hotels and villas, set at discreet intervals from one another down the coast. Many of the hotels in the area are the work of local architect Geoffrey Bawa (see page 122) – it's well worth splashing out to stay in one of his classic creations, whose artful combination of nature and artifice offers an experience both luxurious and aesthetic.

1

DIVING AND WATERSPORTS IN BERUWALA AND BENTOTA

The calm waters of the Bentota lagoon provide a year-round venue for all sorts of **watersports**, including waterskiing, jet-skiing, speedboating, sailing, windsurfing, canoeing, lagoon boat trips, deep-sea fishing and banana-boating. There's also good **diving** along the coast here and decent **snorkelling** at Barberyn reef, near the lighthouse off the northern end of Beruwala beach – trips can be arranged with Malubanna (see below) or with local boatmen who tout for custom along this stretch of beach (around Rs.1500 for the boat plus Rs.600 for snorkelling equipment). The following are the main operators, although there are other smaller outfits dotted around the area.

Malubanna 15/3 River Ave, Aluthgama ☏077 711 7400, ⓦmalubanna.com; map p.114. One of the newer and better watersports operators offering diving, windsurfing, tube riding, banana-boating, canoeing and jet-skiing, as well as river trips and deep-sea fishing. Good for land-based activities too, such as cycling and tours to Beruwala fish market and lighthouse. Also has a good riverside restaurant.

Sunshine Water Sports Center Aluthgama, just north of the Hemadan guesthouse ☏034 428 9379 or ☏077 794 1857, ⓦsrilankawatersports.com; map p.114. Full range of watersports, and particularly good for windsurfing and waterskiing, with tuition available from former Sri Lankan champions. Other offerings include jet-skiing, wakeboarding, bodyboard hire, snorkelling trips, deep-sea fishing, Bentota river cruises and lagoon- and sea-kayaking, as well as diving.

Ypsylon Diving School Ypsylon Tourist Resort, Beruwala ☏034 227 6132; map p.114. One of the area's longest-established dive schools, offering two tank dives daily (€55) and the usual range of PADI courses, plus night dives, introductory "discovery" dives and wreck dives. Also has rooms (fan $38; a/c $45) and offers free pick-up from Beruwala/Bentota.

Despite the number of visitors, Bentota beach remains fairly quiet, particularly south of the station. Unlike Hikkaduwa or Unawatuna, there's virtually no beach life here, and the oceanfront lacks even the modest smattering of impromptu cafés, handicraft shops and hawkers you'll find at Beruwala – it's this somnolent atmosphere that either appeals or bores, depending on which way your boat's pointing. If you're staying at Aluthgama or Beruwala and fancy a day on the beach here, note that you can eat and drink at all the guesthouses and hotels listed; most also allow non-guests to use their pools for a modest fee.

Bentota village

Sprawling under an endless canopy of palm trees between the lagoon and the land side of the busy coastal highway, sleepy **Bentota village** has a smattering of low-key sights, although the place is full of opportunistic locals hanging around waiting to pounce on tourists – harmless but tiresome. You might be offered a village tour, which could include seeing a local toddy tapper in action or a visit to one of the village's many small coir factories, where coconut husks are turned into rope (you'll see huge piles of coconut husks piled up around the village, waiting for processing).

There are also a couple of village temples. At the northern end of the village, next to the lagoon, is the **Wanawasa Raja Mahaviharaya**, a large and unusually ugly building full of kitsch pictures, Day-Glo statues and a memorable model of Adam's Peak equipped with a kind of flushing mechanism which sends water streaming down the mountainside at the tug of a lever. A nearby tunnel, accessed via a gaping lion's mouth, leads into a murraled chamber – part of a wider subterranean network that connects to as many as five other local temples.

Further south, also on the lagoon side, is the more attractive **Galapata Vihara**, a venerable temple which dates back to the twelfth century and sports interesting wall paintings, peeling orange Buddhas and a large boulder outside carved with a long extract from the Mahavamsa, written in Pali.

Bentota Ganga

Trips can be arranged through some Bentota or Aluthgama guesthouses and hotels or through local watersports centres (see page 120) • Around $10 per person per hour in a group of four people, proportionately more in a couple or on your own

The Bentota lagoon is the last section of the broad **Bentota Ganga** and a popular launchpad for boat safaris along the river, which meanders inland for a few kilometres from the Bentota bridge before losing itself in another mazy lagoon dotted with tiny islands and fringed with tangled mangrove swamps. These trips aren't the greatest natural adventure you're likely to have: the boats themselves are usually noisy and smelly, and the standard of guiding rather hit and miss. Even so, you should see a fair selection of aquatic birds – herons, cormorants and colourful kingfishers – as well as a few water monitors, while your boatman might also ferry you right in among the mangroves themselves, a mysterious and beautiful sight as you drift though still, shaded waters beneath huge roots. You're unlikely to see much of interest on a one-hour trip, but the longer the trip and the further upriver you travel, the more unspoiled the scenery becomes. Longer excursions usually include extras such as trips to coconut factories or handicrafts shops, and you may also be taken to visit the Galapata Vihara (see page 120).

Lunuganga

About 6km inland from Bentota along the Elpitiya Rd (turn right at Dedduwa Junction after 4km and ask locally for "Geoffrey Bawa's house") • Garden tours daily 9.30am, 11.30am, 2pm & 3.30pm • Rs.1500 per person or Rs.3100 including a rice and curry lunch (12.30–2.30pm) • ☏ 034 428 7056, ⓦ lunuganga.com

Inland up the Bentota River lie the magical house and gardens of **Lunuganga**, one of the west coast's most beguiling attractions, rambling over two small hills surrounded by the tranquil waters of Dedduwa Lake. Lunuganga was the creation of seminal Sri Lankan architect Geoffrey Bawa (see page 122), who acquired the estate – at that time nothing more than "an undistinguished bungalow surrounded by 25 acres of rubber trees" (according to his biographer David Robson) – in 1948, and gradually transformed it over the subsequent five decades, inspired by the example of his brother Bevis's work at Brief Garden (see page 118). The original house was systematically modified and expanded and new gardens created in place of the old rubber plantation, with intertwining terraces, a sculpture gallery and strategically placed artworks, opening up at moments to reveal carefully planned vistas, such as that over Cinnamon Hill, framing the distant Katakuliya temple. Like much of Bawa's work, Lunuganga manages to feel both captivatingly artful and refreshingly natural at the same time, while the various buildings offer an intriguing overview of the Bawa style in miniature, from the tiny little hip-roofed "Hen House", built sometime during the 1970s, to the serene Cinnamon Hill House of 1992. A recent addition to the site is the magnificent home of artist Ena de Silva, designed by Bawa in 1963 and relocated in pieces from Colombo when it was sold in 2009. At the time of writing it was not yet open to the public.

You can combine a visit to the gardens with tea on the terrace or lunch, although to explore Lunuganga's interior you'll have to stay here (see page 123).

ARRIVAL AND DEPARTURE

BENTOTA

By bus Arriving by bus, it's easiest to get off at the terminal in Aluthgama and catch a tuktuk for the short ride south to Bentota unless you know exactly where you want to be set down.

By train Bentota has its own train station served by some (but not all) express services; alternatively, get off at Aluthgama station and catch a tuktuk.

ACCOMMODATION

For Ayurveda resorts in Bentota, see the "Ayurveda and health resorts on the west coast" box (page 117).

Amal Villa 135 Galle Rd ☏ 034 227 0746, ⓦ amal-villa.com; map p.114. Neat upmarket guesthouse on the land side of the Galle Rd, set amid attractive palm-

1

GEOFFREY BAWA

*We have a marvellous tradition of building in this country that has got lost. It got lost because people
followed outside influences over their own good instincts. They never built right "through" the landscape…
You must "run" with the site; after all, you don't want to push nature out with the building.*
Geoffrey Bawa

One of Asia's foremost twentieth-century architects, **Geoffrey Bawa** (1919–2003) was born
to a wealthy family of Colombo Burghers (see page 144) boasting English, Dutch, German,
Sinhalese and Scottish ancestors – a heady cocktail of cultures which mirrors the eclectic mix
of European and local influences so apparent in his work. Bawa spent a large proportion of
his first forty years abroad, mainly in Europe. Having studied English at Cambridge and law in
London, he finally dragged himself back to Sri Lanka and followed his father and grandfather
into the legal profession, though without much enthusiasm – his only positive experience
of the law seems to have been driving around Colombo in his Rolls-Royce while wearing his
lawyer's robes and wig. After scarcely a year he threw in his legal career and went to Italy,
where he planned to buy a villa and settle down.

Fortunately for Sri Lanka, the Italian villa didn't work out, and Bawa returned, staying with
his brother Bevis at the latter's estate at Brief Garden (see page 118). Inspired by his brother's
example, Bawa decided to do something similar himself, purchasing the nearby house and
gardens which he christened **Lunuganga** (see pages 121 and 123), and beginning to
enthusiastically remodel the estate's buildings and grounds. The architectural bug having finally
bitten, Bawa returned to England to train as a professional **architect**, finally qualifiying at the
advanced age of 38, after which he returned to Colombo and flung himself into his new career.

Bawa's early leanings were modernist, encouraged by his training in London and by
his close working relationship with the Danish architect Ulrik Plesner, a keen student of
functional Scandinavian design. The style of his early buildings is often described as "**Tropical
Modernism**", but local conditions gradually changed Bawa's architectural philosophy. The
pure white surfaces favoured by European modernists weathered badly in the tropics, while
their flat rooflines were unsuitable in monsoonal climates – and in any case, shortages of
imported materials like steel and glass encouraged Bawa to look for traditional local materials
and indigenous solutions to age-old architectural conundrums.

The result was a style in which the strong and simple forms of modernism were softened
and enriched by local influences, materials and landscapes. Bawa revived the huge
overhanging tiled roofs traditionally used by colonial architects in the tropics, whose broad
eaves and spacious verandas offered protection against both sun and rain, while buildings
were designed to blend harmoniously with their surrounding landscape (Bawa often and
famously designed buildings to fit around existing trees, for example, rather than just cutting
them down). In addition, the use of open, interconnecting spaces avoided the need for air-
conditioning as well as blurring the distinction between interior and exterior spaces, allowing
architecture and landscape to merge seamlessly into one.

The arrival of package tourism in the 1960s brought with it the need for modern hotels, a
genre with which Bawa became inextricably associated – see Basics (page 37) for a list of his
principal hotels. His first major effort, the **Bentota Beach Hotel**, whose distinctive pagoda-
style main building still serves as the resort's major local landmark, established a style which
many hotels across the island would subsequently follow. The hotel's main wooden pavilion,
topped by a hipped roof, used natural local materials throughout and paid distant homage
to traditional Kandyan architecture in its overall shape and conception; at its centre lay a
beautifully rustic courtyard and pond set within a cluster of frangipani trees, giving the sense
of nature not only being around the building, but also within.

Around a dozen other hotels followed – most notably the *Kandalama* in Dambulla (now
Heritance Kandalama; see page 297) and the *Lighthouse* in Galle (now *Jetwing Lighthouse*; see
page 149) – as well as major public commissions including the mammoth new **Sri Lankan
Parliament** building in Kotte. Bawa's architectural practice became the largest on the island
during the 1970s, and most of Sri Lanka's finest young architects started their careers working
for him. Many took his influence with them when they left, and buildings (hotels especially)
all over the island continue to show the trappings of the Bawa style, executed with varying
degrees of competence and imagination.

haded gardens with a delectable little infinity pool and small Ayurveda spa. Rooms (all a/c) are comfortable if unremarkable, and the beach is just a couple of minutes' walk away over the road, which is also where you'll find the villa's attractive two-storey pavilion restaurant, as well as a few older, and slightly cheaper rooms. Half board only. ₹18,000

★**Avani Bentota** Hotel Rd ☎034 494 7878, ⊛avanihotels.com; map p.114. Serene Geoffrey Bawa-designed resort, with stylish purple-hued interiors, a big new pool (guests only), smooth spa and very chic rooms (as well as a few fabulous suites) which boast wooden floors and huge 40-inch flatscreen TVs – a far cry from your average bucket-and-spade resort. Slightly more expensive than other places nearby, but worth the extra cash. B&B ₹227

Chami Villa 23 Pitaramba Rd ☎077 974 4265, ⊛chamivillabentota.com; map p.114. Bright white building offering a handful of spotless, high-ceilinged rooms with four-poster bed, a/c, furnished balcony and hot water. They also have a few sunbeds reserved for guests on the beach, accessed via a dusty 100m track that crosses the railway line. ₹65

★**Club Villa** 138/15 Galle Rd ☎034 227 5312, ⊛clubvillabentota.com; map p.114. One of Sri Lanka's most personable small hotels, in a tranquil location at the southern end of Bentota beach. The gorgeous Geoffrey Bawa-designed buildings are full of character, enlivened by strategically placed artworks and colourful furnishings, and there's also a small swimming pool, large garden and an attractive restaurant. B&B ₹225

★**Lunuganga** Dedduwa ☎034 428 7056, ⊛lunuganga.com; map p.114. Geoffrey Bawa's former country house-turned-boutique hotel and its extensive gardens (see page 121) offer a privileged insight into the estate to whose beautification Bawa devoted most of his adult life. There are six sublime yet minimally furnished rooms: three in the main house, plus more expensive lodgings in Bawa's converted private art gallery and the two-room Cinnamon Hill House. ₹250

Nisala Arana 326/1 Yathramulla Rd ☎077 773 3313, ⊛nisalaaarana.com; map p.114. Homely boutique hotel in a secluded fruit and palm garden, 3km inland from the beach. Accommodation is in three colonial-style villas: the gorgeously restored nineteenth-century "Doctor's House" bungalow; the balconied Mango Wing; and the serene Coconut Wing, which opens directly onto the garden. There's also a freshwater pool, inventive gourmet cuisine (outside guests are welcome but should book in advance), and bicycles (or a vintage Morris Minor with driver) for exploring the local area. B&B ₹150

Paradise Road The Villa 138/18-22 Galle Rd ☎034 227 5311, ⊛paradiseroadhotels.com; map p.114. Gorgeous 1880s colonial mansion given a stylish contemporary makeover by Paradise Rd (see page 87)

guru Shanth Fernando, with fifteen well-equipped rooms and suites each individually designed in a variety of styles ranging from smooth contemporary-colonial to funky liquorice-and-peppermint stripes. B&B ₹264

★**Rock Villa** Neelisgewatta Rd, Alawatugoda ☎034 227 5068, ⊛taruvillas.com; map p.114. Gorgeous boutique hotel with four deluxe bedrooms and a two-bedroom suite set in a breathtaking 170-year-old *walauwa* (traditional manor) just 60m from southern Bentota beach. Hammocks are dotted around the palm-spiked grounds, and there's also a lovely pool and amazing food. B&B ₹246

Saman Villas Aturuwella ☎034 227 5435, ⊛samanvilla.com; map p.114. Luxurious boutique hotel, superbly situated on an isolated headland 3km south of Bentota bridge. Rooms are traditionally styled but full of mod cons (including iPhone docks) and the deluxe suites have private plunge pools. The private dining terraces tucked into the cliff's edge are perfect for a honeymoon treat (or for popping the question), and there's also a gorgeous spa and a spectacular swimming pool, seemingly suspended in mid-air above the sea. ₹550

Shangri Lanka Villa 23 De Alwis Rd ☎034 227 1181, ⊛shangrilankavilla.com; map p.114. Welcoming and intimate guesthouse, run by an Anglo–Sri Lankan couple, with five cheerfully furnished rooms (all a/c; one with a little kitchenette) in an attractive little garden with pool. B&B ₹160

★**Sri Lancashire Guest House** Yathramulla Rd ☎077 625 0300, ⊛sri-lancashireguesthouse.com; map p.114. Friendly British-owned guesthouse by the Bentota Ganga with river views and a pretty garden strung with hammocks. Accommodation is in two immaculate, floral rooms – the Jasmine and the Araliya - with plump pillows and optional a/c ($5 extra). Chill out on your private balcony, or head towards the cosy communal living room for cable TV. Amazing value at current rates. B&B ₹48

Susantha's Nikethana Rd ☎034 227 5324, ⊛hotelsusanthagarden.com; map p.114. Set immediately behind the train station around a shady courtyard garden with pool, this well-run guesthouse is one of Bentota's cheapest places. All rooms (fan and a/c, some with kitchenettes) are clean and nicely furnished, and there's also a decent restaurant, plus bargain treatments in the frill-free Ayurveda centre. B&B **Rs.7500**, a/c **Rs.8500**

Vivanta by Taj Southern end of Bentota Beach ☎034 555 5555, ⊛vivantabytaj.com; map p.114. Set in magnificent isolation on a beautiful headland at the southern end of Bentota beach, this vast hotel, all gleaming marble, rather overwhelms its tranquil natural setting, although it has plenty of swanky and rather ostentatious style, and the full range of five-star comforts and facilities, including an attractive spa. B&B ₹380

Waterside Bentota Yathramulla Rd ☎034 227 0080, ⊛bentotawaterside.com; map p.114. Intimate boutique hotel in an attractive cluster of whitewashed,

1

red-tiled buildings overlooking the Bentota river, 1km inland (a 5min ride on the hotel's free boat to the beach). The six rooms are smartly furnished with satellite TV, minibar and a/c, and there are sweeping gardens running down to the water with a good-sized pool, plus an à la carte restaurant. B&B $130

Wunderbar Beach Hotel Robolgoda ☎034 22? 5908, ⓦ hotel-wunderbar.com; map p.114. Pleasa mid-range beachside resort, with very spacious, nicel furnished rooms (all with a/c, satellite TV and minibar plus pool and a rather grand upstairs wooden pavilic restaurant. The more spacious pool-facing luxury room are worth the splurge. B&B $120

EATING

Many visitors here eat at their hotels or guesthouses – the restaurants at *Club Villa*, *Nisala Arana*, *Paradise Road The Villa* and *Amal Villa* are particularly good – while Bentota also boasts a surprisingly good, rather upmarket spread of independent restaurants.

Diya Sisila 2.5km along the Elpitiya Rd ☎077 740 2138, ⓦ diyasisila.com; map p.114. En route to Lunuganga, this lakeside restaurant is a destination in itself, with tables scattered around a pretty courtyard and (better still) on two "island" pavilions perched over the water. The menu focuses on seafood and rice and curry – the owner visits the market every morning so if you want to eat crabs, jumbo prawns and lobsters you're best off ordering the day before. Mains Rs.1200–1850. Daily 10am–11pm.

Golden Grill Restaurant National Holiday Resort ☎078 566 7081, ⓦ goldengrill.lk; map p.114. This long-running lagoon-side restaurant looks disconcertingly like a

Sri Lankan wedding, complete with dressed chairs, a surfe of pink napkins and flowers on every table, and a chunterin soundtrack of *baila* (Sri Lankan dance music) in th background. Food, fortunately, is better than the decor, wit an above-average selection of tourist favourites, includin lots of grilled things – fish, prawns, chicken and sizzlin steaks – plus Sri Lankan standards and seafood. Most main Rs.800–1400. Daily 11am–10pm (last orders).

Malli's Opposite The Surf hotel ☎077 851 4894; ma p.114. Unexpectedly smart little restaurant tucked awa above a line of shops by the railway tracks just down fror the station – pricey, but a distinct cut above your average S Lankan beach restaurant. The menu focuses on internationa fare with an Asian slant – Thai red prawn curry, chicke satay, risotto with mussels, pan-fried mahi-mahi with *rös* and saffron sauce – plus good Sri Lankan curries and fres seafood. Grab a window seat – it's great fun when a trai passes by. Mains around Rs.1500. Daily 10am–11pm.

Induruwa

Immediately south of Bentota, the straggling village of **INDURUWA** is backed by a stretch of wide and beautiful beach which, compared to the more developed stretches of sand further north, remains clean and mercifully tout-free (although it's only a building's width or two away from the road), while an offshore reef makes swimming safer here than in most places further up the coast. This winning combination is attracting more visitors to its increasingly upmarket accommodation, though the general atmosphere remains somnolent.

ARRIVAL AND DEPARTURE

By bus Frequent buses run up and down the Galle Rd past the various hotels and guesthouses; if arriving by bus try to get the conductor to put you off in the right place – the hotels are spread out and can be difficult to spot from the

road as you whizz past.
By train There's a train station in the middle of the villag too, but only slow services stop here.

ACCOMMODATION

There are few decent restaurants or shops in Induruwa, though all hotels serve meals, and the hotels of southern Bentota, including *Club Villa* (see page 123), are only a short tuktuk ride away.

★ **Long Beach Cottage** Next door to Royal Beach Resort ☎034 227 5773; map p.114. This cosy, laidback beachside guesthouse, tenderly looked after by an enchanting elderly Sri Lankan/German couple, has operated pretty much unchanged for well over three decades. The spotlessly white

rooms are comfortable and a real steal – other guesthouse offer half as much for twice the price. Rs.2750

Pandanus Beach Resort and Spa Yalagama ☎03 227 5363, ⓦ pandanusbeach.com; map p.114 Contemporary-styled boutique hotel set on a wide stretc of golden sand. The stylish rooms all have sea view through big picture windows, smooth wood finishes an snazzy bathrooms, and there's a gorgeous pool, nice spa and international cuisine. B&B $200

TURTLE HATCHERIES

A familiar sight along the Galle Road between Bentota and Hikkaduwa, particularly in Kosgoda, are the numerous battered signs for an ever-growing multitude of **turtle hatcheries** set up in recent years in response to the rapidly declining numbers of turtles visiting Sri Lanka's beaches. Staffed by volunteers, and funded by tourist donations, the hatcheries buy the turtles' eggs (at above market value) from local fishermen and rebury them in safe locations; once hatched, the babies are kept in concrete tubs for a few days before being released into the sea. Despite the hatcheries' (mostly) laudable aims however, questions have long been raised over their effectiveness – it is almost impossible to replicate the turtles' natural incubation and hatching conditions, and as a consequence the overwhelming majority succumb to disease or predators – and there is little evidence that they have helped to reverse the turtles' declining fortunes. Two of the longest-running hatcheries are the **Kosgoda Sea Turtle Conservation Project** (ⓦ kosgodaseaturtle.org) beside the Galle Road in Kosgoda, and the **Victor Hasselblad Hatchery** (ⓣ 071 787 9928) reached via the lane next to Kosgoda's police station (both daily 9am–6pm; entry. Rs.500). They also release hatchlings at sunset.

Kosgoda

About 8km south of Induruwa, the 4km stretch of beach close to the village of **KOSGODA** is the most important **sea turtle nesting site** along the west coast – all five species of turtle found in Sri Lanka come ashore to lay their eggs here. Most nights during the season (Jan–May) you should get to see at least one turtle fighting its way up the beach, while in the peak month of April many more might appear. Outside these months, sightings are less reliable.

ACCOMMODATION   KOSGODA

Heritance Ahungalla Ahungalla, 4km south of Kosgoda and 9km north of Ambalangoda ⓣ 091 555 5000, ⓦ heritancehotels.com. This vast Geoffrey Bawa-designed five-star resort sprawls along a considerable section of unspoiled beach to the south of Kosgoda. It's luxurious but surprisingly intimate and low-key given its size, with elegant landscaping, stylish rooms, a fine (if pricey) spa and one of Sri Lanka's most spectacular pools. $\overline{220}$

Hotel Riu Ahungalla, 4km south of Kosgoda (and 9km north of Ambalangoda) ⓣ 091 522 0000, ⓦ heritancehotels.com. This new mega-resort has a whopping 501 spacious rooms, decorated in typical, modern style with vibrantly patterned headboards. Its roster of facilities is hard to beat: three pools, a kids' club and playground, art atelier, gym, spa, five restaurants and four bars, plus a karaoke and disco club. $\overline{316}$

Sankarest Kosgoda ⓣ 077 187 9257, ⓦ sankarest. webs.com. Family-run two-storey guesthouse less than 250m from Kosgoda beach. The three scrupulously clean rooms (two with a/c, and all with TV, DVD player and minibar) open onto cosy lounges overlooking the tropical walled garden and sparkling pool. Good food, too. $\overline{61}$

Balapitiya and the Madu Ganga

Most hotels can arrange a boat for you on the Madu Ganga, or you can take your pick from those stationed around the bridge; 90min trips cost Rs.3500–4000 per boat; if you make your own way there, be aware that tuktuk drivers will take you to whichever operator pays them the most commission, which will probably increase the price of your trip

Some 8km south of Kosgoda, and about 5km north of Ambalangoda, the village of **BALAPITIYA** offers another long stretch of unspoiled beach and is also the starting point for boat safaris along the **Madu Ganga**, a good place to spot water monitors and a wide array of birdlife, including myriad colourful kingfishers. No fewer than 64 islands dot this stretch of river; one is home to a large Buddhist temple adorned with lurid modern paintings and sculptures, another to a cinnamon factory and there's a floating island with fish spa, visits to which (excluding treatments) are included in the cost of a tour.

ACCOMMODATION   BALAPITIYA AND THE MADU GANGA

Balapitiya's Ayurveda-focused *Amba Boutique Hotel* is reviewed in the "Ayurveda and health resorts on the west coast" box (see page 117).

★ **The River House** 70 Uthamanyana Rd ⓣ 091 225 6306, ⓦ theriverhouse.lk. Occupying a fine position above the Madu Ganga, this superb villa houses five large,

1

very stylish suites, each with a private garden and plunge pool – an exquisite blend of traditional craftsmanship and modern comforts. Also has a secluded pool, and activities include boat trips and kayaking. B&B **$400**

Shinagawa Beach 30 Old Guru Niwasa Rd ☎ 011 576 9500, ⊛ shinagawabeach.com. Small and very chilled-out boutique hotel sat close to a rocky headland at the southern end of Balapitiya's sweeping beach, with great sea swimming year-round. The ochre-hued rooms all have sea views, private balconies and plentiful mod cons, and there's an unusual part-indoor pool, lawns plus loungers and a restaurant specializing in Japanese cuisine. B&B **$215**

Ambalangoda and around

Some 25km south of Bentota, the bustling, workaday coastal town of **AMBALANGODA** is the island's major production centre for the demonic wooden **masks** that leer at you from doorways and handicrafts shops across the island. These were originally designed to be worn by performers in exorcism ceremonies and *kolam* dances (see page 127), and although the dances themselves are now rarely performed, the masks have acquired a new lease of life as souvenirs, while many locals hang a Gurulu Raksha mask outside their houses to ward away demons (the Gurulu is a fearsome mythical bird, believed to prey on snakes and related demonic beings). Masks are made out of the light and easily carved Sri Lankan balsa wood, *kaduru* (*Nux vomica*), and come in all sorts of different sizes, costing anything from a few hundred rupees up to several hundred dollars – larger masks can take up to six weeks to carve and paint. Some are artificially aged to resemble antiques, their colours skilfully faded to a lustrous, mellow patina which makes a more aesthetic alternative to the lurid, Day-Glo tones of the standard items.

The main outlets are the two museums-cum-shops (see below) which face one another across the coastal highway at the northern end of the town centre, set up by two sons of the late mask-carver Ariyapala Wijesuriya, who was largely responsible for establishing Ambalangoda as a centre of mask-carving. There are also a number of other mask-making workshops dotted around town.

Ariyapala and Sons Mask Museum

Galle Rd, north end of town • Daily 8.30am–5.30pm • Donation • ⊛ masksariyapalasl.com

The larger and more interesting of the two mask museums, the **Ariyapala and Sons Mask Museum** comprises two well-laid-out rooms focusing on *kolam* dances and *sunni yakuma* healing dances respectively, with masks and photos of performances. The shop upstairs sells the island's biggest selection of masks, featuring all the characters you'll have encountered in the museum. The quality here can be variable. Masks are churned out in the workshop next door (which you can also visit) in industrial quantities for the endless tour groups that stop here, and you might find better craftsmanship in the smaller workshops around town, in Hikkaduwa, or even in Kandy or Colombo.

Ariyapala Traditional Masks

Galle Rd, north end of town • Daily 8.30am–5.30pm • Donation • ☎ 091 225 4899

Opposite the Ariyapala and Sons Mask Museum, the more modest **Ariyapala Traditional Masks** shop-cum-museum is home to a small display featuring large puppets of the last king of Kandy, Sri Wickrama Rajasinha, and his queen, plus a gruesome tableau vivant showing the execution of the family of Prime Minister Ehelepola. The items for sale upstairs are of a similarly variable standard to those over the road.

Dudley Silva Batiks

53 Elpitiya Rd • Daily 9am–6pm • Free • ☎ 091 225 9411

Ambalangoda is also home to the award-winning batik artist **Dudley De Silva**, whose atmospheric antique house is attached to an intimate batik-making workshop, its floors caked with layers of wax. After observing the intricacies of the process, wander indoors to browse some of his beautiful designs.

LOW-COUNTRY DANCING

The masks you'll see at Ambalangoda (and elsewhere around the island) were originally produced to be worn by performers in low-country (southern) dances, either in devil dances or *kolam*. Many Sri Lankans still believe that diseases and illness can be caused by demons, and the purpose of the **devil dance** – more strictly known as an exorcism ceremony (*bali*) or healing dance (*sunni yakuma*) – is to summon up the demons who are causing a person sickness, make offerings to them and then politely request that they leave their victim in peace. There are various groups of demons – five *yakka* demons, twelve *pali* demons and eighteen *sanni* demons – each believed to be responsible for certain diseases, and each represented by its own mask, which is worn by a dancer during the exorcism ceremony (all 35 individual masks are sometimes combined into a single enormous medicine mask). Devil dances are still occasionally performed in rural villages, although you'd have to be very lucky to see one.

The origins of the **kolam** dance-drama are popularly claimed to date back to the mythical Queen Menikpala, who while pregnant developed a craving to witness a theatrical performance. Vishvakarma, the god of craftsmen and artists, is said to have given the king the first *kolam* masks and the plot of the entire entertainment. The traditional *kolam* performance features a sequence of dances held together by a rather tenuous plot based around the visit of the pregnant Queen Menikpala and her husband, King Maha Sammatha, to a village. The performance traditionally comprises a medley of satirical and royal dances, featuring characters such as the king's drunken drummer, a lecherous village clerk, assorted village simpletons, a couple of propitious demons, a lion and, of course, the royal couple themselves. Unfortunately, complete *kolam* performances are no longer staged, so it's impossible to experience this unique Sri Lankan medley of folk tale, demonic superstition and history (laced with a touch of Buddhism) – though you can at least still enjoy the masks.

As well as *kolam* and devil dances, the south is also home to a range of populist **folk dances** – though nowadays you're more likely to see them performed in one of Kandy's nightly cultural shows (see page 228) than anywhere in the south itself. Popular dances include the stick dance (*leekeli*), harvest dance (*kulu*), pot dance (*kalageldi*) and the ever-popular *raban* dance, during which small *raban* drums (they actually look more like thick wooden plates than musical instruments) are spun on the fingers or on sticks balanced on the hands or head – an experienced performer can keep as many as eight *rabans* twirling simultaneously from various parts of his or her body.

Bandu Wijesuriya School of Dance

alle Rd, north end of town • Rehearsals usually take place Tues–Thurs from 2pm, Sat 9–11am & Sun from noon; donation • ☎ 071 961 6955

Dance performances are staged around half-a-dozen times a year at the **Bandu Wijesuriya School of Dance**, adjacent to the Ariyapala and Sons Mask Museum. If no performance is scheduled, you can usually visit the school to see students rehearsing or even enrol in a dance class with Bandu's daughter, Kanchana.

Ambalangoda town and beach

Masks and dancing aside, Ambalangoda also boasts pretty expanses of almost completely untouristed **beaches** and a picturesque fishing harbour. It's also worth wandering down **Main Street**, an interesting and relatively traffic-free little thoroughfare whose southern end is lined by attractive shops selling everything from huge sacks of rice to shiny new motorbikes, and whose pavements are taken over most days by a lively fish, fruit and veg market.

Galagoda Sailathalaramaya Temple

No set hours • Donation (Rs.250) • Karandeniya is on the Elpitiya Rd; the temple itself is off the main road down a tiny road on the left (no sign); take bus #390 (departs hourly) or a tuktuk

About 6km inland from Ambalangoda at the village of Karandeniya, the obscure **Galagoda Sailathalaramaya Temple** is the unlikely home of Sri Lanka's longest reclining Buddha, measuring some 35m in length (the precise dimensions remain unknown, since it's considered sacrilegious to measure it), which fills the entire length of an extremely ramshackle building at the back of the temple. The statue is said to be more than two hundred years old and has now

1

lost most of its original red and saffron paint, though its delicately moulded features – with wide-awake eyes and aquiline nose – remain perfectly preserved.

ARRIVAL AND DEPARTURE
AMBALANGODA AND AROUND

By bus Buses run up and down the coast along the Galle Rd, serving all destinations between Colombo and Galle/Matara. Note that many buses don't actually go into the bus station but simply stop on the road outside.

Destinations Aluthgama (every 15min; 30min); Colombo (every 15min; 2hr); Galle (every 15min; 1hr); Hikkaduwa (every 15min; 20min); Kalutara (every 15min; 1hr).
By train Regular trains on the coastal line stop here – see the timetable (page 32).

ACCOMMODATION AND EATING

Max Wadiya Galle Rd (2km south of Ambalangoda) ☎091 225 7926, ⊛maxwadiya.com. Charming and super-friendly seaside boutique hotel comprising a three-bedroom villa along with two plush suites with kitchenettes and TVs in a newer wing to the side. There's a little Ayurveda garden and delicious food, and nesting turtles often visit the beach. Full board $340

Sanekvin 13 Galle Rd, opposite the IOC petrol shed ☎091 225 5220. A popular local spot dishing out a standard menu of Sri Lankan-Chinese dishes (around Rs.600), plus seafood and a few Western staples; serves alcohol. Mon–Sat 9am–10pm.

Sumudu Tourist Guest House 418 Main St ☎091 225 8832. Very friendly family-run establishment down the side road behind the Ariyapala and Sons Mask Museum with six simple but pleasant, high-ceilinged rooms (fan and a/c), some with hot water, in a characterful old colonial villa. B&B: Rs.3000, a/c Rs.3500

Hikkaduwa and around

Back in the 1970s, **HIKKADUWA** was Sri Lanka's original hippy hangout, its budget guesthouses an alternative to the fancier resort hotels at Beruwala and Bentota. Subsequent decades were not kind to the town: rampant over-development led to the systematic erosion of the beach and the creation of a memorable line of concrete eyesores masquerading as hotels, while its famous Coral Sanctuary was reduced to a circus of boats chasing traumatized fish through a labyrinth of dead coral.

Over the past decade, however, Hikkaduwa has begun to rise, cautiously, from its own ashes, as the tourist hordes have largely ignored the town, flocking to newer and less spoilt destinations further south, allowing it to recapture some of its former sleepy, slightly hippified charm. The much abused beach and Coral Sanctuary are now being gradually rehabilitated, while following the tsunami many of the town's bomb-shelter-style hotels were demolished or newly renovated, meaning that the whole place is now looking better than it has for years.

It's still far from unspoilt, but compared to the somnolent resorts further north Hikkaduwa remains refreshingly lively, with plenty of restaurants, bars and shops to tempt you off the beach, and a crowd of predominantly young and independent travellers keeping things busy. Things are particularly lively during the annual five-day **Hikkaduwa Beach Fest** in July/August when visiting international DJs, musicians and dancers perform nightly for crowds of hedonistic locals and foreigners partying on the beach. Other attractions include reliable local **surf**, plus good **diving** and **snorkelling**. Beach and sea aside, there are also several interesting Buddhist temples **around Hikkaduwa**, as well as a couple of lagoons, all of which are easily reachable by tuktuk or bicycle – though be *very* careful cycling (and even walking) along the treacherous Galle Road.

Hikkaduwa Marine National Park

Daily 7am–6pm • Rs.30; glass-bottomed boat tours Rs.2000 per person (30min); it's cheapest to buy tickets and book tours from the tatty brown national parks ticket booth (other private operators along the beach charge more)

Hikkaduwa Marine National Park (still popularly known as the **Coral Sanctuary**) was established in 1979 to protect the small, shallow area of reef, never more than 5m deep, which stretches from the beach a couple of hundred metres out to sea, now enclosed and protected by a string of rocks. The once-beautiful coral has suffered significant depredations over the years, but

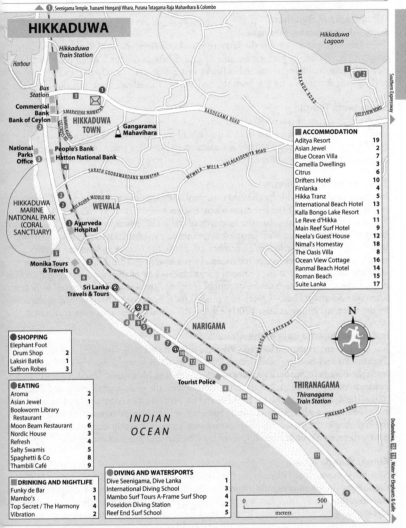

Seenigama Temple, Tsunami Honganji Vihara, Purana Totagama Raja Mahavihara & Colombo

HIKKADUWA

HIKKADUWA TOWN

WEWALA

HIKKADUWA MARINE NATIONAL PARK (CORAL SANCTUARY)

NARIGAMA

THIRANAGAMA

INDIAN OCEAN

■ **ACCOMMODATION**

Aditya Resort	19
Asian Jewel	2
Blue Ocean Villa	7
Camellia Dwellings	3
Citrus	6
Drifters Hotel	10
Finlanka	4
Hikka Tranz	5
International Beach Hotel	13
Kalla Bongo Lake Resort	1
Le Reve d'Hikka	11
Main Reef Surf Hotel	9
Neela's Guest House	12
Nimal's Homestay	18
The Oasis Villa	8
Ocean View Cottage	16
Ranmal Beach Hotel	14
Roman Beach	15
Suite Lanka	17

● **SHOPPING**

Elephant Foot Drum Shop	2
Laksiri Batiks	1
Saffron Robes	3

● **EATING**

Aroma	2
Asian Jewel	1
Bookworm Library Restaurant	7
Moon Beam Restaurant	6
Nordic House	3
Refresh	4
Salty Swamis	5
Spaghetti & Co	8
Thambili Café	9

■ **DRINKING AND NIGHTLIFE**

Funky de Bar	3
Mambo's	1
Top Secret / The Harmony	4
Vibration	2

● **DIVING AND WATERSPORTS**

Dive Seenigama, Dive Lanka	1
International Diving School	3
Mambo Surf Tours A-Frame Surf Shop	4
Poseidon Diving Station	2
Reef End Surf School	5

0   500
meters

N

is now slowly growing back following concerted replanting efforts following the tsunami. Clumps of reviving coral can now be seen in places (they're usually cordoned off to protect them from boats), while the gardens are also home to myriad colourful species of tropical **fish** including parrotfish, unicorn fish, trunkfish, angelfish, grunts, fusilierfish and balloonfish. **Turtles** may also be spotted, especially around the full moon, while a tame trio makes an appearance every morning and evening in front of the *Hikka Tranz* hotel where enterprising locals, armed with bags of seaweed, charge tourists to photograph them.

A popular way of seeing the sanctuary is to take an expensive trip in a **glass-bottomed boat**, although at busy times the flotilla of boats chasing round the waters in search of big fish and turtles lends the park all the charm of a marine motorway. **Snorkelling** is much more eco-friendly, and you'll see more, although the number of boats tearing around can make it a bit unnerving. You can rent snorkelling equipment from one of the dive centres (see page 131).

1

Gangarama Mahavihara
Baddegama Rd, 500m inland from the bus station

The closest temple to town is the attractive, modern **Gangarama Mahavihara**, perched atop a large terrace. Its pretty ensemble of neat, white buildings is often busy with devout locals, including many old ladies in white saris making offerings at the bo tree and various shrines – a far cry from the bedlam of Hikkaduwa town just down the road.

Seenigama Temple
About 2km north of town stands the diminutive **Seenigama Temple**, an eye-catching little white building squeezed onto a tiny island just offshore and accessible by a small ferry. Unusually, the temple is dedicated to Dewol, a malevolent deity who is approached by those seeking revenge.

Tsunami Honganji Vihara
Hikkaduwa was badly hit by the 2004 tsunami, although the scruffy stretch of coast north of town is one of the few areas where evidence of the disaster remains. Around 500m north of Seenigama (on the land side of the main coastal road) stands the **Tsunami Honganji Vihara**, erected with Japanese assistance as a memorial to those who perished in the tragedy and unveiled on December 26, 2006, the second anniversary of the catastrophe. The centrepiece of the memorial is a towering, 18m-high Buddha statue standing on a platform at the centre of a small lake – one of the tallest standing Buddhas in Sri Lanka. The location of the memorial is telling, just a couple of minutes' walk from where the *Samudra Devi* ("Queen of the Sea") train, en route to Matara, was washed away by the tsunami, killing at least 1700 people – the world's worst-ever railway disaster.

Purana Totagama Raja Mahavihara
Just north of the Tsunami Honganji Vihara, a turn-off (at a rather battered sign for the small Tsunami Photo Museum) heads inland for a few hundred metres across the rail tracks to reach the **Purana Totagama Raja Mahavihara**, or Telwatta Monastery. This was a celebrated centre of learning as far back as the fifteenth century – the great teacher and poet Sri Rahula Maha Thera, celebrated both for his verse and for his powers of exorcism, lived here; he's commemorated with a bright modern copper statue. The original temple was destroyed by the Portuguese; the present buildings, which date from 1805, form an atmospheric complex, with well-preserved murals, peeling reclining Buddhas and fine *makara toranas*.

Kumarakanda Vihara
Around 4km south of Hikkaduwa, the traffic-plagued town of **DODANDUWA** is home to the chintzy little **Kumarakanda Vihara**, looking for all the world like a Baroque Portuguese church rather than a Buddhist temple. The temple is on the inland side of the Galle Road just north of the rail line, from where a long flight of brilliant-white steps leads up to the principal shrine, which contains a reclining Buddha and various modern murals.

Rathgama lagoon
Take the road immediately south of the Kumarakanda Vihara and ask for directions • Boat trips cost around Rs.3500 for two people for 2hr

Inland from the Kumarakanda Vihara, a sylvan country lane runs to **Rathgama lagoon**, one of many that dot the southwestern coast. The Blue Lagoon Boat House down by the waterside offers **lagoon trips** in primitive wooden catamarans – late afternoon is the best time to see birds and other wildlife, including monkeys. They'll also take you to the two retreats on the lake, one for men, one for women. You may be offered similar trips but at much higher prices by touts in Hikkaduwa.

ARRIVAL AND DEPARTURE
HIKKADUWA AND AROUND

By bus The bus station is at the northern end of Hikkaduwa town. A tuktuk from here to Wewala will cost around Rs.150, to Narigama around Rs.200 and to Thiranagama around Rs.250–300. Note that many buses heading north don't

WATERSPORTS IN HIKKADUWA

DIVING AND SNORKELLING

Hikkaduwa has the largest selection of **diving schools** in Sri Lanka – the three operators listed below are the most reliable, although other outfits come and go. As usual, the dive season runs from November to April. There's a good range of dives close by, including **reef dives** down to 25m at the labyrinthine Hikkaduwa Gala complex, a well-known spot with swim-through caves, and the rocky-bottomed area of Kiralagala (22–36m deep). There are also some sixteen **wrecks** in the vicinity, including a much-dived old steam-driven oil tanker from the 1860s known as the *Conch*; the nearby *Earl of Shaftesbury* sailing ship, wrecked in 1848; and the less-visited *Rangoon*, which sank near Galle in 1863. The following operators charge $40 for one dive, or $60–70 for two, including all gear, and also rent out **snorkelling** equipment (around $5/hr) – check carefully for leaks.

Dive Seenigama, Dive Lanka 500m north of the Seenigama Temple, 2.5km north of town ☎ 091 494 3659, ⓦ diveseenigamadivelanka.com; map p.129. Diving, snorkelling ($25/boat/hr) and kayaking ($8/hr), among other watersports, with all profits donated to affiliate charity the Foundation of Goodness (ⓦ unconditionalcompassion.org), which provides free technical dive training programmes for local former dynamite fishermen.
International Diving School Coral Sands Hotel ☎ 071 725 1024, ⓦ theinternationaldivingschool.

com; map p.129. Friendly, well-established dive outfit on the beach offering PADI courses and daily dives to some twelve local dive sites.
Poseidon Diving Station Immediately south of the Hikkaduwa Beach Hotel ☎ 091 227 7294, ⓦ divingsrilanka.com; map p.129. A PADI five-star dive centre and one of Sri Lanka's longest-running dive outfits, offering numerous courses, daily boat dives and specialty diving courses such as deep-sea diving and night diving.

SURFING AND OTHER WATERSPORTS

After Arugam Bay and Midigama, Hikkaduwa has some of the best **surfing** in Sri Lanka. Plenty of places along the beach offer tuition, trips and rent out surfboards (from Rs.300/hr or Rs.1000/day) and (slightly cheaper) bodyboards. Some 3km inland from town, the broad, breezy Hikkaduwa lagoon is a popular spot for **wakeboarding**.

Mambo Surf Tours A-Frame Surf Shop Narigama ☎ 077 782 2524, ⓦ mambos.lk; map p.129. Facing the main surf point, this is Hikkaduwa's longest-established surf shop and school. Offerings include board hire, surfing tuition for beginners (Rs.3500; six lessons are recommended) and 24hr board repairs, plus one-day surfing tours along the south coast and two-day surf and safari trips to Yala, among others – count on around $60/person/day.

Reef End Surf School Narigama, next to Rita's guesthouse ☎ 077 704 3559 or ☎ 077 706 9525, ⓦ reefendsurfschool.com; map p.129. Another reliable surf shop, offering surf/bodyboard hire (Rs.1000/800 per day) and running five-day beginner's packages ($150, including two hours' instruction daily) and budget trips to Arugam Bay during Hikkaduwa's off-season.

leave from the bus station itself, but from the oceanside of the main road, about 50m south of the station.
Destinations Aluthgama (every 15min; 45min); Ambalangoda (every 15min; 20min); Colombo (every 15min; 2hr 15min); Galle (every 15min; 30min); Kalutara (every 15min; 1hr 15min).

By train The train station is just north of the bus station; regular trains run up and down the coast (see page 32). There's also a train station at Thiranagama, convenient for the southern end of the beach, although not many services stop here.

GETTING AROUND

By tuktuk When catching a tuktuk look out for vehicles carrying a "Hikkaduwa Tourist Supplier Provided Association Approved Tourist-Friendly Tuktuk" sticker (these tuktuks also have their own parking bays up and down the main road). The scheme was introduced to protect local drivers and visitors from the unscrupulous behaviour of outside

tuktuk drivers descending on the town. All tourist-friendly tuktuks should provide a hassle-free, and possibly cheaper, ride than non-registered vehicles.
By bike A number of places along the main road have knackered old bikes for rent.

1

By car and motorbike Sri Lanka Travels & Tours (☎077 301 6893) hires out cars or jeeps for $35–40/day self-drive, or $70–80/day with driver. They also have a range of mopeds and motorbikes for Rs.1000–3000/day, depending on size; you don't need a licence, but you'll have to leave your passport or plane ticket (should you have one) as a deposit.

ACCOMMODATION

Accommodation in Hikkaduwa is relatively pricey and noisy, as much of it is concentrated along the busy main road. Guesthouses sprawl down the coast for a considerable distance. **Wewala**, immediately south of ramshackle Hikkaduwa town, is the most developed section, with assorted upmarket hotels, restaurants and other amenities. Further south, **Narigama** is more backpacker-oriented, centred on a lively cluster of guesthouses and beach restaurants around *Neela's*. Past here is sleepy **Thiranagama**, notably quieter than areas further north. **Out of season**, room rates can fall by as much as fifty percent though many places (including a few restaurants and surf outfits) close during the summer months and the sea is often rough.

HIKKADUWA TOWN

★ **Camellia Dwellings** Baddegama Rd ☎091 227 7999, ⓦcamelliadwellings.com; map p.129. Immaculately maintained B&B just 150m from the bus station, with four individually designed rooms, all with big mattresses, hot water, a/c and direct garden access (some with private sun loungers), set in a light and breezy 60-year-old family home. Breakfast costs just $2 extra, and guests can visit the owner's cinnamon estate nearby. Excellent value. $40

WEWALA

Blue Ocean Villa 420 Galle Rd ☎091 227 7566, ⓦblueoceaweb.blogspot.com; map p.129. Intimate, modern family house with a Mediterranean feel, painted in pleasing shades of blue and white. The eight rooms (all with hot water and twin beds) are spacious, high-ceilinged and immaculately maintained; best value are the two breezy sea-facing rooms upstairs – and make sure you get a room away from the road. Rs.4000, a/c Rs.7000

Citrus 400 Galle Rd ☎091 556 0001, ⓦcitrusleisure. com; map p.129. Mid-range hotel with good quality standard and "eco-budget" rooms, all well equipped and decorated with an orange theme. They also provide rooms that can be accessed by guests with disabilities. Good medium-size pool with poolside restaurant and bar, as well as Balinese spa. B&B $160

Finlanka 200m inland from the Galle Rd ☎077 306 1068, ⓦfinlanka.net; map p.129. This lovely guesthouse is tucked away from the busy main road (although the train passes close by) and offers five spacious rooms (TV, hot water, optional a/c Rs.500 extra) with four-poster beds and either a balcony or veranda with garden views. B&B Rs.3500

Hikka Tranz Galle Rd ☎091 227 7188, ⓦcinnamonhotels. com; map p.129. In a fantastic location on a palm tree-sheltered headland, this large, long-established hotel has recently been refurbished, with graffiti-style modern art now adorning the walls of the common areas. The spacious a/c rooms are all sea-facing and come with balconies. Facilities include a pool, gym and spa. B&B $360

The Oasis Villa 466 Galle Rd ☎091 227 5202, ⓦoasiskingsley.wixsite.com/theoasisvilla; map p.129. Comfortable, good-value rooms (a/c, more expensive on the upper floor) set slightly back from the Galle Rd in a blue and white building. Downstairs is a nice little restaurant terrace, and the immaculately maintained garden contains a lovely swimming pool. B&B $53

NARIGAMA AND THIRANAGAMA

Drifters Hotel 602 Galle Rd ☎091 227 5692, ⓦdriftershotel.com; map p.129. This pleasant guesthouse is slightly smarter and more expensive than other places nearby but comes with a small pool and attractive beachside restaurant. Rooms are neat and comfortable – the two with private balcony overlooking the beach are the best. $54, a/c $74

International Beach Hotel Galle Rd ☎091 227 7202, ⓦibhsrilanka.com; map p.129. Functional modern guesthouse with a wide spread of rooms, from the simple, with fan only, to pricier ones with a/c, plus a couple of decent value sea-view suites with private balconies. $50, a/c $70

Le Reve d'Hikka 583 Galle Rd ☎077 418 8031, ⓦreve-hikka.com; map p.129. Low-key guesthouse with a handful of cheap rooms in the main house and quieter, more expensive ones in a new block to the back. All have big mattresses and optional a/c (Rs.1500 extra), and there's a chilled-out red-cushioned lounge at the rear. $43

Main Reef Surf Hotel 462/1 Galle Rd ☎091 227 5203, ⓦsrilankasurfholidays.com; map p.129. Small, personable ten-room guesthouse with a buzzy restaurant near Hikkaduwa's main surf break. Rooms (all a/c, except for two) are simple, yet have four-poster beds, hot-water bathrooms and views on the upper floors. Surf tuition available. Rs.5000, a/c Rs6500

★ **Neela's Guest House** 634 Galle Rd ☎091 438 3166, ⓦneelasbeach.com; map p.129. Long-established and very welcoming guesthouse at the heart of the Narigama action – one of Hikkaduwa's stand-out accommodation options. The comfortable and well-maintained rooms are among the best value in town, and there's also a pleasant beachside restaurant. Advance booking recommended. $55, a/c $70

Ocean View Cottage Galle Rd ☎091 227 7237, ⓦoceanviewcottage.net; map p.129. Bright modern guesthouse in a sea-facing block overlooking a grassy garden and decent-sized pool. The spacious tiled rooms come with hot water, minibar and optional a/c ($5 extra); more expensive ones have sea views. $48

Ranmal Beach Hotel Galle Rd ☎091 227 5474, ⓦranmal-rest.com; map p.129. Large guesthouse occupying a couple of blocks built around a garden, with a mix of simple fan rooms and smarter a/c deluxe rooms. All have terrace or balcony plus hot water, and there are also two sea-facing contemporary-styled superior suites (with jacuzzis). $40, a/c $60

★ **Roman Beach** 777/2 Galle Rd ☎091 227 5851, ⓦromanbeach.lk; map p.129. Hikkaduwa's chicest hotel and a real breath of fresh air. The timber-floored rooms, all on the upper floors, are big and sea-facing, with comfy beds, boldly coloured bathrooms, minibars and private balconies. The pricier top-floor rooms also have jacuzzis. There's also a long lush garden with pretty pool, and the ground-floor restaurant gets great reviews. Good value at current rates. B&B $175

Suite Lanka Galle Rd ☎091 227 7136, ⓦsuite-lanka. com; map p.129. Refreshing oasis of old world charm, with bijou sea-facing rooms kitted out with colonial-style furniture (including four-poster beds), a small pool and a shady garden with a Balinese-style curtained pavilion and lounge deck, although overpriced at current rates. €168

AROUND HIKKADUWA

Aditya Resort Rathgama, 5km south of Hikkaduwa ☎091 226 7708, ⓦaditya-resort.com; map p.129.

Intimate and personable – albeit eye-wateringly expensive – small luxury hotel set in a shady, hammock-strewn garden on its own stretch of deserted beach. Each of the sixteen huge suites is a harmonious blend of indoor and outdoor space, with cool, deliciously light interiors featuring distinctive antiques and artwork, and with plunge pools and private gardens or expansive balconies outside. There's also a fine restaurant, glorious pool and a seductive spa. $465

Asian Jewel Field View Rd (off Baddegama Rd), 3km inland ☎091 493 1388, ⓦasian-jewel.com; map p.129. Overlooking the serene Hikkaduwa lagoon, this beguiling little British-run hideaway offers a mix of boutique luxury and homestay hospitality. Accommodation is in five well-equipped a/c rooms (including a family suite) kitted out with chintzy wooden furniture, plus private balcony, TV and DVD. There's also a pool and excellent restaurant (see page 134). B&B $150

Kalla Bongo Lake Resort Off Baddegama Rd, 3km inland ☎091 494 6324, ⓦkallabongo.com; map p.129. Occupying a spacious hilly garden plot with magnificent views over the Hikkaduwa lagoon, this chilled-out place is home to fifteen lagoon-facing rooms (all a/c) in two modern blocks. There's also a lovely pool, and good open-sided restaurant-bar. Rs.14,500

Nimal's Homestay Dodanduwa, 2km south of Thiranagama ☎077 113 6997, ⓦnimalhomestay. wordpress.com; map p.129. Exceptionally welcoming homestay close to the Dodanduwa lagoon, with just three neatly arranged rooms (two share a balcony) and delicious local food (and cooking lessons); perfect for avoiding the hustle and bustle of Hikkaduwa without being too far from the beach. Rs.3000

EATING

★ **Aroma** 285 Galle Rd, Wewala ☎077 447 8644; map p.129. Recently refurbished roadside restaurant with upstairs and downstairs dining areas. The menu offers healthy organic Sri Lankan and Indian cuisine (including naan bread), such as rice and curry (Rs.750), nutritious *gotu kola* (Indian pennywort) soup (Rs.450) and breakfast sandwiches (Rs.600–700). Veggie- and vegan-friendly; no alcohol. Daily 10am–10pm.

Asian Jewel Field View Rd (off Baddegama Rd), 3km inland ☎091 493 1388, ⓦasian-jewel.com; map p.129. The veranda restaurant at this welcoming hotel (see above) is ideal if you've had your fill of rice and curry, with a menu including cottage pie, fish and chips and even Sunday roasts, alongside Indian dishes and Thai curries; diners can also use their inviting pool. Mains around $10–15. Daily 8am–9pm (last orders).

Bookworm Library Restaurant Galle Rd (next to Why Not), Narigama ☎077 622 5039; map p.129. This wins the award for Hikkaduwa's quirkiest restaurant. Downstairs is a library (Rs.300 lending fee) while upstairs a rustic

rooftop provides the venue for home-cooked family-style rice and curry (Rs.700), served throughout the day and evening. Limited seating so it's best to book the day before. Daily 6am–7.30pm.

Moon Beam Restaurant Moon Beam Hotel, 548/1 Galle Rd, Narigama ☎091 545 0657; map p.129. One of Hikkaduwa's nicest beach restaurants, in a big wooden pavilion with a beer garden in the middle and a menu featuring a huge selection of well-prepared, if rather pricey, tourist standards (mains Rs.700–1300). Daily 7.30am–11pm.

Nordic House 339 Galle Rd, Wewala ☎091 227 5970, ⓦfacebook.com/NordicHouseSriLanka; map p.129. Cosy open-fronted restaurant with brightly coloured sofas and adorned with vintage poster prints, serving a wide range of speciality burgers (try the blue cheese topping, Rs.980), salads and sandwiches, plus proper Lavazza coffee and shakes. Daily 10am–10pm.

Refresh 384 Galle Rd, Wewala ☎091 227 7810, ⓦrefreshhikkaduwa.com; map p.129. Set on a romantic lantern-dotted terrace running down to the sea, Hikkaduwa's most famous independent restaurant has a menu the size of a telephone directory, offering everything from gazpacho to gnocchi and enchiladas. The food is pricey (most mains Rs.900–1300) and gets very mixed reviews, although the Thai fried rice, hot butter cuttlefish and chilli crab are reliable. Also has a coffee shop and some smart rooms (from $70) in a block across the road. Daily 9am–11pm.

★ **Salty Swamis** 542 Galle Rd, Wewala ☎077 832 6302, ⓦsaltyswamis.com; map p.129. Hipster café, gallery and surf shop, with in and outdoor seating, serving Hikka's best coffee (Rs.400) made with local roasted beans, plus fresh juices (Rs. 500–800). For hungry surfers there's avocado toast (Rs.960) yogi burgers (Rs. 1300) and the delicious swami bowl (Rs.1100) – veggies, tahini and red rice. Daily 8–4pm.

Spaghetti & Co Galle Rd, Thiranagama ☎077 669 8114; map p.129. Italian-owned and -managed place, occupying an attractive colonial-style villa and garden on the land side of the Galle Rd and dishing up a good range of well-prepared home-made pasta dishes and pizza cooked in a genuine wood-fired oven. Most mains Rs.900–1350. Daily 6–10.30pm.

Thambili Café Galle Rd, Thiranagama ☎077 675 0864, ⓦfacebook.com/thambili; map p.129. This quaint wooden beach café, sprinkled with hammocks and orange beanbags, has plenty of Robinson Crusoe appeal. The menu is surprisingly nutritious, and different – think healthy breakfast shakes, muesli, salads, falafel, hummous (Rs.350–550) and private evening barbecues to order (around Rs.2000). Daily 8am–10pm.

DRINKING AND NIGHTLIFE

The town has a certain amount of tourist-inspired **nightlife** during the season, with a number of crashed-out places to drink along the beach. Most nights out in Hikkaduwa are in any case fairly impromptu and mainly revolve around drinking; for specific events, look out for flyers and posters around the village.

Funky de Bar Galle Rd, Narigama ☎077 752 1003, ⓦfacebook.com/FunkydebarHikkaduwa; map p.129. Tiny venue right over the waves with a diminutive dancefloor hosting a once-weekly house club night (Thurs) and karaoke (Tues). Daily 9pm–3am.

Mambo's Narigama, behind the A-Frame Surf Shop ☎077 782 2524, ⓦmambos.lk; map p.129. Perennially

popular and laidback venue complete with modest dancefloor (with Sat disco; 10pm–6am). Daily 5pm until late.

Top Secret/The Harmony Galle Rd, Narigama ☎091 227 7551; map p.129. Sometimes lively beach bar with nightly DJ playing a mix of pop, house and chill-out at the *Harmony*, a popular beach café. Daily 8pm–late.

Vibration Narigama, land side of Galle Rd near the Moon Beam Hotel ☎091 494 3857, ⓦvibrationhotel.com; map p.129. One of Hikkaduwa's more happening venues. Friday is the big night with local drummers (midnight) and DJs in the yard out back. Fri 9.30pm–6am.

SHOPPING

A load of places along the Galle Rd offer all sorts of collectables, including plenty of *kolam* masks (the quality is actually often as high here as in Ambalangoda) and more unusual wooden sculptures, as well as colourful local art.

Elephant Foot Drum Shop 291B Galle Rd, Wewala ☎076 613 7799, ⓦelephantfootsrilanka.com; map p.129. Elephant Foot is a popular Sri Lankan band, famed for blending drums and percussion with modern music. This shop sells a range of instruments (mostly drums) and CDs, and is *the* place to organize a drum lesson (Rs.1000/30min). Daily 9.30am–9pm.

Laksiri Batiks 400m down Baddegama Rd, behind the bus station (just before the Gangarama Mahavihara), ☎091 227 7255; map p.129. Local batik factory with a showroom selling pieces from Rs.500, plus clothes and sarongs. Mon–Fri 9am–5pm.

Saffron Robes Galle Rd, Wewala ⓦsaffronrobes.com; map p.129. Hikkaduwa's smartest art gallery showcasing the work of talented local painters, with a variety of landscapes, portraits and abstract art. Daily 10am–9pm.

DIRECTORY

Ayurveda There are numerous little ad hoc Ayurveda centres dotted around Wewala and Thiranagama, though they're all very low-key compared with the flashy resorts at Beruwala and Bentota – and also much cheaper.

Banks and exchange There are banks with ATMs in Hikkaduwa town, south of the bus station.

Post office Baddegama Rd, 150m east of the bus station (Mon–Sat 8am–6pm).

Swimming Non-guests can use the pools at *Hikka Tranz* (Rs.1000) and *Ocean View Cottage* (Rs.500).

Travel agents Monika Tours and Travels (☎091 227 5566, ⓔmonika_shyamali@hotmail.com), next to *Refresh*, is one of the more reliable of the many travel agents in town, offering islandwide guided tours for around $100/person/day, including transport and half-board accommodation. The tours arranged by Lalith at *Drifters Hotel* also have a good reputation.

The south

MIRISSA

The south

In many ways, the south encapsulates Sri Lanka at its most traditional. Stretched out along a great arc of sun-baked coastline, much of the area still feels pleasingly rural (at least away from the increasingly developed oceanfront between Galle and Matara): a land of a thousand sleepy villages sheltered under innumerable palms, where the laidback pace of life still revolves around coconut farming, rice cultivation and fishing – the latter still practised in some places by the distinctively Sri Lankan method of stilt-fishing. Culturally, too, the south remains a bastion of Sinhalese traditions, exemplified by the string of temples and giant Buddha statues dotting the coast, and by the colourful festivals celebrated throughout the region, which culminate in the exuberant religious ceremonies enacted nightly at the ancient shrine of Kataragama.

The south's physical distance from the rest of the island, and from the hordes of Indian invaders who periodically overran the north, meant that the ancient kingdom of **Ruhunu** (or Rohana) – a name still often used to describe the region – evolved into one of the heartlands of traditional Sinhalese culture. In later centuries, despite the brief importance of the southern ports of Galle and Matara in the colonial Indian Ocean trade, Ruhunu preserved this separation, and with the rise of Colombo and the commercial decline of Galle and Matara in the late nineteenth century, the south became a relative backwater. Attempts by ex-president Mahinda Rajapakse to transform his unprepossessing home town of Hambantota into a major new commercial centre and tourist hub (complete with international airport and huge new port) have proved spectacularly unsuccessful, although another of his legacies, the **Southern Expressway** (see page 28), has made access to the region easier than it has ever been, cutting travel times from Colombo to Galle from as much as four hours to little over one.

The region's varied attractions make it one of Sri Lanka's most rewarding areas to visit. Gateway to the south – and one of its highlights – is the atmospheric old port of **Galle**, Sri Lanka's best-preserved colonial town, while beyond Galle stretch a string of picture-perfect beaches including **Unawatuna**, **Weligama**, **Mirissa** and **Tangalla**. Nearby, the comparatively little-visited town of **Matara**, with its quaint Dutch fort, offers a further taste of Sri Lanka's colonial past, while ancient **Tissamaharama** makes a good base from which to visit two of the country's finest national parks: the placid lagoons and birdlife-rich wetlands of **Bundala**, and **Yala**, famous for its elephants and leopards. Beyond Tissamaharama lies the fascinating religious centre of **Kataragama**, whose various shrines are held sacred by Buddhists, Hindus and Muslims alike.

Galle

Perched on the coast close to the island's southernmost point, the venerable port of **GALLE** (pronounced "Gaul") has grown from ancient origins into Sri Lanka's fourth largest city. At the heart of the modern city – but strangely detached from it – lies the old Dutch quarter, known as the **Fort**, Sri Lanka's best-preserved colonial townscape, enclosed within a chain of huge bastions which now guard the area from modernization as effectively as they once protected Dutch trading interests from marauding adventurers. The Fort is Sri Lanka at its most magically time-warped, its low-rise streets lined with Dutch-period villas, many of which retain their original

MULKIRIGALA

Highlights

❶ Galle Sri Lanka's most perfectly preserved colonial town, its time-warped streets lined with historic Dutch-colonial villas hidden behind formidable ramparts. See page 138

❷ Unawatuna Crash out on the wide, wave-lapped sands of buzzy Unawatuna Bay, popular with younger travellers and home to a good selection of restaurants and bars. See page 153

❸ Weligama The gentle sandy-bottomed surf breaks off Weligama's wide bay are ideal for beginner board riding. See page 164

❹ Whale-watching, Mirissa Mirissa's picturesque harbour is the jumping-off point for exhilarating boat trips to see one of Sri Lanka's biggest attractions: blue whales. See page 169

❺ Mulkirigala Absorbing sequence of richly decorated cave temples carved into the flanks of a spectacular rock outcrop. See page 180

❻ Yala National Park Sri Lanka's foremost national park, with marvellous scenery and abundant wildlife, from peacocks to leopards. See page 190

❼ Kataragama Join the crowds for the evening puja at Kataragama, one of Sri Lanka's most vibrant religious spectacles, at a shrine held sacred by Buddhists, Hindus and Muslims alike. See page 192

HIGHLIGHTS ARE MARKED ON THE MAP ON PAGE 140

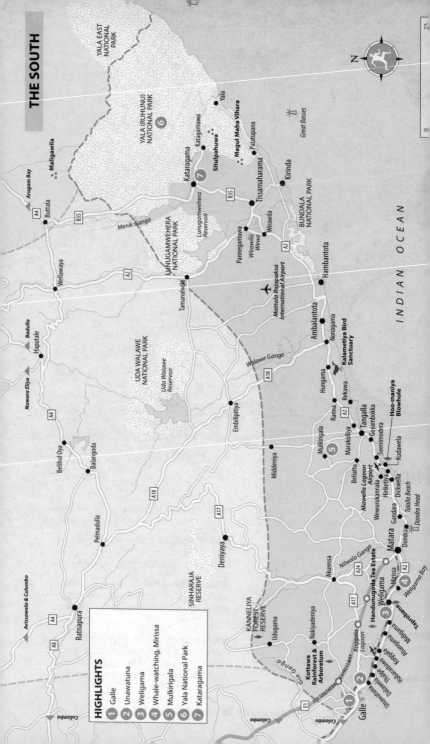

THE SOUTH

HIGHLIGHTS

1. Galle
2. Unawatuna
3. Weligama
4. Whale-watching, Mirissa
5. Mulkirigala
6. Yala National Park
7. Kataragama

YALA EAST NATIONAL PARK

YALA (RUHUNU) NATIONAL PARK ⑥

Maligawila

Arugam Bay

Buttala

Weliwaya

B35

Menik Ganga

Kataragama ⑦

Kdebiliteya

Katagamuwa

Yala

Magul Maha Vihara

Situlpahuwa

Palatupana

Great Basses

B35

Tissamaharama

Kirinda

LUNUGAMWEHERA NATIONAL PARK

Lunugamwehera Reservoir

Panegamuwa

Wirawila Wewa

Wirawila

A2

BUNDALA NATIONAL PARK

Tamanalwila

Mattala Rajapaksa International Airport

Hambantota

I N D I A N   O C E A N

Badulla

Haputale

Nuwara Eliya

A4

UDA WALAWE NATIONAL PARK

Uda Walawe Reservoir

Walawe Ganga

A18

Ambalantota

Nonagama

Kalametiya Bird Sanctuary

Belihul Oya

Balangoda

A18

Embilipitiya

Hungama

Hoo-maniya Blowhole

Middeniya

Mulkirigala ⑤

Rekawa

Ranna

A2

Tangalla

Goyambokka

Seenimodera

Kudawela

Ratnapura

A4

Pelmadulla

A17

A17

Marakolliya

Belatta

Mawella Lagoon Airport

Wewurukannala

Hiriketiya

Dickwella

Dondra

Dondra Head

Talalla Beach

Talalla

Gandara

Matara

Nilwala Ganga

A24

Akuressa

A17

KANNELIYA FOREST RESERVE

Udugama

Ilakiyadeniya

Kottawa Rainforest & Arboretum

SINHARAJA RESERVE

Deniyaya

Handunugoda Tea Estate ③

Weligama ③

Mirissa ④

Weligama Bay

Taprobane

A2

Avissawela & Colombo

A8

Colombo

E1

Gin Ganga

Koggala Lagoon

Unawatuna ②

Galle ①

Dalawella

Thalpe

Habaraduwa

Koggala

Ahangama

Midigama

N

INDIAN OCEAN

0   25

treet-facing verandas and red-tiled roofs, and dotted with a string of imposing
hurches and other colonial landmarks. There's not actually much to see (a few unusual
nuseums excepted): the main pleasure here is just ambling round the atmospheric old
treets and walls, savouring the easy pace of life.

rief history

Galle is thought to have been the biblical **Tarshish**, from whence King Solomon
btained gold, spices, ivory, apes and peacocks, and the combination of its fine natural
arbour and strategic position on the sea routes between Arabia, India and Southeast
sia made the town an important trading emporium long before the arrival of the
uropeans. In 1589, the **Portuguese** established a presence here, constructing a small
ort named Santa Cruz, which they later extended with a series of bastions and walls.
he **Dutch** captured Galle in 1640 after a four-day siege, and in 1663 expanded the
riginal Portuguese fortifications to enclose the whole of Galle's sea-facing promontory,
stablishing the street plan and system of bastions that survive to this day. They also
ntroduced marvels of European engineering such as an intricate subterranean sewer
ystem which was flushed out daily by the tide.

The **British** took Galle in 1796 during the islandwide transfer of power following
Dutch defeat in the Napoleonic Wars (see page 411) – ironically, after all the
ngenuity and labour they had invested in the town's defences, Galle was finally
urrendered with hardly a shot being fired. The city continued to serve as Ceylon's
rincipal harbour for much of the nineteenth century but Colombo's growing
ommercial importance and improvements to its harbour gradually eroded Galle's
rade. By the early twentieth century, it had become an economic backwater, lapsing
nto a tranquil decline which happily, if fortuitously, allowed the old colonial
ownscape of the Fort to survive almost completely intact.

In the years **since independence**, Galle has recovered some of its lost dynamism, with
 dramatic revival in the Fort's fortunes over the past decade as **expats** (mainly British)
nd members of the Colombo elite have bought up and renovated many of the area's
istoric properties. This remarkable influx of foreigners and cash has transformed
he formerly sleepy and slightly scruffy old town into Sri Lanka's most cosmopolitan
nclave, home to a sizeable foreign population and awash with boutique hotels, stylish
illas, convivial cafés and chic shops – a fitting turn of events for Sri Lanka's most
 uropean settlement.

he Fort

he principal entrance to the Fort is through the **Main Gate**, one of the newest parts
f the fortifications, added by the British in 1873 to allow easier vehicular access.
he section of ramparts facing the new town is the most heavily fortified, since it
rotected the Fort's vulnerable land side. The Dutch substantially enlarged the original
ortuguese fortifications here, naming the new defences the **Sun**, **Moon** and **Star**
astions. The sheer scale of these bastions is brutally impressive, if not particularly
esthetic – a fitting memorial to Dutch governor Petrus Vuyst (1726–29), who was
rgely responsible for their construction and whose cruelty and abuse of power was
uch that he was eventually recalled to Jakarta and executed by the Dutch authorities.
he iconic clocktower on top of the bastions was erected by the punctilious British in
883.

From the Main Gate, go left at the roundabout to reach one of the Fort's two main
orth–south thoroughfares, the atmospheric **Church Street** (originally Kerkstraat),
amed after a long-demolished Dutch church.

he National Museum

urch St • Tues–Sat 9am–5pm • Rs.300; camera Rs.250; video camera Rs.2000 • ⓦ museum.gov.lk

2

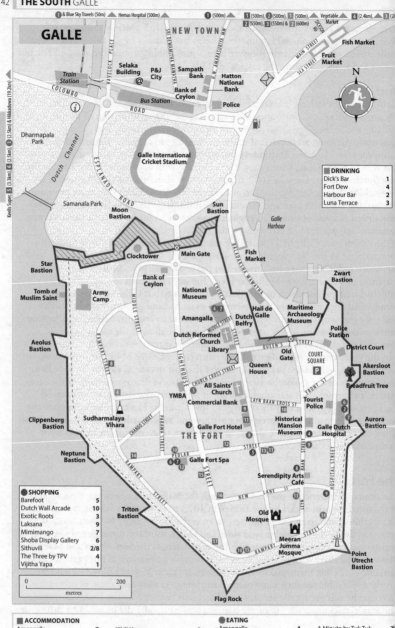

GALLE

DRINKING

Dick's Bar	1
Fort Dew	4
Harbour Bar	2
Luna Terrace	3

SHOPPING

Barefoot	5
Dutch Wall Arcade	10
Exotic Roots	3
Laksana	9
Mimimango	7
Shoba Display Gallery	6
Sithuvili	2/8
The Three by TPV	4
Vijitha Yapa	1

0	200
metres	

ACCOMMODATION

Amangalla	7	Kikili House	3		
Beach Haven	16	Mango House	10		
Closenberg Hotel	4	Pedlar 62	12		
The Dutch House	2	Pedlar's Inn Hostel	15		
Fort Bazaar Hotel	9	Rampart View	17		
The Fort Printers	13	Seagreen Guesthouse	8		
Galle Fort Hotel	11	The Sun House	1		
Jetwing Kurulubedda	5	Weltevreden	14		
Jetwing Lighthouse	6				

EATING

Amangalla	4	A Minute by Tuk Tuk	7
Chambers	8	The Old Railway Café	1
Crepe-ology	9	Pedlar's Inn Café	10
Elita	14	Poonie's Kitchen	12
Fortaleza	5	Royal Dutch Café	13
The Fort Printers	11	The Sun House	2
Indian Hut	15	The Tuna & The Crab	6
Jetwing Lighthouse	3		

GALLE FESTIVALS

Proof of Galle's burgeoning cultural credentials is provided by the string of festivals that have been set up over the last decade. Pride of place goes to the **Galle Literary Festival** (mid-Jan; W galleliteraryfestival.com), founded in 2007, which has established itself as a major item on the global literati circuit. It's held in the historical buildings and hotels of Galle Fort, with various English-language authors giving talks and participating in panel discussions. It's also a great chance to hear more from Sri Lankan writers. Fringe events include live musical performances, film screenings and art exhibitions.

The other big event in town is the **Galle Music Festival** (W facebook.com/GalleMusicFestival), a three-day event alternating between Galle (even-numbered years) and Jaffna (W facebook.com/JaffnaMusicFestival) and showcasing local and international folk musicians, dancers and other performers.

An attractive colonial building near the top of Church Street holds the **National Museum**, a wildly over-optimistic name for three dark rooms of rather sorry-looking exhibits, which give only the faintest sense of the exotic and luxurious items that would formerly have passed through Galle's harbour.

Amangalla

Church St

The large and rather stately white building next door to the National Museum was originally built for the Dutch governor in 1684; it was subsequently converted into the venerable *New Oriental Hotel* in 1863 and then, following a massive makeover, reopened in 2005 as the ultra-luxurious **Amangalla** hotel (see page 147), though the exterior has survived almost unchanged. The spacious and wonderfully atmospheric old veranda is the perfect venue for afternoon tea.

Dutch Reformed Church

Church St • Tues–Sun 9am–5pm • Donation

Galle's most striking colonial building, the graceful **Dutch Reformed Church** (or Groote Kerk) was built on the site of an earlier Portuguese Capuchin convent in around 1755. The delicate, slightly Italianate lines of the facade belie the severity of the **interior**, in which the only decorative concessions are the huge canopy over the pulpit and the attractive organ loft. The floor is covered in ornately carved **memorials** to the city's Dutch settlers, the earlier examples in Dutch (moved here from two earlier Dutch cemeteries which were dismantled by the British in 1853), later ones in English, many of them bearing witness to the lamentably brief life expectancy of Ceylon's early European colonists. Most striking, however, is the carved memorial, hanging on the southern wall, to **E.A.H. Abraham**, Commander of Galle, complete with a miniature skull, a medieval-looking armoured helmet and the remains of his baptism shirt. The church's decaying **belfry** (dated 1701) stands solitarily on the opposite side of the road, close to the junction with Queen Street.

The post office and Queen's House

A few steps further down Church Street is the library, and next to it, an antiquated but still functioning **post office** whose Dickensian-looking interior is worth a peek. Diagonally opposite stands **Queen's House**, dated 1683, and originally the offices of the Dutch city governor; it's still sometimes called the Old Dutch Government House.

All Saints' Church

Church St • Daily 8am–5pm • Donation • W allsaintsgalle.org

Immediately south of the Dutch Reformed Church is the Fort's principal Anglican place of worship, **All Saints' Church**, a Romanesque basilica-style structure whose stumpy steeple provides one of the area's most distinctive landmarks. The church was

2

DUTCH BURGHERS

Many of the tombstones which cover the floor and fill the small churchyard of the Dutch Reformed Church bear Dutch names – Jansz, De Kretser, Van Langenberg and the like – dating from the colonial period right up to modern times. These commemorate the families of Sri Lanka's smallest, and oddest, minority: the **Dutch Burghers** – Sri Lankans of Dutch or Portuguese descent.

At the time of Independence the Burgher community numbered around fifty thousand, based mainly in Colombo. Burghers had held major government posts under the British as well as running many of the island's trading companies, although their numbers declined significantly in the 1950s, when as many as half the country's Burgher families, disillusioned by Sinhalese nationalist laws based on language and religion, left for Australia, Canada or Britain.

Despite their Dutch (or Portuguese) ancestry, the Burghers have for centuries spoken English as their first language. Burgher culture preserves strong Dutch elements, however, and they would be horrified to be confused with the British, despite a certain amount of intermarriage over the years (not only with the British, but also with the Sinhalese and Tamils). Not that there is really such a thing as a single Burgher culture or community. Many of the wealthier Burghers arrived in Ceylon as employees of the Dutch East India Company, while working-class Burghers, more often from Portugal, came to help build the railways and settled largely on the coast between Colombo and Negombo. And to make things a little more confused, there are thousands of Sri Lankans with Dutch or Portuguese names, adopted during the years of occupation, who have no connection at all with Europe.

Over the past five decades, the Burghers have particularly made their mark in the arts, both in Sri Lanka and beyond. Notable figures include: **Geoffrey Bawa** (see page 122); **George Keyt** (1901–93), Sri Lanka's foremost modern painter; **Barbara Sansoni**, founder of the Barefoot company in Colombo; and designer **Ena de Silva**. Overseas, the best-known Burgher is Canada-based novelist **Michael Ondaatje**, whose memoir of island life, *Running in the Family*, gives a wonderful picture of Burgher life in the years before Independence.

---

begun in 1868 on the site of a previous courthouse – the town's gallows might (as a sign outside gruesomely points out) have stood on the site of the current high altar; otherwise, the bare interior gives disappointingly little insight into the history of the British in Galle.

Maritime Archaeology Museum

Queen's St • Daily 8am–5pm • Rs.775 • ⓦ ccf.gov.lk/galle-maritime.htm • No video cameras admitted

Queen's Street, a short walk east from All Saints' Church, is dominated by the imposing bulk of the ochre-coloured **Great Warehouse**, one of Galle's most striking colonial buildings: a long, barn-like structure punctuated by barred windows cloistered behind black shutters, which was formerly used to store ships' provisions and valuable commodities such as cowries, sappan wood and cinnamon.

The warehouse now provides the setting for Galle's dismal **Maritime Archaeology Museum**, without doubt the worst museum in Sri Lanka. The lacklustre exhibits (expect pots, bits of rope, more pots and a few waxwork sailors) plumb impressive depths of dullness, backed by dozens of signboards written in a form of English so mangled, twisted and generally incomprehensible it makes you seasick just looking at them. Save your money.

The Old Gate

Queen's St

On the eastern side of the Maritime Museum stands the **Old Gate**, the only entrance to the Fort until the construction of the Main Gate in 1873. The fully restored arch on the Fort side of the gate is dated 1669 and inscribed with the coat of arms of the **VOC** (Vereenigde Oost-indische Compagnie, or Dutch East India Company). The distinctive VOC symbol at its centre – with the O and C dangling off the arms of

he V – is sometimes claimed to be the world's oldest corporate logo. The mossy arch
n the exterior, port-facing side is decorated with the date 1668 and a British crest,
mblazoned with the words "Dieu et mon droit", which was added in 1796.

Court Square and Zwart Bastion

The northeastern corner of the Fort is occupied by the park-like **Court Square**, which
s almost completely surrounded by handsome old Indian rain trees, one of them
dramatically engulfed by an enormous banyan. Local courts flank either side of the
quare, while south of here, the top of **Leyn Baan Street** (Rope Walk St) is home to
dozens of lawyers' offices, a few still sporting their picturesque old hand-painted black-
nd-white signs.

To the northeast of the square you can glimpse parts of the **Zwart Bastion** (Black Fort)
rom a pathway that leads between the police headquarters and the District Court.
The bastion incorporates the remains of the original Portuguese fortress of Santa Cruz,
making it the town's oldest surviving section of fortification.

Historical Mansion Museum

eyn Baan St • Mon–Thurs, Sat & Sun 9am–6pm, Fri 9am–noon & 2pm–6pm • Donation

One of Galle's quirkier attractions, the entertaining **Historical Mansion Museum** is the
esult of the efforts of a certain Mr Gaffar, who for over fifty years has accumulated an
normous collection of antiques, bric-a-brac and outright junk. The overall effect of
his Aladdin's cave of curiosities is strangely compelling, even when it becomes obvious
hat at least part of the aim of the entire museum is to lure you into Mr Gaffar's gem
hop. The museum also employs a number of local artisans – including a lacemaker,
em-cutter and jewellery-maker – who can be seen at work in the courtyard, and whose
reations are also sold in the shop.

Hospital Street, Galle Dutch Hospital and the eastern ramparts

ounding the eastern side of the Fort, **Hospital Street** flanks another stretch of well-
reserved fort ramparts. Beside it stands the **Galle Dutch Hospital**, an atmospheric
hopping and dining complex arranged around two courtyards and across two floors.
his mammoth colonnaded building with 50cm-thick walls was originally built in the
ighteenth century as a hospital to treat officers serving under the Dutch East India
Company. In the years that followed, it served as a barracks under the British and later
town hall before being painstakingly restored and opening in its current format in
014. Sandwiched between the **Akersloot Bastion** (1789) and the protruding **Aurora
astion**, at the far eastern end of Pedlar Street, the upper floors of the complex offer
narvellous views out across the wide bay towards Rumassala (see page 154).

The Akersloot Bastion was named after the birthplace of Admiral Wilhelm Coster,
he Dutch captain who captured Galle from the Portuguese in 1640. Above it towers
vhat's claimed to be the island's oldest **breadfruit tree**, planted by the Dutch over 300
ears ago, although only its uppermost boughs can be glimpsed as it stands inside an
naccessible government building enveloped by high white walls.

At the southern tip of Hospital Street is **Point Utrecht Bastion**, topped by a slender
vhite **lighthouse** that dates from 1938; the ruined structure standing below it was a
ritish powder magazine. Steps lead down from behind the lighthouse to the fort's only
tretch of sandy **beach**.

Meeran Jumma Mosque

mpart St • Not open to the public (although you might be invited inside if you're lucky)

Jear the lighthouse is the large, early twentieth-century **Meeran Jumma Mosque** –
lthough it actually looks much more like a European Baroque church (and is actually
uilt on the site of the former Portuguese cathedral), with only a couple of tiny
ninarets and a token scribble of Arabic betraying its true function. The mosque stands

2

A WALK AROUND THE RAMPARTS

From the Aurora Bastion, south of the Galle Dutch Hospital, it's possible to **walk** clockwise along the ramparts all the way round to the main town-facing bastions – a good way to get oriented and an enjoyable stroll at any time of day but particularly at sunset, when half the town seems to take to the bastions to fly kites, play cricket, romance under umbrellas or simply shoot the breeze.

at the heart of Galle's **Muslim quarter**, which is often busy with crowds of white-robed, skull-capped locals on their way to or from prayers.

Flag Rock

From the lighthouse the path along the top of the ramparts heads west to **Flag Rock**, usually busy with a few hawkers and the local snake charmer, who will fire his cobra into life at the merest hint of an approaching tourist. At the southernmost point of the Fort is Flag Rock, the most imposing of Galle's bastions – the name derives from the Dutch practice of signalling approaching ships to warn them of offshore hazards hereabouts (the warning signals would have been backed up by musket shots, fired from the huge Pigeon Rock, which you can see just offshore). If you're lucky, you might catch one of the clearly potty "**fort jumpers**" in action, who (anticipating a sizeable tip) fling themselves freestyle off the bastion down the sheer 13m drop into the terrifyingly narrow space between the rampart and the deadly rocks just offshore.

The western bastions

The section of ramparts beyond Flag Rock gives a clear idea of how the original Dutch fortifications would have appeared. Look closely at the stones and you'll see that many are actually formed from coral, which was hewed and carted into place by slaves. The next bastion along, the **Triton**, comes alive around dusk, as the townsfolk turn out en masse to promenade along the walls and take in the extraordinary red-and-purple sunsets.

Guarding the ramparts' southwestern face, the **Neptune** and **Clippenberg bastions** give increasingly fine views over the Fort, with the stumpy spire of All Saints' prominent among the picturesque huddle of red-tiled rooftops. Closer to hand stands the neat white dagoba of the 1889 **Sudharmalaya Vihara**, looking bizarrely out of place in its colonial surroundings. North of here the ramparts are flanked by a wide stretch of parkland, and the pathway inclines between **Aeolus Bastion** and **Star Bastion**; the modest veiled **tomb** of a Muslim saint lies in solitary splendour here below the rampart walls. At Star Bastion, steps lead up to the highest point of the fort, and onto the clocktower-spiked Moon Bastion.

North of the Fort

The lofty grass-tufted ramparts between the Moon and Sun bastions (above the Main Gate) offer a fine view of Galle's compact **Galle International Cricket Stadium**, occupying the site of the former British racecourse, and one of Sri Lanka's three principal Test match venues. To the east, the **harbourside** is normally busy with fishing boats, their owners noisily bartering over piles of tuna, seer and crab.

Beyond the Fort, Galle's **new town** straggles north and eastwards in an indeterminate confusion of hooting buses and zigzagging rickshaws. The most interesting place for a wander is along **Main Street** past the junction with Sea Street, where lines of small shops and local pavement traders cut a colourful dash. At the eastern end of Main Street and next to a small Buddhist stupa, the town's photographic **vegetable market** is set in a 300-year-old Dutch building, with piles of fresh local produce neatly displayed beneath an antiquated columned roof.

ARRIVAL AND DEPARTURE

Galle's **bus and train stations** are in the new town, just north of the fort, and directly linked to one another by a footbridge. A tuktuk from either the train or bus station to any of the Fort guesthouses shouldn't cost more than Rs.150, though drivers will attempt to double that.

By bus Nonstop a/c coaches depart every 15–30min daily (Rs.400) for Colombo, dropping you in the southern suburb of Maharagama, from where it's easy to catch a tuktuk or local bus to central Colombo (see page 84). Services (local and express) in both directions along the slower coastal road leave roughly every 15min. If you're heading to Tangalla, Hambantota or Tissamaharama you may find it quicker to catch a bus to Matara and change there, rather than waiting for a through bus. To reach Sinharaja you'll need to take a direct bus to Deniyaya or opt for one of the more frequent buses to Akuressa where you can then change for Deniyaya (every 30min from Akuressa). Reaching the hill country from Galle is a laborious process. The easiest way to get to Kandy from Galle is to return to Colombo first, while there is one early-morning direct service to Badulla via Bandarawela, and another to Nuwara Eliya. Alternatively, catch the bus to Tissa, then another to Wellawaya, from where there are frequent services to Ella, Haputale and Badulla.

Destinations Akuressa (every 10min; 1hr); Aluthgama (every 15min; 1hr 30min); Badulla (daily; 8hr); Colombo (via coastal highway: every 15min; 3hr; via Southern Expressway: every 15–30min; 1hr 15min); Deniyaya (hourly; 4hr); Hambantota (every 15min; 3hr 30min); Hikkaduwa (every 15min; 30min); Kalutara (every 15min; 2hr 15min); Kataragama (5 daily; 5hr); Matara (every 15min; 1hr 15min); Nuwara Eliya (daily; 8hr); Tangalla (every 30min; 2hr 30min); Tissamaharama (every 30min; 4hr 15min); Weligama (every 15min; 45min).

By train For train times in the south see the timetable in Basics (page 32).

Destinations Aluthgama (7–14 daily; 1hr 30min–1hr 50min); Ambalangoda (7–14 daily; 25min–1hr); Colombo (5–10 daily; 1hr 50min–3hr 25min); Hikkaduwa (6–13 daily; 20–30min); Kalutara (5–11 daily; 1hr–2hr 45min); Matara (6–9 daily; 45min–1hr 15min); Weligama (6–9 daily; 35–45min).

By air Cinnamon Air (see page 31) currently operates daily flights from Koggala Airport, about 12km east of Galle, to Colombo ($237) and Kandy ($176). To reach Galle (and local destinations such as Thalpe, Dalawella and Unawatuna), walk to the main road (300m) and take any bus heading west into the city. Alternatively, take a tuktuk direct (Rs.800–1000).

INFORMATION AND TOURS

Tourist information The Tourist Information Centre (Mon–Fri 9am–4.30pm; ☎091 224 7676, ⓦsrilanka.travel), in the park opposite the train station, is staffed on an ad hoc basis by English-speaking guides, and provides free general information.

Tours Blue Sky Travels (☎077 626 3400, ✉rasikaam@ yahoo.com) at *The Old Railway Café* (see page 149) arrange day-trips and multi-day guided tours across the island for around Rs.12,000/day (excluding food and accommodation). They also rent scooters (Rs.800/day) and motorbikes (from Rs.1000/day), and can help with booking train tickets.

ACCOMMODATION

Galle has a good selection of both **mid-range** and **luxury** accommodation, though there are increasingly lower budget options. Some of the Fort's guesthouses are not clearly signed, so if you take a tuktuk to reach one, check the address to make sure you're actually being taken to the right place; some guesthouse owners will pick you up from the bus or train station if you call in advance.

THE FORT

★**Amangalla** 10 Church St ☎091 223 3388, ⓦamanresorts.com; map p.142. Occupying the premises of the former *New Oriental Hotel*, this superb Aman resort has remained extremely faithful to the decor and style of Galle's most famous colonial hotel (see page 143), with sensitively updated rooms and facilities (including a beautiful pool, library, exquisite Ayurveda spa and gorgeous residents-only

CYCLING AROUND GALLE

Highly enjoyable guided **bike rides** are run in the lush countryside around Galle by Idle Tours (☎077 985 5500, ⓦidletours.com). Trips, on good-quality mountain bikes, range in length from 12km to 40km and offer a variety of terrains – see the website for details. Custom-made tours can also be arranged. If you wish to cover more ground, try the more adventurous three-day (45–80km) "Deep South Bike Tour" run by Moonstone Expeditions (☎077 812 1304, ⓦmoonstone-expeditions.com), which takes in paddy fields, villages and tea estates, with overnight stays in plantation bungalows. Alternatively, Idle Tours' offshoot Idle Boats offers serene punts up the Gin Ganga, west of Galle.

2

VILLAS ALONG THE SOUTH COAST

The past fifteen years have seen a massive explosion in Sri Lanka's **holiday villa** market, with dozens of properties being offered by owners keen to jump onto a potentially lucrative bandwagon. The biggest concentration of villas is in and around Galle (including upwards of twenty historic houses available in the Fort alone, and a dense concentration in Thalpe, about 10km east), though properties dot the coastline as far as Tangalla, and increasing numbers of tea plantation bungalows in the hill country are also becoming available (see page 241). There's plenty of choice, with villas sleeping anything between two and sixteen people and ranging in price from around $250 per night in low season up to $2500 for a large villa over Christmas and New Year. Many occupy stunning natural settings, often on unspoilt stretches of private beach, while some show contemporary Sri Lankan design at its finest. In all, the emphasis is on intimacy, style and self-indulgence. Good places to start browsing include Ⓦvillasinsrilanka.com, Ⓦreddottours.com and Ⓦsrilankainstyle.com, which offer a vast array of properties, many of which can be viewed and booked online.

Sunset Bar) which manage to combine old-world charm with the last word in contemporary luxury – albeit at predictably stratospheric prices. **$960**

★ **Beach Haven** (Mrs N.D. Wijenayake's) 65 Lighthouse St ☎091 223 4663, Ⓦbeachhaven-galle.com; map p.142. Very welcoming and sociable guesthouse right in the middle of the Fort, offering a varied range of squeaky-clean fan and a/c rooms (more expensive upstairs). There's also a pleasant first-floor sitting area and communal veranda overlooking the street – good for idle people-watching. Good value. **Rs.3000**, a/c **Rs.5000**

★ **Fort Bazaar Hotel** 26 Church St ☎077 363 8381, Ⓦteardrop-hotels.com; map p.142. This former merchant's house, dating from the seventeenth century, is one of the newer hotel renovations in the Fort, and the results are outstanding. The eighteen rooms are beautifully designed, cool and peaceful, and the library and garden are relaxing places to enjoy the afternoon. A pool and mini-cinema were under construction at the time of research. B&B **$310**

The Fort Printers 39 Pedlar St ☎091 224 7977, Ⓦthefortprinters.com; map p.142. An immaculately renovated old colonial mansion (formerly the town printers) is the centrepiece of this boutique hotel, which now spreads itself into an adjoining building (Church Street Wing) and a less atmospheric, more contemporary house across the road (Pedlar Street Wing). The huge rooms in the original building are still the best – whitewashed, with creaking teak floorboards, timber ceilings, brightly coloured fabrics and modern artworks. There's also a small pool and an excellent restaurant. B&B **$200**

Galle Fort Hotel 28 Church St ☎091 223 2870, Ⓦgalleforthotel.com; map p.142. Set in a spectacularly restored former gem merchant's mansion, this UNESCO Heritage Award-winning hotel is every bit as memorable as nearby *Amangalla*, and a third of the price. Accommodation is in a mix of elegant rooms and enormous suites, all individually designed, with tasteful neocolonial decor enlivened by quirky personal touches. There's also a restaurant, atmospheric veranda bar and pool. B&B **$310**

Mango House 3 Leyn Baan Cross St ☎091 224 7212, Ⓦmangohouse.lk; map p.142. Tucked down a little side street, this is one of Galle's standout B&Bs, with a handful of luxurious whitewashed a/c rooms (with TV, DVD player and safe; some also have gorgeous balconies/terraces), spacious fuschia-hued living areas, and a lovely courtyard garden scattered with hammocks, loungers and floor cushions. Service is friendly but unobtrusive, and breakfasts are excellent. Highly recommended. B&B **$107**

Pedlar 62 62 Pedlar St ☎077 318 2389, Ⓦpedlar62.com; map p.142. Decent lodgings bang in the middle of the Fort, with big and clean, white rooms with safety boxes and mini-fridges (and some with a/c). Great street views from the modest balcony café, where breakfast is served. B&B: **$75**, a/c **$90**

Pedlar's Inn Hostel 62B Lighthouse St ☎091 22 7443, Ⓦpedlarsinn.com; map p.142. A small, centrally located hostel, resplendent in blue and white, with two small fan-cooled dorms furnished with whitewashed antique four-poster beds (lockers, bedside lights, hot water), plus a couple of a/c en-suite doubles. On the ground floor is a compact kitchen with free tea on offer and a small lounge with satellite TV. Towels and blankets cost $1. Dorms **Rs.1500**, doubles **Rs.6100**

Rampart View 37 Rampart St ☎091 492 8787, Ⓦgalleforttrampartview.com; map p.142. Modern house right by the ramparts with four neat tiled rooms (including more expensive sea- and sunset-view rooms with optional a/c, hot water and a nice little breezy veranda, plus a grassy rooftop terrace with great views over Flag Rock. **Rs.4000**, a/c **Rs.5000**

Seagreen Guesthouse 19b Rampart St ☎091 22 2754, Ⓦseagreen-guesthouse.com; map p.14. Personable little guesthouse in a newish building overlooking the grassy parkland verging the western ramparts. The five comfortable a/c rooms come with cement furnishings and colourful Indian fabrics, while the more expensive have lovely sea views. There's home-cooked food to order and a neat little roof terrace too. **$4**

Weltevreden 104 Pedlar St ☎091 222 2650, ✉piyasena88@yahoo.com; map p.142. Welcoming and peaceful family-run place set in an attractive Dutch house arranged around a neat, flower-filled courtyard garden. Rooms (the cheapest share bathrooms) have seen better days but are fairly priced, and there's tasty home-cooking available. **Rs.2500**

OUTSIDE THE FORT

Closenburg Hotel Megalle ☎091 222 4313, ✉closenburghotel.com; map p.142. Occupying a rambling nineteenth-century villa tucked away on a bay 2km east of Galle, this handsome old colonial-style hotel has modern a/c rooms with sea-facing balconies plus a few atmospheric and old-fashioned "colonial suites" (non-a/c) complete with chunky teak furniture, as well as the attached *Luna Terrace bar* (see page 151). Good value. **$150**

The Dutch House (aka Doornberg) 23 Upper Dickson Rd ☎091 438 0275, ✉thedutchhouse.com; map p.142. Opposite *The Sun House* and under the same management, this meticulously restored Dutch villa of 1712 has four huge suites complete with reproduction antique furniture, plus a cosy book-stuffed lounge, an immaculately manicured garden with croquet hoops and a gorgeous L-shaped infinity pool. B&B **$350**

Jetwing Kurulubedda Dadella ☎091 222 3744, ✉jetwinghotels.com; map p.142. Reached via a short but atmospheric boat ride through the mangroves from *Jetwing Lighthouse*, this magical hideaway feels out in the wilds – though you're just on the edge of the city. Accommodation is in a pair of luxurious private eco-lodges, stylishly designed in dark wood and featuring lap-style

plunge pools and open terraces enveloped by the tree canopy. Another two (near-identical) lodges were under construction at the time of writing. B&B **$315**

Jetwing Lighthouse Dadella ☎091 222 3744, ✉jetwinghotels.com; map p.142. On the main road 2km west of town, this stylish Geoffrey Bawa-designed hotel is perched on a rather wild stretch of coast in an elegantly understated, slightly Tuscan-looking ochre building. The 85 rooms are masterpieces of interior design, complete with all mod cons, and there are plenty of facilities, including two pools, a gym and an attractive spa. Good food, too (see page 150). B&B **$295**

★ **Kikili House** Lower Dickson Rd ☎091 223 4181, ✉kikilihouse.com; map p.142. Superb B&B just north of the centre with five comfortable a/c bedrooms, a sociable lounge, roof terrace and a lush garden. Husband and wife team Hen and Koki are extremely welcoming and always happy to organize local activities and tours. Breakfasts are delicious, and the in-house cook can rustle up fabulous lunches and dinners (think fish pie, pasta, salads, quiches and curries) on demand. A top choice for single female travellers, too. B&B **$125**

★ **The Sun House** 18 Upper Dickson Rd ☎091 438 0275, ✉thesunhouse.com; map p.142. One of Sri Lanka's most magical places to stay, in a restored 1860s planter's villa perched on a hillside and offering memorable views across a sea of palm trees. Rooms are lovingly furnished and brimful of character (albeit a couple are rather small); best is the Cinnamon Suite, occupying the whole first floor of the main house (no a/c). There's also marvellous food (see page 150) and a small pool set in an enchanting, frangipani-studded garden. B&B **$200**

EATING

The ongoing gentrification of the Fort has given Galle a long-overdue injection of culinary sophistication, and there's now a good range of **restaurants**. For those on a budget, most of the Fort's guesthouses dish up good local cooking, as do the growing number of homespun **cafés**, which usually offer lunchtime rice and curry as well as western light meals and snacks. The newly renovated **Galle Dutch Hospital** complex on Hospital St (see page 145) offers a range of cuisines all under one atmospheric roof.

CAFÉS

Crepe-ology Carrousel de Galle, 53 Leyn Baan St ☎091 223 4777, ✉crepe-ology.lk; map p.142. Welcoming first-floor café overlooking the Fort rooftops. The small open kitchen dishes out a consistently good all-day menu of savoury crepes and *rotty* wraps, served with salad and herbed potatoes or chips. The sweet crepes, such as "The Wimbledon" (strawberries and cream), are delicious. Also famed for its icy fruit chillers, good coffee and a relaxed vibe. Mains Rs.600–950. Daily 9am–10pm.

Elita 72 Hospital St ☎077 242 3442; map p.142. Deservedly popular café near the lighthouse where you can either sit beneath umbrellas beside the street or take in the sea views from the ochre-walled fan-cooled dining room upstairs. Serves well-priced Sri Lankan curries, (local) steaks, salads and fried rice (mains Rs.700–1100). Daily 8am–10pm.

Indian Hut 54 Rampart St ☎091 222 7442; map p.142. Inexpensive, no-frills Indian café occupying a breezy upstairs terrace overlooking the ramparts and sea. Serves up a decent range of Indian, Pakistani and Chinese dishes including tandoori kebabs and breads in the evenings from 6pm. Unlicensed. Daily 11am–10pm.

★ **The Old Railway Café** 42 Havelock Place ✉theoldrailwayshop.com; map p.142. Little café on the first floor of British designer Catherine Rawson's brilliant clothing boutique. Squashy sofas and vintage tables set the scene and the delectable menu features fish, seafood, sandwiches, hearty salads, good coffee, English breakfasts and an unbeatable millionaire's shortbread.

2

Mains Rs.700–900. Also a handy place to organize good budget tours (see page 147). Mon–Sat 9am–5.30pm.

Pedlar's Inn Café 92 Pedlar St ☎091 222 5333, ⓦwww.pedlarsinn.com; map p.142. Attractive little café in an old Dutch villa, with seating either on the streetside veranda or in the small courtyard within. The menu features assorted Western breakfasts, sandwiches, salads, snacks and good coffee, plus pasta and other international mains (Rs.650–980). They also sell multiple flavours of authentic Italian ice cream at the *Pedlar's Inn Gelato* (daily 10am–10pm) across the road. Mon–Thurs, Sat & Sun 9am–9.30pm, Fri 9am–noon & 1.30pm–9.30pm.

★ **Poonie's Kitchen** 63 Pedlar St ☎091 224 4030, ⓦon.fb.me/1bzZimU; map p.142. Convivial sun-dappled courtyard café with a wholesome menu of weekly changing dishes prepared from seasonal local organic produce. Standouts include the home-made breakfast granola, soups served with crisp handmade flatbreads, a health-boosting salad thali, imaginative mixes of juices and a deliciously moist carrot cake. Mains Rs.650–1200. Daily 10am–5.30pm.

Royal Dutch Café 72 Leyn Baan St ☎077 177 4949; map p.142. This tiny, quaint veranda café has an unusual hand-drawn menu touting quirky creations like chocolate and coconut sandwiches and flavoured coffees and teas – including the house speciality ginger tea – along with more substantial burianis and rice and curry (Rs.400–900). Owner Fazal is a fount of information about the Fort. Daily 8.30am–9pm.

RESTAURANTS

★ **Amangalla** 10 Church St ☎091 223 3388, ⓦamanresorts.com; map p.142. Even if you can't afford to stay here – and you probably can't (see page 147) – this superb landmark hotel is worth visiting for a meal to lap up something of its dreamy atmosphere. Light lunches go for around $12–15, or come for afternoon tea ($10–20) on the veranda or an evening meal of finely prepared Sri Lankan or international cuisine, including delicious rice and curry (mains $20–45). Daily 7am–10pm.

Chambers 40 Church St ☎091 224 4320, ⓦbit.ly/2H75tQP; map p.142. Originally the law chambers of the owner's grandfather, this restaurant serves delicious but pricey Mediterranean and Middle Eastern dishes, including hot and cold mezzes (Rs.610–1100), shish kebabs (Rs.1570) and an excellent chicken and olive tagine (Rs.1170). Daily 11am–10pm.

DRINKING

Several of the town's hotels make an atmospheric venue for a **sunset drink**, while it's easy enough to head out to Unawatuna, Dalawela or Thalpe for an evening's lounging by the beach; a tuktuk should cost around Rs.500 to Unawatuna (up to Rs.700 for Thalpe)

Fortaleza 9 Church Cross St ☎091 223 341 ⓦfortaleza.lk; map p.142. The coral-walled courtyard restaurant at this bijou boutique hotel is one of the Fort most atmospheric dining spots, serving up an all-day Asia and Western menu including table barbecues, Singapore style burgers and grilled day-fresh fish (mains $7–15 Daily 9am–10pm.

The Fort Printers 39 Pedlar St ☎091 224 797 ⓦthefortprinters.com; map p.142. Eat either in th atmospheric high-ceilinged dining room or romanti courtyard garden of the neat little restaurant of th boutique hotel (see page 148), which serves up a goo range of international dishes with Mediterranean Moroccan influences (mains around Rs.1200 at lunc or Rs.1500–2000 at dinner). Daily noon–3pm & 6.30 10pm.

Jetwing Lighthouse Dadella, 2km west of Gal ☎091 222 3744, ⓦjetwinghotels.com; map p.14 This landmark hotel provides a five-star setting for som excellent Sri Lankan and international cuisine, either in th stylish *Cinnamon Room* restaurant (mains around $10–1 or the less formal *Cardamom Café*, famed for its Saturd night buffet. Cinnamon Room daily 7.30am–9p Cardamom Café daily 24hr.

A Minute by Tuk Tuk First Floor, Galle Dutch Hospita Hospital St ☎091 494 5000, ⓦon.fb.me/1HQtK map p.142. This little restaurant has a fine location rig above the rampart walls – although the east–west fusi dishes satisfy, it's the superb sea views that are the ma attraction. Daily 10am–10pm.

★ **The Sun House** 18 Upper Dickson Rd ☎0 438 0275, ⓦthesunhouse.com; map p.142. Th candlelit garden veranda of this colonial villa provides incomparably romantic setting for daily-changing thre course set meals (around $35), featuring fabulous Lankan cuisine with Indian, Malay, Dutch and Portugue influences. Book by 4pm for dinner. Daily 7–10pm.

The Tuna & the Crab Ground Floor, Galle Dut Hospital, Hospital St ☎091 309 7497; map p.142. Th fine independent restaurant on the ground floor of t Galle Dutch Hospital's eastern wing is one of the comple best. A mash up of its sister-restaurants in Colomb *Ministry of Crab* (see page 89) and *Nihonbashi*, it serv export-quality crab dishes, sushi, sashimi and stea (Rs.1000–2500) in minimalist a/c surroundings. Da noon–10pm.

each way, and (in Unawatuna at least) there are plen hanging around for the return trip until quite late night.

Dick's Bar The Sun House, 18 Upper Dickson Rd ☎0 438 0275, ⓦthesunhouse.com; map p.142. Th intimate and sociable lounge-style bar is stocked with a good range of international beers, single malts and an impressive array of (pricey) cocktails. Daily 10am–11pm.

Fort Dew cnr Rampart and Parawa streets ☎091 222 4365, ⓦfortdew.com; map p.142. The second-floor café-bar of this guesthouse overlooks the western ramparts and ocean, and is lovely for a quiet sunset beer. Service is friendly and there's food too. Daily 8am–11pm.

Harbour Bar Lady Hill Hotel, 29 Upper Dickson Rd ☎091 224 4322, ⓦladyhillsl.com; map p.142. It's well worth the climb up to this hilltop hotel bar before dark, to take in marvellous views on one side out over the red-tiled roofs of the Fort and, on the other, across miles of palm trees stretching away inland to the hill country. Wine, beer and soft drinks only. Daily noon–11pm.

Luna Terrace Closenberg Hotel, Megalle ⓦfacebook. com/lunaterrace; map p.142. This contemporary-styled, often-lively lounge bar is a complete contrast to the rest of the unwaveringly colonial *Closenberg Hotel*, and features a gorgeous infinity pool, tapas menu and sushi bar. Often hosts events and occasional all-night parties featuring local and international DJs. Daily 3pm–midnight.

SHOPPING

Galle, and in particular the Fort, is now firmly established as one of Sri Lanka's **best shopping destinations** outside of Colombo and is home to a diverse array of funky little boutiques and galleries, including over fifty jewellers, with a handful of more upmarket offerings (and posher jewellers) in the Galle Dutch Hospital.

Barefoot 41 Pedlar St ☎091 222 6299, ⓦbarefootceylon.com; map p.142. Galle outpost of the famous Colombo shop, stocking the same distinctive range of clothing, fabrics, stationery, toys and books. Mon–Sat 10am–7pm, Sun 11am–5pm.

Dutch Wall Arcade 54 Rampart St ☎ 091 222 7042, ⓦdutchwallarcade.com; map p.142. This rampart-side old Dutch warehouse houses a fascinating collection of colonial-era bric-a-brac – anything from old phones and cutlery through to religious artefacts and grandfather clocks – picked up from local houses and laid out in glass cabinets. Daily 9am–7pm.

Exotic Roots 50a Lighthouse St ☎091 224 5454; map p.142. Stylish emporium showcasing the colourful paintings and quirky pottery of owner Catherine Hewapathirana and her daughters, with modern takes on traditional Sri Lankan subjects like elephants and stilt fishermen, as well as other crafts including jewellery and homeware, plus a whole floor of fashion. Daily 9.30am–5.30pm.

Laksana 30 Hospital St ☎091 438 1800; map p.142. Of Galle's many jewellers, this is perhaps the most reputable and reliable, crammed full of a wide range of stunning local gems – sapphires in various colours; dazzling quartz and amethysts; and semi-precious stones like moonstone and aquamarine. They also copy designs with a fairly quick turnaround. Daily 9am–6.30pm.

Mimimango 63 Pedlar St ☎091 222 6349, ⓦjoedenmimimango.com; map p.142. A gorgeous a/c boutique selling a beautiful selection of silky cotton cocktail dresses, kaftans, scarves, tops and trousers featuring delicate prints and hand-stitching, sourced in Bali and India, along with a few men's printed shirts, beaded bracelets and Bollywood-printed yoga bags. Daily 9.30am–6pm.

Shoba Display Gallery 67A Pedlar St ☎091 222 4351, ⓦwww.shobafashion.com; map p.142. Women's cooperative showcasing the skills of local lacemakers and other artisans. As well as individual lace pieces there are pretty cotton bags, hand-painted fabrics, patchwork embroidery and toys, and they also run workshops in lacemaking and courses in paper crafts and fabric painting. Daily 9.30am–7pm.

Sithuvili 56 Leyn Baan St & 1st floor, Galle Dutch Hospital ⓦfacebook.com/sithuviligallery; map p.142. Quality Sri Lankan art and crafts by Ambalangoda artist Janaka de Silva, including a good range of masks and well-executed reproductions of Kandyan-style temple paintings – along with a few genuine Kandyan and Jaffna antiques. Both branches daily 9am–6pm.

The Three by TPV 43 Leyn Baan St ⓦthestorebytpv. com/the-home; map p.142. Whitewashed, design-savvy interiors store selling a range of quirky homeware that you won't find anywhere else in Sri Lanka such as papier-mâché-dog lamps, climbing figurines and skull ashtrays. Also sells colourful costume jewellery and a selection of monotone ladies' cocktail attire. Daily 9am–9pm.

Vijitha Yapa 12 Wakwella Rd ☎091 222 4466, ⓦvijithayapa.com; map p.142. Galle branch of the national bookshop chain with a reasonable selection of English-language titles. Mon–Fri 8.30am–6pm.

DIRECTORY

Banks Banks in the new town have ATMs which accept foreign Visa and MasterCards. In the Fort, there are ATMs accepting foreign cards at the Bank of Ceylon on Middle St, and the Commercial Bank on Church St.

Hospital General Hospital, Karapitiya (5km north of Galle) ☎091 223 2267; Hemas Southern Hospital (private), Wakwella Rd ☎091 464 0640, ⓦhemashospitals.com.

2

Internet There are internet cafés in the centrally located Selaka building, opposite the bus station.

Pharmacies Crystal Pharmacy, opposite the Olcott statue, near Abans at the eastern end of Main St (Mon–Sat 8.30am–8pm, Sun 8.30am–1.30pm).

Police The tourist police have an office on Hospital St in the Fort (daily 24hr).

Spas The superb The Baths spa at *Amangalla* is open to non-guests, with steam rooms, saunas and gorgeous

hydrotherapy pools, as well as a full range of massages and treatments, plus Ayurveda rituals. The Galle Fort Spa (☎077 725 2502, ⌨gallefortspa.com) above Mimimango on Pedlar St offers beauty treats and massages at a more affordable price.

Supermarket There's a Cargills supermarket in the P&J City Building in the new town immediately north of the bus station, and a branch of Keells Super along the Galle Rd, around 300m west of the train station.

Inland from Galle

Most visitors to Galle stick to the town and surrounding beaches, although there are a handful of rewarding inland excursions if you fancy a change from the coast, all attesting to Galle's self-proclaimed status as "Rainforest Capital of Sri Lanka". Be aware that leeches can be ferocious in these rainforests during the wet season, and during periods of rainy weather, so bring appropriate gear.

Kottawa Rainforest and Arboretum

Daily 8am–5pm • Rs.700 • Buses run every 15min from Galle to Udugama (30min to Kottawa); the ticket office is located just off the road, down a lane, near the 14km post

Around 17km from the city along the road to Udugama, the compact **Kottawa Rainforest and Arboretum** provides an easily accessible introduction to the Sri Lankan rainforest, with a wide 1km walking trail shaded by giant dipterocarps

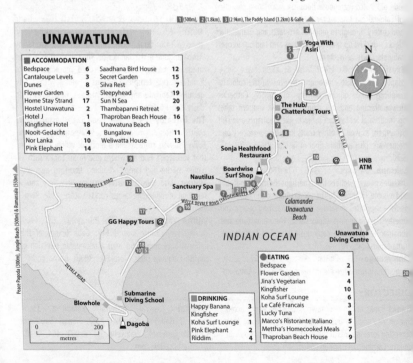

owering up to 45m high. Resident mammals include purple-faced leaf monkeys and giant squirrels, plus rather more shy muntjac and sambur, and there's an impressive array of colourful endemic birds and (rather less polychromatic) reptiles.

Kanneliya Forest Reserve

Daily 8am–5pm • Rs.500 entry; Rs.880 compulsory guide • Rainforest Rescue International (☏ 091 224 6528, Ⓦ rainforestrescuesrilanka.org) offer tours from Galle, including guided trek, park entry, transfers and (optional) lunch for Rs.3000 per person

Kanneliya Forest Reserve, 6km beyond Udugama, is part of the Kanneliya–Dediyagama–Nakiyadeniya (KDN) biosphere reserve and shares similar characteristics with nearby Sinharaja, including its fair share of endemic species. The reserve is a catchment area for the Gin and Nilwala gangas, two of the south coast's primary rivers. Rainforest Rescue International's tours include a two-hour guided hike to a waterfall beneath giant dipterocarps.

Unawatuna

Five kilometres southeast of Galle, the ever-expanding village of **UNAWATUNA** is now firmly established as Sri Lanka's most popular resort for independent travellers and remains a pleasant spot to while away a few days, even if rampant commercialization and ever-growing hordes of visitors have now significantly eroded its former sleepy charm. If you don't mind the increasing hustle and bustle – or the handful of noisy beach discos held a few times each week – there's still plenty to enjoy, including a decent, if heavily developed, stretch of beach, a good selection of places to stay and eat, plus varied activities ranging from surfing and diving through to yoga and cookery classes. The resort remains busy all year round, making it a good place to visit if you're on the west coast during the monsoon.

The beach

Unawatuna **beach** is small and intimate: a graceful, horseshoe-shaped curve of sand, not much more than a kilometre from start to finish, set snugly in a pretty semicircular bay and picturesquely terminated by a dagoba on the rocky headland to the northwest. The sheltered bay offers safe year-round swimming, and a group of rocks 150m offshore further breaks up waves (though it can still get a bit rough during the monsoon). Along its length, rows of sun loungers are laid out expectantly beneath coloured parasols inches from the lapping waves, demarcating the bay's many restaurants, bars and guesthouses.

Over the last decade Unawatuna's famed sands have waxed and waned due to the tsunami, coastal erosion and years of unchecked development. In 2015, heavy machinery was brought in to pump sand from the deep sea onto the eastern half of the bay, widening the denuded beach almost overnight by as much as 15m in some places, although its coarse copper colour is a far cry from the beach's original soft white sands.

At the western end of the beach, a road and a footpath lead up to a small **dagoba** and Buddha statue perched on the rocks above the bay, offering fine views over Unawatuna and great sunset panoramas west to Galle. In the rocks just west of here is a little blowhole, which sporadically comes alive during the monsoon season; steps lead up to it from the *The Blowhole* restaurant.

2

Rumassala

Unawatuna's most striking natural feature is **Rumassala**, an incongruously grand outcrop of rock whose sides rise up green and lush behind the village; it's popularly claimed to be a fragment of the chunk of mountain carried from the Himalayas by the monkey god **Hanuman**. As recounted in the Ramayana, Hanuman was sent by Rama to collect a special herb from the Himalayas which was needed to save the life of Rama's wounded brother, Lakshmana. Arriving in the Himalayas, the absent-minded Hanuman realized he had forgotten the name of the required plant, so ripped up an entire chunk of mountainside in the hope that the necessary plant would be found somewhere on it. He then carried this fragment of mountain back to Sri Lanka, dropping a bit in Ritigala, in the north of the island, and another piece at Unawatuna. The rock still sports a large collection of medicinal herbs as well as entertaining troupes of boisterous macaque monkeys, Hanuman's latter-day relatives, who periodically descend the hill to raid the villagers' papaya trees.

The peace pagoda

The peace pagoda is a 15min drive across Rumassala from Unawatuna (Rs.350 in a tuktuk), though it's much more easily (and prosaically) accessed from the Matara Rd – there's a turning at the 120km post just opposite the cement factory

Around the headland from Unawatuna, high up on the Rumassala hillside, is a gleaming white **peace pagoda** – actually a colossal dagoba – constructed by Japanese Buddhists in 2004. The views from here, particularly at sunset, are magical, with the mosque and clocktower of Galle Fort clearly visible in the distance to the west and, to the east, the carpet of thick jungle that separates the pagoda from Unawatuna.

Jungle Beach

To the north of the Rumassala headland lies a pair of secluded sandy coves, separated by a rocky bluff and collectively known as **Jungle Beach**. Backed by a steep slope of dense jungle, the inviting turquoise sea and golden shoreline here make this a quieter alternative to Unawatuna, although its growing popularity means that it isn't quite the escapist paradise it once was. Most come to Jungle Beach to snorkel (best around the headland facing Galle), although hardly any live coral survives; you're likely to see some colourful fish and perhaps a turtle. Getting to Jungle Beach is half the fun, particularly if you decide to hike the 3km (well-signposted) pathway on foot from Unawatuna through the hilltop village of Rumassala. Alternatively, take a tuktuk to the peace pagoda and follow the steps down to the beach from there. Each bay has its own restaurant, and discos are currently held on Wednesday nights on the (more intimate) eastern beach.

ARRIVAL AND DEPARTURE

By bus Unawatuna is hidden away off the coastal Matara Rd some 5km east of Galle. Take any bus heading east from Galle and ask to be dropped at the turn-off for the village, Wella Devale Rd (also known as Yaddehimulla Rd and Beach Access Rd), which runs from the Matara Rd for 500m down to the beach (no buses actually go into the village itself). The village isn't signposted and is easy to miss – make sure the conductor knows where you're getting off (if you're coming from Galle the turning is just after the

prominently signposted *Nooit-Gedacht*, on the right-hand side of the road). Heading east from Unawatuna, you should be able to flag down a bus to Weligama, Mirissa or Matara along the main Matara Rd. If you're heading west from Unawatuna, it's easiest to take a tuktuk to Galle and pick up a bus or train there.

By tuktuk A tuktuk to or from Galle costs around Rs.400. Tuktuks to Weligama/Mirissa shouldn't cost more than Rs.1000.

ACCOMMODATION

There are heaps of places to stay in Unawatuna, though the resort's ongoing popularity and increasing gentrification has pushed up prices. Note that parts of the beach can be

noisy well into the small hours during high season (Nov to mid-April) if there's a late-night disco going on, and you'll pay over the odds for a beachfront location; the best value accommodation is away from the water. **Seasonal variations** and fluctuations in demand keep prices fluid – outside high season rates fall by up to thirty percent in many places, though at any time of year it's worth bargaining if trade is quiet.

★ **Bedspace** Egodawatta Lane ☎091 225 0156, ⓦbedspaceuna.com; map p.152. New guesthouse with a fabulous restaurant (see page 156) set back from the beach, and close to the highway, though it's mercifully peaceful. There's a mix of clean and comfortable standard, deluxe and family rooms (all a/c), some with balconies. B&B $70

Cantaloupe Levels 500m off the coastal highway at the junction just east of the Holcim cement factory ☎091 751 0570, ⓦcantaloupevillas.com; map p.152. Superbly located boutique hotel perched on the west-facing Rumassala headland with panoramic views across the wide bay to Galle, and just a 10min walk from Jungle Beach. True to its name, the hotel is set across a series of levels with nine stylish rooms (including two suites with ooh-la-la views), a tri-coloured swimming pool edged by lounge beds and lawn terraces for dining plus a magnificent rooftop for sunset gazing. Also has a great fusion menu offering sous-vide steaks and a few Japanese dishes. Doubles $280, suites $445

★ **Dunes** 65b Wella Devale Rd ☎077 742 3636, ⓦfacebook.com/dunesuna; map p.152. This rustic, timbered boutique hotel is just a 2min walk to the beach although its setting, beside a pond shaded by a huge *mara* tree, attracts plenty of wildlife and feels more like a national park than a seaside resort. Rooms (fan only) are small but cosy and atmospheric, with wood floors, good mattresses and hot water, and there's also a two-bedroom cottage in the hammock-strung garden. $50

Flower Garden 14 Wella Devale Rd ☎091 222 5286, ⓦhotelflowergardensrilanka.com; map p.152. Idyllic (if rather pricey) little hideaway set in an abundant flower-filled garden with accommodation divided between simple rooms and neat little chalets (all with hot water and a/c). There's also a decent-sized pool and good European cuisine. Doubles $78, chalets $90

Home Stay Strand 218 Yaddehimulla Rd ☎091 222 4358, ⓦhomestay-strand.net; map p.152. Welcoming guesthouse occupying an attractive 1920s colonial-style house and surrounding modern buildings, all set within a tranquil garden – very peaceful, despite its proximity to the village centre. Rooms come in various styles, sizes and standards (some with hot water, one with a/c); better ones, such as "The Nest" on the first floor, boast attractive period touches. Rs.4000, a/c Rs.7000

Hostel Unawatuna Maharamba Rd, around 1.5km from Unawatuna beach ☎077 468 8699; map p.152. Small, clean and very sociable hostel. The two dorms (no bunks) share a bathroom and open onto a lounge, and

there's an ample kitchen plus tropical garden with paddling pool and hammocks. Sri Lankan breakfast included. To reach it head back towards Galle and it's the first (inland) road on the right (around 300m). Dorms $1500

★ **Hotel J** 165 Matara Road ☎031 223 2999, ⓦhotelj.lk; map p.152. Stylish new budget hotel set behind a lovely old manor house with pool. It's great value for money, with easy access to the beach at Una as well as Galle. All rooms are a/c with flatscreen TVs, comfortable beds and plenty of sockets for recharging. The compact dorm rooms are well designed for maximum privacy and safety, and the converted attic dorm room in the old house sleeps six and is perfect for family groups. The excellent in-house restaurant serves a hearty breakfast. Dorms $12, doubles $50

Kingfisher Hotel Devale Rd ☎091 225 0312, ⓦkingfisherunawatuna.com; map p.152. Unawatuna's leading seafront restaurant, *Kingfisher*, transformed into a modern boutique hotel in 2012 and now offers just four neat and spacious (if rather minimalist) sea-facing rooms (a/c, balconies, TVs and minibars). The restaurant below is flanked by a popular timber bar. $120

Nooit-Gedacht 182 Matara Rd ☎091 222 3449, ⓦnooitgedachtheritage.com; map p.152. Set in spacious gardens with two pools around a delectable colonial mansion of 1735, this long-running Ayurveda resort has bags of character and a wide range of rooms (all with a/c and hot water), from rather uninspiring budget rooms to smart modern accommodation furnished in colonial style in the new wing. The Ayurveda centre here is one of the best on the south coast; a one-week course costs around $1050, inclusive of accommodation, meals and all treatments. B&B: $48, new wing $85

Nor Lanka Peellagoda ☎091 222 6194, ⓦnorlanka.com; map p.152. Set in peaceful gardens a couple of minutes from the beach, this attractive and very professionally run Norwegian/Sri Lankan-owned guesthouse has spacious and attractively furnished rooms, all with fridge, hot water and optional a/c ($10 extra). B&B $65

Pink Elephant Wella Devale Rd ☎072 770 9793, ✉unapinkelephant@gmail.com; map p.152. Set above a lively restaurant-bar, *Pink Elephant*'s no-frills fan-cooled dorm (with small bathroom) is the cheapest place to stay in Unawatuna and great for young sociable types looking to party. Also has a couple of double rooms (with optional a/c for Rs.500 more). Dorm Rs.1000, doubles Rs.3000

Saadhana Bird House Yaddehimulla Rd ☎091 222 4953, ⓦbirdhouse.8k.com; map p.152. Low-key little family homestay surrounded by trees and twittering birds with a small selection of neat, competitively priced fan and a/c rooms of various sizes and standards (some with hot water), including one on the top floor with a nice little balcony. Rs.4000, a/c Rs.5500

2

2

★ **Secret Garden** Wella Devale Rd ☎ 091 224 1857, Ⓦ secretgardenunawatuna.com; map p.152. Exactly as the name suggests, with a tiny door leading into a wonderful concealed walled garden full of trees, birds and the occasional monkey. Accommodation is either in the old colonial villa (all beautifully furnished in period style, with outdoor bathrooms) or in less characterful cottages. There's also a pretty yoga dome (with classes at 9am & 5pm), plus Ayurveda treatments. Cottages $62, villa $82

Silva Rest 55 Wella Devale Rd ☎ 091 222 4933; map p.152. Welcoming and long-standing guesthouse with a range of good-value (and recently refurbished) single and double rooms (some with a/c and hot water) next to the family house. There are also a few newer rooms in a block across the road, plus a two-bedroom apartment. Rs.3500, a/c Rs.4000

Sleepyhead Next to Black Beauty Guesthouse, 200m inland from Sun N Sea ☎ 077 621 6120, Ⓔ sleepyheadunawatuna@gmail.com; map p.152. Two clean and simple rooms finished in smooth polished cement in the two-storey annexe of a family house, plus an upper-floor apartment under construction. The friendly owners offer Sri Lankan cookery classes and can help with onward travel and tours. Rs.3000

Sun N Sea 324 Matara Rd ☎ 091 228 3200, Ⓦ sunnsea.net; map p.152. This small two-storey hotel at the far eastern end of the bay is a favourite with repeat visitors; the eight sea-facing a/c rooms exhibit plenty of polished cement and are clean and unfussy (those upstairs are more private). There's a decent restaurant, which dishes out wood-fired pizzas from 6pm, and the sunsets from this vantage point are hard to beat. The only downside is its close proximity to the noisy main road. $65

★ **Thambapanni Retreat** Yaddehimulla Rd ☎ 091 223 4588, Ⓦ thambapannileisure.com; map p.152. Inviting hotel tucked away in thick jungle at the foot of Rumassala – more rainforest retreat than beachside resort. Accommodation (all with a/c, minibar and satellite TV) ranges from the comfortable but relatively humdrum standard rooms through to more characterful deluxe and superior categories. There's also a small swimming pool, Ayurveda treatments and yoga classes. B&B: standard $85, deluxe $115

Thaproban Beach House Devale Rd ☎ 091 438 1722, Ⓦ thambapannileisure.com; map p.152. Much-loved Unawatuna landmark, right on the beach in the middle of the village. The attractive rooms (all with a/c, minibar and satellite TV) come in various sizes, styles and prices. The cheapest lack sea views; the smarter ones, elegantly furnished in light wood and bamboo, add a touch of boutique style. There's also an excellent restaurant (see page 157). B&B $75

Unawatuna Beach Bungalow Peellagoda ☎ 091 222 4327, Ⓦ unawatunabeachbungalow.com; map p.152. Very pleasant small guesthouse with spotless and very comfortable tiled rooms (a/c and hot water) just a few steps from the beach. $55

Weliwatta House Yaddehimulla Rd ☎ 091 222 6642; map p.152. Friendly family guesthouse with a handful of basic but clean rooms in a gorgeous 115-year-old *walauwa* plus a/c rooms (most with hot water) in a quieter, newer and slightly pricier two-floor block (with balconies) at the end of the garden. Rs.4000, a/c Rs.4500

EATING

Unawatuna is easily the best of the south coast resorts for food, with dozens of inviting **restaurants** lining the beachfront and Wella Devale Rd – the seafood is predictably good.

★ **Bedpace Kitchen** Egodawatta Lane ☎ 091 225 0156, Ⓦ bedspaceuna.com; map p.152. In the leafy garden of the eponymous guest house, with tables set around a busy open kitchen run by an international/ Sri Lankan crew, who use local ingredients and serve up some of the best fusion cuisine on the south coast (mains Rs.1250–1800). Advance booking recommended. Daily 12pm–3.30pm & 6–10pm.

Flower Garden 14 Wella Devale Rd ☎ 091 222 5286, Ⓦ hotelflowergardenunawatuna.com; map p.152. Attractive open-sided restaurant, serving an excellent range of beef steaks, plus pasta and fish, with an extensive wine list. Meals Rs.900–1500 – the price of a main course also includes a starter and a dessert. Daily 7am–10pm.

Jina's Vegetarian Wella Devale Rd ☎ 091 222 6878; map p.152. Long-standing vegetarian café occupying the convivial veranda of an antiquated village house and offering a daily-changing selection of Western dishes and Sri Lankan rice and curry (most mains Rs.695–795), as well as a few standout Indian dishes (thali, dosas and puri). Daily 8am–8pm.

★ **Kingfisher** Devale Rd ☎ 091 225 0301, Ⓦ kingfisherunawatuna.com; map p.152. One of Unawatuna's standout dining options, with candlelit tables on the beach, a chilled vibe and a consistently good menu of pasta, wraps, burgers, grilled seafood – including fresh lobster from the tank – Thai curries, imported Aussie steak and a few in-house specials such as spicy ginger prawns. Mains Rs.800–1400. The adjacent bar serves wines, tropical cocktails and beer. Advance booking recommended. Daily 8am–10.30pm.

Koha Surf Lounge Wella Devale Rd ☎ 077 896 6042, Ⓦ facebook.com/KohaSurfLounge; map p.152. Run by local surfers, and attached to the Boardwise Surf Shop, Koha is a chilled lounge café (and bar) serving tasty wraps, burgers and kebabs to tables scattered along a narrow passageway lined with tropical plants. The floor cushions out front are perfect for people-watching. Mains Rs.650–900. Daily 11am–midnight.

Le Café Francais Wella Devale Rd ✆077 740 1014, 🌐on.fb.me/1JNLRuS; map p.152. Occupying a round pavilion on stilts, this pleasant patisserie dishes up the region's best butter croissants, pains au chocolat, cinnamon rolls, cakes and other French fancies, alongside proper coffee and tea. Doubles up as a boutique, and sells a range of Indian textiles. Daily 8am–7pm.

Lucky Tuna Wella Devale Rd ✆091 225 0288, 🌐luckytunaresort.com; map p.152. This Unawatuna stalwart takes full advantage of the bay's newly replenished beach. The menu (mains Rs.800–1200) is predictable yet good, and the day's catch is displayed every evening and cooked on an outdoor grill. The lively bar stays open late and is a popular place to warm up before Happy Banana's Friday night disco. Also has four very decent boutique-style rooms. Daily 9am–midnight.

Marco's Ristorante Italiano Off Wella Devale Rd ✆077 370 7659, 🌐on.fb.me/1bzqdz8; map p.152.

Small Italian bistro, hidden 200m down a lane behind the Gloria Grand hotel (take a torch as the lane's unlit), with a short menu featuring good if pricier-than-average pizzas (around Rs.1200), pasta, a particularly good sausage-and-mushroom risotto and grilled meats. Mains Rs.800–1600. Daily 5.30–10.30pm.

Mettha's Homecooked Meals Wella Devale Rd ✆077 501 6678; map p.152. The daily-changing rice and curry meals (Rs.600) are the hero of this streetside café, served up on the front porch and in the living room of the owners' home. Daily 11am–9pm.

Thaproban Beach House Devale Rd ✆091 438 1722, 🌐thambapannileisure.com; map p.152. Reliable restaurant with above-average cooking, smooth decor and welcoming service. The reasonably priced menu (mains Rs.700–1200) focuses on seafood, with offerings fresh from the day's catch, plus Sri Lankan classics and a few international offerings ranging from pasta to chicken korma and lamb chops – and the pizzas aren't bad either. Dine either in the attractive dining room or on the beach. Daily 7.30am–10.30pm.

DRINKING

Unawatuna's beach bars mainly cater to a youthful party scene, but there are also some quieter spots for a **drink**. A number of places, including Happy Banana and Riddim, also host regular **discos** in season; if you're interested, ask around when you arrive.

Happy Banana ✆091 225 0252, 🌐happy-banana.com; map p.152. Lively and perennially popular beachfront bar, particularly on Fridays when it hosts a noisy disco (foreigners and women walk in free, otherwise men pay an exorbitant Rs.2000). Daily 11am–late.

Kingfisher Devale Rd ✆091 225 0301, 🌐kingfisherunawatuna.com; map p.152. The beach bar attached to this excellent restaurant is a pleasant place for a quiet drink. It's more expensive than other Una establishments, but there's a reliable cocktail menu and several local beers to choose from (though they're not always in stock). Daily 8am–10.30pm.

Koha Surf Lounge Wella Devale Rd ✆077 896 6042, 🌐facebook.com/KohaSurfLounge; map p.152. Relaxing lounge bar with a great music selection and friendly atmosphere. Get comfortable on a floor cushion and enjoy a tropical-fruit themed cocktail. Daily 11am–midnight.

Pink Elephant Wella Devale Rd ✆072 770 9793, 📧unapinkelephant@gmail.com; map p.152. This lively restaurant and bar attracts a young party crowd, and its enthusiastic staff help keep energy levels up. Daily 6pm–late.

Riddim Next to Unawatuna Diving Centre ✆091 225 0252, 🌐on.fb.me/1KpA7PX; map p.152. Protruding out onto the newly replenished beach at the eastern end of the bay, this timber-and-cement bar hosts regular discos in season as well as impromptu live music evenings (usually followed by an in-house DJ) with expat rock band The Butchers. Good for sunset drinks. Daily 11am–late.

DIRECTORY

Ayurveda and spas Expert Ayurveda treatments are available at the Nooit-Gedacht Ayurveda resort. Another possibility is the excellent Sanctuary Spa, 136 Wella Devale Rd (✆077 307 8583, 🌐sanctuaryspaunawatuna.com; book in advance), tucked away in a pretty garden behind Mettha's, with well-priced Ayurveda, plus spa, reflexology and aromatherapy treatments.

Banks The nearest banks are in Galle, although there is an HNB ATM on the Matara Rd, opposite the turning to Nor Lanka and Unawatuna Beach Bungalow, and a Commercial Bank ATM near the cement factory, towards Galle.

Cookery courses A few places around the village now run half-day cookery classes, usually including a visit to a local market to purchase ingredients. The best are the Sonja Healthfood Restaurant (Rs.3000; ✆077 961 5310) and Nautilus restaurant (Rs.3000/Rs.2500 with/without market visit; ✆077 911 0090). For something a little more upmarket, The Paddy Island (✆077 838 2384, 🌐thepaddyisland.com), an idyllic garden amid rice fields 2km inland from Unawatuna, also offers Sinhalese cooking classes as well as decadent English afternoon teas (which includes a buffalo cart ride to a nearby temple). You'll need to book a day in advance in all places.

2

2

DIVING, SNORKELLING AND SURFING AT UNAWATUNA

Unawatuna has a modest range of diving, snorkelling, surfing and other watersports on offer, with two particularly good diving schools: **Submarine Diving School** (☎077 719 6753, ⓦdivinginsrilanka.com), at the western end of the beach, and **Unawatuna Diving Centre** (☎091 224 4693, ⓦunawatunadiving.com; Oct–April only), on the Matara Road to the east of the bay (look for the blue dolphin). Both offer the usual range of PADI courses, plus single, introductory, wreck and deep dives (there are no fewer than eight wrecks in the vicinity, including an old wooden English ship, the *Rangoon*, lying at a depth of 30m). Diving is best between November and April.

You can **snorkel** off the beach at Unawatuna, although it's not wildly exciting; you might see a few colourful tropical fish, though there is virtually no live coral remaining. The best two snorkelling spots in the area are **Rock Island**, about 1km offshore, and around the headland facing Galle at **Jungle Beach** (see page 154). For the former you can hire a boat from the Submarine Dive School (Rs.3000 for two people for 90min, including snorkelling equipment), which can also be used to reach Jungle Beach (two people Rs.6000 for a 2–3hr trip); both dive operators listed above also offer snorkelling trips to Jungle Beach. Alternatively, Jungle Beach is reachable on foot from Unawatuna (a 45-min well-signposted walk) or you can take a tuktuk to the peace pagoda (Rs.350) and walk down to the beach from there. Submarine rent out expensive snorkelling equipment (Rs.250/hr or Rs.1000/day), as do many of the cheaper shacks on the beach nearby. Check all equipment carefully, as there are plenty of dud masks and snorkels in circulation.

A few locals **surf** at Unawatuna, though the waves aren't nearly as good as at nearby Hikkaduwa, Matara or Midigama. Boards can be rented at the **Boardwise Surf Shop** (daily 11am–9pm; ☎077 154 3063), opposite *Happy Banana* (Rs.400/hr or Rs.1500/day); they also carry out board repairs, offer surf lessons off the shallow beach at nearby Dewata (en route to Galle), below the *Closenberg Hotel*, and at Weligama, and organize local surf tours.

Tour operators At least half-a-dozen travel agents are dotted around the village, all offering general information about the area and assorted local and islandwide tours. Try the long-standing GG Happy Tours, right in the middle of the village (daily 8.30am–8pm; ☎091 223 2838, ⓦgghappytours.com) or the very friendly Chatterbox Tours (daily 9am–8pm; ☎077 793 4430, ⓦchatterboxtoursrilanka.com).

Yoga and meditation *Secret Garden* guesthouse runs daily yoga classes (9am and 5pm) as does *Thambapanni Retreat* (9am), and local instructor Asiri offers daily and private yoga classes (9.30am, plus 6pm Nov–March; ⓦyogawithasiri.com) near Flower Garden.

Dalawela and Thalpe

A few kilometres east of Unawatuna, the beautiful and unspoiled beaches at **DALAWELA** and **THALPE** are becoming increasingly popular with visitors turned off by Unawatuna's hustle and bustle. Dalawela is home to a handful of good mid-range guesthouses and hotels, while a succession of high walls on the ocean side of the Matara Road at Thalpe, 2km further on, conceals a raft of luxury beachfront villas belonging to (mostly) foreigners and available for rent; there are also a few small upmarket hotels.

Accommodation aside, there's very little to either village apart from stretches of beach (though you can only swim at a few of them due to rocks and undercurrents) and a few clusters of fishing stilts (see page 159) – perfect for Robinson Crusoe types who enjoy counting palm trees. The area is also hugely popular with Galle's expats, who flock here to some of the region's buzziest restaurants and beach hangouts.

ARRIVAL AND DEPARTURE

DALAWELA AND THALPE

By bus or tuktuk Buses running along the main coastal highway pass right by all the places listed below, although as most aren't prominently signposted it can be tricky knowing where to get off. It's easier to take a tuktuk from Unawatuna or Galle.

ACCOMMODATION

DALAWELA AND AROUND

EKA Beach 1.5km east of Unawatuna ☎ 077 273 9719, ☎ 091 454 5162, ⓦ ekabeach.com. Bijou boutique B&B with four tastefully furnished rooms of varying sizes, including an a/c master suite, a triple room and a tiny room with enviable ocean views and a private furnished timber deck. B&B: doubles $120, suite $160

Horizon Hilltop Villa 2km east of Unawatuna ☎ 091 225 0443, ⓦ thehorizonvilla.com. Perched on a hilltop just 500m inland from the main coastal road, this new hotel has five smart and spacious rooms, plus a top-floor penthouse, with a/c, hot water and (except for the cheaper "cave" room) fabulously big balconies with far-reaching views over the palm-studded countryside. There's also a pool and a restaurant (with sea views). B&B: doubles $75, penthouse $110

Pittaniya Villa 250m inland from Dalawela ☎ 077 675 707, ⓦ on.fb.me/1Fuavlh. Live out your expat fantasies at this modern, stylishly designed villa set in peaceful gardens with pool. The three rooms feature four-poster beds, sliding glass doors and en-suite modern bathrooms; some have outside showers and gardens. $98

Wijaya Beach 2.5km east of Unawatuna ☎ 077 790 431, ⓦ wijayabeach.com. The nicest place in Dalawela, with a friendly and laidback atmosphere. Rooms include smart, modern ones with a/c in the new wing closest to the road, and a couple more basic, tiled, fan-cooled options in the original building. There's a good beachfront restaurant (see below) and safe swimming thanks to a reef just offshore. *Wijaya Beach* is easy to miss: coming from the west, if you've reached the *Point de Galle* you've gone too far. Rs.8000, a/c Rs.12,000

THALPE

Frangipani Tree 3km past Unawatuna, at the 125km post ☎ 091 228 3711, ⓦ thefrangipanitree.com. Intimate boutique hotel arranged around a spectacular lap pool that extends the length of the immaculate frangipani-studded lawn. Rooms are stylish and minimalist, with built-in cement furniture and, in the garden rooms, outdoor bath tubs. There's also a sliver of sand, and turtles can sometimes be seen. B&B $225

★ **The Owl and the Pussycat** Mihiripenna Beach ☎ 091 228 3844, ⓦ otphotel.com. Exquisite boutique hotel conceptualised by a fervent Edward Lear poetry fan. The luxurious rooms, all individually decorated, look out onto a gorgeous pool and frangipani tree garden, whilst stilt fisherman work in the sea right in front. Fabulous meals are served in seaside *The Runcible Spoon* restaurant (open to outside guests with advance reservation). B&B $540

Why House 4km past Unawatuna, turn at the 124km post, ☎ 091 222 7599, ⓦ whyhousesrilanka. com. A wonderfully secluded boutique hotel set amid beautifully tended gardens complete with a good-size pool, and serving superb seasonally fresh cuisine by the owner in the dining pavilion (if you aren't staying here, you can still dine with an advance reservation). The chic, elegant rooms are based in the main house or small cottages. B&B $250

EATING

Talpe Beach Club 200m east of Why Beach, Thalpe ☎ 091 228 2647, ⓦ talpebeach.com. Well-run, family-friendly restaurant-bar overlooking pretty rock pools with tables sprinkled around an open courtyard with a lovely pool. The menu (mains Rs.900–1800) has an international slant, with fresh seafood, pasta and meat dishes. Grab a spot on the upper lounge for sunset. Tues–Sun 11am–11pm.

★ **Why Beach** Thalpe, 4km east of Unawatuna (there's no sign – look for the large letters "WB" on the entrance doors, set in a big white gateway) ☎ 091 228 2922, ⓦ whybeach.com. Overlooking a gorgeous stretch of beach, this personable Italian-owned restaurant is a fine place to chill either by day or after dark. Their Italian offerings are excellent, ranging from handmade truffle gnocchi and prawn tagliatelle to grilled tuna steaks, plus wicked desserts. Advance bookings are essential, and there are also two chic rooms for rent, if you're really taken with the place. Mains Rs.1000–2500. Daily 10am–10pm.

STILT FISHERMEN

The section of coast between Dalawela and Ahangama is the best place to witness one of Sri Lanka's most emblematic sights: **stilt fishermen**. The stilts consist of a single pole and crossbar planted out in the sea, on which fishermen perch while casting their lines when the currents are flowing in the right direction (most likely to happen between October and December, especially at sunset). Positions are highly lucrative thanks to the abundant supplies of fish, even close to shore. Bear in mind that some fishermen will expect a tip in return for photos.

Wijaya Beach Restaurant Thalpe ☎077 790 3431, ⓦwijayabeach.com. Always lively with local expats, this smooth beachfront restaurant-bar is usually packed out from lunchtime onwards. It dishes up a creative range of daily specials, excellent desserts and the south coast' best wood-fired pizza, as well as good beers, imported cider, wines and cocktails. Mains Rs.800–1200. Dail' 8am–10pm.

Koggala

Around 12km east of Unawatuna lies the small and unprepossessing town of **KOGGALA**, dominated by a pair of military-themed constructions with two very different purposes: an airbase, built here hurriedly during World War II against the threat of Japanese attack, and the spectacular *Fortress* hotel. The town is also home to one of the island's more rewarding museums, erected in honour of the famous Sinhalese writer **Martin Wickramasinghe**, and is close to the **Kataluwa Purvarama Mahavihara** temple, while **Koggala lagoon** is less than a kilometre inland.

Martin Wickramasinghe Museum
Daily 9am–5pm · Rs.200 · ⓦmartinwickramasinghe.info

Directly opposite *The Fortress* hotel, the excellent **Martin Wickramasinghe Museum** is inspired by – and partly devoted to – the life, works and ideas of one of the most important Sinhalese cultural figures of the twentieth century. A prolific writer, Wickramasinghe's novels and non-fiction works – on subjects ranging from Buddhism to cultural anthropology – played an important part in establishing Sinhala as a viable literary alternative to English at a time when the language was particularly threatened by Western influence.

The site is divided into several different sections. The excellent **Folk Museum** houses an absorbing selection of exhibits pertaining to the daily practical and spiritual life of the Sinhalese – everything from catching a fish to chasing off malevolent spirits. You'll also find an excellent collection of traditional masks depicting assorted characters, including an unusual pair of red-faced British officers, and a couple of "sand boards"– trays of sand which were used to practise writing – the Sri Lankan equivalent of a blackboard.

Behind the Folk Museum is a display of traditional modes of transport, including a high-speed bull-racing cart, while at the rear of the grounds stands the **house** in which Wickramasinghe was born and grew up with his nine sisters. The **Hall of Life**, attached to the house, is devoted to his life, though it gives disappointingly little information on the man himself. Wickramasinghe's simple **grave** stands right by the side of the house.

Koggala lagoon

Spreading north of Koggala town, the extensive **Koggala lagoon** is dotted with islands and fringed with mangroves. It's good for birds and **boat trips**, although factories associated with the nearby Free Trade Zone have sullied the waters somewhat. You can easily arrange a boat or catamaran trip here locally (ask around at the Folk Museum in Koggala or one of the hotels, or look out for signs); trips usually stop off at "Bird Island", a serene Buddhist temple, and another island where you can see peelers at work cultivating cinnamon. For a more nature-orientated focus, try one of Rainforest Rescue International's insightful boat safaris (1hr 30min; Rs.4000 for two people; ☎091 224 6528; ⓦrainforestrescuesrilanka.org) through Koggala's mangroves, which demonstrate the current threats to this vital ecosystem.

Kataluwa Purvarama Mahavihara

The temple lies about 1km inland from the coastal highway; various side roads (a couple of them signed) lead to it from the main road, though the road layout is slightly confusing, so you'll have to ask for directions locally

Around 2.5km east of Koggala lies one of the south's most absorbing temples, the **Kataluwa Purvarama Mahavihara**. The temple is interesting principally for the remarkable Kandyan-style **wall paintings** in the main shrine, dating from the late nineteenth century. The four walls were painted by different artists in competition (no one seems to know who won) and illustrate various Jataka and other cautionary Buddhist tales, with detailed crowds of meticulously executed figures including various colonial bigwigs and – strangely enough – a rather lopsided, characteristically dour Queen Victoria, placed here to commemorate her support for native Buddhism in the face of British missionary Christianity. The inner shrine (mind your head: the doors are built purposefully low to force you to bow as you enter the presence of the Buddha) contains further Buddha figures, as well as a black Vishnu and a blue Kataragama.

ACCOMMODATION

KOGGALA

The Fortress 091 438 9400, thefortress.lk. This sprawling super-luxury resort is one of the island's grandest hotel projects, sitting on a prime stretch of beach and occupying a huge verandaed building that looks a bit like an old colonial Dutch villa on steroids – lots of them. The 53 rooms (a few without sea views) come equipped with state-of-the-art amenities, while facilities include a spectacular 74m infinity pool, a fine spa (offering both Ayurveda and Western treatments) and three restaurants. Rates vary wildly, but are never cheap. $330

★ **Kahanda Kanda** Anugulugaha, 5km inland from Koggala 091 494 3700, kahandakanda.com. Perched in a magnificent position above Koggala lagoon, this is one of Sri Lanka's most beguiling small hotels, with ten eclectic, individually designed suites housed in a series of imaginatively landscaped pavilions. Facilities include a fabulous infinity pool, gym and massage room, and there's

also superb food, well worth the trip even if you're not staying (a three-course lunch or dinner costs Rs.3500; non guests are advised to book in advance). B&B $425

Tri Pelassa Rd, Koggala Lake 077 770 8177, trilanka. com. Luxurious eco-resort on the banks of the lake with its own yoga *shala* and spa. Standard rooms are in the water tower, looking out on to cinnamon trees, whilst there are four private villas and a suite close to the lake. $406

Villa Modarawattha Kataluwa, 200m inland from the coastal highway 091 228 3975, villamodarawaththa.com. Idyllic rural bolthole overlooking Koggala lagoon and occupying an attractive 200-year-old (although comprehensively restored) villa in spacious gardens with a small pool. There are just four rooms, all attractively furnished in colonial style, although it's worth paying a bit more ($25) for one of the deluxe rooms. $180

Ahangama and Midigama

The road from Koggala to Midigama runs close to the ocean for much of the way, in many places squeezing the beach into a narrow ribbon of sand between the tarmac and the waves. A few kilometres beyond Koggala, the buzzy town of **AHANGAMA** is famous for having the greatest concentration of **stilt fishermen** (see page 159) along the entire coast (although you can usually see them off Thalpe and Koggala's beaches, too), and it also has some decent surf, while nearby is the fascinating **Handunugoda Tea Estate**.

A couple of kilometres further on, the scattered village of **MIDIGAMA** has some of the best **surfing** on the island, though the village is very small and sleepy and, apart from at its far eastern end, the beach is rather narrow and exposed – unless you're here to surf (which most visitors are), there's not a lot to do.

Handunugoda Tea Estate

Tittagalla, Ahangama • Daily 8am–5pm • Tours free • 077 771 3999, hermanteas.com

The **Handunugoda Tea Estate**, around 4km inland from the Kataluwa junction, is renowned locally for the remarkably high quality of its teas given such low altitude. It's particularly celebrated as one of Sri Lanka's few producers of highly prized white tea

SURFING AT MIDIGAMA

There are three surf shops in Midigama, and most guesthouses can arrange board rental and tuition. Baba at the **Cheeky Monkey** guesthouse (daily 7am–9pm) rents boards at competitive rates (Rs.300/hr, Rs.600/half-day or Rs.1200/day), undertakes board repairs and offers surf lessons (Rs.2500; 1hr 30min) in nearby Weligama; tuktuk transfers are included in the rate. They also rent scooters with surf racks for Rs.800/day. **Indika's**, set back from the road, also rents boards and offers 24hr board repair.

2

or "silver tips") – produced using delicate young buds and leaves which are allowed) wither in sunlight before being lightly processed (without crushing) to avoid the xidation produced during traditional tea-processing techniques. It's also one of he planet's most expensive brews, retailing at around $1500 per kilo. Rubber and innamon, as well as coconuts, are also grown here, and the excellent guided tours 1hr 30min) of the plantation provide an informative overview of the production and reatment of all four crops; the highlight is a tea-tasting session of over twenty varieties with cake) at the main plantation bungalow overlooking the estate.

CCOMMODATION

HANGAMA

There's just one solid choice for accommodation in **Ahangama**, while **Midigama** offers a clutch of low-key guesthouses straggling along the beach and road. The quaint little clocktower at the village's centre makes a useful landmark when you're trying to work out where to et off the bus.

HANGAMA

Café Ceylon 500m west of the 133km post ☏ 011 219 1920, ⌨ cafeceylon.lk. Five neat a/c rooms with hot water a pair of atmospheric colonial bungalows set in spacious ardens on the land side of the coastal highway. There's) pool, but the beach is 50m away, as is "The Rock", a opular local surf break. Also has an excellent restaurant ee below). B&B **$50**

MIDIGAMA

Cheeky Monkey 800m east of the clocktower ☏ 071 12 8686, ⌨ on.fb.me/1QmZiXS. Clean and friendly uesthouse run by a keen surfer, which has just a few fan-oled rooms (hot water) and a rustic first-floor seafood staurant-bar hosting weekly barbecues (Sun 7pm) and vice-monthly discos. B&B **Rs.3000**

Slums Behind Ebb & Flow Jungalows (no sign) 077 009 1575. The four rooms at this homestay beside e railway line are basic, clean and share a cold-water throom. The ladies who run it are super-hospitable

AHANGAMA AND MIDIGAMA

and it's great for long-stayers and female/solo travellers. Downsides are the train noise and lack of wi-fi. B&B **Rs.1500**

Lion's Rest 200m after the 140km post, 100m off the main road ☏ 041 225 0990, ⌨ lions-rest.com. Small, personable and above-average guesthouse on secluded Gurubebila Beach, just east of Midigama, with eight well-furnished rooms, sociable hammock-strewn living areas, a small pool and views to the sea. **€70**

Plantation Surf Inn 700m east of the clocktower ☏ 077 643 8912, ⌨ plantationsurfinn.com. Set back from the main road, rooms (with fans) in this friendly homestay are small yet clean, cosy and comfortable, and there's a nice little garden, home-cooked food and surf tuition available. Also has a few single rooms. B&B **$30**

Ram's Surfing Beach At the 139km post, 300m east of the clocktower ☏ 041 225 2639, ⌨ on.fb.me/1Jxzoii. Lively hangout, perennially popular with visiting surf-dude types, with a mix of cheap and basic rooms (most of which have seen better days) and a sociable restaurant. Expect some road noise. **Rs.1800**

★ **Sun & Soul** 1km east of the clocktower ☏ 077 266 5221, ⌨ sunandsoulsl.com. One of Midigama's more upmarket guesthouses, its five rooms clean and stylishly furnished (hot water, some with a/c). There's also a little garden and café serving breakfast, salads and snacks (Rs.300–650) until 4pm. B&B **$45**, a/c **$55**

ATING

★ **Café Ceylon** 500m west of the 133km post, hangama ☏ 091 228 2729, ⌨ cafeceylon.lk. The ncise international fusion menu at the unassuming afé Ceylon is one of the region's best; many make the lgrimage from across the island just for the super-esh lagoon oysters, but all of the items on the menu

– including steamed whole fish, *gyoza*-style dumplings, sesame-crusted tuna, bone marrow burger and the veggie-friendly baked snake gourd – are delicious, and worth the schlep from Galle (mains Rs.900–2800). A new bar area was under construction at the time of research. Daily 11am–10pm.

Mama's Next to Ebb & Flow Jungalows, Midigama ☎ 077 851 5188. Tiny local restaurant serving sweet and savoury *rottys* (from Rs.50), fried rice, noodles and tasty rice and curr (Rs.300; from 11am onwards). Daily 7am–10pm.

Weligama

Some 23km east of Unawatuna, the increasingly busy fishing town of **WELIGAMA** ("Sandy Village") meanders around a broad and beautiful bay, dotted with rocky outcrops and fringed with fine golden sand. Formerly one of the south coast's quieter destinations, it's become increasingly popular with foreign tourists in recent years (including inexperienced surfers, attracted by the bay's gentle waves), and the beach area gets very crowded during peak season (Jan–March). The arrival of the vast new *Weligama Bay Marriott Resort* hotel, currently looking like a colossal, out-of-place concrete blot on the beach just west of town, has also changed the flavour of the place dramatically.

Weligama village itself is surprisingly attractive as Sri Lankan towns go: quiet and relatively traffic-free, its modest commercial centre trailing off into lush streets of pretty gingerbread villas decorated with ornate *mal lali* wooden fretwork. You'll also often see ladies sitting in front of their houses along the coastal road, hunched over pieces of lace (a local speciality since Dutch times), while the menfolk flaunt baskets of glistening fish on the seafront opposite.

Weligama Bay

The waters of **Weligama Bay** are relatively exposed, and pollution close to town is not unheard of – ask at your guesthouse where's best to swim. The bay's most prominent feature is the minuscule island of **Taprobane**, just offshore, virtually invisible under a thick covering of luxuriant trees. The island was owned during the 1930s by the exiled French Count de Maunay, who built the exquisite white villa that still stands, its red-tiled roof poking up through the trees; the whole lot is available for rent via *The Sun House* in Galle (see page 149). The prettiest part of the bay is around Taprobane, where dozens of colourful outrigger **catamarans** pull up on the beach between fishing expeditions; you may be able to negotiate a trip round the bay with one of the local fishermen, or contact Sri Sail in Mirissa (see page 170), who offer lovely cruises of the bay.

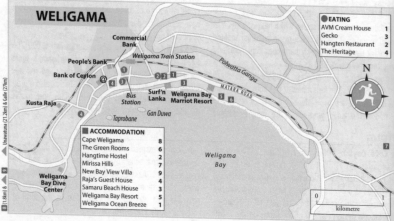

WELIGAMA

EATING
AVM Cream House	1
Gecko	3
Hangten Restaurant	2
The Heritage	4

Commercial Bank
People's Bank
Weligama Train Station
Bank of Ceylon
Potwatta Ganga
Bus Station
Surf'n Lanka
Weligama Bay Marriott Resort
MATARA ROAD
Kusta Raja
Taprobane
Gan Duwa
Weligama Bay Dive Center
Weligama Bay

ACCOMMODATION
Cape Weligama	8
The Green Rooms	6
Hangtime Hostel	2
Mirissa Hills	7
New Bay View Villa	9
Raja's Guest House	4
Samaru Beach House	3
Weligama Bay Resort	5
Weligama Ocean Breeze	1

Unawatuna (21.2km) & Galle (27km)
(1.8km) &
Mirissa (3.6km) & Matara (15.2km)

0 — kilometre — 1

SURFING AND DIVING AT WELIGAMA

There's some good (beginners') **surfing** in the centre of the bay between November and April; the beach in front of *Weligama Ocean Breeze* is littered with places offering competitively priced board rental and surf instruction (boards from Rs.300/hr; lessons from Rs.2000 for 1hr 30min); a good option is Surf'n Lanka (☎077 605 6196, ⓦsurfnlanka.com), who also offer six-day surf packages with full-board accommodation in their guesthouse across the road (€299). Virtually all hotels and guesthouses also offer or can arrange board rental and instruction.

Diving can be arranged through the Weligama Bay Dive Center, on the side road leading to the *Fisherman's Bay* hotel (☎041 225 0799, ⓦscubadivingweligama.com) who offer twice-daily trips to local coral reefs and the spectacular underwater Yala Rock complex.

Kusta Raja

At the western edge of Weligama, near the rail line, stands a large megalith carved probably sometime during the eighth or ninth centuries) with a 3m figure known as Kusta Raja, the "Leper King", usually thought to show an unknown Sinhalese monarch who was miraculously cured of leprosy by drinking nothing but coconut milk for three months. An alternative theory claims it as a depiction of a Mahayana Bodhisattva, possibly Avalokitesvara or Samantabhadra – a claim lent credence by the carvings of meditating Buddhas in the figure's tiara.

ARRIVAL AND DEPARTURE WELIGAMA

By bus Buses stop at the bus station in the centre of Weligama, a block inland from the bay. Few services originate in Weligama (most are in transit between Galle, Matara and Colombo), so you'll have to take your chances with what's passing through. If you're heading to Colombo, you're best off first taking a bus to Matara or Galle and picking up an express highway bus from there.

Destinations Akuressa (for Deniyaya and Sinharaja; hourly; 1hr 30min); Colombo (via coastal highway every 15min; 1hr 45min); Galle (every 15min; 45min); Hambantota (every 15min; 3hr); Matara (every 10min; 30min) Tangalla (every 15min; 1hr 45min); Tissamaharama (every 30min; 3hr 20min).

By train Weligama is a major stop on the Matara–Colombo railway; the train station is in the town centre a block inland from the bus station. See the timetable (page 32) for details.

Destinations Aluthgama (4–6 daily; 1hr 20min–2hr); Ambalangoda (4–6 daily; 1hr–1hr 40min); Colombo (4–6 daily; 2hr 20min–3hr); Galle (5–11 daily; 30min–1hr); Hikkaduwa (4–5 daily; 50min–1hr 10min); Kalutara (4–6 daily; 1hr 40min–2hr 30min); Matara (5–9 daily; 15–30min).

ACCOMMODATION

Weligama has a decent range of fairly pricey accommodation, spread out along the beach, and there are also a few more accommodation options in Bandrawatta, 5km southwest of town.

Cape Weligama 46/38 Nawam Mawatha ☎011 774 700, ⓦcapeweligama.com; map p.164. Sibling to the famed *Ceylon Tea Trails* bungalows in the hill country, this swanky 40-room resort-style hotel has an unbeatable location atop a palm-spiked cape, a couple of headlands west of Weligama. Rooms are immaculately presented and range from luxe suites to two-bedroom residences with their own pools, while facilities include an idyllic 60m clifftop pool and kid's pool, a gym, spa and well-equipped dive centre. Rates are predictably sky-high but do at least include two meals, alcohol and daily activities. Suites **787**, two-beds **$885**

The Green Rooms New Bypass Rd ☎077 111 9896, ⓦthegreenroomssrilanka.com; map p.164. Pleasantly laidback beach hangout, aimed mainly at surfers, directly opposite Weligama's best break. Accommodation is in five cute but fairly basic mango-wood cabanas (some with open bathroom) while activities include expensive surfing tuition (and packages), yoga and cookery lessons. Ten percent of profits go to local causes, although it's still very pricey for what you get. **Rs.11,200**

★Hangtime Hostel 540 Weligama Bypass Road ☎076 525 8933, ⓦhangtimehostel.com; map p.164. Wildly popular hostel right in the middle of the beachside action with private rooms (with unusual "fishing boat" beds) on the ground floor (a/c Rs.1000 extra), as well as female-only and mixed dorms (one with a/c for Rs.500 extra). The facilities are geared towards surfing and yoga enthusiasts, and it's also a great hub for local travel info. The rooftop restaurant (see page 166) is an added bonus. Dorms **Rs.1500**, doubles **Rs.4500**

Mirissa Hills Turn-off from the coastal road signed between km147 and 148 ☎041 225 0980, ⓦmirissahills.com; map p.164. Superb retreat set on a working cinnamon plantation on a hillside 2km inland from the beach. Accommodation is spread over three buildings: The Bungalow, a restored *walauwa*; The Museum, four (rather overpriced) rooms and an infinity pool; and, best (and most expensive), the superb Mount Cinnamon villa (sleeps eight; you can rent the whole thing for $1200), complete with stunning views and contemporary Sri Lankan artworks galore (including an extraordinary sculpture by Laki Senanayake). Museum rooms $262

New Bay View Villa Bandrawatta ☎041 226 0078, ⓦnewbayviewvilla.com; map p.164. This guesthouse is located west of Weligama on an out-of-the-way hillside overlooking a shallow bay (good for swimming and snorkelling). Rooms are fairly similar (fans, TVs, hot water) and a tad overpriced, but those upstairs are more private, have a/c and better sea views. Avoid the ground-floor rooms overlooking the rustic timber-frame restaurant. Rs.6500, a/c Rs.9750

Raja's Guest Home 248/4 First Lane, Weligama Bypass Rd ☎041 571 2263, ⓔenterthex@hotmail.com; map p.164. The cosy rooms (tiny singles for Rs.1000 and smallish doubles, all en-suite) at this welcoming guesthouse tucked down a quiet side lane between town and beach are a steal at current rates. Also has a nice front veranda and good, if pricey, home-cooked food. Rs.1500

Samaru Beach House 544 New Bypass Rd ☎04⬛ 225 1417, ⓦsamarubeachhouseweligama.com; ma⬛ p.164. A popular guesthouse, right on the beach, with spotless modern rooms outside the main building an⬛ darker and simpler rooms inside – not particularly goo⬛ value, but comfortable nonetheless. They have a hug⬛ range of surfboards for rent (Rs.400/hr) and can arrang⬛ surfing lessons, as well local trips such as Polwatta Gang⬛ boat cruises. $65, a/c $90

Weligama Bay Resort Matara Rd ☎041 225 392⬛ ⓦweligamabayresort.com; map p.164. This high-en⬛ low-rise hotel (flanked by the towering *Marriott*) is hom⬛ to luxurious lodgings stylishly decorated in black an⬛ white, ranging from rooms and suites in the main buildin⬛ to larger and pricier garden villas (all with TV, DVD playe⬛ and minibar) leading down to the inviting beachside poo⬛ There's also a good restaurant serving international cuisin⬛ B&B: doubles $180, villas $230

Weligama Ocean Breeze 487 New Bypass Rd ☎04⬛ 454 5005, ⓦweligamaoceanbreeze.com; map p.16⬛ This new hotel is one of the best-value mid-range place⬛ to stay, and a stone's throw from the beach. Rooms a⬛ clean, cheerfully decorated and have hot-water bathroom⬛ (upper-floor rooms cost $10 more) – opt for a poolsid⬛ room, away from the noisy main road. B&B $50

EATING

All hotels and guesthouses offer food (the restaurant at the *Weligama Bay Resort* is particularly good) although great restaurants are still thin on the ground.

AVM Cream House Opposite the bus station ☎041 490 4546; map p.164. This unassuming grocery store-cum-food joint sells fresh juices concocted from ingredients ranging from dates and dragon fruit to *gotu kola* and rosewater (Rs.160–400). Also sells super-cheap (halal) food – burgers, fried rice and *shwarma* from Rs160. Daily 8am–8pm.

Gecko Beach Rd; map p.164. This cosy little roadside café champions fresh, locally sourced ingredients, and serves numerous breakfast options (including muesli and marmite toast), along with salads, pasta, sandwiches, fish and chips, burgers and a range of delicious home-made

cakes, cookies and buffalo-curd ice creams. Mains Rs.700⬛ 1200. Daily 8am–8pm.

★ **Hangten Rooftop Restaurant** 540 Weligam⬛ Bypass Road ☎076 525 8933, ⓦhangtimehostel.com⬛ map p.164. Offering fabulous views of the bay, this ope⬛ sided rooftop restaurant serves up delicious breakfast⬛ lunches and dinners, including wraps, sandwiches, salac⬛ and burgers. Vegetarians and vegans are also well-catere⬛ for, and there's great coffee too. Mains Rs.650–1800. Mo⬛ Tues & Thurs–Sun 7.30am–9.30pm. Wed 7.30am⬛ 6pm.

The Heritage Matara Rd ☎041 521 001⬛ ⓦchcresthouses.com; map p.164. The restaurant a⬛ this traditional rest house on the seafront is a good spo⬛ for lunchtime rice and curry (from Rs.600) or an afternoo⬛ snack. Daily 7am–10pm.

DIRECTORY

Banks There are branches of the Commercial Bank, People's Bank and Bank of Ceylon in the town centre, all of which have ATMs accepting foreign cards.

Boat trips Several guesthouses also offer boat trips on the Polwatta Ganga (Rs.4000 per boat for the 2hr trip), which flows behind the town a few hundred metres inland.

Internet First-floor Nenasala, east of the Bank of Ceylo⬛ on Main St (daily 8.30am–5.30pm; Rs.80/hr).

Swimming Non-guests can use the pool at the *Weligam⬛ Bay Resort* for Rs.1000.

Mirissa

Just a couple of kilometres beyond Weligama, picturesque **MIRISSA** is one of the most appealing places to spend a few days next to the sea in southern Sri Lanka. The beach here is one of the nicest along this stretch of coast, with a fine swathe of sand tucked away into a pretty little bay, backed by a dense thicket of coconut palms – particularly lovely at night, when the lights go on and the sands transform into a magical tangle of fairy lights. It's not quite the well-kept secret it used to be, admittedly, but despite increasing visitor numbers and the construction of new accommodation, the beach itself remains largely unspoiled, with rustic restaurants fronting modest guesthouses and a merciful absence of big resorts. The lively but pleasantly low-key atmosphere attracts a youngish crowd of mainly independent travellers, and while the growing number of noisy beach discos means things aren't quite as sleepy as they once were, the whole place strikes a nice balance between party nights and peaceful wave-gazing by day.

Mirissa is also Sri Lanka's leading **whale-watching centre** (see page 169), with excellent chances of seeing blue and sperm whales close to shore. There's reasonable **swimming**, especially in the quieter bays east of Parrot Rock, though the strong currents and big waves off the main portion of the beach can be dangerous, so it's worth asking at your guesthouse about where's safe to swim before venturing into the water. You can also **surf, bodyboard** and **snorkel** here, though you won't see much apart from the occasional pretty fish.

ARRIVAL AND DEPARTURE
MIRISSA

Mirissa village is mostly packed into a compact area between the harbour to the west, headland to the south and Matara Road to the north and east.

By bus Buses whizz up and down the Matara Road through Mirissa every few minutes; when arriving, make sure the conductor knows to let you off, since Mirissa is easily missed. When leaving, you'll have to flag something down along the main road.

Destinations Colombo (via coastal highway; every 15min; 4hr 10min); Galle (every 15min; 1hr); Hambantota (every 15min; 2hr 25min); Matara (every 10min; 25min); Tangalla (every 15min; 1hr 40min); Tissamaharama (every 30min; 3hr 15min).

By train The village has its own train station, though only slow services stop here and it's quite a distance from the village. It's faster and more convenient to get off the train at Weligama or Matara stations, and catch a bus to Mirissa.

ACCOMMODATION

Mirissa's broad range of accommodation is strung out along the **beach** or, more peacefully (given the increase in discos and late-night activity on the beach during the season), inland **in the village** itself. There are also an increasing number of options hugging the emerging coastal villages of Talaramba and Kamburugamuwa, off the main coastal highway into Matara.

Celestial Inn 150m inland from the Matara Rd ☎041 225 3759, ⍟celestialinnmirissa.com; map p.168. Friendly family-run and above-average guesthouse whose tidy rooms (some a/c) in a neat modern block are equipped with four-poster beds, hot water and private garden terraces. Rs.5000, a/c Rs.7000

Dream Palace Matara Rd ☎041 225 1772, ⍟on. fb.me/1GBrgcV; map p.168. This cute ninety-year-old antique house on the main road, 30m from the beach, is hardly palatial but its simple, comfortable rooms spiralling off a central courtyard are equipped with thick mattresses, en-suite hot water bathrooms and garden views. Handy for the bus. Rs.3000

Giragala Village Matara Rd ☎041 225 0496, ⍟giragala.com; map p.168. Refreshingly breezy location on the grassy defile at the eastern end of the beach, with comfortable if rather pricey rooms (with a/c and hot water) dotted around attractive gardens, plus a small spa. The bay to the east is safe for swimming and snorkelling, and snorkelling gear is available for hire. They also have a few cheaper rooms (Rs.7500) in a less atmospheric building across the road, so make sure you know what you're getting when you book. Rs.10,000

Handagedara Resort Harbour Rd ☎041 225 4770, ⍟facebook.com/handagedara.com; map p.168. Located midway between the beach and Mirissa Harbour (handy for whale-watching), this restored century-old *walauwa* has a few standard rooms in the main house (including a couple of basic fan-cooled singles) and more spacious and contemporary deluxe a/c rooms ($20 extra) in an adjacent annexe overlooking the swimming pool. B&B $60

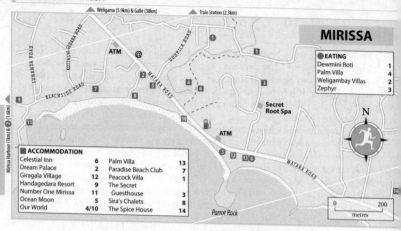

MIRISSA

● **EATING**
Dewmini Roti	1
Palm Villa	4
Weligambay Villas	2
Zephyr	3

Secret Root Spa

Parrot Rock

■ **ACCOMMODATION**
Celestial Inn	6	Palm Villa	13
Dream Palace	2	Paradise Beach Club	7
Giragala Village	12	Peacock Villa	1
Handagedara Resort	9	The Secret	
Number One Mirissa	11	Guesthouse	3
Ocean Moon	5	Sira's Chalets	8
Our World	4/10	The Spice House	14

Number One Mirissa Turn off Beach Access Rd near Palace Mirissa ☎ 041 225 4884, ⓦ numberonemirissa.com; map p.168. Mirissa's most upmarket, boutique-style option is spectacularly perched on the western, palm-studded headland with views across the bay. Suites, in a whitewashed two-storey building, have four-poster beds, modern bathrooms and private sea-view terraces (best on the upper floor though they cost $80 more). There's also a (small) infinity pool, restaurant and sunbathing terrace just above the surf. $250

Ocean Moon Matara Rd ☎ 041 225 2328, ⓔ oceanmoon46@gmail.com; map p.168. Friendly place on the beach with a selection of above-average and fairly priced concrete cabanas and a few cheaper and more basic rooms, plus a restaurant and bar. Rs.4000, a/c Rs.5000

Our World Matara Rd ☎ 041 225 0036, ⓦ ourworldsrilanka.wordpress.com; map p.168. Budget-conscious option with a choice of super-cheap although rather grubby rooms with shared bathrooms right on the beach adjoining a little café, or nicer, cleaner and quieter rooms in a small guesthouse 150m inland. Beach Rs.2000, inland Rs.1700

Palm Villa Matara Rd ☎ 041 225 0022, ⓦ palmvillamirissa.com; map p.168. The eight rooms (a/c Rs.1500 extra) at this well-run guesthouse are a mixed bag; basic ones are located in the main building (a little gloomy, and with no view) while neater, pricier ones to the front are just a few footsteps from the sea. There's good swimming in the bay in front, a decent restaurant and daily yoga classes. Rs.5500, sea view Rs.8000

Paradise Beach Club Beachside Rd ☎ 041 225 0380, ⓦ paradisemirissa.com; map p.168. This popular, laidback establishment is Mirissa's only proper resort. Accommodation ranges from simple, slightly cramped concrete cabanas (some a/c) scattered around attractive gardens by a wide stretch of beach, to deluxe rooms in a two-storey a/c block beside the pool, and super deluxes in a new four-storey block; all face the ocean. The main drawback is the very average buffet food (served, bizarrely enough – given the lovely beachfront – in a second-floor restaurant, and compulsory half board. Cabanas $68, doubles $100

Peacock Villa 500m inland from the coastal highway, signposted from almost opposite the Ocean Moon guesthouse ☎ 041 225 1200, ⓦ peacockvilla.lk; map p.168. Some distance from the beach, but the idyllic rural location, surrounded by lush gardens full of birds and the occasional monkey, is ample compensation. Of the five cement-floored rooms, those on the ground floor have a/c while the upper-floor rooms have fans and balconies with views across jungle and farmland. Extras include a shared fridge and pantry, books and board games. Rs.6400

★ **The Secret Guesthouse** 250m inland from the coastal highway, turn opposite Palm Villa ☎ 077 329 4332, ⓦ secretguesthouse.com; map p.168. Located up a side road opposite *Palm Villa*, this is one of Mirissa's nicest places to stay. Secluded, tranquil and with very friendly owners, it's an upmarket homestay with just three very comfortable fan-cooled rooms (all hot water), as well as an idyllic self-catering family bungalow ($60 handsomely located next to their Secret Root Spa (see opposite). $40

Sira's Chalets 220/5 Matara Rd ☎ 041 225 0750, ⓦ siraschaletsmirissa.lk; map p.168. Clustered around a sandy garden, the scrupulously clean chalets (a/c, cable TV, hot water, tea/coffee, comfy beds) here are among the nicest rooms on the beach. Friendly owner Charith is a mine of local info, and can source bodyboards, scooters or anything else you might need. B&B Rs.10,500

★ **The Spice House** 1km east towards Matara ☎ 077 351 0147, ⓦ thespicehousemirissa.com; map p.168. The a/c guest rooms at this gorgeous rural hideaway 100m from the beach, are completely unique. Choose

WHALE-WATCHING IN MIRISSA

Over the past decade, Sri Lanka has emerged as one of the world's major **whale-watching destinations**, thanks largely to the work of pioneering British marine biologist Charles Anderson, who in 1999 first proposed the theory that there was an annual migration of blue and sperm whales between the Bay of Bengal and around the coast of Sri Lanka to the Arabian Sea (heading west in April, and returning in the opposite direction in December and January). Anderson's theory led to the dramatic discovery that Sri Lanka was sitting alongside one of the world's great cetacean migratory routes, with sightings of these majestic creatures almost guaranteed for large parts of the year, and the possibility of seeing both sperm and blue whales (as well as spinner dolphins) in a single trip.

Mirissa is perfectly placed for whale-watching expeditions, being where the continental shelf on which Sri Lanka sits is at its narrowest, with ocean depths of 1km within 6km of the coast – ideal whale country. Sightings are most regular from December to April (with December and April being the best months). A large number of operators around the village offer **whale-watching trips** in a variety of boats, seating anything from eight to fifty or more people. Most trips leave early in the morning (around 6–7am), last 3–5hr and cost around $50–80 per person – touts on the beach sell trips for as low as Rs.2500, but such excursions often show little regard either for the whales or your own safety (boats are often overloaded) and are best approached with caution.

The main operators are located in or at the entrance to **Mirissa Harbour**, around 1km west of the beach. For more on the island's whales and dolphins, see page 444.

RECOMMENDED OPERATORS

Blue Water Cruise ☎077 497 8306, ⓦgoo. gl/0c30vW. Currently the best option, with a big modern boat (trips for Rs.7000) and a smaller, nippier eight-person speedboat (Rs.80,000/person).

Mirissa Water Sports ☎077 359 7731, ⓦmirissawatersports.lk. Mirissa's original whale-watching operator with big fit-for-purpose boats and a reliable reputation (Rs.8000 per person).

Raja & the Whales ☎071 333 1811, ⓦrajaandthewhales.com. Experienced family-run outfit with two boats; breakfast is prepared on board (Rs.6000/person).

ne in the fretwork-adorned main house (some with sea iews), in the smaller building in the lower garden or, nore unusually, go for the two-bedroom mud house or the elevated cabin for the best valley views. The lush, steeply terraced tropical garden is home to plenty of wildlife and there's also a pool. B&B: doubles $86; cabins $100

EATING

he beach is backed by a long string of low-key **café-estaurants**, particularly pretty after dusk when tables re set out on the sands and hundreds of fairy lights twinkle n the darkness. Most places are much of a muchness, and ood at most is generally reliable rather than spectacular, with all the usual seafood suspects and other touristy lassics, although the freshness of the produce usually can't e faulted. Many places lay out big trays of iced seafood to empt you inside – huge jumbo prawns, deep crimson red napper, pointy snouted barracuda, butterfish, seer fish, ed and white mullet, calamari, and so on. For nightlife, *ephyr* is a good place to hang out, while a few restaurants ost regular discos during the season.

Dewmini Roti On the south side of the road leading o Peacock Villa ☎071 516 2604, ⓦdewminirotishop. wordpress.com; map p.168. Peaceful and deservedly opular little garden café serving up a great selection of asty *rottys* (Rs.80–300) in many guises – plain, coconut, ineapple, chocolate, chicken, and so on – plus *kottu*, fried rice, rice and curry, as well as Western and Sri Lankan breakfasts (mains Rs.180–400). They also run cookery courses (Rs.2000; book the day before). No alcohol. Daily 8am–10pm.

Palm Villa Matara Rd ☎041 225 0022, ⓦpalmvillamirissa.com; map p.168. Nice seaside restaurant to the east of Mirissa's main beach, serving an above-average menu of light lunches (Rs.350–650) and, for dinner, full fish, seafood and rice and curry (Rs.750–900). Daily 12.30–3.30pm & 7.30–10pm.

Weligambay Villas Mirissa Harbour ☎041 225 4750, ⓦweligambayvillas.lk; map p.168. The 300-degree views from this navy-owned resort restaurant are hard to beat, overlooking Mirissa Harbour and the wide arc of Weligama Bay and stretching far inland – spectacular at sunset. The wide-ranging food and drink offering is surprisingly cheap given the picturesque setting (mains Rs.300–800). Daily 9am–10.30pm.

★**Zephyr** Matara Rd ☎041 454 5044, ⓦfacebook.com/zephyrmirissa; map p.168. This grass-roofed restaurant is currently the coolest restaurant/bar/chill-out spot on the beach. Tables top an elevated deck, with coloured beanbags on the sands below. The menu (mains Rs.600–1600) stands out from the crowd, being small and concise – think burgers, *rotty* wraps, melts, pasta, grilled fish, slow-cooked pork, chilli jaggery beef and seafood curries. Also has a fab selection of cocktails and shots. Daily 10am–11.30pm.

DIRECTORY

Banks There are no banks in Mirissa, although there are a couple of ATMs along the main road that accept foreign cards.

Bike hire Your guesthouse should be able to help you with bicycle and scooter rentals.

Sailing and watersports Snorkelling "safaris" and sport fishing, as well as sunrise and sunset coastal cruises can be arranged with Blue Water Cruise (see page 169). Sri Sail (☎071 440 5000, ⓦsrisail.com), also based at the harbour, offer fabulous cruises too (3hr), aboard *Pearl*, snazzy catamaran equipped with snacks and drinks ($30) or in nippy RIBs ($35), as well as two-day sailing lessons in *dhonis* or *minibees* ($120). There are jet skis for hire in front of *Suduweli* restaurant (Rs.3500/15min).

Spa Secret Root Spa, near *The Secret Guesthouse* (see page 168), inland from the main road opposite *Giragala Village*.

Yoga *Palm Villa* hosts Kundalini yoga classes (Rs.2000 1.5hr; ⓦmirissayoga.com) every day except Sun.

Matara and around

Close to the southernmost point of the island, the bustling town of **MATARA** (pronounced "*maat*-rah", the middle syllable is virtually elided) provides a taste of everyday Sri Lanka that may (or may not) be welcome if you've spent time in the coastal resorts. Sitting at the terminus of both the southern rail line and Southern Expressway, the town is an important transport hub and a major centre of commerce – a lively place given a youthful touch by the presence of students from the nearby **Ruhunu University**. Matara preserves a few Dutch colonial buildings, an atmospheric old fort area and an attractive seafront (though you wouldn't want to swim here). A couple of kilometres east of town, the low-key beachside suburb of **Medawatta** offers good beginners' surfing while the waves at **Madiha**, a similar distance west, are better suited to experienced board riders; in between the two is **Polhena**, which is good for snorkelling. Further afield are a handful of little-visited sights, including the giant Buddha at **Weherehena**.

Matara itself (from Mahatara, or "Great Harbour") is an ancient settlement, though no traces of anything older than the colonial era survive. The Portuguese used the town intermittently, but it was the Dutch, attracted by the deep and sheltered estuary of the Nilwala Ganga, who established a lasting presence here, fortifying the town and making it an important centre for cinnamon and elephant trading.

As at Galle, Matara divides into two areas: the **modern town** and the old Dutch colonial district, known as the **Fort**. The two are separated by the **Nilwala Ganga**, a fine and remarkably unspoiled stretch of water, edged by thick stands of palm trees.

The Fort

Matara's main **Fort** lies on the narrow spit of land south of the river, its eastern side bounded by a long line of stumpy **ramparts**, built by the Dutch in the eighteenth century and topped by the inevitable ugly white British clocktower of 1883. At the north end of the ramparts, a dilapidated **gateway** (dated 1780) marks the original entrance to the Fort, while a short walk brings you to the restored **Dutch Reformed Church**, one of the earliest Dutch churches in Sri Lanka – a large and rather austere gabled structure sheltered beneath a huge pitched roof.

The rest of the Fort comprises an interesting district of lush, tree-filled streets dotted with fine old colonial-era houses in various stages of picturesque disrepair: some are surprisingly palatial, with grand colonnaded facades and sweeping verandas, although heavy-handed development is beginning to seriously erode the area's character. At the far west end of the Fort, the peninsula tapers off to a narrow spit of land at the confluence of the Nilwala Ganga and the sea, where there's a pretty little harbour.

The Star Fort

Mon & Wed–Sun 8am–4.30pm • Free

On the north side of the river the diminutive **Star Fort** is the smaller of Matara's two Dutch strongholds, a quaint little hexagonal structure built to protect the river crossing to the main Fort area and surrounded by a dirty-green moat in which the Dutch once kept crocodiles. The entrance gate is emblazoned "Redoute Van Eck 1763", commemorating the governor under whose administration it was constructed, and sports a fully working wooden drawbridge. A circuit of the tiny ramparts offers fine views over the cacophony of modern Matara and its unruly traffic below.

The fort's interior houses a small **museum**, with modest exhibits on the history of the fort and Matara featuring the usual mishmash of Kandyan artefacts, antique ola-leaf books, tablet inscriptions and a selection of Dutch period glass.

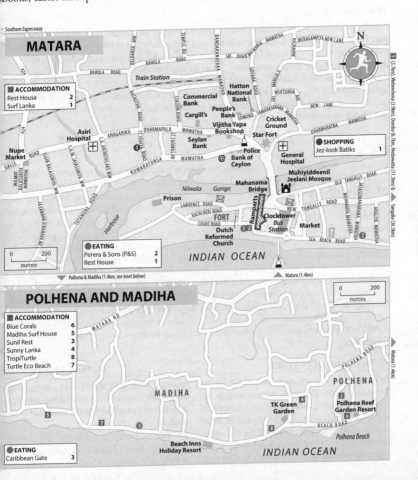

2

WATERSPORTS AROUND MATARA

A couple of kilometres west of the centre of Matara, the rather down-at-heel beachside suburb of **Polhena** has some good **snorkelling** straight off the beach, with lots of colourful fish and a small section of live coral; swimming conditions and visibility are best outside the monsoon period. Snorkelling equipment can be rented from *Sunil Rest* for Rs.400 per day, and the knowledgeable local snorkelling guides Titus (c/o *Hotel TK Green Garden*; ☎ 041 222 2603) and Nishantha (c/o *Blue Corals*) charge around Rs.800 per hour (including equipment).

In recent years the **surf** breaks at **Madiha**, an idyllic and still unspoiled series of shallow bays on Polhena's western boundary, have gained popularity as in-the-know surfers flock to enjoy the consistent year-round swell and tranquillity of this quiet backwater. **Medawatta**, at the picturesque eastern end of Matara Bay, about 1.5km east of the town, is also popular with long-term surfers coming to ride waves of up to 4m at **Secret Point**, best between November and March. The surf off the beach is also a good place for beginners. Surfboards (Rs.1000/day) can be hired from *Neutral Wind* guesthouse and *Surf Lanka* hotel; *Neutral Wind* also organizes surf lessons ($30).

PADI courses and fun **dives** can be arranged through the *Beach Inns Holiday Resort* in Madiha (🌐 beach-inns.com).

The new town

North of the Star Fort, the **new town** sprawls away in all directions. Continue straight past the prominent Buddhist temple to head down **Anagarika Dharmapala Mawatha**, the area's principal thoroughfare, a heaving, gridlocked confusion of vehicles and pedestrians. About 500m west along here, an unprepossessing house in a small side street hides **Jez-look Batiks** (see page 174), while some 500m further on (at the traffic lights, opposite the expressway access road) you'll reach the striking old **Nupe Market**, a quaint, T-shaped pavilion with heavy red-tiled roof and stumpy white pillars, built by the Dutch sometime around 1780.

Weherehena

Daily 6am–6pm • Bus #349 from Matara bus station (every 10min; 20min) or a tuktuk (around Rs.800 return, including waiting time)

A few kilometres east of Matara and a couple of kilometres inland, the tiny village of **WEHEREHENA** is home to one of the island's largest Buddha statues, the focal point of a sprawling modern temple complex constructed on the site of a hidden underground temple built in the seventeenth century to escape the evangelical attentions of the Portuguese. Some 39m tall and set within a rather ugly shelter, the giant Buddha figure itself, shown in the seated *samadhi* position, is a thing of impressive size if no particular beauty. Most of the temple is actually buried underground, with endless corridors decorated with around twenty thousand cartoon-style depictions of various Jatakas. Right underneath the giant Buddha, a monk will take your donation (Rs.200 is "suggested") and point out a mirror below in which you can see reflected a cache of precious gold and stone Buddhas buried in an underfloor vault. From here steps lead up to the giant Buddha itself – you can climb all the way up to the head, although there's not much to see. A big **perahera** is held here on the Unduvap poya day in early December.

ARRIVAL AND DEPARTURE

MATARA AND AROUND

By bus Matara is the south's major transport hub. The bus station (next to the old ramparts and convenient for the *Rest House*) is unusually orderly, with clearly marked bays and a helpful information office (not signposted) in the outside corridor in the corner near the statue of a woman holding a baby. Eastbound services leave from the eastern side of the terminal; westbound services from the west.

Heading to Kandy, you're best off taking a bus to Colombo and then one bound for Kandy from there. As ever, it pays to check the latest schedules in the information office in advance.

Destinations Akuressa (for Deniyaya and Sinharaja; every 10min; 45min); Badulla (2 daily; 6hr); Bandarawela (4 daily; 6hr); Colombo via Southern Expressway (every

15min; 2hr) or via the coastal route (every 15min; 4hr); Deniyaya (3 daily; 3hr); Ella (3 daily; 5hr 30min); Embilipitiya (every 20min; 2hr 30min); Galle (every 10min; 1hr 15min); Hambantota (every 15min; 2hr 30min); Kandy (daily; 10hr); Kataragama (5 daily; 3hr 30min, alternatively change at Tissa); Monaragala (daily; 5hr); Nuwara Eliya (2 daily; 8hr); Ratnapura (3 daily; 4hr); Tangalla (every 15min; 1hr 30min); Tissamaharama (every 15min; 3hr); Weligama (every 10min; 30min).

By train Matara stands at the end of the southern rail line from Colombo (see page 32). The train station is just north of the town centre.

Destinations Aluthgama (5–6 daily; 2hr–2hr 30min); Ambalangoda (5–6 daily; 1hr 20min–2hr); Colombo (5–6 daily; 2hr 40min–3hr 30min); Galle (5–10 daily; 40min–1hr 15min); Hikkaduwa (3–5 daily; 1hr–1hr 30min); Kalutara (4–6 daily; 2hr–2hr 45min); Weligama (5–11 daily; 15–30min).

2

ACCOMMODATION

Matara town suffers from a chronic lack of places to stay, and most visitors stay in the suburbs of **Polhena** and **Madiha**, 2–3km west of town, or **Medawatta**, about 1.5km east.

MATARA TOWN
Rest House Fort ☏041 222 2299, ⓦresthousematara.com; map 171. Painstakingly rebuilt following the tsunami, this attractive seafront rest house still has plenty of old-school charm, with attractively furnished rooms (all with hot water), shady verandas, a decent restaurant and refreshing sea breezes. Rs.2500, a/c Rs.4000

POLHENA
Blue Corals 36 Beach Rd ☏077 760 0803, ⓔbluecoralspolhena@yahoo.com; map p.171. Two modern, cheap yet rather shabby tiled rooms close to the beach, as well as a couple of slightly nicer ones on the beachfront itself. The owner, Nishantha, runs snorkelling trips (see page 172), rents out motorbikes (Rs.900/day) and bikes (Rs.300, or free for guests) and can also arrange boat tours along the Nilwala Ganga (Rs.8000/six-person boat). Rs.2000, beachfront Rs.3000

Sunil Rest 29 Second Cross Rd ☏041 222 1983, ⓔsunilrestpolhena@yahoo.com; map p.171. Polhena's friendliest and best-organized guesthouse, with a mix of inexpensive rooms, a range of day-trips and bikes for hire (Rs.300/day). If the guesthouse is full, Sunil might offer a comfy room at his parent's house nearby, or at the more expensive *Residence Riviera* on the seafront. Rs.2000

Sunny Lanka Polhena Rd ☏041 222 3504, ⓔsunnyamare@yahoo.com; map p.171. Long-running

budget stalwart, with large, clean and nicely furnished rooms – very good value at current prices. Rs.2300, a/c Rs.3500

TropiTurtle 123 Beach Rd ☏077 376 2625, ⓦtropiturtle.com; map p.171. An intimate hostel with just four double rooms and a dorm (with bunk beds and lockers), shared bathrooms, a basic communal kitchen, living room (with cable TV) and sea-view lounge on the upper floor. Arranges tours, rents snorkels (Rs200) and bikes (Rs1000). Dorm Rs.900; doubles Rs.2000

MADIHA
Madiha Surf House Pubudu Mawatha ☏077 903 0998, ⓦfacebook.com/madihasurfhouse; map p.171. A modern, surfer-run guesthouse with seven tidy rooms (all with fans) and a chilled vibe, just 50m from two of Madiha's best breaks. Rs.4000

Turtle Eco Beach Beach Rd ☏041 222 3377, ⓦturtleecobeach.com; map p.171. Pleasant, low-key village-style resort set amid lush tropical gardens, a stone's throw from the beach. Rooms edge a gorgeous 24m lap pool, and are bright, clean and comfortable (a/c and hot water). Also a restaurant, and massages available on request. $80

MEDAWATTA
Surf Lanka S.K Town ☏041 222 8190, ⓦsurf-lanka.com; map p.171. The smartest place in Medawatta, with a range of bright and spacious rooms in a functional white building right above Secret Point; more expensive ones have a/c, hot water, TV and jacuzzis. Rs4000, a/c Rs5500

EATING

MATARA TOWN
Perera & Sons (P&S) Sea Beach Rd ☏041 437 4708, ⓦpereraandsons.com; map p171. Outlet of a popular fast-food national chain that sells short eats, cakes and snacks all day out front and inside, tasty Sri Lankan breakfasts (Rs.130) and lunches (Rs.240), as well as *kottu rotty*, *lamprais* and Indian-style dishes for dinner. Daily 6.30am–9am, 11am–2.30pm & 6.30–9pm.

Rest House Fort ☏041 222 2299, ⓦresthousematara.com; map 171. Sedate, old-fashioned dining room with a well-prepared selection of all the usual Sri Lankan classics, as well as Western mains and a decent club sandwich with fries and coleslaw. Good, but definitely not the cheapest in town. Mains around Rs.400–900. Licensed. Daily 8am–11pm.

MADIHA

Caribbean Gate Madiha ☎041 222 1521, ⓦfacebook.com/Caribbean.Gate; map p.171. It's well worth the schlep from town to this welcoming palm-thatched restaurant, with tables placed beneath parasols right on the beach. The menu lists all the usual Sri Lankan staples (fried rice, devilled noodles), and the portions are generous. Rs.300–600. Daily 11am–11pm.

SHOPPING

Jez-look Batiks 12 St Yehiya St ☎041 222 2142; map p.171. One of the best batik workshops in the island, run by the charming Jezima Mohamed in her own home. The batiks produced here are far superior to the usual tourist junk, with a wide range of striking original designs, and they also make gorgeous silk and even jute batiks, as well as clothes. Jezima's girls can also make up pieces according to your own designs if you fancy, and you can even stay and study batik-making here if you get really enthused. Daily 9am–6pm or later.

Dondra and around

Around 5km southeast of Matara, the sleepy little town of **DONDRA** was formerly one of the south's most important religious centres, known as Devi Nuwara ("City of the Gods") and home to the great Tenavaram temple, among the most magnificent on the island until it was destroyed by the Portuguese in 1588. Nothing of the temple now survives apart from one ancient shrine, the **Galge**, a small, plain rectangular structure thought to date back to the seventh century AD, making it the oldest stone building in Sri Lanka. The shrine lies half a kilometre inland from the main crossroads in the middle of Dondra; turn left down a narrow lane just after the clocktower. After 400m you'll reach a rather flouncy modern white temple; the Galge lies up a short flight of steps in a grassy field on the slope immediately above.

The diminutive Galge pales into insignificance next to modern Dondra's main temple, the sprawling roadside **Devi Nuwara Devalaya**, which is right in the middle of town by the main road, and comes complete with a huge standing Buddha (a copy of the Aukana Buddha; see page 299), and with an elephant or two usually on display grazing in the grounds. One of the south's major festivals, the **Devi Nuwara Perahera**, is held annually at the temple on the Esala poya day (late July/early Aug).

Dondra lighthouse

Daily 9am–6pm; closed at the time of research

Just over a kilometre south of Dondra, the 50m-high **Dondra lighthouse**, built in 1889, marks the **southernmost point** in Sri Lanka (although the lighthouse was closed at the time of writing and it was unclear when it would re-open – check ahead if you're keen to visit). If you do manage to get inside you can climb the 222 steps to the top of the lighthouse for huge views up and down the coast, as well as a close look at the beam's beautifully maintained colonial machinery, still used to illuminate Dondra Head for the benefit of local shipping. South of here, there's nothing but sea between you and Antarctica, over fifteen thousand kilometres distant.

Talalla Beach

A few kilometres beyond Dondra, close to the small fishing village of Gandara, **Talalla Beach** a near 2km curve of champagne-coloured sand. Backed by palms, this is one of the south coast's most unspoiled beaches and a favourite with surfers and beachcombers looking for a more tranquil alternative to Tangalla or Mirissa. For the time being at least the bay is blissfully devoid of development, with just a scatter of colourful fishing catamarans sprinkling the bay, a few simple guesthouses and the fabulous Talalla Retreat.

Dickwella Lace

Naotunna South • Daily 9am–5pm • ☎ 076 685 7380

Dickwella Lace is a women's cooperative set up to protect and revive the art of *beeralu*, or bobbin lacemaking, one of the area's traditional industries. Women from local villages are trained up here and provided with the skills to earn an income from their craft. As well as demonstrations of lacemaking techniques, there's also a small shop with beautifully made bags, dolls, toys, tablecloths and linen, as well as lace trimming, for sale.

ARRIVAL AND DEPARTURE

By bus To reach Dondra and Talalla, take any bus heading east from Matara; for the lighthouse, you'll have to alight

DONDRA AND AROUND

at the clocktower in Dondra and walk or take a tuktuk from there.

ACCOMMODATION AND EATING

Talalla Retreat Gandara, 4km east of Dondra ☎ 041 225 171, ⓦ talallaretreat.com. Wonderfully tranquil retreat set in extensive gardens next to Talalla's gorgeous stretch of unspoilt beach. Accommodation is in bungalows and attractive two-storey chalets, with plenty of simple rustic chic and outdoor bathrooms throughout, and there's also a dorm. Also has a simple spa, surfing equipment, and runs a variety of yoga and surfing classes. Rates fall by around 25 percent during low season. Dorm $20, doubles $69

★ **Zephyr** Naotunna, 5km east of Dondra ☎ 077 338 6606, ⓦ facebook.com/zephyrtalalla. Gorgeous new villa on a quiet stretch of beach. There are only four a/c rooms – all with stunning views of the garden and beach. Its restaurant (daily 10am–10pm) and in-house bakery are highlights, serving super-fresh seafood salads, delicious prawn burgers (Rs.750–1600) and refreshing mango and coconut smoothies (Rs.600) in an attractive dining pavilion (open to non-guests). B&B $130

Dickwella and around

Around 15km east of Dondra on the coastal highway, the small town of **DICKWELLA** is home to a pretty curved beach and an attractive resort (see page 176). From here, it's just 8km east to the Hoo-maniya blowhole (see page 179), en route to Tangalla. Nearby, the village of **Hiriketiya** and its horseshoe-shaped beach is becoming one of the south coast's most popular surfing destinations – at the moment it's very small scale with just a few guesthouses, but this may change very soon.

Wewurukannala Temple

1km north of Dickwella • Rs.200 • Buses between Matara and Tangalla via Beliatta pass directly by the temple; alternatively, take any bus along the coastal highway and get off at Dickwella, then cover 2km on foot or by tuktuk

Just inland from Dickwella, the entertainingly kitsch **Wewurukannala Temple** is home to the largest Buddha statue on the island, a 50m concrete colossus constructed in the late 1960s. The rather supercilious-looking Buddha is shown in the seated posture, draped in golden robes with his head crowned by a gaudy, polychromatic *siraspata* (the Buddhist equivalent of the halo) – supposedly representing the flame of wisdom, though on this occasion it looks more like an enormous dollop of ice cream. Immediately to the rear of the statue is a seven-storey building, which the Enlightened One appears to be using as a kind of backrest. You can walk up the steps inside the building, past a big collection of cartoon-style Jataka paintings, and peer into the Buddha's head.

The main **image house** dates from the late nineteenth century and contains an impressive ensemble of huge Buddhas in various poses. Outside and to the left of the main shrine is the oldest part of the temple, a small shrine some 250 years old, decorated with faded murals and housing a seated clay Buddha. Next door, another image house contains a kind of Buddhist **chamber of horrors** showing the punishments awaiting wrongdoers in the afterlife. The gruesome collection of life-size statues here portray assorted unfortunates being tormented by rather jolly-looking devils, and paintings depict various sins – everything from slapping your mother to urinating in front of a temple – and the corresponding punishments.

ACCOMMODATION AND EATING

DICKWELLA AND AROUND

Dickwella Resort & Spa Coastal highway, between km179 and 180 ☎ 041 225 5271, ⓦ brownshotels. com/dickwella. Mid-range resort in a superb location on a headland flanked by two gorgeous beaches, with stylish rooms scattered around extensive gardens. Diving and watersports are available, and there's a large saltwater swimming pool, a spa and good food including a Neapolitan-standard pizzeria. Half-board rates only. $200

★ **Dots Bay House** 2.5km east of Dickwella ☎ 077 793 5593, ⓦ dotsceylon.com. *Dots* is the main hub for live music, great food and surf-related socialising in Hiriketiya, and the lively but chilled-out atmosphere attracts a colourful local and international clientele. It has a/c and non-a/c rooms, plus bungalows and mixed dorms, with some more dorm rooms also in their surf café up the road. Eco-friendly policies mean plastic bottles and straws are banned, while the new surf shop also sells boards, clothing and other items, and can arrange surf lessons and tours. Dorms $13, doubles $50

Hiriketiya Beach House 2.5km east of Dickwella ☎ 077 102 5527, ⓦ surfteamsrilanka.com. There are just four light and airy cement-finished rooms (all a/c, some with outside bathrooms) at this laid-back boutique guesthouse. Also has a beachfront café and bar, and organizes surf-orientated tours. B&B $95

★ **Verse Collective** Pehebiya Road, south end of Dickwella beach ☎ 076 776 8163, ⓦ verse-collective. com. Swanky hotel, café and surf shop in a former wedding hall, with plenty of breezy open spaces. Downstairs are eight dorm beds with fans, while upstairs there are suite rooms with a/c – two also have balconies. The café serves all-day breakfasts (Rs.700–1400) plus *rottys* (Rs.1300). B&B: Dorms $25, doubles $65

Tangalla

Strung out along one of the south's most stunning stretches of coastline, **TANGALLA** (or **Tangalle**) is among the region's more developed beach destinations, with a string of simple guesthouses – and a handful of upmarket hotels and villas – dotted along the coves and beaches that line the oceanfront here. Tourism has never taken off quite as much as the entrepreneurial locals would like, however, and Tangalla remains resolutely low-key compared to the resorts further west. What gives the place added appeal, however, is the number of rewarding attractions in the surrounding countryside, including Sri Lanka's premier site for turtle-watching and the south's finest rock temple (see page 180).

The beaches

Tangalla's beaches stretch for several kilometres either side of **Tangalla town**, a busy but unremarkable provincial centre with a dusty selection of shops and cafés plus the obligatory clocktower and anarchic bus station. The most developed section of coast, though still very somnolent, is to the east of town, along **Medaketiya and Medilla beaches**, a long, straight stretch of golden sand lined with a string of guesthouses opened in anticipation of a flood of tourists who have yet to arrive. Beyond Medilla, around 4km northeast of Tangalla town, the coastline tapers to little more than a

SWIMMING AT TANGALLA

Swimming in Tangalla can be hazardous: Kapuhenwala, Medaketiya and Medilla beaches shelve steeply into the sea and there are dangerous currents in places, though there is now a good swimming spot in front of *Blue Horizon*, between Medaketiya and Medilla, thanks to a recently constructed breakwater. The coves south of town at Pallikaduwa and Goyambokka are pleasantly sheltered. Always check at your guesthouse before venturing into the water: conditions vary considerably even within a few hundred metres.

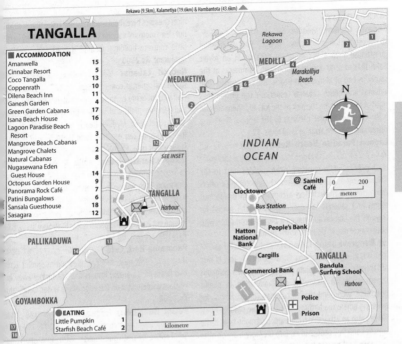

TANGALLA

■ ACCOMMODATION	
Amanwella	15
Cinnabar Resort	5
Coco Tangalla	13
Coppenrath	10
Dilena Beach Inn	11
Ganesh Garden	4
Green Garden Cabanas	17
Isana Beach House	16
Lagoon Paradise Beach Resort	3
Mangrove Beach Cabanas	1
Mangrove Chalets	2
Natural Cabanas	8
Nugasewana Eden Guest House	14
Octopus Garden House	9
Panorama Rock Café	6
Patini Bungalows	7
Sansala Guesthouse	18
Sasagara	12

● EATING	
Little Pumpkin	1
Starfish Beach Café	2

andspit at idyllic Kapuhenwala beach in **Marakolliya**, backed by the mangrove-fringed Rekawa lagoon.

Though just as sleepy, the coast immediately west of town, known as **Pallikaduwa**, is quite different in character, made up of a sequence of rocky coves interspersed with swathes of sand. The most picturesque section of Tangalla coastline can be found a couple of kilometres further west at the village of **Goyambokka**, where a superb rocky promontory is flanked by two beaches. To the west of the headland, Godellawela Beach (or "Silent Beach", as it's popularly known) is an absolute picture, though you'll have to share it with guests from the superb *Amanwella* hotel.

ARRIVAL AND DEPARTURE

TANGALLA

By air Cinnamon Air (see page 31) currently operate daily flights from Dickwella Airport, about 10km southwest of Tangalla on the Mawella Lagoon, to Colombo ($260) and Kandy ($229). The landing spot is 500m south of the coastal highway. Buses run frequently east into Tangalla or west to Dickwella (6.5km).

By bus Buses stop at the station right in the middle of town by the clocktower.

Destinations Colombo via Southern Expressway (hourly; 3hr 30min) or via the coast (every 15min; 5hr); Embilipitiya (every 30min; 1hr 30min); Galle (every 15min; 2hr 30min); Hambantota (every 15min; 1hr 30min); Matara (every 15min; 1hr 30min); Tissamaharama (every 15min; 2hr); Weligama (every 15min; 1hr 45min).

ACCOMMODATION

The biggest concentration of budget guesthouses is north of Tangalla at **Medaketiya**, while, further north, **Medilla** and particularly Kapuhenwala beach at **Marakolliya** (accessed by car from the main road only; take the small side road between the km200 and 201 posts) boast some more characterful alternatives. South of Tangalla there are

further options at **Pallikaduwa** and **Goyambokka** – the rustic accommodation (and restaurants) at the latter are significantly more expensive given the secluded locale and neighbouring beaches. The idyllic bays of Seenimodera (Sugar Bay) and Mawella, 6km **west of Tangalla**, are largely the preserve of private villas.

MARAKOLLIYA

Ganesh Garden Medilla Rd ☏ 047 224 2529, ⓦ ganeshgarden.com; map p.177. Well-established guesthouse with a big range of cabanas in an idyllic palm-shaded sand garden strung with hammocks at the southern end of Marakolliya Beach. The clay-walled mud cabanas and beach cabanas (especially the pricier ones right at the front) are the pick of the lot, and there are also a few cheaper "natural" cabanas by the lagoon. Also has a restaurant, and can arrange local tours. $75

Lagoon Paradise Beach Resort Kapuhenwala Rd ☏ 047 224 2528, ⓦ lagoonparadisebeachresort.com; map p.177. Set in rambling palm gardens next to the Rekawa lagoon, this largish resort-style complex offers comfortable if characterless accommodation in spacious rooms and cabanas (all a/c). Kayaks can be rented for trips on the lagoon and there's a big pool complete with underwater music. Doubles $60, cabanas $90

★ **Mangrove Beach Cabanas** Hambantota Rd ☏ 077 790 6018, ⓦ beachcabana.lk; map p.177. This is one of Tangalla's most appealing places to stay, on a gorgeous stretch of beach and with accommodation in quaint beachside wood-and-thatch cabanas (*douze points* for guessing where the bathroom is) and more swanky villas. There's also an attractive restaurant, and night-time turtle watches and free canoes to explore the lagoon are on offer – or take a catamaran trip with a local fisherman. Cabanas €45, villas €80

Mangrove Chalets Hambantota Rd ☏ 077 790 6018, ⓦ beachcabana.lk; map p.177. *Mangrove Chalets* is located 200m away across the lagoon from sister hotel *Mangrove Beach Cabanas*. It has free-standing rooms in a palm-spiked sand garden, a big pavilion-style restaurant and safe swimming in a natural rock pool in front of the resort. €45

MEDAKETIYA AND MEDILLA

Cinnabar Resort Medilla Rd ☏ 077 965 2190, ⓦ cinnabarresort.wordpress.com; map p.177. Seven imaginatively designed rooms (one is a tree house with branches protruding from the floor, others are made from clay or wood), plus two standard rooms with sea-view balconies and a second tiny tree house, fashioned from mangrove palms, above the restaurant. $50

Coppenrath 61 Vijaya Rd ☏ 076 727 5844, ⓦ coppenrathhouse.com; map p.177. One of the better Medaketiya guesthouses, with clean and bright rooms (some with tubs) in two sea-facing orange blocks behind a pleasant timber restaurant (good food), from where tables spill onto the narrow stretch of beach opposite. The top-floor rooms have a/c and good sea views. Rs.6000, a/c Rs7500

Dilena Beach Inn 65 Vijaya Rd ☏ 047 224 2240, ✉ dilenabeachinn@yahoo.com; map p.177. One of the nicer cheapies hereabouts, with a small collection of simpl[e] but clean rooms of varying sizes (all with hot water) in tw[o] little concrete buildings behind the attractive seafron[t] restaurant. Rs.2500

Natural Cabanas Medilla Rd ☏ 077 993 6454, ⓦ naturalcabanas.com; map p.177. Cute an[d] characterful ochre bungalows, decorated with rope buoy[s] and hanging shells and set in a pretty hammock-strew[n] garden between Medilla Beach and the lagoon. Th[e] friendly family can organize local tours, bicycle hire an[d] lagoon boat trips. Rs.3000

Octopus Garden House Medilla Rd ☏ 077 302 2276, ⓦ octopusgardenhouse.com; map p.177. A simple ye[t] charming B&B, whose five spotless rooms (one with a/c) have sea views, pillared verandas and direct access onto grassy lawn that's sprinkled with sun loungers. There's [a] lounge out back and the beach is less than 50m away. B&E Rs.6500, a/c Rs7500

Panorama Rock Café Medilla Rd ☏ 077 762 0092; map p.177. Six neat, modern, tiled rooms spread acros[s] two floors plus a breezy little restaurant tucked away in verdant garden right on the edge of the water. Good value Rs.5000

Patini Bungalows Medilla Rd ☏ 077 740 2038, ⓦ patinibungalows.com; map p.177. French[-] Sri Lankan-owned guesthouse with five sparklingl[y] clean, attractively furnished beach bungalows se[t] amid lush palm-shaded gardens on peaceful Medill[a] beach. The owners can arrange kayaking on the lagoo[n] (Rs.1500/90min), and also rent bicycles (Rs.500/day) an[d] scooters (Rs.1000/day). Only drawbacks: hot water cost[s] a bizarre Rs.250 per person per night extra, and there's n[o] food. Rs.5500

Sasagara Near Frangipani Hotel ☏ 077 792 0346; ma[p] p.177. Very welcoming homestay that's a 2min stro[ll] from the beach, with just three tidy tiled rooms (hot water[)] opening onto a furnished courtyard. Great budget optio[n] Rs.2000

PALLIKADUWA AND GOYAMBOKKA

★ **Coco Tangalla** 355 Mahawella Rd ☏ 081 720 1115, ⓦ cocotangalla.com; map p.177. Located just to th[e] west of Tangalla town, this well-run, stylishly designe[d] boutique hotel is home to just six small, well-equippe[d] a/c rooms; four are in the atmospheric main house and th[e] other two in a more modern adjacent annexe. Also has [a] lovely pool, garden and excellent food. $190

★ **Green Garden Cabanas** Goyambokka Beach ☏ 07[7] 624 7628, ⓦ greengardencabanas.com; map p.177. This guesthouse has an assortment of rooms and concret[e] cabanas scattered among attractive gardens, just [a] couple of minutes' walk from a slim stretch of beach. The restaurant serves delicious wood-fired pizza. Doubles $30, a/c $34; cabanas $40

Nugasewana Eden Guest House Mahawela Rd ☎ 047 224 0389, ⓦ nugasewana.com; map p.177. The setting, right next to the main road, isn't great, but rooms all with hot water, some with a/c) are among the best in town at this price: modern, tiled, nicely furnished and scrupulously clean. There's also a new sea-facing pool and ab tree house ($90). **$28**, a/c **$55**

Gansala Guest House Goyambokka Beach ☎ 077 601 693, ✉ surangalanka0@gmail.com; map p.177. Just two spacious, tiled en-suite rooms with four-poster beds and hot water, in a family-run guesthouse on a hillside; each has a nice veranda overlooking the garden below, and there's good home-cooked food. **Rs.3000**

WEST OF TANGALLA

★ **Amanwella** Godellawela Beach ☎ 047 224 1333, ⓦ amanresorts.com; map p.177. Set on sublime Godellawela Beach (or "Silent Beach", as it's generally known), this utterly captivating if uber-expensive resort offers a model of how beach hotels in Sri Lanka should be done, with a stylishly understated, low-impact design which blends magically with the surrounding palm trees and water. The rooms are works of art in themselves, with all mod cons including large plunge pools and superb ocean views through huge French windows, plus a sensational infinity pool overlooking the beach. In low season rates drop by 25 percent. **$1364**

Isana Beach House Seenimodera Beach ☎ 047 224 4033, ⓦ isanabeachhouse.com; map p.177. Small six-room boutique hotel on an idyllically peaceful stretch of beach west of Tangalla. Rooms follow a minimal Japanese aesthetic, flaunting monotone furnishings, and have sea views. Serves good Italian cuisine, and has a small garden with a grassy lawn and direct beach access. **$100**

EATING

The nicest places to eat are the string of seafront guesthouses in Medaketiya and Medilla – the restaurants at Dilena, Ganesh Garden and Mangrove Beach Cabanas also serve reliably good food and a range of drinks.

Little Pumpkin Marakolliya Beach ☎ 072 787 6539; map p.177. Deservedly popular little seaside restaurant with tables on a raised, curved timber deck. Serves Sri Lankan meals and seafood; jumbo prawns, chips and salad costs Rs.1000. Daily 8am–10pm.

Starfish Beach Café Medilla Rd ☎ 047 224 1005; map p.177. Small *rotty* shop attached to a guesthouse perched midway between Medaketiya and Medilla beaches, with a few tables on a little platform by the sea. Serves sweet and savoury *rottys* (chocolate and banana, cheese, vegetable; Rs.150–600) as well as *kottu* concoctions (Rs.500–650). Daily 8am–9pm.

DIRECTORY

Banks The ATMs at Commercial Bank, People's Bank and Hatton National Bank in the middle of town accept foreign cards.

Internet Samith Café, 150m east of the clocktower on Medaketiya Rd (next to *Damith Homestay*), is handy for getting online (daily 8am–8pm; Rs.120/hr).

Watersports and fishing Bandula Surfing School, 130 Beach Rd (☎ 077 635 7734) offers surf lessons for $44, as well as snorkelling ($20) and fishing ($60 per tour). They can arrange pick-up from wherever you're staying.

Around Tangalla

A rewarding half-day trip from Tangalla combines the **Hoo-maniya blowhole**, the Wewurukannala Temple (see page 175) with its enormous Buddha statue, and the absorbing rock temples of **Mulkirigala**. All local guesthouses should be able to arrange a combined round trip by tuktuk to these three places; the current going rate is around Rs.3500 for two people. Other interesting local excursions include evening trips to spot turtles coming ashore at **Rekawa**, while Tangalla can also be used as a base for trips to the little-visited wetlands of the **Kalametiya Bird Sanctuary** en route to Hambantota.

Hoo-maniya blowhole

Kudawela · Rs.500 · Take a direct Tangalla–Matara bus along the coast road and get off at the turn-off to Kudawela, just beyond Nakulugamuwa, then cover the 2km on foot or by tuktuk

Around 8km west of Tangalla, the **Hoo-maniya blowhole** is one of the south's more uncomplicated tourist attractions – the fanciful name derives from the low, booming "Hoo" sound it produces prior to spouting water. The blowhole is formed from a deep, narrow cleft in the cliff which funnels plumes of water up into the air in great jets by some mysterious action of water pressure – it's most impressive during the monsoon (May–Sept; June is reckoned to be best), when the jets can reach heights of 15m. At other times it can be underwhelming, though a push-button contraption at the **visitor centre** gives an entertaining re-creation of the blowhole's jetstream even when the real thing has decided not to perform.

Mulkirigala

Daily 6am–6pm (last entry 5pm) • Rs.500 (guide Rs.1000) • Bus from Tangalla to Beliatta (every 15min; 30min), then catch any onward bus to Middeniya, taking you directly past the turn-off to the site; a round trip by tuktuk costs Rs.3000 including waiting time

Sixteen kilometres north of Tangalla lies the remarkable temple-monastery of **Mulkirigala**, the only monument in the south to rival the great ancient Buddhist sites of the Cultural Triangle. Mulkirigala (also spelt "Mulgirigala") consists of a series of **rock temples** carved out of the face of a huge rock outcrop which rises sheer and seemingly impregnable for over 200m out of the surrounding palm forests. The temples date back to the third century BC, but were completely restored during the eighteenth century under the patronage of the kings of Kandy.

Terrace one

Immediately to the left of the ticket office lies **terrace one**, home to two rock temples and a small dagoba; the unusual structures standing on elephants outside are oil lamps. The temple nearest the entrance contains a reclining Buddha, plus paintings (along the side wall nearest the entrance) of Vishnu, Kataragama (by the door) and Vibhishana (the demonic blue figure with fangs). The second cave here is one of Mulkirigala's finest, with vivid Kandyan-style paintings dating back to the eighteenth-century restoration – the wall between the two doors, decorated with Jataka stories, is particularly striking.

Terraces two and three

Retrace your steps past the ticket office to reach the steep flight of steps that lead up to **terrace two**, which has a single rock temple housing a reclining Buddha flanked by two disciples. Further steps lead up to **terrace three**, where there are four temples, ranged side by side, and a small rock pool at the left-hand end with a half-submerged Sinhala inscription. Immediately behind the pool is the smallest of the four temples (you have to go through the adjacent temple to reach it), the so-called **Naga** or **Cobra temple**, named after the fearsome snake painted on the door at the rear.

The next temple along sports a gaudy reclining Buddha in its inner shrine, while the third temple, known as the **Raja Mahavihara**, is Mulkirigala's finest. The vestibule, paved with old Dutch floor tiles and supported by Kandyan-style wooden pillars, contains an antique chest which was once used to hold ola-leaf manuscripts of religious and other texts. It was in this chest, in 1826, that the British official and antiquarian **George Turnour** discovered a clutch of ancient manuscripts which enabled him to translate the Mahavamsa (see page 402), the first time Sri Lanka's famous historical chronicle had been deciphered in the modern era. The shrine itself holds yet another sleeping Buddha, its feet intricately decorated. The fantastically kitsch final temple is home to Mulkirigala's only *parinirvana* Buddha – that is to say a dead, rather than a merely sleeping, Buddha (see page 435), surrounded by a lurid tableau of grieving figures.

Terrace four

Next to the Raja Mahavihara, steps lead up again, past a set of treacherously narrow and steep rock-cut steps, to **terrace four**, at the very summit of the site. The main attraction here is the wonderful view – scramble down the path to the left of the dagoba down to the open rock for an unobstructed panorama over a sea of palms.

Rekawa

1km off the coastal highway, signposted just east of the 203km post • Nightly turtle watches start around 8pm from the Turtle Watch Visitor Centre (☎ 076 685 7380, ⓦ turtlewatchrekawa.org) on Rekawa beach • Rs.1000 • A tuktuk from Tangalla (and back) will cost around Rs.1500

The 2km beach at **REKAWA** village, 10km east of Tangalla, is home to one of the most important **sea turtle nesting sites** in Sri Lanka, visited by five different species which lay their eggs in the sand here most nights throughout the year (see page 181). The nesting sites along the beach are protected by Turtle Watch Rekawa, run by the Nature Friends of Rekawa (NFR) – an offshoot of the Turtle Conservation Project (TCP), which was established in 1993 to conduct research into visiting turtles. Local villagers are paid to protect the turtle eggs from poachers and some are trained as tourist guides. **Turtle watches** are held nightly, with NFR members keeping watch up and down the beach for their arrival. The **best time** to see the animals is between March and June; periods when there's a full or fullish moon are also good throughout the year, because there are more turtles and there's also more light to see them by. Rekawa's record is apparently 23 turtles in one night, and most nights from March to June at least one will appear, though you might have to wait in the dark until around midnight for a sighting, most likely in the company of many other tourists.

ACCOMMODATION
REKAWA

To get to the beachside village of Rekawa, turn off the coastal highway at the Netolpitiya junction, and follow the signs to Turtle Watch.

Green Turtle Wellawathugoda Rd ☎ 070 267 5929, ⓦ bit.ly/2EM6v1H. Recently opened guesthouse in a pleasant garden run by two friendly brothers, opposite Buckingham Place (see below). Currently there are just two spacious a/c rooms, in a separate chalet-style building. Meals are served in a dining pavilion. With easy access to the beach, this is a great location for turtle-watching enthusiasts. B&B $55

Buckingham Place Wellawathugoda Rd ☎ 047 348 9447, ⓦ buckingham-place.com. Striking, modern boutique resort, a stone's throw from Rekawa's turtle beach, with rooms and suites in a series of elegant cube-shaped buildings attractively situated on a bluff above the lagoon. The cool, minimalist rooms feature lots of polished stone and crisp white walls enlivened with colourful artworks and fabrics. There's also a rather mediocre restaurant (open to non-guests with advance reservation) and bar, plus two swimming pools, free bikes for guests, canoe trips and turtle-watching. Doubles $265, suites $325

TURTLE NESTING AT REKAWA

The chance to see **turtles** laying their eggs (and if you're lucky, hatching) at Rekawa, by the light of the moon, is one of the south coast's natural highlights. When one appears (the vast majority are green turtles), it first crawls across the beach, away from the sea, leaving behind a remarkable trail which looks as if a one-wheeled tractor has driven straight out of the water. This takes an exhausting thirty minutes, since turtles are very badly adapted for travel on land. Having reached the top of the beach, the turtles then spend about another 45 minutes digging a huge hole; you'll hear periodic thrashings and the sound of great clouds of sand being scuffed up. As laying begins, you're allowed in close to watch, although all you actually see is the turtle's backside with eggs – looking just like ping-pong balls – periodically popping out in twos and threes. The eggs are then taken by staff to be **reburied** in a secure location. The turtle then rests, fills in the hole and eventually crawls back down to the sea. It's an epic effort, the sight of which makes the whole evening-long experience worthwhile.

Kalametiya Bird Sanctuary

Daily 24hr • Free • Catamaran trips cost around Rs.4000 for up to four people

Roughly equidistant between Tangalla and Hambantota, the **Kalametiya Bird Sanctuar** (best Nov–March) comprises an area of coastal lagoons and mangroves, similar to that found in Bundala, and rich in marine and other birdlife. There are various entrances to the sanctuary, perhaps most conveniently from the road leading to the *Turtle Bay* reso and *Mamboz Beach Cabanas* (see below), both of which can organize catamaran trips on the sanctuary's pretty **Lunama lagoon**.

ACCOMMODATION   KALAMETIYA BIRD SANCTUAR

To reach the places listed, take the turning off the main coastal highway towards the coast at Gurupokuna junction, 2km west of Hungama (signed Kalametiya; it's very close to the 214km post). After 3km you'll come to a fork: turn right for *Back of Beyond* (followed by another right after 700m), and keep left for *Mamboz* and *Turtle Bay*.

Back of Beyond Kahandamodera ☎077 395 1527, ⓦbackofbeyond.lk. The handful of clay-coloured cottages at this rustic eco-retreat engulfed by lagoon-edged scrub jungle reveals the area at its most tranquil. The extensive grounds brim with dry-zone produce that's used in the lodge's nutritious, local-style meals. Cottages display plenty of wood and polished cement, sleep 2–6, and have breezy private terraces. Activities include walking, kayaking and night-time turtle watches on the local beach (a 10min walk away). B&B $120

★ **Mamboz Beach Cabanas** ☎047 492 1702, ⓦmambozbeach.com. Set in a sandy palm garden

strewn with hammocks on an endless stretch of desert beach, this idyllic retreat has just two simple rooms (share bathrooms) and three comfortable, fan-cooled wood cabanas. Owner Matthew is hugely welcoming, and al an experienced Thai masseur. The food is outstanding a dinner is served communally. Closed May–Sept. Half boa only: doubles $104, cabana $159

Turtle Bay ☎047 788 7853, ⓦturtlebay.lk. Sere boutique hotel in an idyllic, picture-perfect setting Kalametiya beach, with sweeping coastal views and very peaceful Robinson Crusoe ambience. There are ju seven rooms, kitted out with suave modern wooden dec and most mod cons (but no TVs), plus a small garden a neat little pool. Turtles can often be spotted on the bea here during season (Nov–April), and it's just 5min walk Kalametiya Bird Sanctuary. B&B $140

Hambantota

The area dividing Tangalla and Hambantota marks the transition between Sri Lanka's wet and dry zones, where the lush palm forests of the southwest give way to the arid and scrub-covered savanna that characterizes much of the island. Some 53km east of Tangalla, the dusty provincial capital of **HAMBANTOTA** is the unlikely beneficiary of a remarkable economic regeneration programme sponsored by former president Mahinda Rajapakse (who hails from Hambantota District) focused aroun the construction of the island's second international airport (see page 25), the dredging of a huge new Chinese-sponsored port, and a $15 million International Convention Centre that's hardly been used. Other ambitious projects include an international cricket ground, an inconvenient 27km north of town (and predictably named after the former president), and a 300-acre botanic gardens at Mirijjawila, 15km distant. Despite all of this, Hambantota remains, for the time being at least, an indomitably sleepy little place with little obvious tourist potential, except for avi bidwatchers and as an alternative base to Tissamaharama from which to visit Bunda or Yala national parks. The modest attractions of the town itself are easily covered in an hour's walk.

   Hambantota is the **salt** capital of Sri Lanka. Salt is produced by letting sea water into the **lewayas**, the often dazzlingly white saltpans which surround the town, and allowin it to evaporate, after which the residue is scraped up and sold.

A MALAY ENCLAVE

Hambantota was originally settled by Malay seafarers (the name is a corruption of "Sampan-tota", or "Sampan Port", alluding to the type of boat in which they arrived) and the town still has the largest concentration of **Malay-descended people** in Sri Lanka, with a correspondingly high proportion of Muslims and mosques – you really notice the call to prayer here. A few inhabitants still speak Malay, and although you probably won't notice this, you're likely to be struck by the occasional presence of a local face with pure Southeast Asian features.

The fish market and harbour

Starting from the lively **fish market** opposite the bus station, follow the coastal road south, edging the pretty breakwater-fringed **harbour**. The views over the beach, usually lined with colourful fishing boats, and along the coast to the grand, saw-toothed hills around Kataragama away in the distance are magnificent, though the beach itself is scruffy, and strong currents make swimming dangerous.

Old Hambantota

Beyond the harbour, the road meanders around the headland to the attractive old *Rest House*, at the centre of a time-warped little cluster of recently renovated government buildings and crumbling old villas that is all that survives of colonial Hambantota. The buildings here were formerly home to Hambantota's British government agents, among them **Leonard Woolf**, future husband of Virginia, who spent several years here in the pay of the Ceylon Civil Service – his name is recorded on a board outside the District Secretariat – before returning to England, where following his marriage he published the classic *The Village in the Jungle*, an extraordinarily depressing tale of life in the Sri Lankan backlands. Nearby sits a neglected old British **Martello tower**, and a black-and-white-striped **lighthouse**.

Magampura Ruhuna Heritage Museum

Daily 9am–4pm · Rs.500 · ⓦ museum.gov.lk

Based in the restored former District Secretariat offices, this museum has an interesting perspective on both the ancient and modern history of the area. Exhibits range from photos and models of ruins to large portraits of Leonard Woolf (see page 183) and R.L. Spittel (Sri Lankan surgeon and Veddha expert), with mentions of their connections to Hambantota and the "admiration" they received from the local people.

ARRIVAL AND DEPARTURE | HAMBANTOTA

By bus Buses stop at the terminal right in the middle of town. There are branches of Hatton National Bank, just up from the harbour on Main St, and the People's Bank, opposite the *Rest House*.

Destinations Colombo, via the coastal highway (every 15min; 6hr) or via the Southern Expressway (every 1hr 30min; 4hr); Embilipitiya (every 15min; 1hr 30min); Galle (every 15min; 3hr 30min); Matara (every 15min; 2hr 30min); Monaragala (every 15min; 3hr); Tangalla (every 15min; 1hr 30min); Tissamaharama (every 15min; 45min); Weligama (every 15min; 3hr).

ACCOMMODATION

Happy Beach 91/2 Murray Rd ⓣ 077 678 3090. Friendly beachside guesthouse with unobstructed views of the coastline. The five rooms are clean but very basic; all have fans and two are a/c. There's also a cabana hut with two beds for shoestring travellers (Rs.2000). The main reason to stay here is the splendid location. B&B **Rs.3000**

Peacock Beach Hotel 1km along the old road to Tissa ⓣ 047 567 9032, ⓦ peacockbeachonline.com. One of Hambantota's golden oldies, set behind luxuriant gardens on a rather wild stretch of beach (not safe for swimming) with a pool tucked to one side. Accommodation (all with a/c and satellite TV) comprises a mix of older standard rooms and much nicer deluxe rooms. The *Monara Restaurant* dining room has a fantastic peacock-inspired ceiling and seventies aesthetic. They can arrange jeeps to Bundala (Rs.4700) and Yala (Rs.7800). B&B **$90**

2

2

Rest House Murray Rd ☎047 222 0299, ⓦhambantotaresthouse.com. Renovated in 2015, this fine old guesthouse has a charming, colonial character and is superbly located on a headland overlooking the harbour, with views of the parched coastline and distant hills from the veranda. Rooms in the atmospheric old wing are huge and stuffed full of creaking old furniture; the cheaper rooms in the "new" wing are less characterful, but still neat and comfortable; all are a/c. B&B Rs.9000

★ **Shangri-La Hambantota Golf Resort and Spa** Chitragala, Ambalantota ☎047 788 8888, ⓦshangri-

la.com. This vast luxury resort is the largest in Sri Lanka with an eighteen-hole golf course and no fewer than three pools and a water slide. The 300 opulent rooms are divided into five animal-themed blocks, with either beach or golf course views. There are three restaurants, as well as a gorgeous lounge bar that's particularly atmospheric at night. The resident naturalist can advise on wildlife excursions and organize fascinating jungle boat safaris. B&B $244

EATING AND DRINKING

Jade Green Opposite the Peacock Beach Hotel ☎047 222 0692. This is a rather drab-looking restaurant beside the salt pans, but it offers a good range of Sri Lankan and Western breakfasts and snacks, plus the usual local staples (Rs.400–1200) and an above-average lunchtime rice and curry buffet (Rs.660). Daily 8am–10pm.

Lihiniya Bar 1km along the old road to Tissa ☎047 567 9032, ⓦpeacockbeachonline.com. The terrace of the *Monara Restaurant* in the *Peacock Beach Hotel* is

a pleasant and breezy place for a drink at sunset. Daily 10am–midnight.

Rest House Murray Rd ☎047 222 0299. The attractive colonial-style dining room at Hambantota's *Rest House* is the prettiest spot in town for lunch or dinner, but the short menu has only the usual array of rice and curry and other Sri Lankan standards, plus pasta and noodles. Mains Rs.400–1100. Daily 7am–10pm.

DIRECTORY

Banks Several banks along or just off the main road have ATMs accepting foreign cards.

Internet P&H Communications, Wilmot St, next to the bus station (daily 8am–8pm; Rs.80/hr).

Bundala National Park

Daily 6am–6pm • $10, plus the usual additional charges and taxes (see page 50)

Accessed around 15km east of Hambantota (and a similar distance west of Tissa), **Bundala National Park** is one of Sri Lanka's foremost destinations for **birdwatchers**, protecting an important area of coastal wetland famous for its abundant aquatic (and other) birdlife, as well as being home to significant populations of elephants, crocodiles, turtles and other fauna. Although it doesn't have quite the range of wildlife or scenery of nearby Yala National Park, Bundala is much quieter, and makes a good alternative if you want to avoid Yala's crowds.

The park stretches along the coast for around 20km, enclosing five shallow and brackish **lagoons**, or *lewayas* (they sometimes dry up completely during long periods of drought), separated by thick low scrubby forest running down to coastal dunes. Almost two hundred bird species have been recorded here, their numbers swelled by seasonal visitors, who arrive between September and March. The lagoons attract an amazing variety of **aquatic birds**, including ibis, pelicans, painted storks, egrets and spoonbills, though sadly greater flamingos, formerly present in huge flocks, are now rarely seen due, it's thought, to freshwater contamination of the *lewayas* which killed off the tiny insect larvae they used to feed on. These days, the park's most visible avian residents are its many **peacocks** (or Indian peafowl, as they're correctly known): a memorable sight in the wild at any time, especially when seen perched sententiously among the upper branches of the park's innumerable skeletal *palu* (rosewood) trees.

Bundala is also home to 32 species of **mammals**, including (most commonly seen) excitable troupes of grey langur **monkeys**. There are also **elephants**, including a few permanent residents and a few more semi-residents; larger seasonal migratory herds

of up to sixty, comprising animals that roam the Yala, Uda Walawe and Bundala area, also visit the park. You'll probably also come across large **land monitors** and lots of enormous **crocodiles**, which can be seen sunning themselves along the sides of the park's lagoons and watercourses.

The **best time to visit** is between September and March, when the migratory birds arrive; early morning is the best time of day, though the park is also rewarding in late afternoon. Take binoculars, if you have them.

ARRIVAL AND DEPARTURE

BUNDALA NATIONAL PARK

By tour Bundala is about a 20min drive from both Hambantota and Tissa; drivers charge around Rs.5000–6500 for a half-day jeep tour from either. Tours are most easily arranged in Tissa (see page 188) or via the *Peacock Beach Hotel* in Hambantota or the *Lagoon Inn* (see page 186).

ACCOMMODATION

Lagoon Inn Bundala Junction, midway between Hambantota and Tissa ☎ 071 631 0173, ✉ lagooninn@yahoo.com. Set back from the main Hambantota–Tissa road around 2km from Bundala, this family homestay (run by an avid birdwatcher) has simple, clean rooms (the best are on the first floor overlooking scrubby marshland) and home-cooked meals, while jeeps to Bundala (Rs.4500) and Yala (Rs.8000) can be arranged. No wi-fi. **Rs.2000**

Tissamaharama

Beyond Bundala National Park the main highway turns away from the coast towards the pleasant town of **TISSAMAHARAMA** (usually abbreviated to **Tissa**). Tissa's main attraction is as a base for trips to the nearby national parks of Yala and Bundala or the temple town of Kataragama, but it's an agreeable place in its own right, with a handful of monuments testifying to the town's important place in early Sri Lankan history when, under the name of **Mahagama**, it was one of the principal settlements of the southern province of Ruhunu. Mahagama is said to have been founded in the third century BC by a brother of the great Devanampiya Tissa (see page 402) of Anuradhapura, and later rose to prominence under **Kavan Tissa**, father of the legendary Dutugemunu (see page 330).

Tissamaharama and Sandagiri dagobas

Standing amid lush paddy fields just north of the town centre is the most impressive of Tissa's various dagobas, the **Tissamaharama dagoba**, allegedly built by Kavan Tissa in the second century BC, with a "bubble"-shaped dome topped by an unusually large and lavishly decorated *harmika* and broad spire – a strangely squat and top-heavy-looking construction unlike any other dagoba in the island.

A second, much more obviously ancient (and bare brick) stupa, the **Sandagiri dagoba**, stands close by, comprising a big, square, high brick base and a slope-shouldered stupa in the "heap-of-paddy" shape (see page 436), although the *harmika* has completely vanished. The scant remains of the monastery that formerly stood here can be seen scattered hereabouts.

Tissa Wewa and around

About 1km north of the modern town lies the beautiful **Tissa Wewa**, an expansive artificial lake thought to have been constructed in the second or third century BC – the shore nearest the town is often busy with crowds of people bathing and flocks of aquatic birds including bitterns, herons and egrets. A rewarding walk leads along the massive **bund** (embankment) which bounds the lake's southern shore and is lined by majestic old Indian rain trees which were planted throughout the island by the British to provide shade along major trunk roads and are home to thousands of bats. At the

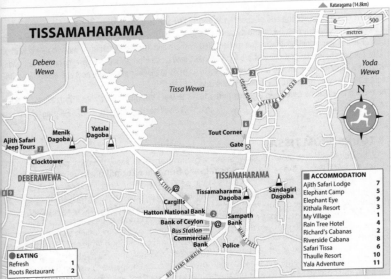

far end a track leads to the smaller adjacent lake of **Debera Wewa**, another haven for birdlife, its surface prettily covered in water lilies.

From the southwest corner of the Tissa Wewa, a short walk along the road back towards the town centre takes you past two large dagobas dating back to the second century BC. The first of these is the **Yatala dagoba**, surrounded by a wall faced with sculpted elephant heads, while 400m further down the road is the similar **Menik dagoba**.

ARRIVAL AND DEPARTURE

TISSAMAHARAMA

By bus Tissa is a major terminus for buses travelling east along the coastal road, which stop here before heading back west (meaning that you should be able to get a seat); most are old SLTB rust buckets. To head back to Colombo, it's faster and more comfortable to change onto a highway bus in Tangalla or Matara. Buses stop at the bus station in the middle of the town; a tuktuk to the guesthouses around Tissa Wewa will cost Rs.150–200. If you're staying around Tissa Wewa and going to Kataragama (every 10min; 20min), there's no need to go into the bus station in town; just stand on the main road here, which is also the road to Kataragama, and flag down anything that passes. Tissa is also a convenient place to head up into the

hills, though to get there you may have to change buses at Pannegamuwa, a small town located on a major road intersection 5km west of Tissa, and/or at Wellawaya, from where there are plenty of buses to Ella or Haputale. There are also a few services to Monaragala, from where you can catch a bus to Arugam Bay.

Destinations Colombo (every 30min; 7hr); Ella (3 daily; 2hr); Galle (8 daily; 4hr–4hr 30min); Hambantota (every 15min; 45min–1hr); Ella (3 daily; 2hr); Kandy (daily; 7hr); Matara (every 15min; 3hr); Monaragala (daily; 2hr); Polonnaruwa (daily; 6hr); Tangalla (every 15min; 2hr); Weligama (every 15min; 3hr 20min); Wellawaya (hourly; 1hr 30min).

ACCOMMODATION

Most accommodation in Tissa is north of the town proper, surrounding the tranquil **Tissa Wewa**. There are also few appealing alternatives near the small temple town of **Kirinda** (see page 190) and on the far banks of the very tranquil **Yoda Lake**, 2.5km east of town, far from the madding safari crowds yet conveniently en route to Yala.

TISSA WEWA AND AROUND

★ **Ajith Safari Lodge** Near the clocktower in Deberawewa ☏ 047 223 7557, ⓦ yalawild.com; map above. New lodge that's super convenient for early morning safari excursions if you've booked with Ajith Safari – you can just tumble out of bed and into the jeep. The nine a/c rooms are squeaky clean and comfortable, and the food is delicious. B&B **Rs.4200**

2

Elephant Camp Opposite the end of Court Rd ☎047 223 7231, ⓦelephantcampguest.blogspot.co.uk; map p.187. Friendly family guesthouse with five spotless tiled rooms (all with hot water and optional a/c for Rs.2000 extra) in a modern house on the main road (meaning slight traffic noise at the front). The food is superb and the evening meal has no fewer than eighteen curries to sample. Rs.2000

Kithala Resort Kataragama Rd ☎047 223 7206, ⓦkithalaresort.com; map p.187. Upmarket hotel with suave and attractively furnished modern rooms with all mod cons and private balconies overlooking the lush paddy fields to the rear, plus a nice pool and garden area. B&B $140

★ **My Village** Court Rd ☎077 350 0090, ⓦmyvillageelk.com; map p.187. Relaxing guesthouse

TOURS FROM TISSA

A horde of local operators offer a wide range of trips from Tissa. Easily the most popular are the half- (7hr) and full-day (12hr) trips to **Yala** and **Bundala national parks**, which are best started at either 5.15am or 2.30pm, to be in the parks for dawn or dusk. Some operators also offer **overnight camping trips**; these usually leave at 2pm and return at 10.30am the next morning and include one or two park drives, plus tent, dinner, breakfast and tea. Camping trips don't come cheap (upwards of $150/person, including entrance fees), although staying the night in the park gives you the chance to see nocturnal animals, including snakes, crocs, owls, wild pigs, porcupines (rare) and nocturnal birds. You can arrange similar trips to stay in the buffer zone around the edge of Yala; the terrain is similar, and you might see a bit of wildlife, but by and large this is a watered-down experience compared to visiting the park itself, and costs the same (apart from not having to pay park entrance fees).

Another popular option is the half-day excursion to the rock temple at **Situlpahuwa** followed by a visit to **Kataragama** for the evening puja. The journey to Situlpahuwa passes through the fringes of Yala (though you don't have to pay the entrance fee), so you might spot some wildlife en route, but this is much less interesting than a proper trip to the main portion of the park. Some drivers also offer a combined tour of five different local **tanks**, including Tissa Wewa, Debera Wewa and Wirawila Wewa, all rich in birdlife (assuming the tanks haven't dried up, as happens frequently in periods of low rainfall). There's also a third national park nearby, **Lunugamwehera** (entered off the Wellawaya–Tissa road close to the km282 post) although this lacks the appeal of either Yala or Bundala and sees very few visitors.

TOUR OPERATORS AND PRICES

Almost all the town's guesthouses and hotels can fix up tours, though it may be Rs.500–1000 cheaper to organize one yourself with one of the drivers at **tout corner**, by the archway at the southeastern corner of Tissa Wewa, or at the Yala Junction with the Kirinda Road (on the way into Kirinda), where a second rabble of jeep drivers is stationed. It's worth chatting to a few drivers to gauge their level of English, and their knowledge of the park and its wildlife.

A half-day trip to Yala or Bundala in a standard jeep (seating up to six people) currently costs Rs.4500–5000 or Rs.9000–10,000 for a full day, plus entry ticket and tip (prices are about Rs.500 more to Lunugamwehera National Park). If you're after a more luxurious ride, try **Ajith Safari Jeep Tours** (☎047 223 7557, ⓦyalawild.com), near the clocktower in Deberawewa, which has a fleet of quieter and more comfy front-facing jeeps that will set you back around $145/$190 for a half/full day-trip for two (including park entry tickets, breakfast and snacks) to Yala or $105/$180 for a half/full day tour to Bundala. Other half-day trips – such as to Situlpahuwa combined with Kataragama or around five different local lakes – also cost around Rs.4500.

SCAMS AND ANNOYANCES

It's been known for rogue drivers to collect the Yala entrance fee from their passengers, then to drive them around the edge of the park on the pretence that they're inside it, allowing the driver to pocket the hefty entrance fee. Only ever hand over entrance fees at the park's visitor centre, to the relevant official. Note too that in recent years, an increase in visitors and jeep operators mean that at certain times of the year Yala gets overrun with vehicles. Lazy and inexperienced drivers, often in anticipation of a good tip, share leopard sightings by mobile phone, meaning that you might be in one of many jeeps crowding around a leopard in a noisy, diesel-filled gridlock of fumes. Better operators avoid the crowds as much as possible and seek out leopards (and other wildlife) in quieter areas of the park.

spread across two floors of a pair of buildings, beneath a shady roof. The restaurant downstairs serves excellent rice and curry, and the seven rooms (all a/c with hot water) are cool, smart and surprisingly stylish for the price – those upstairs are best. A new pool and three new rooms were under construction at the time of writing. **$50**

Rain Tree Hotel ☎047 223 8125, ⚲theraintreehotel.com; map p.187. New mid-range hotel in a shady lakeside location with over twenty spacious and stylishly decorated rooms. The highlight is the rooftop viewing deck, where it's possible to see thousands of birds – and the hundreds of bats that fly in at sunset to roost in the trees. B&B **$135**

★ **Richard's Cabanas** ☎077 606 6739, ⚲richardscabanas.com; map p.187. Three sought-after a/c cottages with terraces overlooking a small gurgling river in tranquil surroundings. Each is spacious and adorned with colourful handloom bedspreads. The owner knows Yala inside out, and can arrange overnight camping trips. **Rs.7000**

Safari Tissa Kataragama Rd ☎047 567 7620, ⚲thesafarihotel.lk; map p.187. Set right next to Tissa Wewa, this smartly refurbished former guesthouse has the most scenic position in town. The fifty rooms have modern decor and all mod cons, plus pleasant views of the lake. Also has a good-sized pool and spa. B&B **$163**

TISSA TOWN AND DEBERAWEWA

Elephant Eye 350m off the Tissa Rd (turn off beside Seylan Bank), 750m south of the Deberawewa clocktower ☎047 223 8901, ⚲elephanteyeyala.com; map p.187. In a quiet location, directly opposite Riverside Cabanas, this new hotel tends to attract bus tour groups. The smart but simply furnished rooms have flat screen TVs

as well as tea and coffee making facilities. There's also a pool. B&B **$60**

Riverside Cabana 350m off the Tissa Rd (turn off beside Seylan Bank), 750m south of the Deberawewa clocktower ☎077 358 3468, ⚲riversidecabana.com; map p.187. The highlights of this friendly guesthouse are its rustic palm-thatched treehouses perched above the river, including the new four-storey en-suite option that's perfect for families – if the kids can handle the ladders ($79). Facilities are basic (though clean), but accommodation in Tissa doesn't get quirkier (or friendlier) than this. Also has two simple en-suite rooms. Free pick up from the clocktower. **$36**, treehouse **$50**

YODA WEWA

Thaulle Resort 4km southeast of town ☎047 223 7901, ⚲thaulle.com; map p.187. This upmarket hotel offers fabulous views, utter tranquillity and some of the town's smartest accommodation – even if the orange colour scheme isn't quite in keeping with the lush riverside locale. Rooms range from comfortable budget options to fabulous suites with unrivalled lake vistas ($300) – all featuring timber floors, colourful handlooms and plenty of mod cons. Also has a pool, bar and restaurant, plus an eye-catching ceiling mural in reception. Breakfast included. **$195**

Yala Adventure 2km beyond Thaulle Resort ☎077 390 6666, ⚲thayalaadventure.lk; map p.187. A great off-the-beaten-track lakeside lodge, offering standard rooms in a tall "tower", deluxe cottages ($130) and, best of all, gorgeous a/c tents complete with snazzy en-suite bathrooms ($175). Safaris aside, the friendly staff can arrange many other activities including rappelling, archery, cycling, trekking and kayaking. Breakfast included. **$80**.

EATING

Refresh Kataragama Rd ☎047 223 7357, ⚲refreshhikkaduwa.com; map p.187. Virtually every tourist piles in at some point to the popular Refresh, a big, slick operation with seating under a cavernous open-air pavilion. The wide-ranging menu majors on seafood, and there's also a good spread of pasta and pizza, plus Sri Lankan and Chinese standards and a few other international dishes. The food gets mixed reviews and is a bit pricey (mains from Rs.1000, some seafood dishes

significantly more) although the huge rice and curry spread is always a good option. There's also a full bar, Lavazza coffee and shisha. Daily 5am–10pm.

Roots Restaurant Just off Main St ☎077 570 1844; map p.187. Pleasant open-sided restaurant serving up a reasonable selection of cheap Chinese and Sri Lankan food (mains Rs.250–750), including all the usual suspects: simple rice and curry, devilled dishes, fried rice and noodles, plus assorted sandwiches and snacks. Daily 10am–10pm.

DIRECTORY

Banks Various banks along Main St have ATMs accepting foreign cards.

Swimming Non-guests can use the pools at The Safari, Chandrika and Priyankara hotels for Rs.500 (free at the Priyankara if you have a meal).

Kirinda

Some 15km south of Tissa, and around 12km from the entrance to Yala National Park, the village of **KIRINDA** is famous in Sri Lankan folklore as the landing place of Queen Viharamahadevi (see page 190), and among divers as the jumping-off point for **Great Basses and Little Basses**, two of the island's most spectacular and challenging dive sites. Diving the Basses is for advanced divers only and conditions are such that it is usually only possible to dive here from mid-March to mid-April.

Kirinda village itself runs along a wild stretch of shore, dramatically dotted with huge rocks interspersed with stretches of sand. Sitting atop one of the biggest rock outcrops is the attractive **Kirinda Maha Vihara** – a picturesque cluster of white buildings plus dagoba and Buddha statue, perched high above the sea with sweeping views up and down the coast. Another rocky outcrop to the west, **Nidangala**, towers above a particularly striking stretch of sandy beach and is well worth the climb to the top – though swimming in the sea here is treacherous.

ACCOMMODATION

Nikara Yala Nidangala Beach ☎072 692 1169, ⓦ nikarayala.com. Kirinda's swankiest accommodation, located right on Nidangala Beach. The seven contemporary-style rooms are well equipped (balconies, a/c, satellite TVs, minibars, electric blinds and coffee machines), and some proffer sea views; the two villas have private plunge pools. There's a lovely long swimming pool amid the shaded gardens, and staff can organize local tours and comfy jeeps for Yala trips. B&B: doubles $200, pool villa $260

Suduveli 2km outside Kirinda towards Tissa, 200m off the main road (look for the orange wall) ☎072 263 1059, ⓦ beauties-of-nature.net. Friendly and homely little guesthouse in a very peaceful spot with accommodation either in simple rooms in the main house (a couple with shared bathroom; Rs.4500) or in more appealing cabanas in the rambling gardens (Rs.6500). There are free bikes for guests, motorbike rental, plus jeep hire for Yala trips (Rs.6000/half-day). Breakfast included. $35

Yala National Park

Daily 6am–6pm (closed Sept 1–Nov 1 most years) • $15, plus the usual additional charges and taxes (see page 50)

Yala National Park (or Ruhunu National Park) is Sri Lanka's most visited and most rewarding wildlife reserve. Yala covers an area of 1260 square kilometres, although four-fifths of this is designated a Strict Natural Reserve and closed to visitors. On the far side of the Strict Natural Reserve is Kumana (Yala East) National Park (see page

---

QUEEN VIHARAMAHADEVI

Early Sinhalese history has many heroes but very few heroines – with the notable exception of the legendary **Queen Viharamahadevi**. According to tradition, Viharamahadevi's father – a certain King Tissa of Kelaniya – unjustly put to death a Buddhist monk, whereupon the waters of the ocean rose up and threatened to submerge his kingdom. The waters abated only when he sacrificed his pious and beautiful young daughter to the sea, placing her in a fragile boat and casting her off into the waves. The brave young princess, who had patiently submitted to this ordeal for the sake of her father's kingdom, was carried away around the coast and finally washed ashore in Kirinda. The local king, the powerful **Kavan Tissa**, came upon the delectable princess as she lay asleep in her boat, fell in love with her, and promptly married her. Their first son, **Dutugemunu** (see page 330), became one of the great heroes of early Sinhalese history.

Quite what the story of Viharamahadevi's sea journey symbolizes is anyone's guess (although following the 2004 tsunami the part of the story describing the catastrophic flooding of Kelaniya – which was previously regarded as a piece of colourful but entirely fanciful storytelling –acquired a new significance and credibility). Whatever the legend's basis, it provided the Sinhalese's greatest warrior-king with a suitably auspicious parentage, and created Sri Lanka's first great matriarch in the process.

WILDLIFE IN YALA

Yala's most famous residents are its **leopards** – the park boasts a higher concentration of these elusive felines than anywhere else in the world (block 1 of the park, the main section open to visitors, is thought to be home to around fifty animals) and sightings are reasonably common, though you'll stand a much better chance if you spend a full day in the park, which allows you to reach less touristed areas and evade the crowds. Leopards can be seen year round, though they might be slightly easier to spot during the latter part of the dry season, when the ground vegetation dies back. Adult leopards are mainly active from dusk until dawn. Most daytime leopard sightings are of cubs and sub-adults, who are dependent on their mother for food. These confident and carefree young animals can provide hours of viewing, often showing themselves to visitors in the same spot for several days running.

Much more visible than leopards are the resident **elephants**, which can be seen on most trips, though they can be a bit easier to spot during the dry season (May–Aug), when they congregate around the park's waterholes. Other resident **mammals** include sambar and spotted deer, wild boar, wild buffaloes, macaque and langur monkeys, sloth bears, jackals, mongooses, pangolins, porcupines, rabbits and (rare) wild cats, as well as **crocodiles**.

Yala also offers outstanding **birdwatching** year round, while from October to March visitors have the added bonus of seeing thousands of migratory species arrive to escape the northern winter. Around 130 species have been recorded here including the endemic jungle fowl, a singularly inelegant, waddling creature, like a feral hen, which has been adopted as the national bird of Sri Lanka.

71), which is only accessible via Arugam Bay. There's no public transport to Yala, and you're only allowed into the park in a vehicle, so you'll have to hire a jeep – many visitors pick one up at Tissamaharama, 27km to the northwest (see page 188).

The park's dry-zone **landscape** is impressively wild and unspoiled, especially when viewed from the vantage points offered by the curious rock outcrops which dot the park. From these you can look out over a seemingly endless expanse of low scrub and trees dotted with brackish lakes next to the dune-covered coastline – particularly magical from Situlpahuwa.

Situlpahuwa and Magul Maha Vihara

Yala also has significant historic interest. The remains of extensive settlements that once dotted the area during the Ruhunu period can still be seen, most notably the monastery at **Situlpahuwa**, which may once have housed over ten thousand people and remains an important site of pilgrimage en route to nearby Kataragama. The temple comprises two rock-top dagobas separated by a small lake, although the main draw is the temple's lost-in-the-jungle setting and the marvellous views it affords of pretty much the entire park. South of Situlpahuwa are the very modest remains of the first-century BC **Magul Maha Vihara**. Although these two temples lie within the national park, you can visit them without paying the entrance fee; combined with Kataragama, they make a good half-day excursion from Tissa (see page 188).

ARRIVAL AND INFORMATION

YALA NATIONAL PARK

Visiting the park The main entrance to the park is at Palatupana, 27km from Tissa (about a 45min drive), where there's a well-designed and informative visitor centre. There is also a second entrance north of the park, 4km east of Kataragama, from which tours can also be arranged.

Park rules All vehicles entering the park are assigned an obligatory ranger (although at busy times of the year there aren't always enough to go around). You're meant to stay inside your vehicle (except on the beach), keep your jeep's hood up, stick to roads and avoid all noise, although you are allowed to drive freely around the park, following whichever track takes your fancy. At the time of research, a new law had just come into force banning the use of plastic bottles in Yala.

2

ACCOMMODATION

Cinnamon Wild Yala ☎ 047 223 9450, ⓦ cinnamonhotels.com. Low-rise complex a couple of kilometres from the main park entrance, with appealing chalets (beach chalets cost $40 more) equipped with all mod cons (in case you get bored of looking for elephants from the hotel's elevated observation deck) scattered around ten acres of jungle between the sea and lagoon. $255

Jetwing Yala ☎ 047 471 0710, ⓦ jetwinghotels.com. This modern, ninety-room hotel 3km from the main park entrance doesn't quite blend into its natural surroundings, but it does offer exceptional panoramic views over them, across a sweeping coastline softened by sand dunes. Rooms are smart, opulent and have private terraces, and

the romantic a/c "tented villas" – slightly away from the rest of the hotel – offer similar levels of comfort amid the scrub and dunes. Also has a 50m pool, spa and ocean-view bar, and plenty of outdoor space for lounging. B&B $220

★ **Leopard Safaris** ☎ 077 780 0030, ⓦ leopardsafaris. com. A luxury safari campsite 6km from the park's less busy northern Katagamuwa entrance (near Kataragama), with gorgeous tented rooms featuring big beds, en-suite hot-water bathrooms and furnished porches, as well as communal lounge and alfresco dining, all set in pleasantly rural wildlife-filled environs. It's expensive, but rates are fully inclusive of all meals, drinks and safaris with experienced guides. All-inclusive $990

Kataragama

Nineteen kilometres further inland from Tissa lies the small and remote town of **KATARAGAMA**, one of the three most venerated religious sites in Sri Lanka (along with Adam's Peak and the Temple of the Tooth at Kandy), held sacred by Buddhists, Hindus and Muslims alike – even Christians sometimes pop along in search of divine assistance. The most important of the town's various shrines is dedicated to the god **Kataragama** (see below), a Buddhist-cum-Hindu deity who is believed to reside here.

Kataragama is easily visited as a day-trip from Tissa, though staying the night means you can enjoy the evening puja in a leisurely manner and imbibe some of the town's backwater charm and laidback rural pace. It also makes a good base from which to visit Yala, since the park's second entrance at Katagamuwa is just 14km away and usually much less congested than the main Tissa gate.

KATARAGAMA

Perhaps no other deity in Sri Lanka embodies the bewilderingly syncretic nature of the island's Buddhist and Hindu traditions as clearly as the many-faceted **Kataragama**. The god has two very different origins. To the Buddhist Sinhalese, Kataragama is one of the four great protectors of the island. Although he began life as a rather unimportant local god, named after the town in which his shrine was located, he gained pan-Sinhalese significance during the early struggles against the South Indian Tamils and is believed to have helped Dutugemunu (see page 330) in his long war against Elara. To the Hindu Tamils, Kataragama is equivalent to the major deity **Skanda** (also known as Murugan or Subramanian), a son of Shiva and Parvati and brother of Ganesh. Both Buddhists and Hindus have legends which tell how Kataragama came to Sri Lanka to battle against the *asuras*, or enemies of the gods. While fighting, he became enamoured of Valli Amma, the result of the union between a pious hermit and a doe, who became his second wife. Despite Kataragama's confused lineage, modern-day visitors to the shrine generally pay scant attention to the god's theological roots, simply regarding him as a powerful deity capable of assisting in a wide range of practical enterprises.

Kataragama is often shown carrying a vel, or trident, which is also one of Shiva's principal symbols. His colour is red (devotees offer crimson garlands when they visit his shrines) and he is frequently identified with the peacock, a bird which was sacrificed to him. Thanks to his exploits, both military and amorous, he is worshipped both as a fearsome warrior and as a lover, inspiring an ecstatic devotion in his followers exemplified by the wild *kavadi*, or peacock dance (see page 195), and the ritual self-mutilations practised by pilgrims during the annual Kataragama festival (see page 193) – a world away from the chaste forms of worship typical of the island's Buddhist rituals.

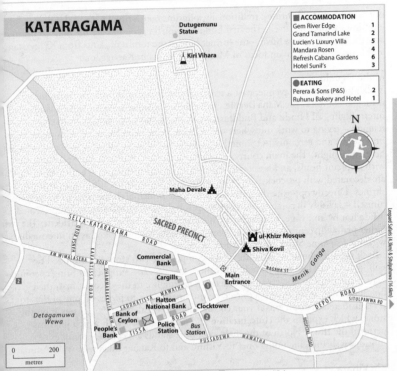

Kataragama is at its busiest during the **Kataragama festival**, held around the Esala poya day in July or August. The festival is famous for the varying forms of physical mortification with which some pilgrims express their devotion to Kataragama, ranging from crawling from the river to the Maha Devale to gruesome acts of self-mutilation: some penitents pierce their cheeks or tongue with skewers; others walk across burning coals – all believe that the god will protect them from pain. During the festival devotees flock to the town from all over Sri Lanka, some walking along the various pilgrimage routes which converge on Kataragama from distant parts of the island – the most famous route, the **Pada Yatra**, leads all the way down the east coast from Jaffna, through the jungles of Yala, and is still tackled by those seeking especial religious merit. Most of today's visitors, however, come on the bus.

Kataragama town spreads out over a small grid of tranquil streets shaded by huge Indian rain trees – outside poya days and puja times, the whole place is incredibly sleepy, and its quiet streets offer a welcome alternative to the dusty mayhem that usually passes for urban life in Sri Lanka. During the **evening puja** (see page 195), Kataragama is magically transformed. Throngs of pilgrims descend on the Sacred Precinct, while the brightly illuminated stalls which fill the surrounding streets do a brisk trade in garlands, fruit platters and other colourful religious paraphernalia, as well as huge slabs of gelatinous oil cake and other unusual edibles.

The Sacred Precinct

The town is separated by the Menik Ganga ("Gem River") from the so-called **Sacred Precinct** to the north, an area of sylvan parkland overrun by inquisitive grey langurs and dotted with myriad shrines; traditionally, pilgrims take a ritual bath in the river before entering the precinct itself. The first buildings you'll encounter are the **ul-Khizr mosque** and the adjacent **Shiva Kovil** – the former houses the tombs of saints from Kyrgyzstan and India and is the main focus of Muslim devotions in Kataragama.

Maha Devale

Walk along the main avenue, past a string of gaudy minor shrines, to reach the principal complex, the **Maha Devale**. This exhibits a quintessentially Sri Lankan intermingling of Hindu and Buddhist, with deities and iconography from each religion – trying to work out where one religion begins and the other ends is virtually impossible, and certainly not something which troubles the pilgrims who congregate here every night. The main courtyard is surrounded by an impressive wall decorated with elephant heads, and is entered through an ornate metal gate – both wall and gate are decorated with peacocks, a symbol of the god Kataragama. Inside are three main shrines. Directly opposite the entrance gate is the **principal shrine**, that of Kataragama himself – lavishly decorated, although surprisingly small. **Kataragama** is represented inside not by an image, but simply by his principal symbol of a *vel*, or trident. The two rather plain adjacent shrines are devoted to **Ganesh**, often invoked as an intermediary with the fearsome Shiva, and the **Buddha**.

Back towards the main entrance to the complex are two **stones** surrounded by railings, one marked by a trident, the other with a spear – supplicants bring coconuts here as offerings to Kataragama, sometimes setting fire to the coconut first, then holding it aloft while saying a prayer, before smashing it to pieces on one of the stones. It's considered inauspicious if your coconut fails to break when you throw it on the stone, which explains the concentration and determination with which pilgrims perform the ritual. North of the main enclosure stands a secondary complex of subsidiary shrines, including ones to Vishnu and to Kataragama's wife, Valli Amma.

Kiri Vihara

From the rear of the Maha Devale, a road leads 500m past lines of stalls selling lotus flowers to the **Kiri Vihara**, an alternative focus for Buddhist devotions at Kataragama – it's basically just a big dagoba, its only unusual feature being the two sets of square walls which enclose it – but it's a peaceful place, surrounded by parkland and usually far less busy than the Maha Devale. A modern statue of King Dutugemunu astride his faithful elephant Kandula stands just behind.

ARRIVAL AND INFORMATION

KATARAGAMA

By bus Kataragama is a 30min bus journey north of Tissa (with departures every 10min or so; 20min). The bus station is right in the centre of town on the Tissa Rd, a 5min walk south of the temples.

By tour Most guesthouses can arrange jeep safaris to Yala; the price is similar to Tissa – around Rs.5000 per jeep.
Information ⦿ kataragama.org is an absolute treasure trove of weird and wonderful information about the shrine

ACCOMMODATION

It's best to book ahead during the Kataragama festival and on weekends.

★ **Gem River Edge** 300m off the Sella Rd (turn at the 3km sign post on Sella Road, look for a stone with a yellow star), 1.5km west of town ⦿ 047 223 6325, ⦿ gemriveredge.com; map p.193. An idyllic eco-homestay on the banks of the Menik Ganga, offering just six clean rooms (two en-suite; $50) in a rustic cottage complete with cobbled floors and breezy verandas. The *cadjan*-thatched dining area is attached to a traditional Sri Lankan kitchen where real magic happens – using organic

rice and locally sourced produce, the kitchen team produce exceptional and truly authentic pure-veg meals, cooked over an open hearth (Rs.1500; outside guests welcome with advance reservation). The owners are a fount of knowledge on Kataragama and offer Yala safaris, free bicycles and maps. If you'd rather just cool off, you can take a dip in the river. No alcohol. B&B $40
Grand Tamarind Lake Raja Mawatha ⦿ 047 223 6377, ⦿ tamarindlake.lk; map p.193. Recently opened luxury hotel with one block still under construction at the time of writing. The spacious rooms have high ceilings, as well as

THE EVENING PUJA

Kataragama's Sacred Precinct springs to life at **puja** times. Flocks of pilgrims appear bearing the fruit platters as offerings to Kataragama, and many smash coconuts in front of his shrine (see above). As the puja begins, a long queue of pilgrims line up to present their offerings, while a priest makes a drawn-out sequence of obeisances in front of the curtained shrine and a huge ringing of bells fills the temple. Musicians playing oboe-like *horanavas*, trumpets and drums perambulate around the complex, followed by groups of pilgrims performing the **kavadi**, or peacock dance, spinning around like dervishes while carrying *kavadis*, the semicircular hoops studded with peacock feathers after which the dance is named. The music is strangely jazzy, and the dancers spin with such fervour that it's not unusual to see one or two of the more enthusiastic collapsing in a dead faint on the ground. Eventually the main Kataragama shrine is opened to the waiting pilgrims, who enter to deposit their offerings and pay homage to the god, while others pray at the adjacent Buddha shrine or bo trees.

The evening puja starts at 6.30pm. There's also an early-morning puja at around 4.30am plus another at 10am on Saturdays, though these are pretty low-key compared to the evening ceremonies.

2

balconies with excellent lake views. The lakeside pool is fringed by frangipani trees, and there's also a restaurant and bar (though the license is pending). B&B **$120**

Lucien's Luxury Villa Tissa Rd, next to Jayasumanaraya Monastery, 4km out of town ☎ 047 223 5500; map p.193. This homestay, run by the jovial Lucien, is light on luxury but has some basic, comfortable rooms (the cheapest share cold-water bathrooms; one has hot water and a/c) off a central living area. There's a big and sociable restaurant (mains Rs.270–590), free bicycles for rent and plenty of advice on local tours and safaris. **Rs.4000**, a/c **Rs.5000**

Mandara Rosen Tissa Rd, Detagamuwa, 1.5km out of town ☎ 047 223 6030, ⓦ rosenhotelsrilanka.com; map p.193. This smart four-star looks a bit out of place in sleepy Kataragama but makes a good base from which to explore the area. Rooms (all with a/c, satellite TV and minibar) are set in a pretty building modelled on a traditional pilgrim's

rest house and there's also a decent-size swimming pool complete with underwater music, a spa, an upmarket restaurant and more informal roadside café. B&B **$150**

Refresh Cabana Gardens Tissa Rd, 3.5km out of town ☎ 047 223 6357, ⓦ refreshhikkaduwa.com; map p.193. A little oasis on the Tissa Rd into Kataragama, with eight big cottages set in their own gardens – each is airy, well furnished and equipped with a/c, TV, minibar and modern bathroom. Also serves good food in the attached restaurant, plus there's a new pool. B&B **Rs.7500**

Hotel Sunil's Tissa Rd ☎ 047 567 7172, ⓦ facebook. com/HotelSunilsKataragama; map p.193. Ten clean, tiled rooms in a small and friendly family-run guesthouse – the more modern a/c rooms come with private balconies overlooking the neighbouring paddy fields. Also arranges tours to Yala National Park. No alcohol. **Rs.2500**, a/c **Rs.4000**

EATING

All the guesthouses do **food** and there are plenty of simple local places in town and along Sella Rd serving dirt-cheap rice and curry and short eats. As well as its fine-dining restaurant, *Mandara* also has a roadside café serving pastries, cheap local staples, salads and sandwiches – handy if you're just day-tripping to Kataragama. Note that **alcohol** is prohibited close to the Sacred Precinct: if you can't do without booze, head just outside town to the *Mandara*, *Okrin* or *Chamila* hotels, which are always happy to indulge spiritually imperfect foreign tourists.

Perera & Sons (P&S) Tissa Rd, next to the bus station ☎ 047 493 8146; map p.193. Shiny new branch of the

island-wide chain attached to the revamped *YMBA Pilgrim Rest*, with an extensive menu of Sri Lankan favourites including hoppers, *kottu*, buriani and even *lamprais* (Rs. 160–380). Daily 7am–9pm.

Ruhunu Bakery and Hotel Abhaya Mawatha; map p.193. Bustling cafeteria serving rice and curry (Rs.110–150), a wide range of fried rice dishes (Rs.220–450) and the usual array of short eats. It's also decent place for a cup of tea (Rs.15). Lots of good options here for vegetarians. Daily 6.30am–9pm.

DIRECTORY

Banks The ATMs at the Hatton National Bank and Bank of Ceylon, both just west of the bus station, accept foreign cards, as does the Commercial Bank next to Cargills.

Swimming Non-guests are permitted to swim in the pools at the *Mandara Rosen* (Rs.500).

Kandy and the hill country

NUWARA GIYA

Kandy and the hill country

Occupying the island's southern heartlands, the sublime green heights of the hill country are a world away from the sweltering coastal lowlands – indeed nothing encapsulates Sri Lanka's scenic diversity as neatly as the short journey by road or rail up from the humid urban melee of Colombo to the cool altitudes of Kandy or Nuwara Eliya. The landscape here is a beguiling mixture of nature and nurture. In places the mountainous green hills rise to surprisingly rugged and dramatic peaks; in others, the slopes are covered in carefully manicured tea gardens whose neatly trimmed lines of bushes add a toy-like quality to the landscape, while the mist and clouds which frequently blanket the hills add a further layer of magic.

The hill country has been shaped by two very different historical forces. The northern portion, around the historic city of **Kandy**, was home to Sri Lanka's last independent kingdom, which survived two centuries of colonial incursions before finally falling to the British in 1815. The cultural legacy of this independent Sinhalese tradition lives on today in the city's distinctive music, dance and architecture, encapsulated by the **Temple of the Tooth**, home to the island's most revered Buddhist relic, and the exuberant **Kandy Esala Perahera**, one of Asia's most spectacular festivals.

In contrast, the southern hill country is largely a product of the British colonial era, when tea was introduced to the island, an industry which continues to power the economy of the region today. At the heart of the tea-growing uplands, the time-warped town of **Nuwara Eliya** preserves many quaint traces of its British colonial heritage and also provides the best base for visiting the misty uplands of **Horton Plains** and **World's End**. Southeast of here, in Uva Province, a string of small towns and villages – most notably **Ella** and **Haputale** – offer marvellous views and walks through the hills and tea plantations, while to the west the spectacular summit of **Adam's Peak** remains an object of pilgrimage for devotees of all four of the island's principal religions. Further south, the gem-mining town of **Ratnapura** is the jumping-off point for visits to the **Sinharaja** reserve, a rare and remarkable pocket of tangled tropical rainforest, and **Uda Walawe National Park**, home to one of the island's largest elephant populations.

Colombo to Kandy

The 110km journey from **Colombo to Kandy** provides a neat snapshot of Sri Lanka's dramatic scenic contrasts, taking you within just three hours from sweltering coastal lowlands to cool inland hills. Many visitors make the journey **by train**, a classic journey along one of south Asia's most spectacularly engineered tracks, first opened in 1867, which weaves slowly upwards through long tunnels and along narrow ledges blasted by Victorian engineers out of solid rock, with vertiginous drops below (sit on the right-hand side en route to Kandy for the best views). Perhaps even more spectacular, however, is the journey **by road** (another legacy of British engineering skills, completed in 1825), as the main A1 highway rolls uphill and down before making the final, engine-busting climb up into Kandy, giving a much more immediate sense of the hills' scale and altitude than the railway line's carefully graded ascent.

The major caveat concerning the road is the traffic, which is now more or less permanently gridlocked in the environs of Kandy. The new **Central Expressway** (see

SINHARAJA

Highlights

❶ **Kandy** Hidden away amid the beautiful central highlands, Sri Lanka's second city and cultural capital is a vibrant showcase of traditional Sinhalese art, architecture and crafts. See page 207

❷ **Esala Perahera, Kandy** The island's most spectacular festival, with immense processions of drummers, dancers and richly caparisoned elephants. See box, page 210

❸ **Kandyan dancing** Watch lavishly costumed dancers performing to an accompaniment of explosively energetic drumming. See box, page 229

❹ **Horton Plains and World's End** Hike across the uplands of Horton Plains to the vertiginous cliffs of World's End, which plunge sheer for almost a kilometre to the plains below. See page 250

❺ **Adam's Peak** The classic Sri Lankan pilgrimage, climbing to the summit of one of the island's most spectacular mountains. See page 252

❻ **Ella** The island's most beautifully situated village, with superb views and country walks. See page 263

❼ **Sinharaja** This unique tract of undisturbed tropical rainforest is a botanical treasure trove of global significance. See page 273

HIGHLIGHTS ARE MARKED ON THE MAP ON PAGE 200

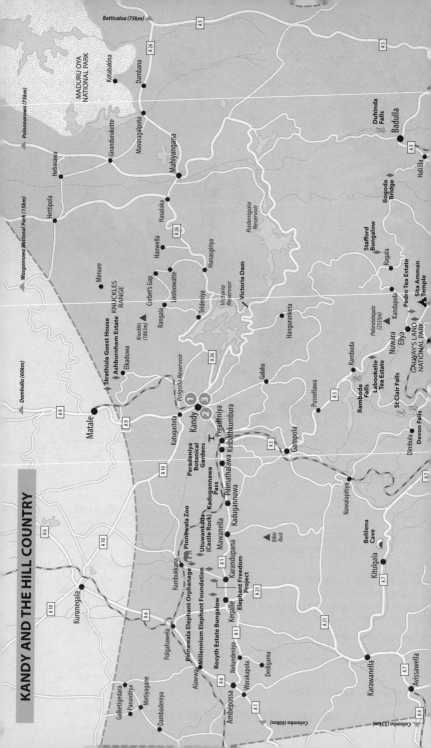

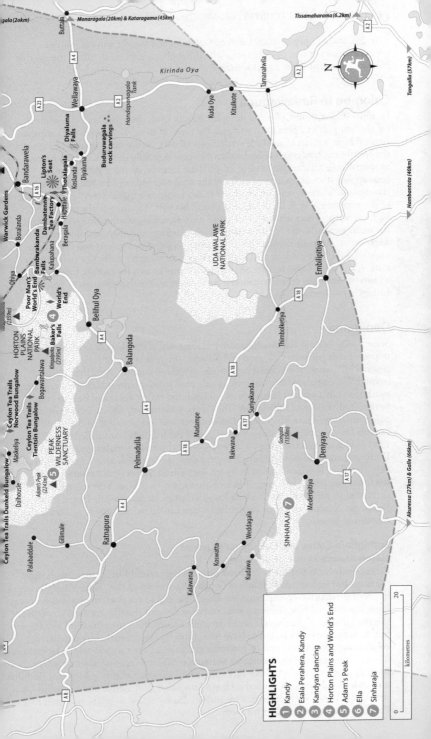

page 28), due to open in 2020 between Colombo and Kandy, will cut journey times between the two cities significantly, although it's unlikely to match the existing highway's levels of white-knuckle drama.

Colombo to Radawaduna

Heading inland from Colombo along the Kandy road, the urban sprawl continues for the best part of 25km until you pass the turn-off to the large town of Gampaha. Beyond here, a series of roadside settlements (shown on the map on page 66) exemplify the continuing tendency for Sri Lankan villages (especially in the Kandyan region) to specialize in a particular craft or crop. These include, in order, **Belummahara** (pineapples, stacked up in neat racks by the roadside) followed by **Nittambuwa** (rambutans, when in season); the latter is also home to a striking memorial to former prime ministers S.W.R.D. Bandaranaike and his wife, Sirimavo (right next to the highway at the 39km marker). Next, and most famous, is **Kadjugama** (cashew nuts – the name means "Cashew Nut Village"), where a long line of colourfully dressed female *kadju*-sellers stand by the roadside attempting to flag down drivers and flog them cashews – the best place in Sri Lanka to experience what it's really like to be driven nuts. A couple of miles further on, **Radawaduna** is known for its cane industry, with all sort of ingenious creations ranging from chairs and shelves through to beautiful lantern-style lampshades.

Dedigama

Some 10km beyond Radawaduna, around the town of **Warakapola** (roughly at the midway point between Colombo and Kandy), the appearance of steep-sided, forest-covered hills marks the gradual beginnings of the hill country. A further 10km beyond Warakapola, at Nelundeniya, a side road from the main highway heads 3km south through a verdant landscape of rubber trees, paddy fields and banana palms to the sleepy village of **DEDIGAMA**. The village was formerly the capital of the semi-autonomous southern kingdom of **Dakkinadesa** and served as one of the island's capitals for a decade or so during the reigns of the brothers Bhuvanekabahu IV (r. 1341–51) and Parakramabahu V (r. 1344–59), who ruled simultaneously from Dedigama and Gampola, although sources disagree on which king reigned from which city. The place is better known, however, for its associations with **Parakramabahu the Great** (see page 314), king of Polonnaruwa, who was born here and who later succeeded to the throne of Dakkinadesa – although he quickly hot-footed it off to Panduwas Nuwara, where he established a new capital before launching his bid for islandwide power.

Suthighara Cetiya and Dedigama Museum

Dedigama Museum Mon & Wed–Sun 8am–4pm • Free

Parakramabahu is popularly credited with having created Dedigama's major sight, the huge but unfinished **Suthighara Cetiya** (also known as the "Kota Vihara"), whose impressive remains – comprising the huge base and lower portion of a dagoba on a high, three-tiered base – seem totally out of scale with the tiny modern-day village. On the far side of the stupa, a secondary mini-stupa built into the third tier (signed, but in Sinhalese only) is said to have been built by Parakramabahu's parents in celebration of his birth, and to mark the exact site of the room in which he was born

Next to the dagoba, the **Dedigama Museum** contains a cache of objects recovered from the dagoba's relic chamber including a fine sequence of tiny gold-plated Buddhas and an unusual elephant-topped oil lamp (*ath pahana*). A simple bowl (labelled "A recede clay bowl" – whatever that means) on display is said to be the one used to wash Parakramabahu himself after his birth.

Dambadeniya

Some 20km north of Warakapola, the small town of **DAMBADENIYA** was once home to the first of the short-lived Sinhalese capitals established following the fall of Polonnaruwa in 1212. The new capital was founded by **Vijayabahu III** (r. 1232–36) and also served as the seat of his son, **Parakramabahu II** (r. 1236–70), whose long reign saw a brief renaissance in Sinhalese political power. Parakramabahu II succeeded in expelling the Indian invader Magha with Pandyan help, after which his forces reoccupied the shattered cities of Anuradhapura and Polonnaruwa. This purely symbolic victory was followed by further turmoil, and his son, Vijayabahu IV (r. 1270–72), lasted only two years before being assassinated by Bhuvanekabahu, who then moved the capital to Yapahuwa.

The Royal Palace

Daily 24hr • Free

Around 1km south of the main road lie the remains of Dambadeniya's old **Royal Palace**. There's not much left of the palace itself, although the location is dramatic, perched on a huge granite outcrop, with a beautiful old stone-cut stairway running through pristine jungle up to the top. A stiff fifteen-minute climb will get you to the palace, where you can still make out the brick foundations of the council chamber. A further five-minute scramble through trees brings you the summit itself, from where there are stunning views, only slightly marred by the huge factory directly below.

Vijayasundara Vihara

A couple of minutes' drive from the palace is the rambling **Vijayasundara Vihara** –"Beautiful Vijaya Temple", named in honour of Vijayabahu III, who founded it. In the middle of the complex sits the temple's rustic central shrine, a rough-and-ready structure supported by rudimentary stone columns; this formerly housed the island's famous Tooth Relic, kept in a room in the (now vanished) third storey. The remains of Kandyan-era murals can be seen on the exterior, with the plaster peeling away in places to reveal even older (but badly eroded) pictures etched into the blackened walls beneath. There are also some fine Kandyan-era strip paintings inside the shrine's upstairs room, although you'll have to get the head monk to unlock it for you. Next to the shrine stands an unusual roofed dagoba reminiscent of the one at Gadaladeniya (see page 233). Fragments of ancient stone carvings (including some old guardstones), probably dating back to the thirteenth century, lie scattered around the temple, while the brick foundations of a monastery sit to one side.

Panavitiya

The turn-off to Panavitiya is in the village of Metiyagane, 4.5km northeast of Dambadeniya; from here, turn north (left) along Danggolla Road for 1.7km, then go left at the black archeological department sign to Panavitiya for 1.5km to reach the ambalama, just past the main village temple (Mahamuni Vihara).

North of Dambadeniya, the village of **PANAVITIYA** is home to an interesting little **ambalama** (rest house), built to provide shelter for travellers along the road (this was the old highway to Anuradhapura). The tiny but intricately carved rosewood structure is richly decorated with assorted Kandyan-style carvings, similar to those found at the Embekke Devale and Padeniya Raja Mahavihara, including a mahout with elephant and stick, wrestlers, dancers and drummers, demons, coiled snakes, peacocks and many other human and animal figures.

East from Kegalle to Kandy

East from Warakapola, the main highway from Colombo to Kandy climbs steeply to reach the bustling town of **KEGALLE**, crammed into a single hectic main street along the side of an elevated ridge – the top of the town's cute yellow clocktower is said to be modelled on the hat of a British governor.

SARADIEL: SRI LANKA'S ROBIN HOOD

The spectacular rock-topped peak of Utuwankanda is famous in local legend as the hideout of the Sri Lankan folk hero, **Deekirikevage Saradiel** (or Sardiel), who terrorized traffic on the main Kandy to Colombo highway throughout the 1850s and early 1860s, and whose exploits in fleecing the rich while succouring the poor have provoked inevitable comparisons with Robin Hood, whose flowing locks and predilection for remote forest hideouts Saradiel shared.

Based in the impenetrable jungle around **Utuwankanda**, Saradiel's gang waylaid carriages, regularly disrupting traffic on the Kandy Road and forcing the British authorities into a massive manhunt to track down the elusive bandit. Saradiel was eventually lured to Mawanella and captured by a detachment of the Ceylon Rifles following a shoot-out, during which his companion, Mammalay Marikkar, shot dead a certain Constable Shaban, the first Sri Lankan police officer to die in action – an event still commemorated annually by the island's police. Saradiel and Marikkar were taken to Kandy, sentenced to death, and **hanged** on May 7, 1864. Thousands thronged the streets of the city to catch a glimpse of the notorious criminal, but were surprised to see a slim and pleasant-looking figure rather than the ferocious highwayman they had expected – a police statement described him as just 5ft 3in tall, with long hair and hazel eyes.

Just over 3km beyond Kegalle a turn-off heads north to the **Pinnewala Elephant Orphanage, Pinnewala Zoo, Millennium Elephant Foundation** and **Elephant Freedom Project** (see page 206), beyond which are immediate views of the dramatically steep and densely forested mountain of **Utuwankanda** (also known by its British name of Castle Rock), the former stronghold of the infamous robber **Saradiel** (see above). The road then climbs steeply again, giving increasingly grand views of craggy, densely wooded hills, including the prominent, flat-topped **Bible Rock** to the right, which acquired its pious name thanks to dutiful local Victorians on account of its alleged resemblance to a lectern.

Past Bible Rock the road enters **Mawanella**, beyond which it runs past assorted spice gardens before it hairpins upwards again, with increasingly spectacular views, to the famous viewpoint at **Kadugannawa Pass**, the most dramatic point along the highway, with spectacular views of Bible Rock and surrounding peaks – a panorama which brings home the ruggedness and scale of the hill-country terrain and makes you realize why the Kingdom of Kandy was able to hold out against European invaders for so long. The road up cuts through a short rock-hewn tunnel before reaching the top of the pass, where there's an imposing monument to British engineer **W.F. Dawson** (d.1829), who oversaw the construction of the Kandy road.

Just past the monument, an incongruous array of antiquated railway carriages and steam engines lined up alongside the highway announce the presence of the **National Railway Museum** (daily 9am–4pm; Rs.500), housing an interesting collection of colonial-era rolling stock and other railway-related paraphernalia ranging from station furniture to safety equipment, including a striking fire-cart with a gleaming copper water tank. There's also a short film about the history of trains in Sri Lanka, screened in a beautifully restored wooden carriage.

Further old mechanical relics can be found another 6km down the road at the **Highway State Museum** in the village of Kiribathkumbura, a rather grand name for a collection of five old colonial-era steamrollers, plus a replica of the Bogoda Bridge, laid out along the side of the road.

Just down the road is the large town of **Peradeniya** (now more or less fused with Kandy), home to Kandy's university and famous botanical gardens (see page 230), on the outskirts of Kandy proper.

Pinnewala Elephant Orphanage

Daily 8.30am–6pm • Rs.2500 (or Rs.3000 combined ticket with Pinnewala Zoo) • ⓦ nationalzoo.gov.lk/elephantorphanage

Due west of Kandy, situated in the rolling hills around the Ma Oya river, the **Pinnewala Elephant Orphanage** remains one of Sri Lanka's most popular tourist attractions. Set up in 1975 to look after five orphaned baby elephants, Pinnewala now has around eighty, making it home to the world's largest group of captive elephants. The animals include orphaned and abandoned elephants, as well as those injured in the wild (often in conflicts with farmers).

Sadly, despite its laudable original aims, ongoing concerns have been raised over the past decade about the treatment of Pinnewala's elephants, including repeated allegations of systematic **animal cruelty**. Various malpractices have been described, culminating in 2011 when one of the orphanage's male elephants died after apparently being stabbed 96 times with an elephant goad (*ankus*). Other concerns include the sheer number of **visitors** to the orphanage and the ways animals are hemmed in during bathing and feeding times.

Although still the target of innumerable negative comments online, it should be noted that the orphanage has made efforts to clean up its act in recent years. CCTV cameras have been installed to prevent clandestine cruelty to elephants, while births at the orphanage have also dried to a trickle (one argument against the place was that elephants were deliberately being bred here for a life in captivity, or for onward sale). In addition, fewer mahouts nowadays seem to be soliciting **tips** in return for a chance to touch or be photographed with one of the beasts, and no **elephant rides** are offered, either. For more on the rights and wrongs of Pinnewala see ⓦbit.ly/Pinnewala or ⓦbit.ly/Pinnewala2.

The herd are kept for most of the time in a 30-acre enclosure at the back of the complex, and are allowed to wander at will – visitors are kept at one end behind a fence. If you want to see the animals up close, you'll have to time your visit to coincide with one of the regular **feeding sessions**, an entertaining sight as the older elephants stuff their faces with trunkloads of palm leaves, while youngsters guzzle enormous quantities

3

ANIMAL RIGHTS AND WRONGS

The Pinnewala Orphanage – and indeed the holding of elephants in captivity generally – is a complex and emotive issue. Elephant welfare is of course paramount, although it shouldn't be forgotten that there's a very human dimension to the management of elephants in Sri Lanka, given that around a hundred villagers are killed annually by wild elephants.

The use of **elephant chains** is a frequent bone of contention. One problem concerns restraining practices applied to male elephants, who become extremely aggressive and dangerous when in heat (*musth*) and who have to be isolated and restrained – if you see a visibly distressed elephant chained up on its own at Pinnewala, this is probably the reason (not a great sight, admittedly, but better than a dead elephant – or dead people). Other elephants are sometimes lightly chained for various reasons, such as new arrivals being trained, or the matriarch elephant during bathing times to stop her wandering off and leading the herd with her. Used appropriately, elephant chains are no more cruel (perhaps less) than putting a lead on a dog, and are a lot more comfortable than rope or cord since they don't – when used correctly – cut into the skin, and also allow it to breathe. Conversely, the incorrect use of elephant chains can lead to intense distress and deep flesh wounds as elephants struggle against their bonds. The same applies to the use of the **ankus** (elephant goad), which can in the wrong hands serve as a lethal weapon, but which, when correctly employed, provides a humane and painless way of controlling the animals.

Less ambiguity surrounds the issue of **elephant rides**, which have been rightly boycotted by tour operators worldwide over recent years. Putting a *howdah* (elephant seat) on the back of an elephant and loading it up with as many as four or five people is unquestionably cruel. Harnesses used to secure *howdahs* frequently result in deep flesh wounds, while the sheer weight of people which some elephants are obliged to carry is akin to torture – some Asian elephants have simply dropped dead beneath their loads after being systematically overworked. The only humane way to ride an elephant is for a single rider to sit bareback on its neck, as Asian mahouts traditionally do. Any other form of elephant riding should be completely avoided.

Some people also wonder why elephants like the ones at Pinnewala can't simply be **released** back into the wild. Unfortunately, many would not survive, while others – being so habituated to humans, and accustomed to receiving food from them – would most likely descend on the nearest village, with potentially catastrophic results.

of milk out of oversized baby bottles (general feeding sessions at 9am and 12.15pm; bottle feeding at 9am, 1.15pm & 5pm). Twice a day the elephants are driven across the road to the Ma Oya river for a leisurely **bath** (10am–noon & 2–4pm) – you can observe their antics from the riverbank or, in greater comfort and for the price of a drink, from the terraces of the *Pinnalanda* or *Elephant Park Hotel* restaurants above the river.

Pinnewala Zoo

Daily 8.30am–6pm • Rs.1000 (or Rs.3000 combined ticket with the elephant orphanage) • ⓦ nationalzoo.gov.lk

Some 500m south of the elephant orphanage, the recently opened **Pinnewala Zoo** was established to provide a more spacious and state-of-the-art alternative to the dated and impossibly cramped Dehiwala Zoo in Colombo (see page 82). It's still very much a work in progress and rather lacking in wildlife so far, and the leopard enclosure, despite the amount of land available, still feels depressingly cramped. Leopards apart there's not a great deal to see bar a few impressive saltwater and mugger crocs in the central lake, and lots of local ungulates, including a few impossibly cute mouse deer.

The Millennium Elephant Foundation

Daily 8am–5pm • Rs.5000 (or Rs.6000 with lunch); advance booking by phone or via the website advised • ☎ 076 900 8388, ⓦ millenniumelephantfoundation.com

A few kilometres down the road from Pinnewala towards Kandy, the **Millennium Elephant Foundation** offers intimate and insightful elephant interactions. With the exception of the young Pooja, who was born at the foundation in 1986 (the only birth here to date), the nine elephants here are all former working animals rescued from logging, tourist elephant rides and temples. Visits (2–3hr; maximum 10 people per elephant) include guided 45min **walks** with chain-free elephants and the chance to feed and have a bath in the river with them, plus a tour of the foundation's small **museum** and a visit to an elephant-paper factory (see page 207). You can also sign up to do **voluntary work** here for any length of time from one day upwards. All ages are welcome, with prices starting from Rs.9000/day full board and falling the longer you stay.

The Elephant Freedom Project

Daily 9am–5pm (advance booking required) • Half-day visit Rs.5500, one-day visit Rs.10,500 (plus $25 full board to stay the night) • ☎ 077 212 1305, ⓦ volunteersatwork.org/en

Further pachyderm possibilities can be found 1km south of the Millennium Foundation at the new **Elephant Freedom Project**, which provides a refuge to two elephants, Sita and Nilami, who were previously used for logging. Visitors get to spend an extended period in close contact with the animals, helping to feed, wash and accompany them during their regular walks (but no elephant rides), and with a maximum of ten visitors per elephant. The project also has some neat and cosy rooms in a comfortable, modern house ($18 per person half board) if you fancy staying overnight.

ARRIVAL AND DEPARTURE

PINNEWAL

Pinnewala is on a side road a few kilometres north of the Colombo to Kandy highway, just east of Kegalle. With your own vehicle the journey from Kandy should take around an hour, or perhaps slightly less depending on traffic. The orphanage can also be visited from **Colombo** by train or bus. From **Negombo**, a day-trip to the orphanage by taxi will cost around $55–60.

By taxi or tuktuk The return trip by taxi from Kandy costs around $25–30. It's also possible to get a tuktuk from Kandy (around $20), though it's a smelly and uncomfortable ride, and not really worth the small saving.

By bus Take a service from the Goods Shed terminal in Kand towards Kegalle (every 30min; 1hr–1hr 30min) and get c at Karandupana, a few kilometres before Kegalle. From her catch a bus for Rambukkana and get off at Pinnewala (ever 20min; 10min) or catch a tuktuk (around Rs.300). Fro Colombo, catch any bus to Kandy and get off at Karandupan **By train** Rambukkana, 3km from the orphanage, served by slow trains from Kandy to Colombo – there a approximately 5 trains daily from each city, which will g you to Rambukkana during opening hours (1hr 30m from Kandy, 1hr 50min–2hr 10min from Colombo). Fro Rambukkana you can either hop on a bus or take a tuktu

SHIT HAPPENS: ELEPHANT PAPER

You won't visit many tourist shops in Sri Lanka without finding at least a few examples of the local **elephant paper**: paper made from elephant dung. As well as their many remarkable abilities, elephants are also a kind of paper factory on legs. During feeding, they ingest huge amounts of fibre (roughly 180kg per day) which is then pulped in the stomach and delivered (around sixteen times daily) in fresh dollops of dung, ready prepared for the manufacture of paper. Dung is dried in the sun to kill bacteria, then washed and boiled with margosa leaves, and the resultant pulp is used to make high-quality stationery. The texture and colour vary according to the elephants' diet, while other ingredients including tea, flowers, paddy husks and onion peel are also added according to the required finish. More than just a novelty stationery item, pachyderm paper could prove an important source of income to locals – and thus a significant help in conservation measures.

A number of places along the elephant bathing road in Pinnewala specialize in elephant paper stationery, most notably **Maximus** (W ecomaximus.com), one of the pioneers of the process and winners of numerous international awards. Staff demonstrate how the entire process works in a room at the back, equipped with assorted paper presses, drying racks and vats of the gloopy-looking liquid made as the dung is mixed with water to create the precious paper pulp.

3

ACCOMMODATION

Elephant Park Elephant Bath Rd, right next to the elephant bathing spot T 035 226 6171, W hotelelephantpark.com. The nicest option in the village, in an unbeatable riverside location. Rooms (all a/c and with hot water) are comfortable and modern, and some also have balconies with beautiful river views right above the elephant bathing spot for a roughly $20 surcharge. $50

Greenland Guest House Elephant Bath Rd T 035 226 5668, W greenlandguesthouse.blogspot.co.uk. The cheapest place in the village, tucked away on the side road leading to the elephant bathing spot, with a range of neat and nicely furnished wood-panelled rooms. Rs.3500, a/c Rs.4000

SHOPPING

Numerous **handicraft shops** are found around the village (especially along the road leading from the orphanage to the river), with a wide range of stock, including leather goods and elephant paper (see above). There are also heaps of **spice gardens** en route to Pinnewala.

Kandy

Hidden away amid precipitous green hills at the heart of the island, **KANDY** is Sri Lanka's second city and undisputed cultural capital of the island, home to the **Temple of the Tooth**, the country's most important religious shrine, and the **Esala Perahera**, its most exuberant festival. The last independent bastion of the Sinhalese, the Kingdom of Kandy clung onto its freedom long after the rest of the island had fallen to the Portuguese and Dutch, preserving its own customs and culture which live on today in the city's unique music, dance and architecture, while the city as a whole maintains a somewhat aristocratic air, with its graceful old Kandyan and colonial buildings, scenic highland setting and pleasantly temperate climate. The only real downside is the city's hideous traffic, with far too many cars crammed into not nearly enough road space – major roads in and out of town are frequently gridlocked, with all the noise and pollution that entails.

Brief history

Kandy owes its existence to its remote and easily defensible location amid the steep, jungle-swathed hills at the centre of the island. The origins of the city date back to the early thirteenth century, during the period following the collapse of

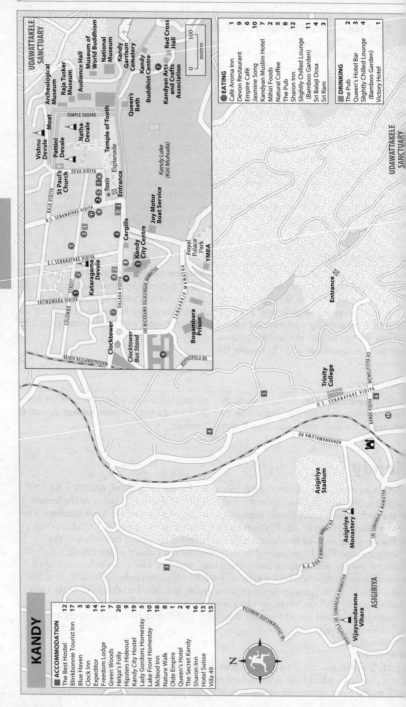

KANDY

■ ACCOMMODATION
The Best Hostel	12
Blinkbonnie Tourist Inn	17
Blue Haven	3
Clock Inn	6
Expeditor	14
Freedom Lodge	11
Green Woods	7
Helga's Folly	20
Hipsters Hideout	9
Kandy City Hostel	19
Lady Gordons Homestay	5
Lake Front Homestay	10
Mcleod Inn	18
Nature Walk	8
Olde Empire	1
Queen's Hotel	2
The Secret Kandy	4
Sharon Inn	16
Hotel Suisse	13
Villa 49	15

● EATING
Café Aroma Inn	1
Devon Restaurant	9
Empire Café	6
Jasmine Song	10
Kandyan Muslim Hotel	7
Mihiri Foods	2
Natural Coffee	5
The Pub	8
Sharon Inn	12
Slightly Chilled Lounge (Bamboo Garden)	11
Sri Balaji Dosa	4
Sri Ram	3

■ DRINKING
The Pub	2
Queen's Hotel Bar	3
Slightly Chilled Lounge (Bamboo Garden)	4
Victory Hotel	1

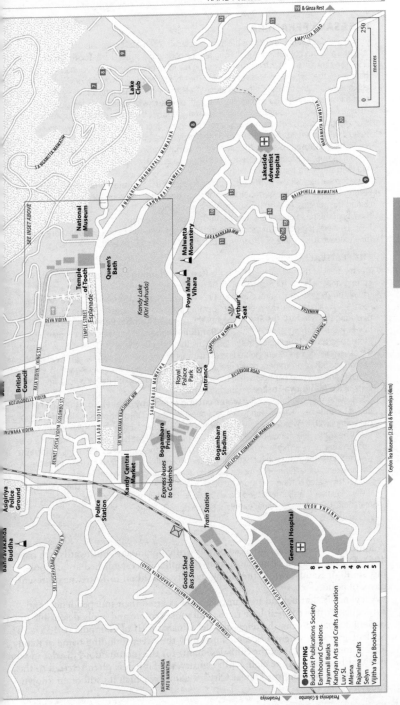

3

● SHOPPING

Buddhist Publications Society	8
Earthbound Creations	1
Jayamali Batiks	6
Kandyan Arts and Crafts Association	3
Luv SL	4
Mlesna	9
Rajanima Crafts	2
Selyn	7
Vijitha Yapa Bookshop	5

THE ESALA PERAHERA

Kandy's ten-day **Esala Perahera** is the most spectacular of Sri Lanka's festivals, and one of the most colourful religious pageants in Asia. Its origins date back to the arrival of the **Tooth Relic** (see page 215) in Sri Lanka in the fourth century AD, during the reign of Kirti Siri Meghawanna, who decreed that the relic be carried in procession through the city once a year. This quickly developed into a major religious event – the famous Chinese Buddhist Fa-Hsien, visiting Anuradhapura in 399 AD, described what had already become a splendid festival, with processions of jewel-encrusted elephants.

These celebrations continued in some form throughout the thousand years of upheaval which followed the collapse of Anuradhapura and the Tooth Relic's peripatetic journey around the island. Esala processions continued into the Kandyan era in the seventeenth century, though the Tooth Relic lost its place in the procession, which evolved into a series of lavish parades in honour of the city's four principal deities: Vishnu, Kataragama, Natha and Pattini, each of whom had (and still has) a temple in the city.

The festival took shape in 1775, during the reign of **Kirti Sri Rajasinha**, when a group of visiting Thai clerics expressed their displeasure at the lack of reverence accorded to the Buddha during the parades. To propitiate them, the king ordered the Tooth Relic to be carried through the city at the head of the four temple processions: a pattern that endures to this day. The Tooth Relic itself was last carried in procession in 1848, since when it's been considered unpropitious for it to leave the temple sanctuary – its place is now taken by a replica.

THE FESTIVAL

The ten days of the festival begin with the **Kap Tree Planting Ceremony**, during which cuttings from a tree – traditionally an Esala tree, though nowadays a Jak or Rukkattana are more usually employed – are planted in the four *devales* (see page 219), representing a vow (*kap*) that the festival will be held. The procession (perahera) through the streets of Kandy is held nightly throughout the festival: the first five nights, the so-called **Kumbal Perahera**, are relatively low-key; during the final five nights, the **Randoli Perahera**, things become progressively more spectacular, building up to the last night, the Maha Perahera, or "Great Parade", featuring a massive cast of participants including as many as a hundred brilliantly caparisoned elephants and thousands of drummers, dancers and acrobats walking on stilts, cracking whips, swinging fire pots and carrying banners, while the replica casket of the Tooth Relic itself is carried on the back of the **Maligawa Tusker** elephant (see page 217).

Following the last perahera, the **water-cutting ceremony** is held before the dawn of the next day at a venue near Kandy, during which a priest wades out into the Mahaweli Ganga and "cuts" the waters with a sword. This ceremony symbolically releases a supply of water for the coming year (the Tooth Relic is traditionally believed to protect against drought) and divides the pure from the impure – it might also relate to the exploits of the early Sri Lankan king, **Gajabahu** (reigned 114–136 AD), who is credited with the Moses-like feat of dividing the waters between Sri Lanka and India in order to march his army across during his campaign against the Cholas.

After the water-cutting ceremony, at 3pm on the same day, there's a final "**day**" perahera (Dawal Perahera), a slightly scaled-down version of the full perahera. It's not as spectacular as the real thing, though it does offer excellent photo opportunities.

Polonnaruwa, when the Sinhalese people drifted gradually southwards (see page 406). During this migration, a short-lived capital was established at Gampola, just south of Kandy, before the ruling dynasty moved on to Kotte, near present-day Colombo.

A few nobles left behind in Gampola soon asserted their independence, and subsequently moved their base to the still more remote and easily defensible town of **Senkadagala** during the reign of Wickramabahu III of Gampola (r. 1357–74). Senkadagala subsequently became known by the sweet-sounding name of **Kandy**, after Kanda Uda Pasrata, the Sinhalese name for the mountainous district in which it lay (although from the eighteenth century, the Sinhalese often referred to the city as Maha Nuwara, the "Great City", a name by which it's still often known today).

THE PROCESSION

The perahera is a carefully orchestrated, quasi-theatrical event – there is no spectator participation here, although the astonishing number of performers during later nights give the impression that most of Kandy's citizens are involved. The perahera actually comprises five separate processions, which follow one another around the city streets: one from the Temple of the Tooth, and one from each of the four *devales* – a kind of giant religious conga, with elephants. The exact route changes from day to day, although the procession from the Temple of the Tooth always leads the way, followed (in unchanging order) by the processions from the Natha, Vishnu, Kataragama and Pattini *devales* (Natha, as a Buddha-to-be, takes precedence over the other divinities). As its centrepiece, each procession has an elephant carrying the insignia of the relevant temple – or, in the case of the Temple of the Tooth, the replica Tooth Relic. Each is accompanied by other elephants, various dignitaries dressed in traditional Kandyan costume and myriad dancers and drummers, who fill the streets with an extraordinary barrage of noise. The processions each follow a broadly similar pattern, although there are slight differences. The Kataragama procession – as befits that rather unruly god – tends to be the wildest and most free-form, with jazzy trumpet playing and dozens of whirling dancers carrying *kavadis*, the hooped wooden contrivances, studded with peacock feathers, which are one of that god's symbols. The Pattini procession, the only one devoted to a female deity, attracts mainly female dancers. The beginning and end of each perahera is signalled by a deafening cannon shot.

PERAHERA PRACTICALITIES

The perahera is traditionally held over the last nine days of the lunar month of Esala, finishing on Nikini Poya day – this usually falls during late July and early August, though exact **dates** vary according to the vagaries of the lunar calendar. Dates can be checked on ⓦ sridaladamaligawa. lk and ⓦ daladamaligawa.org. **Accommodation** during the Esala Perahera can get booked up months in advance, and prices in most places double or even triple – be sure to reserve as far in advance as possible.

The perahera itself begins between 8pm and 9pm. You can see the parade for free by grabbing a spot on the **pavement** next to the route. During the early days of the perahera it's relatively easy to find pavement space; during the last few nights, however, you'll have to arrive four or five hours in advance and then sit in your place without budging – even if you leave for just a minute to go to the toilet, you probably won't get your spot back. Not surprisingly, most foreigners opt to pay to reserve one of the thousands of **seats** which are set out in the windows and balconies of buildings all along the route of the perahera. There are a number of websites selling tickets online for the best seats around the *Queens Hotel* (usually $75–125), although you should be able to find much cheaper seats either through your guesthouse/hotel or simply by asking around in town – although many of these are crammed into the upper floors of streetside buildings and may have restricted views (and beware unscrupulous touts who might simply disappear with your money – If possible, ask to see exactly where you'll be seated before handing over any cash). Count on around $20–40 depending on the night, although much depends on luck and your own persistence and bargaining skills.

The rise of the Kandyan kingdom

By the time the Portuguese arrived in Sri Lanka in 1505, Kandy had established itself as the capital of one of the island's three main kingdoms (along with Kotte and Jaffna) under the rule of Sena Sammatha Wickramabahu (r. 1473–1511), a member of the Kotte royal family who ruled Kandy as a semi-independent state. The Portuguese swiftly turned their attentions to Kandy, though their first expedition against the city ended in failure when the puppet ruler they placed on the throne was ousted by the formidable **Vimala Dharma Suriya**, the first of many Kandyan rulers who tenaciously resisted the European invaders. As the remainder of the island fell to the Portuguese (and subsequently the Dutch), the Kandyan kingdom clung stubbornly to its independence, remaining a secretive and inward-looking place, protected by its own inaccessibility – Kandyan kings repeatedly issued orders prohibiting the construction of bridges or the widening of footpaths into the city, fearing that they would become conduits for foreign attack. The city was repeatedly besieged and captured by the Portuguese (in 1594, 1611, 1629 and 1638) and the Dutch (in 1765), but each time the Kandyans foiled their attackers by burning the city to the ground and retreating into the surrounding forests, from where they continued to harry the invaders until they were forced to withdraw to the coast. Despite its isolation, the kingdom's prestige as the final bastion of Sinhalese independence was further enhanced during the seventeenth and eighteenth centuries by the presence of the **Tooth Relic** (see page 215), the traditional symbol of Sinhalese sovereignty, while an imposing temple, the Temple of the Tooth, was constructed to house the relic.

The Nayakkar dynasty

The last Sinhalese king of Kandy, Narendrasinha, died in 1739 without an heir, after which the crown passed to his Indian wife's brother, Sri Viyjaya Rajasinha (r. 1739–47), so ending the Kandyan dynasty established by Vimala Dharma Suriya and ushering in a new Indian **Nayakkar** dynasty. The Nayakkar embraced Buddhism and cleverly played on the rivalries of the local Sinhalese nobles who, despite their dislike of the foreign rulers, failed to unite behind a single local leader. In a characteristically Kandyan paradox, it was under the foreign Nayakkar that the city enjoyed its great Buddhist revival. **Kirti Sri Rajasinha** came to the throne in 1747 and began to devote himself – whether for political or spiritual reasons – to his adopted religion, reviving religious education, restoring and building temples and overseeing the reinvention of the **Esala Perahera** (see page 210) as a Buddhist rather than a Hindu festival. These years saw the development of a distinctively Kandyan style of architecture and dance, a unique synthesis of local Sinhalese traditions and southern Indian styles.

Kandy under the British

Having gained control of the island in 1798, the **British** quickly attempted to rid themselves of this final remnant of Sinhalese independence, although their first expedition against the kingdom, in 1803, resulted in a humiliating defeat. Despite this initial reverse, the kingdom survived little more than a decade, though it eventually fell not through military conquest but thanks to internal opposition to the excesses and cruelties of the last king of Kandy, **Sri Wickrama Rajasinha** (r. 1798–1815). As internal opposition to Sri Wickrama grew, the remarkable **Sir John D'Oyly** (see page 219), a British government servant with a talent for languages and intrigue, succeeded in uniting the various factions opposed to the king. In 1815, the British were able to despatch another army which, thanks to D'Oyly's machinations, was able to march on Kandy unopposed. Sri Wickrama fled, and when the British arrived, the king's long-suffering subjects simply stood to one side and let them in. On **March 2, 1815**, a convention of Kandyan chiefs signed a document handing over sovereignty of the kingdom to the British, who in return promised to preserve its laws, customs and institutions.

The colonial era and after

Within two years, however, the Kandyans had decided they had had enough of their new rulers and **rebelled**. The uprising soon spread across the entire hill country and the British were obliged to call up troops from India in order to put down the rebellion. Fears of resurgent Kandyan nationalism continued to haunt the British during the following decades – it was partly the desire to be able to move troops quickly to Kandy which prompted the construction of the first road to the city in the 1820s, one of the marvels of Victorian engineering in Sri Lanka. Despite the uncertain political climate, Kandy soon developed into an important centre of British rule and trade, with the usual hotels, courthouses and churches servicing a burgeoning community of planters and traders. In 1867, the **railway** from Colombo was completed, finally transforming the once perilous trek from the coast into a comfortable four-hour journey, and so linking Kandy once and for all with the outside world.

Post-colonial Kandy has continued to expand, preserving its status as the island's second city despite remaining a modest little place compared to Colombo. It has also managed largely to avoid the civil war conflicts which traumatized the capital, suffering only one major LTTE attack, in 1998, when a **truck bomb** was detonated outside the front of the Temple of the Tooth, killing more than twenty people and reducing the front of the building to rubble.

Kandy Lake (Kiri Muhuda)

Ioy Motor Boat Service, at the western end of the lake, offers fifteen-minute spins around it (daily 8.30am–6.30pm; Rs.2500/boat seating up to ten people)

Kandy's centrepiece is its large artificial **lake**, created in 1807 by Sri Wickrama Rajasinha in an area of the town previously occupied by paddy fields. Although it is nowadays considered one of Kandy's defining landmarks, at the time of its construction the lake was regarded by the city's put-upon inhabitants as a huge white elephant and conclusive proof of their king's unbridled delusions of grandeur – a number of his subjects who objected to labouring on this apparently useless project were impaled on stakes on the bed of the lake. Rajasinha named the lake the **Kiri Muhuda**, or Milk Sea, and established a royal pleasure house on the island in the centre. The more practically minded British subsequently converted this into an ammunition store, but also added the attractive walkway and parapet (the *walakulu bemma*, or "cloud wall") that encircles the lake. The walk around the lake is still (despite the manic traffic) the most enjoyable in the city, particularly along the south side, with the long white lakeside parapet framing perfect reflections of the Temple of the Tooth and old colonial buildings around the *Queen's Hotel*.

Malwatta Monastery and Poya Malu Vihara

The south side of the lake is dotted with assorted religious buildings. These include the **Malwatta Monastery**, with its distinctive octagonal tower, built in imitation of the Pittirippuva at the Temple of the Tooth on the opposite side of the lake. The temple is reached from the lakeside through an impressive stone arch decorated with creatures both real (lions, geese, birds) and imaginary (*makana toranas*, centaurs). A tiny circular monks' bathing house stands right by the lakeside pavement, close to the gate.

A hundred metres along the lakeside road back towards town (go up the broad steps to the building signed Sri Sangharaja Maha Pirivena) is another cluster of monastic buildings belonging to the **Poya Malu Vihara**, including an interesting square colonnaded **image house**, with a colourfully painted upper storey and a finely carved stone doorway very similar to one in the Temple of the Tooth's main shrine.

Royal Palace Park

Daily 8am–5pm • Rs.100

From the southwestern corner of the lake, steps ascend to the entrance to Rajapihilla Mawatha and the entrance to the modest **Royal Palace Park**, also known as Wace Park, another of Sri Wickrama Rajasinha's creations. The small ornamental gardens at the top of the park provide an unlikely setting for a Japanese howitzer, captured in Myanmar (Burma) during World War II and presented to the city by Lord Mountbatten (who had his wartime headquarters here in the *Hotel Suisse*). Beyond the ornamental gardens, a series of terraced footpaths wind down a bluff above the lake, offering fine views of the water and Temple of the Tooth – usually chock-full of snogging couples hiding in every available corner.

There are better views over the lake and into the green ridges of hills beyond from **Rajapihilla Mawatha**, the road above the park – the classic viewpoint is from the junction of Rajapahilla Mawatha and Kirthi Sri Rajasinghe Mawatha – popularly known as "**Arthur's Seat**" in honour of the famous Edinburgh viewpoint – from where one can look down over the entire town below, laid out at one's feet as neatly as a map.

The Temple of the Tooth

Daily 5.30am–8pm · Rs.1500 (plus Rs.100 to leave your shoes) · ⓦ sridaladamaligawa.lk and ⓦ daladamaligawa.org

Posed artistically against the steep wooded hills of the Udawattakele Sanctuary, Sri Lanka's most important Buddhist shrine, the **Temple of the Tooth**, or Dalada Maligawa, sits on the lakeshore just east of the city centre. The temple houses the legendary **Buddha's Tooth** (see page 215), which arrived here in the sixteenth century after various peregrinations around India and Sri Lanka, although nothing remains of the original temple, built around 1600. The main shrine of the current temple was originally constructed during the reign of Vimala Dharma II (r. 1687–1707) and was rebuilt and modified at various times afterwards, principally during the reign of Kirti Sri Rajasinha (r. 1747–81). It was further embellished during the reign of Sri Wickrama Rajasinha, who added the moat, gateway and Pittirippuva; the eye-catching golden roof over the relic chamber was donated by President Premadasa in 1987.

The temple was badly damaged in 1998 when the LTTE detonated a massive **truck bomb** outside the entrance, killing more than twenty people and reducing the facade to rubble. Restoration work was swift and thorough, however, and no visible evidence left of the attack, although crash barriers now prevent vehicular access to the temple.

Be sure to **dress respectfully**, with shoulders and legs covered, or you won't be allowed in. **Guides** of varying standards hang around at the entrance; count on around Rs.1000 for a thirty-minute tour. Some are very informative, but check how good their English is first and always agree a price before starting. **Pujas** (lasting around 1hr) are held at 5.30am, 9.30am and 6.30pm, although the temple can get absolutely swamped with tourists during the 9.30am and 6.30pm pujas. The main attraction of the three pujas is the noisy drumming which precedes and accompanies the ceremony. Most of the actual ceremony is performed behind closed doors, although at the end of each puja the upstairs room housing the Tooth Relic is opened to the public gaze. You're not actually allowed into the Tooth Relic chamber, but you are permitted to file past the entrance and look inside for a cursory glance at the big gold casket containing the relic.

The Pittirippuva

The temple's exterior is classically plain: a rather austere collection of unadorned white buildings whose hipped roofs rise in tiers against the luxuriant green backcloth of the Udawattakele Sanctuary. The most eye-catching exterior feature is the octagonal tower, the **Pittirippuva**, projecting into the moat that surrounds the temple. Sri Wickrama Rajasinha used the upper part as a platform from which to address his people, and it's now where all new Sri Lankan heads of state give their first speech to the nation.

The Maha Vahalkada

Access to the temple is through the **Maha Vahalkada** (Great Gate), which was formerly the main entrance to the royal palace as well as the temple. Beyond the gateway, further steps covered by a canopy painted with lotuses and pictures of the perahera lead up to the entrance to the temple proper, via a gorgeously carved stone door adorned with moonstone, guardstones and topped by a *makara torana* archway.

The shrine

The interior of the temple is relatively modest in size, and something of an architectural hotchpotch. In front of you lies the **drummers' courtyard** (Hewisi Mandapaya), into which is squeezed the two-storey **main shrine** itself. The exterior of the shrine has a strangely ad hoc appearance: some portions have been lavishly embellished (the three doors, for instance), but many of the painted roundels on the walls have been

3

THE BUDDHA'S TOOTH

Legend has it that when the Buddha was cremated in 543 BC at Kushinagar in North India, various parts of his remains were rescued from the fire, including one of his **teeth**. In the fourth century AD, as Buddhism was declining in India in the face of a Hindu revival, the Tooth was smuggled into Sri Lanka, hidden (according to legend) in the hair of an Orissan princess. It was first taken to Anuradhapura, then to Polonnaruwa, Dambadeniya and Yapahuwa. In 1284, an invading Pandyan army from South India captured the Tooth and took it briefly back to India, until it was reclaimed by Parakramabahu III some four years later.

During these turbulent years the Tooth came to assume increasing **political importance**, being regarded not only as a unique religious relic but also as a symbol of Sri Lankan sovereignty – it was always housed by the Sinhalese kings in their capital of the moment, which explains its rather peripatetic existence. After being reclaimed by Parakramabahu III, it subsequently travelled to Kurunegala, Gampola and Kotte. In the early sixteenth century, the Portuguese captured what they claimed was the Tooth, taking it back to Goa, where it was pounded to dust, then burnt and cast into the sea (Buddhists claim either that this destroyed Tooth was simply a replica, or that the ashes of the Tooth magically reassembled themselves and flew back to Sri Lanka). The Tooth finally arrived in Kandy in 1592 and was installed in a specially constructed temple next to the palace, later becoming the focus for the mammoth Esala Perahera.

The exact nature and **authenticity** of the Tooth remains unclear. Bella Sidney Woolf, writing in 1914 when the Tooth was still regularly displayed to the public, described it as "a tooth of discoloured ivory at least three inches long – unlike any human tooth ever known", unconsciously echoing the sentiments of an earlier Portuguese visitor, a certain de Quezroy, who in 1597 claimed that the Tooth had actually come from a buffalo. Whatever the truth, the Tooth remains an object of supreme devotion for many Sri Lankans. Security concerns mean that it is no longer taken out on parade during the Esala Perahera, though it is put on display in the Temple of the Tooth for a couple of weeks once or twice every decade.

eft unfinished, giving the whole thing the effect in places of a job only half done – lthough the overall effect is still undeniably impressive.

Three doors lead into the ground floor of the shrine: the main doors are flanked by lephant tusks and made out of gorgeously decorated silver (though they're usually idden behind a curtain except during pujas), with two intricately carved stone doors n either side. The walls are decorated with a tangled confusion of lotuses, vines and ions, and dotted with painted medallions of the **sun and moon**, a symbol of the kings f Kandy – the image of the twinned heavenly orbs representing the light-giving and he eternal nature of their rule. A quirky touch is supplied by numerous paintings of ares curled up inside some of the moons (see page 216), while the overhanging eaves re also embellished with a fine sequence of paintings. What's perhaps strangest about ll this decoration, however, is its largely royal and secular content: Buddha images, in his holiest of Sri Lankan temples, are notable largely by their absence.

he Pirit Mandapa and Tooth Relic Chamber

 set of stairs to the left (as you face the main shrine) from the drummers' courtyard eads to the upper level; halfway up you'll pass the casket in which a replica of the ooth Relic is paraded during the Esala Perahera, along with golden "flags" and mbrellas which are also used during the procession. At the top of the steps is the **Pirit Mandapa** (Recitation Hall), a rather plain space whose unusual latticed wooden walls end it a faintly Japanese air. This leads to the entrance of the **Tooth Relic Chamber** itself, n the upper level of the main shrine. You can't actually go into the relic chamber, and he entrance is railed off (except during pujas), although you can make out some of the etails of the fantastically ornate brass doorway into the shrine, framed in silver and ecorated in a riot of embossed ornament, with auspicious symbols including dwarfs, ome holding urns of plenty, plus entwined geese, peacocks, suns, moons and dagobas.

HARES IN THE MOON

The paintings of hares in the moon shown on the exterior of the Tooth Relic shrine refer to one of the most famous of the **Jataka** stories, describing the previous lives of the Buddha before his final incarnation and enlightenment. According to the Jataka story of the Hare in the Moon, the future Buddha was once born as a hare. One day the hare was greeted by an emaciated holy man, who begged him – along with a fox and a monkey, who also happened to be passing – for food. The fox brought a fish, the monkey some fruit, but the hare was unable to find anything for the holy man to eat apart from grass. Having no other way of assuaging the ascetic's hunger, the hare asked him to light a fire and then leapt into the flames, offering his own body as food. At this moment the holy man revealed himself as the god Indra, placing an image of the hare in the moon to commemorate its self-sacrifice, where it remains to this day.

The Jataka fable may itself be simply a **local version** of a still more ancient Hindu or Vedic myth – traditions referring to a hare in the moon can be found as far away as China, Central Asia and even Europe, while the story also appears, in slightly modified form, in one of the Brothers Grimm fairy tales.

Paintings to either side of the door show guardstone figures bearing bowls of lotuses, surmounted by *makara toranas*.

The **interior** of the Tooth Relic chamber is divided by golden arches into three sections, though the chamber is kept shut except during pujas, and even then you'll only be able to get a brief glimpse as you're hurried past the door amid the throngs of visitors. The Tooth Relic is kept in the furthest section, the **Vedahitina Maligawa** (Shrine of Abode), concealed from the public gaze in a dagoba-shaped gold casket that is said to contain a series of six further caskets, the smallest of which contains the Tooth itself.

Alut Maligawa

At the back of the Drummers' Courtyard, the **Alut Maligawa** (New Shrine Room) is a large and undistinguished building completed in 1956 to celebrate the 2500th anniversary of the Buddha's death. The interior, as if to compensate for the lack of Buddhist imagery in the main section of the temple, is filled with a glut of Buddha statues, many donated by foreign countries, which offer an opportunity to compare different Asian versions of traditional Buddhist iconography, with images from Thailand (in the middle), China, Sri Lanka, Japan, Korea and Taiwan. Set in a pair of miniature dagobas at either side of the central Thai image are two holographic Buddha faces from France, which appear to turn their heads to follow you as you move around the room.

A sequence of 21 **paintings** hung around the chamber's upper walls depict the story of the Tooth Relic from the Buddha's death to the present day. The Buddhas below were a gift from Thailand to commemorate the fiftieth anniversary of Sri Lanka's independence.

Sri Dalada Museum (Tooth Relic Museum)

Entrance included in main temple ticket

On the first and second floors of the Alut Maligawa building, the **Sri Dalada Museum** (reached via the rear exit from the ground-floor shrine room) contains a medley of objects connected with the Tooth Relic and temple. The **first floor** is dominated by a sequence of large and solemn busts of all the *diyawardene nilambe* (temple chiefs) from 1814 to 1985. Other exhibits include photos of the damage caused by the 1998 bombing, along with assorted precious artefacts from the temple collections including ancient palm-leaf manuscripts, items used in religious rituals and a selection of the enormous ceremonial handkerchiefs designed for the kings of Kandy.

The **second floor** is largely occupied by the bewildering assortment of objects offered to the Tooth Relic at various times, including several donated by former Sri Lankan presidents. The highlight is the gorgeous silk Buddha footprint which is said to have been offered to the temple in the reign of Kirti Sri Rajasinha by a visiting Thai monk on behalf of the king of Siam.

Exiting the Sri Dalada Museum you may want to detour first to the **Museum of World Buddhism** (see page 218), just a few steps away – not actually part of the temple, but included in the entrance ticket.

The Royal Palace and around

The Temple of the Tooth originally lay at the heart of the sprawling **Royal Palace**, a self-contained complex of buildings immediately surrounding the temple and housing various royal residences, audience chambers and associated structures. Significant sections of the original palace complex survive, although it's difficult to get a very clear sense of how it would originally have looked, thanks to the many additions and alterations made to the area since 1815.

The Audience Hall

Immediately north of the temple (and reached via a side exit from it, or from the exit from the Sri Dalada Museum) lies the imposing **Audience Hall**, an impressively complete Kandyan pavilion set on a raised stone plinth, open on all sides and sporting characteristic wooden pillars, corbels and roof, all intricately carved. The hall originally dated from 1784, though it was set on fire by the Kandyans during the British attack of 1803 – the conservation-minded British invaders obligingly put out the fire and subsequently restored the building. It was here that the Kandyan chiefs signed the treaty that handed over power to the British on March 2, 1815.

Raja Tusker Museum

Daily 8am–5pm • Entrance with Temple of the Tooth ticket

Just north of the Audience Hall stands the **Raja Tusker Museum**, devoted to the memory of Sri Lanka's most famous elephant, **Raja**. The main attraction is the stuffed remains of Raja himself, now standing proudly in state in a glass cabinet. Raja died in 1988 after fifty years' loyal service as Kandy's **Maligawa Tusker** – the elephant that carries the Tooth Relic casket during the Esala Perahera (see page 210). Such was the veneration in which he was held that his death prompted the government to order a day of national mourning, while the animal's remains are now an object of devotion to many Sinhalese, who come to pray at Raja's glass case. The museum also has photos of Raja in various peraheras, plus sad snaps of him surrounded by anxious vets during his final illness.

MALIGAWA TUSKERS

No single elephant has yet proved itself able to fill Raja's considerable boots, and at present the role of **Maligawa Tusker** is shared between various elephants. All Maligawa Tuskers must fulfil certain physical requirements. Only male elephants are permitted to carry the relic and, most importantly, they must be **Sathdantha** elephants, meaning that all seven parts of their body – the four legs, trunk, penis and tail – must touch the ground when they stand upright. In addition, the tusks must be formed in the curved shape of a traditional winnow, and the elephant must have a flat back and reach a height of around twelve feet. It has proved increasingly difficult to find such "high-caste" elephants locally, although the temple already owns several suitable beasts, including ones donated by notables, among them various prime ministers of Sri Lanka and India, as well as the king of Thailand.

Archeological Museum

Daily 8am–5pm • Entrance with Temple of the Tooth ticket

Immediately north of the Raja Tusker Museum in the former **palace** of King Vimala Dharma Suriya (r. 1591–1604), Kandy's dusty **Archeological Museum** comprises a modest collection of assorted pots, bits of masonry, fragments of carved stones and old wooden pillars. It's all fairly humdrum, although the former palace building is impressive: a long, low, barn-like structure sporting an ornate gateway and doors decorated with the sun and moon symbol of the kings of Kandy, along with other auspicious symbols.

Museum of World Buddhism

Daily 8am–7pm • Entrance free with Temple of the Tooth ticket, otherwise Rs.500

Directly behind the Temple of the Tooth (and just north of the National Museum – see below) is the imposing British-era Neoclassical building which formerly housed the city's High Court. This now provides a grand setting for the entertainingly strange **Museum of World Buddhism**, one of Sri Lanka's most enjoyable museums, showcasing Buddhist beliefs and artefacts from across Asia. The museum's **ground floor** features an excellent sequence of galleries with assorted displays on Sri Lankan Buddhism, a colourful recreation of a Bhutanese shrine, displays on Gandharan-era Buddhism from Pakistan, Indian statues and murals, plus further rooms devoted to Nepal and Bangladesh, all intelligently presented and explained.

Things really fire into life in the **upstairs galleries**, however, which are stuffed full of a weird, occasionally wonderful and unquestionably random selection of displays and artefacts focusing on the Buddhist heritage of countries from Indonesia to Japan. Many of the displays appear to have been donated as PR exercises by the various countries involved, and the general impression is not so much of a curated museum as an international travel fair, with assorted promotional videos looping endlessly in the background. It's not without a certain bizarre appeal, and some of the exhibits are undeniably impressive, including a room full of shiny gilded Buddhas from Myanmar (Burma) and a fine array of Chinese, Tibetan and Thai artefacts. Elsewhere, things become decidedly haphazard, such as the photos of Mahinda Rajapakse in the Japan gallery (including one in which he appears to be receiving treatment for lice) and the entire Vietnamese room, which bears an uncanny resemblance to a Hong Kong seafood restaurant.

The National Museum and around

Tues–Sat 9am–5pm • Rs.600

Immediately behind the Temple of the Tooth, though not directly accessible from it lies the Kandy branch of the **National Museum**, set in a low white building set around a flagstoned courtyard which was formerly the Queen's Palace (or "King's Harem", as it's also described). The well-presented collection showcases a treasure-trove of Kandyan traditional artefacts, with exhibits attesting to the high levels of skill achieved by local craftsmen – jewellery, fabrics, musical instruments, lacquerware and so on, plus a fine display of minutely detailed ivory objects (look for the cute figurines of various Kandyan bigwigs).

Next door to the National Museum is the modest **Queen's Chamber**, a discreet low white structure with tiny balustraded windows and stone pool inside. Close by, just southwest of the museum on the edge of the lake, sits the **Queen's Bath** (Ulpenge), a grand but rather dilapidated structure, looking a bit like a boathouse; the upper storey was added by the British.

The Kandy Garrison Cemetery

Garrison Cemetery Rd (signposted from beside the National Museum) • Mon–Sat 8am–6pm • Donation

The evocative **Kandy Garrison Cemetery** was established in 1817, shortly after the British seized control of Kandy, to provide a final resting place for expired British colonists. Having fallen into complete dereliction, the cemetery has been painstakingly restored and now offers a moving memorial to Ceylon's former colonial master. Shockingly few of the people buried here made it to the age of 30, and even those who avoided the usual hazards of tropical diseases and hostile natives found unusual ways to meet their maker, such as John Spottiswood Robertson (d. 1856), trampled to death by a wild elephant; David Findlay (d. 1861), killed when his house collapsed on top of him; and William Watson Mackwood (d. 1867), who somehow managed to impale himself on a stake while dismounting from his horse.

The most notable burial, however, is **Sir John D'Oyly**, the remarkable colonial official who brokered the surrender of the city to the British in 1815. D'Oyly was one of the most fascinating figures in the history of colonial Ceylon – at once a supreme diplomat who manipulated the Kandyan nobility with almost Machiavellian genius, and also a kind of proto-hippy who became a strict vegetarian, avoided European society and devoted himself to the study of Sinhala and Buddhism. As an observer remarked in 1810: "He lives on plantain, invites nobody to his house, and does not dine abroad above once a year. When I saw him… I was struck with the change of a Cambridge boy into a Cingalese hermit." Despite his brilliant orchestration of the bloodless coup at Kandy, D'Oyly's subsequent attempts to protect the Kandyans from British interference and Christian missionaries were little appreciated, and by the time of his death from cholera in 1824, he had become a lonely and marginalized figure – not that you'd realize it, judging by the size of his memorial, the largest in the cemetery, topped by a broken Greek pillar. It's on your left as you come in, quite close to the entrance.

The devales and St Paul's Church

Kandy traditionally lies under the protection of four gods, each of whom is honoured with a temple (*devale*) in the city. Three of these temples, the **Pattini**, **Natha** and **Vishnu** *devales*, sit next to one another just in front of the Temple of the Tooth – a fascinating and picturesque jumble of shrines, dagobas and bo trees. The fourth *devale*, dedicated to **Kataragama**, lies a couple of blocks west in the city itself. Besides their obvious artistic merits, the *devales* offer a fascinating lesson in the way in which Hindu and Buddhist beliefs shaded into one another in Kandy, as throughout Sri Lankan history: two of the four *devales* are dedicated to adopted Hindu gods, while the principal shrine of the Natha *devale* is housed in a building that wouldn't look out of place in South India.

Pattini Devale

The **Pattini Devale** is the simplest of the four temples. The cult of the goddess **Pattini** (see page 220) was introduced from South India in the second century AD by King Gajabahu (r. 114–136 AD); she remains a popular deity among poorer Sri Lankans, thanks to her lowly origins. Her golden ankle bracelet, brought back from India by Gajabahu, is said to be kept here (though you can't see it). Entering from Deva Vidiya, you're confronted by the **Wel-Bodhiya**, a huge bo tree, perched on an enormous, three-tiered platform; it's believed to have been planted by **Narendrasinha**, the last Sinhalese king of Kandy, in the early eighteenth century.

The actual shrine to Pattini is off to the right, set in a modest little enclosure entered through gorgeous embossed brass doors decorated with the usual sun and moon symbols, *makara toranas* and guardstone figures. The shrine itself is set in a small but beautiful Kandyan wooden pavilion, and is usually the most popular of all the *devales* among visiting worshippers. To either side stand subsidiary shrines to the Hindu deities Kali and Mariamman – the latter, like Pattini, is a female deity of humble South Indian origins who is believed to protect against disease. You may be approached by a temple flunkey at this point asking for a donation; he'll most likely show you a book in which previous donations are listed, many of which appear to have been wildly inflated by the addition of surplus zeros.

PATTINI

Pattini (originally named Kannaki) was a humble Indian girl from the city of Madurai who married a certain **Kovalan**, an errant spouse with a weakness for dancing girls. Despite Pattini's considerable charms, the feckless Kovalan abandoned his wife and bankrupted himself in pursuit of one particular amour until, ashamed and penniless, he returned to Pattini to beg forgiveness. The pliable Pattini welcomed him back without even a word of reproach and handed over her last possession, a golden ankle bracelet, for him to sell. The unfortunate Kovalan did so, but was promptly accused of stealing the bracelet by the king's goldsmith and executed. The distraught Pattini, legend states, descended upon the royal palace, tore off one of her breasts, caused the king to drop dead and then reduced his palace to ashes before being taken up into the heavens as a goddess.

Pattini's cult was originally introduced to Sri Lanka by **King Gajabahu** in the second century BC, but enjoyed its heyday during the Kandyan era, when the kingdom's Hindu rulers revived her cult and built her Kandy temple. Pattini is now revered as the ideal of the chaste and devoted wife: pregnant women come here to pray for a safe delivery (rather inexplicably, since Pattini was childless), while she is also thought to protect against infectious diseases such as chickenpox, smallpox and measles.

Natha Devale

A gate leads from the Pattini Devale directly through to the **Natha Devale**. **Natha** is the most purely Buddhist of the gods of the four *devales*, and thus the most important in the city, being considered a form of the Mahayana Bodhisattva **Avalokitesvara**, who is still widely worshipped in Nepal, Tibet, China and Japan. Natha was thought to have influence over political events in the kingdom – new kings of Kandy were obliged to present themselves at the shrine on attaining the throne – although the god's exalted status means that his shrine is rather less popular with the hoi polloi than that of humble Pattini next door.

Away to your right at the end of the enclosure is the **Natha Shrine** itself, built by Vikramabahu III in the fourteenth century, and thus the oldest building in Kandy. This low *gedige* (stone shrine), topped with a small *shikhara* dome, is very reminiscent in style of similar Indian-style temples at Polonnaruwa (the fact that the city's most Buddhist deity sits in its most Hindu-looking temple seems pretty much par for the course given Kandy's pick-'n'-mix attitude towards foreign gods). Inside, the walls of the shrine are covered with beautifully embossed brass sheets, while in front stands a much later pavilion sporting beautifully carved wooden pillars.

Close by, a **Buddha shrine** sits in the centre of the enclosure, with two elaborately railed bo trees to the rear. Exit the temple through the archway to the north, its exterior wall richly carved and painted with *makara torana* and guardstone figures.

Vishnu Devale

From the back of the Natha Devale, steps lead up through a wooden pavilion into the third of the *devales*, the **Vishnu Devale** (also known as the Maha Devale, or "Great Temple"). The first building you come to is an open-sided **digge** pavilion, in which drummers and dancers would once have performed in honour of the deity – you can still occasionally see trainee dancers being put through their paces here. Past the *digge*, further steps lead up to the main **Vishnu shrine**. The Vishnu image here is thought to come from Dondra on the south coast, though it's usually hidden behind a curtain; ceremonial objects used in Esala Perahera line the sides of the shrine. Behind and to the left of the Vishnu shrine stands a subsidiary shrine to **Dedimunda** (a local god of obscure origins), his image framed by a gorgeously embossed gilded arch featuring the ubiquitous sun and moon motif.

St Paul's Church

Immediately north of the Pattini Devale, the quaint neo-Gothic **St Paul's Church** (1843) offers a homesick and thoroughly incongruous memento of rustic English nostalgia amid the Buddhist monuments – indeed, the irreverent insertion of such a large Christian building into such a sacred Buddhist precinct says much about British religious sympathies, or lack of. The **interior** is a piece of pure English Victoriana (although sadly it's usually kept locked), with beautiful wooden pews, floor tiles decorated with floral and fleur de lys patterns, wooden rood-screen and choir stalls, naff stained glass, brass eagle lectern and a grand piano, all tenderly preserved. The various monuments date back to the 1840s, recording deaths in parts of the empire as far flung as Bombay, Port Said, Wei-Hai-Wei and South Africa.

Opposite the church, the walls of the buildings along Deva Vidiya are all but buried underneath a surfeit of **signs** in English and Sinhala advertising the services of local lawyers, whose offices stand along the street, occupying a former Victorian-era army stables and barracks.

The rest of the city

Away from the Temple of the Tooth, Royal Palace and *devales*, most of Kandy has a largely modern appearance, although a fair number of crusty old colonial-era buildings survive. The centre of the modern city spreads out around **Dalada Vidiya**, confined, thanks to the hilliness of the surrounding terrain, into a compact grid of low-rise streets lined with small shops and retaining a engagingly small-town atmosphere given that it's at the heart of the nation's second-biggest city. The most interesting area is along

---

ROBERT KNOX AND SEVENTEENTH-CENTURY KANDY

In 1660, a party of English sailors who had gone ashore near the mouth of the Mahaweli Ganga were taken prisoner by soldiers of the king of Kandy, Rajasinha II. Among them was a 19-year-old Londoner named **Robert Knox**. Knox's subsequent account of his nineteen years as a hostage of the king was eventually published as *An Historical Relation of Ceylon*, a unique record which offers a fascinating snapshot of everyday life in the seventeenth-century Kingdom of Kandy. The book later served as one of the major sources of Daniel Defoe's *Robinson Crusoe*, and something of Knox's own industrious (if rather dour) character may have crept into Defoe's self-sufficient hero.

Upon arriving in Kandy, Knox was surprised to discover that he and his shipmates were not the only **European "guests"** being detained at Rajasinha's pleasure – also in Kandy were prisoners of war, shipwrecked sailors, army deserters and assorted diplomats. Knox seems to have admired many of the qualities of his hosts, though he did object (as have so many subsequent Western travellers to Asia) that "They make no account nor conscience of lying, neither is it any shame or disgrace to them, if they be catched in telling lies; it is so customary." He also recorded (with puritan disapproval) the kingdom's **liberal attitude** to sex: "Both women and men do commonly wed four or five times before they can settle themselves." Married women appeared free to have affairs with whoever took their fancy, so long as they were of an equal social rank, sometimes even leaving their husbands at home to look after the children. When important visitors called, husbands would offer them the services of their wives and daughters "to bear them company in their chamber". Men were allowed to have affairs with lower-caste women, but not to sit or eat with them. Polyandry, in which a wife was shared between two or more brothers, or in which one man married two or more sisters, was also accepted, while incest was reputedly common among beggars. If nothing else, the kingdom's sex drive was impressive. As Knox observed of the Kandyan women: "when their Husbands are dead, all their care is where to get others, which they cannot long be without."

In terms of **material possessions**, the life which Knox recorded was simple. Most Kandyans contented themselves with the bare necessities, encouraged in their indolence by the fact that the moment they acquired anything it was taken away by the king's mob of tax collectors. Justice was meted out by a court of local chiefs, but appeared to favour whoever was able to present the largest bribe – those convicted of capital offences were trampled to death by an elephant.

the eastern end of **Bennet Soysa Vidiya** (generally known by its old name of Colombo Street), where fruit and veg sellers ply their wares from the narrow and congested pavements.

At the far end of Dalada Vidiya stands Kandy's unusually ornate **clocktower**, complete with golden elephant friezes and a cute, hat-like top. Just south of here is the **Kandy Central Market**, set around a pair of grassy courtyards ringed with small shops stuffed with dried fish, cheap spices, all sorts of seasonal fruits, and bananas of every conceivable size shape and colour, while there are also a number of touristy souvenir shops – including the excellent Jayamali Batiks (see page 228) – on the upper level.

Kataragama Devale

The fourth of the city's principal *devales*, the **Kataragama Devale**, sits buried away in the city centre, somewhat separate from the other *devales*, entered through a lurid blue gateway on Kotugodelle Vidiya (though it's surprisingly easy to miss amid the packed shopfronts). This is the most Hindu-influenced of Kandy's temples, right down to the pair of resident Brahmin priests. The attractive central Kataragama shrine is topped by a broad wooden roof and protected by two intricately gilded doors, with a pair of Buddha shrines behind and to the left. The right-hand side of the enclosure has a very Indian flavour, with a line of shrines housing images of Durga, Krishna, Radha, Ganesh and Vishnu – those at the back have ornate gold doors with tiny bells on them which devotees ring to attract the gods' attention.

The Bahiravakanda Buddha

Daily 6am–8pm • Rs.200

West of the city centre, the immense white **Bahiravakanda Buddha** stares impassively over central Kandy from its hilltop perch. The statue was constructed at the behest of the religiously minded **President Premadasa**, who also contributed the striking golden roof of the principal shrine of the Temple of the Tooth, as well as various other religious edifices around the island – though these many pious acts didn't save him from being blown to smithereens by an LTTE suicide bomber in 1993.

You can walk up to the statue – a stiff 15–20-minute hike – although in truth it's hardly worth the effort and the views, although extensive, aren't as attractive as those from Rajapahila Mawatha, which is much less of a climb, and also free.

Udawattakele Sanctuary

The entrance to the park is a steep hike from town: go up past the post office along Kandy Vidiya and then Wewelpitiya Road; the easy-to-miss entrance is next to the Sri Dalada Thapowanaya temple • Daily 7am–5.30pm • Rs.660

On the opposite (north) side of the lake, providing a dense green backdrop to the Temple of the Tooth, is **Udawattakele Sanctuary**, formerly a royal reserve, subsequently preserved and protected by the British. The sanctuary sprawls over two square kilometres of densely forested hillside, with imposing trees, plenty of birdlife, snakes, and a few mammals including monkeys, porcupines and pigs – as well as lots of leeches if it's been raining. Two main paths, Lady Horton's Drive and Lady Gordon's Road (both named after the wives of British governors) wind through the reserve, with a few smaller paths and nature trails branching off them.

ARRIVAL AND DEPARTURE KANDY

Thanks to its position roughly in the centre of the island, Kandy is within fairly easy striking distance of pretty much everywhere in the country (and will be even more so when the **Central Expressway** – see page 28 – opens), although if you're heading to the south coast, it's normally easiest to go back to Colombo and start from there. Heading into the hill country, the **train** connects Kandy with most

places you're likely to want to go, while to the north, the sites of the Cultural Triangle are no more than two three hours away by road. For **Katunayake Airport**, note that all buses to Negombo pass the turn-off to the airport about 2km from the terminal itself; alternatively, take a (non-intercity) Colombo train to Veyangoda, then catch a bus or tuktuk for the thirty-minute trip to the airport.

By air Cinnamon Air (see page 31) operate flights from Kandy's Polgolla Reservoir (about 5km northeast of the centre) to Colombo and other destinations. Travelling to Colombo it probably works out almost as quick to take the train, although the bird's-eye views of the hills are spectacular. Fares range between $175 and $230 one-way.
Destinations: Colombo (1 daily; 30min); Dickwella (1 daily via Hambantota; 1hr); Hambantota (1 daily; 30min); Koggala (1 daily via Hambantota and Dickwella; 1hr 30min).

By bus Most long-distance bus services depart from Kandy's main bus station, the truly horrible Goods Shed Bus Terminal opposite the train station (the Clocktower Bus Stand, south of the clocktower at the west end of the city centre, is used for local departures only). If you can't find the bus you're looking for, ask at one of the various wire-mesh information kiosks along the central aisle. For Ella, you'll probably have to travel via Bandarawela, and for Haputale via Nuwara Eliya and/or Bandarawela; in both instances it's easier (if not necessarily quicker) to take the train. All buses to Polonnaruwa travel via Habarana and Giritale. Most buses to Jaffna travel overnight, although there are a couple of early morning services too.

Destinations Anuradhapura (every 30min; 3hr 30min); Badulla (every 45min; 3hr); Bandarawela (8 daily; 4hr); Colombo (express services every 30min; 3hr 30min; these leave from the roadside on Station Rd about halfway between the Goods Shed terminal and the clocktower); Dambulla (every 20min; 2hr); Jaffna (8–10 daily; 10hr); Kegalle (for Pinnewala; every 30min; 1hr–1hr 30min); Kurunegala (every 30min; 1hr 30min); Negombo (hourly; 3hr; or catch a bus to Kurunegala and change there); Nuwara Eliya (every 30min; 2hr 30min); Polonnaruwa (every 45min; 3hr 30min); Ratnapura (hourly; 3hr 30min); Sigiriya (1 daily at 7.30am; 2hr 30min; otherwise change at Dambulla); Trincomalee (hourly in the morning; 6hr).

By train Kandy's train station sits close to Goods Shed bus station on the southwest edge of the city centre; various services run on this line (see page 32). The ride through the hills up to Nanu Oya (for Nuwara Eliya), Haputale, Ella and Badulla is slow but unforgettable – travelling to Colombo, sit on the south side of the train (the left-hand side, as you face the front) for the best views.
Destinations Badulla (3 daily; 7hr 30min); Colombo (7 daily; 2hr 30min–3hr 30min); Ella (3 daily; 6hr 30min); Haputale (5 daily; 5hr 30min); Hatton (3 daily; 2hr 30min); Nanu Oya (for Nuwara Eliya; 3 daily; 4hr).

3

GETTING AROUND

Although greater Kandy sprawls for miles over the surrounding hills, the centre is extremely compact, and easily covered **on foot**. Places around the lake and Udawattakele Sanctuary are all within walking distance of the centre,

although if you're staying further afield (in Ampitiya, for example) you'll need to catch a tuktuk – although be aware that the city's **tuktuk** drivers are possibly the most rapacious in Sri Lanka, so be prepared to haggle hard.

ACCOMMODATION

There's a huge selection of **accommodation** in all price ranges in and around Kandy, although budget accommodation is increasingly hard to find. Note that the **temperature** in Kandy is markedly cooler than along the coast – you probably won't need air-conditioning, but you probably will want hot water (all the following places have this unless stated otherwise). In general, the better the view, the further from town – and the more taxing the walk from the centre. If you're staying on Rajapihilla Mw note that there's a useful **shortcut** up to the road from the top of Saranankara Rd: go up the steps on the left side of the *Highest View* guesthouse.

CITY CENTRE

Olde Empire 21 Temple St ☎ 081 222 4284; map p.208. Bang in the centre, this is one of Kandy's oldest places to stay, and still one of the best cheapies in town, with a charmingly antiquated wood-panelled interior, picturesque streetside veranda and restaurant, and nineteen basic white rooms (some with shared bathroom; cold water only) – no particular frills, but clean and well-

maintained. No wi-fi. Shared bathrooms Rs.1500, en suites Rs.3300

Queen's Hotel 45 Dalada Vidiya ☎ 081 223 3026, ⓦ queenshotel.lk; map p.208. Dating back to the 1860s, this venerable hotel is one of central Kandy's most famous landmarks, and still has a certain old-world style. The spacious a/c rooms have plenty of colonial character, although most overlook busy roads and so are rather noisy – the inward-facing pool rooms are quieter, although the views aren't as interesting. Facilities include a rather antiquated pool plus an endearingly old-fashioned bar and restaurant (although with uninspiring food). $150

SOUTH OF THE LAKE

Blinkbonnie Tourist Inn 69 Rajapihilla Mw ☎ 081 222 2007; map p.208. Reliable guesthouse in a fine position high above town. Good range of comfortable modern rooms (all with optional a/c); those downstairs come with superb views through big French windows. Free pick-up from bus/train station and has scooters/motorbikes for rent (Rs.1500/2500 per day). Rs.4400, a/c Rs.4950

3

TOURS FROM KANDY

The main **taxi stand** (minivans and cars) is opposite the Clocktower Bus Stand at the west end of the centre. Sample prices are around Rs.4000 to Pinnewala, Rs.3000 for the three-temples circuit; and around Rs.6000 for the two combined. Almost all the city's guesthouses can arrange **tours**; count on $40–50 per day for the hire of a car and driver. Alternatively, contact the reliable **Blue Haven Tours and Travels** (☏081 222 9617, ☏077 737 2066, ⊛bluehaventours.com), who can arrange inexpensive local and islandwide tours.

The vastly experienced **Sumane Bandara Illangantilake** (c/o *Expeditor* guesthouse, Saranankara Rd ☏077 260 6069, ☏071 720 4722, ⊛trekkingexpeditor.com) and his team of ten highly trained guides offer island-wide tours, plus all sorts of trips and hikes around Kandy including an unusual full-day off-road version of the three-temples walk for ($50 per person); all walks can be customized to suit different levels of physical fitness. Sumane is also the island's leading guide to the Knuckles Range, with a range of 1- to 3-day treks around the region; an authority on the Veddhas; and can arrange visits to pretty much anywhere you might fancy going, including more off-the-beaten-track national parks like Wasgomuwa and Gal Oya, plus "camping on water" stays (featuring tents on rafts) at Sorabora Lake. For tours, count on around $65–75 per person per day (in a group of 2–4), excluding entrance fees; a proportion of profits is returned to local communities.

Ravi Desappriya (☏071 499 7666, ⊛srilankatrekking.com) is another good local guide, organizing a similar range of tours including dedicated birding trips (see ⊛srilankabirdwatching.com), Knuckles expeditions (see ⊛knucklesrange.com), Wasgamuwa excursions and visits to the dramatic Alagalla range 20km west of Kandy, plus night safaris and wilderness camping.

Expeditor 41 Saranankara Rd ☏081 223 8316, ⊛expeditorkandy.com; map p.208. Smart modern guesthouse, owned by Kandy's leading tour guide (see page 224) and with a wide range of rooms, from a couple of downstairs cheapies with shared bathroom to upstairs en-suite rooms with high wooden ceilings and fine lake views – all nicely furnished, extremely comfortable and very competitively priced. Shared bathrooms Rs.2000, en suites Rs.2500, a/c Rs.6000

Freedom Lodge 30 Saranankara Rd ☏081 222 3506, ✉freedomomega@gmail.com; map p.208. Excellent and very professionally run family guesthouse offering a very friendly welcome and accommodation in ten smart and comfortable modern rooms (including family accommodation), plus good home-cooking, a roof terrace and kitchen for guests' use. B&B Rs.5500

★ **Helga's Folly** Off Mahamaya Mw ☏081 223 4571, ⊛helgasfolly.com; map p.208. Utterly maverick and magical place, set high above Kandy in a rambling old house whose former house guests have included Gandhi, Nehru and Laurence Olivier – not to mention Stereophonics frontman Kelly Jones, who penned a song ("Madame Helga") in honour of the place. The extraordinary interior is a riot of colourful invention, from the eye-popping yellow lounge, with petrified dripping candles, deer heads, Indonesian puppets and colonial photos, to the individual bedrooms (all a/c), each with its own unique design featuring any combination of wacky murals, colonial furniture and unusual *objets d'art*. Facilities include a small cinema and a (very shallow) pool. $100

Lake Front Homestay 26 Cyril Jayasundara Ave (Lake Round) ☏081 222 7135, ✉info@lakefrontkandy.com; map p.208. Not actually on the lake front, but still a good choice, in a very quiet side road with six simple but spacious rooms and efficient service – although the manager might try to sell you a tour. Breakfast is served in the sunny dining room, with nice views to accompany. Rs.3000

★ **Mcleod Inn** 65A Rajapihilla Mw ☏081 222 2832 or ☏071 682 0914, ⊛mcleodinnkandy.com; map p.208. Kandy's best bargain, perched in a peerless location high above town and with very friendly and super-efficient service from the husband-and-wife owners. The ten rooms are clean, modern and attractively furnished. All come with satelite TV, while two (Rs.1000 extra) have views to dream of through enormous French windows, as does the dining room. Also offers a handy laundry service. Excellent value. Rs.4000

Sharon Inn 59 Saranankara Rd ☏081 222 2416, ✉sharon@sltnet.lk; map p.208. Ever-expanding edifice at the very top of Saranankara Rd with attractive furnished rooms (including interconnecting family rooms for Rs.12,000) with a/c and satellite TV – all bright, white, scrupulously clean and with marvellous bird's-eye views over town from private balconies. Also cooks up the best rice and curry in town (see page 227), served nightly at the rooftop restaurant. B&B Rs.6500

Hotel Suisse Sangaraja Mw ☏081 223 3024, ⊛hotelsuisse.lk; map p.208. This gracious old hotel served as Mountbatten's Southeast Asian headquarters during World War II and retains much of its time-warped olonial charm. Rooms (some lake-facing for $40 extra; all with a/c, satellite TV and minibar) are spacious and neatly urnished, and the attractive public areas include a cosy ar, a billiards room and a pool. **$158**

NORTH OF THE LAKE

The Best Hostel 11, 1st Lane, Dharmaraja Mw ☏ 081 223 223, ✉ thebesthostel.kandy@gmail.com; map p.208. One of the best hostels in Kandy (we'll say that for it), in a quite central but very quiet location with accommodation in a mix of female, male and mixed four- and eight-bed dorms, plus a couple of basic doubles. It's a bit bare and lacking in facilities (although it does have a kitchen and lounge), but you can hardly complain given the absolutely rock-bottom price. B&B: dorms **$6pp**, doubles **$15**

Green Woods 34A Sangamitta Mw ☏ 081 223 2970, ✉ greenwoodsinfo@gmail.com; map p.208. Tucked away in a surprisingly rural setting not far from the centre, with simple but comfortable fan rooms in a beautifully secluded location overlooking Udawattakele Sanctuary, whose birdlife can be ogled for free from the veranda or attractive communal lounge. B&B **Rs.3500**

Hipsters Hideout 117/3 Angarika Dharmapala Mw ☏ 081 222 9222, ⓦ facebook.com/thehostelkandy; map p.208. Lively, central hostel. There's a great, and often kicking, little restaurant and bar in the courtyard, plus daily yoga classes. Dorms (one 8-bed mixed, one 14-bed female) and rooms are pretty basic and a bit grubby, but also very cheap. B&B: dorms **$7pp**, doubles **$15**

Nature Walk 9 Sangamitta Mw ☏ 077 771 7482, ⓦ naturewalkhr.net; map p.208. Attractive small hotel with spacious and nicely decorated modern a/c rooms, plus a few non a/c budget rooms. A couple of standard rooms at the front (no surcharge) come with balcony and hill views through big French windows, and there's also a surprisingly stylish open-sided restaurant on the top floor. B&B: budget **30**, standard **$55**

Villa 49 49 Louis Peiris Mw ☏ 081 224 1142, ⓦ villa49. weebly.com; map p.208. Attractive little boutique guesthouse, with six very comfortably furnished and well-equipped rooms with a/c, TV, fridge, safe, kettle and balcony – or spend an extra $10 to get one of the slightly larger and fancier deluxe rooms, decorated with colourful Indian fabrics. B&B **$80**

NORTH OF THE CENTRE

Blue Haven 30/2 Poorna Lane, Asigiriya ☏ 081 222 0617, ✉ bluehavtravels@gmail.com; map p.208. In a pleasantly semi-rural setting on the edge of the centre, with bright tiled rooms, an attractive upstairs veranda, a terrace restaurant looking out over the tree tops, and a pool. Choose between top-floor "deluxe" rooms with a/c and hot water and cheaper fan rooms downstairs (optional a/c $5). There's free pick-up from town. Good value at

current rates, and *Rough Guides* readers are promised a ten-percent discount on room prices. B&B: **$23**, a/c **$35**

Clock Inn 11 Kande Vihara (Hill St) ☏ 081 223 5311, ⓦ clockinn.lk; map p.208. In a quaint colonial verandahed building right in the heart of the city, this is Kandy's most upmarket hostel, with crisp, six-bed a/c dorms (each bed with its own light and socket), plus neat and cosy double rooms. B&B: dorms **$13pp**, doubles **$50**

★ **The Elephant Stables** 46 Nittawela Rd ☏ 081 742 3201, ⓦ elephantstables.com; map p.231. Very stylish new boutique hotel, set in a beautifully updated colonial villa with fine views towards the Knuckles Range. There are just six gorgeous and very comfortable colour-coded rooms (plus cottage and luxury tent) in a kind of contemporary country-house style, with vibrant decor, heaps of comfy furniture and a real home-from-home feel. Facilities include an attractive decked pool in the neat garden, a cosy bar and lounge, plus cute little library, with city tours in the hotel's classic cars available on request. B&B **$350**

Lady Gordons Homestay 116/4 Lady Gordon's Drive ☏ 081 220 1354, ✉ ladygordonshomestay@gmail.com; map p.208. A real home-from-home, hidden away in the pleasantly quiet and leafy streets below Udawatakele, with a very welcoming owner and five simple but comfortable rooms in an enjoyably old-fashioned villa – and at a very affordable price. **Rs.3000**

The Secret Kandy 25 Lady Gordon's Drive ☏ 081 220 4280, ⓦ thesecrethotels.com/kandy; map p.208. Lovely little boutique guesthouse in a stylishly updated 125-year-old bungalow, combining colonial character and contemporary comforts. All five rooms come with a/c, TV, minibar and bathtub and facilities include a small courtyard pool and suave little courtyard café. B&B **$170**

EAST OF THE CENTRE

Ginza Rest 92E Ampitiya Rd ☏ 081 565 6667 or ☏ 077 268 4702; map p.231. This slightly ramshackle family house has just a handful of huge, bare rooms, each sleeping four or five. Absolutely no frills, and not much furniture either, although the owner is a delight and rates are among the lowest in town. B&B **Rs.2000**

Kandy City Hostel 76 Ampitiya Rd (on the right, just past the 2km post) ☏ 077 444 9182, ⓦ hostelslanka. com; map p.208. Cheap lodgings in three well-equipped six- to eight-bed dorms (plus one six-bed female dorm for $10pp and one double for $35) – all beds come with individual fans, nets and lockers with plugs in, and there's also a kitchen, washing machines and rooftop movie screenings some nights (but no restaurant). A tuktuk from the bus/train station should cost Rs.300. B&B **$8pp**

AROUND KANDY

Bougainvillea Retreat Rajawella ☏ 077 029 1896, ⓦ bv-retreat.com; map p.231. One of several upmarket

3

places to stay around the Victoria Golf Club, this boutique-retreat offers wonderful views over the surrounding hills and waters of the nearby Victoria Reservoir, and very peaceful and comfortable accommodation in nine rooms dotted around spacious gardens and a big pool. B&B $\overline{\$220}$

Cinnamon Citadel 2km west of Kandy ☎081 223 4365, ⓦcinnamonhotels.com; map p.231. Occupying an attractive perch above the Mahaweli Ganga, this low-rise four-star is one of the best looking (and often best value) of the big hotels around Kandy, with spacious and stylish rooms (all with minibar, safe, satellite TV and balcony) and a large pool. $\overline{\$120}$

Jungle Tide Metiyagolla, Uduwela (around 45min drive from Kandy) ☎077 981 0631, ⓦjungletide.com; map p.231. Modern guesthouse built in the style of a traditional plantation bungalow in a remote location up in the Hantana hills south of Kandy, with lovely gardens, a good-sized pool, spotless and very comfortable rooms, and stunning views towards the Knuckles Range. B&B $\overline{\$100}$

★ **The Kandy House** Gunnepana, 5km east of Kandy ☎081 492 1394, ⓦthekandyhouse.com; map p.231. Magical boutique guesthouse, set in a wonderfully atmospheric old traditional Kandyan *walauwa* (manor house). Rooms are sumptuously equipped with antique-style furniture, four-poster beds, Victorian bathtubs and colourful fabrics; outside, gorgeous landscaped gardens run down to a beautiful little infinity swimming pool. Minimum two-night stay. $\overline{\$290}$

★ **Kandy Samadhi Centre** Kukul Oya Rd, 23km east of the city ☎081 447 0925, ⓦthekandysamadhicentre.com; map p.231. Beautiful and serene retreat, a 40min drive east of the city in an unspoilt area of mountainous jungle. The emphasis is on simplicity and tranquillity, offering holistic balm to both body and soul, with organic, home-grown food and a range of Ayurveda and yoga packages available. Accommodation is in a variety of elegantly rustic rooms, pavilions, a quaint rock house and a pair of "mud houses" (much nicer than the name suggests) scattered around the idyllic grounds. B&B $\overline{\$110}$

Richmond House Heerassagala, 5km from Kandy ☎081 221 8495, ⓦtherichmondhousekandy.com; map p.231. Nestled amid the hills between Kandy and Peradeniya, this attractive guesthouse offers bright and well-equipped modern tiled rooms (all with bathtub, a/c, satellite TV and minibar) with a hint of slightly chintzy old-world charm, including colonial repro furniture, four-poster beds and a Hollywood staircase. B&B $\overline{\$65}$

Theva Residency Hantana Rd, 3km from Kandy ☎081 738 8296, ⓦtheva.lk; map p.231. Perched in a fine position high above town, this striking modern hotel sports stylish – if very minimalist – arctic-white rooms (more expensive deluxe rooms with fine views). There's also small pool (if it's warm enough to swim), and an attractive dining room. B&B $\overline{\$189}$

★ **Villa Rosa** Asigiriya, 2km west of Kandy ☎081 221 5556, ⓦvillarosa-kandy.com; map p.231. Gorgeous boutique hotel in a stunning location high above the Mahaweli Ganga, with spacious and stylish rooms (some from $235, with wonderful river views). The attractive, soothing orangey-pink decor complements the very serene atmosphere, while yoga and meditation teaching can also be arranged and massages and shirodhara are available in the rustic wellness centre, while guests get free use of the pool at the nearby *Cinnamon Citadel*. There's also free tuktuk transport to town, plus a VW Beetle for short joyrides. Minimum two-night stay. B&B $\overline{\$140}$

MEDITATION

Kandy is the best place in Sri Lanka to study **meditation**, with numerous centres dotted around the countryside nearby (though none right in the city itself). The Buddhist Publications Society (see page 230) has a list of all the various centres in the area.

Dhamma Kuta Vippassana Meditation Centre Hindagala, 7km from Peradeniya ☎081 238 5774, ⓦdhamma.org/en/schedules/schkuta or ✉info@kuta.dhamma.org. Caters to experienced meditators only, with intensive ten-day courses (no talking). Free, but donations welcome. Book well in advance.

International Buddhist Meditation Centre Hondiyadeniya, Wegirikanda, 10km from Kandy on the road to Nuwara Eliya ☎081 380 1871, ⓦrockhillsrilanka.com. Runs challenging courses in Vipassana meditation during which students are required to adopt the ascetic lifestyle of a Buddhist monk.

Nilambe Meditation Centre Near Galaha, around 22km from Kandy ⓦnilambe.net. This long-running centre is the place most popular among foreign visitors, set in a beautifully tranquil spot in the hills. Potential visitors are advised to contact the centre at least two weeks in advance. Courses last 6–11 days and cost Rs.1500/day, including basic vegetarian food and lodging. All levels are welcome, from novices to experienced meditators. To reach the centre, take the Deltota or Galaha bus from Kandy's Goods Shed bus station and ask the conductor to put you off at Nilambe Office Junction, from where it's a 45min walk (or catch a tuktuk). Bring a torch (there's no electricity), umbrella, alarm clock and warm clothing.

EATING

Kandy has a disappointingly limited number of good places to eat given its size, and don't necessarily expect to enjoy a glass of wine or a beer with your meal – none of the following serve alcohol except *The Pub*, *Sharon Inn* and *Slightly Chilled*.

Café Aroma Inn 98 Sir Benet de Soyza St (Colombo St) ☎ 081 222 9950; map p.208. Bright white modern bakery-cum-restaurant serving up cakes and good coffee alongside a wide and well-prepared selection of international food including light meals (pasta, stir-fries and so on) for around Rs.800, and more substantial meat mains (Rs.1400). Good breakfast selection too. Daily 9am–10pm.

Devon Restaurant 11 Dalada Vidiya ☎ 081 222 2537; map p.208. No-frills modern local restaurant constantly packed with locals thanks to its good selection of Sri Lankan staples, including hoppers, string hoppers, burianis, *lamprais* and devilled dishes (mains Rs.400–500), plus Western and Sri Lankan breakfasts. Portions are large, though the food can be hot. Daily 7.30am–8pm.

Empire Café 21 Temple St ☎ 081 563 8006, facebook.com/EmpireCafeKandy; map p.208. Colourful little café on the ground-floor of the *Olde Empire* hotel serving up a wide range of international dishes – rice and curry, salads, mac and cheese, and assorted burgers, plus good juices and smoothies. Food above-average and attractively presented, though portion sizes are a bit minimalist. Mains Rs.500–825. Daily 8.30am–9pm.

Jasmine Song 169 Kotugodelle Vidiya ☎ 081 223 2888, jasminesong.com; map p.208. Quiet Sri Lankan-style Chinese restaurant, serving up a big and reasonably well-prepared menu of Cantonese meat, fish and veg classics (mains Rs.600–950). Daily 11.30am–10.30pm.

Kandyan Muslim Hotel Dalada Vidiya ☎ 081 222 4129; map p.208. This classic slice of Kandyan café culture is somewhere you either love or hate – famous for its old-school hygiene standards (or, rather, lack of) and service which ranges from brilliant to disastrous. Served in a rather gloomy upstairs dining room, food features a big range of meat-heavy Muslim-style Sri Lankan cuisine including rice and curry, burianis and *kottu*. Prices aren't exactly dirt cheap (that's mainly on the floor), but reasonable for what you get. Daily 6am–9pm.

Mihiri Foods Colombo St; map p.208. Great selection of reviving juices (a bargain Rs.80) including pineapple, papaya, lime, wood apple, soursop and passion fruit, plus lipsmackin' faluda and shakes (Rs.100). Daily 8.30am–8pm.

Natural Coffee 5 Temple St ☎ 081 220 5734, ⓦ naturalcoffee.lk; map p.208. Cosy little café with seating upstairs and down serving up good pure Arabica coffee from Kotmale, plus a bizarrely eclectic selection of snacks and sweet items (around Rs.400). Daily 7.30am–7pm.

The Pub 36 Dalada Vidiya (above the Bake House; the entrance is easily missed) ☎ 081 223 4341; map p.208. Touristy place serving up an eclectic selection of reasonably prepared if slightly pricey continental standards including pastas, fish, pork chops and steak (though hardly any vegetarian options). Also a good spot for a drink (see page 227). Most mains Rs.1200–1500. Daily 11am–11pm.

★ **Sharon Inn** 59 Saranankara Rd ☎ 081 222 2416; map p.208. The best rice and curry in town (Rs.1300) – indeed one of the best in the island – served buffet-style daily at 7.30pm and comprising a sumptuous spread of fifteen or so dishes usually featuring a gourmet array of unusual Sri Lankan vegetables, plus chicken. Non-guests should reserve in advance by 4pm latest.

Slightly Chilled Lounge (Bamboo Garden) 29A Anagarika Dharmapala Mw ☎ 081 223 8267, ⓦ slightly-chilled.com; map p.208. Kandy's coolest nightspot (see page 228), *Slightly Chilled* is best for a drink but also does a passable range of Sri Lankan-style Chinese food, covering all the usual meat, veg and seafood Cantonese bases, plus assorted salads, sandwiches and pasta and chicken dishes. Most mains around Rs.1000. Daily 11am–9.30pm (last orders); bar shuts 2–5pm.

Sri Balaji Dosa 9 DS Senanayake Vidiya ☎ 222 4593; map p.208. A good, inexpensive place for lunch during a tour of the centre, serving up a tasty range of pure-veg South Indian grub including good thalis (Rs.170) and a virtuoso range of dosas (around Rs.200). Daily 7.30am–9.30pm.

Sri Ram 87 Bennet Soysa Vidiya (Colombo St) ☎ 081 567 7287; map p.208. A more upmarket alternative to *Sri Balaji*, but serving up a similar range of South Indian standards including cheap lunchtime thalis and burianis (Rs.300–650) as well as a few North Indian offerings plus more unusual Chettinad (Tamil Nadu-style) veg and meat curries (around Rs.500). No alcohol. Daily 9.30am–9.30pm.

DRINKING

The Pub 36 Dalada Vidiya ☎ 081 223 4341; map p.208. The outdoor terrace overlooking Dalada Vidiya at this touristy restaurant (see page 227) is one of the nicest spots in town for a drink, and is backed up with a decent drinks list, including refreshingly cheap beer. Daily 11am–2pm & 5–11pm.

Queen's Hotel Bar Queen's Hotel, Dalada Vidiya; map p.208. Atmospheric, colonial-style drinking hole under a huge veranda at the back of the stately *Queen's Hotel*, with an old wooden bar, armchair seating and long rows of fans whirling gently overhead. Daily 9am–11pm.

3

3

Slightly Chilled Lounge (Bamboo Garden) 29A Anagarika Dharmapala Mw ☎ 081 223 8267; map p.208. Kicking bar-restaurant (see page 227) set high above the lake, with an above-average drinks list accompanied by a smooth soundtrack. Daily 11am–2pm & 5pm–midnight.

Victory Hotel 79 Colombo St ☎ 081 222 2526; ma p.208. This smart (if rather smokey) upstairs bar attrac a noisy mix of tourists and locals, with cheap beer and passable range of simple food to go with it – althoug service can sometimes be a bit Basil Fawlty-esque. Dail 8am–10pm.

ENTERTAINMENT

Five places in town put on nightly shows of Kandyan **dancing and drumming** (all starting at 5pm, lasting around 1hr and costing Rs.1000). All are touristy but fun, with a fairly standard range of dances, generally including snippets of both southern as well as Kandyan dances and usually culminating in a spot of fire walking. Touts will try very hard to sell you tickets in advance, although there are pretty much always seats available on the door for all the shows if you simply show up ten minutes before curtain up. **Kandyan Arts Association** Sangaraja Mw, southeast of the Temple of the Tooth. The long-running show here is the biggest, ritziest and most touristy of the dance shows, with flashy but fun performances drawing coach parties galore.

Kandy Buddhist Centre East of the temple. Energeti performances in a mid-sized venue just behind the Templ of the Tooth.

Lake Club Sangamitta Mw. The second smallest c the five venues, although lacking either the appealin intimacy of the YMBA or the pizzazz of the larger shows.

Red Cross Hall Next door to the Kandyan Art Association. Almost next door to the crowd-pullin Kandyan Arts Association, and also with a fair bit c razzamatazz.

YMBA Rajapihilla Mw. The most intimate of the fiv shows, held in a much smaller auditorium and allowin you to get much closer to the performers.

SHOPPING

Kandy is one of Sri Lanka's main artisanal centres: many local villages still specialize in particular **crafts** (metalware, lacquerware, leatherwork and so on) and the city is perhaps the best place in the island to pick up traditional souvenirs. One place worth a look is the ramshackle **Kandy Central Market** (just south of the clocktower) whose upper floor is stuffed with souvenir and craft shops selling bags, batiks, cheap clothes, wallhangings, woodcarvings and so on, while shops below sell spices, plus fruit and veg. In complete contrast, the glitzy **Kandy City Centre** on Dalada Vidiya is the city's prime upscale retail destination. Most of the shops are pretty run of the mill, although there are branches of local chains including Odel, the Cotton Collection and the Vijitha Yapa bookshop, plus a large foot court up top. There's a handy (but often hectic) Cargills **supermarket** on Dalada Vidiya, and a slightly more peaceful Keells supermarket in the basement of Kandy City Centre (both open daily 8.30am–9pm); both have good selections of local tea and spices.

ARTS, CRAFTS AND TEXTILES

Earthbound Creations Yatinuwara Vidiya ☎ 081 222 7122, ⊛ ebcsl.com; map p.208. Brilliant selection of colourful crafts made from recycled newspapers and magazines, including pencils, placemats, bowls and ingenious beaded jewellery, as well as a range of other quality contemporary crafts, clothes and collectibles. Daily 9am–9pm.

Jayamali Batiks 1st Floor, 196 Central Market ☎ 077 783 3938, ⊛ jayamalibatiks.com; map p.208. Quality

batiks in a range of original designs by Upali Jayakod Pieces range from traditional Kandyan-style batiks throug to striking contemporary creations, including signatu angelfish and tea-picker designs. Upali has been th subject of numerous commission rackets by unscrupulou rickshaw drivers and other types, so greatly appreciate visitors who arrive independently, or only with a truste guide. Daily 10am–6.30pm.

Kandyan Arts and Crafts Association (Kandya Cultural Centre) Sangaraja Mw ☎ 081 222 310 ⊛ facebook.com/KandyanArtAssociation; map p.20 In a 300-year-old building which once housed the ol British Military Hospital, this government-supported pla showcases the full range of Kandyan crafts – metalwor lacquerware, drums and so on – all relatively inexpensiv and of a decent quality. Local artisans can often be see at work around the veranda, working looms, brushes ar needles. Daily 9am–5pm.

Luv SL Dalada Vidiya, next to Pub Royale; map p.20 Kandy branch of this ever-expanding chain (an offshoot the Odel store in Colombo), selling chic clothes plus assorte souvenirs, ranging from teas and Ayurvedic produc through to funky painted elephants and other assorte bric-a-brac. There's a branch of Odel proper (selling cloth only) in Kandy City Centre. Daily 10am–9pm.

Selyn 7 Temple St ☎ 081223 7735, ⊛ selyn.lk; ma p.208. Made in their factory in Kurunegala, Selyn's han woven fair-trade cottons are some of the finest textil the island has to offer, patterned with vivid slabs of colo and transformed into a wide range of clothes (includin

KANDYAN DANCING AND DRUMMING

Kandyan dancing and drumming is Sri Lanka's iconic performing art, and you're unlikely to spend long in the city without seeing a troupe of performers going about their (rather noisy) business, clad in elaborate traditional costumes, with dancers twirling, stamping and gyrating to a pulsating accompaniment of massed drumming. The art form originated as part of an all-night ceremony in honour of the god Kohomba, an elaborate ritual featuring some fifty dancers and ten drummers. This ceremony flourished under the patronage of the kings of Kandy and reached such heights of sophistication that it was eventually adopted into local religious ceremonies, becoming a key element in the great Esala Perahera festival. Many temples in the Kandyan area even have a special columned pavilion, or **digge**, designed specifically for performances and rehearsals by resident dancers and drummers.

KANDYAN DANCING

There are five main **types of Kandyan dance**. The four principal genres are the *ves*, *pantheru*, *udekki* and *naiyandi*, all featuring troupes of flamboyantly attired male dancers clad in sumptuous chest plates, waistbands and various other neck, arm and leg ornaments which jangle as the dancers move about. The most famous is the **ves** dance, which is considered sacred to the god Kohomba. It's at once highly mannered and hugely athletic, combining carefully stylized hand and head gestures with acrobatic manoeuvres including spectacular backflips, huge high-kicking leaps and dervish-like whirling pirouettes. In the more sedate **pantheru** dance, the turbaned performers play small tambourines, while during the **udekki** dance they beat tiny hourglass-shaped drums.

The fifth and final style of Kandyan classical dance is the **vannam**. This began life as songs, before evolving into stylized dances, each of which describes a certain emotion or object from nature, history or legend – the most popular are the various animal-derived *vannams*, including those inspired by the movements of the peacock (*mayura*), elephant (*gajaga*), lion (*sinharaja*) and cobra (*naga*). *Vannams* are usually performed by just one or two dancers (and sometimes by women), unlike other Kandyan dances, which are ensemble dances featuring four or five performers, always men.

As well as the traditional Kandyan dances, the city's cultural shows usually include examples of a few characteristic **southern dances** such as the *kulu* (harvest dance) and the ever-popular *raban* dance (see page 127).

KANDYAN DRUMMING

All genres of dance are accompanied by **drumming**, which can reach extraordinary heights of virtuosity – even if the finer points pass you by, the headlong onslaught of a Kandyan drum ensemble in full flight leaves few people unmoved. The archetypal Sri Lankan drum is the *geta bera* (literally "boss drum"), a double-headed instrument carried on a strap around the drummer's waist and played with the hands. *Geta bera* are made to a fixed length of 67cm, with different types of skins (monkey and cow, for example) at either end of the drum to produce contrasting sounds. The double-headed *daule* drum is shorter but thicker, and is played with a stick in one hand and the palm of the other. The *tammettana bera* is a pair of tiny drums (a bit like bongos) which are tied together and played with a pair of sticks. A *horanava* (a kind of Sri Lankan oboe) is sometimes added to the ensemble, providing a simple melodic accompaniment.

Like the dancers they accompany, Kandyan drummers perform in **traditional costume**, dressed in a large sarong, a huge red cummerbund and a white tasselled turban – significant musical points are marked by a toss of the head, sending the tassel flying through the air in a delicate accompanying flourish.

---

arves, shawls, blouses, aprons and lunghis) as well as bleware, pencil cases, cuddly toys and other trinkets. hey also sell a good selection of upcycled jewellery and her fun bric-a-brac. Daily 9.30am–6pm.

ajanima Crafts 173 Rajapahilla Mw ☏ 081 495 0347, rajanima.com; map p.208. Good-quality selection of local crafts including *kolam* masks (painted in either chemical or – more expensive – natural dyes), Buddha and elephant carvings in sandalwood, teak and mahogany, drums, chess sets and carrom boards and so on (bargaining possible). You can also watch craftsmen at work in the adjacent factory. Daily 8am–5.30pm.

BOOKSHOPS

Buddhist Publications Society Sangaraja Mw; map p.208. Enormous selection of Buddhist titles, plus a few books on Sri Lankan history. Mon–Sat 9am–4.30pm.

Vijitha Yapa Bookshop Level 2, Kandy City Centre; map p.208. Reasonable selection of English-language and Sri Lankan titles from the island's leading booksto■ chain. Daily 9am–6pm.

TEA

Mlesna Dalada Vidiya; map p.208. Posh tea sho■ selling a good range of gift tea sets, fancy teapots an■ other upmarket tea-making kit. Daily 8.15am–6pm.

DIRECTORY

Ayurveda A number of hotels in and around Kandy have Ayurveda centres or spas: those at the *Amaya Hills* and *Earl's Regency* are both good.

Banks There are heaps of banks in the city centre (see map, page 208), the majority on Dalada Vidiya, most with ATMs that accept foreign cards, plus a couple of authorized moneychangers in the basement of Kandy City Centre.

Cricket Kandy is one of the island's three Test-match venues (along with Colombo and Galle). Matches are now held at the custom-built Pallekele International Cricket Stadium, 15km outside the city. Aficionados might also enjoy a visit to the city's former Test-match arena, the Asigiriya Stadium, shoe-horned into the hills just west of the centre and often described as the most beautiful cricket ground in the world.

Golf The magnificent eighteen-hole, par-73 course at the Victoria Golf Club (☎ 071 737 6376, ⓦ golfsrilanka.com) is around 20km east of Kandy at Rajawella, tucked in scenic spot between the Knuckles Range and the Victori■ Reservoir. Green fees are Rs.9000/round.

Hospital Lakeside Adventist Hospital, 40 Sangaraja M■ (☎ 081 222 3466), on the lakeshore 100m beyond the *Hot Suisse*; there's also a dental clinic here.

Internet The Prince of Wales internet café, next to th■ *Queen's Hotel* (daily 8am–9pm; Rs.120/hr) is reliable an■ well equipped.

Pharmacy There's a well-stocked pharmacy at the back ■ Keells supermarket in the basement of Kandy City Cent■ (Mon–Sat 8.30am–8pm, Sun 8.30am–7.30pm).

Post office The main post office is opposite the tra■ station (Mon–Sat 7am–8pm). There's also a handy po■ office counter in the basement of Kandy City Centre.

Swimming Non-guests can use the pools at the *Queen■ Hotel* (Rs.250) and *Hotel Suisse* (Rs.500 for 2hr).

Around Kandy

The countryside around Kandy is full of attractions, featuring an interesting blend of the cultural and the natural – elephants, historic temples, hill walking and more. Top of most visitors' lists is the famous **Pinnewala Elephant Orphanage** (see page 204), usually followed by the idyllic **Peradeniya Botanical Gardens**. There's also a fascinating collection of Kandyan-era **temples** scattered around the countryside, while the dramatic **Knuckles Range** boasts some of the island's finest wilderness trekking.

Commonwealth War Cemetery

Lady Magdalene Drive • Daily 7am–4pm • Free • ⓦ cwgc.org

West of Kandy, the moving **Commonwealth War Cemetery** is set amid beautiful gardens tucked into a peaceful little hollow in the hills next to the Mahaweli Ganga. The cemetery is home to around 200 immaculately maintained graves of servicemen who died in Sri Lanka during World War II, including army, navy and air-force personnel from across the British Empire – Britain, Canada, India, East Africa, plus 26 Sri Lankans from the Ceylon Light Infantry, Ceylon Pioneers, Ceylon Engineers and other regiments.

Peradeniya Botanical Gardens

6km southwest of Kandy • Daily 7.30am–6pm • Rs.1500 • A tuktuk to the gardens costs around Rs.400 one way from Kandy; alternatively take bus #644 (every 10–15min) from the Clocktower Bus Stand

Enclosed within a meandering loop of the Mahaweli Ganga, the **Peradeniya Botanical Gardens** are among the largest and finest in Asia, covering almost 150 acres and stuffed

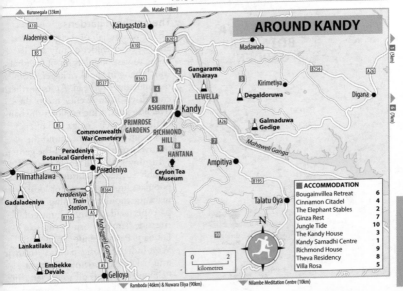

with a bewildering variety of local and foreign tree and plants (many of them labelled). The history of the site dates right back to the fourteenth century, when Wickramabahu III established a royal residence here. The park itself was created during the eighteenth century by King Kirti Sri Rajasinha to serve as a pleasure garden for the Kandyan nobility. It was transformed into a botanical garden by the British in 1821 during the enterprising governorship of Edward Barnes, who had Sri Lanka's first tea trees planted here in 1824, though their full commercial potential wasn't to be realized for another half-century.

Royal Palm Avenue and the Great Lawn

Running from the entrance, the principal thoroughfare, stately **Royal Palm Avenue**, bisects the gardens, heading in an arrow-straight line north to the Mahaweli Ganga. At the southern end of the avenue, the **Great Lawn** is home to Peradeniya's most majestic sight: a huge Javan fig whose sprawling roots and branches create a remarkable natural pavilion. (There's also an overpriced **restaurant** near here, and cheaper drinks in a kiosk next door.)

Running along the southern side of the Great Lawn, **Double Coconut Palm Avenue** is flanked with a cluster of stumpy coco de mer trees, native to the Seychelles, whose massively swollen coconuts – the heaviest ever recorded weighed 42kg – hold the record for the world's largest wild fruit. There are also a few stunning kauri pines here from Queensland (they're actually broadleaved trees, not pines), while a long line of strangely twisted Cook's pines, looking rather like oversized pipe-cleaners, flank the east side of the lawn.

The Great Circle and memorial trees

North of here is the Great Circle, its eastern side dotted with a sequence of **memorial trees** planted at various times by assorted international bigwigs. The first was planted by the Prince of Wales in 1875 (his successor came back and planted another one in 1922), with subsequent contributions from the Tsar of Russia (1891 – the tree has lasted rather longer than the tsar), Queen Elizabeth (1954 – a sickly looking *ficus krishnae*), Joseph Tito (1959) and Yuri Gagarin (1961), along with various post-independence Sri Lankan and other Asian leaders.

3

The northern gardens

The northern half of the gardens has an altogether wilder quality and is home to vast populations of **fruit bats**, which hang in spooky clusters from the branches overhead. At its northern end, Royal Palm Avenue meets the **riverside walk**, which follows the bank of the Mahaweli Ganga and offers a pleasant circuit right round the relatively peaceful edges of the garden.

Turning left you'll reach a cute, wobbly **suspension bridge** – a popular climbing frame for local macaque monkeys. Turning right, past spectacularly large clumps of riverside bamboo, brings you to **Cabbage Palm Avenue**, lined with West Indian cabbage palms with their unusual greenish trunks. **Palmyra Palm Avenue** leads off to the left, lined with very tall and slender palmyra palms with their distinctively spiky tops, a familiar sight to anyone who has visited the Jaffna Peninsula, where they are the dominant palm species, though they're much less common elsewhere in the island.

South of here is a marvellous group of **Java almonds** (follow the path towards Canarium Row and the Orchid House), whose huge buttressed roots line the side of the path. Returning to Cabbage Palm Avenue and continuing south brings you to **Cannon Ball Avenue**, lined with beautiful cannon ball trees, wreathed in creepers from which hang the characteristically large, round fruits, after which the artillery-loving British named the tree. The Sinhalese (who call them *sal* trees) hold their beautiful flowers sacred, since they appear to comprise a tiny dagoba, shaded by a cobra's hood and surrounded by tiny florettes, which are thought to represent a crowd of worshippers. Beyond here, the avenue curves around away from the river, before returning you to the entrance.

The southern gardens

South of the Great Lawn lies a small but picturesque Sri Lanka-shaped **lake**, covered in water lilies and overlooked by a classical rotunda and an enormous clump of giant bamboo. Continuing south brings you to a small area of carefully laid out medicinal and aquatic plants, plus various types of grass. Next to these is a line of far more striking **talipot palms**, identifiable by the unusual crisscross bark pattern at the foot of the trunk (the remains of old leaves) and by their huge leaves – the trees as a whole look rather like enormous toilet brushes. Beyond here, at the southernmost edge of the gardens, is the pretty little **Students' Garden**, featuring over 350 plant species neatly laid out and labelled, surrounded by weird cycads and ferns.

The three-temples loop

The countryside around Kandy is dotted with dozens of historic Kandyan-era **temples**, most of them still largely unvisited by foreign visitors. The most interesting are the **Embekke Devale**, **Lankatilake** and **Gadaladeniya**, which lie some 10km west of Kandy and make for a rewarding half-day walk (see page 234) popularly known as the **three-temples loop**; they can be visited rather more quickly but less memorably by car or tuktuk. All three temples were constructed during the fourteenth century, in the early days of the nascent Kandyan kingdom, when the region was ruled from Gampola and Tamil influence was strong. There's a further trio of temples to the east of Kandy (see page 234).

Embekke Devale

Daily 8am–6pm • Rs.300 • Buses to Embekke depart from the Clocktower bus station (every 30min; 1hr)

Dating from the fourteenth century, the rustic little Embekke Devale, dedicated to Kataragama, is famous principally for the fine **digge** (drummer's pavilion) fronting the main shrine. The *digge*'s intricately decorated wooden pillars were apparently brought here from another temple at Gampola; each bears a different design, with an entertaining jumble of peacocks, entwined swans, wrestlers, dragons, dancers, horsemen, soldiers and bodhisattvas (shown as composite figures: half man, half bird). One of the most famous panels depicts an elephant and lion fighting; another shows what looks curiously like a Habsburg double-headed eagle.

Two quaint lions flank the entrance to the **main shrine** behind, topped by a delicate tower. To the left of the main building stands a rustic **granary** (signed "Ancient Paddy Barn") raised on stones above the ground to protect its contents from wild animals.

Lankatilake

Daily 8am–6pm • Rs.300 • Buses to Lankatilake depart from the Goods Shed bus station (every 30min; 1hr)

Built on a huge rock outcrop, the imposing **Lankatilake** is perhaps the finest temple in the district. Founded in 1344, its architecture is reminiscent of the solid, gedige-style stone temples of Polonnaruwa rather than the later and more decorative Kandyan-style wooden temples. The building was formerly four storeys tall, though the uppermost storeys collapsed in the nineteenth century and were replaced by the present, badly fitting wooden roof. The gloomy central **shrine**, with eighteenth-century Kandyan paintings, is magically atmospheric: narrow but tall, and filled with a great seated Buddha under a huge *makara torana*, with tiers of gods rising above. The massive exterior walls contain a sequence of small shrines containing statues of Saman, Kataragama, Vishnu and Vibhishana (often kept locked, sadly), punctuated by majestic low-relief carvings of elephants. To the left of the temple, carved onto the ground, is a gigantic rock inscription, one of the largest in Sri Lanka, which records the details of the temple's construction.

Gadaladeniya

Daily 8am–6pm • Rs.300 • To reach Gadaladeniya by bus, take any of the numerous non-express buses heading west along the road to Kegalle and Colombo and ask to be set down at the Gadaladeniya turn-off in Pilimathalawa

Gadaladeniya dates from the same year – 1344 – as Lankatilake. The principal **shrine** is built on a rock outcrop at the top end of the site, and the style of the corbelled roof and carvings of dancers and drummers have a pronounced South Indian flavour, having been designed by a Tamil architect, a certain Ganesvarachari. The interior houses a fine gold Buddha (with oddly close-set eyes) under a marvellous *makara torana*. The whimsical subsidiary shrine, in the middle of the compound, consists of a cruciform building, each wing housing a tiny Buddha shrine and topped by a minuscule dagoba, with the entire structure being surmounted by a larger dagoba – one of the island's most unusual religious buildings.

3

3

WALKING THE THREE-TEMPLES LOOP

Embekke, Lankatilake and Gadaladeniya temples can all be visited (albeit with some difficulty) by bus or, far more conveniently, by taxi (count on around Rs.3000 for the round trip, or Rs.2000 by tuktuk). The best way to visit, however, is to **walk** at least part of the way between the three, starting at the Embekke Devale and finishing at the Gadaladeniya (or vice versa).

To reach the **Embekke Devale** and the start of the walk, take bus #643 from the Goods Shed bus station (every 30min; 1hr) – the bus tends to leave from the left-hand side of the station in front of the row of shops rather than from one of the actual bus stands. All being well you'll be dropped off on the main road through **Embekke village**, from where a black sign points down a side road to the Embekke Devale. Walk down this road for 800m then turn right and you'll see the Embekke Devale directly in front of you.

Continue along the road past the Embekke Devale and go left at the T-junction. The road begins climbing steeply for around 1km until you reach the edge of the village, marked by a gorgeous bo tree and paddy fields. Go straight on for a further 500m until the road forks. Keep right and continue over the brow of a hill and down the other side. You'll now catch your first glimpse of the **Lankatilake**, almost obscured by trees on the steep little hillock ahead on your left. Turn left down the short road next to a line of small pylons to reach the base of the hill, from where a magnificent flight of ancient rock-cut steps (alongside a less treacherous set of modern stone steps) leads precipitously up to the temple itself.

From the Lankatilake temple, return to the road by the pylons and go left, walking uphill (again) to reach a larger road and a few shops. Turn left again and follow this road for about 1km to reach the village of **Pamunuwa** and then continue another 2km to reach the **Gadaladeniya temple** (next to the road on the left). This part of the walk is less special – the road is bigger, there's more traffic and you might prefer to just jump into a tuktuk (if you can find one) to reach Gadaladeniya. The area is also a major metalworking centre, and you'll pass dozens of shops selling traditional oil lamps, looking a bit like overblown cake stands.

Beyond Gadaladeniya, carry on along the road for a further ten to fifteen minutes past numerous metalworking shops to reach the busy town of **Pilimathalawa** on the main Colombo–Kandy highway. Turn right along the highway and walk through town for about 200m and you'll find a bus stop in front of Cargills and the Commercial Bank. Buses back to Kandy pass every minute or so – just flag one down.

Temples east of Kandy

Just east of the city there's another rewarding trio of temples dating from the Buddhist renaissance experienced under Kirti Sri Rajasinha (see page 212), who built all three.

Gangarama Viharaya

Daily 8am–6pm • Donation

About 2km east of Kandy (head east along the Mahiyangana road, then turn north towards Madawela) on the banks of the Mahaweli Ganga, lies the **Gangarama Viharaya**. This small monastery is notable mainly for its fine two-storey **image house**, decorated with Kandyan-era paintings and home to an 8m-tall standing Buddha statue, carved out of the natural rock outcrop around which the shrine is built. (You can see the rock outcrop poking out of the back of the image house, carved with an extensive rock inscription in Sinhala recording details of the temple's construction.) The walls inside are decorated with hundreds of tessellated sitting Buddhas, while the lower sections of the wall show Jataka stories and scenes from the Buddha's life, delicately painted in characteristic Kandyan style in narrow panels using a predominantly red palette. A small **digge** stands opposite the entrance to the image house.

Degaldoruwa

Daily 8am–6pm • Donation

The most interesting of this group of temples, **Degaldoruwa** is built in and around a large rock outcrop about 2km northeast of the Gangarama Viharaya. The temple consists of three small connected chambers: the first two – the *digge* and antechamber – are built outside the rock and topped by crumbling old wooden roofs, while the third, the main shrine, is hollowed out of the rock itself, and invisible from the outside. The **digge** has a few old wooden pillars and a couple of drums hanging from the rafters; it's unusual in being directly attached to the rest of the temple, rather than occupying a separate pavilion, as is usually the case. Old wooden doors lead into the **antechamber**, which preserves a fine moonstone and a sequence of murals showing scenes from the Jataka stories, painted in five vivid red panels.

From here, doors (whose metal fittings were formerly studded with jewels) lead into the **main shrine**. The main image inside is a large reclining Buddha, his head resting on a pillow inlaid with a glass copy of a huge amethyst – according to tradition, the painters who decorated the shrine worked by the light generated by this enormous jewel. The murals here are some of Sri Lanka's finest, though they're rather dark and difficult to make out, having formerly been covered in a thick layer of soot from fires lit inside the shrine – a tiny square of black wall has been left just next to one of the doors to show what the walls looked like before restoration. The wall opposite the reclining Buddha is painted with Jataka scenes and pictures of dagobas at Sri Lanka's principal pilgrimage sites, but the finest painting is on the ceiling, a magnificent depiction of the **Buddha's battle with Mara**, dating from the 1770s and rivalling the far better-known example at Dambulla.

Outside stands a belfry, apparently built in imitation of a Christian church tower. Steps to the left of the temple lead up to a large platform, where a stupa and bo tree stand facing one another above the temple.

Galmaduwa Gedige

The extremely unusual **Galmaduwa Gedige** is the main attraction at the village of Kalapura (signposted north off the Mahiyangana road about 5km east of the turn-off to the Gangarama and Degaldoruwa temples). The bizarre shrine here is enclosed in a cloister-like stone structure (the gedige) and topped by a stone pyramid – an odd but endearing Kandyan version of a traditional South Indian temple. Apparently, the gedige was left unfinished, and its exact purpose remains unclear (the image house at the back was only added during a restoration in 1967). Old ola-leaf manuscripts suggest that the innermost section was originally built as a jail to contain a single prisoner of noble birth who had offended the king, and that the surrounding ambulatory was added later.

Ceylon Tea Museum

Tues–Sat 8.30am–4pm, Sun 8.30am–3pm • Rs.800 • ⊕ ceylonteamuseum.com

South of Kandy, the small Hantana Road climbs steeply up into the hills through run-down tea estates, with sweeping views back to the city. Four kilometres along the road is the mildly interesting **Ceylon Tea Museum**, housed in an attractively converted tea factory. The ground and first floors hold various imposing pieces of colonial-era machinery collected from defunct factories around the hill country, including assorted rollers, sifters, drying furnaces, withering trays and even a tractor, plus a cute little working model of a tea factory. The second floor has displays on two of Sri Lankan tea's great pioneers, with a small collection of the frugal personal effects (pipe, plate and walking stick) of James Taylor, who established the island's first commercial tea estate, and a display on the much more flamboyant career of Thomas Lipton (see box, p.442), who did so much to publicize Sri Lankan tea. There are also exhibits of other tea-related colonial-era bits and pieces, including Sri Lanka's oldest packet of tea, dating from 1944 and "Guaranteed by the Ceylon Tea Propaganda Board". The top two floors host a small café plus tea shop.

East of Kandy

The hill country **east of Kandy** remains far less developed than the area to the west of the city – a refreshingly untamed area of rugged uplands which still preserves much of its forest cover. Two main highways run east from Kandy to Mahiyangana on either side of the sprawling **Victoria Reservoir and Dam**, opened in 1989 as part of the huge Mahaweli Ganga Project and one of the island's major sources of electricity. A **visitor centre**, just off the highway, offers fine views of the spectacular dam itself. Much of the densely forested area around the reservoir is protected as part of the Victoria-Randenigala Sanctuary (no entrance), and you might even spot the occasional elephant sticking its trunk out of the forest while you're travelling down the road.

Hanguranketa

Around 8km south of the southern road around Victoria Reservoir, and roughly 40km from Kandy, the sleepy little town of **HANGURANKETA** formerly served as a refuge for the kings of Kandy, who built a large palace here to which they would retreat during times of internal rebellion or external threat. The original palace was destroyed by the British in 1818 (or 1803, according to some sources) and its remains used to construct the **Potgul Maliga Vihara** ("Temple Library"), now home to an important collection of ola-leaf manuscripts, protected in their sumptuous original copper and silver covers. The temple as a whole is a good example of the high Kandyan style, with a fine central image house surrounded by smaller shrines and an unusual, mural-covered dagoba.

The Knuckles Range

The second of the two main roads east from Kandy, the rougher but dramatic **A26** twists and turns through the hills, skirting the northern edge of the Victoria Reservoir and running around the southern outliers of the **Knuckles Range**, the hill country's last great wilderness, though its tourist potential is only slowly beginning to be tapped. The rugged peaks of the Knuckles (Dumbara Hills) – named by the British for their resemblance to the knuckles of a clenched fist – cover a rugged and still largely untouched area of great natural beauty and biodiversity. The steeply shelving mountain terrain reaches 1863m at the summit of the main Knuckles peak itself (the sixth highest in Sri Lanka) and includes stands of rare dwarf cloudforest. The area is home to leopard, various species of deer (sambar, barking and mouse), monkeys (purple-faced langur and macaque), giant squirrels, rare species of lizard such as the horned black-lipped lizard, and an exceptionally fine collection of endemic bird species.

Exploring the Knuckles

An entrance fee of Rs.675 per person per day is charged to enter the conservation area

The most straightforward approach to the Knuckles is from the main Kandy to Mahiyangana Road. Some 27km east of Kandy, at **Hunasgiriya**, turning on the left takes you up into the range on hairpin bends via the village of Looloowatte (1065m) to reach **Corbet's Gap**, from where there are magnificent views of the main Knuckles directly ahead. The central parts of the range – described as a "super biodiversity hotspot" – are protected as a conservation forest and in 2010 were added to the list of World Heritage Sites along with Horton Plains National Park (the eighth place in Sri Lanka to achieve World Heritage status). There are all sorts of intriguing **trekking** possibilities in the Knuckles, although you'll really need to go with a guide (see page 224) if you plan on doing any extended walks.

ACCOMMODATION   THE KNUCKLES RANGE

Amaya Hunas Falls Elkaduwa, 27km north of Kandy ☎ 081 494 0320, ⓦ amayaresorts.com. One of the most spectacularly located hotels in Sri Lanka, perched way up in the hills on the western edge of the Knuckles Ranges, a bumpy 1hr drive from Kandy. It's all surprisingly luxurious, despite the remote setting, with good food and plush rooms, while facilities include an Ayurveda centre and small golf course. B&B **$220**

Green View Elkaduwa ☎ 077 781 1880, ⓔ bluehavtravels@gmail.com. Shangri-La guesthouse set in a very peaceful spot way up in the hills some 22km

from Kandy (a 45min drive; a pick-up can be arranged for $12). The thirteen rooms are simple but comfy enough, with superb views through big picture windows out over the mountains, and there's also a pool. B&B **$23**

Rangala House Teldeniya, 25km west of Kandy ☎ 081 240 0294, ⓦ rangalahouse.com. Cosy modern boutique guesthouse – more like staying in a friend's country house than in paying accommodation. The location up in the Knuckles Range, a 50min drive from Kandy, is beautiful, and it's also very convenient for the nearby Victoria Golf Club. **$178**

East to Mahiyangana

East of Hunasgiriya, the A26 gives increasingly fine views of the Knuckles Range to the north, with sheer rock faces towering above the road and further craggy peaks rising beyond – Sri Lanka at its most alpine. Another thirty minutes' drive brings you to the dramatic escarpment at the eastern edge of the hill country, from where there are marvellous views of the dry-zone plains almost a kilometre below. The highway descends through a precipitous sequence of seventeen numbered hairpins – this stretch of the A26 is popularly known as Sri Lanka's most dangerous road, and although it's fairly small beer compared to Himalayan or Andean highways, the local bus drivers do their best to keep the adrenaline flowing. At the bottom of the hills, the village of **Hasalaka** is the starting point for a 45km road north to the little-visited Wasgomuwa National Park.

Mahiyangana

Lying spread out across the plains at the foot of the dramatic Knuckles Range, the small town of **MAHIYANGANA** (pronounced "my-*yan*-gana") is famous in Buddhist legend as the first of the three places in Sri Lanka which the Buddha himself is said to have visited (the others are Kelaniya and Nainativu). The large **Rajamaha Dagoba**, a kilometre or so south of town, is held to mark the exact spot at which the Buddha preached, and is also believed to enshrine a lock of his hair. The dagoba's origins are lost in antiquity; it's said to have been rebuilt by King Dutugemunu, and has been restored many times since. The present bell-shaped structure, picturesquely set against a backdrop of hill-country escarpment, sits atop a large platform studded with elephant heads and approached by an impressively long walkway. The town's other eye-catching building is the striking replica of the famous **Mahabodhi Stupa** at Bodhgaya in India, erected at the behest of the late President Premadasa, which sits next to the main road on the west side of town.

ARRIVAL AND DEPARTURE   MAHIYANGANA

By bus Mahiyangana is something of a crossroads town between Polonnaruwa, Kandy, Badulla, Monaragala and Ampara, with reasonably frequent bus connections to all

these places. The town itself is rather spread out, sprawling west from the Mahaweli Ganga.

ACCOMMODATION

The Nest Padiyathalawa Rd, 2km east of town ☎ 077 519 9511, ⓦ nest-srilanka.com. Welcoming little place with five comfortable, modern rooms (all with optional a/c for Rs.750) and good Sri Lankan food. The owner can organize trips to local Veddha villages and other local excursions. **Rs.3000**

Sorabora Gedara Hotel Sorabora Wewa Rd ☎ 055 225 8307, ⓦ soraboragedara.com. Neat, modern hotel in spacious grounds with comfy a/c doubles, a swimming pool, plus bar and restaurant. **Rs.5450**

Kotabakina

The country east of Mahiyangana is one of the last strongholds of Sri Lanka's ever-diminishing number of **Veddhas** (see page 239), who live in the area around the village of **Dambana**, some 25km further along the A26. From Dambana, a rough track leads north a couple of kilometres to the principal Veddha village of **KOTABAKINA** ("King's Village", also often referred to as Dambana, although properly speaking this name refers to the Sinhalese village on the main highway). The village itself is a beautifully sylvan spot, with picturesque little bamboo-framed, mud-walled huts hemmed in by lush paddy fields. Men will be welcomed to the village with the traditional double-handed handshake (Veddha propriety means that female visitors are not handled, out of respect), after which you can have a look round and talk to the village chief and other male villagers – instantly recognizable with their wispy uncut beards, shoulder-length hair and brightly polished little axes, which they carry over their shoulders. You won't meet any women, however, since all females retreat to their huts so as not to be seen by outsiders, and will stay there for the duration of your visit. You'll need to pick up an **interpreter** en route to the village, however (there are usually lots of volunteers offering their services for a consideration), since the Veddhas cannot – or perhaps will not – speak either English or standard Sinhalese, but stick doggedly to their own "Veddha language" (although whether it's a proper language or merely a strange sub-dialect of Sinhalese remains a moot point; native Sinhalese speakers can usually understand around a third of it).

Although undeniably interesting, visits to Kotabakina can also, sadly, be gratingly false. The Veddhas are used to entertaining passing coach parties with displays of dancing, singing, fire-making and bow-and-arrow shooting, and have become adept at extracting large sums of money for their services. Visits can be rather demeaning for all concerned, and may well end in unedifying disputes over money. If you do agree to watch some dancing or anything else, make sure you agree a sum in advance, and don't expect to pay less than about $30 for the pleasure, or perhaps significantly more. Even if you don't, expect to hand over $10 or so to look around the village (plus a few dollar for your interpreter). Alternatively, you might be able to find some cut-price Veddhas along the main A26 at **Mavaragalpota**, a few kilometres back toward Mahiyangana, who offer similar displays at about a quarter of the price. Fake Veddhas have also been known to offer their services to unwary tourists along the road and around the temple in Mahiyangana. If you have a genuine interest in the Veddhas, contact Sumane Bandara Illangantilake (see page 224), who can arrange visits to Kotabakina on a more rewarding and equitable footing.

Maduru Oya National Park

Daily 6am–6pm • $12 per person, plus the usual additional charges and taxes (see page 50) • The most common way to get to the park is to use the southern entrance, via Dambana (see page 238); you can also get there via the village of Mannampitiya (14km east of Polonnaruwa on the main road to Batticaloa) from where a road leads 25km south to the entrance

Flanking the road inland between Mahiyangana and Batticaloa, the huge and remote **Maduru Oya National Park** was established in 1983 to protect the catchment area of the enormous **Maduru Oya Reservoir** and four smaller reservoirs (at least fifteen percent of the park area is usually made up of water, depending on recent rainfall levels). Much of Maduru Oya's predominantly low-lying terrain was previously used for slash-and-burn agriculture, and is now mostly covered by open grasslands and secondary vegetation, although there are a few rocky mountains in the southwest corner reaching elevations of 685m. The usual range of fauna can be seen here: various species of monkeys and deer, abundant birdlife, rare sloth bears and even rarer leopards. It's also good for elephants, at least during the dry season, when up to three hundred descend on the park to drink at its lakes.

THE VEDDHAS

The **Wanniyala-aetto** ("People of the forest"), more usually known by the name of **Veddhas** (meaning "hunter"), were the original inhabitants of Sri Lanka, and are ethnically related to the aborigines of India, Sumatra and Australia. The Veddhas may have arrived in the island as far back as 16,000 BC, and developed a sophisticated matrilineal hunter-gatherer culture based on ancestor worship and an intimate knowledge of their forest surroundings, the latter allowing them to coexist in perfect harmony with their environment until the arrival of the Sinhalese in the fourth century BC. Veddhas feature extensively in early Sinhalese legend, where they are described as *yakkas*, or demons, and this common perception of them as demonic savages has persisted through the centuries. One memorably smug Victorian colonial official described them as a:

strange and primitive race [whose] members are but a degree removed from wild beasts. They know nothing of history, religion or any art whatever. They cannot count, know of no amusement save dancing, and are popularly supposed not to laugh. During the Prince of Wales's visit, however, one of those brought before him managed to grin when presented with a threepenny piece. The Veddhas have, however, of late years shown some signs of becoming civilised under British influence.

Faced by successive waves of **colonizers**, the Veddhas were forced either to assimilate with the majority Sinhalese or Tamils, or retreat ever further into their dwindling forests. Despite the best attempts of successive British and Sri Lankan governments to "civilize" them, however, an ever-diminishing population of Veddhas still cling obstinately to their traditions – about 350 pure Veddhas are now left in seven villages, mainly in the area east of Mahiyangana, and a small number have attempted to continue their traditional hunter-gatherer existence (even if they now use guns rather than bows and arrows), and also farm rice and other crops to supplement their diet and income. The creation of **national parks**, alongside government development and resettlement schemes and agricultural projects, have further encroached on traditional Veddha lands – in recent years they have campaigned vigorously for recognition and for the right to continue hunting on land now protected by the Maduru Oya National Park. Some "reserved" areas have now been set aside for their use, though their struggle for proper recognition continues.

For more on the Veddhas, see ⓦ vedda.org.

The southern hill country

The **southern hill country** is the highest, wildest and in many ways the most beautiful part of Sri Lanka. Although the area was an integral part of the Kandyan kingdom, little physical or cultural evidence survives from that period, and most of what you now see is the creation of the British colonial period, when the introduction of **tea** here changed the economic face of Sri Lanka forever. The region's attractions are self-evident: a whimsical mixture of ruggedly beautiful scenery and olde-worlde colonial style, with sheer green mountainsides, plunging waterfalls and mist-shrouded tea plantations enlivened by quaint British memorabilia – clunking railways, half-timbered guesthouses, Gothic churches and English vegetables. A further, unexpected twist is added by the colourful Hindu temples and saris of the so-called "Plantation Tamils", who have been working the tea estates since colonial times.

South from Kandy to Nuwara Eliya

The journey south from Kandy to Nuwara Eliya is spectacular both by train and by bus. The **bus** is far more direct and significantly quicker, cutting up through the hills and swinging round endless hairpins, passing the magnificent waterfalls, which plunge over the cliffs in two adjacent 100m cataracts, at the village of **RAMBODA** en route. Around 3km south of Ramboda, the **Bluefield Tea Gardens** (ⓦ bluefieldteagardens. om) offers interesting free guided tours of its tea factory, plus tea shop, restaurant, and attractive walks through the surrounding plantations. From here, it's a short drive on to the Labookelie Tea Factory (see page 249) and Nuwara Eliya.

The **train** is significantly slower, but makes for a quintessentially Sri Lankan experience, as the carriages bump and grind their way painfully up the interminable gradients towards Nuwara Eliya (and occasionally lose traction and slither a yard or so back downhill again). The track climbs slowly through pine and eucalyptus forest into a stylized landscape of immaculately manicured tea plantations which periodically open up to reveal heart-stopping views through the hills, nowhere more so than above the village of **Dimbula**, at the centre of a famous tea-growing area, where the line passes high above a grand, canyon-like valley between towering cliffs.

Kitulgala

West of the train line between Kandy and Nuwara Eliya (and roughly equidistant from both), is the village of **KITULGALA**, nestled in the dramatic valley of the Kelani Ganga, with sheer-sided, forest-covered hills plunging down to the wild waters of the river below.

Kitulgala's original claim to fame is as the location for David Lean's classic 1957 film **Bridge on the River Kwai**. If you know the film you'll probably recognize some of the locations down along the river. About 1.5km east of the *Plantation Hotel*, a white sign saying "Bridge Road of Kwai Rever" (and a blue sign saying "Bridge on the Riverqua Road") point to a small path. Follow this as it goes down a few steps then curves left around a cluster of small houses and on to the river, currently in the throes of building works associated with the new dam (see page 236). A guide may magically materialize to show you the way and point out a few locations used in shooting.

Nowadays, however, Kitulgala is best known as the site of Sri Lanka's best **whitewater rafting**, with grade two and three rapids some 5km upriver from the village, offering exhilarating descents of the foaming Kelani Ganga. **Rafting trips** can be organized through all the town's hotels and guesthouse (around $20–30/person for 1hr 30min–2hr). The construction of two new dams as part of the Broadlands Hydropower Project (due for completion in 2020/21) may adversely affect rafting here over the coming years, and although the government had said the dam will only be closed at night, leaving daytime waterflows unaffected, whether it will actually honour this promise, particularly during periods of low rainfall, remains to be seen.

Kitulgala's final claim to fame is the nearby **Belilena Cave**, around 8km north of town one of prehistoric Sri Lanka's best-known sites thanks to the discovery in the late 1970s of ten of the oldest human skeletons found on the island, thought to date by to around 30,000 BC. Adventure Base Camp (see below) arrange cycling trips here, although there's not much to see.

TOURS KITULGALA

Adventure Base Camp ☎ 077 306 9903, ⓦ adventurebckitulgala.com. A good resource if you want to do a bit more than just rafting whilst in Kitulgala (although they do that too), with trips including half-day cycling tours to Belilena cave ($15), local birdwatching trips and two-day treks to Dahousie ($75).

ACCOMMODATION

Borderlands Main Rd, 250m west of the Plantation Hotel ☎ 011 441 0110, ⓦ discoverborderlands.com. Half eco-resort and half adventure-sports centre, with accommodation in fifteen smallish tents and nicer (but identically priced) cabanas on a river-facing platform with gorgeous views, plus three en-suite "VIP" rooms ($36 extra). Activities include rafting, canyoning, waterfall abseiling, kayaking, guided hikes and mountain biking. Rates include two activities daily. Full board **$294**

Hotel Breeta's Garden Main Rd, near the 49km post, 5km past the Plantation Hotel ☎ 051 224 2020, ⓦ breetasgarden.com. Far and away Kitulgala's best mid-range option, in an attractively airy modern building with spacious and very nicely furnished fan rooms with hot water and thick mattresses, all at a sensible price. Facilities include a nice restaurant and pool set amid surrounding tea plantations, and cut-price rafting trips can be arranged on request. **Rs.5700**

Plantation Hotel Main Rd, 1.5km east of the Rest House ☎ 036 228 7575, ⓦ plantationgrouphotels.com. Attractive 11-room hotel occupying a fine old colonial villa set in leafy grounds shelving down to the river. Room re nicely furnished in pseudo-colonial style, while the uite-sized superior rooms ($80) come with river view – bargain at current rates. There's also a decent riverside estaurant, although it often gets absolutely overrun with assing coach parties at lunchtime. The hotel also provides

a home for the quaint little Anton Jayasuriya Memorial Automobile Museum, home to a fun medley of vintage cars including a pair of Rolls Royces and an unsual Porsche tractor (though sadly no "My other tractor is also a Porsche" sticker). **$60**

ATING

itulgala Rest House Main Rd ☎ 036 228 7528. Set a drop-dead gorgeous riverside location, the good-ooking old colonial dining room in Kitulgala's elegant rest ouse scores top marks for style, although the lacklustre nd overpriced selection of European (Rs.1400–1800)

and cheaper Asian (around Rs.900) mains hardly sets the tastebuds racing. You can also stay here, although rooms are mediocre and seriously overpriced. Daily 12.30–3.30pm & 7–10pm.

luwara Eliya

ri Lanka's highest town, **NUWARA ELIYA** lies at the heart of the southern hill country, et amid a bowl of green mountains beneath the protective gaze of Pidurutalagala, ri Lanka's tallest peak. Nuwara Eliya (pronounced, as one word, something like Nyur-*rel*-iya") was established by the British in the nineteenth century, and the own is often touted as Sri Lanka's "Little England", a quaint Victorian relic complete 'ith municipal park, golf course, boating lake, a trio of fine old colonial hotels and 'equent, very British, showers of rain.

3

TEA ESTATE BUNGALOWS

For a true taste of the colonial lifestyle of old Ceylon, you can't beat a stay in one of the sumptuous **tea estate bungalows** that dot the southern highlands. Built for British estate managers in the nineteenth and early twentieth centuries, many offer beautiful and atmospheric lodgings, often in spectacular locations (and at similarly spectacular prices). The following are just a small selection of what's available – further properties can be found at ⓦ boutiquesrilanka.com and ⓦ reddottours.com.

Ashburnham Estate Elkaduwa ☎ 07921 724439 (UK), ⓦ toniclankacollection.com. Affordable option in the Knuckles Range about an hour's drive east of Kandy, with six rooms in a gracious old 1930s bungalow on a working tea estate. B&B **$149**

Ceylon Tea Trails ☎ 011 774 5700, ⓦ resplendentceylon.com/teatrails. Five superb bungalows of contrasting characters, all in working tea estates in the beautiful Bogawantalawa valley, close to Adam's Peak. Full board from **$800**

Jetwing Warwick Gardens Ambewella, about 20km south of Nuwara Eliya ☎ 052 353 2284, ⓦ jetwinghotels.com. Plush bungalow in its own six-acre estate deep in the heart of the southern hill country. B&B **$340**

Kirchhayn Bungalow Aislaby Estate, around 3km from Bandarawela ☎ 057 492 0556, ⓦ kirchhaynbungalow.com. Characterful old bungalow owned by the last remaining British planting family in Sri Lanka. B&B **$175**

Rosyth Estate House Kegalle ☎ 071 533 7765, ⓦ rosyth.lk. Colonial character meets contemporary

chic at this 1926 planter's bungalow, set in a working tea and rubber plantation a few kilometres north of Kegalle (and close to the elephant sanctuaries). Half-board (including afternoon tea) **$375**

Stafford Bungalow Ragala, 20km northeast of Nuwara Eliya ☎ 011 473 1307, ⓦ staffordbungalow. com. In a small working tea plantation, this four-room Scottish planter's bungalow of 1884 has been stylishly updated but retains plenty of period character. Half-board (including afternoon tea) **$400**

Strathisla Guest House Alwatta ☎ 077 760 2403, ⓦ strathislaguesthouse.com. About 15min drive south of Matale, this is one of the island's oldest estate bungalows, dating back to the 1860s, when it formed part of a coffee estate. Attractively affordable, too. B&B **$140**

Thotalagala Dambatenne, Haputale ☎ 077 204 0981, ⓦ thotalagala.com. Uber-luxurious (but wallet-wrenchingly expensive) lodgings in a gorgeously restored nineteenth-century plantation bungalow next to the Dambatenne tea plantation. All inclusive **$750**

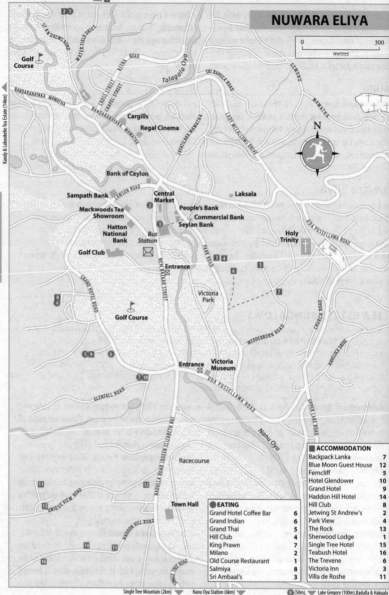

NUWARA ELIYA

0 _____ 300
metres

N

ACCOMMODATION
Backpack Lanka	7
Blue Moon Guest House	12
Ferncliff	5
Hotel Glendower	10
Grand Hotel	9
Haddon Hill Hotel	14
Hill Club	8
Jetwing St Andrew's	2
Park View	4
The Rock	13
Sherwood Lodge	1
Single Tree Hotel	15
Teabush Hotel	16
The Trevene	6
Victoria Inn	3
Villa de Roshe	11

EATING
Grand Hotel Coffee Bar	6
Grand Indian	6
Grand Thai	5
Hill Club	4
King Prawn	7
Milano	2
Old Course Restaurant	1
Salmiya	8
Sri Ambaal's	3

Single Tree Mountain (2km) ▼   Nanu Oya Station (6km) ▼   ⊙ (50m), ▼ Lake Gregory (100m),Badulla & Hakgala

Parts of Nuwara Eliya still live up to the hype, with a medley of doughty British-era landmarks whose misplaced architecture – from jaunty seaside kitsch to solemn faux-Tudor – lend some corners of the town an oddly English (or perhaps Scottish) air, like a crazily transplanted fragment of Brighton or Balmoral. Much of modern Nuwara Eliya is, admittedly, far less of a period piece than the publicity would have you believe while the unpredictable weather can add a further dampener. That said, if you take it with a pinch of salt, Nuwara Eliya still has a certain charm, especially if you can afford to stay in one of the town's grand old colonial hotels, and it also makes an excellent base for **excursions** into the spectacular surrounding countryside and tea estates.

Brief history

Although there's evidence of Kandyan involvement in the region, Nuwara Eliya is essentially a British creation. The Nuwara Eliya region was "discovered" by the colonial administrator John Davy in 1819, and a decade later governor **Edward Barnes** recognized its potential, founding a sanatorium and overseeing the creation of a road from Kandy, which he hoped would encourage settlement of the area. Barnes's plans slowly bore fruit, and during the 1830s the town gradually developed into a commercial and coffee-planting centre, with a largely British population. In 1847, **Samuel Baker** (who later distinguished himself by discovering Lake Albert in Africa and helping to identify the sources of the Nile) had the idea of introducing English-style agriculture to the area, laying the foundations for the town's market-gardening industry: vegetables grown here are still exported all over the island, while many of the area's local Tamil tea plantation workers supplement their incomes by growing vegetables in their own allotments.

With the gradual failure of the coffee crop during the 1870s, local planters turned their attention to the beverage which would radically change the physical and social face of the region: **tea**. The first experimental plantation was established in 1867 by Sir James Taylor at the Loolecondera Estate, between Kandy and Nuwara Eliya, and its success led to Nuwara Eliya becoming the centre of Sri Lanka's tea-growing industry. British influence went beyond quaint architecture and golf, however. Whereas the coffee industry had required only seasonal labour, tea required year-round workers, and this led to the arrival of massive numbers of Tamil migrant workers from South India – the so-called **Plantation Tamils** – who settled permanently in the area and decisively changed the region's demographic make-up; about sixty percent of the population here is now Tamil.

New Bazaar Street

There's nothing very historic about the centre of modern Nuwara Eliya, with its featureless procession of concrete shops strung out along **New Bazaar Street**, although it's worth sticking your nose into the determinedly local **Central Market**, a picturesque little covered alleyway of fruit and veg stalls stuffed full of local horticultural produce. Small-scale market-gardening (introduced during the British era) remains one of the mainstays of the modern town's economy and the odd spectacle of dark-skinned Tamils dressed up like English farm labourers in padded jackets and woolly hats, while carting around great bundles of turnips, swedes, marrows, radishes and cabbages, is one of Nuwara Eliya's characteristic sights, adding a pleasantly surreal touch to the town's out-of-focus English nostalgia.

Just west of the Central Market, the **Mackwoods Fine Tea showroom** (second floor, Queen Elizabeth Plaza; daily 8.30am–7pm; free) is home to a fun little display featuring miniature versions of the various machines found in most tea factories and an admirably clear and concise explanation of the entire tea-production process. They also have a shop downstairs selling some of their own leaves.

Victoria Park

Entrance on Uda Pussellawa Rd • Daily 7am–7pm • Rs.300

South of the Central Market, the immaculate, British-style **Victoria Park** boasts wide swathes of pristine lawn, beautiful ornamental gardens, a children's park and some of the tallest eucalyptuses you'll ever see. The park also has an unusual ornithological distinction: despite its proximity to the polluted town centre, it's something of an ornithological hotspot, being visited by a number of rare Himalayan migrant **birds**,

SPRING IN NUWARA ELIYA

A popular resort among Sri Lankans, Nuwara Eliya is at its busiest during the Sinhalese–Tamil **new year** in April, when spring comes to the hill country, the flowers bloom and the Colombo smart set descends. For ten days the town gets overrun and accommodation prices go through the roof, while visitors are entertained by a succession of events, including horse racing, golf tournaments, motor-cross (motorcycles), clay-pigeon shooting and a mini-carnival.

including the Kashmir flycatcher, Indian blue robin and the pied thrush, as well as Sri Lankan endemics such as the Sri Lanka white-eye, yellow-eared bulbul and the dusky-blue flycatcher.

Next to the southern entrance to the park the small **Victoria Museum** (same ticket) showcases an interesting selection of photographs from the 1860s through to the 1940s including old shots of the town, assorted cricket matches and horse races, and pictures of the railway line and tea plantations under construction.

South of the centre

Opposite Victoria Park, Nuwara Eliya's sylvan **golf course** (see page 248) adds a further welcome splash of green, while to the south lies the town's scrubby **racecourse**, the scene of Sri Lanka's only horse-racing meetings, held here in April, August and December; each meeting lasts for a day, with ten to fifteen races.

Beyond the racecourse, **Lake Gregory** (created by governor Sir William Gregory in 1873) stretches between low hills to the southern end of town. New footpaths, boardwalks and lawns have been laid out along the west side of the lake (foreigners pay a Rs.200 entrance charge) and there are also horse rides, swan pedalos and loads of kiosks serving up drinks and snacks – a fun place to watch locals at play, although otherwise not wildly exciting.

Single Tree Mountain

If you want to get a bird's-eye view out over the surrounding hills, there's a pleasant short walk, starting near the racecourse, to **Single Tree Mountain**. Go straight up the road immediately before the *Clifton Inn*, and walk up through tea plantations to the electricity station at the top, from where (in clear weather) there are marvellous views out to Hakgala and beyond.

Pidurutalagala

At the northern end of town rises the thickly forested mountain of **Pidurutalagala** (whose tongue-twisting name was transformed by the linguistically challenged British into the cod-Spanish Mount Pedro). The highest peak in Sri Lanka at 2555m, the summit (home to an array of militarily sensitive telecommunications masts used by the army, civil aviation authority and others) has recently been reopened to the public after decades off limits. Count on around 45 minutes' drive each way to the top from Nuwara Eliya (around Rs.3000 return by taxi) – you're not allowed to walk up due to security concerns and the risk, it's said, of leopard attacks. It's a fine drive, twisting up through dense cloudforest and with marvellous views, assuming the clouds hold off. You'll need to collect a (free) security pass just before your reach the summit – bring your passport.

ARRIVAL AND DEPARTURE

By train Nuwara Eliya doesn't have its own train station; the nearest stop is at Nanu Oya, about 8km down the road, with regular connections (see page 32) east to Haputale, Ella and Badulla, and west to Kandy and Colombo. Buses to Nuwara Eliya meet all arriving trains (despite what waiting touts and tuktuks driver might tell you); alternatively, tuktuk or taxi will cost around Rs.600, or possibly more depending on how few vehicles there are around.

By bus The bus station is right in the middle of town. There are occasional direct services to Ella and Haputale

TOURS FROM NUWARA ELIYA

The best place to organize **local tours** is *Single Tree Hotel* (contact Aruna on ☎077 356 0116 or ☎045 2222 3009, or email ✉ krishanthagamage@ymail.com) where you can arrange various activities including tea factory visits, guided mountain biking, horseriding, fishing, canoeing and an interesting full-day waterfall tour (Rs.10,000 per vehicle seating up to six), visiting up to sixteen cascades (or slightly fewer in the dry season) – a good way to get to see some of the hidden corners of the surrounding hill country. They can also arrange a car or van to take you up Pidurangala (Rs.3000). Further afield, the return trip to Horton Plains costs Rs.4000 per vehicle (single travellers and couples might also be able to get discounted transport for Rs.1000 per person by taking a ride in a shared vehicle arranged by the hotel). The journey to Horton Plains and then on to Haputale or Ella will cost around Rs.7000, while the trip to Adam's Peak (leaving at 10.30pm) goes for Rs.10,000.

There are also several good **walking guides** attached to *Single Tree*, including the excellent Raja (Neil Rajanayake, contactable via *Single Tree*), who leads various one-day walks throughout the area (around Rs.3000 per group, plus any transport costs). These include the fine hike up to Shantipura and Uda Radella (15km); an exhilarating downhill walk from Ohiya to Haputale (15km); another one-day walk from Bomburuwela (4km from Nuwara Eliya) to Welimada (17km); and a 20km hike up Great Western mountain, near Nanu Oya. Another good local guide is Deen (☎077 646 243, ⚐trekkingsrilanka.com or ⚐srilankatrekkingclub. com), who leads treks throughout the southern hill country, and also runs the *Misty Mountain Lodge* (see page 256) in Ohiya.

3

---

alternatively, change at Welimada (every 30min; 1hr), from where there are frequent onward services to Bandarawela, with regular onward connections to Haputale and Ella – although in general it's easier (if not necessarily faster) to take the train.

Destinations Badulla (every 30min; 3hr); Bandarawela (6 daily; 1hr 45min, or change at Welimada); Colombo (hourly; 5hr); Ella (4 daily; 2hr 15min); Galle (2 daily; 8hr); Hatton (7 daily; 2hr); Kandy (every 30min; 2hr 30min); Matara (2 daily; 8–9hr); Nanu Oya (every 15–30min; 15min).

ACCOMMODATION

Although accommodation in Nuwara Eliya is plentiful, prices are high and many places are aimed more at Sri Lankan than foreign visitors – come the weekend or holiday periods, many cheaper places get overrun by parties of hormonal teenage boys or drunken locals. Wherever you stay, make sure you've got reliable hot water and blankets – Nuwara Eliya can get surprisingly cold at night. Many places hike rates at weekends, especially over "long" weekends when the Friday or Monday is a poya day. Rates also rise steeply during December and Christmas, and over the "mini-season" during the school vacations in August, while rates in most places can triple or quadruple during the April new year period (see page 244).

Backpack Lanka 18 Wedderburn Rd ☎052 222 4383, ⚐backpacklanka.com; map p.242. In a nice old one-storey villa offering basic accommodation in two simple and rather poky six-bed dorms and a few uninspiring rooms, although the public areas are nice, and there's a handy kitchen. Dorms **Rs.1200pp**, doubles **Rs.3500**

Blue Moon Guest House 7 Ranasinghe Mw, off Badulla Rd ☎071 746 7497; map p.242. One of Nuwara Eliya's better bargains, with cosy pine-panelled rooms with TV, quality mattresses and smart modern bathrooms, efficiently run and at a very competitive price. **Rs.3500**

★ **Ferncliff** Wedderburn Rd ☎052 222 2516, ⚐ferncliff.lk; map p.242. Built for celebrated British governor Edward Barnes in 1831, this is one of Nuwara Eliya's most picture-perfect colonial bungalows, surrounded by a lovely wraparound veranda and enclosed in immaculate gardens. The interior has been sensitively updated but retains bags of period character, with just four attractively furnished rooms, plus cosy lounge and restaurant. B&B **$210**

Hotel Glendower 5 Grand Hotel Rd ☎052 222 2501, ⚐hotelglendower.com; map p.242. One of the town's better mid-range options, this atmospheric half-timbered establishment makes a decent halfway alternative to the town's posh hotels and retains oodles of period character, including a pub-style bar, a pleasant lounge and billiards table, and cosy rooms, plus the added bonus of the good in-house *King Prawn* Chinese restaurant (see page 248). B&B **Rs.$110**

Grand Hotel Grand Hotel Rd ☎052 222 2881, ⚐tangerinehotels.com; map p.242. Doughty half-timbered pile, over a century old, which appears to have been lifted wholesale from a golf course in Surrey. The gorgeous public areas are painfully redolent of Blighty, with gracious old wooden decor and creaking furniture, and there are plenty of facilities including three good restaurants, bar, wine bar and a billiards room. As a period piece it's difficult to beat, although rooms are small and relatively undistinguished, and pricey for what you get. **Rs250**

Haddon Hill Hotel 24/3 Haddon Hill Rd ☎052 222 2087; map p.242. Bland but comfortable modern hotel, with smart, spotless and cheerfully bright tiled rooms and efficient service, although not much character. **Rs.6600**

★ **Hill Club** Off Grand Hotel Rd ☎052 222 2653, ⓦhillclubsrilanka.lk; map p.242. Founded in 1876, this baronial-looking stone and half-timbered structure is Sri Lanka's most famous exercise in nostalgia, with one of the island's best-preserved colonial interiors, complete with a cosy lounge, billiards room, a pair of bars and a fine old dining room. Rooms are homely, with creaky wooden floors, dark wood furniture and bathtubs, and rather incongruous-looking satellite TVs. Excellent value at present rates, and even if you're not staying it's worth coming for dinner or a drink (see page 248). B&B **Rs150**

★ **Jetwing St Andrew's** 10 St Andrew's Drive ☎052 222 2445, ⓦjetwinghotels.com; map p.242. In a late Victorian former country club overlooking a swathe of immaculate lawn and the golf course, this serene colonial-style hotel is the smartest place in town. Rooms are spacious, well equipped and pleasantly old fashioned, while public areas – including an oak-panelled restaurant (see page 248), billiards room and cosy lounge – retain a delightful Edwardian ambience. Also offers a good range of walks and tours with the hotel naturalist. B&B **Rs220**

Park View Off Park Rd, behind the Victoria Inn ☎072 230 4220; map p.242. A new budget offshoot of the nearby *Trevene*, offering five simple but very competitively priced rooms (with hot water), plus a nice little lounge and balcony overlooking Victoria Park. **Rs2000**

The Rock 60 Unique View Rd ☎052 567 9002, ⓦtherock.lk; map p.242. Small, mid-range guesthouse, a steep 10min walk up the hill from town, though compensated for by fine views. Rooms are comfortably furnished in British B&B style and well equipped with heater, TV, minibar and DVD player. There's a cosy little in-house restaurant and bar, and half-board rates ($85) are good value. B&B **Rs75**

Sherwood Lodge 22 Waterfield Drive ☎077 734 5715, ⓔsherwoodlodge@yahoo.com; map p.242. Attractive modern guesthouse with cosy rooms in a pair of A-frame buildings high above town (plus one inside the main house) and fine views through big picture windows. **Rs30**

Single Tree Hotel 1/8 Haddon Hill Rd ☎052 222 3009, ☎077 356 0116; map p.242. Comfortable and reasonably priced guesthouse spread across two buildings – the wood-panelled rooms in the main building are particularly cosy on chilly nights. Also a great place to arrange tours (see page 245). Free pick-up from train or bus station. **Rs.4000**

Teabush Hotel 29 Haddon Hill Rd ☎052 222 2345 ⓦteabush-hotel.com; map p.242. Small hotel set in a gracious colonial bungalow with comfortable rooms attractively kitted out with old-fashioned wooden furniture (plus two "super-deluxe" rooms in an ugly building outside). There's also a comfortable lounge to crash out in and a nice restaurant and bar with panoramic views. Good value. B&B **Rs55**

★ **The Trevene** 17 Park Rd ☎072 230 4220 ⓦhoteltrevenenuwaraeliya.com; map p.242 Attractive guesthouse set in an atmospheric 200-year-old colonial bungalow complete with cosy old lounge and sunny veranda. The attractively time-warped rooms at the front have old wooden floors and period furniture; those at the back are simpler and cheaper. Free pick up from train/bus station if you book direct, and local tours and transport can be arranged including inexpensive transport to Horton Plains. Good value. **Rs.3500**

Victoria Inn Park Rd ☎077 475 6258; map p.242. Long-running budget stalwart with basic but just about adequate rooms in a nice central location overlooking the park, although quoted rates can fluctuate according to demand – try bargaining. **Rs.2500**

Villa de Roshe 60 Unique View Rd ☎052 745 1655, ⓦvilladeroshe.com; map p.242. In a smart modern mock-Tudor building perched high above town, this upmarket new guesthouse offers something a bit different from your usual old-world Nuwara Eliya-style accommodation, with three surprisingly chic rooms and fine views over town from the attractive lounge and terrace. B&B **Rs65**

AROUND NUWARA ELIYA

Amaya Langdale Radella, Nanu Oya, 12km southwest of Nuwara Eliya ☎052 492 4959, ⓦamayaresorts com. Set in beautiful tea country high above Nuwara Eliya, this soothing black and white boutique hotel set in an old plantation owner's residence has plenty of old-world charm, very comfortable rooms and a beautiful pool and spa. **Rs240**

★ **Heritance Tea Factory** Kandapola, 14km east of Nuwara Eliya ☎052 555 5000, ⓦheritancehotels com. Set on a hilltop surrounded by rolling tea estates this spectacular five-star hotel was created out of the old Hethersett Estate Tea Factory, which closed in the 1970s. The factory's original exterior has been completely preserved, with corrugated-iron walls and green windows and it's not until you step inside the stunning interior atrium that you realize the place isn't a working factory at all, although there's still plenty of old machinery lying around, giving the place a kind of industrial-retro-chic look. Rooms are stylish and extremely comfortable, with stunning views to all sides, and there are loads of facilities including a plush spa. **Rs240**

EATING

Several decent **restaurants** in the larger hotels offer good food and heaps of colonial charm. Many guesthouses and hotels also have convivial little **bars** – those at the *Hill Club* and *Jetwing St Andrew's* are particularly nice, and outsiders can also use the great little bar at the Golf Club. It's also fun to have **high tea** (usually served around 3–5pm) on the lawns of one of the Big Three hotels, either *St Andrew's* ($7), the *Grand Hotel* ($8) or, most spectacularly, the *Hill Club* ($20).

Grand Hotel Coffee Bar Grand Hotel Drive ☎ 052 222 2881; map p.242. In the other half of the building shared with the *Grand Indian*, this place serves up good coffee and fresh juices along with decent cakes and short eats. Daily 7am–7pm.

Grand Indian Grand Hotel Drive ☎ 052 222 2881; map p.242. This low-key little place at the foot of the *Grand Hotel* driveway isn't nearly as grand as its name suggests but still gets packed most nights thanks to its crowd-pleasing selection of North Indian classics (mains Rs.900–1200, plus cheaper veg options) – no culinary surprises, but well prepared and reasonably priced. They don't accept reservations, so arrive early or expect to queue. Daily noon–3.30pm & 6.30–10pm.

Grand Thai Grand Hotel ☎ 052 222 2881; map p.242. Another in the *Grand Hotel*'s growing restaurant portfolio, with plush decor and a decent selection of mainstream curries, stir-fries and soups. Surprisingly inexpensive given the setting. Mains mostly Rs.900–1100 (meat), Rs.700 (veg). No reservations accepted, so arrive early. Daily noon–3pm & 6.30–10pm.

★ **Hill Club** Off Grand Hotel Drive ☎ 052 222 2653; map p.242. Dining at this atmospheric old hotel offers a heady taste of the colonial lifestyle of yesteryear, complete with discreetly shuffling, white-gloved waiters. Men need to wear a jacket and tie to eat in the main dining room; you can borrow the requisite clobber from the club wardrobe. Ladies are expected to don "formal dress". Food is either à la carte from a varied international menu (mains $9–12) or sign up for the daily-changing five-course set dinner ($25) or three-course set lunch ($20), usually featuring classic old-school cuisine – think roast leg of pork, rhubarb crumble and so on. (The hotel's "casual" *Lily Restaurant* serves exactly the same food and doesn't require you to dress up, but it's nowhere near as atmospheric as the main restaurant). Alternatively, just come for a drink in one of the cosy "Mixed Bar" (formal dress required after 7pm). A temporary club membership fee of Rs.100 must be paid to use either restaurant or bar. Daily noon–10.30pm.

King Prawn Hotel Glendower, 5 Grand Hotel R ☎ 052 222 2501; map p.242. Cosy so-called "Chinese" restaurant, with an extensive menu of meat, fish and vegetarian Cantonese dishes (around Rs.900) prepared Sri Lankan-style with great hunks of chilli. The food actually quite tasty, albeit overpriced and about as authentic as a dancing dodo, but OK if taken with a large pinch of spice. Daily noon–3pm & 6–10pm.

Milano 24 New Bazaar St ☎ 052 222 2763; map p.242. Lively local upstairs restaurant serving up passable food from a mainly Chinese menu (mains Rs.550–660). The downstairs café area is also open from breakfast for drinks and snacks. Daily 12.30–9.30pm.

Old Course Restaurant Jetwing St Andrew's hotel, 1 St Andrew's Drive ☎ 052 222 2445; map p.242. Set in the oak-panelled dining room of Nuwara Eliya's smartest hotel (plus a much less atmospheric overflow dining area next door) with a mainly Sri Lankan and Indian menu (mains Rs.1200–1600), plus a few pricier continental dishes, all well-prepared and attractively presented. Daily 12.30–3pm & 7–10pm.

Salmiya 122 Badulla Rd ☎ 077 913 5263; map p.242. This dark-green corrugated-iron shack provides an unlikely setting for some of the best Italian food in the hill country featuring delicious thin-crust pizza (Rs.800–1200) plus a few pasta dishes. Slight lake views offset the functional decor, while the air is so heavy with garlic it's almost a meal in itself. Daily 11.30am–8.30pm.

Sri Ambaal's New Bazaar St; map p.242. Cheery little South Indian-style vegetarian café serving up cheap and tasty dosas (Rs.140–220), string hoppers and banana-leaf rice-and-curry meals along with assorted short eats, *vada* and sweets. *Ambaal's* restaurant, diagonally opposite, is very similar. Daily 6am–8.30pm.

DIRECTORY

Banks The ATMs at the Commercial, Sampath and Hatton banks all accept foreign Visa and MasterCards; those at the Seylan and People's banks accept Visa only.

Bicycle hire *Single Tree Hotel* have loads of bikes for hire (Rs.1500/day).

Golf The gorgeous, 125-year-old Nuwara Eliya Golf Club course (☎ 052 222 2835; ⓦ nuwaraeliyagolfclub.com) winds through the town centre, beautifully landscaped with magnificent old cypresses, pines and eucalyptus. round (including green fees, club hire, caddy and balls) costs around $33 on weekdays and $41 at weekends.

Post office In the quaint half-timbered building on New Bazaar St, just south of the town centre (Mon–Sat 7am–8pm).

Taxis Taxis can be found lined up along New Bazaar St.

Around Nuwara Eliya

The main reason for visiting Nuwara Eliya is to get out into the surrounding countryside, which boasts some of the island's highest and most dramatic scenery. The most popular and rewarding trip is to **Horton Plains National Park** and **World's End**, while you could also, at a push, use Nuwara Eliya as a base for visiting **Adam's Peak** – although you'll need to leave Nuwara Eliya before midnight in order to reach the summit for dawn.

Pedro Tea Estate and around

Daily 8–11am & 2–4pm • Rs.200 • Bus #715 to Kandapola (every 30min–1hr) goes past the factory, or catch a tuktuk

Set beneath a flank of Mount Pedro about 3km east of Nuwara Eliya, the **Pedro Tea Estate** offers a convenient introduction to the local tea industry. The factory building and tea fields are less picturesque than others in the highlands (there's rather too much suburban clutter, and pylons straggle impertinently across the views), but the easy accessibility and informative guides make it a worthwhile short excursion. Established in 1885, the estate remained under British ownership until being nationalized in 1975 (it was reprivatized in 1985); its factory is still home to a few impressive pieces of old British machinery, some still in operation.

In the same area, the **Lover's Leap** waterfall is the most impressive cataract in the immediate environs of Nuwara Eliya, tumbling over a thickly wooded cliff at the foot of Pidurutalagala. The falls can be reached on foot from the Pedro Tea Factory, a pleasant 2km walk – ask for directions locally.

Galway's Land National Park

1.5km southeast of the centre between Havelock Drive and Upper Lake Rd • Daily 6am–5pm • $10, plus additional taxes (see page 50)

Keen birders might be interested in visiting the tiny **Galway's Land National Park**, just southeast of the city centre near the village of Hawa Eliya. The park's forty acres play host to twenty-odd rare migrants including Indian blue robins, pied thrush and Kashmir flycatchers, plus assorted native species, among them endemic species including the dull-blue flycatcher, Sri Lanka white-eye and yellow-eared bulbul.

Labookelie Tea Estate

Kandy–Nuwara Eliya highway • Daily 8.30am–6.30pm • Free • ⓦ facebook.com/DamroLabookellieTeaLounge

Around 20km north of Nuwara Eliya lies the expansive **Labookelie Tea Estate**, set in gorgeous rolling countryside at an elevation of around 2000m. The Labookelie tea gardens are much more photogenic, and the countryside much more unspoiled, than at the Pedro estate, and the whole place is well set up for visitors, with a swish café and free **tours** of the busy factory, albeit these can be a bit rushed and uninformative compared to those at the nearby Bluefield Tea Gardens (see page 239). It's also easy to reach, since buses between Nuwara Eliya and Kandy pass right by the entrance.

Hakgala Botanical Gardens

Daily 8am–5pm • Rs.1500 • Take any bus heading to Welimada or Badulla (every 15min; 20min)

Some 10km southeast of Nuwara Eliya, **Hakgala Botanical Gardens** lie beneath the towering **Hakgala Rock**, with majestic views across the hills of Uva Province receding in tiers into the distance. The rock is allegedly one of the various pieces of mountain scattered by Hanuman on his return from the Himalayas (see page 154) – Hanuman apparently carried this bit of mountain in his mouth, hence its name, meaning "Jaw Rock". The gardens were first established in 1861 to grow **cinchona**, a source of the anti-malarial drug quinine, and were later expanded to include a wide range of foreign species. They're also well known for their **roses** (in bloom from April to August).

The gardens sprawl up the steep hillside, ranging from the anodyne ornamental areas around the entrance to the far wilder and more interesting patches of forest up the hill where you'll find many majestic Monterey cypresses from California, plus fine old cedars, a section of huge tree ferns, stands of Japanese camphor, and pines and eucalyptus, including a shaggy cluster of bark-shedding Australian melaleucas. You might also glimpse one of the gardens' elusive **bear monkeys**, while this is also an excellent place to spot endemic montane **bird** species, including the dull-blue flycatcher, Sri Lanka whistling thrush and Sri Lanka bush warbler.

The Sita Amman Temple

About 1.5km along the main road from Hakgala Botanical Gardens towards Nuwara Eliya, the **Sita Amman Temple** is said to be built at the spot where Rawana held Sita captive, as related in the Ramayana – although the same claim is also made for the Rawana Cave in Ella (see page 265) – the strange circular depressions in the rock by the adjacent stream are supposed to be the footprints of Rawana's elephant. The small temple – the only one in Sri Lanka dedicated to Sita – boasts the usual gaudy collection of statues, including a couple of gruesome Kali images, though there's not really much to see.

Waterfalls west of Nuwara Eliya

The area west of Nuwara Eliya around the tiny village of **DIMBULA** is one of the most scenically spectacular parts of the island, though its tourist potential remains largely unexploited. The easiest way to get a taste of the area is to go on one of the "waterfall tours" run by the *Single Tree* hotel in Nuwara Eliya (see page 245), which usually include the Ramboda falls (see page 239) along with several picturesque cascades in the Dimbula area – notably the broad, two-tiered **St Clair Falls** and the taller and more precipitous **Devon Falls**, which lie less than 2km apart just north of – and clearly visible from – the A7 highway.

Horton Plains National Park

Daily 6am–4pm · $15 per person, plus additional service charge and taxes (see page 50)

Perched on the very edge of the hill country midway between Nuwara Eliya and Haputale, **Horton Plains National Park** covers a wild stretch of bleak, high-altitude grassland bounded at its southern edge by the dramatically plunging cliffs that mark the edge of the hill country including the famous **World's End**, where the escarpment falls sheer for the best part of a kilometre to the lowlands below. Set at an elevation of over two thousand metres, Horton Plains are a world apart from the rest of Sri Lanka, a misty and rainswept landscape whose cool, wet climate has fostered the growth of a unique but fragile ecosystem. Large parts of the Plains are still covered in beautiful and pristine stands of **cloudforest**, with their distinctive umbrella-shaped *keena* trees, covered in a fine cobweb of old man's beard, and whose leaves turn from green to red to orange as the seasons progress. The Plains are also one of the island's most important watersheds and the source of the Mahaweli, Kelani and Walawe rivers, three of the island's largest.

The park's **wildlife** attractions are relatively modest. The herds of elephants which formerly roamed the Plains were all despatched long ago by colonial hunters, while you'll have to be incredibly lucky to spot one of the 45-odd leopards which are thought to still live in the area. The park's most visible residents are its herds of sambar deer, while you might see rare bear monkeys (see page 441). The park is also one of the best places on the island for **birdwatching**, and an excellent place to see montane endemics such as the dull-blue flycatcher, Sri Lanka bush warbler, Sri Lanka whistling thrush and the pretty yellow-eared bulbul. You'll probably also see beautiful lizards, some of them boasting outlandishly fluorescent green scales, though their numbers are declining as the result of depredations by crows, attracted to the park (as to so many other parts of the island) by the piles of litter dumped by less environmentally aware visitors.

xploring the park

Vehicles aren't allowed into the park, making this the only major national park in Sri Lanka which you can explore on foot. The only track open to visitors is the 9km circular trail around the park, starting from the visitor centre by the entrance and walkable at a gentle pace in two to three hours. There's also a much longer (22km return) trek to the top of **Kirigalpota** from here, as well as an easy shorter trail (6km return) to the summit of **Totapolakanda**, which starts a few kilometres back down the main road to Nuwara Eliya (although you'll still have to pay the park entrance fee for if you want to walk either of these trails). If you haven't come with a guide, it's fairly easy to find your own way around – you may be able to pick up a guide at the entrance, but don't count on it. Wherever you go, remember that the Plains can get cold and very wet: take a thick sweater, stout shoes and something waterproof.

From the visitor centre, the circular trail around the park leads for 500m through rolling plains covered in patana grass and dotted with rhododendron bushes; the altitude here is over 2000m and the air quite thin – fortunately, most of the trail is more or less flat. This opening section of the trail gives a good view of the park's strange patchwork flora, with alternating stretches of bare patana grassland interspersed with densely wooded cloudforest. According to legend, the grasslands were created by Hanuman during the events described by the Ramayana. Tradition states that Hanuman, to avenge the kidnapping of Sita, tied a burning torch to his tail and swept it across the plains, creating the areas of treeless grassland which can still be seen today, although the prosaic explanation is that they're the result of forest clearances by prehistoric farmers – these areas were still being used to grow potatoes as recently as the 1960s. Beyond the grasslands, the path leads for 2km through a superb stretch of cloudforest: a tangle of moss-covered *keena* trees and *nellu* shrubs, along with many medicinal herbs and wild spices such as pepper, cardamom and cinnamon. From here, it's another couple of kilometres to reach the cliffs which bound the southern edge of the park and the first viewpoint, **Small World's End**.

World's End

Beyond Small World's End the path continues through another 1.5km of cloudforest, dotted with numerous clumps of dwarf bamboo, before reaching **World's End** proper (2140m). From here, the cliffs plunge almost vertically for 825m, revealing enormous views across much of the southern island; the large lake in the near distance is at Uda Walawe National Park, while on a clear day you can see all the way down to the coast. There are also marvellous views along the craggy mountains which line the escarpment, including Sri Lanka's second- and third-highest peaks, **Kirigalpota** (2395m) and **Totapolakanda** (2359m), which stand at the edge of the park (and which are reachable by the trails mentioned above). Another 200m beyond World's End, the path turns inland towards Baker's Falls. If you ignore this turning for a moment and continue along the cliff edge for a further 100m you'll reach another viewpoint from the overhanging rock ledge – it's said that no fewer than ten star-crossed couples have leapt to their deaths from here over the years.

From here, retrace your steps back to the main track and follow it as it loops back towards the visitor centre, through open patana grassland with cloudforest set back on both sides.

Baker's Falls

A couple of kilometres from World's End you pass **Baker's Falls**, named after the pioneering Samuel Baker (see page 243). It's a steep and slippery scramble down to the beautiful little falls themselves, after which you'll have to scramble back up again. The final couple of kilometres are relatively humdrum, crossing open patana grassland back to the entrance, and enlivened during the early morning by the resonant croaking of thousands of frogs in the surrounding grasses and trees.

Poor Man's World's End

Just outside the entrance to the park on the Ohiya side, a track leads off the road to **Poor Man's World's End**, named back in the days when it was possible to come here to enjoy the view without having to pay the national park entry fee. The viewpoint is reachable along the plantation road which divides the national park itself from the Forestry Department land on the other side; look for the DWC stone post roughly 1km before the Ohiya-side ticket office. It's a five-minute walk to the viewpoint, although you can carry on along the plantation road for several kilometres, a superb little hike through tea plantations strung out along the edge of the ridge. It's a fine panorama, offering an interestingly different perspective of the dramatically plunging escarpment, and there are further sensational views of World's End from the road beyond as it plunges down towards Ohiya.

ARRIVAL AND INFORMATION   **HORTON PLAINS NATIONAL PARK**

Note that the view from World's End is generally obscured by **mist** from around 10am onwards, especially during the rainy months from May to July, so you'll have to **arrive early** to stand a realistic chance of seeing anything – most drivers will suggest you leave around 5.30am to reach the park entrance by 7am, and World's End by 8.30am. One other way of getting into Horton Plains is to tackle the strenuous paths leading up from Bambarakanda and Belihul Oya (page 255).

By car You can reach Horton Plains from either Nuwara Eliya or Haputale; the return trip from either takes around 1hr 30min and currently costs around Rs.4000/vehicle, including waiting time. Single travellers and couples may be able to save money by taking a ride in a shared van organized by *Single Tree Hotel* (see page 246). The plains are bisected by a single road running between Pattipola (on the park's Nuwara Eliya side) and Ohiya (Haputale side); entrance fees are collected at ticket offices next to this road on either side of the park. (Note that although the road is publicly owned

and maintained, tourists now have to pay the national park entrance fee just to drive along it, even if you've no intention of going walking in the Plains themselves. It's a 3km drive from either ticket office up to the main entrance into the park.

By train It's also possible – with difficulty – to reach the park by public transport and on foot. The easiest place to start is Haputale; catch the first train (currently leaving at 7.45am) to Ohiya (arrive 8.22am), from where it's an 11km walk (around 3hr uphill, and 2hr back down) up the road to the national park entrance, a pleasant hike with fine views. Make sure you check latest train times before starting out to make sure you don't get stranded – if you miss the 4.51pm train the next one's not until 8pm.

Tourist information The smart visitor centre at the park entrance has some interesting displays on the Plains' history, flora and fauna. There are a few places to stay dotted around the edge of the park, including a couple of remote options around Bambarakanda Falls (see page 256).

Adam's Peak

Poking up from the southwestern edge of the hill country, the soaring summit of **Adam's Peak** (Sri Pada) is one of Sri Lanka's most striking natural landmarks and also one of its most celebrated pilgrimage destinations – a miniature Matterhorn which stands head and shoulders above the surrounding hills, giving a wonderful impression of sheer altitude (even though, at 2243m, it's actually only Sri Lanka's fifth-highest peak). The mountain has accumulated a mass of legends centred around the curious depression at its summit, the **Sri Pada** or Sacred Footprint. The original Buddhist story claims that this is the footprint of the Buddha himself, made at the request of the local god **Saman** (see page 253); different faiths subsequently modified this to suit their own contrasting theologies. Sometime around the eighth century, Muslims began to claim the footprint to be that of **Adam**, who is said to have first set foot on earth here after being cast out of heaven, and who stood on the mountain's summit on one leg in penitence until his sins were forgiven. Hindu tradition, meanwhile, claimed that the footprint was created by **Shiva**. Many centuries later, the colonial Portuguese attempted to rescue the footprint for the Christian faith, claiming that it belonged to **St Thomas**, the founder of the religion in India, though no one seems to have ever taken this random assertion very seriously.

SAMAN

Saman is one of the four great protective divinities of Sri Lanka, and the one who boasts the most modest and purely Sri Lankan origins. He is believed originally to have been a pious Indian trader (or possibly a king) who, thanks to the merit he had acquired, was reborn as a god residing at Sumanakuta (as Adam's Peak was originally called). According to the quasi-mythological chronicle of Sri Lankan history, the Mahavamsa, Saman was among the audience of gods to whom the Buddha preached during his visit to Mahiyangana, and upon hearing the Buddha, he immediately entered on the path of Enlightenment. When the Buddha returned to Sri Lanka on his final visit, Saman begged him to leave a footprint atop Sumanakuta to serve as a focus for worship; the Buddha duly obliged. Saman is still believed to reside on the mountain, and to protect pilgrims who climb it. He is usually shown in pictures with a white elephant, holding a red lotus, with Adam's Peak rising behind.

Despite all these rival claims, Adam's Peak remains an essentially Buddhist place of worship (unlike, say, the genuinely multi-faith pilgrimage town of Kataragama). The mountain has been an object of pilgrimage for over a thousand years, at least since the Polonnaruwan period, when Parakramabahu and Vijayabahu constructed shelters here for visiting pilgrims. In the twelfth century, Nissanka Malla became the first king to climb the mountain, while later foreign travellers including Fa-Hsien, Ibn Battuta, Marco Polo and Robert Knox all described the peak and its associated traditions with varying degrees of fanciful inaccuracy.

When to go

The ascent of Adam's Peak is traditionally made **by night**, allowing you to reach the top in time for dawn, which offers the best odds of seeing the extraordinary views free from cloud as well as a chance a glimpsing the peak's enigmatic **shadow** (see page 254).

Most visitors climb the mountain during the **pilgrimage season**, which starts on the Duruthu poya day in December or January and continues until the Vesak Poya in May. During the season the weather on the mountain is at its best, and the chances of a clear dawn at the summit highest; the steps up the mountainside are also illuminated, and little tea shops open through the night to cater to the throngs of weary pilgrims dragging themselves up. It's perfectly possible, if less interesting, to climb the mountain out of season, though most of the tea shops are closed and the lights are turned off, so you'll need to bring a decent torch. Note, too, that the summit itself might be locked, although you may be able to summon a resident monk to let you in.

Although most people climb by night, you can also go up the mountain **by day**, but the summit is often obscured by cloud and, even if it's clear, you won't see the famous shadow, or (assuming you're visiting during the pilgrimage season) be able to enjoy the spectacle of the night-time illuminations and all-night tea shops on the way up.

Finally, don't despair if you arrive in Dalhousie and it's **pouring with rain**. The daily deluge which usually descends on the village out of season (and sometimes in season as well) often stops at around midnight, allowing you a clear run at the summit during the night, although the path will be wet and the leeches will be out in force.

Routes up the Peak

The easiest ascent, described below, is from **Dalhousie**. An alternative, much longer and little used route (15km; around 7hr), ascends from the **Ratnapura** side of the mountain via **Palabaddale** (see page 271). An interesting walk, if you could arrange the logistics, would be to ascend from Dalhousie and then walk down to Palabaddale. Another possibility is to take a tour from **Nuwara Eliya** (see page 241), climbing the peak from Dalhousie, although this makes for a very long night.

However fit you are, the Adam's Peak climb is **exhausting** – a taxing 7km up mainly stepped footpath (there are around 5500 steps) which can reduce even seasoned hill walkers to quivering wrecks. Dawn is at around 6am, and most people make the ascent in anywhere between two hours, thirty minutes and four hours, depending on your speed, levels of fitness, and how many tea shops you stop off in on the way (although at particularly busy times, such as poya days, the crowds can seriously slow your progress). A 2am start should therefore get you to the top in time for sunrise. The eastern side of the summit (facing the rising sun) can get jam-packed at dawn, and you might struggle to find a place to stand – arrive early if you want to be sure of finding a spot. The western side of the summit (facing the shadow) is generally emptier. It can get bitterly cold at the summit: take warm clothing. **Guides** are available (around Rs.2500), though you'll only really need one if you're attempting the climb out of season at night, when the mountain can be a very cold and lonely place.

The climb

The track up the mountain starts at the far end of Dalhousie village, passing a large standing Buddha, crossing a bridge and looping around the back of the large pilgrim's rest hostel (if you reach the *Green House* guesthouse you've gone wrong). For the first thirty minutes the path winds gently through tea estates, past Buddha shrines and through the big *makara torana* arch which marks the boundary of the sacred area. Beyond here the path continues to run gently uphill to the large **Peace Pagoda**, built with Japanese aid during the 1970s. In wet weather the cliff face opposite is spectacularly scored with myriad waterfalls.

Beyond the Peace Pagoda, the climb – and the steps – start in earnest; not too bad at first, but increasingly short and steep as you progress. By the time you reach the leg-wrenchingly near-vertical section equipped with handrails you're within about 1500 steps of the summit, although by then it's a real physical struggle. The path is very secure and enclosed, however, so unless you suffer from unusually bad vertigo, this shouldn't be a problem (unlike at Sigiriya, for example) – and obviously at night you won't be able to see anything on the way up in any case. The upper slopes of the mountain are swathed in dense and largely undisturbed stands of cloudforest which are home to various species of colourful montane birdlife such as the Sri Lanka white-eye and Eurasian blackbird, the sight of which might offer some welcome distraction during the slog up or down.

The summit and descent

The **summit** is covered in a huddle of buildings. The **footprint** itself is surprisingly unimpressive: a small, irregular depression, sheltered under a tiny pavilion and painted in gold – although tradition claims that this is actually only an impression of the true footprint, which lies underground. Upon reaching the summit, pilgrims ring one of the two bells (tradition stipulates that pilgrims ring a bell once for every ascent of the mountain they have made).

The views are as spectacular as you would expect, while as dawn breaks you may also see the mysterious **shadow** of the peak – a spooky, almost supernatural apparition which seems to hang magically suspended in mid-air in front of the mountain for around twenty minutes, given a clear sunrise (most visitors face east in order to watch the sunrise – to see the shadow you'll have to go right up to the rear side of the summit and face west). One of the mysteries of Adam's Peak is the shadow's perfectly triangular outline, which doesn't correspond to the actual – and far more irregular – shape of the summit itself. The Buddhist explanation is that it's not actually the shadow of the peak at all, but a miraculous physical representation of the "Triple Gem" (a kind of Buddhist equivalent to the Holy Trinity, comprising the Buddha, his teachings and the community of Buddhist monks). Locals reckon you've got an eighty percent chance of seeing the shadow during the pilgrimage season, falling to around forty percent (or less) at other times of year.

The **descent** is much quicker though no less painful, since by now your legs will have turned to jelly. A low-key Siddhalepa spa at the bottom of the track offers muscle-soothing post-climb massages (10min/Rs.400).

ARRIVAL AND DEPARTURE   ADAM'S PEAK

The main base for the ascent of Adam's Peak is the modest village of **Dalhousie** (pronounced "Del-house"; also increasingly known by its Tamil name of **Nallatanniya**). It's usually busy with visitors during the pilgrimage season, but can seem rather desolate at other times. Dalhousie lies just over 30km southwest of the busy town of **Hatton**, which is on the main rail line through the hill country (see timetable, page 32).

By bus During the pilgrimage season once-daily (sometimes more) buses run to Dalhousie from Colombo and Kandy; alternatively, take a bus or train to Hatton, from where there are regular buses (hourly; 1hr 30min) to Dalhousie in season. Outside the pilgrimage season there are a few direct buses from Hatton to Dalhousie (6 daily – usually 3 in the morning and 3 late afternoon); alternatively, take a bus from Hatton to Maskeliya (hourly; 45min), and then pick up one of the battered old minibuses which ply between Maskeliya and Dalhousie (every 30min; 45min). A taxi from Hatton to Dalhousie will cost around Rs.3000; a tuktuk costs around Rs.1500 – all the guesthouses listed should be able to arrange a pick-up.

ACCOMMODATION

There's a reasonable spread of **accommodation** in Dalhousie, although rates are high and rooms are at a premium over public holidays and poyas during the season, so it pays to book in advance. Outside the season, it should be possible to score a discount on quoted prices. In addition to the places listed, there are also the four superb Tea Trail bungalows (see page 241) dotted around the countryside nearby. All the following places in Dalhousie are lined up along the main road into the village, starting with the *Wathsala Inn* (around 500m from the village) and finishing with the *Punsisi Rest*, almost in the centre.

Grand Adam's Peak (formerly the Achinika Holiday Inn) ☎052 205 5510, ⓦadamspeakholidayinn.com. This ever-expanding place is one of the biggest in the village, with a bewildering array of 40-odd rooms starting with budget basement cheapies and progressing through a selection of progressively smarter and pricier rooms, with increasingly fine views, as you climb the floors, culminating in a handful of flash new rooftop cabanas for a cool $150. There's also a sauna and jacuzzi in which to revive aching legs. $15

★ **Hugging Clouds** ☎052 205 5529, ⓦhuggingclouds.com. A blissfully small-scale and personable contrast to the faceless concrete monstrosities now mushrooming across Dalhousie, with just five rustic, colourfully decorated rooms and a pleasantly intimate restaurant – plus fine views from the attached balcony. B&B $30

Punsisi Rest Middle of village ☎051 492 0313, ⓦpunsisirest.com. Another of Dalhousie's ever-expanding hotels. The cheapest rooms (little more than simple tiled boxes) are in the old hotel building at the bottom, with a string of increasingly upmarket "cottages" mushrooming on the hillside above, the most expensive going for around $100, smartly decorated and with stunning views. It's a stiff climb up to the higher cottages (a staggering 340-odd steps to reach the highest ones, and the last thing you'll want after climbing the peak), although a road around the back means hotel staff can drive you up to your room on request. B&B Rs.4500

Slightly Chilled Guest House ☎052 205 5502, ⓦslightlychilledhotel.com. Spacious and very comfortably furnished rooms in an attractive riverside setting, plus mountain bikes for rent and information about local hikes. Rates include an excellent buffet rice and curry dinner. Half board $60

Wathsala Inn ☎052 205 5505, ⓦadamspeakhotels.com. A range of rooms of varying standards in a peaceful riverside setting (all with some sort of view) – nothing to write home about, but comfortable enough. Staff can arrange rafting, canoeing and other excursions. Rs.4500

White Elephant ☎052 205 5511, ⓦhotelwhiteelephant.com. Large, functional-looking place with a handful of small but cosy and very competitively priced budget doubles. Avoid the vast standard rooms, which are drab and expensive – albeit big enough to swing an entire sackful of cats. B&B: budget Rs.2500, standard Rs.6550

Belihul Oya and around

Tucked away in the lushly wooded valley of the Belihul Oya river at the foot of the hill country escarpment immediately below Horton Plains, the little town of **BELIHUL OYA** sits in an attractive but still largely untouristed corner of the hill country. Belihul

Oya is also the nearest jumping-off point for the **Bambarakanda Falls**, which tumble out of the dramatic hills below the towering escarpment of World's End. The long, slender cascade has a total drop of 241m, making it the highest in Sri Lanka and five times taller than Niagara – although it can be slightly underwhelming during periods of low rainfall. The falls are 5km north of the main A4 highway between Haputale and Belihul Oya at the village of **Kalupahana**; lots of buses pass through Kalupahana, from where you should be able to pick up a tuktuk to take you up the tiny road which hairpins to the falls. Bambarakanda is also the starting point for a taxing 17km hike, known as the "Colonial Trail", up to **Horton Plains**.

ACCOMMODATION
BELIHUL OYA AND AROUND

The places in **Belihul Oya** below are all situated on the main road fairly close to one another along the main A4 highway, around 4–5km west of town. The places listed under **Bambarakanda Falls** are among the most remote and dramatically situated in Sri Lanka – though you'll have to brave steep, twisting and nerve-racking roads to reach them.

BELIHUL OYA
The Glenrock Ulugalathenna, 3.5km north of town (turn off by the Rest House) ☎076 920 5305, ⌨glenrock.lk. Luxurious nature retreat hidden away on the rocky Belihul Oya river at the foot of Horton Plains, with lush jungle surroundings and sweeping hill views. Accommodation is in a mix of stylish suites and more rustic cabanas, with balconies and big windows making the most of the superb riverside setting. B&B $175

Jungle Rest 500m up the road behind the Rest House ☎045 490 2952. The beautiful setting, amid tropical gardens with drop-dead gorgeous views over river and paddy fields below, is the reason to come here, although the whole place is badly in need of some major TLC, with gloomy and damp dark-green rooms (fan only; hot water Rs.500 extra), shabby furniture and the general sense that the whole place is slowly falling to bits. The restaurant promises "lump rice", "lasaniya" and "pitza". Rs.1800

Landa Holiday Homes 1.5km west of the Rest House ☎045 228 0288. Set in lush gardens running down to the river, with five attractive cabanas in a mix of chunky stone and orange-painted brick dotted around the hillside, all attractively furnished and very tranquil. B&B $75

Pearl Tourist Inn Just east of the 157km post, and 300m east of the Rest House ☎045 228 0157. The

cheapest place in town, with large, old-fashioned and slightly musty rooms (with hot water) – dated but comfortable, and at a good price. Rs.2000

AROUND BAMBARAKANDA FALLS
Hill Safari Eco-Lodge Off the road between Bambarakanda and Ohiya ☎071 277 2451 or ☎011 264 7582. Set in the middle of a tea estate in a dramatic location (reached via a hair-raisingly steep access road) below the towering escarpment of World's End, the rooms are simple but comfortable, and there are also two fancier "luxury" rooms (half board Rs.7000/8000) with observation deck offering views all the way to the south coast. Half board Rs.5000

Misty Mountain Lodge Udawariya Hospital Rd, Ohiya (6km from Ohiya train station) ☎077 764 6243 or ☎057 561 9772, ⌨facebook.com/ mistymountionlodgeohiya. Run by leading local trekking guide B. M. Mohideen ("Deen"), this bungalow up in the mountains above Ohiya offers a good taste of upland Sri Lanka at its wildest. Rooms (with hot water) are simply but comfortably furnished, and treks can be arranged in the vicinity of the lodge and elsewhere across the hill country. Half board Rs.6000

World's End Lodge ☎057 567 6977. Perhaps the most spectacularly situated place to stay in Sri Lanka; look for the turn-off from the A4 highway between Haldumulla and Kalupahana, just east of the Bambarakanda Falls turning. From here, it's 4km up a very steep and rough road of hairpin bends – passable, but only just, in a normal car. Rooms are simple and rather spartan, with verandas from which to enjoy the wild and beautiful views, when not blanketed by mist. You can walk from here up to Horton Plains in around four hours. Half-board Rs.11,000

EATING

Rest House Main Rd ☎045 228 0156. Easily the nicest place to eat hereabouts, with a lovely old colonial-style terrace restaurant overlooking the foaming waters of the Kudu Oya. Set Western and Sri Lankan lunches (Rs.900–

1100) pull in the coach parties, and there's also a small à la carte selection (mains Rs.700–1100) – nothing special but decent value, and in a setting that can't be beat. Daily 7am–10pm.

Haputale and around

One of the most spectacularly situated of all Sri Lankan towns, **HAPUTALE** (pronounced "ha-*poo*-tah-lay") is perched dramatically on the crest of a ridge at the southern edge of the hill country with bird's-eye views in both directions – south to the plains and coast, and inland across the jagged lines of peaks receding away to the north. The town itself is a busy but fairly humdrum little commercial centre with a mainly Tamil population, though the mist that frequently blankets the place adds an enjoyably mysterious touch to the workaday shops that fill the centre.

As with Ella (see page 263), the principal pleasure of a stay in Haputale is the chance to get out and walk in the surrounding hills – most notably up to (or down from) the magnificent viewpoint at **Lipton's Seat**. Specific sights around town include the tea factory at **Dambatenne**, the evocative old country mansion of **Adisham** and the impressive **Diyaluma Falls** (see page 270). The major drawback to Haputale is the **weather**, exacerbated by its exposed position. The marvellous views usually disappear into mist by midday, while the town receives regular afternoon showers of varying severity for much of the year – September to December is the wettest period.

Views excepted, **Haputale** has little to detain you. The town comprises a small but lively mishmash of functional concrete shops and cafés, while a small fruit and vegetable market straggles along the approach to the train station, offering the slightly surreal sight of crowds of loquacious Tamil locals in saris and woolly hats haggling over piles of very English-looking vegetables.

Sadly little remains of Haputale's Victorian past. The principal memento is **St Andrew's**, a simple neo-Gothic barn of a building with a rustic wooden interior which lies just north of the town centre along the main road to Bandarawela. The churchyard is full of memorials to nineteenth-century tea planters, along with the grave of Reverend Walter Stanley Senior (1876–1938), author of the once-famous *Ode to Lanka*, Victorian Ceylon's great contribution to world literature.

Dambatenne Tea Factory

Mon–Sat 8am–5pm • Tours Rs.250 • Buses run every 30min to the factory from the south side of the bus stop in the centre of Haputale; a tuktuk will cost around Rs.600/1000 one-way/return

East of Haputale, a scenic road leads 10km along the edge of the escarpment through beautiful tea estates to the rambling **Dambatenne Tea Factory**, built in 1890 by the famous tea magnate **Sir Thomas Lipton** (see page 447). The long white factory building is one of the most impressive in the highlands and preserves some of its original colonial-era equipment, which demonstrates the extent to which the tea-making process (and often the actual machinery as well) has remained unchanged for a hundred years or more. Factory tours explain the tea-making process from leaf to

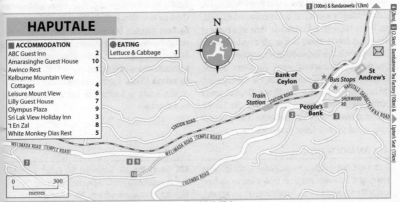

HAPUTALE

ACCOMMODATION

ABC Guest Inn	2
Amarasinghe Guest House	10
Awinco Rest	1
Kelburne Mountain View Cottages	4
Leisure Mount View	6
Lilly Guest House	7
Olympus Plaza	9
Sri Lak View Holiday Inn	3
't En Zal	8
White Monkey Dias Rest	5

EATING

Lettuce & Cabbage	1

Beragala (5km) & Belihul Oya(27km)

packet, although disappointingly, there's no tea for sale, either to take home or drink on the premises. Note that you've got more chance of seeing the entire factory in operation if you visit before noon, after which things slow down.

Lipton's Seat

Rs.50 • Around Rs.1000/1300 one-way/return by tuktuk from Haputale

From Dambatenne, a marvellous walk leads up to **Lipton's Seat**, one of the finest viewpoints in the country – the equal of World's End, but minus the hefty entrance fee. The road offers increasingly expansive views the higher you go, leading steeply up through a perfect landscape of immaculately manicured tea plantations with scarcely a leaf out of place, connected by flights of stone steps and enclosed in fine old drystone walls. It's quite a strenuous hike to the seat – about 7km by road, though you can avoid the lengthy hairpins made by the tarmac and so reduce the overall distance by taking short cuts up the stone steps. Lipton's Seat itself – named after Sir Thomas Lipton (see page 447), who often came here to admire the view – sits perched at the edge of a cliff, offering an almost 360-degree overview of the surrounding countryside; you can see all the way to the coast on a clear day. Taking a taxi up to Lipton's Seat then walking back down (either to Dambatenne Tea Factory or all the way back to Haputale) is one of Sri Lanka's finest, but most effortless, short hikes. As with World's End, the viewpoint clouds over most days from about 10am, so it's best to arrive early. The walk from here down to Dambatenne takes around two hours.

Adisham

3km west of Haputale along Welimada Rd • Sat & Sun, poya days and school holidays 9am–4.30pm • Rs.100 • ⓦ adisham.org

Just west of Haputale, the grand colonial mansion of **Adisham** offers a misty-eyed moment of English nostalgia in the heart of the tropics. Adisham was built by **Sir Thomas Villiers**, who named it after the Kent village in which he was born. No expense was spared in the construction of the rather dour-looking building, with its rusticated granite walls and vaguely Tudor-style windows. The house was bought by the Benedictine monastic order in the 1960s and now functions as a monastery. Only the sitting room and library are open to visitors, complete with their musty original fittings; the monastery shop, selling home-made pickles, chutneys, sauces and cordials, is particularly popular with locals. Adisham is about 4km west of Haputale: go down Welimada Road from the town centre and follow the signs.

ARRIVAL AND GETTING AROUND

HAPUTALE AND AROUND

By bus Buses stop right in the centre of town, although as hardly any bus services originate in Haputale it's pot luck whether or not you'll get a seat, and as there's no actual bus station finding the right bus can be trickier than usual. For Ella, you'll need to change at Bandarawela. There are a couple of direct buses daily to Nuwara Eliya, or take a bus to Welimada (or Bandarawela, then Welimada) and change there.

Destinations Bandarawela (every 20–30min; 30min); Badulla (hourly; 1hr 30min; or change at Bandarawela); Belihul Oya (every 30min; 1hr 30min); Colombo (every 30min; 6hr 30min); Nuwara Eliya (2 daily; 2hr 15min); Ratnapura (every 30min; 3hr); Wellaya (5 daily, or catch a bus to Beragala and change there; 1hr).

By train Haputale's train station is right in the town centre, with direct connections to Ella, Bandarawela Badulla, Nanu Oya (for Nuwara Eliya), Kandy and Colombo Check the timetables in "Basics" (see page 32).

By tour Haputale is a good place from which to visit Horton Plains – most guesthouses can arrange transport for around Rs.4000–4500, as well as vehicles to visit local attractions such as Lipton's Seat.

By tuktuk All local guesthouses can arrange a tuktuk (or possibly a taxi) to Dambatenne, Lipton's Seat and other local attractions.

ACCOMMODATION

Accommodation in Haputale is good value. All the following places have hot water and serve food; a few rooms have fans, although none have a/c (totally unnecessary up here).

ABC Guest Inn Off Sherwood Rd ☎ 057 226 8630 ✉ abcguestinn.haputale@gmail.com; map p.257 Well-run guesthouse right in the centre of town with neat and very competitively priced rooms – some of the cheapest with shared bathroom; more expensive ones have some sort of view. **Rs.1200**

★ **Amarasinghe Guest House** ☎057 226 8175 or ☎077 776 3397, ✉agh777@sltnet.lk; map p.257. Established in 1978, Haputale's oldest guesthouse is still one of its best, centred on a very cosy lounge-cum-restaurant with a good rice and curry served nightly. Rooms are spacious and nicely furnished and come with little balconies, and there are also three newly refurbished doubles (Rs.3800) with fancier décor and big thick mattresses. The guesthouse can be reached on foot by following the tiny footpath from the road by the rail tracks next to *Susantha Stores*, just east of the *Olympus Plaza hotel*; alternatively, you can drive up from the Colombo Rd, although the access road is nerve-janglingly narrow and twisty. Free tuktuk from train or bus station. **Rs.2500**

Awinco Rest Badulla Rd ☎057 226 8620, �🌐awincorest.blogspot.co.uk; map p.257. Pleasant family guesthouse with six varied rooms (including two family rooms) of various sizes, standards and prices, plus communal TV area, lounge and fine views from the terrace outside. Free cooking classes for guests. **Rs.1500**

Kelburne Mountain View Cottages 1km east of Haputale, off Dambatenne Rd ☎011 257 3382, 🌐kelburnemountainview.com; map p.257. Three pretty colonial-style cottages (each with two or three bedrooms) in a breezy hillside location just outside Haputale, surrounded by tea gardens and with sweeping views. **$220**

Leisure Mount View Off Welimada Rd (signed on left about 750m past the Olympus Plaza hotel) ☎057 226 8327; map p.257. Mixed guesthouse-cum-hotel, with four simple rooms at rock-bottom prices in the cosy family house and five attractively furnished upmarket rooms in the big new annexe – the latter with superb views south. Old block (room only) **Rs.1500**, new block B&B **Rs.4500**

Lilly Guest Inn 35 Lilly Ave ☎077 475 9753, ✉lillyguestinn@gmail.com; map p.257. Immaculate and good-value modern guesthouse, run by a charming Muslim family. Rooms are squeaky clean and nicely furnished; those upstairs have views and slightly fancier furnishings for Rs.1000 extra. **Rs.3500**

Olympus Plaza 75 Welimada Rd ☎057 226 8543, 🌐olympusplazahotel.com; map p.257. This ugly but comfortable mid-range hotel is Haputale's only non-budget option. Rooms are spacious and nicely (if rather chintzily) furnished, with private balconies and fine views over the hills below, plus hot water and satellite TV. There's also a so-so restaurant, a surprisingly chic little bar, gym and kids' play area. B&B **$77**

★ **Sri Lak View Holiday Inn** Sherwood Rd ☎057 226 8125; map p.257. The best option in the town centre, with a wide range of spotless, modern tiled rooms, some with marvellous views south, of varying sizes and standards (getting more expensive as you go up the building) and a nice little restaurant from which to watch the clouds roll by. **Rs.2500**

★ **'t En Zal** 79A Welimada Rd ☎077 7586 584, 🌐tenzal.com; map p.257. A stay in this unique boutique guesthouse is almost like sleeping in a museum. The tall, stone-clad exterior is striking, but it's the interior which really boggles, stuffed full of an astonishing array of antique wooden furniture and fittings salvaged by the Dutch owner from across the island, along with beautiful old carpets, prints and other colonial memorabilia. Just

---

THE WALK TO IDALGASHINA

A fine walk leads west from Adisham along the ridgetop towards the village of **Idalgashina** through the **Tangamalai** (or Tangmale) nature reserve (open access; free), home to plentiful birdlife and wildlife including lots of monkeys. The path starts just to the left of the Adisham gates and runs for 3km through patches of dense subtropical jungle full of grey-barked, moss-covered *weera* trees alternating with airy stands of eucalyptus. The track is reasonably easy to follow at first, though it becomes indistinct in places further on (the directions below should suffice, though). After about 1km, the path comes out to the edge of the ridge with panoramic hill views stretching from Pidurutalagala and Hakgala near Nuwara Eliya to the left, Bandarawela below, and right towards the distinctive triangular-shaped peak of Namunakula, south of Badulla. Below you can see Glenanore Tea Factory and (a little later) the rail tracks far below (they will gradually rise to meet you).

From here on, the path sometimes sticks to the edge of the ridge, sometimes turns away from it, undulating slightly but always keeping roughly to the same height. After a further 1.5km you'll see the rail tracks again, now much closer. Over the next 500m the path winds down the edge of the ridge to meet the ascending rail line, at which point there's a wonderful view south, with impressive sheer cliffs to the left framing views of the lines of hills descending to the south, and the flat, hot plains beyond. From here you can either continue along the tracks to Idalgashina (about 6km) and catch a train back, or return to Haputale along the tracks (about 4km).

three rooms, all beautiful, and with great views too. B&B <u>$120</u>

★ **White Monkey Dias Rest** Dambatenne Rd ☎072 409 3534, ✉diasrest@yahoo.com; map p.257. Enjoying one of the most spectacular locations of any Sri Lankan guesthouse, clinging to the escarpment 3km east of Haputale (10min/Rs.200 by tuktuk). Rooms (some with stunning views) are spread over three buildings, including a trio of simple, inexpensive doubles, a pair of family rooms and two fancier deluxe rooms, and the ultra-helpful owner can arrange tours islandwide including hikes and jungle camping in Koslanda, Idyalume and Bambarakanda. All meals available (with mains from just Rs.350). <u>Rs.1800</u>

AROUND HAPUTALE

Living Heritage Koslanda Naulla, Koslanda ☎077 935 5785, ⓦkoslanda.com. Lovely back-to-nature boutique retreat in a gorgeous location midway between Haputale and Wellawaya (and close to Diyaluma Falls), centred on a beautiful infinity pool and surrounded by forest and tea plantations. Design mixes traditional architecture with modern facilities and comforts, with accommodation in a mix of beautiful suites and a handful of *ambalama*-style "forest pavilions". Pavilions <u>$185</u>, suites <u>$325</u>

Melheim Resort Lower Blackwood, Beragala-Diyaluma Rd, 6km from Haputale, 2km from Beragala ☎057 567 5969, ⓦmelheimresort.com. A marvellous location right on the edge of the hill country escarpment is the big draw at this attractive boutique hotel, with sweeping views south and the lights of Hambantota on the coast sometimes visible after dark. Rooms are bright and spacious, with attractive wooden furnishings, private balconies and big picture windows. Terraced gardens run down to a pool and kids' play area, and there are free bikes. <u>$150</u>

EATING

Lettuce & Cabbage Station Rd ☎077 776 3397; map p.257. Haputale's first independent tourist restaurant offers an incongruous dash of city cool right in the ramshackle heart of town, with minimalist modern décor and a wide-ranging menu of well-prepared, very inexpensive international fare including a good rice and curry (just Rs.325) alongside European dishes like chicken schnitzel and fish 'n' chips (Rs.750). No alcohol, although you can bring your own. Daily 10am–9.30pm.

Bandarawela

Midway between Ella and Haputale, the scruffy little town of **BANDARAWELA** lacks either the rural charm of the first or the dramatic setting of the latter. The only real reason to stay here is to spend a night at the time-warped *Bandarawela Hotel*, although you might well find yourself changing buses here en route to somewhere else.

ARRIVAL AND DEPARTURE

BANDARAWELA

By bus Buses to Ella, Wellawaya and Badulla leave from opposite the HNB Bank on the east side of town. All other buses leave from the new bus station in the middle of town. For Nuwara Eliya, it's generally easier to catch a

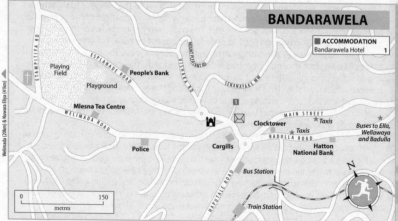

bus to Welimada, from where there are frequent onward services.

Destinations Badulla (every 15min; 1hr); Colombo (every 30min; 7hr); Ella (every 10min; 30min); Haputale (every 20–30min; 30min); Kandy (8 daily; 4hr); Matara (3 daily; 7hr); Nuwara Eliya (6 daily; 1hr 45min); Ratnapura (every

30min; 3hr 30min); Welimada (every 30min; 45min); Wellawaya (every 30min; 1hr 15min).

By train Bandarawela is on the main hill-country train line midway between Ella and Haputale. For timetables see Basics (page 32).

ACCOMMODATION

★ **Bandarawela Hotel** 14 Welimada Rd ☎ 057 222 2501, ⊚ aitkenspencehotels.com; map p.260. Easily the best place to stay in Bandarawela, occupying a lovely old planters' clubhouse of 1893. The personable, rambling old wooden building is brimful of charm (albeit stronger on

colonial atmosphere than modern creature comforts), with polished wooden floorboards, colonial fittings, bathtubs and quaint old metal bedsteads. Probably the best bargain in Sri Lanka at current rates. B&B $\overline{\$60}$

Badulla and around

Set on the eastern edge of the hill country, the bustling modern town of **BADULLA** is capital of Uva Province and its most important transport hub – you might pass through en route between the hill country and the east coast, and if you do get stuck here overnight, you'll find a couple of modest attractions to while away a few hours. Thought to be one of the oldest towns on the island, Badulla became a major centre on the road between Polonnaruwa and the south, though the old town has vanished without trace. Badulla thrived under the British, developing into a vibrant social centre complete with racecourse and cricket club, though there's almost nothing left to show from those days now. Nearby **Dunhinda Falls** (see page 262) and the unusual **Bogoda Bridge** (see page 263) are also both worth a look.

Kataragama Devale

Entrance from Devale St

Easily the most striking building in town is the eighteenth-century **Kataragama Devale**. Centrepiece of the temple is the quaint Kandyan-style **main shrine**, a rustic little structure with tiled wooden tower and the extensive remains of murals on the exterior walls showing scenes from a perahera. The shrine is entered via a colonnaded walkway leading to a cluster of finely carved columns and an elaborate door topped by a carving

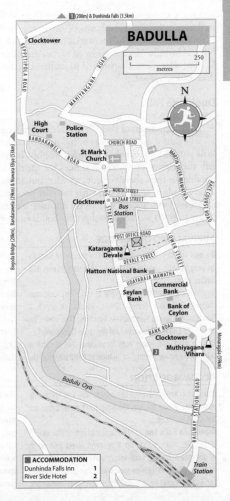

BADULLA

ACCOMMODATION
Dunhinda Falls Inn	1
River Side Hotel	2

of a buxom figure in a tiara, flanked by two elephants – possibly a bodhisattva. Inside, the principal image of Kataragama is, as usual, hidden behind a curtain except during pujas, and flanked by statues of a pink Saman, holding an axe and flag, and Vishnu, bearing a conch shell and bell.

There's a smaller subsidiary shrine to **Pattini** (see page 220) to the right of the main shrine, with another finely carved wooden door, pillars and the slight remains of old murals.

The rest of town

At the southern end of town stands the **Muthiyangana Vihara**, whose origins are believed to date back two thousand years to the reign of Sri Lanka's first Buddhist king, Devanampiya Tissa. It's a tranquil, if unremarkable, spot, occasionally enlivened by the presence of a rambling temple elephant.

Elephants are unlikely to be seen in the vicinity of the modest little **St Mark's Church**, one of the few mementoes of Badulla's colonial-era past, which flanks the roundabout at the northern end of King Street. Inside, a prominent tablet memorializes the infamous soldier and sportsman **Major Thomas William Rogers**, who is said to have shot well over a thousand elephants before being torched by a timely bolt of lightning at Haputale in 1845. The memorial concludes, appropriately enough, with the traditional biblical homily, "In the midst of life we are in death" – a sentiment with which Major Rogers, who alone despatched so many of island's most majestic creatures, would no doubt have agreed.

Dunhinda Falls

Daily 7am–5pm • Rs.200

Around 7km north of Badulla tumble the majestic, 63m-high **Dunhinda Falls**, reached via a beautiful drive from town, followed by a pleasant 1.5km scramble along a rocky little path during which you cross a wobbly, Indiana Jones-style suspension bridge. The falls themselves, fed by the Badulla Oya, are the island's seventh highest, but are most notable for their sheer volume, spewing out an impressive quantity of water which creates great clouds of spray as it crashes into the pool below. **Buses** running past the path to the falls leave town about every thirty minutes; alternatively, hire a tuktuk (around Rs.300 return). Avoid weekends and public holidays, when the falls are thronged with locals.

ARRIVAL AND DEPARTURE

BADULLA AND AROUND

By bus The bus station is bang in the middle of Badulla on King St, with regular services to all nearby towns and further afield.

Destinations Bandarawela (every 15min; 1hr); Colombo (hourly; 8hr); Ella (every 30min; 45min; or catch a Bandarawela bus to Kumbalwela Junction, 3km from Ella, where the Ella Road branches off the main Bandarawela–Badulla road, and either wait for another bus or catch a tuktuk); Haputale (hourly, or change at Bandarawela; 1hr

30min); Kandy (every 45min; 3hr); Monaragala (every 30min; 3hr); Nuwara Eliya (every 30min; 3hr); Wellawaya (every 45min; 1hr 30min).

By train Badulla sits at the terminus of the hill country railway line from Kandy (see page 32). The train station is on the southern edge of the centre.

Destinations Colombo (4 daily; 10–11hr); Ella (5 daily; 1hr); Haputale (5 daily; 2hr); Hatton (5 daily; 5hr); Kandy (3 daily; 7hr); Nanu Oya (for Nuwara Eliya; 5 daily; 3hr 45min)

ACCOMMODATION

Badulla has a modest range of places to stay. You'll probably **eat** where you're staying; the only other possibilities are the usual local cafés.

Dunhinda Falls Inn 35/10 Bandaranayake Mw ☏ 055 222 3028; map p.261. On a peaceful street just north of the town centre, with large, comfortable and well-maintained old-fashioned rooms with fan (plus hot water for Rs.500 extra) or a/c and hot water, plus restaurant.

The helpful manager can arrange interesting local tours. Rs.2200, a/c Rs.3850

River Side Hotel 27 Lower King St ☏ 055 222 2090; map p.261. Close to the centre, with pleasant if slightly battered-looking and overpriced modern rooms with hot water and optional a/c (Rs.1000 extra) and a passable rooftop restaurant, though the view of the massed pylons next door probably isn't what you came to Sri Lanka to see. Rs.4500

Bogoda

Some 20km west of Badulla lies the remote village of **BOGODA**, squirrelled away in a deeply rural setting on the banks of the small Galanda Oya amid the undulating fringes of the hill country. Steep steps lead from the village down to an unusual **roofed bridge**, a quaint little toy-like structure, with delicately balustraded sides and tiled roof elegantly balanced on a single wooden pier plunged into the rocky rapids below. The bridge lies on a pilgrimage route that connects with Mahiyangana and the Dowa Temple near Ella – there's thought to have been a bridge here since the twelfth century, though the present structure dates from around 1700. Next to the bridge is the **Raja Maha Vihara** temple, an attractive little whitewashed structure built into a large rock outcrop. The temple dates back to the eighteenth century and houses a large reclining Buddha, but not much else.

ARRIVAL AND DEPARTURE   BOGODA

By bus It's slightly tricky to reach Bogoda by public transport from Badulla. First, catch a Bandarawela-bound bus to Hali-Ela. In Hali-Ela, buses leave from outside the post office (on the side road on your right as you enter the village) to Katawela, from where it's a 4km walk or tuktuk ride (around Rs.600 return) to the bridge. A few buses go all the way from Hali-Ela to Bogoda. Alternatively, bus #312 goes directly to Katawela from Badulla. You could also visit the bridge from Bandarawela or Ella.

Ella and around

The southern hill country's major tourist honeypot, **ELLA** is highland Sri Lanka at its photogenic best, surrounded by idyllic green hills blanketed in tea plantations and enjoying a pleasantly temperate climate midway between the heat of the plains and the chills of the hills – as well as serving up one of the finest views in Sri Lanka.

The village itself has changed dramatically over recent years, with new buildings mushrooming on every available plot and skyrocketing visitor numbers making the whole place feel a bit like some kind of Unawatuna in the hills, with hordes of tourists roaming up and down the main drag and cafés pumping music out until approaching midnight. Still, it's easy enough to escape the crowds, and Ella remains a fine place to walk and unwind, particularly if you get a bed away from the heart of the village, such

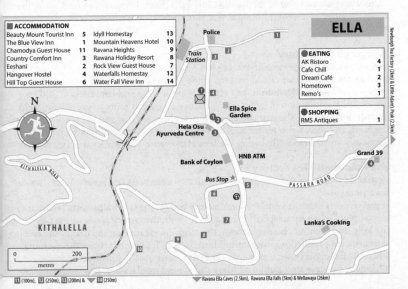

■ **ACCOMMODATION**
Beauty Mount Tourist Inn	5	Idyll Homestay	13
The Blue View Inn	1	Mountain Heavens Hotel	10
Chamodya Guest House	11	Ravana Heights	9
Country Comfort Inn	3	Rawana Holiday Resort	8
Eeshani	2	Rock View Guest House	7
Hangover Hostel	4	Waterfalls Homestay	12
Hill Top Guest House	6	Water Fall View Inn	14

ELLA

● **EATING**
AK Ristoro	4
Cafe Chill	1
Dream Café	2
Hometown	3
Remo's	1

● **SHOPPING**
RMS Antiques	1

Police

Train Station

Ella Spice Garden

Hela Osu Ayurveda Centre

HNB ATM

Bank of Ceylon

Bus Stop ★

Grand 39

PASSARA ROAD

Lanka's Cooking

KITHALELLA ROAD

KITHALELLA

N

0   200
metres

Newburgh Tea Factory (2km) & Little Adam's Peak (2.5km)

11 (100m), 12 (250m), 13 (200m) & 14 (250m)

Ravana Ella Caves (2.5km), Rawana Ella Falls (5km) & Wellawaya (26km)

3

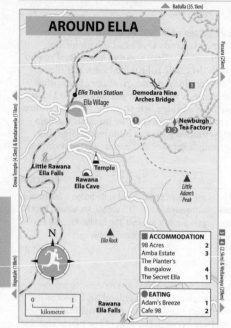

as in the neighbouring hamlet of Kithalella.

There's not much to Ella itself bar a single street meandering gently downhill, past innumerable guesthouses, cafés and shops before reaching the edge of the escarpment, just below the *Grand Ella Motel*, from where you can see the classic view past the towering bulk of **Ella Rock** on the right and through a cleft in the hills – the so-called **Ella Gap** – to the plains far below.

Little Adam's Peak

One of the best ways to spend a morning in Ella is to tackle the beautiful short walk up to the top of **Little Adam's Peak** (aka "Mini Adam's Peak"). The walk is largely flat, apart from a short climb at the end – count on around 2–3hr return. Start by heading down **Passara Road** for 1km. Just past the 1km marker (and *Adam's Breeze* restaurant) a small but clearly signed road goes off on the right, running through beautiful tea plantations. Keep left whenever there's a choice of routes, following the path as it loops around a ramshackle tea pickers' village. After another 500m you'll see two gated tracks heading off on the right close to one another. Take the second (signed to Mini Adam's Peak), and follow it for the final kilometre and climb the 300-odd steps up to the top, from where there are marvellous views of Ella Rock, Ella Gap, the Newburgh Tea Factory and the very top of the Rawana Ella Falls. From here another track switchbacks along the ridge to a second hilltop about 1km distant, with further views over the lowlands below.

Newburgh Tea Factory

Passara Rd, about 250m past the 98 Acres resort • Mon–Sat 8.30am–5pm • Rs.500 •

Further down the Passara Road past the Little Adam's Peak turn-off, endless fields of green enclose the **Newburgh Tea Factory**, built in 1903 and converted in 2009 for the exclusive production of green tea. Whistle-stop guided tours (every 30min) help explain differences in the manufacturing process between this and the black variety of the brew, and there's also tea for sale, although if you've not been round a tea factory previously you're better off visiting the Uva Halpewatte Tea Factory first (see below).

Uva Halpewatte Tea Factory

Badulla Rd, 6km from Ella • Mon–Sat 8am–4pm • Rs.450 • ☎ 057 222 8599 • ⌨ halpetea.com • Take a tuktuk for Rs.1200–1500 return including waiting time

If you've never seen the inside of a tea factory before, the **Uva Halpewatte Tea Factory** is a good place to get up to speed. Dating from 1940, the factory is one of the biggest in the hills, and the tours here are among the most informative on the island, unravelling the entire tea-production process from bush to bag. It's best to visit in the morning, when the factory is busiest, and note the factory isn't usually fully operational on a Monday (or days after public holidays and some Saturdays too, depending on

WALKING TO DEMODARA BRIDGE

For an enjoyable and not-at-all-strenuous two-hour walk around Ella, the hike to the landmark Demodara Bridge ticks all the right boxes. Head out along Passara Rd, past the Newburgh Tea Factory (see page 264). About 100m past the factory you'll see three small roads going off to the left (the middle leads to *The Secret Ella*). Take the left-hand road and walk downhill for twenty minutes to reach the railway line, then turn left and cross the impressive **Demodara Nine Arch Bridge** (if you just want to see the bridge without the walk you can catch a tuktuk here from Ella for around Rs.800 return). Just past here the tracks pass through a short tunnel (about 100m long – a bit gloomy, and with a few bats in the middle) before emerging back into daylight. From here, carry on along the railway track, which will bring you back to Ella station in another 30–40 minutes or so. If you want to extend the walk, it's easily combined with the hike up Little Adam's Peak (see page 264). There are several places for drinks and food en route, including *Adam's Breeze* and *Cafe 98* (see page 268).

3

production levels), although there are still guides on hand to show you round. Tours (roughly every 30min) last around 45min, after which visitors are invited to exit through the well-stocked gift shop and café.

Rawana Ella Falls

Ella is famous in Sri Lankan folklore for its Ramayana connections: according to one tradition, the demon king Rawana brought the captive Sita here and hid her away in a cave a couple of kilometres outside the present-day village. Rawana's name is now memorialized in the names of various village guesthouses, as well as in the dramatic **Rawana Ella Falls** (also known as the Bambaragama Falls), which plunge magnificently for some 90m over a series of rock faces 6km below Ella down the Wellawaya Road. It's an impressive sight, and you can clamber some way up the rocks to one side of the falls. To reach the falls, catch any bus heading down towards Wellawaya.

Rawana Ella Cave

To reach the cave, head down the Wellawaya Road from the village for about 2km, from where a path on the right heads up to the cave – it's easiest to find the start of the path by catching a tuktuk from Ella (around Rs.250)

En route to Rawana Ella Falls, a few kilometres out of Ella, lies the **Rawana Ella Cave**, in which Rawana is claimed to have held Sita captive, as related in the Ramayana – although a similar claim is made for the Sita Amman Temple (see page 250) near Nuwara Eliya. It's a punishing climb up to the cave, including over 600 steps, and sections can be treacherously slippery after rain (there's a very welcome tea shack

WALKING UP ELLA ROCK

The most rewarding, and most taxing, hike around Ella is the ascent of the majestic **Ella Rock**, which looms over the village. It's around a four-hour hike in total, with an interesting mix of rail track, tea plantation, and some steep stuff near the summit. Carry food, water and good footwear, and take care in wet weather, when tracks can get slippery – and be aware, too, that mist and rain can descend quickly at the top.

There are several different possible **routes** – it's a good idea to ask at your guesthouse for latest information before setting out. Most begin by following the rail line south out of the village for about 1.5km until the tracks cross a rickety bridge near the top of **Little Rawana Ella Falls**. From here, various paths strike up towards the top of the rock – quite possibly, a local villager will materialize to guide you up, for a consideration, or you could simply try to make your own way by following the likeliest-looking path (although scams involving fake signs and deliberate misdirection have been reported). Alternatively, most guesthouses should be able to arrange a guide for around Rs.1500–2000.

around two-thirds of the way up). The sweeping views at least partly compensate, although there's not much to see in the cave itself – bring a torch.

Dowa Temple

10km southwest of Ella, 6km from Bandarawela • No set hours • Donation

Next to the main road between Ella and Bandarawela, the small **Dowa Temple** is set in a secluded and narrow wooded valley and boasts a striking low-relief Buddha, carved into the rock face which overlooks the temple. It's similar in style to the figures at Buduruwagala (see page 269), and may represent Maitreya, the future Buddha of the Mahayana pantheon who also appears at Buduruwagala. The temple itself is of some antiquity, though there's not much to show for it now apart from some fairly uninteresting paintings and a reclining Buddha. All buses from Ella to Bandarawela run past the temple.

ARRIVAL AND DEPARTURE
ELLA AND AROUND

BY BUS

Buses drop passengers off at the road junction outside the *Curd and Honey Shop* in the centre of the village, close to most of the guesthouses. No buses originate in Ella, so finding a seat when leaving can sometimes be tricky.

Hill country Both Haputale or Nuwara Eliya are easier (although not necessarily quicker) to reach by train; heading to Haputale by bus, you'll have to change at Bandarawela. Heading towards Badulla, you might find it easier to catch any bus heading to the main Badulla–Bandarwela road, about 3km from the village (or take a tuktuk to the junction), and pick up a bus there.

Destinations Badulla (every 30min; 45min); Bandarawela (every 10min; 30min); Kandy (2 daily; 6hr; alternatively go to Badulla, from where there are Kandy services every 30min); Nuwara Eliya (1 daily at 9.30am; 2hr 15min; alternatively go to Bandarawela, from where there are services onto Welimada every 15min, and then on to Nuwara Eliya).

South coast Ella is a convenient jumping-off point for the south coast, with regular services to Matara via Pamegamuwa

Junction (for Tissa), Tangalla and Hambantota. There's one direct bus daily to Tissa and Kataragama; alternatively, take any Matara bus to Pamegamuwa and change there. For Galle, change at Matara.

Destinations: Kataragama (1 daily at 8.30; 2hr 30min); Matara (8 daily; 6hr); Tissamaharama (1 daily at 8.30am; 2hr); Wellawaya (every 30min; 45min).

BY TRAIN

It's generally more comfortable and enjoyable to leave Ella by train, especially if you're heading to Haputale or Nuwara Eliya – and railway buffs will also enjoy the famous loop which the train tracks make to gain height just east of Ella en route to Badulla. The train station is on the north side of the village. See Basics for timetables (see page 32).

Destinations Badulla (5 daily; 1hr); Colombo (3 daily; 9–10hr); Haputale (5 daily; 1hr–1hr 40min); Hatton (4 daily; 4–5hr); Kandy; 4 daily; 6hr–10hr 40min); Nanu Oya (for Nuwara Eliya; 5 daily; 2hr 40min–4hr 20min).

INFORMATION AND TOURS

Information The *Dream Café* is a good source of local information, including bus times.

Tours Most of the village's guesthouses can arrange taxis and tours. Alternatively, the *Dream Café* (☎057 222 8950) runs various excursions including day-trips to Horton Plains (Rs.7500 for vehicle only) and two enjoyable one-day tours, the first combining Buduruwagala, Rawana

Falls, Haputale, Diyaluma Falls, Dowa Temple and the Uva Halpewatte Tea Factory (Rs.7500 for a minivan seating up to five, plus Rs.1000 extra to add in Lipton's Seat), the second combining Uva Halpewatte, Dunhinda Falls, Bogoda Bridge, Dowa and the Demodara railway loop (Rs.8500 for vehicle only). They also have 90cc scooters for rent (Rs.1500/day).

ACCOMMODATION

Ella has a huge range of accommodation for such a small place, although real bargains are hard to find – and you'll pay a premium for anywhere with a view. There are plenty of options in the **village** itself, plus a growing number of places above the village along the railway tracks in **Kithalella** – much more peaceful, and often with superb views, although a little way from the action. All

of the following have hot water, although a/c isn't usually provided, and isn't really needed.

Beauty Mount Tourist Inn Main Rd ☎077 679 1168, ✉ nimalibeautymountcottage@gmail.com; map p.263. Neat and very good-value rooms in a steep-side garden bang in the centre of the village. Good food, and cooking classes on request, plus scooters for hire. **Rs.2500**

The Blue View Inn Off Police Station Rd ☎ 077 695 243; map p.263. Welcoming guesthouse house tucked away in a central but very peaceful location, a 5min walk from the village, with five neat, bright modern rooms nestled amongst the trees. B&B **Rs.4200**

Country Comfort Inn 32 Police Station Rd ☎ 057 222 8532, ⓦ hotelcountrycomfort.lk; map p.263. Small hotel on quiet Police Station Rd. Rooms in the main building are pleasant but overpriced, although the two budget doubles in the pretty old garden villa are a bargain. Garden rooms **Rs.2000**, main building **Rs.7500**

Eeshani 22/3 Police Station Rd ☎ 057 222 8703, ⓔ eeshaniguestinn@yahoo.com; map p.263. Five small rooms in a very cosy little family guesthouse, central but very peaceful, and at a sensible price. **Rs.3500**

Hangover Hostel 16 Police Station Rd ☎ 077 313 7797, ⓦ hangoverhostels.com; map p.263. Upmarket hostel in a smart two-storey house with beds in cool and spacious 6- and 8-bed mixed a/c dorms, each with its own in-dorm bathroom. Beds come with individual lights and sockets, thick mattresses and big lockers, and there are also daily yoga sessions (Rs.1000), a nice chillout deck, plus free tea and coffee. **$14**

Hill Top Guest House Off Main Rd ☎ 057 222 8780, ⓔ hilltopella@hotmail.com; map p.263. Perched at the top of a short but steep hill just above the main road, with fine views of Ella Gap from the upper storey and attractive hammock-strewn veranda. Rooms are spacious and neatly furnished, although slightly pricey for what you get, and you'll pay around Rs.2000 extra for a view. B&B **Rs.4800**

★ **Ravana Heights** ☎ 057 222 8888, ⓦ ravanaheights.com; map p.263. One of the nicest places to stay in Ella, set amid a lovely little garden just below the village. The three bright modern rooms come with picture-perfect views of Ella Rock and the Gap, and there are also two smart new family suites and a rooftop apartment. The owner can also arrange hiking excursions (around $15 plus transport) and serves up superior Thai food. *Rough Guides* readers are promised a discount of around ten percent when booking directly (contact the guesthouse for details). B&B **$150**

Rawana Holiday Resort ☎ 057 222 8794, ⓦ rawanaholiday.com; map p.263. Decent selection of clean and comfortable rooms, reasonably priced, plus good home-cooking in the large restaurant with fine views of Ella Gap. Also offers cookery classes. **Rs.3500**

Rock View Guest House ☎ 057 222 8561, ⓔ rockviewh@gmail.com; map p.263. One of the longest-established places in the village, with a marvellous view of Ella Rock and good-value accommodation – choose between the spacious and attractively refurbished rooms in the main house or the three smaller but newer ones with balcony in the annexe outside. **Rs.3000**

KITHALELLA

Chamodya Guest House ☎ 078 535 4726, ⓔ chamodyahomestay@hotmail.com; map p.263. Super-friendly family guesthouse offering five smart and attractively decorated rooms worthy of a mid-range hotel at a well below-average price, plus gorgeous views, particularly from upstairs, of the rock and falls. **$40**

Idyll Homestay ☎ 057 2050 834, ☎ 071 911 3701, ⓦ ellagoodneighbours.com; map p.263. Tiny and very friendly little family guesthouse with five bright and quite smart modern rooms with big picture windows and a small terrace facing the Little Rawana Ella Falls. B&B **Rs.5000**

Mountain Heavens Hotel ☎ 057 492 5757, ⓦ mountainheavensella.com; map p.263. Small modern hotel with a jaw-dropping view right down the middle of Ella Gap, offering spacious modern rooms with private balcony or terrace and big French windows through which to enjoy the scenery. Nice, although rates are steep verging on silly. B&B **$190**

★ **Waterfalls Homestay** ☎ 057 567 6933, ⓦ waterfalls-guesthouse-ella.com; map p.263. In a wonderfully peaceful location opposite Little Rawana Ella Falls, this Australian-owned hideaway feels more like a homestay than a conventional guesthouse, with just three colourful and very comfortable rooms (including one triple/family room) and a lovely terrace from which to watch the falls, There's also a small Ayurvedic massage parlour downstairs, and cooking lessons are available on request, and dinner is available at the adjacent *Water Fall View Inn* restaurant (see below). B&B **Rs.6500**

Water Fall View Inn ☎ 077 996 1971, ⓔ ellawaterfallview@gmail.com; map p.263. Small, very welcoming family guesthouse with four rooms (including a family room), all with hot water, big windows and verandas facing the Little Rawana Ella Falls. The small attached restaurant serves up a good rice and curry buffet (Rs.900) at 7.30pm nightly. B&B **Rs.4500**

AROUND ELLA

★ **98 Acres** Passara Rd (next to 2km post) ☎ 057 205 0050, ⓦ resort98acres.com; map p.264. Gorgeous eco-resort set amid the rolling tea-bushes of the Uva Greeland Estate. Accommodation is in a string of rustic-chic stone-thatched cabanas, perched on the ridge at the top of the estate, with stylish rooms up and down and stunning views of nearby Little Adam's Peak and Ella Rock. Facilities include the eye-catching *Cafe 98* (see page 268), plus gym, spa and a skinny little pool, while activities include yoga, archery, birdwatching, trekking and biking. B&B **$190**

Amba Estate Ambadandegama (30–40min drive south of Ella) ☎ 057 357 5489, ⓦ ambaestate.com; map p.264. Idyllic rural retreat, far from the madding crowds of Ella, set in an organic farm amid stunning scenery. Accommodation is in either the old estate bungalow, full of

COOKING CLASSES IN ELLA

Virtually every guesthouse in the village now seems to offer **cookery classes**. Classes usually last 2–3hr, cost Rs.2000–2500 and feature between three and five traditional Sri Lankan dishes which you get to eat at the end of the class. The places below are three of the best – be sure to book in advance.

Ella Spice Garden Down the path next to Café Chill ☏ 075 236 3636. Three-hour morning and afternoon classes (Rs.2500), including recipe book and a tour of the attached spice garden (which is also open daily 8am–5pm for guided tours; Rs.100pp).

Grand 39 Passara Rd ☏ 076 709 9200. Well-regarded classes run by local chef Iran featuring five veg curries,

plus chicken/fish and a dessert (classes on request; Rs.2500).

Lanka's Cooking Signed south off Passara Road ☏ 077 695 7495. Perhaps the most authentic classes in the village, featuring five dishes cooked in traditional clay pots over wood fires in a pleasantly rural setting slightly southwest of the village (Rs.2000; daily at 5pm).

wonderfully time-warped country-house character, or the modern Clove Tree Cottage, while activities include cooking lessons and some great local hikes. Advance reservations essential. $\underline{\$65}$

★ **The Planter's Bungalow** Wellawaya Rd, 10km south of Ella ☏ 055 205 5600, ⊛ plantersbungalow. com; map p.264. Lovely colonial-style boutique guesthouse in a superbly restored tea planter's bungalow of 1889 surrounded by lush wooded gardens. Accommodation is in three stylish rooms in the bungalow itself, a small cottage, plus six stylish and slightly pricier modern rooms with stunning views spread around the garden, and there's also a pool and excellent and

authentic hill-country-style Sri Lankan food using home-grown organic vegetables. Good value at current rates B&B $\underline{\$105}$

The Secret Ella Sutherland Estate, Namunukula R ☏ 057 222 6333, ⊛ thesecrethotels.com/ella; map p.264. Lovely boutique guesthouse in a gorgeously updated 1855 tea plantation bungalow, set in fourteen acres of immaculate garden amid the Sutherland Te Estate, with sweeping hill views at the rear. The fiv beautifully appointed rooms are luxurious but full o character, and there's also a pool and various activitie including croquet, minigolf, bike rides and tours of th Sutherland estate. B&B $\underline{\$248}$

EATING

Ella is well stocked with places to eat, mainly strung out along Main St, while there's often good home-cooking in the various guesthouses as well. Rice and curry is generally king, although there are also several places serving up good international cuisine.

Adam's Breeze Passara Rd (just before the 1km post and the path off to Little Adam's Peak) ☏ 077 506 6560; map p.264. A nice place for a drink or food on the way to or from Little Adam's Peak, with a well-prepared and inexpensive range of Sri Lankan and Western breakfasts, rice and curry (Rs.600 veg, Rs.750 meat), plus snacks including lots of sweet and savoury *rottys*. Daily 8.30am–10pm.

★ **AK Ristoro** 37 Grand View, Passara Rd ☏ 057 205 0676; map p.263. Not at all what you'd expect to find down a dusty Ella back road, this funky restaurant – with cool warehouse-style stripped-brick decor and food to match – brings something a bit different to Ella's rice-and-curry-centric dining scene. The innovative menu features unusual local and international tapas (Rs.100–350) plus a good Japanese selection (Rs.850–1250) and excellent authentic pasta (Rs.600–900) – or there's always the obligatory rice and curry (Rs.600), given a nice contemporary twist. Daily 11am–10pm.

Cafe Chill Main St ☏ 077 180 4020; map p.263 At the heart of the main drag, this kicking restaurar is usually the liveliest place in the village, and often th last place to close, with seating either on the streetsid veranda or around the back by the open kitchen – or ju have a drink on the rooftop terrace under a spectacula thatched roof. Food comprises a decent spread of loca and international fare – the pizza (from Rs.1100) i good, as is the eight-dish rice and curry (Rs.770), an there's also real coffee and very cheap beer. Arriv early or expect to queue. Kitchen closes at 10pm. Dail 10am–12.30am.

Cafe 98 Passara Rd ☏ 057 205 0050; map p.264. In th beautiful *98 Acres* resort (see page 267), this attractiv pavilion restaurant, topped by a huge thatched roo and with wonderful views from the decked seating are outside, makes a good pit stop en route to or from Adam Peak or Demodara Bridge. Drinks include a fine selection o single-estate teas from the nearby Halpewatte estate, an there's also a wide range of Sri Lankan and international mains (from Rs.1000). Daily 7.30am–10.30pm.

Dream Café Main St ☏ 057 222 8950; map p.263. Thi sprawling two-floor café in the middle of the village ha become a bit too big for its own good, but still serves uj ome of the best food in Ella, with a well-prepared range of ocal and international dishes (mains mostly Rs.700–1000) - anything from rice and curry through to pasta, burgers, raps and salads, plus some of the best pizza in the island. ood breakfasts, too, either Western or Sri Lankan. Daily am–10pm.

Hometown 17 Main St ☎071 292 4507; map p.263. ang in the middle of the village but easily overlooked, his unprepossessing little café is highly rated by locals r its very good, very inexpensive rice and curry spreads

(Rs.350–550), and also serves up tasty sweet rottys and above-average breakfasts. Daily 10am–10pm.

Remo's 7 Main St (on the first floor and easily missed; access is via the Lanka Grand Herbal arch) ☎057 454 5073; map p.263. A great place for inexpensive rice and curry featuring a mouthwatering array of dishes for a bargain Rs.500. Good Sri Lankan and Western breakfasts too, plus assorted snacks, all delivered with tremendous enthusiasm by Remo and his exceptionally chipper staff. Daily 8.30am– 10pm.

SHOPPING

MS Antiques 5 Police Station Rd ☎077 929 7811; map 263. Small shop selling an interesting range of antiques

sourced by the owner from around the island, alongside some attractive modern crafts and bric-a-brac. Daily 10am–7pm.

DIRECTORY

Ayurveda The best of the various Ayurveda centres round Ella, the small and very rustic little Hela Osu (☎071 1 0010) in the middle of the village offers assorted assages, herbal baths and shirodhara at bargain rates s.2000–4000). Avoid the Suwamadura centre on Passara d, which has a dreadful reputation.

Banks There's a small Bank of Ceylon beneath the *Jade reen Restaurant* with a single, temperamental ATM, and a

more reliable HNB machine slightly further down the road. Both accept Visa and MasterCard.

Internet The EzTaxi office, just south of the bus stop, has a couple of machines (daily 7am–9pm; Rs.200/hr).

Laundry There are several places offering cheap laundry services along Police Station Rd.

Wellawaya and around

Standing in the dry-zone plains at the foot of the hills of Uva Province, **WELLAWAYA** is, strictly speaking, not part of the hill country at all, though it's an important transport hub and provides regular connections to Ella, Haputale and beyond. The town itself s eminently forgettable, though there are a few worthwhile sights nearby – although it's also perfectly possible to visit these from Ella or Haputale. There are also a couple of excellent eco-lodges in the area around the town of **Buttala**, about 15km east of Wellawaya (see page 269).

Buduruwagala rock carvings

aily 7am–6pm • Rs.200 • Daily 24hr • A tuktuk from Wellawaya will cost around Rs.500 return; head 5km south of Wellawaya along the main road towards Tissa, then turn right onto a signed side road for another 5km

Just south of Wellawaya lie the magical rock carvings of **Buduruwagala**, in a patch of beautifully unspoilt dry-zone forest populated by abundant birds and butterflies. The site features a series of seven figures carved in low relief into the face of a large rock outcrop (whose outline is sometimes fancifully compared to that of an elephant lying down). The figures are some of the largest in the island (the biggest is 16m tall), and are thought to date from the tenth century – they're unusual in displaying Mahayana Buddhist influence, which enjoyed a brief vogue in the island around this time. The large central standing **Buddha** in the *abhaya* ("have no fear") pose still bears traces of the stucco which would originally have covered his robes, as well as faint splashes of his original paint.

On the left-hand side of the rock stand a group of three figures. The central one, which retains its white paint and red halo, is generally thought to represent **Avalokitesvara**, one of the most important Mahayana divinities. To the left stands an unidentified attendant, while the female figure to his right in the "thrice-bent" pose is **Tara**, a Mahayana goddess. The three figures on the right-hand side of the rock are much more Hindu in style. The figure on the right is generally thought to represent the

Tibetan bodhisattva **Vajrapani**, holding a thunderbolt symbol (a *dorje* – a rare instance of Tantric influence in Sri Lankan Buddhist art); the central figure is **Maitreya**, the future Buddha, while the third figure is **Vishnu**. The presence of square-cut holes in the rock above some figures – particularly the central Buddha – suggests that they would originally have been canopied.

Handapanagala Tank

Head 8km south of Wellawaya along the main road towards Tissa (3km past the Buduruwagala turn-off), then 1.5km along a track on the le

Just beyond Buduruwagala lies the beautiful **Handapanagala Tank**. There are gorgeous views from here, especially if you scramble up the rock at the far end of the path that runs along the south side of the tank, with the great wall of Uva mountains spread out on one side and the arid dry-zone plains towards Tissa on the other. Although the tank is worth visiting just for the views, there's the possible added bonus of spotting wild **elephants**, who sometimes come to the tank to drink (late afternoon is usually th best time). It might also be possible to arrange a **catamaran trip** on the lake with local boatmen (around Rs.2000).

Diyaluma Falls

Reached by any bus running between Wellawaya and Beragala/Haputale

Around 12km west of Wellawaya and 30km from Haputale, the **Diyaluma Falls** are the second-highest in Sri Lanka, tumbling for 220m over a sheer cliff face in a single slender cascade. A circuitous walk (allow 1hr each way) to the top of the falls starts from the main road a few hundred metres east, next to the km 207/5 marker. Follow the track he uphill for around twenty minutes until you reach a small rubber factory, where you'll need to stop and ask someone to point out the very faint and rough path up the steep and rocky hillside behind – if in doubt just keep on heading straight up. It's a steep and tiring hike (and you can't actually see the falls properly from the top), although you can cool off with a dip in one of the large natural rock pools near the summit of the falls.

The pleasant *Diyaluma Falls Inn* on the main road below the falls, has fine views of the cascades and is a pleasant spot for lunch or a drink.

ARRIVAL AND INFORMATION — WELLAWAYA AND AROUN

By bus The bus stand is in the middle of town. Wellawaya is a major transport hub between the south coast and hill country, with good services in all directions, although if travelling to Kandy or Nuwara Eliya you might prefer to take a bus to Ella and then catch the train from there. A lot of southbound services bypass Tissamaharama, calling at Pannegamuwa Junction, a short bus or tuktuk ride from Tissa itself. For Kataragama, change at Buttala.

Destinations Bandarawela (every 30min; 1hr 15mi Badulla (every 30min; 1hr 30min); Buttala (every 15m 40min); Ella (every 30min; 45min); Embilipitiya (4 daily; 3h Haputale (5 daily, or take one of the hourly buses to Berag and change there; 1hr); Kandy (2 daily; 6hr); Matara (eve 30min; 4hr); Monaragala (every 15min; 1hr 15min); Nuw Eliya (5 daily; 3hr 30min); Tissamaharama (hourly; 2hr).

Banks The Commercial, HNB and People's banks all ha ATMs which accept foreign cards.

ACCOMMODATION

Little Rose Inn 1km south of town on the Tissa Rd ⓣ077 657 3647, ⓦlittlerosewellawaya.com. The best of Wellawaya's scant accommodation options, this family-run guesthouse has clean, bright and spacious rooms in the modern garden annexe plus a few slightly older but well-k ones inside the house itself – smarter rooms come with a hot water and satelite TV. There's also bike rental, and owners can arrange local excursions. **Rs.2500**, a/c **Rs.450**

Ratnapura

Nestled among verdant hills at the southwestern corner of the hill country, **RATNAPUR** (literally "City of Gems") is famous for its **precious stones**, which have been mined here in extraordinary quantities since antiquity. Naturally, the town makes a big deal this, with plenty of touts offering trips to gem mines and stones for sale, though unle ou have a specialist interest in gemology, this alone isn't really a sufficient reason to isit the place. If you are interested in learning more, ask your guesthouse or touts in own, who may be able to arrange a visit to a working mine. *Ratna Gems Halt* (see page 72) run a convenient trip combining a visit to a gem mine, gem museum and Saviya Street (Rs.1000pp), and even run a five- and ten-day gem-cutting course if the subject eally grabs your imagination.

Ratnapura does have other attractions, however. The town makes a possible base for isits to **Sinharaja** and **Uda Walawe national parks**; trips to both involve a long (4hr-lus) return drive, making for a big day. Local guesthouses (including *Ratna Gems Halt*) an arrange trips: the going rate for a minivan or jeep is around $50–60 to either park. Ratnapura is also the starting point for an alternative ascent of **Adam's Peak**, though it's ignificantly longer and tougher than the route up from Dalhousie. The path starts from he village of **Palabaddale**, from where it's a climb of five to seven hours to the summit. Buses run to Palabaddale via Gilimale during the pilgrimage season; alternatively, ransport can be arranged through *Ratna Gems Halt* and *Deer Park Inn* (see page 272).

Ratnapura also has the distinction of being one of the **wettest places** in Sri Lanka, vith an annual rainfall sometimes exceeding four metres – and even when it's not aining, the climate is usually humid and sticky.

aviya Mawatha and around

. major regional commercial centre, Ratnapura is a busy and rather exhausting place, even efore you've dealt with the attentions of touts trying to flog you gems or get you on visits to ocal mines. The heart of the town's gem trade is **Saviya Mawatha** (also spelt Zavier, Zaviya nd Zavia), about 150m east of the clocktower, which presents an entertaining scene of

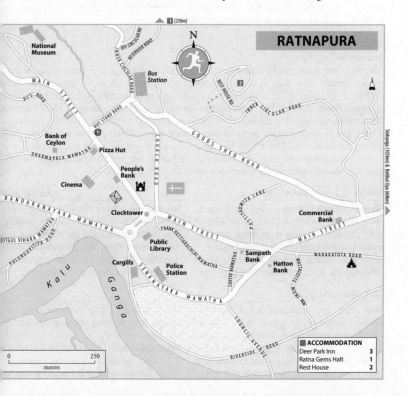

crowds of locals haggling over handfuls of uncut stones; the shops of a few small dealers line the street (the town's traditional jewellers' shops are mainly located at the clocktower end of Main St). Trading takes place on weekdays until around 3pm. You're likely to be offered stones to buy – it should go without saying that unless you're an expert, steer well clear.

Ratnapura Gem Bureau

Potgul Vihara Mw • Mon–Fri 9.30am–4.30pm • Rs.100

If you want a detailed look at the area's mineral riches, head out to the **Ratnapura Gem Bureau**, usually simply referred to as the "Gem Museum", a couple of kilometres west of town on Potgul Vihara Mawatha. Intended as an altruistic and educational venture (although they might make a gentle attempt to flog you a few stones), the museum's centrepiece is a colourful display of minerals and precious stones from around the world, including interesting Sri Lankan gems in both cut and uncut states. There are also displays of other handicrafts – stone carvings, metalwork and so on.

National Museum

Main St • Tues–Sat 9am–5pm • Rs.300, camera Rs.250

There's surprisingly little coverage of the town's gem-mining heritage at the lacklustre **National Museum**, off Main Street on the northwest side of the town centre, located in a fine old *walauwa* of 1814. Exhibits here run through the predictable gamut of Sri Lankan arts and crafts, the usual depressing collection of pickled and stuffed wildlife, plus assorted rocks, fossilized bones, the fossilized shells of snails on which prehistoric Ratnapura man presumably feasted, and a few lion and pig teeth (also fossilized). The surrounding grounds have been turned into the so-called **Paleobiodiversity Museum Park** – a rather fancy name for what is basically a few fibre-glass prehistoric hippos, elephants and so on, already looking decidedly mildewed.

Maha Saman Devale

Horana Rd • Free

The most interesting sight hereabouts is the impressively large and harmonious **Maha Saman Devale**, 3km west of town, the most important temple in the island dedicated to Saman (see page 253), who is said to reside on nearby Adam's Peak. There has been a temple here since the thirteenth century. It was rebuilt by the kings of Kandy during the seventeenth century, destroyed by the Portuguese, then rebuilt again during the Dutch era (a carving to the right of the entrance steps, showing a Portuguese invader killing a Sinhalese soldier, recalls European attacks against the town and temple).

A big **Esala Perahera** takes place here during July or August. Numerous local **buses** run past the entrance to the temple, or you can catch a tuktuk.

ARRIVAL AND DEPARTURE RATNAPUR

By bus Good roads head east and west from Ratnapura, served by regular buses. Heading north into the central hill country or south to the coast is significantly more time-consuming however, given the lack of good direct roads.

Destinations Akuressa (for Galle; 4 daily; 4hr 30min); Avissawella (for Hatton and Nuwara Eliya; every 10min;

1hr); Bandarawela (every 30min; 3hr 30min); Colom (every 30min; 3hr 30min); Deniyaya (for Sinharaja; daily; 2hr 30min); Embilipitiya (every 30min; 2hr 30mi Haputale (every 30min; 3hr); Kalawana (for Sinhara every 30min; 1hr); Kandy (hourly; 3hr 30min); Matara daily via Deniyaya, or change at Embilipitiya; 5hr).

ACCOMMODATION

Deer Park Inn Muwagama ☎045 223 1403, ⓦdeerparkratnapura.com; map p.271. Tranquil guesthouse in a large modern house south of the Kalu Ganga river (about 1km from the centre). There's a mix of simple but very neat and clean fan and a/c rooms (some with shared bathrooms), plus a small pool inserted

beneath the house, and the owners can arrange vario activities including cycling excursions and Adam's Pe trips. $30

Ratna Gems Halt 153/5 Outer Circular Rd ☎0 222 3745, ⓦratnapura-online.com; map p.2 Varied collection of simple but extremely good-va

GEMS OF SRI LANKA

Sri Lanka is one of the world's most important sources of precious stones, and its gems have long been famous – indeed one of the island's early names was **Ratnadipa**, "Island of Gems". According to legend, it was a Sri Lankan ruby which was given by King Solomon to the Queen of Sheba, while Marco Polo described a fabulous ruby – "about a palm in length and of the thickness of a man's arm" – set in the spire of the Ruvenveliseya dagoba at Anuradhapura. The island also provided the "Blue Belle" sapphire which now adorns the crown of the British queen, while in 2003 a 478-carat Sri Lankan sapphire – larger than a hen's egg – fetched $1.5m at auction.

Gems are actually found in many parts of Sri Lanka, but the **Ratnapura** district is the island's richest source. The origin of these gems is the geological rubble eroded from the central highlands, which is washed down from the hills along the valleys which crisscross the area – a gravelly mixture of eroded rock, mineral deposits, precious stones and muddy alluvial deposits known as *illam*. Gem mining is still a low-tech, labour-intensive affair. Pits are dug down into riverbeds and among paddy fields, and piles of *illam* are fished out, which are then washed and sieved by experts who separate the precious stones from the mud. The mining and sorting is traditionally carried out by the Sinhalese, though gem cutters and dealers tend to be Muslim.

The most valuable precious stones found in Sri Lanka are **corundums**, including sapphires and pink rubies. Other stones mined locally include garnets, cat's eyes, alexandrite, tourmalines, quartz, spinel and zircon. The greyish moonstone (a type of feldspar) is a particular Sri Lankan speciality, though these aren't mined in the Ratnapura area.

ooms, getting nicer (and more expensive) as you go up he building, from the rather poky, but also very cheap, round-floor offerings to the bright, modern and spacious ooms (with a/c and hot water) on the top floor. They also un a good local gem-mining tour (Rs.1000), plus other nteresting local excursions, and have a small Ayurveda entre attached. **Rs.1250**, a/c **Rs.3000**

Rest House Rest House Rd ☎045 222 2299; map p.271. Imposing old colonial rest house in a wonderful position on a hilltop above town and with fine views. Rooms, of various sizes and standards (all a/c), are clean and spacious, albeit pricey for what you get and with some furniture so dated it's almost retro. The in-house restaurant (mains from Rs.600) is the nicest in town. **Rs.6050**

Sinharaja and around

aily 6.30am–6pm • Rs.660; Rs.1000/group for an obligatory guide (unless you bring your own), who will lead you on walking tours (3hr)

The largest surviving tract of undisturbed lowland rainforest in Sri Lanka, **Sinharaja** is one of the island's outstanding natural wonders and a biodiverse treasure box of global significance (recognized by its listing as a UNESCO World Heritage Site in 1989). This is the archetypal rainforest as you've always imagined it: the air thick with humidity (approaching ninety percent in places) and alive with the incessant noise of birds, cicadas and other invisible creatures; the ground choked with a dense understorey of exotic ferns and snaking lianas wrapped around the base of towering tropical hardwoods, rising towards the forest canopy high overhead.

According to tradition, Sinharaja was formerly a royal reserve (as suggested by its name, meaning "Lion King"). The first attempts to conserve it were made as far back as 1840, when it became property of the British Crown. Logging began in 1971, until being banned in the face of national protests in 1977, when the area was declared a national reserve. Sinharaja is now safely protected under UNESCO auspices, using a system whereby inhabitants of the twenty-odd villages which surround the reserve have the right to limited use of the forest's resources, including tapping kitul palms for jaggery and collecting rattan for building.

Sinharaja stretches for almost 30km across the wet zone at the southern edges of the hill country, enveloping a series of switchback hills and valleys ranging in altitude from just 300m up to 1170m. To the north and south, the reserve is bounded by two sizeable rivers, the Kalu Ganga and the Gin Ganga, which cut picturesque, waterfall-studded courses through the trees.

INFORMATION SINHARAJA AND AROUND

Visiting the reserve The closest starting points for visits to Sinharaja are Deniyaya, on the eastern side of the reserve, and Kudawa, on its northern edge. It's also possible to arrange visits from guesthouses in Ratnapura or with a couple of tour operators in Unawatuna, though it would be a long day by the time you've driven to and from the reserve.

Entry points There are two entrances to the reserve. The most popular approach is via the northern entrance at Kudawa. The less frequently used eastern entrance is at Mederipitiya, about 11km east of Deniyaya; the rainforest here is denser and more dramatic than on the Kudawa side, though it makes bird- and wildlife-spotting correspondingly more difficult. The road from Deniyaya ends just short of the reserve, from where it's a pleasant

1.5km walk through tea plantations. The path isn't signposted (go right at the fork by the gravestones near the beginning).

Walking There are no driveable roads in the reserve, so you have to walk (which is, indeed, one of the pleasures of a visit). Waterproofs are advisable: Sinharaja receives up to 5m of rain annually. Leeches are abundant after rain.

Guides What you get out of a visit to Sinharaja relies on having a good guide – the rainforest is dense and difficult to decipher. Many of the reserve's guides speak very little English, although some may be able to turn up some interesting birdlife even so. A fail-safe option is to sign up for a tour with Bandula or Palitha Ratnayake, based at the *Sinharaja Rest* in Deniyaya (see page 275).

Kudawa

The village of **KUDAWA** is the most popular base for visiting Sinharaja. There's a better range of accommodation in the area on this side of the reserve, including a couple of top-end options, but it's more difficult to reach by public transport, so is likely to be of interest mainly to those with their own vehicle.

Note that Kudawa and the area immediately around the reserve is one of the few places in Sri Lanka which doesn't have **mobile phone** coverage.

ARRIVAL AND DEPARTURE KUDAWA

By car It's a slow and bumpy drive to Sinharaja from Ratnapura. With your own vehicle it's likely to take the best part of 2hr to reach Kudawa, or slightly over an hour to reach Kalawana and Koswatte.

By bus There are frequent buses from Ratnapura to Kalawana (15km north of Kudawa), from where there are infrequent (around four daily) buses to Kudawa itself.

ACCOMMODATION

There's not much choice of accommodation in Sinharaja, and prices are high. Accommodation on the Kudawa side of the reserve can be found in **Kudawa** itself and in the nearby villages of **Weddagala**, about 6km from

the reserve entrance, and **Koswatta**, a further 10km back up the road, and about 2km from the town of Kalawana.

SINHARAJA'S WILDLIFE

A staggering 830 of Sri Lanka's endemic species of flora and fauna are found in Sinharaja, including myriad birds, reptiles and insects, while no less than sixty percent of the reserve's trees are endemic too. The reserve's most common **mammal** is the purple-faced langur monkey, while you might also encounter three species of squirrel – the dusky-striped jungle squirrel, flame-striped jungle squirrel and western giant squirrel – along with mongooses. Less common, and very rarely sighted, are leopards, rusty spotted cats, fishing cats and civets. There's also a rich **reptile** population, including 21 of Sri Lanka's 45 endemic species, among them rare snakes and frogs. Many of the reserve's bountiful population of **insects** are yet to be classified, although you're likely to see various colourful spiders and enormous butterflies, while giant millipedes are also common.

Sinharaja has one of Sri Lanka's richest **bird** populations: 21 of the country's 26 endemic species have been recorded here (although some can only be seen in the reserve's difficult-to-reach eastern fringes). The density of the forest, and the fact that its birds largely inhabit the topmost part of the canopy, means that actually seeing them can be tricky, especially if entering via the Mederipitiya entrance, where the forest is particularly thick – as ever, a good guide (see below) is of the essence.

KALAWANA

Lakmini Luxury Lodge Just south of the side road to the Boulder Garden Resort ☏ 045 225 6110. Attractive little six-room family guesthouse in a trim modern house surrounded by lush forest. Rooms are simple but very comfortable, with thick mattresses, and there's even a small pool. Good value. **$40**

KOSWATTA

Boulder Garden Koswatta ☏ 045 225 5812, ⌨ bouldergarden.com. Small eco-resort in a captivating natural setting some 16km from Sinharaja (a 45min drive), nestled between huge boulders and patches of rainforest. It's a lovely concept, if you don't mind the rather sombre expanses of slate-grey stone which give the rooms a slightly coal mine-like ambience. Facilities include a striking open-air restaurant underneath a huge rock overhang and a (very shallow) swimming pool. B&B **$275**

Ingraj Rest Koswatta ☏ 045 225 5201. Quiet – verging on moribund – guesthouse, with a selection of modern rooms of various sizes and standards (including a couple with a/c for a hefty supplement). Uninspiring, but easily the cheapest place in the area. **Rs.2000**, a/c **Rs.4000**

KUDAWA

Blue Magpie Lodge Kudawa ☏ 045 492 8284, ⌨ bluemagpie.lk. In a perfect location close to the ticket office in Kudawa, with nicely furnished modern rooms grouped around a patch of lawn and a nice natural swimming area in the river below. Good value by Sinharaja standards. **$60**

Forest View (Martin Wijesinghe's Guest House) Kudawa ☏ 045 568 1864 or ☏ 045 791 3323. Long-established guesthouse run by a knowledgeable former Sinharaja ranger and on the edge of the reserve; staying here is the closest you can get to spending a night in the forest itself, and the after-dark cacophony of cicadas and other nocturnal creatures is extraordinary. Accommodation is in a handful of very basic but clean rooms, with simple meals (bring your own booze). It's around 3km by road from the ticket office – walkable in 15–20min via a tricky-to-find off-road shortcut, or arrange a jeep (around 20min drive, or longer during rainy months; Rs.3500 return). A memorable experience, although very expensive given the basic accommodation on offer, especially if you pay for a jeep to get there. Half board **Rs.8100**, full board **Rs.9600**

WEDDAGALA

Rock View Motel Rakwana Rd, Weddagala, 8km from Sinharaja (signed 2km off road on left, 6km before you reach Sinharaja, past Rainforest Edge) ☏ 077 771 4024. Pleasant but overpriced hotel with attractively furnished, high-ceilinged modern a/c rooms with hot water and private balconies offering fine views over the wooded hills opposite. Note that there's a reception hall downstairs, however, so it can be noisy if there's a function in progress. B&B **Rs.8000**

Deniyaya

The small town of **DENIYAYA** offers an alternative base for visiting Sinharaja if you haven't got your own vehicle; it can be reached either from Galle or Matara on the south coast or from Ratnapura to the north (although bus services are surprisingly skimpy).

ARRIVAL AND DEPARTURE   DENIYAYA

By bus The bus station is right in the middle of town. Moving on from Deniyaya, there are irregular direct buses to Matara and Galle (roughly every 2hr). Otherwise change at Akuressa (every 30min; 1hr 30min), from where there are frequent onward connections to both these places. Transport northwards is much more infrequent, with about four buses to Pelmadulla and Ratnapura daily.

ACCOMMODATION

Deniyaya Guesthouse Ihalagama Rd ☏ 071 353 0895, ⌨ facebook.com/deniyaya.guesthouse. Super-cheap, great-value lodgings in a lovely little family guesthouse close to the town centre and bus stop, with cheerily painted rooms and good rice-and-curry spreads. **Rs.2000**

Natural Mystic Sanctuary Naindawa Estate, Batandura Road, ☏ 078 882 2328, ⌨ naturalmysticsanctuary.com. A 15min walk from the nearest driveable road (unless you have 4WD or a motorbike), this is a real rural escape, deep in the heart of nature on an old tea estate currently being restored to its former forested splendour. Accommodation is in two spacious guest rooms and a pair of pretty mud huts, with great organic food straight from the garden. B&B **$51**

Rain Forest View Villas Mederiditiya ☏ 041 491 8651 or ☏ 071 801 0700, ⌨ rainforestviewvillas.com. Just 5min walk from the Mederipitiya entrance to Sinharaja (45min by tuktuk from Deniyaya), this is a good place to soak up the forest atmosphere, with beds in a handful of rustic but well-made wooden cabanas and good home cooking. B&B **$51**

Sinharaja Rest 500m north of the bus station ☏ 041 227 3368. Six simple but comfortable rooms, plus organic food. It's owned and managed by local guides Bandula and Palitha Ratnayake, who run day-trips to

3

Sinharaja for Rs.6000/person (including entrance fees), entering the reserve through Mederipitiya and walking 12–14km. Shorter trips can also be arranged, as can longer excursions, such as the seven-hour hike over to Kudawa or the two-day (27km) trek across the entire reserve to Lion Rock. B&B Rs.4000

Uda Walawe National Park and around

Entrance on the Embilipitiya–Tanamal road at km-post 7 • $15 per person, plus the usual additional charges and taxes (see page 50)

Sprawling across the lowlands due south of the towering cliff faces of Horton Plains, **Uda Walawe** has developed into one of Sri Lanka's most popular national parks mainly thanks to its large and easily spotted population of elephants – it's the best place on the island to see pachyderms in the wild, although in other respects it doesn't have the range of fauna and habitats of Yala or Bundala. The park is beautifully situated just south of the hill country, whose grand escarpment provides a memorable backdrop, while at its centre lies the **Uda Walawe Reservoir**, whose catchment area it was originally established to protect. Most of Uda Walawe lies within the dry zone, and its terrain is flat and denuded, with extensive areas of grassland and low scrub (the result of earlier slash-and-burn farming) dotted with the skeletal outlines of expired trees, scratched to death by the resident elephants. The actual landscape of the park is rather monotonous during dry periods, although the lack of forest cover makes it easier to spot wildlife than in any other Sri Lankan park, and the whole place transforms magically after rain, when temporary lagoons form around the reservoir, drowning trees and turning the floodplains an intense, fecund green.

The principal attraction is, of course, **elephants**, of which there are usually around six hundred in the park; animals are free to migrate along an elephant corridor between here and Lunugamvehera National Park, though most stay here. There are also hundreds of **buffaloes**, plus macaque and langur monkeys, spotted and sambar deer and crocodiles, while other rarely sighted residents include leopards, giant flying squirrels, jungle cats, sloth bears and porcupines. Uda Walawe is also good for **birds**, including a number of endemics and some birds of prey, while the reservoir also attracts a wide range of aquatic birds including the unmistakable lesser adjutant, Sri Lanka's largest – and ugliest – bird, standing at well over a metre tall.

Elephant Transit Home

Daily feeding sessions 9am, noon, 3pm and 6pm • Rs.500

About 5km west of the park entrance on the main road is the engaging **Elephant Transit Home** – usually referred to as the "Elephant Orphanage". Founded in 1995, the orphanage is home to around 25 baby elephants rescued from the wild after the loss of their parents. As at the better-known orphanage at Pinnewala, elephants here are bottlefed milk until the age of 3 and a half, after which they're given a diet of grass. At the age of 5, most are released into the national park (around 110 so far). You can't get quite as close to the elephants as at Pinnewala; outside feeding times the elephants are allowed to wander, so there's usually nothing to see.

ARRIVAL AND DEPARTURE | UDA WALAWE NATIONAL PARK AND AROUND

By tour Uda Walawe's central location makes it accessible from a number of different places, and you can arrange tours here from as far afield as Ratnapura, Hambantota, Tissa and even Unawatuna (see the relevant town accounts for more details), although all these involve long drives to reach the park. The closest starting point is Embilipitiya 20km distant.

By bus and jeep Half-hourly buses from Embilipitiya to Tamanalwila go right past the entrance, where you can hire a jeep (seating 6–8) for around Rs.4000 for a few hours' drive.

ACCOMMODATION

There's plenty of accommodation on (or slightly off) the main road along the south of the park, plus further places in nearby Embilipitiya. If you want to stay inside the park itself, note that upmarket **tented safaris** are run by Kul Safaris, Mahoora and Big Game Camps and Lodges (see p.51).

Grand Udawalawe Safari Resort Thanamalwila Rd (1.5km east of Thimbolketiya junction) ☎047 223 2000, ⦵udawalawesafari.com. This impressive modern four-star is the area's fanciest address, occupying an eye-catching orange building set around a narrow garden inside a lush walled compound. Rooms are a tad bare but come with all mod cons, while facilities include a spa, gym, and a large kidney-shaped pool (plus kids' pool). B&B $140

Kalu's Hideaway Walawegama Rd, 15min from the park entrance ☎077 805 0600, ⦵kalushideaway.com. Chic boutique hotel owned by World Cup-winning former cricketer Romesh Kaluwitharana, with lots of cricketing memorabilia on display and fourteen smooth modern a/c rooms either in the main building or in an incongruous-looking three-storey block in the garden, plus two-room chalet. Facilities include a fine decked restaurant, and a small pool plus spa in the lovely grounds. B&B $110

Silent Bungalow Behind the army camp, 1.3km south of the main road (turn off 1km past the Grand Uda Walawe Safari Resort, and around 10km from the park entrance) ☎071 271 8941. Welcoming and reliable budget option, set in gorgeously lush gardens, with five simple but spacious and spotless rooms, plus competitively priced safaris and good food. Rs.3000

Walawa Cottage Behind the army camp, 1.6km south of the main road (near Silent Bungalow) ☎071 213 5152, ⦵walawacottage.com. Another good budget option, set in a peaceful family villa with neat, clean and very well-kept rooms at a bargain price. Rs.3000

Superson Family Guest House Walawegama Rd ☎047 347 5172, ✉supersonfg@gmail.com. One of the few reasonably priced options close to the park – the house looks a bit of a mess and rooms are fairly basic, but the veranda and garden is pleasant, and the home-cooking can't be faulted. Rs.2500

Embilipitiya

Halfway between Ratnapura and the coast, the medium-sized town of **EMBILIPITIYA** is the closest base for visits to Uda Walawe, 20km distant. There's not much to Embilipitiya itself apart from the scenic Chandrika Wewa which stretches south of town – actually a modern man-made reservoir rather than a natural lake.

ARRIVAL AND DEPARTURE   EMBILIPITIYA

By bus Buses arrive at the station about 100m south of the clocktower at the centre of town. If you're heading towards the southeastern hill country, catch a bus to Tamanalwila, from where you can pick up a bus to Wellawaya, which has frequent connections with Ella, Haputale, Bandarawela and Badulla. To reach Deniyaya (for Sinharaja) you'll need to catch one of the early-morning buses from Embilipitiya

to Suriyakanda (a two-hour journey; check latest times the night before), from where infrequent buses head south. For Tissa, change at Hambantota.

Destinations Hambantota (every 15min; 1hr 30min); Matara (every 30min; 2hr 30min); Ratnapura (every 30min; 2hr 30min); Tamanalwila (every 30min; 1hr); Tangalla (every 30min; 1hr 30min).

ACCOMMODATION AND EATING

You'll most likely **eat** where you're staying, unless you fancy venturing out to the *Centauria Lake Resort*. All the place listed can also arrange half-day trips to Uda Walawe for around Rs.4500.

Centauria Lake Resort South of town (signposted off the west side of the main road slightly south of Sarathchandra Rest, then 1.5km down this road) ☎047 223 0514, ⦵centauriahotel.com/lake. Pleasant resort hotel, surprisingly well-appointed for dusty little Embilipitiya. Accommodation is in a comfortable scatter of modern a/c rooms and slightly pricier villas, most with fine views of adjacent Chandrika Wewa, and there's also a decent restaurant, pool and Ayurveda centre. $100

Frozen Villa Ratnapura Rd, Udagama ☎077 713 7041, ⦵frozen.lk. On the north side of town, this recently opened guesthouse is a cut above most other places in Embilitpitiya, with immaculate bright white rooms (all

with a/c and satelite TV), plus decent food, a funky little pool and a small gym – but, sadly, no reindeer. $37

Pavana Resort 250m down the side road running east off the main road just south of Sarathchandra Rest ☎077 351 6838, ⦵pavanaresort.lk. A more modern alternative to the nearby *Sarathchandra Rest*, with twelve neat modern rooms (pricier ones with a/c and hot water) and a teensy pool. Free use of bikes, but no meals except breakfast. Rs.4000, a/c Rs.5000

Sarathchandra Rest On the main road 100m south of the bus station ☎047 223 0044. Well-run hotel with comfortable modern a/c rooms, all spacious and attractively furnished, plus fancier new "deluxe" rooms in the block opposite. There's also a good little restaurant downstairs, plus a rather rowdy local bar. Rs.3500, a/c Rs.7000

3

The Cultural Triangle

POLONNARUWA

The Cultural Triangle

North of Kandy, the tangled green hills of the central highlands tumble down into the plains of the dry zone, a hot and denuded region of dense jungle and thorny scrub interspersed with isolated mountainous outcrops towering dramatically over the surrounding flatlands. Despite the unpromising natural environment, these northern plains served as the crucible of the island's earliest civilizations, spawning the great kingdoms of Anuradhapura and Polonnaruwa along with vast irrigation works which transformed the face of the land. Physical evidence of this history survives in the region's extraordinary surfeit of ancient monuments (including five of the island's eight World Heritage Sites), now collectively protected as the so-called "Cultural Triangle" and still serving as a potent reminder of the golden age of Sinhalese art and architecture.

The largest of the Triangle's myriad attractions is the huge ruined city of **Anuradhapura**, capital of the island from the third century BC to 993 AD and one of medieval Asia's great metropolises, dotted with vast monasteries, elaborate palaces, enormous tanks and a trio of monumental dagobas, surpassed in scale in the ancient world only by the Egyptian pyramids. The remains of **Polonnaruwa**, the island's second capital, are more compact but equally absorbing, while few visitors miss the chance to climb the spectacular rock citadel of **Sigiriya**, perhaps Sri Lanka's single most extraordinary sight. Other leading attractions include the marvellous cave temples of **Dambulla**, a magical treasure box of Buddhist sculpture and painting, and the religious centre of **Mihintale**, scene of the introduction of Buddhism to the island.

Major attractions aside, the Cultural Triangle is peppered with other intriguing but relatively little-visited ancient monuments, including the abandoned cities of **Yapahuwa** and **Panduwas Nuwara**; the great Buddha statues of **Aukana** and **Sasseruwa**; the absorbing temples of **Aluvihara** and **Ridi Vihara**; and the haunting forest monasteries of **Arankele** and **Ritigala**. And there is no shortage of natural attractions, either, at the national parks of **Minneriya**, **Kaudulla** and **Wasgomuwa**.

GETTING AROUND   THE CULTURAL TRIANGLE

Planning an itinerary The major Cultural Triangle sites are all relatively close to one another, and there are all sorts of different permutations when it comes to planning an itinerary or choosing where to stay. One possibility is to base yourself in or around Dambulla, Sigiriya or Habarana, from where it's possible to visit all the other major sights on day-trips, assuming you have your own transport.

Public transport Regular buses connect Kandy, Dambulla, Sigiriya, Anuradhapura and Polonnaruwa, while occasional trains run from Colombo, via Kurunegala, to both Anuradhapura and Polonnaruwa. All the major monuments can be easily reached by public transport; smaller sites are trickier to access without your own car, although local buses will get you to most of them in the end if you don't mind sometimes time-consuming and laborious journeys.

Kurunegala

The biggest town between Colombo and Anuradhapura, busy **KURUNEGALA** sits athwart a major junction on the roads between Colombo, Dambulla, Anuradhapura and Kandy, so you may well change buses here – although there's no huge reason to stay. The town enjoyed a brief moment of pre-eminence in Sri Lankan affairs during the late thirteenth and early fourteenth centuries when it served as the capital of

THE WATER GARDENS, SIGIRIYA

Highlights

❶ Rock temples, Dambulla An extraordinary Aladdin's cave of Buddhist art, packed with hundreds of statues and decorated with the finest murals in the country. See page 292

❷ Sigiriya The spectacular rock outcrop of Sigiriya was the site of Sri Lanka's most remarkable royal capital and palace, complete with water gardens, paintings of celestial nymphs and 1300-year-old graffiti. See page 300

❸ "The Gathering", Minneriya National Park Asia's largest gathering of wild elephants, as three-hundred-plus pachyderms congregate around the retreating waters of Minneriya Tank during the northern dry season. See page 310

❹ Polonnaruwa Polonnaruwa is home to some of Sri Lanka's finest ancient stupas and shrines, dating back to its brief but brilliant period as the island's capital. See page 311

❺ Anuradhapura The remains of the vast ancient city of Anuradhapura are one of the island's most compelling historical sites, as well as a major place of Buddhist pilgrimage. See page 326

❻ Mihintale Revered as the place where Buddhism was introduced to the island, Mihintale boasts an interesting collection of religious monuments scattered across a beautiful hilltop location. See page 339

HIGHLIGHTS ARE MARKED ON THE MAP ON PAGE 282

Sinhalese kings Bhuvanekabahu II (ruled 1293–1302) and Parakramabahu IV (r. 1302–26), though hardly anything remains from this period.

On the northern side of the centre, attractive lakeside walkways ring the breezy **Kurunegala Tank**, with views of the huge bare **rock outcrops** that surround the town and lend the entire place a strangely lunar air. The inevitable legend professes that these are the petrified bodies of a strange menagerie of giant animals – including an eel, tortoise and elephant – who were threatening to drink the lake dry, only to be turned to stone by a demoness who inhabited the waters.

If you've an hour or so to kill, it's worth heading up to the enormous seated Buddha statue atop **Etagala** (Elephant Rock), signed "Samadhi Buddha Statue Athugala 1.9km" along a twisting road behind the People's Bank. The **statue** itself was finished in 2003

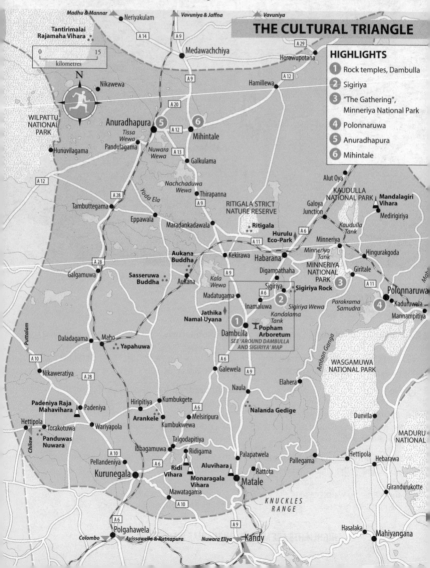

THE CULTURAL TRIANGLE

HIGHLIGHTS

1. Rock temples, Dambulla
2. Sigiriya
3. "The Gathering", Minneriya National Park
4. Polonnaruwa
5. Anuradhapura
6. Mihintale

TRIANGULAR VISION

The plains of northern Sri Lanka have been known for millennia as **Rajarata**, "The King's Land", although nowadays the traditional name has largely lapsed and the region is generally referred to as the **Cultural Triangle** (its monuments run under the auspices of the government's Central Cultural Fund, ⓦ ccf.gov.lk). The origins of the name – perhaps inspired by the "golden triangles" of Thailand and India – date back to the 1970s when the Sri Lankan government and UNESCO first began restoring the region's great monuments and promoting them to the international tourist market. The three points of this imaginary triangle lie at the great Sinhalese capitals of Kandy in the south, Anuradhapura in the north and Polonnaruwa in the east, although in fact, this tourist-oriented invention presents a rather warped sense of the region's past, given that the history of Kandy is quite different and separate – both chronologically and geographically – from that of the earlier capitals.

and stands 27m high, although it's the superb views over town and surrounding countryside that really impress.

ARRIVAL AND DEPARTURE   KURUNEGALA

By bus Buses arrive at the overcrowded station bang in the town centre.
Destinations Anuradhapura (every 20min; 3hr); Colombo (every 20min; 2hr); Dambulla (every 15min; 2hr); Kandy (every 15min; 1hr); Negombo (every 30min; 1hr 30min).

By train The train station is just over 1km southeast of the bus station on Kandy Rd.
Destinations Anuradhapura (8 daily; 2–3hr); Colombo (11–14 daily; 2hr); Maho (for Yapahuwa; hourly; 40min–1hr 40min).

4

ACCOMMODATION

Most of Kurunegala's small selection of accommodation is clustered around **Kurunegala Tank**, north of the town centre, although most places are more used to local wedding parties than to foreign tourists. Another possibility is the upmarket *Brook Boutique Hotel & Spa* (see page 297), midway between Kurunegala and Dambulla.

IN TOWN

Hotel Kamrel 604 Malkaduwawa ☎037 494 7504, ⓦ hotelkamrel.com; map p.284. Clean, modern hotel with thirty comfortable and well-equipped rooms, all with a/c, flatscreen satellite TV and tea- and coffee-making facilities. There's also an in-house restaurant and bar. B&B $50

Richards Welangola Rd ☎037 222 5087, ⓔ richardsguesthousekurunegala@gmail.com; map p.284. This friendly guesthouse is the most comfortable place to stay in Kurunegala. The en-suite rooms are small and clean, with mosquito nets and free toiletries, and

there's a spacious communal lounge area. B&B: $20, a/c $30

Seasons 7 North Lake Rd ☎037 222 3452, ⓔ diyadahara@sltnet.lk; map p.284. In a fancy new building directly opposite the *Diya Dihara* restaurant, this hotel currently has six spacious, modern rooms with a/c, TV, coffee machine and fridge, as well as two function halls. More rooms, as well as a pool and rooftop lounge, are currently under construction. B&B $60

AROUND KURUNEGALA

Littlemore Estate Bungalow 8km northwest of Kurunegala (3km west off the A10 highway from Pellandeniya village) ☎076 696 9383, ⓦ facebook. com/littlemoreestate; map p.284. Three attractive rooms done up in cool colonial style, set inside a gracious old verandaed bungalow nestled in the middle of a working coconut plantation, with a large pool. B&B $120

EATING

There are few good places to eat in Kurunegala, and not many places to get a drink, either – for a sundowner, the lake-side terrace of the *Diya Dihara* is the best option.

Diya Dahara 7 North Lake Rd ☎037 526 6662; map p.284. Kurunegala's nicest place to eat, occupying a garden terrace overlooking the lake and serving up a competently prepared range of Sri Lankan, Chinese and Continental dishes. Often closes for functions, however,

and some days there's a buffet only. Mains around Rs.850. Daily 6am–11pm.

In & Out Puttalam Rd; map p.284. Smart, modern bakery near the bus station dishing up a wide selection of cakes and short eats along with a few simple hot meals (Rs.300–400), served in the small dining area at the back. Daily 6am–10pm.

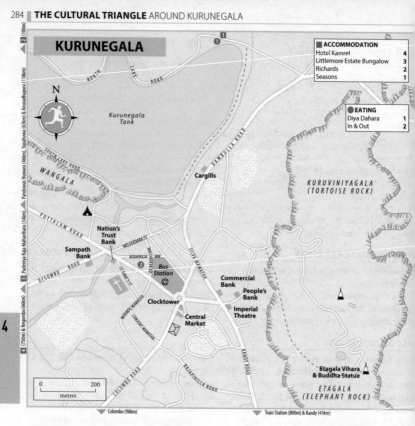

Around Kurunegala

The little-visited area north of Kurunegala is home to an intriguing range of attractions: the abandoned cities of **Yapahuwa** and **Panduwas Nuwara**; the absorbing forest monastery of **Arankele**; the beautiful Kandyan-era temples at **Padeniya** and **Ridi Vihara**; and a striking Buddha statue at the **Monaragala Vihara** near Ridigama. If you have your own transport, all of these sites could be visited in a leisurely day's excursion, either as a round trip from Kurunegala or en route to Anuradhapura. (If you don't want to pay for a car all the way to Anuradhapura, ask to be dropped at Daladagama, from where it's easy to pick up a bus.)

Ridi Vihara

2km outside Ridigama village • No set hours • Donation • Take a bus from Kurunegala to Ridigama (hourly; 45min) then either walk or take a tuktuk; by car, the temple is easily reached from either the Kurunegala–Dambulla highway (turn off at Talgodapitiya) or the Kandy–Dambulla highway (turn off at Palapatwela)

Tucked away in beautiful rolling countryside around 20km northeast of Kurunegala, the cave temple of **Ridi Vihara** is well worth hunting out if you have your own transport (although difficult to reach if you don't). According to legend, Ridi Vihara, or "Silver Temple", was built by the legendary King Dutugemunu (see page 330). Dutugemunu lacked the money to complete the great Ruwanwelisaya dagoba at Anuradhapura until the discovery of a rich vein of silver ore at Ridi Vihara allowed the king to finish his masterpiece – he expressed his gratitude by creating a temple at the location of the silver lode.

Varakha Valandu Vihara

When you enter the complex, bear left in front of a cluster of modern monastery buildings and a fine old bo tree to reach the diminutive **Varakha Valandu Vihara** ("Jackfruit Temple"), a pretty little structure built up against a small rock outcrop. Originally constructed as a Hindu temple, the building was converted into a Buddhist shrine around the eleventh century but still looks decidedly South Indian in style, with heavy rectangular columns overhung by a very solid-looking stone roof.

The main temple

Beyond the Varakha Valandu Vihara lies the main temple, built beneath a huge rock outcrop said to resemble the shape of a cobra's hood. The temple is in two parts. The older **Pahala Vihara** (Lower Temple) is built into a cave beneath the rock. An exquisite ivory carving of five ladies stands next to the entrance door, while inside a series of huge statues pose solemnly in the semi-darkness. A huge sleeping Buddha occupies the left-hand side of the cave, in front of which is a platform inset with blue-and-white Flemish tiles, donated (it's said) by a Dutch ambassador to the Kandyan court and showing pictures of village life in the Netherlands along with a few biblical scenes – a sneaky bit of Christian proselytizing in this venerable Buddhist shrine. The weather-beaten statues at the far end of the temple include one eroded image said to be of Dutugemunu himself.

To the right of the Pahala Vihara, steps lead up to the eighteenth-century Upper Temple, or **Uda Vihara** – the work of Kandyan king Kirti Sri Rajasinha (see page 212). The main chamber has an impressive seated Buddha set against a densely peopled background (the black figures are Vishnus), while the entrance steps outside boast a fine moonstone flanked by elephant-shaped balustrades. Note, too, the door to the small shrine behind, topped with an unusual painting of nine women arranged in the shape of an elephant. Outside, a dagoba sits almost completely covered under another part of the overhanging rock.

Back at the entrance to the monastery, more than a hundred steps, some cut into bare rock, lead up to a small restored **dagoba**, from which there are fine views across the surrounding countryside.

Monaragala Vihara

Ambadagalla village, about 5km south of Ridigama (and 4km south of Ridi Vihara) down the Keppetigalla Rd • No set hours • Donation • ⊕ samadhibuddhastatue.lk

Worth a visit if you're in the Ridigama area is the **Monaragala Vihara**, home to a gigantic **Samadhi Buddha** statue, begun in 2003 in response to the destruction of the famous Bamiyan Buddhas in Afghanistan and finished in 2014. Carved out of a huge rock outcrop and standing (or, rather, sitting) around 22m tall, the image is variously claimed to be the world's largest Buddha statue in the *samadhi* (meditation) pose and also the largest rock-carved Buddha in Sri Lanka, outstripping even the famed statues at Polonnaruwa's Gal Vihara.

Arankele

Between Hiripitiya and Kumbukwewa, 2km down the small back road connecting the two • Daily 6am–6pm • Free • Driving (there's no public transport to Arankele), the back road to the site is unsurfaced on the Hiripitiya side, although passable in a car, and signage is minimal, so you may have to ask for directions; approaching from Kurunegala and Kumbukwewa, the road passes the rear entrance to the site (where the modern monastery is) first, before reaching the main entrance around 1km further down the road

Hidden away on a jungle-covered hillside some 25km north of Kurunegala, the ruined forest hermitage of **Arankele** is one of the Cultural Triangle's least-visited but most intriguing sites. Arankele was occupied as far back as the third century BC, although most of what you see today dates from the sixth to eighth centuries AD, while extensive parts of the site have yet to be excavated. A community of *pamsukulika* monks (see page 308) who have devoted themselves to a reclusive, meditative life still live at the monastery at the back of the site.

The monastery ruins

Just before you reach the entrance to the site, note the fine **Jantaghara** (literally "hot water bath" – perhaps some kind of monastic hospital similar to the one in Mihintale), which has a fine old stone bathing tank enclosed in stout rectangular walls.

The main monastery

Immediately beyond the entrance lie the extensive ruins of the **main monastery**, distinguished by their fine craftsmanship and the staggeringly large chunks of stone used in their construction – the fact that early Sinhalese engineers and craftsmen were able to transport and work such huge rocks slightly beggars belief. Major structures here include the impressive chapter house, surrounded by a large moat to help cool the air, and, beside it, a large step-sided pond. Nearby you'll find the monastery's main reception hall, floored with just four enormous slabs of granite; an elaborate stone toilet; and, next to it, a small meditation walkway, which was originally roofed – the only one of its kind in Sri Lanka. The roof is long gone, although the footings that supported the columns which formerly held it up can still be seen.

Meditation walkway

Beyond the main monastery begins Arankele's remarkable main **meditation walkway**: a long, perfectly straight, stone walkway, punctuated by small flights of steps, its geometrical neatness making a strange contrast with the wild tropical forest through which it runs. At the time of research, small lamp posts were being inserted along the path, suggesting that night walks may be possible in the future. After some 250m you reach a miniature "roundabout" on the path, popularly believed to have been built to allow meditating monks to avoid walking into one another, although it more likely served as a rest area, covered with a (long since vanished) roof. Close by stand the remains of the principal monk's residence, with the base of a large hall, a stone toilet and (below) a jumble of pillars, partly collapsed, which would have supported an open-air meditation platform.

The meditation walkway continues a further 250m or so, ending at a small **cave-shrine** built beneath a rock outcrop. This is the oldest part of the ruins, dating back to the third century BC – the original drip-ledge and the holes where a projecting canopy was once fixed can still be seen. Inside, a small Buddha shrine sits flanked by two tiny meditation cells.

Beyond here the path continues to the **modern monastery**, with a long covered walkway leading to the rear entrance to the site.

Padeniya Raja Mahavihara

Catch any bus travelling from Kurunegala to either Anuradhapura or Puttalam and get off in Padeniya – although the temple's only really worth visiting if you've got your own transport

Some 25km northwest of Kurunegala, right in the centre of the village of **PADENIYA**, the **Padeniya Raja Mahavihara** is one of Sri Lanka's most attractive Kandyan-era temples, and well worth a halt. The unusual **main shrine** is set on a small rock outcrop and enclosed by fine walls, topped with cute lion statues. Inside, the fine old wooden roof is supported by around thirty beautifully carved wooden **pillars** showing various figures including a double-headed swan, a lion, an elephant, a man smoking a pipe, a Kandyan drummer and a dancing girl.

Next to the shrine sits a beautiful pond and a fine old **bo tree** growing out of an imposing three-tiered platform – the roots of the tree have worked their way down through the bricks, with marvellously photogenic results.

Panduwas Nuwara

Daily 24hr • Free • Buses run approximately every hour from Kurunegala to Chilaw, passing through Panduwas Nuwara village, from where it's a 1km walk to the site

Buried away in little-visited countryside around 35km from Kurunegala, midway to Chilaw, are the ruins of the ancient city of **Panduwas Nuwara**. The city is popularly believed to date back to the very earliest days of Sinhalese civilization, taking its name – "Town of Panduwas" – from the legendary Panduvasudeva (see page 403), and said to be the location of the mythical Ektem Maligaya (see page 288), although as with much early Sinhalese history the line between fact and fiction is somewhat blurred, if not totally smudged.

Most of the surviving ruins date from the reign of **Parakramabahu I** (see page 314), the royal adventurer who established his first capital here before eventually seizing Polonnaruwa. The city that Parakramabahu created at Panduwas Nuwara is often seen as a trial run for his spectacular achievements at Polonnaruwa, and although the individual remains are relatively low-key in comparison, the overall scale of the place is undeniably impressive, and exudes an Ozymandias-like aura of vanished splendour.

The citadel

The ruined city sprawls over an area of several square kilometres. At its centre lies the **citadel**, surrounded by sturdy walls, protected by a (now dried-up) moat and pierced by just a single, east-facing entrance. Inside the citadel, facing the entrance, the main ruin is the two-tiered **royal palace**, reminiscent in layout of Parakramabahu's royal palace at Polonnaruwa – not much of it survives, although you can still see the footings for pillars which would have supported the long-since-vanished wooden palace building. At the top of the steps on the left a table inscription records a visit by the bumptious Nissankamalla (see page 317), while at the rear right-hand side of the same terrace are the remains of an ingenious medieval latrine with a water channel leading into a well-like cesspit.

The slight remains of a few further buildings around the palace have been neatly restored, but the rest of the citadel remains unexcavated, with the mounds of numerous old buildings still buried under established woodland.

The monasteries

South of the citadel are the extensive remains of a trio of **monasteries**. The first is some 500m south, with a ruined brick dagoba, bo tree enclosure (*bodhigara*) and the ruins of a pillared image house (only the Buddha's feet survive). Immediately south lies a second monastery, with a Tamil pillar inscription at its entrance, plus two more ruined dagobas and further monastic buildings.

Some 250m further south lies the third, and perhaps most impressive of the trio, with the remains of an imposing stupa on a huge raised square base facing a smaller vatadage (on a round base), a high-walled *bodhigara* and the remains of a *tampita* (a shrine raised on pillars).

Further south lies a fourth, much more modern monastery, still very much in use. The core of the monastery dates back to the Kandyan period, and has a rustic *tampita* fronted by an old wooden pavilion and surrounded by a cluster of colourful modern buildings.

Ektem Maligaya

Just a few metres from the modern monastery lies Panduwas Nuwara's most enigmatic and intriguing site, comprising the foundations of a small round building at the exact centre of a large, partially walled and perfectly circular depression – a structure completely unlike anything else on the island. According to popular legend, this is nothing less than the remains of the legendary **Ektem Maligaya** (see page 288), although the more plausible historical explanation is that it served as a place where Parakramabahu received oaths of loyalty, the circular space symbolizing the universe, with the king at its centre.

UNMADACHITRA

Daughter of the legendary King Panduvasudeva (see page 403), **Unmadachitra** (which loosely translates as "she whose beauty drives men mad") was one of the great *femmes fatales* of early Sri Lankan history. When she was still a girl, a prophecy foretold that her future son would kill his uncles and usurp the throne. Panduvasudeva, anxious to prevent such an occurrence, had Unmadachitra shut up in a windowless circular tower, the **Ektem Maligaya**. As is generally the case with young princesses locked up in tall towers, however, Unmadachitra rapidly contrived to meet and fall in love with an eligible young prince, a certain Digha-Gamini. The young couple were allowed to marry on condition they give up any son born to them, although when their first child, named **Pandukabhaya**, arrived he was instead spirited away into hiding. Coming of age, Pandukabhaya revealed himself and went into battle against his uncles, all of whom were duly killed with the exception of a certain **Anuradha**, the only one who desisted from taking up arms against the upstart nephew, and in whose honour Pandukabhaya subsequently named his new city: Anuradhapura.

Panduwas Nuwara Museum

Mon & Wed–Sun 8am–4.30pm • Free

On your way out of the complex it's worth dropping by the modest **Panduwas Nuwara Museum**, which displays finds from the site. Highlights include an unusual polished-stone mirror and a tiny metal figurine of Parakramabahu posed in a very similar style to that of the famous statue of the king at the Potgul Vihara (see page 323) in Polonnaruwa.

Yapahuwa

Daily 7am–6pm • Rs.620

Around 45km north of Kurunegala, just off the road to Anuradhapura, lies the magnificent citadel of **Yapahuwa**, built around a huge granite rock rising almost 100m above the surrounding lowlands. One of the short-lived capitals established during the collapse of Sinhalese power in the thirteenth century, Yapahuwa was founded by **Bhuvanekabahu I** (r. 1272–84), who transferred here from the less easily defensible Polonnaruwa in the face of recurrent attacks from South India, bringing the Tooth Relic (see page 215) with him. The move proved to be of no avail, however. In 1284, Yapahuwa was captured by the army of the South Indian Pandyan dynasty, who carried off the Tooth Relic to Madurai in Tamil Nadu. Following its capture, Yapahuwa was largely abandoned and taken over by monks and hermits, and the capital was moved to Kurunegala.

The palace stairway

Yapahuwa's outstanding feature is the marvellous **stone stairway**, which climbs with Maya-like steepness up to the palace – its neck-cricking gradient apparently designed to protect the Tooth Relic at the top from potential attackers. Its top flight is a positive riot of decoration. Statues of elephants, *makara toranas*, dwarfs, goddesses and a pair of goggle-eyed stone lions flank the stairs, which are topped by a finely carved doorway and windows. Panels around the base and sides of each window are embellished with reliefs of dancers and musicians, one playing a Kandyan drum, the oldest pictorial record of Sri Lanka's most famous musical instrument. The quality of the craftsmanship and material (solid stone, rather than plebeian brick) is strikingly high, and doesn't suggest the residence of a king on the run – although the decidedly Indian style pays unintentional tribute to the invaders who had driven Bhuvanekabahu here in the first place.

The Lion Terrace

At the top of the palace stairway, the so-called **Lion Terrace** is deeply anticlimactic after the grandiose approach. This was the site of the Temple of the Tooth itself, though there's not much to see now. At the rear left-hand side of the terrace, a rough path, crisscrossed with trailing tree roots, leads to the **summit** of the rock – a breathless ten-minute scramble offering panoramic views.

Around the rock

The extremely modest remains of the **rest of the city** lie scattered around the base of the rock, including the foundations of various buildings dotted across the area at the bottom of the palace stairway, bounded by a limestone wall and surrounded by a dried-up moat.

Close to the site entrance and ticket office is a gorgeous old Kandyan-style wooden barn (on the right as you come in) with a quaint bell tower attached. Behind this is a **cave temple**, its entrance projecting from the rock outcrop, inside which are some extremely faded Kandyan-era frescoes plus assorted old plaster, wood and bronze Buddha images. The temple is usually locked, though someone from the ticket office may offer to open it for you.

ARRIVAL AND DEPARTURE   **YAPAHUWA**

By bus Catch any bus travelling between Anuradhapura and Kurunegala and get off at Daladagama, 8km west of the site, from where you can pick up a tuktuk for the return trip to Yapahuwa.

By train Yapahuwa is 5km from Maho train station, which is served by regular local trains from Kurunegala and by fast trains between Colombo and Anuradhapura. Trains run roughly hourly throughout the day.

Destinations Anuradhapura (7 daily; 1hr 15min–2hr); Colombo (11 daily; 3–4hr); Kurunegala (hourly; 40min–1hr 40min).

ACCOMMODATION

Yapahuwa Paradise 1.5km west of the site ☎037 397 5055, ⓦhotelyapahuwaparadise.com. This cheery place, complete with obligatory stone lions, makes a more luxurious base than any of the guesthouses in Kurunegala for exploring the local area. Accommodation is in bright and comfortable rooms (all with a/c, satellite TV and minibar) in attractive white cottages dotted around the garden. There's also a large pool and a new beer garden. B&B $100

North from Kandy to Dambulla

From Kandy, most visitors heading for the Cultural Triangle plough straight up the main road north to Dambulla, Sigiriya and beyond. If you have your own transport, however, there are several interesting sites en route. Two of these – the famous monastery of **Aluvihara** and the wonderful little temple at **Nalanda** – are right on the main highway.

The main road between Kandy and Dambulla is also littered with innumerable **spice gardens**. The temperate climate of the region – halfway in altitude between coastal plains and the hill country – offers ideal horticultural conditions, and if you're interested in seeing where the ingredients of Sri Lankan cuisine come from, now is your chance. Entrance is generally free, but you'll be encouraged to buy some spices at inflated prices in return for a look at the various plants and shrubs.

Matale

Around 25km north from Kandy, the bustling town of **MATALE** (pronounced *mah*-ta-lay) and surrounding area is an important centre for the production of traditional Sri Lankan **arts and crafts** (Matale itself is famous for its lacquerware) – and also a major traffic bottleneck when travelling to or from Kandy.

Sri Muthumariamman Thevasthanam

Main St • Daily 7am–11.45am & 5–7.45pm (although you can still see the temple exterior outside these hours) • Rs.200

Modern Matale is unremarkable apart from the huge **Sri Muthumariamman Thevasthanam**, right next to the main road through town. This is one of the biggest Hindu temples in Sri Lanka outside the north, east and Colombo, and is dedicated to the goddess Mariamman (Mari meaning *shakti*, or female energy and power, and *amman* meaning "mother"), the major female deity in South Indian and Sri Lankan Hinduism. The temple itself is characteristically cavernous and colourful, while a couple of rickety corrugated-iron garages in the surrounding courtyard are used to store the towering chariots used in the temple's annual festival. The entrance fee helps support local social projects, including the little pre-school around the back.

Aluvihara

Daily 6am–6pm • Rs.250 • All buses heading north from Kandy to Dambulla go right past the entrance • No photography

Sitting right next to the main Kandy–Dambulla highway, 2km north of Matale, the small monastery of **Aluvihara** is of great significance in the global history of Buddhism as the place where the most important set of Theravada Buddhist scriptures, the Tripitaka ("Three Baskets"), were first committed to writing. During the first five centuries of the religion's existence, the vast corpus of the Buddha's teachings were simply memorized and passed orally from generation to generation. Around 80 BC, however, fears that the Tripitaka would be lost during the upheavals caused by repeated South Indian invasions prompted the industrious King Vattagamani Abhaya (who also created the Dambulla cave temples and founded the great Abhayagiri monastery in Anuradhapura) to establish Aluvihara, staffing it with five hundred monks who laboured for years to transcribe the Pali-language Buddhist scriptures onto ola-leaf manuscripts. Tragically, having survived for almost two thousand years, this historic library was largely destroyed by British troops when they attacked the temple in 1848 to put down a local uprising.

Cave temples

The heart of the complex consists of a sequence of **cave temples**, tucked away in a picturesque jumble of huge rock outcrops and linked by flights of steps and narrow paths between the boulders. From the first temple (home to a 10m-long sleeping Buddha), steps lead up to the main level, where a second cave temple conceals another large sleeping Buddha and various pictures and sculptures demonstrating the lurid punishments awaiting wrongdoers in the Buddhist hell – a subject which seems to exert a ghoulish fascination on the ostensibly peace-loving Sinhalese. Opposite, another cave houses a similarly gruesome tableau vivant showing bloodthirsty punishments meted out by Sri Wickrama Rajasinha (see page 212), the last king of Kandy.

From here, steps lead up past the side of the second temple to another cave temple behind, which is devoted to the great Indian Buddhist scholar **Buddhaghosa**, who worked at Anuradhapura during the fifth century AD (though there's no evidence that he ever visited Aluvihara), producing a definitive set of commentaries on the Tripitaka. A statue of Vattagamani Abhaya stands in the corner of the cave, offering the scholar an ola-leaf manuscript, while a brilliant gilded Buddhaghosa image from Thailand stands sentry outside. From here, a final flight of steps leads up past a bo tree (apparently growing out of solid rock) to the very top of the complex, where a dagoba and terrace offer fine views across the hills and over to a huge golden Buddha (also a gift from Thailand) which surveys the entire complex from a hillside far above.

International Buddhist Library and Museum

Daily 7am–5pm

Just up the hill to the left of the temple complex, the **International Buddhist Library and Museum** houses a few random objects including a vast antique ola-leaf copy of the *Tripitaka* in many volumes. A resident monk may also be on hand to demonstrate the ancient and dying art of writing upon ola-leaf parchment (for a small donation): the words are first scratched out with a metal stylus, after which ink is rubbed into the leaf causing the invisible words to magically appear.

Nalanda Gedige

km east of the main highway to Dambulla • Daily 6am–5pm • Any bus from Kandy to Dambulla will drop you at the turn-off to the temple on the main road, from where it's a 10min walk

Some 25km north of Matale stands the **Nalanda Gedige**, a little gem of a building and one of the most unusual monuments in the Cultural Triangle. The gedige (Buddhist image house) occupies a scenic location overlooking a tank, with fine views of the steep green surrounding hills – it originally stood nearby at a lower level among paddy fields but was painstakingly dismantled and reconstructed in its present location in 1980, when the Mahaweli Ganga hydroelectricity project led to its original site being flooded. The building is named after the great Buddhist university at Nalanda in northern India, though its origins remain mostly obscure – different sources date it anywhere between the sixth and tenth centuries. According to tradition, it's claimed that Nalanda is located at the exact centre of Sri Lanka, although a glance at any map shows that it's actually rather closer to the west coast than the east.

The gedige

The **gedige** is pure South Indian in style, and looks quite unlike anything else in Sri Lanka. Constructed entirely of stone, it's laid out like a Hindu temple, with a pillared antechamber, or *mandapa* (originally roofed), leading to an inner shrine encircled by an ambulatory. There's no sign of Hindu gods, however, and it appears that the temple was only ever used as a Buddhist shrine. The **main shrine** is entered through a fine square stone door topped by an architrave comprising a line of miniature buildings. To the side, the southern tympanum of the unusual horseshoe-shaped roof features a carving of Kubera, the god of wealth, and the other walls are also richly carved, with many small faces in roundels. The carvings are now much eroded, although if you look carefully you may be able to find the erotic Tantric carving which adorns the southern face of the base plinth on which the entire gedige stands – the only example in Sri Lanka of a typically Indian sculptural motif. The brick base of a ruined (but much more modern) dagoba stands close by.

A tiny **museum** in the car park area houses a few more heavily eroded pillars and a pillar inscription recovered from the site.

4

ACCOMMODATION

NALANDA GEDIGE

Between Matale and Dambulla there are lush valleys of coconut and tea plantations. It's a lovely area to spend a few quiet days unwinding before or after touring the Cultural Triangle or the Hill Country via Kandy.

★ **Jim's Farm Villas** 9km south of Nalanda Gedige and 3km west of Madawala Ulpotha ☎ 077 782 8395, ⓦ jimsfarmvillas.com. Three luxurious boutique villas, with single, double and family rooms, set on a hill overlooking a coconut and mango plantation. There's also a pool, yoga pavilion, spa and excellent restaurant (open to non-guests with advance reservation) serving fresh organic produce from the farm. B&B $180

Wasgamuwa National Park

Daily 6am–6pm • $12, plus the usual additional fees and taxes (see p.00)

Wasgamuwa National Park is one of the most unspoiled of all Sri Lanka's reserves, enjoying an isolated position and being largely enclosed – and offered a measure of protection – by two large rivers, the Mahaweli Ganga and Amban Ganga, which bound it to the east and west. Straddling the northeastern edge of the hill country, the park ranges in elevation from over 500m to just 76m along the Mahaweli Ganga, and comprises mainly dry-zone evergreen forest along the main rivers and in the hills, and open plains in the southeastern and eastern sections. The usual cast of Sri Lankan fauna can be found here, including up to 150 **elephants**, best seen from November to May (especially in February, March and April); at other times they tend to migrate to Minneriya and Kaudulla national parks). Other wildlife includes sambar and spotted deer, buffalo and rarely sighted leopards and sloth bears, plus around 150 species of bird, including a number of endemics.

ARRIVAL AND INFORMATION

Getting to Wasgamuwa is half the fun, with a range of scenic **approach routes** to the park providing views of pristine countryside and wildlife-spotting opportunities. The park's entrance is along its southern flank, about 20km north of the village of **Hettipola**, where all the roads converge. Most visitors approach from Kandy, although the park is also reachable from Polonnaruwa/Giritale and Dambulla. The most convenient way to get the park entrance is with your own vehicle. Alternatively, take a bus to Hettipola and change there for a service to Handungamuwa, which is about 1km from the park entrance. At the entrance, it's possible to hire a jeep with a guide to enter the park.

From Kandy via Mahiyangana/Hasalaka The easiest approach from Kandy is to head east to Mahiyangana and then north along the Mahiyangana–Polonnaruwa road, turning off at either Girandurukotte or Hebarawa to reach Hettipola via the Japan (Nippon) Bridge over the Mahaweli Ganga. This road is in good condition all the way

WASGAMUWA NATIONAL PARK

to Hettipola. A more direct approach is to turn north of the Kandy–Mahiyangana road at Hasalaka, from where heavily pot-holed road leads up to Hettipola via the broa Rathna Falls.

From Kandy via Matale An alternative but slowe approach from Kandy is to head north to Matale and the east, along a minor road which climbs over the norther part of the Knuckles Range and through the villages c Rattota and Pallegama to reach Hettipola.

From Dambulla/Polonnaruwa via Elahera Fror Dambulla, head south down the Kandy road to Naula, the turn east to reach Hettipola via the village of Elahera, whic is also connected by a reasonable road to Polonnaruwa vi Giritale.

Guides Sumane Bandara Illangantilake (☏ 077 260 606; ⊛ trekkingexpeditor.com) and Ravi Desappriya (☏ 071 49 7666, ⊛ srilankatrekking.com) in Kandy are both exceller guides to the park.

ACCOMMODATION

There are a couple of places to stay overlookin **Dunvila Lake**, a popular spot with local elephant about 5km from the main gate in the park southeastern corner. Mahoora (⊛ mahoora.lk) also ru mobile tented safari camps in the park.

Wasgamuwa Safari Village Dunvila Lake ☏ 07 796 0361, ⊛ safarivillagehotels.com. Rustic pla with a dozen thatched en-suite cabanas (fan onl overlooking the lake. B&B **$30**

Willys Safari Hotel Dunvila Lake ☏ 071 689 339 ⊛ willyssafari.com. Basic hotel catering to trekke with comfortable a/c rooms in a low-slung mode building, plus a fair-sized pool. Half board **Rs.9000**

Dambulla and around

More or less at the heart of the Cultural Triangle, the bustling little town of **DAMBULLA** is famous for its remarkable **cave temples**: five magical dimly lit grottoes crammed with statues and decorated with exquisite murals, offering a picture-perfect snapshot of Sinhalese Buddhist art at its finest.

Dambulla stands at an important junction of the Colombo–Trincomale and Kandy–Anuradhapura roads, and makes a convenient base for exploring the area. The **town** itself is

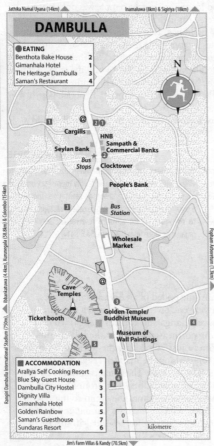

DAMBULLA

● **EATING**
Benthota Bake House	2
Gimanhala Hotel	1
The Heritage Dambulla	3
Saman's Restaurant	4

Jathika Namal Uyana (14km) ▲

Inamaluwa (8km) & Sigiriya (18km) ▲

N

Cargills

HNB

Sampath & Commercial Banks

Seylan Bank

Bus Stops

Clocktower

People's Bank

Bus Station

Wholesale Market

Cave Temples

Ticket booth

Golden Temple/ Buddhist Museum

Museum of Wall Paintings

Ibbankatuwa (4.4km), Kurunegala (58.8km) & Colombo (154km) ◀

Rangiri Dambulla International Stadium (750m) ◀

Popham Arboretum (1.3km) ▶

■ **ACCOMMODATION**
Araliya Self Cooking Resort	4
Blue Sky Guest House	8
Dambulla City Hostel	3
Dignity Villa	1
Gimanhala Hotel	2
Golden Rainbow	5
Saman's Guesthouse	7
Sundaras Resort	6

0 ———— 1
kilometre

Jim's Farm Villas & Kandy (70.5km) ▼

ne of the least attractive in the region, however, strung out along a single long, dusty nd traffic-plagued main road. The centre is marked by the usual clocktower, north of which stretches the main run of shops. South of the clocktower lies the bus stand, an njoyably anarchic wholesale **market** and most of the town's guesthouses.

Dambulla cave temples

bout 2km south of Dambulla centre • Daily 7am–6pm; ticket office 7am–5pm • Rs.1500; buy your ticket at the office in the car park ehind the main road)

Dambulla's **cave temples** enjoy a privileged position, set halfway up an enormous granite outcrop which rises more than 160m above the surrounding countryside, offering majestic views across the dry-zone plains as far as Sigiriya, over 15km distant. t's a ten- to fifteen-minute walk up to the temples from the entrance – make sure you buy your ticket at the office at the bottom before climbing the steps up.

It's best to visit the caves in **reverse order**, starting at the end (Cave 5) and working backwards – this way you get to see the caves in gradually increasing degrees of magnificence, culminating in the wonderful Cave 2.

Brief history

The cave temples date back to the days of **Vattagamini Abhaya** (also known as Valagambahu or Valagamba; reigned 103 BC and 89–77 BC). Just five months after becoming king Vattagamini lost his throne to a group of Tamil invaders and was forced into hiding for fourteen years, during which time he found refuge in these caves. Having reclaimed his throne, Vattagamini had temples constructed here in gratitude for the shelter the rock had offered him – the individual "caves" are actually man-made, created by building partition walls into the space beneath what was originally a single huge rock overhang. The cave temples were further embellished by Nissankamalla (see page 317) – while comprehensive restorations and remodellings were carried out by the **Kandyan kings** Senerat (r. 1604–35) and Kirti Sri Rajasinha (r. 1747–82) – the latter also created the magnificent Cave 3 and commissioned many of the vast number of **murals** that now adorn the interiors. Most of what you now see dates from the reigns of these last two kings, although precise dating of individual paintings is made difficult since these were traditionally repainted on a regular basis when their colours faded, and further changes and embellishments were added right through to the twentieth century.

Cave 5

The small and atmospheric Cave 5, the **Devana Alut Viharaya** ("Second New Temple"), is the most modern of the temples. The statues here are made of brick and plaster, unlike the site's other images, most of which were carved out of solid rock. A 10m reclining Buddha fills most of the available space, while on the wall behind its feet are paintings of a dark Vishnu flanked by Kataragama (see page 192) plus peacock, to the right, and Bandara, a local deity, to the left. To the right of the door as you exit is a mural of a noble carrying lotus flowers, perhaps the patron who originally endowed the temple.

Cave 4

Cave 4, the **Paccima Viharaya** ("Western Temple" – although Cave 5, constructed later, is actually further west), is relatively small. Multiple identical figures of seated Buddhas in the meditation pose sit around the walls, along with a few larger seated figures, one (curtained) under an elaborate *makara torana* arch. A small dagoba stands in the middle; the crack in its side is said to be the work of treasure-hunters who believed the dagoba contained the jewellery of Vattagamini Abhaya's wife, Queen Somawathie. As in Cave 5, the walls are covered with pictures of Buddhas and floral and chequered decorative patterns, most of which were heavily repainted in the early twentieth century.

4

Cave 3

Cave 3, the **Maha Alut Viharaya** ("Great New Temple") was constructed by Kirti Sri Rajasinha and is on a far grander scale, lined with over fifty standing and seated Buddhas; the sloping ceiling reaches a height of up to 10m and gives the cave the appearance of an enormous tent. To the right of the entrance stands a statue of **Kirti Sri Rajasinha**, with four attendants painted onto the wall behind him. The meditating Buddha, seated in the middle of the cave, and the sleeping Buddha by the left wall, are both carved out of solid rock – an extraordinary feat in an age when every piece of stone had to be hacked off using rudimentary chisels.

The murals

Cave 3 has several interesting murals. Two ceiling paintings show the future Buddha, **Maitreya**, preaching in a Kandyan-looking pavilion. In the first (look up as you enter the cave), he preaches to a group of ascetic disciples; in the second (to the right of the entrance) he addresses a gathering of splendidly adorned gods in the Tusita heaven, where he is believed to currently reside pending his arrival on earth roughly five billion years hence. To the left of the door as you exit (behind a pair of seated Buddhas) is another interesting mural showing an idealized **garden** with square ponds, trees, elephants, cobras and Buddhas – a folksy nineteenth-century addition to the original Kandyan-era murals.

Cave 2

Cave 2, the **Maharaja Vihara** ("Temple of the Great Kings"), is the biggest and most spectacular at Dambulla, an enormous, sepulchral space measuring over 50m long and reaching a height of 7m. Vattagamini Abhaya is credited with its creation, though it was altered several times subsequently and completely restored in the eighteenth century. The cave is named after the statues of two kings it contains. The first is a painted wooden image of **Vattagamini Abhaya** himself (just left of the door furthest away from the main steps up to the caves); the second is of **Nissankamalla**, hidden away at the far right-hand end of the cave and almost completely concealed behind a large reclining Buddha – a rather obscure fate for this most vainglorious of Sinhalese kings (see page 317).

The sides and back of the cave are lined with a huge array of Buddha statues. The main Buddha statue on the left of the cave, set under a *makara torana* in the *abhaya* ("Have No Fear") *mudra*, was formerly covered in gold leaf, traces of which can still be seen. To either side stand wooden statues of Maitreya (left) and Avalokitesvara or Natha (right). Against the wall behind the main Buddha are statues of Saman (see page 253) and Vishnu, while images of Kataragama and Ganesh are painted onto the wall behind, an unusually varied contingent of Theravada, Mahayana and Hindu gods within such a small space.

The murals

The ceiling and walls of Cave 2 are covered in a fabulous display of murals – the finest in Sri Lanka. On the ceiling at the western end of the cave (to the left as you enter), Kandyan-style strip panels show pictures of dagobas at Sri Lanka's holy places and scenes from the Buddha's life (you can just make out the small white elephant which appeared in a dream to the Buddha's mother during her pregnancy, symbolizing the remarkable qualities of her future child). These murals pale in comparison, however, with the three adjacent ceiling panels showing the **Defeat of Mara**, which depict the temptations meted out to the Buddha during his struggle for enlightenment at Bodhgaya. In the first he is shown seated under a beautifully stylized bo tree while crowds of hairy grey demons attack him with arrows (one technologically advanced devil even carries a musket), supervised by a magnificent Mara riding on an elephant. This attempt to break the Buddha's concentration having failed, the next panel, the **Daughters of Mara**, shows him being tempted by bevies of seductive maidens. The Buddha's triumph over these stupendous feminine wiles is celebrated in the next panel, the **Isipatana**, which shows him delivering his first sermon to a vast assembly of splendidly attired gods.

Across the cave, a wire-mesh enclosure in the right-hand corner contains a pot fed constantly by drips from the ceiling which is said never to run dry, even in the worst drought.

Cave 1

Cave 1, the **Devaraja Viharaya** ("Temple of the Lord of the Gods") is named in honour of Vishnu, who is credited with having created the caves; a Brahmi inscription outside the temple to the right commemorates the temples' foundation. Inside, the narrow space is almost completely filled by a 14m-long sleeping **Buddha**, carved out of solid rock, which preserves fine traces of beautiful gold gilding on his elbow (often covered). By the Buddha's head, images of Vishnu and other figures are hidden behind a brightly painted wooden screen, while a statue of the Buddha's most faithful disciple, Ananda, stands at his feet. The cave's unusual **murals** are quite badly eroded in places. Some are said to be the oldest at the site, though constant repainting over the centuries has dulled any clear sense of their antiquity; the bright frescoes behind Ananda's head (including a weird tree sporting an Italian-style cherub) are clumsy twentieth-century additions.

Golden Temple

At the bottom of the steps up to the cave temples stands the bizarre **Golden Temple**, a shamelessly kitsch building topped by a 30m seated **golden Buddha**. A nearby sign claims this to be the largest Buddha statue in the world – although in fact it's not even the biggest in Sri Lanka (the actual largest Buddha statue in the world, at Henan in China, stands over four times as tall at 128m).

Golden Temple Buddhist Museum

Daily 7am–6pm • Free

At the foot of the golden Buddha statue sits the **Golden Temple Buddhist Museum**, entered through the golden mouth of an enormous lion-like beast. The museum itself is large but rather lacking in exhibits apart from some dull copies of the cave temple paintings, a few Buddhas donated from around the world and a sprinkling of other artefacts, none of which is labelled.

Museum of Wall Paintings

Some 100m south of the Golden Temple (the easy-to-miss entrance is on the building's ground floor) • Daily 7.30am–4pm • Rs.310 ⓦ ccf. gov.lk

The recently spruced-up **Museum of Wall Paintings** offers a fascinating overview of the development of Sri Lankan art, showing the development of the island's rock paintings and wall murals from the stick-figure scribbles of the Veddhas through to the genre's golden era during the Kandyan period and on to the European-influenced work of colonial-era artists such as George Keyt. The seven dimly lit but absorbing rooms consist of an expertly executed series of copies (on canvas) of paintings from cave temples, shrines and other locations around the island, gathering together under a single roof a compendium of Sri Lankan art from widely scattered and often remote and inaccessible locations; the copies manage to superbly mimic the cracked and flaking plaster effects of the older murals, and in many cases you get a much better view of the paintings here than in their original settings.

Ibbankatuwa Burial Site

Around 5km southeast of Dambulla town centre, along the Kurunegala road • Daily 7am–5pm • Rs.310 • ☎ 066 306 3323, ⓦ ccf.gov.lk• Buses from Dambulla run every 20–30min past the entrance; alternatively, a tuktuk from Dambulla will cost around Rs.400–500 each way

Dating from the sixth century BC, the **Ibbankatuwa Burial Site** is the largest burial ground discovered in Sri Lanka so far. Opened to the public in 2017, the site exhibits

4

the three major stages of excavation that took place here, beginning in the 1970s through to 2015, which uncovered forty-seven burial chambers enclosing stone urns containing ashes, as well as metal implements and a variety of bead and gemstone necklaces. None of the originals are on display at the site, although large colour photos of the finds can be seen at the entrance.

Popham Arboretum

Around 3km east of the cave temples, along the Kandalama road · Daily 6am–6pm · Rs.1000 (including guided walk if you book ahead or if a member of staff is available to show you around); evening guided walks from 7pm Rs.1500 · ☎ 077 726 7951, ⓦ facebook.com/sampophamarboretum · Buses from Dambulla run every 20–30min past the entrance; alternatively, a tuktuk from Dambulla will cost around Rs.300–400 each way (ask to be taken to the "Suddage Waththa", as the arboretum is known locally)

The **Popham Arboretum** was the creation of British tea planter and keen dendrologist Sam Popham. Dismayed by the destruction of Sri Lanka's dry-zone forests, Popham established the arboretum in 1963 as an experiment in reforesting an area of scrub jungle with minimal human interference, and it now preserves almost three hundred tree and plant species, including seven endemics, in a peaceful 36-acre stretch of woodland crisscrossed by a network of paths.

Visitors can explore the arboretum's colour-coded walking trails on their own or alternatively call to book a **guided walk**; these start from the arboretum's rustic **visitor centre**, a modest bungalow originally designed as Popham's quarters by his friend Geoffrey Bawa. Evening guided walks (best to book in advance) offer an excellent chance of spotting some of the arboretum's elusive wildlife, including loris, spotted and mouse deer and the rare pangolin, and there are even a couple of simple cottages (Rs.3000/2500) if you fancy staying overnight.

ARRIVAL AND DEPARTURE
DAMBULLA AND AROUND

By bus The bus station is towards the southern end of town, a Rs.200–300 tuktuk ride from the various guesthouses. Many through buses however don't actually go into the station but pick up and drop off on the main road, usually at the stops outside and opposite the *Benthota Bake House*, a bit further north along the road. Leaving Dambulla, it's almost always quicker to catch a bus on the main road than at the station itself.

Destinations Anuradhapura (every 30min; 1hr 30min); Colombo (every 20min; 4hr); Habarana (every 20min; 45min); Inamaluwa Junction (every 15min; 20min); Kandy (every 20min; 2hr); Kurunegala (every 20min; 2hr); Polonnaruwa (every 30min; 1hr 45min); Sigiriya (every 30min; 30min).

ACCOMMODATION

DAMBULLA

★ **Araliya Self Cooking Resort** Lihiniya, Kandalama Rd ☎ 077 785 0829; map p.292. If you want to learn the basics of traditional Sri Lankan home cooking, this welcoming guesthouse is a great place to learn. Located in the suburbs of Dambulla, its five basic but clean rooms (fan only) look out on to a pleasant garden. The kitchen is in a separate building with a wood stove, and the lessons are included in the cost of the meal (Rs.350–600). Rs.1500

Blue Sky Guest House 44 Mile Post Kandy Road ☎ 077 785 0829, ⓦ dambullaguesthouse.com; map p.292. One of Dambulla's best cheapies, offering competitively priced rooms with hot water, remote-controlled wall fans, mosquito nets, bottled water and optional a/c (Rs.1000). The friendly owner can organize budget tours to the surrounding sites. Rs.1500

★ **Dambulla City Hostel** 320/25 Kurunegala Rd ☎ 076 561 6223, ⓦ hostelslanka.com; map p.292. Lively backpacker hostel in a stately old home with garden that's a great hub for travel information and an excellent budget choice. There are communal kitchen and laundry facilities, and there's also a comfortable TV lounge with a good selection of movies. Dorm beds come either mixed or women-only, and there are two doubles with kitchen and lounge rooms attached. Camping facilities were also in the works at the time of research. Dorms $10, a/c doubles $30

Dignity Villa 29 Yaya Rd, Sampath Watta (700m down the side road next to Cargills supermarket) ☎ 066 493 5335 or ☎ 077 518 0902, ⓦ thesimpletraveler.com; map p.292. Neat little guesthouse with a friendly-family atmosphere in a quasi-rural setting within five minutes' walk of the town centre. Rooms overlook a rectangle of lush lawn. The owner (a former pro chef) can rustle up Western and Sri Lankan meals on request, served on the attractive garden veranda. $16, a/c $25

Gimanhala Hotel Anuradhapura Rd ☎ 066 228 4864, gimanhala.com; map p.292. Attractive modern building in the centre of town, with pleasantly large and nicely decorated rooms, all with a/c, hot water and satellite TV. There's also a decent-sized pool and an attractive pavilion restaurant (see page 297). B&B $70

Golden Rainbow Off Kandy Rd ☎ 077 307 9437, rainbowguesthousedambulla.com; map p.292. Three neat, inexpensive fan rooms in a pretty modern house hidden amid trees in a very quiet location just south of the cave temples, plus a wooden cabin (Rs.3500) and two new "luxury" a/c doubles (around Rs. 4500) currently under construction. Call for a free pick-up when you arrive. Rs.2000

Saman's Guesthouse Kandy Rd ☎ 077 435 3484, facebook.com/samansrestaurantandguesthouse; map p.292. Long-running guesthouse, with nine attractive modern rooms, all with hot water, smart bathrooms and big frame-nets. Excellent value – although optional a/c (Rs.1000) bumps up the price considerably. Also has a good in-house restaurant (see page 298). Rs.4500

Sundaras Resort 189 Kandy Rd ☎ 072 708 6000, sundaras.com; map p.292. Recently expanded mid-range hotel with comfortable and attractively furnished rooms, including two popular family suites ($100), located round a central garden with pool and bar. There's also an Ayurvedic spa on site, and a gym. $45

AROUND DAMBULLA

Amaya Lake 9km east of Dambulla ☎ 066 446 8100, amayaresorts.com; map p.298. Stylish resort in a beautiful rural location next to Kandalama Lake. The main building (with reception and restaurant) occupies a pair of striking interlocking wooden pavilions, while accommodation is in a string of stylishly decorated villas dotted around the extensive grounds. Facilities include a huge pool and seductive Ayurvedic spa, and birdwatching and boat trips on the lake can be arranged. $210

Brook Boutique Hotel & Spa Melsiripura, off A6 highway 30km southwest of Dambulla (25km northeast of Kurunegala) ☎ 066 750 0500, brook. lk; map p.298. Idyllic rural hideaway and popular honeymoon destination, tucked away in a lovely 80-acre fruit farm, with fine views over the surrounding hills. Understated luxury and designer tranquillity are the order of the day, with rocking chairs on each veranda, a pillow menu and plenty of garden in which to unwind. Stylish rooms come with all mod cons; more expensive villas also have private gardens and plunge pools, and there's also a huge coconut-shaded pool and excellent food. B&B $250

★ **Heritance Kandalama** 9km east of Dambulla ☎ 066 555 5000, heritancehotels.com; map p.298. One of Sri Lanka's most celebrated hotels, in a stunning location on Kandalama Lake and with sweeping views towards Sigiriya and beyond. Designed by Geoffrey Bawa (see page 122), the whole place manages to be simultaneously huge but almost invisible, built into a hillside and largely concealed under a lush jungle canopy, so that nature is never far away. Rooms are stylishly furnished and well equipped, with big picture windows and marvellous views, while facilities include three excellent restaurants, a spectacular infinity pool, a gym and a gorgeous Six Senses spa. $285

★ **Jetwing Lake** Yapagama, 5km south of Dambulla ☎ 066 204 0700, jetwinghotels.com; map p.298. All the rooms at this new lakeside resort have superb views of either the mountain ranges to the south, or Sigiriya to the northeast. The sprawling grounds include a 70m-long pool, a spa and a nature trail for birdwatching. There are also two in-house dining options – a Sri Lankan and international buffet and a Chinese restaurant. $200

Thilanka Resort and Spa Kandy Rd, 7km south of Dambulla ☎ 066 446 8001, thilankaresortandspa. com; map p.298. This boldly simple luxury hotel and spa – all clean lines and right angles – is dominated by its dazzling pool, which flows almost into reception, and magnificent expanse of paddy. Rooms are bright and stylish, with huge picture windows, eye-catching oversized prints, DVD players, big TVs and private plunge pools. At the time of writing, a new wing of 24 rooms was under construction. $125

EATING

Benthota Bake House Kandy Rd; map p.292. The lovely *Benthota Bake House* dishes up the usual short eats and cheap helpings of rice and curry (Rs.350–500). There's plenty of seating and it's a good place to take a break if you're on a long car trip, or just need to wait for a bus. Daily 8am–10.30pm.

Gimanhala Hotel Anuradhapura Rd ☎ 066 228 4864, gimanhala.com; map p.292. If you've built up an appetite and want to enjoy a variety of Sri Lankan, Chinese and Western-style dishes, the *Gimanhala's* breakfast (Rs.750)

or lunch (Rs.1500) buffet, including tea or coffee, offers a delicious and filling selection. Dinner is à la carte only, with a good range of mains from Rs.700. Daily 6.30am–9.30pm.

The Heritage Dambulla Kandy Rd ☎ 011 558 5858, chcresthouses.com/dambulla; map p.292. A surprisingly chic little café for dusty Dambulla, and a convenient stop before or after a visit to the cave temples. Well-presented fare includes breakfasts, sandwiches, soups and salads, plus more substantial Sri Lankan and European-style mains (Rs.600–800). Daily 6am–10pm.

4

Saman's Restaurant Saman's Guesthouse, Kandy Rd ☎077 435 3484, ⓦfacebook.com/samansrestaurantandguesthouse; map p.292. This long-running restaurant is best known for its huge rice

and curry spreads (Rs.800), often featuring unusual loca vegetables and with plenty of authentic flavour and a fa bit of spice too. Also a good place for both Western and S Lankan breakfasts (Rs.500). Daily 7am–11pm.

DIRECTORY

Ballooning Sun Rise Ballooning (ⓦsrilankaballooning. com) operate daily excursions departing just after sunrise (weather permitting) in the Dambulla/Sigiriya area from Nov to April for $210.

Banks The northern end of town has plenty of banks with ATMs accepting foreign cards.

Cricket The impressive modern Rangiri Dambulla International Stadium, southwest of the centre, hosts regular international one-day matches (but no test fixtures).

Internet Try Excellence, opposite the post office (dail 9am–6pm; Rs.100/hr), and Kopi Kade (daily 9am–8pm Rs.100/hr), at the northern end of town near th *Gimanhala* hotel.

Swimming Non-guests get free use of the pleasant poc at the *Gimanhala Transit Hotel* when they spend Rs.1000 o food and drink in the hotel.

Northwest of Dambulla

The area **northwest of Dambulla**, en route to Anuradhapura, conceals the little-visited **Jathika Namal Uyana**, with its remarkable ironwood forest and rose-quartz hills, plus two of the island's finest ancient Buddhas, at **Aukana** and **Sasseruwa**, all three of which can be easily combined into a rewarding short day-trip if you have your own vehicle.

Jathika Namal Uyana

Adiyagala road, 7km west of Madatugama junction on the Dambulla–Anuradhapura road • Daily 6am–6.30pm • Rs.500

Around 15km north of Dambulla is the remarkable **Jathika Namal Uyana** forest reserve. According to legend, the forest was originally planted by Devanampiya Tissa

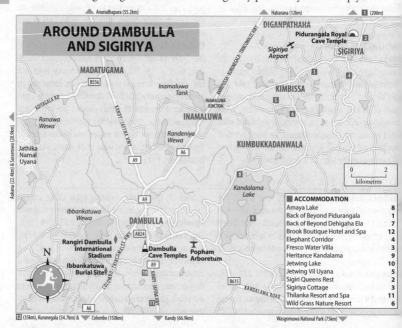

AROUND DAMBULLA AND SIGIRIYA

▲ Anuradhapura (55.2km)   ▲ Habarana (12km)   ▲ ◨ (200m)

DIGANPATHANA

Pidurangala Royal Cave Temple ◨ 2

✈ Sigiriya Airport

SIGIRIYA

MADATUGAMA

B556

◨ 3   ◨ 4

Inamaluwa Tank

INAMALUWA JUNCTION

KIMBISSA

◨ 5

INAMALUWA

◨ 6

Ranawa Wewa

Randeniya Wewa

A6

KUMBUKKADANWALA

Jathika Namal Uyana

A9

◨ 8

Kandalama Lake

0   2
kilometres

Ibbankatuwa Wewa

A9

DAMBULLA

AB24

◨ 9

Rangiri Dambulla International Stadium

Dambulla Cave Temples

Popham Arboretum

N

A9

Ibbankatuwa Burial Site

◨ 10

B615

KANDALAMA ROAD

◼ ACCOMMODATION	
Amaya Lake	8
Back of Beyond Pidurangala	1
Back of Beyond Dehigaha Ela	7
Brook Boutique Hotel and Spa	12
Elephant Corridor	4
Fresco Water Villa	3
Heritance Kandalama	9
Jetwing Lake	10
Jetwing Vil Uyana	5
Sigiri Queens Rest	2
Sigiriya Cottage	3
Thilanka Resort and Spa	11
Wild Grass Nature Resort	6

◨ (35km), Kurunegala (54.7km) & ▼ Colombo (150km)   ▼ Kandy (66.9km)   Wasgomuwa National Park (75km) ▼

◀ Aukana (22.4km) & Sasseruwa (28.9km)

(see page 339) and later became a religious retreat – various monastic remains are dotted around the site. The reserve now protects Sri Lanka's largest extant forest of the indigenous **ironwood** (*na*), the country's national tree, often planted close to Buddhist temples where its fragrant, four-petalled white flowers are a popular offering during puja. Also contained within the reserve is an impressive range of 550-million-year-old **rose-quartz** hills, the biggest such deposit in South Asia, which rise lunar-like from the verdant woodland – tradition claims that Mughal emperor Shah Jahan himself had stone imported from here for use in the construction of the Taj Mahal.

From the entrance, a path leads for about 1km though the forest, at its prettiest from April to June when the *na* trees are in bloom, to a ranger's hut, the ruins of a moss-covered **dagoba**, surrounded by a low wall decorated with pink-quartz stones, and a few other hard-to-decipher ruins. From here another trail climbs gently up the hillside (ask a ranger the way), the forest increasingly giving way to quartz outcrops. It's about a ten-minute hike across the pinky-grey rock face above the tree canopy to the pleasantly breezy **summit** of the first low mountain, surmounted by a small pink fibreglass Buddha, from where there are magnificent views across to Dambulla.

Aukana Buddha

Daily 7.30am–7.30pm • Rs.1000 • Aukana is difficult to reach by public transport; the best option is to catch one of the buses that run from Dambulla to Anuradhapura, get off at Kekirawa, then catch a local bus or tuktuk to Aukana

One of the island's most iconic monuments, the magnificent **Aukana Buddha** statue (or Avukana Buddha, as it's increasingly spelled), 30km northwest of Dambulla, offers a superb example of Sri Lankan religious art at its classical best. The 12m-high statue stands in the small village of Aukana, close to the vast **Kala Wewa** tank created by the unfortunate King Dhatusena (see page 404) in the fifth century, although the Buddha itself may date from some three or four centuries later, contemporaneous with the images at Buduruwagala, Maligawila and Polonnaruwa's Gal Vihara and Lankatilaka.

The brief craze for such monumental statues may have been the result of Indian Mahayana influence, with its emphasis on the Buddha's superhuman, transcendental powers. Like many of the finest Sinhalese statues, the Aukana image succeeds in striking a delicate balance between realism and symbolism in its portrayal of the Buddha, creating a figure at once recognizably human but also unquestionably divine – and also providing an interesting contrast with the more realistic but altogether lumpier Sasseruwa Buddha nearby.

The statue is in the unusual (for Sri Lanka) *asisa mudra*, the blessing position, with the right hand turned sideways to the viewer, as though on the point of delivering a swift karate chop. The figure is carved in the round, just connected at the back to the stone from which it's cut, though the lotus plinth it stands on is made from a separate piece of rock. The walls at the foot of the statue would originally have enclosed a vaulted image chamber.

Sasseruwa Buddha

Daily 7am–7pm • Donation • Sasseruwa is difficult enough to find even with your own transport (follow the signs to Reswehera), and all but impossible by public transport

The remote and little-visited **Sasseruwa Buddha** (also known as the Reswehera Buddha), 11km west of Aukana, is only slightly smaller than the much better-known image at Aukana, though apparently uncompleted. The figure stands in the *abhaya mudra* ("have no fear" pose) and, as at Aukana, was originally concealed inside its own image house, as shown by the holes cut into the rock around it.

The statue was once part of a **monastery** established, according to legend, by Vattagamini Abhaya, who found refuge here during his years in hiding from Tamil invaders (see page 293). Assorted monastic remains can still be seen around the statue

A TALE OF TWO BUDDHAS

Two legends connect the **Sasseruwa and Aukana Buddhas**. The first, and more prosaic, says that cracks in the Sasseruwa Buddha (which can be seen in the torso) started appearing during its construction, and that it was therefore abandoned in favour of a new statue being created at Aukana. A second and more poetic legend relates that the two Buddhas were carved at the same time in competition between a master and his student. The master's Aukana Buddha was finished first and the frustrated student, realizing his own limitations, abandoned the Sasseruwa image in disappointment. A third, and perhaps more convincing, theory has it that the two statues were created at completely separate times, with the Sasseruwa Buddha perhaps dating from as early as the third century AD, some five hundred years before the Aukana image, and reflecting the Greek-influenced Gandharan style of sculpture, which originated in present-day Afghanistan and provided a model for early Buddha images across South Asia. Certainly the Sasseruwa Buddha's realistic but rather ungainly square head and heavy features are in striking contrast to the much more delicate and expressive face of the Aukana image.

including a pair of cave temples, one with a large reclining Buddha and another with Kandyan-era paintings and further Buddha images.

Sigiriya and around

Around 15km northeast of Dambulla, the spectacular citadel of **SIGIRIYA** rises sheer and impregnable out of the plains of the dry zone, sitting atop a huge outcrop of gneiss rock towering 200m above the surrounding countryside. The shortest-lived but the most extraordinary of all Sri Lanka's medieval capitals, Sigiriya ("Lion Rock") was declared a World Heritage Site in 1982 and is the country's most memorable single attraction – a remarkable archeological site made unforgettable by its dramatic setting.

Brief history

Inscriptions found in the caves that honeycomb the base of the rock indicate that Sigiriya served as a place of religious retreat as far back as the third century BC, when Buddhist monks established refuges here. It wasn't until the fifth century AD, however, that Sigiriya rose briefly to pre-eminence in Sri Lankan affairs, following the power struggle that succeeded the reign of **Dhatusena** (r. 455–473) of Anuradhapura. Dhatusena had two sons, **Mogallana**, by the most important of his various queens, and **Kassapa**, his son by a lesser consort. Upon hearing that Mogallana had been declared heir to the throne, Kassapa rebelled, driving Mogallana into exile in India and imprisoning his father. Threatened with death if he refused to reveal the whereabouts of the state treasure, Dhatusena agreed to show his errant son its location if he was permitted to bathe one final time in the great Kala Wewa tank, whose creation he had overseen. Standing in the tank, Dhatusena poured its water through his hands and told Kassapa that the water, and the water alone, was all the treasure he possessed. Kassapa, none too impressed, had his father walled up in a chamber and left him to die.

Mogallana, meanwhile, vowed to return from India and reclaim his inheritance. Kassapa, preparing for the expected invasion, constructed a new residence on top of Sigiriya Rock – a combination of pleasure palace and impregnable fortress, which he intended would emulate the legendary abode of Kubera, the god of wealth, while a new city was established around its base. According to tradition, the entire extraordinary structure was built in just seven years, from 477 to 485.

The long-awaited **invasion** finally materialized in 491, Mogallana having raised an army of Tamil mercenaries to fight his cause. Despite the benefits of his unassailable fortress, Kassapa, in an act of fatalistic bravado, descended from his rocky eminence and rode boldly out on an elephant at the head of his troops to meet the attackers on the plains below. Unfortunately for Kassapa, his elephant took fright and bolted at the height of the battle. His troops, thinking he was retreating, fell back and left him cut off. Facing certain capture and defeat, Kassapa killed himself.

Following Mogallana's reconquest, Sigiriya was handed over to the Buddhist monks, after which its caves once again became home to religious ascetics seeking peace and solitude. The site was finally abandoned in 1155, after which it remained largely forgotten until modern times.

Sigiriya Rock

Daily 7am–6pm; last entrance 5pm • $30 • The ticket booth for foreign tourists is in Sigiriya Museum • Ⓦ ccf.gov.lk

You'll need two or three hours to explore **Sigiriya Rock**; it's best to visit in the early morning or late afternoon, when the crowds are less dense and the temperature is cooler – late afternoon also brings out the rock's extraordinary ochre colouration, like a kind of Asian Ayers Rock. The site is best avoided at weekends (especially Sundays) and on public holidays, when its narrow staircases and walkways can become unbearably congested. The ascent of the rock is a stiff climb, and vertigo sufferers might find some sections unpleasant, though it's less gruelling than you might imagine when standing at the bottom of the towering cliff face. **Guides** can usually be hired at the entrance, though it pays to ask a few questions to check their knowledge and level of English before committing to anyone.

4

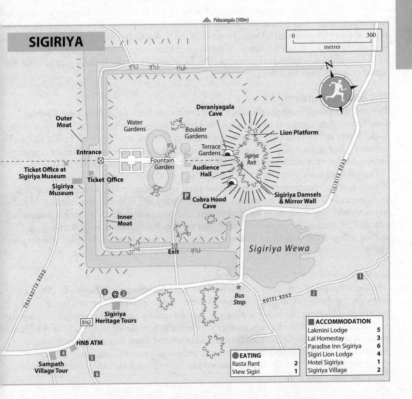

The site divides into two sections: the **rock** itself, on whose summit Kassapa established his principal palace; and the area **around the base** of the rock, home to elaborate royal pleasure gardens as well as various monastic remains pre-dating Kassapa's era. The entire site is a compelling combination of wild nature and high artifice – exemplified by the delicate paintings of the Sigiriya Damsels which cling to the rock's rugged flanks. Interestingly, unlike Anuradhapura and Polonnaruwa, there's no sign here of large-scale monasteries or religious structures – Kassapa's Sigiriya appears to have been an almost entirely secular affair, perhaps a reflection of its unhallowed origins.

Sigiriya Museum

Included in Sigiriya Rock ticket, otherwise $5 • Daily 8.30am–5.30pm • ⓦ ccf.gov.lk

Close to the site entrance, the lacklustre **Sigiriya Museum** showcases assorted prehistoric archeological finds alongside various artefacts discovered at the site. There's also a bird's-eye scale model of the rock and re-creations of the frescoes and a section of Mirror Wall.

The Water Gardens

From the entrance, a wide, straight path arrows towards the rock, following the line of an imaginary east–west axis around which the whole site is laid out. This entire side of the rock is protected by a pair of broad moats, though the Outer Moat is now largely dried out. Crossing the Inner Moat, you enter the **Water Gardens**. The first section comprises four pools set in a square which create a small island at their centre when full, connected by pathways to the surrounding gardens.

Beyond here is the small but elaborate **Fountain Garden**. Features include a serpentine miniature "river" and limestone-bottomed channels and ponds, two of which preserve their ancient fountain sprinklers. These work on a simple pressure-and-gravity principle and still spurt out modest plumes of water after heavy rain – after almost 1500 years of disuse, all that was needed to restore the fountains to working order was to clear the water channels that feed them.

The Boulder Gardens

Beyond the Water Gardens the main path begins to climb up through the **Boulder Gardens**, constructed out of the huge boulders that lie tumbled around the foot of the rock. Many of the boulders are notched with lines of holes – they look rather like rock-cut steps, but in fact they were used as footings to support the brick walls or timber frames of the numerous buildings built against or on top of the boulders.

The gardens were also the centre of Sigiriya's monastic activity before and after Kassapa, with around twenty **caves** once used by resident monks, some containing inscriptions dating from between the third century BC and the first century AD. The caves would originally have been plastered and painted, and traces of this decoration can still be seen in a few places; you'll also notice the dripstone ledges that were carved around the entrances to many of the caves to prevent water from running into them.

Deraniyagala Cave and Cobra Hood Cave

The **Deraniyagala Cave**, just to the left of the path shortly after it begins to climb up through the gardens (no sign), has a well-preserved dripstone ledge and traces of old paintings including the faded remains of various *apsaras* (celestial nymphs) very similar to the famous Sigiriya Damsels further up the rock. On the opposite side of the main path up the rock, a side path leads to the **Cobra Hood Cave**, named for its uncanny resemblance to that snake's head. The cave preserves traces of lime plaster, floral decoration and a very faint inscription on the ledge in archaic Brahmi script dating from the second century BC.

Audience Hall and Asana Cave

Follow the path up the hill behind the Cobra Hood Cave and up through "Boulder Arch no. 2" (as it's signed), then turn left to reach the so-called **Audience Hall**. The wooden walls and roof have long since disappeared, but the impressively smooth floor, created by chiselling the top off a single enormous boulder, remains, along with a 5m-wide "throne", also cut out of the solid rock. The hall is popularly claimed to have been Kassapa's audience hall, though it's more likely to have served a purely religious function, with the empty throne representing the Buddha. The small **Asana Cave** on the path en route to the Audience Hall retains colourful splashes of various paintings on its ceiling (though now almost obliterated by idiotic contemporary graffiti) and is home to another throne, while a couple more thrones can be found carved into nearby rocks.

Terrace Gardens

From the Asana Cave, you can carry on back to the main path, then head on up through "Boulder Arch no. 1". The path – now a sequence of walled-in steps – begins to climb steeply through the **Terrace Gardens**, a series of rubble-retaining brick and limestone terraces that stretch to the base of the rock itself, from where you get the first of an increasingly majestic sequence of views back down below.

The Sigiriya Damsels

No flash photography

At the base of the rock, two incongruous nineteenth-century cast-iron spiral staircases lead to and from a sheltered cave in the sheer rock face above which you'll find Sri Lanka's most famous sequence of frescoes, popularly referred to as the **Sigiriya Damsels**. These busty beauties were painted in the fifth century and are the only non-religious paintings to have survived from ancient Sri Lanka; they're now one of the island's most iconic – and most relentlessly reproduced – images. It's thought that these frescoes would originally have covered an area some 140m long by 40m high, though only 21 damsels now survive out of an original total of some five hundred (a number of paintings were destroyed by a vandal in 1967, while a few of the surviving pictures are roped off out of sight). The exact significance of the paintings is unclear: they were originally thought to depict Kassapa's consorts, though according to modern art historians the most convincing theory is that they are portraits of *apsaras*, which would explain why they are shown from the waist up only, rising out of a cocoon of clouds. The portrayal of the damsels is strikingly naturalistic, showing them scattering petals and offering flowers and trays of fruit – similar in a style to the famous murals at the Ajanta Caves in India and a world away from the much later and more stylized paintings at nearby Dambulla. An endearingly human touch is added by the slips of the brush visible here and there: one damsel has three hands, while another sports an extra nipple.

The Mirror Wall

Just beyond the damsels, the pathway runs along the face of the rock, bounded on one side by the **Mirror Wall**. This was originally coated in highly polished plaster made from lime, egg white, beeswax and wild honey; sections of the original plaster survive and still retain a marvellously lustrous sheen. The wall is covered in **graffiti**, the oldest dating from the seventh century, in which early visitors recorded their impressions of Sigiriya and, especially, the nearby damsels – even after the city was abandoned, the rock continued to draw a steady stream of tourists curious to see the remains of Kassapa's fabulous pleasure dome. Taken together, the graffiti form a kind of early medieval visitors' book, and the 1500 or so decipherable comments give important insights into the development of the Sinhalese language and script.

BEST BEE-HAVIOUR

The small wire-mesh cages you can see standing on Sigiriya's Lion Platform were built as a refuge in the event of **bee attacks** – several of which have occurred in recent years despite efforts (using a mixture of chemicals and exorcism rituals) to evict the offending insects from their nests, which can be seen clinging to the underside of the rock overhang above, to the left of the stairs. Local Buddhist monks claim that such attacks are divine retribution for the impious behaviour of visiting tourists. The site is closed in the event of an attack – and tickets are not refunded.

Beyond the Mirror Wall, the path runs along a perilous-looking iron walkway bolted onto the sheer rock face. From here you can see a huge **boulder** below, propped up on stone slabs. The popular explanation is that, in the event of attack, the slabs would have been knocked away, causing the boulder to fall onto the attackers below, though it's more likely that the slabs were designed to stop the boulder inadvertently falling down over the cliff.

The Lion Platform

As you continue up the rock, a flight of limestone steps climbs steeply up to the **Lion Platform**, a large spur projecting from the north side of the rock, just below the summit. From here, a final staircase, its base flanked by two enormous paws carved out of the rock, leads up across all that remains of a gigantic **lion statue** – the final path to the summit apparently led directly into its mouth. Visitors to Kassapa were, one imagines, suitably impressed both by the gigantic conceit of the thing and also by the heavy symbolism – lions were the most important emblem of Sinhalese royalty, and the beast's size was presumably meant to reflect Kassapa's prestige and buttress his questionable legitimacy to the throne.

The whole section of rock face above is scored with countless notches and grooves which once supported steps up to the summit: in a supreme irony, it appears that Kassapa was afraid of heights, and it's thought that these original steps would have been enclosed by a high wall – though this isn't much comfort for latter-day vertigo sufferers, who have to make the final ascent to the summit up a narrow iron staircase attached to the bare rock.

The summit

After the tortuous path up, the **summit** seems huge. This was the site of Kassapa's palace, and almost the entire area was originally covered with buildings. Only the foundations now remain, though, and it's difficult to make much sense of it all – the main attraction is the fabulous view down to the Water Gardens and out over the surrounding countryside. The **Royal Palace** itself is now just a plain, square brick platform at the very highest point of the rock. The upper section is enclosed by steep terraced walls, below which is a large tank cut out of the solid rock; it's thought that water was channelled to the summit using an ingenious hydraulic system powered by windmills. Below here a series of four further terraces, perhaps originally gardens, tumble down to the lower edge of the summit above Sigiriya Wewa.

The path down takes you along a slightly different route – you should end up going right past the Cobra Hood Cave (useful if you missed it earlier) before exiting the site to the south.

Pidurangala Royal Cave Temple

Daily 5am–6pm • Rs.300 (if there's anyone around to sell you a ticket)

A couple of kilometres north of Sigiriya, another large rock outcrop is home to the fifth century AD **Pidurangala Royal Cave Temple**, offering superb views of Sigiriya Rock and an increasingly popular sunrise-viewing spot. According to tradition, the monastery here dates from the arrival of Kassapa, when the monks who were then living at Sigiriya were relocated to make room for the royal palace – the king provided new dwellings and a temple at Pidurangala to compensate them.

It's a pleasant short bike or tuktuk ride to the foot of Pidurangala rock: head down the road north of Sigiriya and continue for about 750m until you reach a modern white temple, the **Pidurangala Sigiri Rajamaha Viharaya** (about 100m further on along this road on the left you'll also find the interesting remains of some old monastic buildings, including the ruins of a sizeable brick dagoba). Behind the Pidurangala Viharaya take either of the two paths to the right, both of which come out on a terrace just below the summit of the rock (a stiff 15min climb), where you'll find the Royal Cave Temple itself, although despite the rather grand name there's not much to see apart from a long reclining Buddha under a large rock overhang, its upper half restored in brick. The statue is accompanied by figures of Vishnu and Saman and decorated with very faded murals.

From here you may be able to find the rough path up to the **summit** of the rock (a five-minute scramble), but you'll need to be fit and agile, and take care not to lose your way when coming back down, which is surprisingly easy to do. The reward for your efforts will be the best view of Sigiriya you can get short of chartering a balloon: the far more irregular and interestingly shaped northern side of the rock, which you don't get to see when climbing up it, the ant-like figures of those making the final ascent to the summit (which you're almost level with) just visible against the huge slab of red rock.

4

ARRIVAL AND DEPARTURE SIGIRIYA AND AROUND

BY PLANE

It's possible to fly to Sigiriya with Cinnamon Air, whose daily Colombo–Trincomalee flight touches down at Sigiriya's airport, 4km due west of the rock, en route between the two cities; the fare is currently $229 one-way.

BY BUS

From Dambulla Regular buses (every 30min; 30min) connect Sigiriya with Dambulla.

From Polonnaruwa Take any bus heading to Dambulla and get off at Inamaluwa Junction, 10km west of Sigiriya on the main Dambulla–Trincomalee highway, from where

you can pick up a tuktuk (around Rs.800) or wait for the half-hourly bus from Dambulla.

From Anuradhapura It's probably easiest to take a bus to Dambulla, then pick up the Sigiriya bus from there. Alternatively, take a bus to Habarana, then another bus to Inamaluwa Junction.

Onward travel from Sigiriya If you're heading up to Anuradhapura or Polonnaruwa, you will have to flag something down on the main road at Inamaluwa Junction, or alternatively go to Dambulla (every 30min; 30min) and take a bus from there. There are also twice-daily, early-morning services direct to Kandy (2hr 30min).

ACTIVITIES AND TOURS

Village tours Sampath Village Tour (☏077 666 7110) near *Sigiri Lion Lodge* can organize unusual village tours (Rs.1500 per person) including a ride in a traditional bullock cart, a 20min boat trip on Sigiriya Wewa, traditional lunch and visit to local cottage workshops, before returning by tuktuk.

Wildlife Sigiriya is a convenient base for trips to Minneriya and Kaudulla national parks. Most of the accommodation

options listed here can arrange jeeps for visits to either park (around Rs.4500–5000/half-day), or alternatively you can try Sigiriya Heritage Tours in the middle of the village (☏077 675 4595).

Ballooning Sun Rise Ballooning (☏077 352 2013, ⓦ srilankaballooning.com) run daily rides departing just after sunrise (weather permitting) in the Sigiriya/Dambulla area from Nov to April for $210.

ACCOMMODATION

There's a growing range of accommodation in all price ranges, both in Sigiriya village itself and scattered around the surrounding countryside – though you'll need a car, tuktuk or bicycle to reach the rock itself if staying outside the village.

During the dry season elephants can often be seen wandering at night on their way to a nearby tank along a local elephant corridor running roughly parallel with the Inamaluwa road, past the back of the *Lakmini Lodge* or *Sigiri Lion Lodge*.

SIGIRIYA VILLAGE

★ **Lakmini Lodge** 50m off Main Rd, opposite the post office ☎071 709 8128, ⊛lakminilodge.com; map p.301. Stylish and well-run guesthouse with a varied range of accommodation, from cheaper rooms in the old main building to smart, good-value modern rooms (some with superb views of Sigiriya) in a new block next door; all have optional a/c for Rs.1000. Their newly opened restaurant with resident chef serves sandwiches, smoothies and a wide selection of mains. Old block **Rs.3000**, new block **Rs.7500**

★ **Lal Homestay** 209 Main Rd ☎077 704 5386, ✉lalhomestay@gmail.com; map p.301. Friendly, family-run guesthouse with exceptionally clean and comfortable rooms (all with fans, one with a/c) looking onto a pretty garden. The beautifully prepared curry dinners (Rs.700) made with seasonal ingredients are a standout. Lal, the owner, is an excellent source of travel information. **Rs.2000**, a/c **Rs.2500**

Paradise Inn Sigiriya (also known as Sigiriya Paradise Inn) 75m off Main Rd, opposite the post office ☎072 433 7890, ⊛sigiriyaparadiseinn.com; map p.301. Bright, modern and welcoming family guesthouse in a lovely setting next to a rice paddy, with nine rooms, including four deluxe and two family-sized ones, all with hot water, quality mattresses and optional a/c (Rs.700). A little pricier than other nearby places, but reasonable value given the quality. **Rs.3000**

Sigiri Lion Lodge 186 Main Rd ☎066 228 6368, ⊛sigirilionlodge.com; map p.301. Centrally located family guesthouse, arranged around a small square of garden down a peaceful side road. Rooms are spacious and spotlessly maintained, and breakfast is served on the veranda in front of the rooms. Good value unless you take the pricey optional a/c (Rs.1000 extra). **Rs.3000**

Hotel Sigiriya Hotel Rd ☎066 493 0500, ⊛serendibleisure.com; map p.301. Appealing and good-value resort-style hotel, set in a rambling collection of low-slung buildings topped with red-tiled roofs. The stylish a/c rooms come with TV and minibar, while amenities and activities include an Ayurveda centre, a swimming pool with fine views of the rock and nature walks with the resident naturalist. A major renovation is scheduled for 2019. B&B **$140**

Sigiriya Village Hotel Rd ☎066 228 6804, ⊛sigiriyavillage.com; map p.301. Quaint chalet-style accommodation scattered around thematic cultural clusters including a small rice paddy and a temple. There's also a pool and an Ayurveda centre, and birdwatching trips can be arranged on request. A refurbishment is expected to begin by late 2018. B&B **$120**

AROUND SIGIRIYA

Back of Beyond Pidurangala – Kurulu Uyana Pidurangala ☎077 395 1527, ⊛backofbeyond.lk; map p.298. Idyllic eco-retreat set in bird-rich jungle at the base of the Pidurangala. Accommodation is in three colourful little cottages and one larger three-bedroom bungalow, all comfortably appointed with hot water and fan, while staff rustle up good Sri Lankan food and serve as ad hoc nature guides. B&B **$110**

Back of Beyond – Dehigaha Ela Alakolawawe village, 6km from Sigiriya village ☎077 395 1527, ⊛backofbeyond.lk; map p.298. Robinson Crusoe in the jungle, with three rustic tree houses and two "boulder cottages" (built around natural rocks) in pristine forest – as close to nature as it's possible to get in a bed. B&B **$130**

Elephant Corridor 1.5km south of Sigiriya village ☎066 228 6950, ⊛elephantcorridor.com; map p.298. This fancy boutique hotel boasts plenty of rather gimmicky opulence, with lavish suite-style rooms, all with private plunge pool, plus a fancy spa, although the real attraction is the setting in pristine dry-zone scrub, with stunning views of Sigiriya. B&B **$260**

Fresco Water Villa Kimbissa (2km west from Sigiriya along the Inamaluwa Rd) ☎066 228 6160, ⊛oakrayhotels.com/fresco-water-villa-sigiriya; map p.298. Large resort hotel, with accommodation in pale grey three-storey buildings set around a large slab of garden. The minimalist-verging-on-dull architecture and international-bland interior design hardly set the pulse racing, although rooms are comfy and well equipped and it's a reasonable deal. Nice big pool, too, plus restaurant and bar. **$110**

★ **Jetwing Vil Uyana** 3.5km east of Inamaluwa Junction ☎066 492 3585, ⊛jetwinghotels.com; map p.298. The island's most audacious hotel project, born from an ambitious scheme to create an artificial wetland out of abandoned agricultural land, using ancient Sri Lankan irrigation techniques combined with modern know-how. It's a fascinating, and very peaceful, environment, with its five habitats – marsh, paddy, forest, garden and lake – attracting plenty of wildlife. Accommodation is in a scatter of luxuriantly thatched villas, modelled on traditional Sinhalese dwellings, combining state-of-the-art mod con with the homeliness of an über-luxurious Japanese ryokan and facilities include a magnificent infinity pool and serene spa. **$510**

Sigiri Queens Rest Pidurangala, 2.5km from Sigiriya village ☎071 368 6671, ✉sigiriqueens@gmail.com; map p.298. Simple family-run establishment in beautifully unspoiled setting. There are three basic rooms in an older building, plus five simple, rustic treehouses of various sizes (some with a/c) scattered amongst the trees. It's also possible to camp here. Organic food is served fresh from the garden and there are bikes for rent. **$30**

Sigiriya Cottage Ehalagala, 1.5km west of Sigiriya village ☎ 072 751 3122; map p.298. Attractive mid-range option, arranged around huge, immaculate gardens, and with a neat pavilion restaurant. Accommodation is in stylish and spacious a/c bungalows, attractively furnished with repro-colonial touches and high wooden ceilings. Free bikes or drop-off by tuktuk to the rock or village are included. B&B $50

Wild Grass Nature Resort Kumbukkadanwala, south of Kimbissa village ☎ 066 567 0680; map p. Idyllic but pricey boutique eco-retreat set in thirty acres of unfenced jungle – you may find yourself sharing the resort with elephants, deer or wild boar, plus a wide variety of birds. Accommodation is in five chic modern villas spread out around the grounds, all with private lounge, terrace and huge picture windows framing stunning views. B&B $280

EATING

Rasta Rant Main Rd, Sigiriya village ☎ 077 794 2095; map p.301. Chilled-out riverside reggae bar with lounge eating and a "top secret" cocktail menu (from Rs. 450), fresh juices (from Rs.250) and a nightly BBQ (Rs.550). They also have the only espresso machine in the village (Rs.300). Daily 12pm–late.

View Sigiri 129 Main Rd, Sigiriya village ☎ 077 293 4497; map p.301. Large, friendly restaurant with great views of the rock, serving up Western and Sri Lankan standards with lunch buffet spreads (Rs.600), an à la carte selection in the evening, plus a nightly BBQ (Rs.800–900). Satisfied customers have written their reviews in multiple languages all over the walls. Daily 7am–10pm.

DIRECTORY

Banks There's a HNB ATM in the village next to the turn off to Sigiri Lion Lodge, and a Bank of Ceylon ATM at the rock.
Bike rental Bikes are available from some guesthouses. Alternatively try TMS Tours, next door to Croissant Hut in the village (Rs400/day).

Swimming Non-guests can use the pools at the Hotel Sigiriya (Rs.400), Sigiriya Village (Rs.350) and Fresco Water Villa (Rs.1000).

4

Habarana and around

Sitting on a major road junction almost equidistant between Polonnaruwa, Anuradhapura and Dambulla (and close to Sigiriya and Ritigala), the large village of HABARANA is situated near the fine **Habarana Lake**, which is home to plenty of resident

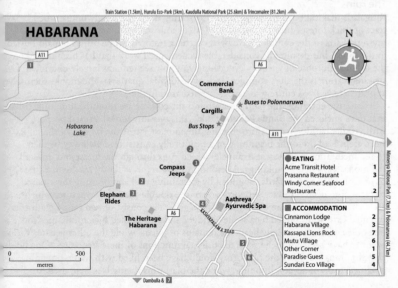

Train Station (1.5km), Hurulu Eco-Park (5km), Kaudulla National Park (25.6km) & Trincomalee (81.2km)

HABARANA

N

A11

A6

Commercial Bank

Buses to Polonnaruwa

Cargills

Habarana Lake

Bus Stops

A11

Compass Jeeps

Elephant Rides

Aathreya Ayurvedic Spa

The Heritage Habarana

A6

KASHYAPAGAMA ROAD

0   500
metres

Minneriya National Park (7km) & Polonnaruwa (4a.7km)

Minneriya National Park (17km) & Polonnaruwa (4a.7km)

● EATING	
Acme Transit Hotel	1
Prasanna Restaurant	3
Windy Corner Seafood Restaurant	2

■ ACCOMMODATION	
Cinnamon Lodge	2
Habarana Village	3
Kassapa Lions Rock	7
Mutu Village	6
Other Corner	1
Paradise Guest	5
Sundari Eco Village	4

Dambulla & 7

birds and wildlife. It has a good range of accommodation, making it a convenient base from which to visit any of the Cultural Triangle's major sights. It's also the handiest point of departure for trips to **Minneriya and Kaudulla national parks**, which offer some of the island's best elephant-spotting, as well as the magical forest monastery of **Ritigala**, one of the Triangle's most atmospheric but least-visited attractions.

Ritigala

On a dirt track 8km north of the main Habarana–Anuradhapura highway, signposted 11km west of Habarana • Daily 7am–5pm • Rs.310 • Ⓦ ccf.gov.lk

North of Habarana, on the slopes of a densely wooded mountainside protected by the Ritigala Strict Nature Reserve, lie the mysterious remains of the forest monastery of **Ritigala**. The mountainside on which it sits is thought to be the Ramayana's Aristha, the place from which Hanuman leapt from Lanka back to India, having discovered where Sita was being held captive. According to popular belief, Hanuman later passed by Ritigala again, carelessly dropping one of the chunks of Himalayan mountain which he was carrying back from India for its medicinal herbs (other fragments fell to earth at Unawatuna and Hakgala); this is held to account for the unusually wide range of plants and herbs found at Ritigala, although the mundane explanation is that the area, being higher and wetter than the surrounding plains, supports a correspondingly wider range of plant species.

Ritigala's remoteness appealed to solitude-seeking **hermits**, who began to settle here as far back as the third century BC. In the ninth century, the site became home to an order of reclusive and ascetic monks known as *pamsukulikas*, who devoted themselves to a life of extreme austerity – *pamsukulika*, meaning "rag robes", refers to the vow taken by these monks to wear only clothes made from rags either thrown away or recovered from corpses. The order seems to have started as an attempt to return to traditional Buddhist values in reaction against the self-indulgent living conditions enjoyed by the island's clergy. So impressed was Sena I (r. 833–853 AD) with the spirit of renunciation shown by the order that he built them a fine new monastery at Ritigala, endowing it with lands and servants. Most of the remains you see today date from this era.

The ruins

Ritigala is magical but enigmatic, while the setting deep in a totally undisturbed tract of thick forest (not to mention the lack of tourists) lends an additional sense of mystery. Parts of the complex have been carefully restored, while others remain buried in the forest, but despite the considerable archeological work that has been done here, the original purpose of virtually everything you now see remains largely unknown. One striking feature is the site's complete lack of residential quarters – the monks themselve appear to have lived entirely in caves scattered around the forest.

Beyond the entrance, the path turns around the edge of the tumbled limestone bricks that once enclosed the **Banda Pokuna** tank – this possibly served a ritual purpose, with visitors bathing here before entering the monastery. At the far end of the tank, steep steps lead up to the beginning of a beautifully constructed **walkway** (similar to the meditation walkway at Arankele) which runs through the forest and links all the monastery's major buildings. After around 200m the walkway reaches the first of several **sunken courtyards**, bounded by a retaining wall and housing three raised terraces. The nearest terrace supports one of the **double-platform** structures which are a characteristic feature of Ritigala. These generally consist of two raised platforms oriented east–west, linked by a stone "bridge" and surrounded by a miniature "moat"; one of the platforms usually bears the remains of pillars, while the other is bare. Variou theories have been advanced as to the original functions of these structures. One holds that the "moat" around the platforms would have been filled with water, providing a natural form of air conditioning, while the platforms themselves were used for meditation – communal meditation on the open platform and individual meditation in the building on the linked platform opposite. A few metres to the right-hand (east) end of this enclosure is a second sunken courtyard, usually described as a **hospital**, although it may have been an almshouse or a bathhouse.

Beyond here, the pavement continues straight ahead to reach one of the "**roundabouts**" that punctuate its length – perhaps formerly a covered rest area, like the similar roundabout at Arankele. About 20m before reaching the roundabout, a path heads off to the right, leading through enormous tree roots to the so-called "**Fort**", reached by a stone bridge high above a stream, and offering fine views over the forests below.

As you continue past the roundabout, a couple of **unexcavated platforms** can be seen off the path in the woods to the left, looking exactly as they must have appeared to British archeologist H.C.P. Bell when he first began exploring the site in 1893. After another 500m you reach two further sunken courtyards. The **first courtyard** contains a substantial double-platform structure, one of the largest buildings in the entire monastery. The left-hand side of the courtyard is bounded by two **stelae**; according to one theory, monks would have paced between these while practising walking meditation. A few metres beyond lies the **second courtyard** and another large double platform.

Hurulu Eco-Park

8km north of Habarana along the Trincomalee road • Daily 2–6.30pm • $10

When the season is not right for wildlife-spotting at Minneriya and Kaudulla, jeep operators often run trips to **Hurulu Eco-Park**, on the edge of the vast Huluru Biosphere Reserve that stretches west of the Habarana–Trincomalee road. There's no lake here and the park's terrain is more reminiscent of Uda Walawe, dominated by long grass that makes elephant-spotting easy: from January to March you stand a chance of seeing herds of thirty or more of the beasts, though you're unlikely to see much other wildlife.

Kaudulla National Park

km off the main Habarana–Trincomalee road • Daily 6am–6pm • $12, plus the usual additional fees and taxes (see p.51); ask at the visitor centre at the entrance to arrange paddle boats for birdwatching on the tank • Jeep tours to Kadulla can be arranged through guesthouses and hotels in Habarana, Polonnaruwa and Sigiriya

Some 22km north of Habarana, **Kaudulla National Park** provides a link in the migratory corridor for **elephants**, connecting with Minneriya and Wasgamuwa national parks to the south, and Somawathiya National Park to the north and east – elephants move freely up and down the corridor, and local safari operators should know whether it's best to head to Kaudulla or Minneriya at any one particular time.

As at Minneriya, the centrepiece is a lake, the **Kaudulla Tank**, where elephants collect when water dries up elsewhere. The best time to visit is between August and December, with elephant numbers peaking in September or October (slightly later than Minneriya's "Gathering") when up to two hundred congregate at the tank. Outside the dry season much of the park is under water, and elephants can be more difficult to spot. Other **wildlife** inhabiting the park's mix of grasslands and scrubby forest includes sambar deer, monkeys and (very rarely seen) leopards and sloth bears, plus a characteristically wide array of birdlife.

Minneriya National Park

m east of Habarana on the Polonnaruwa road • Daily 6am–6pm • $15, plus the usual additional fees and taxes (see p.51) • Most hotels and guesthouses in Habarana, Polonnaruwa, Giritale and Sigiriya can arrange trips, while Mahoora (🌐 mahoora.lk) also run mobile tented safari camps in the park

Just a ten-minute drive east of Habarana, **Minneriya National Park** is one of Sri Lanka's most popular and interesting nature reserves, centred around the large **Minneriya**

Tank, created by the famous tank-builder and monk-baiter Mahasena (see page 331). Despite its relatively small size, the park boasts an unusually wide range of habitat types, from dry tropical forest to wetlands, grasslands and terrain previously used for slash-and-burn (*chena*) agriculture. Much of the area around the entrance is covered in superb dry-zone evergreen forest dotted with beautiful satinwood, *palu* (rosewood), *halmilla* and *weera* trees – though the thickness of the forest cover can make wildlife-spotting difficult.

The principal attraction here is **elephants**. Minneriya forms part of the elephant corridor that joins up with Kaudulla and Wasgomuwa national parks, and large numbers of the beasts can be found here at certain times of year during their migrations between the various parks – local safari operators should know whether there are more elephants here or in Kaudulla at any given time. They are most numerous from July to October, peaking in August and September when water elsewhere dries up and as many as three hundred or more come to the tank's ever-receding shores from as far away as Trincomalee to drink, bathe and feed on the fresh grass that grows up from the lake bed as the waters retreat – as well as to socialize and search for mates. This annual event has been popularly dubbed "**The Gathering**", the largest meeting of Asian elephants anywhere in the world. At other times, you may spot only a few elephants, which in fact are often more easily seen from the main Habarana–Polonnaruwa road that runs along the park's northern edge. Other **mammals** found in the park include sambar, spotted deer, macaque and purple-faced langur monkeys, plus sloth bears and around twenty leopards (although these last two are very rarely sighted), plus an enormous number of **birds**.

4

ARRIVAL AND DEPARTURE

By bus Habarana is located on a major road junction at the crossroads of the Dambulla, Anuradhapura, Polonnaruwa and Trincomalee roads. Buses stop at (or close to) the junction itself, at the northern end of the town centre. Though Habarana sees a lot of passing buses, not many originate here, so you may struggle to get a seat.
Destinations Anuradhapura (every 45min; 1hr 30min); Colombo (hourly; 5hr); Dambulla (every 20min; 45min); Giritale (every 20min; 30min); Kandy (every 30min; 2hr 45min); Polonnaruwa (every 20min; 1hr); Trincomalee (every 30min; 1hr 30min).

By train Habarana station is 2.5km north of the village o the Trincomalee road. As well as the trains below, there also a service (2hr 30m) to Trinco (plus a second service Colombo) but these leave and/or arrive in the middle of th night.
Destinations Batticaloa (2 daily; 3hr 30min–5hr 20min Colombo (1 daily; 5hr 40min); Polonnaruwa (1hr 15min 2hr 25min); Valaichchennai (2 daily; 2hr 40min–4 20min).

TOURS

Jeep tours Most local hotels and guesthouses, along with several local safari outfits, arrange jeep tours of the national parks; prices start from around Rs.3500–4000 for a 3hr jeep trip to either park (transport only); some places also offer inclusive ticket-and-transport deals starting

from around Rs.4500 per person to Kaudulla or Rs.6000 Minneriya per person in a group of at least two (in genera the larger the group, the lower the price). Compass Jee (☏ 077 717 1660), on the main road just south of th *Prasanna* café, is a reliable and inexpensive operator.

ACCOMMODATION

HABARANA

★ **Cinnamon Lodge** Dambulla Rd ☏ 066 227 0011, ⊛ cinnamonhotels.com; map p.307. One of the Cultural Triangle's most appealing places to stay, this stylish five-star occupies an idyllic setting spread out across superb grounds running down to the beautiful Habarana Lake. Accommodation is in spacious, good-looking rooms in a string of attractive two-storey cottages scattered around

the grounds, while facilities include a large pool, open-¤ pavilion restaurant and the Azmaara spa (which it shar with *Chaaya Village*). B&B $250
Habarana Village Dambulla Rd ☏ 066 227 004 ⊛ cinnamonhotels.com; map p.307. Traditional reso style hotel close to the lake, with large, comfortable roo in chalets dotted around sylvan grounds and an unusu fan-shaped pool. There's also the stylish Indonesi

Azmaara spa, though overall it lacks the class of its sister establishment, *Cinnamon Lodge*, next door. B&B **$110**

Mutu Village Kashyapagama Rd ☎077 269 4579, ⓦmutuvillage.com; map p.307. Smart, modern guesthouse in a wonderfully quiet location with seven bright modern rooms (all with a/c and hot water) boasting high ceilings and big French windows, plus a rather expensive but very nice "treehouse" (actually just an upstairs room made entirely of wood; $70). Their Ayurvedic spa includes a traditional herbal sauna. B&B **$40**

Other Corner Anuradhapura Rd ☎077 374 9904, ⓦtocsrilanka.com; map p.307. Gorgeous (if slightly pricey) little eco-resort set amid sylvan gardens running down to the lake, complete with organic vegetable plots, fruit trees and a small pool. Accommodation is spread around the grounds in a string of faux-mud-brick thatched cabanas (all a/c with hot water) – beautifully rustic outside but very comfortable within – plus a couple of cute rooms on stilts. There's also a good-looking thatched restaurant, and free nature walks with the resident naturalist. B&B **$143**

Paradise Guest Kashyapagama Rd ☎066 227 0227; map p.307. Three very spacious, cool, and spotlessly clean tiled rooms (all with hot water) set alongside a sandy square of garden. Good value, unless you take the startlingly expensive optional a/c (Rs.3500 extra). **Rs.2500**

Sundari Eco Village Kashyapagama Rd ☎066 227 0099, ⓦsundariecovillage.com; map p.307. Formerly the *Mihipiya Guest House*, this place has been spruced up with a new wing of stylishly appointed rooms with a/c, although it's still unclear how "eco" it is. The older fan rooms, including three with no hot water, are rather grim in comparison. There's also a new pavilion-style restaurant and a pleasant gazebo seating area. Fan **Rs.2000**, a/c **Rs.5000**

SOUTH OF HABARANA

Kassapa Lions Rock Digampathaha, 7km from Habarana ☎066 567 7440, ⓦkassapalionsrock.com; map p.307. Low-key resort hotel with attractively furnished rooms (all with TV, a/c and open-air showers) in attractive bungalows dotted around carefully manicured grounds with pool, spa and fine views of Sigiriya – although a new two-storey accommodation currently under construction may somewhat diminish its quasi-rural appeal. Good value, and with very inexpensive half- and full-board rates too. B&B **$115**

EATING

Acme Transit Hotel Polonnaruwa Rd, 500m from Habarana junction, ☎066 227 0280; map p.307. A big green eyesore from the outside but pleasantly cosy within, with good Sri Lankan standards including big lunchtime rice and curry spreads and tasty devilled dishes. Mains Rs.700–1200. Daily 8am–8pm.

Prasanna Restaurant Dambulla Rd ☎066 227 0026; map p.307307. Friendly little no-frills place serving up simple lunchtime rice and curries (Rs.300) plus inexpensive noodles, fried rice and short eats throughout the day. Hoppers are available at breakfast time. No alcohol. Daily 7am–10pm.

Windy Corner Seafood Restaurant Dambulla Rd ☎066 565 8239; map p.307307. Small a/c restaurant that's a great place to stop for a rice and curry lunch (Rs.700) but the real surprise is how good the seafood meals are (from Rs. 800). They also serve burgers, fried rice and devilled dishes. Daily 7am–10pm.

DIRECTORY

Ayurveda Aathreya Ayurvedic Spa on Kashyapagama Rd (☎066 227 0303, ✉athreyaayurvedaspa@gmail.com) is a beautifully rustic little Ayurveda centre, with pretty little palm-thatched, mud-walled treatment rooms and 1–3hr packages (Rs.4500–12,000) featuring various combinations of body and facial massages, body scrubs, herbal steam baths and shirodhara.

Banks There's a branch of the Commercial Bank with an ATM accepting foreign Visa cards at the main road junction, where the A6 meets the A11.

Polonnaruwa and around

The great ruined capital of **POLONNARUWA** is one of the undisputed highlights of the Cultural Triangle – and indeed the whole island. The heyday of the city, in the twelfth century, represented one of the high watermarks of early Sri Lankan civilization. The Chola invaders from South India had been repulsed by King Vijayabahu and the Sinhalese kingdom he established at Polonnaruwa enjoyed a brief century of magnificence under his successors Parakramabahu and Nissankamalla, who planned the city as a grand statement of imperial pomp. They transformed it briefly into one of the great urban centres of South Asia, before their own hubris and excess virtually bankrupted the state. Within a century, their enfeebled successors had been driven south by new waves of invaders from southern India and Polonnaruwa had been abandoned to the jungle, where it remained, unreclaimed and virtually unknown, for seven centuries.

Polonnaruwa's extensive and well-preserved remains offer a fascinating snapshot of medieval Sri Lanka and are compact enough to be thoroughly explored in a single

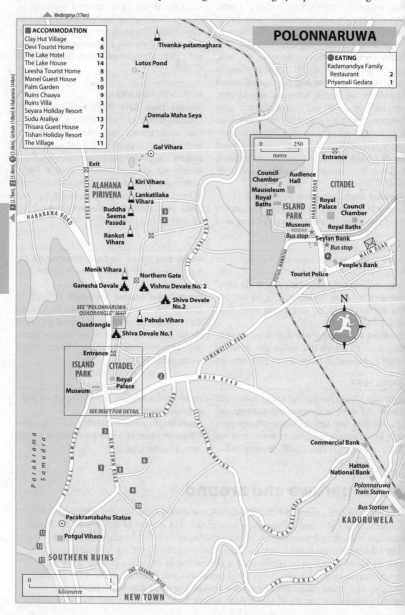

POLONNARUWA

▲ Medirigiriya (37km)

ACCOMMODATION
Clay Hut Village	4
Devi Tourist Home	6
The Lake Hotel	12
The Lake House	14
Leesha Tourist Home	8
Manel Guest House	5
Palm Garden	10
Ruins Chaaya	9
Ruins Villa	3
Seyara Holiday Resort	1
Sudu Araliya	13
Thisara Guest House	7
Tishan Holiday Resort	2
The Village	11

EATING
Kadamandiya Family Restaurant	2
Priyamali Gedara	1

Tivanka-patamaghara

Lotus Pond

Demala Maha Seya

Gal Vihara

Exit

ALAHANA PIRIVENA
Kiri Vihara
Lankatilaka Vihara
Buddha Seema Pasada
Rankot Vihara

Menik Vihara
Ganesha Devale
Northern Gate
Vishnu Devale No. 2
Shiva Devale No.2
Pabula Vihara
Quadrangle
Shiva Devale No.1

SEE "POLONNARUWA QUADRANGLE" MAP

HABARANA ROAD

RATAMUNA ROAD

1ST CANAL ROAD

Entrance
ISLAND PARK
CITADEL
Royal Palace
Museum

SEE INSET FOR DETAIL

Parakrama Samudra

SOMAWATIYA ROAD

MAIN ROAD

CIRCULAR ROAD

POTGUL MAWATHA

NEW TOWN ROAD

ISIPATHANA MAWATHA

Parakramabahu Statue
Potgul Vihara

SOUTHERN RUINS

4TH CHANNEL ROAD

Commercial Bank

Hatton National Bank

Polonnaruwa Train Station

Bus Station

KADURUWELA

2ND CHANNEL ROAD

2ND CANAL ROAD

NEW TOWN

0   1
kilometre

Inset:
0   250
metre

Entrance
Council Chamber
Audience Hall
Mausoleum
Royal Baths
ISLAND PARK
Museum
Bus stop
CITADEL
Royal Palace
Council Chamber
Royal Baths
Seylan Bank
Bus stop
People's Bank
Tourist Police

HABARANA ROAD
POTGUL MAWATHA
MAIN ROAD

N

POLONNARUWA OR ANURADHAPURA?

Many visitors to Sri Lanka only have the time or the archeological enthusiasm to visit one of the island's two great ruined cities, but given how different the two are it's difficult to call decisively in favour of either. The ruins at **Polonnaruwa** cover a smaller area, are better preserved and offer a more digestible and satisfying bite of ancient Sinhalese culture – and there's nowhere at Anuradhapura to match the artistry of the Quadrangle and Gal Vihara. That said, **Anuradhapura** has its own distinct magic. The sheer scale of the site and the number of remains means that, although much harder to get to grips with, it preserves a mystery that much of Polonnaruwa has lost – and it's far easier to escape the coach parties. In addition, the city's status as a major pilgrimage centre lends it a vibrancy lacking at Polonnaruwa.

albeit busy) day. Remains aside, Polonnaruwa is also a good jumping-off point for the national parks at Minneriya and Kaudulla (see page 309).

Brief history

The **history** of Polonnaruwa stretches far back into the Anuradhapuran period. The region first came to prominence in the third century AD, when the creation of the Minneriya Tank boosted the district's agricultural importance, while the emergence of Gokana (modern Trincomalee) as the island's major port later helped Polonnaruwa develop into an important commercial centre. As Anuradhapura fell victim to interminable invasions from India, Polonnaruwa's strategic advantages became increasingly apparent. Its greater distance from India made it less vulnerable to attack and gave it easier access to the important southern provinces of Ruhunu, while it also controlled several crossings of the Mahaweli Ganga, Sri Lanka's longest and most important river. Such were the town's advantages that four rather obscure kings actually chose to reign from Polonnaruwa rather than Anuradhapura, starting with Aggabodhi IV (r. 667–683).

Polonnaruwa's golden age

Throughout the anarchic later Anuradhapuran era, Polonnaruwa held out against both Indian and rebel Sinhalese attacks until it was finally captured by **Rajaraja**, king of the Tamil Cholas, following the final sack of Anuradhapura in 993. Rajaraja made it the capital of his short-lived Hindu kingdom, but in 1056 the city was recaptured by the Sinhalese king **Vijayabahu** (r. 1055–1110), who retained it as the new Sinhalese capital in preference to Anuradhapura, which had been largely destroyed in the earlier fighting. Vijayabahu's accession to the throne ushered in Polonnaruwa's golden age, although most of the buildings date from the reign of Vijayabahu's successor **Parakramabahu** (see page 314). Parakramabahu developed the city on a lavish scale, importing architects and engineers from India (whose influence can be seen in Polonnaruwa's many Hindu shrines). Indian influence continued with Parakramabahu's successor, **Nissankamalla** (see page 317), a Tamil from the Kalinga dynasty and the last king of Polonnaruwa to enjoy any measure of islandwide power.

Decline and fall

Nissankamalla's death ushered in a period of chaos. Opposing Tamil and Sinhalese factions battled for control of the city – the next eighteen years saw twelve changes of ruler – while at least four invasions from India threatened the stability of the island at large. This era of anarchy culminated with the seizure of the increasingly enfeebled kingdom by the notorious Tamil mercenary **Magha** (r. 1215–36). Under Magha the monasteries were pillaged, and onerous taxes imposed, while his soldiers roamed the kingdom unchecked and the region's great irrigation works fell into disrepair, leading to a decline in agricultural produce and a rise in malaria. Magha was finally driven out of Polonnaruwa in 1236, but the damage he had inflicted proved irreversible

PARAKRAMABAHU THE GREAT

The Sri Lankan monarch most closely associated with Polonnaruwa is **Parakramabahu I**, or Parakramabahu the Great (r. 1153–86), as he's often styled. Parakramabahu (a grandson of Vijayabahu) was born at Dedigama (see page 202), capital of the minor kingdom of Dakkinadesa, which was ruled by his father. Upon becoming ruler of Dakkinadesa, Parakramabahu established a new capital at **Panduwas Nuwara** (see page 287) before rising up against the king of Polonnaruwa, his cousin Gajabahu. After an extended series of military and political manoeuvrings, Parakramabahu finally triumphed and was crowned king of Polonnaruwa in 1153, although it took a brutal and protracted series of military campaigns before the entire island was finally subdued.

Even while Parakramabahu was mopping up the last pockets of resistance in the south, he began to embark on the gargantuan programme of building works and administrative reforms which transformed **Polonnaruwa** into one of the great cities of its age, as well as finding the time to launch a couple of rare military offensives overseas, first in Burma and then India. According to the Culavamsa, the new king built or restored over six thousand tanks and canals, including the vast new **Parakrama Samudra** in Polonnaruwa, as well as restoring the three great dagobas at Anuradhapura and rebuilding the monastery at Mihintale. It was at his new capital, however, that Parakramabahu lavished his greatest efforts, supervising the construction of a spate of imposing new edifices including the Royal Palace complex, the majestic Lankatilaka, and the beautiful Vatadage, the crowning achievement of medieval Sinhalese architecture.

4

and Polonnaruwa was finally abandoned in 1293, when Bhuvanekabahu II moved the capital to Kurunegala. The city was left to be swallowed up by the jungle, until restoration work began in the mid-twentieth century.

The ancient city

Daily 7.30am–5.30pm (last entrance) • $25; note that tickets (valid for one day only) aren't sold at the entrance to the site itself and must be bought at the Polonnaruwa Museum in the village (ticket office open daily 7.30am–5pm) • Bikes are available from virtually all the town's guesthouses for Rs.300–400/day • ⓦ ccf.gov.lk

The **ruins of Polonnaruwa** are scattered over an extensive area of gently undulating woodland about 4km from north to south. You can see everything at Polonnaruwa in a single long day, but you'll have to start early to do the city justice. The site is rather too large to cover by foot; the best idea is to rent a bike.

Polonnaruwa was originally enclosed by three concentric walls and filled with parks and gardens. At the heart of the city lies the **Royal Palace** complex, while immediately to the north is the city's most important cluster of religious buildings, the so-called **Quadrangle**, containing the finest group of remains in Polonnaruwa – and, indeed, in Sri Lanka. Polonnaruwa's largest monuments are found in the northern part of the city, comprising the buildings of the **Menik Vihara**, **Rankot Vihara**, **Alahana Pirivena** and **Jetavana** monasteries, including the famous Buddha statues of the **Gal Vihara** and the soaring **Lankatilaka** shrine.

Although Polonnaruwa doesn't have the huge religious significance of Anuradhapura, the city's religious remains are still held sacred and signs outside many of the ruins ask you to **remove your shoes** as a token of respect – quite painful, unless you're accustomed to walking barefoot over sharp gravel, while the ruins' stone floors can often reach oven-like temperatures in the midday sun. Wimps wear socks.

Parakrama Samudra

To the west of the city lies the great artificial lake, the **Parakrama Samudra** ("Sea of Parakramabahu"), providing a beautiful backdrop. The lake was created by the eponymous king, Parakramabahu, though sections of the irrigation system date right back to the third century AD. Covering some 26 square kilometres, it provided the medieval city with water, cooling breezes and an additional line of defence, and also irrigated over ninety square kilometres of paddy fields. The tank fell into disrepair after its walls were breached in the late thirteenth century, and was restored to its original size only in the 1950s.

The Polonnaruwa Museum
Daily 8.30am–5pm • Entrance with site ticket only • No photography

Close to the lakeshore on the northern edge of Polonnaruwa town is the modern **Polonnaruwa Museum**, one of the best in the country and well worth a look before setting off around the ruins. Exhibits include some fascinating **scale models** showing how the city's buildings might have looked in their prime, notably a fine mock-up of the Vatadage and a rather more conjectural model of Parakramabahu's Royal Palace. There's also an excellent collection of **bronzes** and **sculptures** recovered from the site – many are elaborately carved images of Hindu deities, proof of the huge influence which southern India exerted on the ancient city's culture.

The Citadel

At the heart of the ancient city lie the buildings of the **Citadel**, surrounded by a (heavily restored) circuit of walls. At the centre of the complex lie the remains of Parakramabahu's **Royal Palace** (Vijayanta Prasada). According to the Culavamsa, the palace originally stood seven storeys high and boasted a thousand rooms, although this was probably an exaggeration. The remains of three brick storeys have survived (any further levels would have been built of wood and have long since disappeared), although they don't give much idea of how the building would originally have looked – the ruins now appear more like a medieval European castle than a Sinhalese royal palace. The holes in the walls were for floor beams, while the vertical grooves up to the

4

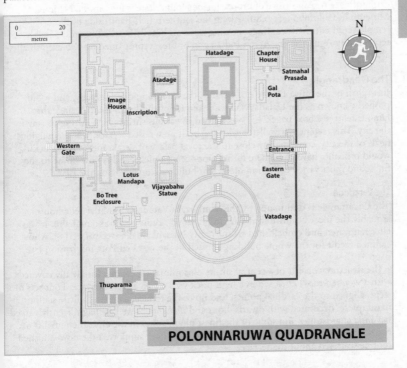

POLONNARUWA QUADRANGLE

first floor would have held wooden pillars; numerous patches of original plaster also survive.

Just east of the Royal Palace stand the remains of Parakramabahu's **Council Chamber** (Raja Vaishyabhuganga), where the king would have granted audiences to his ministers and officials. The wooden roof has vanished, but the imposing base survives, banded with friezes of dwarfs, lions and galumphing elephants. The sumptuous steps are embellished with *makara* balustrades, a pair of fine moonstones, and topped with two of the rather Chinese-looking lions associated with Sinhalese royalty during this period – other examples can be seen at Nissankamalla's Audience Chamber (see page 303) and at Yapahuwa.

Just east of here are the **Royal Baths** (Kumara Pokuna), designed in an unusual geometric shape (a square superimposed on a cross) and fed by two spouts carved with eroded *makaras*. Next to here stands the impressive two-tiered base of what is thought to have been the royal changing room, decorated with the usual lions and moonstone.

Shiva Devale no. 1

About 300m north of the Citadel lies the quaint little **Shiva Devale no. 1**, one of many temples at Polonnaruwa dedicated to either Vishnu or Shiva. The shrine dates from the Pandyan occupation of the early thirteenth century, following the collapse of Sinhalese power; the fact that the Indian invaders saw fit to construct an unabashedly Hindu shrine so close to the city's most sacred Buddhist precinct says much about their religious sympathies, or lack of.

The temple is made of finely cut, slate-grey stone, fitted together without the use of mortar. The bottom halves of two rudely truncated guardian figures stand by the doorway into the inner shrine, inside which stands a rather battered lingam – the extraordinary treasure-trove of **bronze images** found here is now in the National Museum in Colombo (see p.80). Along the southern (left-hand) side of the temple stand cute little carvings showing a pair of heavily bearded figures, possibly representing Agni, the pre-Aryan Indian god of fire, accompanied by two even smaller attendants.

The Quadrangle

Just north of the Shiva Devale no. 1 stands the **Quadrangle** – originally, and more properly, known as the Dalada Maluwa ("Terrace of the Tooth Relic"), since the famous relic (see box, page 215) was housed in various shrines here during its stay in the city. This rectangular walled enclosure, built on a raised terrace, was the religious heart of the city, conveniently close to the royal palace of Parakramabahu – the king would probably have come here for religious ceremonies – and is now home to the finest and most varied collection of ancient buildings anywhere on the island.

The Vatadage

The Quadrangle is dominated by the flamboyant **Vatadage** (circular relic house), arguably the most beautiful building in Sri Lanka. Built by Parakramabahu, it was later renovated and embellished by the crafty Nissankamalla (see page 317), who claimed credit for the whole building himself in the vast Gal Pota inscription (see page 317).

The structure consists of a central shrine plus miniature dagoba (originally covered with a wooden roof) enclosed in a high brick wall set on a raised terrace. Four sets of steps, aligned to the cardinal points, lead up to the terrace, each one a little sculptural masterpiece, decorated with dwarfs, lions and *makaras*, as well as magnificently carved *nagaraja* guardstones and some of the finest moonstones in the city. The remains of further pillars and carved capitals that would once have supported the now vanished roof lie scattered about the terrace.

NISSANKAMALLA THE VAINGLORIOUS

Following Vijayabahu and Parakramabahu, **Nissankamalla** (r. 1187–96) is the third of the famous trinity of Polonnaruwan kings. A Tamil prince, Nissankamalla originally hailed from South India, but married into the Sinhalese nobility by wedding a daughter of Parakramabahu, and then succeeded in attaining the throne after a brief political skirmish following the death of his father-in-law.

Nissankamalla was notable chiefly for being the last king of Polonnaruwa to exercise real power over the whole island, even feeling secure enough to launch military expeditions against the Pandyans of South India. Perhaps conscious of his foreign birth, he seems to have endeavoured to become more Sinhalese than the Sinhalese, making a great show of his religious orthodoxy, purging the Sangha of disreputable monks and becoming the first king to make the pilgrimage to the summit of Adam's Peak. He is also known to have embarked on extensive tours of the island to discover the conditions under which his subjects were living, rather in the manner of a contemporary politician at election time – not that Nissankamalla would have worried much about public opinion, since he considered himself (as did many later Sinhalese kings) a living god.

For all his genuine achievements, however, Nissankamalla is best remembered for the long trail of **inscriptions** he left dotted around Polonnaruwa and other places in Sri Lanka, recording his own valour, wisdom, religious merit and other outstanding qualities. The king's bombastic scribbles can be found in Polonnaruwa at the Gal Pota, Hatadage and Vatadage in the Quadrangle, and at the Rankot and Kiri viharas (plus a couple more in the Polonnaruwa Museum), though some historians regard the claims made in them as somewhat dubious, while Nissankamalla also stands accused of having stolen the credit for many of the building works carried out by Parakramabahu.

The only image of Nissankamalla stands in the Maharaja cave temple at Dambulla (see page 293). Ironically for this great self-publicist, it's tucked away in a corner, and almost completely hidden from sight.

From the terrace, further steps, aligned with those below, lead up into the central shrine through four entrances, each presided over by a seated Buddha, to the eroded remains of the central brick dagoba in which the **Tooth Relic** may have been enshrined – strangely enough, the inner sanctum is virtually unadorned, in striking contrast to the remainder of the building.

The Hatadage

Opposite the Vatadage stand the rather plain remains of the **Hatadage**, said to have been so named due to the fact that it was built in just sixty (*hata*) hours – which seems highly unlikely. Commissioned by Nissankamalla (who placed a long inscription just inside the main entrance on the right), the Hatadage may have been constructed to house the Tooth Relic and was originally two storeys high, though the upper storey has long since crumbled away. It now houses three Buddha statues, possibly intended to represent the Buddhas of the past, present and future; the central one is positioned to line up through the shrine's doorway with the Buddha directly opposite in the Vatadage.

The Gal Pota

Immediately east of the Hatadage stands the **Gal Pota** ("Book of Stone"), an enormous slab of granite, some 9m long, covered in a densely inscribed panegyric praising the works of the bumptious Nissankamalla (see page 317) – an astonishing display of self-publicity that would put even a modern politician to shame. The stone itself, according to the inscription, weighs 25 tons and was brought over 90km from Mihintale, though exactly why this particular slab was considered so remarkable that it had to be dragged all the way here remains unclear. On the end of the stone facing the Vatadage a carving shows the Hindu goddess Lakshmi being given a shower by two elephants, a traditional symbol of wealth.

The Satmahal Prasada

Next to the Gal Pota stands the strange **Satmahal Prasada** (the name means "seven-storey temple", though only six storeys survive). The ziggurat-like structure is unique in Sri Lanka and its original function remains unclear, although it may have been an unusual kind of step-sided stupa similar to those found in Southeast Asia – it's been hypothesized that Khmer (Cambodian) craftsmen may have been involved in the construction of the building, although no one really knows. The heavily eroded figures of a few deities and fragments of original white plaster can still be seen on its walls.

Just to the west of the Satmahal Prasada are the slight remains of a seventh-century **Chapter House** – just a tiny brick outline and a few pillars, including one in the unusual "thrice-bent" style of the Lotus Mandapa (see below).

The Atadage

On the other side of the Hatadage, the **Atadage** is one of the oldest structures in the city, having been constructed by Vijayabahu to house the Tooth Relic, although all that now remains are a few finely carved pillars and a delicate Buddha, standing contemplatively atop a lotus plinth in the middle of the now-derelict structure. A **tablet inscription** immediately to the west records details of the building's construction and the arrival of monks from Burma, on the far side of which are the remains of an **image house** – the brick plinth inside would have supported a now-vanished reclining Buddha.

The Lotus Mandapa

As you continue anticlockwise, the next building is the exquisite **Lotus Mandapa** (also known as the Latha Mandapaya or Nissankalata), a small open-air pavilion for religious rituals built by Nissankamalla. The *mandapa* features an unusual latticed stone fence, reminiscent of the Buddhist Railing at the Jetavana monastery in Anuradhapura, and a small platform surmounted by stone pillars shaped as thrice-bent lotus buds on stalks, a beautiful and very unusual design whose sinuous organic lines look positively Art Nouveau. In the centre of the platform are the remains of a tiny dagoba which was, according to different interpretations, either used to hold holy relics or which served as a seat for Nissankamalla during religious ceremonies (though not, presumably, both). In front of the Lotus Mandapa stands an armless **statue**, popularly thought to represent Vijayabahu, though it might be a bodhisattva.

The Thuparama

In the southwest corner of the Quadrangle stands one of its oldest structures, the **Thuparama**, an exceptionally large and well-preserved shrine thought to date back to the reign of Vijayabahu. The building's original name is unknown; it was confusingly christened the Thuparama ("The Stupa") by the pioneering British archeologist H.C.P. Bell, though it isn't actually a stupa at all but a gedige, a type of rectangular image house with a vaulted brick roof. At the time of research, it was covered in scaffolding for restoration work, but it was still possible to enter.

The exterior walls are decorated with elaborately carved *vimanas* (miniature representations of the dwellings of the gods). Inside, the shrine preserves part of its sturdy vaulted roof and traces of its original plasterwork, as well as exceptionally thick brick walls whose massive dimensions keep the interior pleasantly cool – the walls are so thick that the architects were actually able to construct a staircase inside them (you can see the doorway set in a recess on the left). At the back of the shrine are eight beautiful old standing and seated crystalline limestone Buddhas, which sparkle magically when illuminated.

Shiva Devale no. 2 and Pabula Vihara

The road north from the Quadrangle runs through attractive light woodland and past a scatter of minor monuments. The most interesting is the diminutive **Shiva Devale no. 2**, the oldest surviving structure in Polonnaruwa, dating back to the original eleventh-century Chola occupation. An inscription states that it was built in memory of one of his queens by the great Chola emperor Rajaraja, whose army destroyed Anuradhapura in 993. The pretty little domed building is pure Indian in style, boasting the same distinctive rounded capitals and niche windows that adorn the Shiva Devale no. 1. Four headless Nandis (Shiva's bull) stand guard around the shrine.

Just to the southwest of the Shiva Devale no. 2 stands the **Pabula Vihara** ("Red Coral Shrine"), named by H.C.P. Bell after the red corals he discovered during excavations here. Said to have been built by a certain Rupavati, one of Parakramabahu's wives, the vihara's main structure is a large brick dagoba, the third largest in Polonnaruwa, though restorations have reduced it to a strange two-tier stump which gives no clue as to its original form. The remains of various brick image houses and Buddha statues lie scattered around the base.

The Northern Gate and around

Continuing north along the main track brings you to the remains of the **Northern Gate**, which marked the limits of the central walled city. The **Vishnu Devale no. 2** and **Ganesha Devale** stand on the main track opposite one another on the south side of the gate. The former has a fine Vishnu image and the remains of stone (rather than brick) walls, though little remains of the latter. Immediately south of the Ganesha Devale are the equally slight ruins of another **Shiva Devale**, comprising the base of a tiny one-room shrine enclosing a battered lingam.

The city's monastic areas begin immediately north of the northern gate with the scattered and rather scant remains of the **Menik Vihara**. Little survives other than heavily restored foundations of assorted monastic buildings, a few armless (and sometimes also headless) Buddha statues, and the remains of a small brick dagoba whose top has crumbled away, exposing the relic chamber within.

Rankot Vihara

North of the Menik Vihara stands Nissankamalla's monumental **Rankot Vihara**, an immense red-brick dagoba rising to a height of some 55m. The fourth largest such structure in Sri Lanka, it's surpassed in size only by the three great dagobas at Anuradhapura, in imitation of which it was built, although its unusually steep sides and flattened top (it looks as though someone very large has sat on it) are less graceful than its Anuradhapuran antecedents. An inscription to the left of the entrance pathway describes how Nissankamalla oversaw work here, testifying to his religious devotion and the spiritual merit he presumably expected to gain from the stupa's construction – whether the forced labourers who were obliged to raise this gargantuan edifice shared the king's sense of religious idealism is not recorded.

Alahana Pirivena

A few hundred metres beyond the Rankot Vihara stretch the extensive remains of the **Alahana Pirivena** ("Monastery of the Cremation Grounds"), named after the royal cremation grounds established in this part of the city by Parakramabahu – the many minor stupas scattered about the area would have contained the relics of royalty or prominent monks. The monastery was one of the most impressive in the ancient city, and the remains here are some of the finest at the site.

Lankatilaka Vihara

At the heart of the Alahana Pirivena stands the majestic **Lankatilaka Vihara** ("Ornament of Lanka"), one of the city's finest monuments, with towering brick walls enclosing a huge – though now sadly headless – standing Buddha. The shrine as a whole emphasizes the change in Buddhist architecture and thought from the abstract symbolic form of the dagoba to a much more personalized and devotional approach, in which attention is focused on the giant figure of the Buddha (more than 14m high) that fills up the entire space within.

Built by Parakramabahu, the Lankatilaka is (dagobas excepted) one of the biggest, and certainly the tallest, building to survive from ancient Sri Lanka, and still an imposing sight, despite the loss of its roof and much of its original decoration. The entrance is approached by two sets of steps; the outer face of the upper left-hand balustrade sports an unusually fine lion carving. More unusual are the intriguing low-relief **carvings** on the exterior walls showing a series of elaborate multistorey buildings, probably intended to represent the celestial dwellings (*vimanas*) of the gods.

Kiri Vihara

Next to the Lankatilaka is the so-called **Kiri Vihara**, the best preserved of Polonnaruwa's dagobas, believed to have been constructed at the behest of one of Parakramabahu's wives, a certain Queen Subhadra. *Kiri* means "milk", referring to the white lime plaster that covers the building and which was almost perfectly preserved when the dagoba was rescued from the jungle after seven hundred years – and which recent restoration has now returned to something approaching its original milkiness. As at the Rankot Vihara, Kiri Vihara boasts four *vahalkadas* and an unusual number of brick shrines around its base, while on its south side an inscription on a raised stone plinth records the location at which Nissankamalla worshipped.

Buddha Seema Pasada

South of the Lankatilaka is the **Buddha Seema Pasada**, the monastery's chapter house, substantial building which might originally – judging by the thickness of its outer wall – have supported several upper storeys of brick or wood. In the middle of the building is a square pillared hall with a raised dais at its centre, surrounded by monks' cells and connected to the surrounding courtyard by four entrances, each with its own exquisite moonstone. Urns on pillars (symbolizing plenty) stand in the outer courtyard.

Gal Vihara

A short distance north of the Buddha Seema Pasada lies the magnificent **Gal Vihara** ("Stone Shrine"; also known as the Kalugal Vihara, or Black Stone Shrine), the undisputed pinnacle of Sri Lankan rock carving. The four Buddhas here, all chiselled from the same massive granite outcrop, originally formed part of the Alahana Pirivena monastic complex, with each statue formerly housed in its own enclosure – you can still see the sockets cut into the rock behind the standing image into which wooden beams would have been inserted. (Sadly, the modern answer to protecting the carvings from the elements is a pair of huge metal shelters which have plunged the statues into permanent twilight.)

The massive **reclining Buddha**, 14m long, is the most famous of the statues, a huge but supremely graceful figure which manages to combine the serenely transcendental with the touchingly human; the face, delicately flecked with traces of natural black sediment, is especially beautiful. The 7m-tall **standing Buddha** next to it is the most unusual of the set: its downcast eyes and the unusual position of its arms led some to consider it an image of Ananda, the Buddha's disciple, grieving for his departed master though it's now thought to represent the Buddha himself in the weeks following his enlightenment.

Two splendid **seated Buddhas** complete the group, posed against elaborately detailed backdrops which are rather unusual by the austere standards of Sri Lankan Buddhist art. The smaller of the two, unfortunately now kept behind a metal grille and fibreglass

shield, is placed in a slight cave-like recess (the other three would have been housed in brick shrines), seated in the *dhyani mudra* (meditation posture); other deities stand in the background, along with a distinctive arch modelled after the one at the great Buddhist shrine at Sanchi in India. Tiny strips of the beautifully detailed murals that once covered the interior of the cave can be seen hidden away in each corner.

The larger seated Buddha is also posed in *dhyani mudra* and entirely framed by another Sanchi-style arch, with tiny Buddhas looking down on him from their celestial dwellings – perhaps showing a touch of Mahayana Buddhist influence, with its belief in multiple Buddhas and bodhisattvas.

Demala Maha Seya

A kilometre north of the Gal Vihara, a rough side track leads to the **Demala Maha Seya** (or Damilathupa), an unfinished attempt by Parakramabahu to build the world's largest stupa using labour supplied by Tamil (*damila*, hence the dagoba's name) prisoners of war captured during fighting against the Pandyans. The dagoba is actually constructed on top of a natural hill: a retaining wall was built around the hill and the gap between filled with rubble, though it seems the dagoba was never finished. The remains of the structure had been completely buried under dense forest, although a short section of the massive three-tiered base was excavated and restored. A complete restoration of the entire structure is now underway, though the staggering scale of the project means that it will most likely take years to complete.

North to the Tivanka-patamaghara

Around 500m north of the Demala Maha Seya, just to the west of the main track, is an unusual **lotus pond** (*nelum pokuna*), formed from five concentric rings of stone finely carved in the shape of stylized lotus petals. The pond may have been used as a ritual bath for those entering the **Tivanka-patamaghara** image house, an exceptionally large and sturdy gedige-style brick structure a further 400m on at the far northern end of the site, now protected from the elements by a huge metal shelter. Along with the lotus pond, the Tivanka-patamaghara is one of the few surviving structures of the **Jetavana monastery**. *Tivanka* means "thrice-bent", referring to the graceful but headless Buddha image inside which is in a position (bent at the shoulder, waist and knee) usually employed only for female images.

The interior is also home to a sequence of outstanding (but rather difficult to see) **frescoes**, depicting scenes from the Buddhist Jatakas and lines of very finely painted Hindu-looking deities in sumptuous tiaras. The **exterior** shows the influence of South Indian architecture perhaps more clearly than any other Buddhist building in Sri Lanka with densely pillared and niched walls decorated with the usual friezes of lions, dwarfs and *vimanas*. The overall effect is richly exuberant, and a world away from the chaste Buddhist architecture of Anuradhapura. Restoration work continues inside and out.

Ruins beyond the main site

Two further complexes of ruins lie outside the main site: the **Island Park**, on a promontory jutting out into the lake a little north of the museum, and the **southern ruins**, a scenic fifteen-minute walk south along the raised bank of the lake. Although of lesser interest, they're still worth a visit and, as entry to them is free, you don't have to try to cram seeing them and the rest of the site into a single day.

Island Park

Daily 24hr • Free

Reachable from behind either the museum or the *The Lake House* (see page 324), the modest ruins of the **Island Park** (Dipanyana) complex comprise Parakramabahu's former pleasure gardens along with a string of later buildings constructed during the reign of Nissankamalla. The most interesting structure here is Nissankamalla's **Council Chamber**, similar to that of Parakramabahu (see page 314). The roof has vanished, but the raised base survives, studded with four rows of sturdy columns, some inscribed with the titles of the dignitaries who would have sat next to them during meetings with the king. A marvellous stone **lion** stands at the end of the plinth marking the position of Nissankamalla's throne.

Another of Nissankamalla's interminable **inscriptions** sits on the south side of the Council Chamber, while close by, the overgrown remains of a many-pillared **summer house** jut out into the lake. On the other side of the Council Chamber lie the slight remains of a large building, possibly Nissakamalla's **Audience Hall** (as it's signed), although it may have been his royal palace.

Just south of the Council Chamber are the remains of a small, square brick-built structure (signed "White Edifice"), possibly some kind of royal **mausoleum**, and sometimes said to mark the site of Nissankamalla's cremation. The surviving walls reach heights of around 5m and retain traces of red and white paint on their exterior – surprisingly bright and well preserved in places, considering that it's more than eight hundred years old. Nearby lie the remains of the extensive sunken **Royal Baths**.

The southern ruins
Daily 24hr • Free

Polonnaruwa's final group of remains, the modest **southern ruins**, lie 1.5km south of the Island Park along the lakeshore. The best-preserved building here is the **Potgul Vihara**, a circular image house surrounded by four small dagobas and the pillared ruins of monastic living quarters. The central room is thought to have housed a monastic library where the city's most sacred texts would have been stored, protected by massive walls that reach a thickness of around 2m at ground level.

The principal attraction, however, lies about 100m to the north: an imposing 3.5m-high **statue** of a bearded figure, thought to date from the ninth century, which has become one of Polonnaruwa's most emblematic images. It's usually claimed that the statue is a likeness of **Parakramabahu** himself, holding an object thought to be either a palm-leaf manuscript, representing the "Book of Law", or a yoke, representing the burden of royalty (the less reverent claim that it's a slice of papaya). Another theory holds that the statue could be the sage named Pulasti, a hypothesis lent credence by its position near the monastic library.

Mandalagiri Vihara
33km north of Polonnaruwa, and 3km northeast of Medirigiriya town • Daily 7.30am–6pm • Free • Buses run every 15min from Polonnaruwa to the village of Hingurakgoda, 13km north, where you can change onto a second bus, or take a tuktuk, for the bumpy 30min ride to Medirigiriya; hiring a vehicle from Polonnaruwa should cost around $30

The remains of **Mandalagiri Vihara**, which was built and flourished during the heyday of Polonnaruwa, are interesting, but the bother of reaching it mean that unless you have a particularly strong interest in Sinhalese Buddhist architecture, you probably won't find it worth the effort. The main attraction here is the fine eighth-century **vatadage**, similar in size and design to the vatadage at Polonnaruwa, though the quality of the workmanship is of a far lower level. The remains of other **monastic buildings** lie around the vatadage, including the base of a sizeable brick dagoba, a couple of tanks and assorted shrines and Buddha statues, many of them now headless.

ARRIVAL AND DEPARTURE	POLONNARUWA AND AROUND
By bus The main bus station is in the town of Kaduruwela, 4km east along the road to Batticaloa. If you arrive by bus, ask to be put off at Polonnaruwa "Old Town"; buses stop close to the Seylan Bank, within spitting distance of the	central guesthouses. Leaving Polonnaruwa you can hop on a bus at the stop on the main road, but to be sure of a seat it's easiest to take a tuktuk to the station at Kaduruwela (around Rs.300) and catch a bus there.

Destinations Anuradhapura (hourly; 2hr 30min); Batticaloa (every 30min; 2hr 30min); Colombo (every 30min; 6hr); Dambulla (every 30min; 1hr 45min); Giritale (every 15min; 30min); Habarana (every 20min; 1hr); Kandy (every 30min; 3hr 45min).

By train The train station is close to the main bus station in Kaduruwela.

Destinations Batticaloa (4 daily; 2hr 20min); Colombo (2 daily; 6hr 50min).

TOURS

Jeep tours Polonnaruwa is a convenient starting point for trips to Minneriya and Kaudulla national parks; most guesthouses and hotels can arrange a jeep to either park for around Rs.4500–5500.

Tuktuk tours It's also possible to visit the sites in Polonnaruwa and around by tuktuk. Nuwan Tuktuk Service (**☎** 072 444 3599) is reliable and very reasonably priced, with day trips starting at Rs.1000.

ACCOMMODATION

Polonnaruwa has an ever-growing selection of budget and mid-range **accommodation**, but few luxury options. There are a couple of more upmarket hotels 15km down the road at the village of **Giritale**, perched on the edge of the beautiful Giritale Lake; a third, the long-running *Royal Lotus* hotel, was closed for major (and much-needed) renovations at the time of writing. From Giritale there are frequent buses to Polonnaruwa, or tuktuks for around Rs.1000 each way.

POLONNARUWA

Clay Hut Village Rankot Vihara Rd **☎** 077 747 0560, **⊕** clayhutvillage.com; map p.312. Halcyon little place virtually in the shadow of the Rankot Vihara – the nearest you can get to actually staying in the ancient city. Set in a beautiful garden with its own small lake, the four spacious chalets resemble traditional village mud huts from the outside but are modern, tiled and very comfortable within; all have hot water and a/c. There's also a pretty little stilted restaurant, and excellent food. Note that although there is a gate to the ancient city close by, you may not be able to enter or exit here. <u>Rs.3500</u>, a/c <u>Rs.4500</u>

★ **Devi Tourist Home** 31 New Town Rd **☎** 027 222 3181, **⊕** facebook.com/devitouristhome; map p.312. Long-running guesthouse and still one of the nicest in Polonnaruwa, set in a peaceful location 1km south of town with five comfy rooms (three with a/c and hot water), good home-cooking and a very friendly welcome. <u>Rs.2000</u>, a/c <u>Rs.3000</u>

The Lake Hotel Off Potgul Mw **☎** 027 222 2411, **⊕** thelakehotel.lk; map p.312. Set in a fine lakeside location, this dated old hotel (formerly the *Seruwa*) has been given a thorough interior refurb, with glassed-in restaurant, smooth modern rooms (all with lake view) and a postage-stamp-sized pool. Uninspiring, but decent value. B&B <u>$105</u>

The Lake House Island Park, behind the museum **☎** 027 222 2299, **⊕** thelakehouse.lk; map p.312. Attractive boutique hotel in a superb lakeside location, with a sleek modern design and spacious white rooms

with beautiful lake views and dark wood-plus-saffron trimmings. The hotel sits on the plot of land previously occupied by Polonnaruwa's historic colonial rest house, although all that survives of the old building is the iron bathtub rescued from the room in which Queen Elizabeth II stayed in 1954, now taking pride of place in the Queen Suite. B&B <u>$300</u>

★ **Leesha Tourist Home** 105/A New Town Rd **☎** 071 334 0591, **⊕** leeshatouristhome.com; map p.312. Run by the affable and energetic Upali, this guesthouse offers simple, clean and comfortable rooms in a great location. The newer rooms at the rear of the property are quieter. This is a good place to get information on safari tours and other travel destinations. A rooftop restaurant was under construction at the time of research. <u>Rs.2000</u>, a/c <u>Rs.3000</u>

Manel Guest House New Town Rd **☎** 027 222 2481, **⊕** manelguesthouse.com; map p.312. One of Polonnaruwa's biggest guesthouses. Cheaper rooms in the old building (with hot water and fan) are functional but perfectly OK. The big, bright rooms in the smart new building at the back come with balconies and fine views over surrounding paddy fields. Old building <u>Rs.2000</u>, new building <u>Rs.3500</u>

Palm Garden 2nd Canal Colony, 1km from town **☎** 027 222 2622, **⊕** palmgarden.lk; map p.312. Low-key place in an attractively rural setting on the edge of town with four modern en-suite rooms, all with hot water and optional a/c (Rs.1000), plus two cheaper upstairs rooms sharing one bathroom (Rs.1500). Free pick-up/drop-off from town, and the owners can also arrange catamaran trips on the lake. <u>Rs.2500</u>

Ruins Chaaya 2nd Canal Colony **☎** 027 222 6999, **⊕** ruinschaaya.com; map p.312. Fancy new resort set amid lush gardens next to a paddy field. There are currently twelve tastefully furnished deluxe rooms, with TVs and fridges. The bathrooms are rather narrow with shower only. Good value for the price range. <u>$89</u>

★ **Ruins Villa** 99 Sri Nissankamallapura **☎** 071 861 9465, **⊕** ruinsvilla.com; map p.312. Four clean and spacious tiled rooms (two with a/c) in a newly built guesthouse stranded in the middle of a field. The welcome's very friendly, and the setting very peaceful. Note that although this guesthouse is close to the ancient city, you may not be able to enter or exit at the nearby gate. Rs.2500, a/c Rs.3250

Seyara Holiday Resort Bendiwewa, 3km west of Polonnaruwa (signed around 250m north of the main road) ☏027 222 3990, ⓦseyaraholiday.com; map p.312. Friendly and well-run family guesthouse with fourteen bright modern rooms, all nicely furnished and very comfortable; most have a/c and hot water, while some also have small balconies. Rs.3000, a/c Rs.5000

Sudu Araliya Potgul Mw, New Town ☏027 222 5406, ⓦhotelsuduaraliya.com; map p.312. Polonnaruwa's biggest hotel is in a fabulous lakeside location. Elephants regularly pass by in the late afternoon and there's a treehouse where you can view more wildlife or request to have your dinner. The large a/c rooms are perfectly comfortable and there's also a big pool and rustic little spa. B&B $110

★ **Thisara Guest House** New Town Rd ☏027 222 2654, ⓦthisaraguesthouse.com; map p.312. One of the nicest of Polonnaruwa's ever-expanding array of guesthouses, with spacious, comfy and very competitively priced rooms (all with hot water, plus optional a/c Rs.3500) set amid a large garden including a nice little outdoor restaurant with paddy-field views. The evening buffet is open to outside guests (call ahead to reserve). Rs.2000

Tishan Holiday Resort Bendiwewa, 4km west of Polonnaruwa (just west of the 64km post, on south side of the main road) ☏077 932 9451, ⓦtishanholidayresort.com; map p.312. On a peaceful side road overlooking paddy fields, this welcoming family guesthouse is slightly plusher (and pricier) than most of the competition, offering very comfortable rooms with hot water, TV and optional a/c (Rs.500). The gardens are spacious and there's also an attractive new pool area. B&B Rs.3000

The Village Potgul Mw, New Town ☏027 222 3366, ⓦthevillagehotel.org; map p.312. Charming, very low-key hotel set around attractive gardens and a decent-size pool. Rooms (all with a/c, hot water and satellite TV) are modestly decorated and squeaky clean. Although it's looking a bit dated, overall it's a very reasonable deal for the price. Rs.5500

GIRITALE

★ **The Deer Park** Giritale ☏027 777 7777, ⓦdeerparksrilanka.com. Giritale's most appealing address, with accommodation in a string of cute little buildings scattered around beautiful wooded grounds with fine lake views. Choose between the recently refurbished spacious rooms and even larger two-storey cottages, all with nice open-air showers. Facilities include a tranquil two-tier pool, gym and Ayurveda centre. B&B $150

Giritale Hotel Giritale ☏027 224 6311, ⓦgiritalehotel.com. The longest-running of Giritale's hotels with a commanding position high above Giritale Tank. All rooms have superb views. A major renovation is scheduled for mid-2018, which will no doubt bump up the price but improve the facilities. The excellent Ayurvedic health centre is open to outside guests. B&B $130

EATING

Kadamandiya Family Restaurant Main Rd ☏027 205 4438; map p.312. Roadside restaurant in a rustic two-storey hut, serving the usual array of Sri Lankan dishes, some European standards (mains Rs.300–900) and a good daily buffet (Rs.450) of rice and curry. The sign is in Sinhala, so look out for "family restaurant". Daily 8am–10pm.

Priyamali Gedara Bendiwewa, 3km from town ☏071 721 6480; map p.312. Traditional rice and curry meals, served in the rustic *gedara* (house) of hosts Priya and Mali. The daily lunch spread (Rs.950) features around ten seasonally changing curries including chicken and fish, plus local fruit and veg (such as jackfruit, breadfruit, drumsticks and longbean), all cooked over firewood (imparting extra flavour, it's claimed) and served with red rice on cute rattan plates and banana leaves. Best to reserve in advance for lunch, and they'll also open for dinner (Rs.1100) if you book by 5pm. To find it, follow the dirt road by the big Buddha on the north side of the main road, opposite the side road to the *Gimanhala Hotel*, and follow the signs; it's around 500m north of the road. Daily 11.30am–4pm & 6.30–8pm.

DIRECTORY

Bank The Seylan and People's banks both have ATMs accepting foreign cards.

Bike hire All the guesthouses and hotels listed above have bikes for hire for around Rs.300–400/day.

Internet Try KIT-PIC Computer Shop (daily 8am–8pm; Rs.100/hr) on the main road in the middle of town.

Swimming Non-guests can use the large and attractive pool at the *Sudu Araliya* hotel for Rs.500 or the slightly smaller pool at the adjacent *The Village* hotel for Rs.300, or free if you have a drink at the poolside bar.

Anuradhapura

For well over a thousand years, the history of Sri Lanka was essentially the history of **ANURADHAPURA** (see page 402). Situated almost at the centre of the island's northern plains, the city rose to prominence very early in the development of Sri Lanka, and maintained its pre-eminent position for more than a millennium until being laid waste

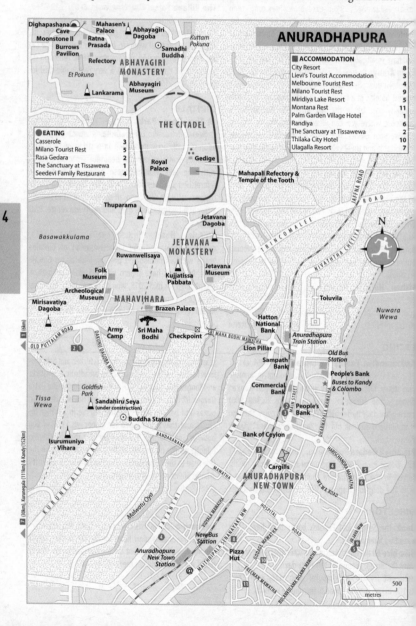

ANURADHAPURA

■ ACCOMMODATION

City Resort	8
Lievi's Tourist Accommodation	3
Melbourne Tourist Rest	4
Milano Tourist Rest	9
Miridiya Lake Resort	5
Montana Rest	11
Palm Garden Village Hotel	1
Randiya	6
The Sanctuary at Tissawewa	2
Thilaka City Hotel	10
Ulagalla Resort	7

● EATING

Casserole	3
Milano Tourist Rest	5
Rasa Gedara	2
The Sanctuary at Tissawewa	1
Seedevi Family Restaurant	4

ANURADHAPURA ORIENTATION

The vast scatter of monuments and ruins contained within Anuradhapura's **Sacred Precinct** can be seriously confusing. The easiest way to get a mental handle on the area is to think of it in terms of its three great monasteries: the **Mahavihara**, and the **Jetavana** and **Abhayagiri** monasteries – about two-thirds of the main sights belong to one of these complexes.

The obvious place to start is the Mahavihara, at the physical and historical centre of the ancient city, beginning at the **Ruwanwelisaya dagoba** and walking south to **Sri Maha Bodhi**, before doubling back towards the **Thuparama**. From here you can either head east to the Jetavana monastery or north to the Abhayagiri complex.

There are further important clusters of sights at the **Citadel**, between the Mahavihara and Abhayagiri monasteries; and **south of the Mahavihara**, between the Mirisavatiya dagoba and Isurumuniya Vihara. The major dagobas provide useful landmarks if you get disoriented, though beware confusing the Ruwanwelisaya and Mirisavetiya dagobas, which can look very similar when seen from a distance.

by Indian invaders in 993. Largely forgotten until its "rediscovery" by the British in the nineteenth century, Anuradhapura remains a magical place today. The sheer scale of the ruined **ancient city** – and the thousand-plus years of history buried here – is overwhelming, and you could spend days or even weeks ferreting around among the ruins.

At its height, Anuradhapura was one of the greatest cities of its age, functioning as the island's centre of both temporal and spiritual power, and dotted with dozens of **monasteries** populated by as many as ten thousand monks – one of the greatest monastic cities the world has ever seen. The kings of Anuradhapura oversaw the golden age of Sinhalese culture, and the temples and enormous **dagobas** they erected were among the greatest architectural feats of their time, surpassed in scale only by the Great Pyramids at Giza. The city's fame spread to Greece and Rome and, judging by the number of Roman coins found here, appears to have enjoyed a lively trade with the latter.

The tanks

Anuradhapura lies nestled between a trio of **tanks** – the lifeblood of the ancient city, although from the fifth century onwards their waters were supplemented by those from larger and more distant reservoirs such as the Kala Wewa. West of the Sri Maha Bodhi is the city's oldest tank, the **Basawakkulama**, created by King Pandukabhaya around the fourth century BC. South of the city is the **Tissa Wewa**, built by Devanampiya Tissa (250–210 BC), while to the east lies the largest of the three, the **Nuwara Wewa**, completed in around 20 BC and significantly expanded by later kings to reach its present imposing dimensions. The raised bunds (lakeside embankments) on the west and south sides of Nuwara Wewa are perfect for an evening stroll and some birdwatching, while there are wonderful views of the city's dagobas from the north shore of the Basawakkulama.

The Mahavihara

The centre of ancient Anuradhapura was the **Mahavihara**, the oldest of the city's monasteries and for many centuries its most important. The monastery was founded around the **Sri Maha Bodhi** by Devanampiya Tissa, who also built Sri Lanka's first dagoba here, the **Thuparama**, although this is now dwarfed by the great **Ruwanwelisaya**. The Mahavihara is still a living place of pilgrimage rather than an archeological site, with pilgrims flocking to the Ruwanwelisaya and Sri Maha Bodhi – the latter is still considered one of the world's most important Buddhist relics, rivalled in popularity in Sri Lanka only by the Tooth Relic in Kandy.

WATER WORLD: IRRIGATION IN EARLY SRI LANKA

The map of Sri Lanka is studded with literally thousands of man-made reservoirs, or **tanks**, as they're usually described (*wewa* in Sinhalese, pronounced, and occasionally spelt, "*vava*"), ranging in size from modest lakes to huge expanses of water many kilometres wide – a remarkable feat of landscape engineering without parallel in the ancient world. The early Sinhalese obsession with tank-building was primarily a result of the island's challenging climate, with its brief monsoonal deluges separated by long periods of drought. The ability to capture monsoon rains and then transport the stored waters where needed during the ensuing dry season was the major factor underpinning the economy of Anuradhapura, transforming the island's arid northern plains into an enormous rice bowl capable of supporting one of early Asia's most vibrant civilizations.

The first, modest examples of **hydraulic engineering** date back to around the third century BC, when farmers began to dam rivers and store water in small village reservoirs. As royal power increased, Sri Lanka's kings began to take an active role in irrigation schemes, overseeing the highly evolved bureaucracy and engineering expertise necessary to maintain and develop the system. The first giant reservoirs were constructed in the reign of **Mahasena** (r. 274–301), who oversaw the construction of some sixteen major tanks, including the Minneriya tank, and **Dhatusena** (r. 455–473), who constructed the remarkable Jaya Ganga canal, almost 90km long and maintaining a steady gradient of six inches to the mile, delivering water to Anuradhapura from the huge Kala Wewa – whose waters ultimately hastened that unfortunate king's demise (see page 300). Further tanks and canals were built during the reigns of **Mogallana II** (r. 531–551), whose Padaviya tank, in Vavuniya district, was the largest ever constructed in ancient Sri Lanka, and **Aggabodhi II** (r. 604–614), who was responsible for the tank at Giritale, among other works.

Waters stored in these huge tanks allowed a second rice crop and other produce to be grown annually, supporting far higher population densities than would otherwise have been possible. The surplus agricultural produce and taxes raised from the system were also major sources of royal revenue, allowing expansive building works at home and military campaigns overseas, culminating in the reign of Polonnaruwan king **Parakramabahu the Great** (see page 314), who famously declared that "not one drop of water must flow into the ocean without serving the purposes of man" and who oversaw the creation of the vast Parakrama Samudra at Polonnaruwa, one of the last but greatest examples of the Sinhalese genius for watering and greening the land.

Sri Maha Bodhi

Not included in the Sacred Precinct ticket; you may be asked for a donation of around Rs.200

At the spiritual and physical heart of Anuradhapura stands the **Sri Maha Bodhi**, or Sacred Bo Tree. According to popular belief, this immensely venerable tree was grown from a cutting taken from the original bo tree in Bodhgaya, India, under which the Buddha attained enlightenment, and brought to Sri Lanka by Princess Sangamitta, the sister of Mahinda (see page 339). The original bo tree in India was destroyed not long afterwards, but the Sri Maha Bodhi survived. New trees from cuttings taken from it have been grown all over the island and at temples in other Southeast Asian countries, providing a living link with the religion's decisive founding event.

The Sri Maha Bodhi sits at the centre of a large and elaborate enclosure, festooned with prayer flags and dotted with dozens of younger bo trees, some of which have grown, Angkor-style, out of (or even right through) the enclosure's stone walls. A series of elaborate terraces decorated with gold railings have been built up around the trunk of the Sri Maha Bodhi, although the tree itself is disappointingly unimpressive, appearing neither particularly large nor old (despite one large trailing branch propped up on gilded metal supports). Far more interesting is the general scene in the enclosure, usually full of devout white-robed pilgrims, while during poya days huge crowds flock here to make offerings.

The Brazen Palace

Closed to visitors, although you can see it through the fence

Just north of the Sacred Bo Tree stand the remains of the **Brazen Palace** ("Loha Pasada"), named on account of the copper roof which once covered it. The "palace" was built by Dutugemunu, though despite its name it only ever served as a monastic, rather than a royal, residence – the Mahavamsa describes a nine-storeyed structure with a thousand rooms (though the second part of this claim is doubtless hyperbole, and perhaps the first as well). Unfortunately, since most of the palace was made of wood, it burnt down just fifteen years after its construction and on a number of occasions thereafter, and had to be repeatedly rebuilt, most recently by Parakramabahu the Great in the twelfth century. Little remains now apart from a dense forest of plain, closely spaced **columns** – some 1600 in total – which would have supported the first floor. Confusingly, many of these did not belong to the Brazen Palace itself but were salvaged from other buildings at Anuradhapura. The only hint of decoration is on the fallen capitals, carved with dwarfs, that lie scattered around the ground in the southeast corner of the palace.

Ruwanwelisaya dagoba and around

North of the Brazen Palace stands the huge white **Ruwanwelisaya** (also known as the Maha Thupa, or "Great Stupa", though it's actually only the third largest in the city), commissioned by **Dutugemunu** (see page 330) to commemorate his victory over Elara. It's popularly believed to enshrine various remains of the Buddha, and is thus the most revered in the city.

The dagoba now stands 55m high, rather less than its original height, with the entire base encircled by a strip of coloured ribbon almost 300m long. According to tradition, the dagoba's original shape was inspired by the form of a bubble – a perfect sphere – though the effects of subsequent renovations have flattened its outline slightly. It stands on a terrace whose outer face is decorated with life-sized elephant heads (most are modern replacements). Symbolically, the elephants support the platform on which the dagoba is built, just as, in Buddhist cosmology, they hold up the earth itself (at a more prosaic level, elephants also helped in the construction of the stupa, being used to stamp down the dagoba's foundations). Four subsidiary dagobas stand in each corner of the terrace – considerable structures in their own right, but completely dwarfed by the main stupa.

From the entrance, steps lead up to the huge terrace on which the dagoba stands. Four **vahalkadas** mark the cardinal points around the base: tall, rectangular structures decorated with bands of elephant heads and, above, friezes of lions, bulls and elephants carved in low relief – the one on the western side is the oldest and yet to be restored. Walking clockwise around the dagoba you immediately reach a modern **shrine** holding five standing Buddha statues. The four identical limestone figures date back to the eighth century and are thought to represent three previous Buddhas and the historical Buddha; the fifth (modern) statue is of the future Buddha, Maitreya, wearing a tiara and holding a lotus. Continuing clockwise brings you to an extremely eroded limestone **statue** in a small glass pavilion, facing the

---

SACRED PRECINCT TICKETS

Most (but not all) of the sites at Anuradhapura are covered by a single **ticket** ($25), which can be bought at the Jetavana, Abhayagiri and Archeological museums, and at the ticket office at the northern entrance to the Jetavana dagoba. The ticket is only valid for one day which means (in theory) that if you want to spend more time exploring the site you'll have to shell out $25 on a fresh ticket, although the whole area is actually open access and ticket checks are rare except at the museums and the Samadhi Buddha. Most visitors tend to cram all Anuradhapura's sights into a day in any case, although this isn't really long enough to get the full flavour of the place. Note that the **Isurumuniya** and **Folk Museum** aren't covered by the main ticket, while you may also be asked for a donation when visiting the Sri Maha Bodhi.

DUTUGEMUNU THE DISOBEDIENT

Of all the two hundred or so kings who have ruled Sri Lanka over the past millennia, none is as revered as the semi-legendary **Dutugemunu** (r. 161–137 BC), the great warrior prince turned Buddhist king whose personality – a compelling mixture of religious piety and anti-Tamil nationalism – continues to provide inspiration for many Sinhalese today.

Dutugemunu grew up during the reign of the Tamil general **Elara**, who seized control of Anuradhapura in around 205 BC and reigned there for 44 years. Much of the island remained outside the control of Anuradhapura, however, being ruled by various minor kings and chiefs who enjoyed virtual autonomy, although they may have professed some kind of token loyalty to Elara. The most important of these subsidiary kings was **Kavan Tissa**, husband of the legendary Queen Viharamahadevi (see page 190). From his base in the city of Mahagama (modern Tissamaharama), Kavan Tissa gradually established control over the whole of the south. Despite his growing power, the naturally cautious king demanded that his eldest son and heir, Gemunu, swear allegiance to Elara. On being asked to make this oath, the 12-year-old Gemunu allegedly threw his rice bowl from the table in a fury, saying he would prefer to starve rather than declare loyalty to a foreign overlord, and subsequently demonstrated his contempt for his father by sending him items of women's clothing – all of which unfilial behaviour earned him the name of Dutugemunu, or "Gemunu the Disobedient".

On the death of Kavan Tissa, Dutugemunu acceded to the **throne**, raised an army and set off to do battle armed with a spear with a Buddhist relic set into its shaft, accompanied by a large contingent of monks – like the leader of some kind of Buddhist jihad. The subsequent campaign was a laborious affair. For fifteen years Dutugemunu fought his way north, conquering a succession of minor kingdoms until he was finally able to engage Elara himself at Anuradhapura. After various preliminary skirmishes, Elara and Dutugemunu faced one another in single combat. A mighty tussle ensued, at the end of which Dutugemunu succeeded in spearing Elara, who fell lifeless to the ground.

As the leader who evicted the Tamils and united the island under Sinhalese rule for the first time, Dutugemunu is still regarded as one of Sri Lanka's **great heroes** (at least by the Sinhalese). Despite his exploits, however, the fragile unity he left at his death quickly collapsed under subsequent, less able rulers, and within 35 years, northern Sri Lanka had once again fallen to invaders from South India.

dagoba's south side and popularly believed to represent Dutugemunu contemplating his masterpiece.

Kujjatissa Pabbata

A couple of hundred metres east of the Ruwanwelisaya is the **Kujjatissa Pabbata**, the remains of a small dagoba on a stone base with well-preserved guardstones. The structure dates from around the eighth century, but probably occupies the site of an earlier building – it's been suggested that this was the place, just outside what was once the south gate into the city, where Dutugemunu buried Elara and raised a memorial in honour of his fallen adversary.

Thuparama and around

North of the Ruwanwelisaya, a broad walkway leads 300m to the **Thuparama**. This was the first dagoba to be built in Sri Lanka (its name means simply "The Stupa"), though by later Anuradhapuran standards it's a modest affair, standing less than 20m high. It was constructed by Devanampiya Tissa shortly after his conversion to Buddhism at the behest of Mahinda (see page 339), who suggested that the new Sinhalese faith be provided with a suitable focus for worship. A monk was despatched to Ashoka, the Buddhist emperor of India, who obligingly provided Devanampiya Tissa with two of his religion's most sacred relics: the Buddha's right collarbone and alms bowl. The bowl was sent to Mihintale (and subsequently disappeared), while the bone was enshrined in the Thuparama, which remains a popular pilgrimage site to this day.

By the seventh century, the original structure had fallen into ruins; Aggabodhi II had it restored and converted into a **vatadage** (circular relic house), a uniquely Sri Lankan form of Buddhist architecture, with the original dagoba being enclosed in a new roof, supported by four concentric circles of pillars of diminishing height – an excellent model in the Archeological Museum (see page 331) shows how it would all have looked. The roof has long since disappeared and the surviving pillars now topple unsteadily in all directions, though you can still make out the very eroded carvings of geese (*hamsas*, a protective bird) which adorn their capitals. The dagoba itself is actually a reconstruction of 1862, when it was restored in a conventional bell shape – the original structure was built in the slightly slope-shouldered "heap of paddy" form.

Around the Thuparama

The area just south of the Thuparama is littered with the remains of buildings from the Mahavihara monastery, including numerous living units arranged in the quincunx pattern (like the five dots on the face of a die) which is characteristic of so many of the city's monastic dwellings. About 100m south of the Thuparama is a pillared shrine set on an imposing brick platform, with one of the most magnificent **moonstones** at Anuradhapura, though sadly it's protected – as are most of the city's best moonstones – by an ugly metal railing. The outer faces of the balustrades flanking the entrance steps are decorated with unusual carvings showing canopied panels filled with deer, hermits, monkeys, delicately sculpted trees and a pair of large lions. Their meaning remains unclear, though they may be intended to depict an ideal Buddhist realm in which creatures of all persuasions live harmoniously together.

4

The Archeological Museum

daily 8.30am–4.30pm; kiosk daily 8am–5.30pm • Entrance only with site ticket • No photography

West of the Ruwanwelisaya dagoba lies a pair of museums, although they can't be reached directly from the dagoba; you have to follow the road that runs north of Ruwanwelisaya and west to Basawakkulama, and then turn south along the lakeside road. Housed in a fine old colonial British administrative building, the **Archeological Museum** was still closed after a year-long restoration at the time of research, and it was unclear when it would re-open. In the meantime, you can still buy tickets to visit the Sacred Precinct from the kiosk by the entrance. Some exhibits from the museum's rooms are on display in open pavilions in the garden and include numerous sculptures from Anuradhapura and beyond, an interesting cutaway model of the Thuparama (see page 318), a reconstruction of the relic chamber from a dagoba at Mihintale, and colourful fragments of ancient murals recovered from inside the relic chamber of the great dagoba at Mahiyangana.

Folk Museum

Tues–Sat 8.30am–5pm • Rs.300; camera Rs.250

A little further north along the same road as the Archeological Museum, west of the Ruwanwelisaya dagoba, is the less interesting **Folk Museum**, which explores rural life in the North Central Province, with some rather dull displays of cooking vessels, handicrafts and the like. Save your time and money.

Jetavana monastery

The last of the three great monasteries built in Anuradhapura, the **Jetavana monastery** was raised on the site of the Nandana Grove – or Jotivana – where Mahinda (see page 339) once preached, and where his body was later cremated. The monastery was founded during the reign of the great tank-building king, **Mahasena** (r. 274–301), following one of the religious controversies that periodically convulsed the ancient city. Relations between Mahasena and the Mahavihara monastery had been strained ever since the king had disciplined some of its monks. They retaliated by refusing to accept alms from the king, who responded by pulling down some of the Mahavihara's buildings and then establishing the new Jetavana monastery on land owned by the Mahavihara. The king gave the monastery to a monk called Tissa – who was then promptly expelled from the Sangha for breaking the rule that individual monks should not own any private property. Despite this, the new monastery continued under a new leader, becoming an important rival source of Theravada doctrine within the city.

The Jetavana dagoba

The centrepiece of Jetavana is its monumental red-brick **dagoba**. Descriptions of this massive edifice tend to attract a string of statistical superlatives: in its original form the dagoba stood 120m high and was at the time of its construction the third-tallest structure in the world, surpassed only by two of the Great Pyramids at Giza in Egypt. It was also the world's biggest stupa and is still the tallest and largest structure made entirely of brick anywhere on earth, having taken a quarter of a century to build and containing more than ninety million bricks – enough, as the excitable Victorian archeologist Emerson Tennant calculated, to build a 3m-high wall from London to Edinburgh (though why anyone would wish to erect such a pointless construction at this exact height and between these two particular cities has never been satisfactorily explained). The dagoba has now lost its topmost portion, but still reaches a neck-wrenching height of 70m – similar to the Abhayagiri dagoba. **Vahalkadas** stand at each of the cardinal points; the one facing the entrance on the southern side is particularly fine, studded with eroded elephant heads, with *naga* stones to either side and two figures to the right – the top is a *nagaraja*, the lower one an unidentified goddess.

The rest of the monastery

The area south of the dagoba is littered with the extensive remains of the **Jetavana monastery**, all carefully excavated and landscaped. The monastery would once have housed some three thousand monks, and the scale of the remains is impressive, although except in a few places only the bases of the various structures survive. Most of what you see today dates from the ninth and tenth centuries.

Immediately behind the Jetavana Museum (see page 332) lies a deep and beautifully preserved **bathing pool** and the unusual latticed **Buddhist Railing**, which formerly enclosed either a bo tree shrine or an image house; the three tiers of the fence are claimed to represent Buddhism's "Three Jewels" (see 427). Slightly east of here stands the **Uposathagara** (chapter house), with dozens of roughly hewn and very closely spaced pillars; these probably supported upper storeys, since a room with this many pillars crowded into it would have been of little practical use.

To the west of the dagoba is the **Patimaghara** (image house), the largest surviving building at Jetavana: a tall, slender door leads between 8m-high walls into a narrow image chamber, at the end of which is a lotus base which once supported a standing Buddha. Below this is a latticed stone "**relic tray**" consisting of 25 holes in which relics or statues of various deities would have been placed; further examples are on show in the Jetavana Museum. Around the image house are more extensive remains of monastic residences – many are laid out in the characteristic quincunx pattern, with a large central building, in which the more senior monks would have lived, surrounded by four smaller structures, the whole enclosed by a square brick wall.

Jetavana Museum

Daily 7am–5.30pm • Entrance with site ticket only • No photography

The interesting **Jetavana Museum** holds a striking collection of objects recovered during decades of excavations around the monastery. The first of the three rooms contains fine fragments of decorative friezes and carvings from the site, including assorted Buddhas, a well-preserved guardstone and an unusually large relic tray. The second room is the most absorbing, filled with an assortment of finely crafted personal items that give a rare glimpse into the secular life of Anuradhapura, with displays of jewellery and precious stones. Next door is a less engaging collection of pottery, though look out for the ingenious three-tiered urinal pot. A pavilion outside has more stone sculptures: friezes, elephants and guardstones, although no descriptions or information.

The Citadel

The area north of the Thuparama, between the Mahavihara and Abhayagiri monasteries, is occupied by the **Citadel**, or Royal Palace area. This was the secular heart of the city, enclosed by a moat and thick walls, which perhaps reached a height of 5m.

Royal Palace

At the southern end of the complex lie the remains of the **Royal Palace**, one of the last buildings to be erected in the Sacred Precinct, commissioned by Vijayabahu I after his victory over the Cholas in 1070 – although by this time power had shifted to Polonnaruwa and the palace here was no more than a secondary residence. Little of the palace remains apart from the terrace on which it stood and a few bits of wall, although two fine **guardstones** survive, flanking the main steps up to the terrace and featuring a couple of unusually obese dwarfs (a similar pair guard the steps on the far side). A wall on the terrace, protected by a corrugated-iron shelter, bears a few splashes of paint, all that remains of the frescoes that once decorated the palace.

Mahapali Refectory

About 100m east of the Royal Palace, on the opposite side of the road, are the remains of the **Mahapali Refectory**, or Royal Alms Hall. The huge stone trough here would have been filled with rice for the monks by the city's lay followers and could have fed as many as five thousand – any monk could find food here, even during periods of famine. Next to the refectory is an impressively deep stepped **well**.

Temple of the Tooth and around

Immediately north of the Mahapali Refectory are the remains of a building studded with a cluster of columns reaching up to 4m high; this is thought to be the very first **Temple of the Tooth**, constructed to house the Tooth Relic (see page 215) when it was originally brought to the island in 313. The columns may have supported a second storey, and it's been suggested that the Tooth Relic was kept on the upper floor, thus setting the pattern for all the shrines that subsequently housed it. The Tooth Relic was taken annually in procession from here to the Abhayagiri in a ceremony which was the ancestor of today's great Esala Perahera at Kandy.

Just north of here are the partially reconstructed remains, reaching up to 8m high, of a brick **gedige**, with several original stone doorways and some of its window frames intact.

Abhayagiri monastery

The third of Anuradhapura's great monasteries, **Abhayagiri** was founded by King Vattagamini Abhaya (r. 89–77 BC), the creator of the Dambulla cave temples (see page 293), in 88 BC. According to the Mahavamsa, Vattagamini had earlier lost his throne to a group of invading Tamils but subsequently returned with an army and drove them out. Upon returning to Anuradhapura he quickly established a new Buddhist monastery in the place of the existing one, naming it after the second part of his own name (meaning "fearless" – as in the *abhaya*, or "Have No Fear", *mudra*).

Abhayagiri rapidly surpassed the older Mahavihara as the largest and most influential monastery in the country. By the fifth century it was home to five thousand monks and had become an important source of new Buddhist doctrine, and a flourishing centre of artistic activity and philosophical speculation. Although it remained within the Theravada tradition, elements of Mahayana and Tantric Buddhism were taught here (much to the disgust of the ultra-conservative clergy of the Mahavihara, who labelled the monks of Abhayagiri heretics), and the monastery established wide-ranging contacts with India, China, Myanmar (Burma) and even Java.

Abhayagiri is in many ways the most interesting and atmospheric part of the city. One of the great pleasures here is simply in throwing away the guidebook and wandering off at random among the innumerable ruins that litter the area – getting lost is half the fun. The sheer scale of the monastic remains is prodigious, while their setting, scattered amid beautiful light woodland, is magical – and particularly memorable early in the morning or at dusk.

Abhayagiri Museum
Daily 8.30am–5.30pm • Entrance with site ticket only • No photography

At the centre of the complex, the small but informative **Abhayagiri Museum** gives a detailed account of the monastery's history backed by an interesting selection of well-preserved artefacts including a fine (though armless) Buddha, and an unusually large *nagaraja*, both very eroded. Further stone sculptures are displayed on the veranda outside, including an impressive collection of guardstones and urinal stones.

Lankarama

Just south of the museum on the main road are the remains of the first-century BC **Lankarama** vatadage, thought to have originally formed part of the Abhayagiri nunnery. The vatadage's unusually square central dagoba has been thoroughly rebuilt in modern times, though many of the original pillars which formerly supported the vatadage's wooden roof have survived around it, some retaining their finely carved capitals.

Abhayagiri dagoba

As at Mahavihara and Jetavana, Abhayagiri's most striking feature is its great **dagoba**, said to mark the spot where the Buddha left a footprint on one of his three visits to Sri Lanka, standing with one foot here and the other on top of Adam's Peak. The dagoba was originally built by Vattagamini Abhaya and enlarged during the reign of Gajabahu I (r. 114–136); it formerly stood around 115m tall, only slightly smaller than the Jetavana dagoba, making it the second tallest in the ancient world – though the loss of its pinnacle has now reduced its height to around 70m.

Flanking the main entrance stand two guardian statues of **Padmanidhi** and **Samkanidhi**, two fat and dwarfish attendants of Kubera, the god of wealth. The statues have become objects of devotion in their own right, with pilgrims tying prayer ribbons to the grilles of the ugly little concrete sheds in which they are ignominiously confined. At the top of the steps stand a pair of the incongruously Grecian-looking urns, symbolizing prosperity, which can be found at several points around the monastery, while just beyond is a modern temple with a large reclining Buddha.

The dagoba's four **vahalkadas** are similar in design to those at the Ruwanwelisaya. Most interesting is the eastern *vahalkada*, flanked by unusual low-relief carvings showing elephants, bulls and lions, all jumping up on their hind legs, plus two winged figures looking like a pair of angels who've flown straight out of the Italian Renaissance.

The Samadhi Buddha

Around 250m east of the dagoba lies the so-called **Samadhi Buddha**, one of Anuradhapura's most celebrated images, now sheltered by a large concrete structure. A classic early example of Sinhalese sculpture, the figure was carved from limestone in the fourth century AD and shows the Buddha in the meditation (*samadhi*) posture. The Buddha was originally one of a group of four statues (the base and seated legs of another figure can be seen opposite it); it's thought that all four were originally painted, and sported gems for eyes.

Kuttam Pokuna

Northeast of the Buddha lie the superbly preserved **Kuttam Pokuna** ("Twin Baths"), constructed in the eighth century for monks' ritual ablutions. Standing at the far end of the smaller pond and looking to your right you can see a small stone pool at ground level. Water would have been fed into this and the sediment left to settle, after which the cleaned water would have been released into the smaller bath through the conduit with the eroded lion's head on one side. The superb *naga* (snake) stone next to this conduit was a symbol of good fortune, while the urns at the top of the stairs down into the bath symbolize plenty. Water passed from the smaller to the larger bath through small holes connecting the two.

West to Et Pokuna

The area **west of the Abhayagiri dagoba** is particularly rich in small monuments, while copious signs help make some sense of the bewildering profusion of remains that litter the forest hereabouts. West of the dagoba, a side road (signed "Elephant Pool and Refectory") leads past a second *samadhi* Buddha statue (similar to but less finely carved than the main Samadhi Buddha, and now missing its arms) to reach the Abhayagiri's **refectory**, complete with the usual huge stone trough – more than big enough to hold food for the monastery's five-thousand-odd monks.

A short distance further along stands the so-called **Burrows Pavilion**, a neat little stone structure named in honour of S.M. Burrows, archeological surveyor of Sri Lanka from 1884 to 1886, author of the *Buried Cities of Ceylon* and a leading figure in the nineteenth-century "discovery" of Anuradhapura. Nearby stand two impressive tenth-century pillar **inscriptions** recording various monastic rules and administrative details. The pavilion forms a kind of entrance to an extensive bo tree enclosure, signed **Bodhi Tree Shrine III**. The original tree has vanished, but the enclosing walls and a cluster of stone-slab seats survive largely intact along with another *samadhi* Budda, numerous *sri pada* carvings and a stone floor studded with lotus-shaped pillar bases.

From here it's a short walk south to the colossal **Et Pokuna** ("Elephant Pool"). Dug out of the bedrock, this is the largest bathing pool in the ancient city and quite big enough to hold a whole herd of elephants, should the need arise.

Ratna Prasada

Northeast of the Burrows Pavilion rise the slender pillars of the ruined **Ratna Prasada** ("Gem Palace"; signed as "Guardstone"), built in the eighth century to serve as the main chapter house of the Abhayagiri monastery, and originally standing five storeys tall. The main attraction here is the magnificent **guardstone** next to the building's entrance showing the usual *nagaraja* standing on a dwarf, shaded by a seven-headed cobra and carrying various symbols of prosperity: lotus flowers, a flowering branch and an urn. The **arch** that frames this figure shows an extraordinary chain of joined images, with four *makaras* swallowing two tiny human couples and two equally microscopic lions, separated by four flying dwarfs; an unimpressed elephant stands to one side. Not surprisingly, the symbolism of this strange piece of sculpture remains obscure.

Mahasen's Palace and around

A short distance north of Ratna Prasada, on the other side of the main track through this part of the monastery, lies **Mahasen's Palace** (signed as "Moonstone I"), though it's not actually a royal residence at all but an image house dating from the eighth or ninth century. It's famous principally for its delicately carved **moonstone**, sadly enclosed within a metal railing. Behind this rises a flight of finely carved steps supported by the inevitable dwarfs, squatting like tiny sumo wrestlers.

About 100m west of here is another magnificent (and unfenced) **moonstone** (signed as "Moonstone II"), almost the equal of the one at Mahasen's Palace, with further portly dwarfs supporting the steps behind.

Dighapashana Cave
Northeast of Moonstone II lies the **Dighapashana Cave** (signed "Sudassana Padhanaghara"), comprising the remains of a rudimentary brick structure nestled beneath a giant boulder. On the right-hand side of the cave, steps lead up to a long Pali inscription, carved into the rock.

The southern city
If you have the energy after seeing the rest of the site, make for the cluster of interesting remains that lie west and south of the Sri Maha Bodhi along the banks of the **Tissa Wewa**.

Mirisavatiya dagoba
Around 1km west of the Sri Maha Bodhi stands the **Mirisavatiya dagoba**, a huge structure that was the first thing to be built by Dutugemunu after he captured the city, very similar to – and only slightly smaller than – the Ruwanwelisaya dagoba. The obligatory legend recounts how the new king went to bathe in the nearby Tissa Wewa, leaving his famous spear (in which was enshrined a Buddhist relic) stuck in the ground by the side of the tank. Having finished bathing, he discovered that he was unable to pull his spear out – an unmistakable message from the heavens. At the dagoba's consecration, Dutugemunu dedicated the monument to the Sangha, offering it in compensation, the great king declared, for his once having eaten a bowl of chillies without offering any to the city's monks, a small incident which says much about both the island's culinary and religious traditions.

The dagoba was completely rebuilt by Kassapa V in the tenth century and is surrounded by various largely unexcavated monastic ruins. To its northeast you may be able to find the remains of a monks' **refectory**, furnished with the usual enormous stone rice troughs.

Goldfish Park
South of the Mirisavatiya dagoba, on the banks of the Tissa Wewa, lie the royal pleasure gardens, known as the **Goldfish Park** after the fish that were kept in the two **pools** here. The pools were created in the sixth century and used water channelled from the tank; the northern one has low-relief carvings of bathing elephants very similar to those at the nearby Isurumuniya temple, cleverly squeezed into the space between the pool and the adjacent rock outcrop.

Isurumuniya Vihara
Daily 6am–6pm; museum daily 8am–6pm • Rs.200
Some 500m south of Goldfish Park is the **Isurumuniya Vihara**, a venerable rock temple that dates right back to the reign of Devanampiya Tissa in the third century BC. Though it's a bit of a hotchpotch architecturally, it's worth a visit for its interesting stone **carvings**.

The main shrine and around
The steps leading up to the **main shrine** (on your right as you enter) are embellished with the usual fine, though eroded, guardstones and moonstone, while to the right, just above the waterline of the adjacent pool, are low-relief carvings of elephants in the rock, designed so that they appear to be bathing in the waters. To the right of the shrine door is an unusual carving showing a man with a horse looking over his

FESTIVALS IN ANURADHAPURA

The ancient city is crowded with pilgrims at weekends and, especially, on poya days, and is also the focus of several festivals. The largest, held on **Poson Poya** day (June), commemorates the introduction of Buddhism to Sri Lanka with enormous processions.

houlder, while inside the shrine a gilded Buddha sits in a niche carved directly into the ock.

To the left of the main shrine is a small **cave** inhabited by an extraordinary number of ery noisy bats.

urumuniya Vihara Museum

he temple's **museum** (in the modern building on your left as you enter) is home to number of its most celebrated carvings, all rather Indian in style. Perhaps the most mous is the fifth-century sculpture known as **The Lovers**, probably representing ither a bodhisattva and his consort or a pair of Hindu deities, though the figures are opularly thought to represent Prince Saliya, the son of Dutugemunu, and Asokamala, ne low-caste girl he fell in love with and married, thereby giving up his right to the rone. Another carving (labelled "King's Family") depicts a palace scene showing five gures, said to include Saliya, Asokamala and Dutugemunu.

he viewing platforms

queezed between the museum and bat cave, steps lead up to the two small rock utcrops looming above the temple, offering sweeping **views** north to the Jetavana agoba, and west over Tissa Wewa, best at sunset. Close by you can also see the base f the **Sandahiru Seya** ("Triumphant Stupa"; ⊕defence.lk/sadahiruseya), a gargantuan ew dagoba begun in 2014 to commemorate soldiers who gave their lives fighting the TTE, and which will contain an estimated thirty million bricks and stand 95m high hen finished.

4

RRIVAL AND DEPARTURE　　　　　　　　　　　　　　**ANURADHAPURA**

y bus There are two main bus stations in uradhapura: the New Bus Station, at the southern d of Main St is where most services arrive and depart, hile the Old Bus Station, off the northern end of Main , is the terminus for all public and private buses from Kandy via Dambulla as well as Colombo via runegala (although many buses call at both stations). hen leaving, check at your guesthouse to make sure u're going to the right bus station. For Sigiriya, take Kandy bus to Dambulla and pick up a connection from ere. For Polonnaruwa, it's often quicker to catch a bus Habarana and pick up a connection there. For Jaffna, u'll have to change at Vavuniya. For Trinco, if you can't t a direct bus catch a service to Horowupotana from nere there are frequent onward connections.

Destinations Colombo (every 30min; 5hr 30min); Dambulla (every 30min; 1hr 30min); Habarana (every 45min; 1hr 30min); Horowupotana (hourly; 2hr); Jaffna (via Vavuniya, every 45min; 5hr); Kandy (every 30min; 3hr 30min); Kurunegala (every 20min; 3hr); Mannar (hourly; 3hr); Polonnaruwa (every 45min until noon, then every 1hr 30min; 2hr 30min); Trincomalee (2 daily; 3hr); Vavuniya (every 45min; 1hr 30min).

By train The principal train station is on Main St just north of the centre of the New Town, a short tuktuk ride from the Harischandra Mw guesthouses. The subsidiary Anuradhapura New Town Station lies at the southern end of Main St, though not all services stop here.

Destinations Colombo (8 daily; 3hr 30min–5hr); Jaffna (4 daily; 2hr 45min–4hr 45min); Kurunegala (8 daily; 2–3hr); Vavuniya (6 daily; 50min–1hr 15min).

ETTING AROUND

bike The Sacred Precinct is much too big to cover on ot, and it's far easier to explore by bicycle; these can hired from virtually all the town's guesthouses for

Rs.400–500/day, though note that bikes (and indeed all types of vehicle) aren't allowed anywhere near the Sri Maha Bodhi.

INFORMATION AND TOURS

Guides Guides hang out mainly at the Jetavana Museum (see page 332). If you go with a guide, you might like to check their accreditation (they should be in possession of a Sri Lanka Tourism site guide's licence for Anuradhapura) to make sure you're getting someone genuine. Expect to pay around $15–20 for half a day, though you may be able to bargain.

Wildlife tours Anuradhapura makes a convenient bas for a trip to Wilpattu National Park; tours can be arrange through some of the local guesthouses, including *Milar Tourist Rest* and *Lievi's* – the latter currently offer day-trip at Rs.16,000 for two people or Rs.24,000 for four peopl including transport and all entry fees.

ACCOMMODATION

Anuradhapura has a good and growing spread of budget and mid-range accommodation, though a relative paucity of upper-range options – for something more upmarket you're better off heading to one of the two fine resorts west of the city.

IN THE CITY

City Resort 242 National Housing (behind the Hotel Dulyana) ☏071 992 3400, ☼bit.ly/cityresortap; map p.326. Smart guesthouse close to the bustling main road and bus station. There are five cool, white rooms with a/c, hot water and TVs, plus two new mixed and women-only dormitories. Meals are served on the tiny outdoor terrace, though at the time of research there was also a new restaurant in the works. They also offer night city tours and sunset trips to Mihintale at very reasonable prices. Dorms Rs.1100, doubles Rs.3800

★ **Lievi's Tourist Accommodation** 319/1 Vidyala Mw ☏077 320 6073, ☼lievistourist.com; map p.326. This well-run, centrally located guesthouse is one of the best places to stay in Anurdhapura. It has spacious, comfortable rooms at a very competitive price (Rs.1000 extra for a/c and hot water), while the beautiful L-shaped garden veranda is a fine place for a beer or meal. The friendly owner, Ranjan, can help organize safari tours. B&B Rs.2500

Melbourne Tourist Rest 388/28 Harischandra Mw ☏025 223 7843, ☼melrest.com; map p.326. Attractive little low-slung hotel in a quiet side street close to the centre of town. The modern rooms (all with hot water; a/c Rs.750 extra) are bright, spacious and comfortable enough if you don't mind the naff furniture, and the lovely garden patio at the front is a nice place to catch some rays. Rs.3500

★ **Milano Tourist Rest** J.R. Jaya Mw ☏025 222 2364, ☼milanotouristrest.com; map p.326. One of the town's standout cheapies, with bright budget rooms (all with hot water and satellite TV; a/c Rs.500 extra) at very competitive rates, plus very comfortable and nicely furnished deluxe a/c rooms in a second building over the road. There's also a good restaurant (see opposite) and free pick-up from the bus/train stations. Rs.1500, a/c Rs.3950

Miridiya Lake Resort Wasaladantha Mw ☏025 222 2112, ☼miridiyahotel.lk; map p.326. Recently expanded resort-style hotel arranged around attractive gardens running down to Nuwara Wewa. The rooms (a with a/c, TV, fridges and attractive outdoor bathrooms) a bright and stylishly furnished, and there's also a good-size pool. B&B $80

Montana Rest Off Freeman Mw ☏025 222 048 ☼montanarest.com; map p.326. Occupying a sma modern building in a quiet, leafy side street, this mi range guesthouse has a quiet atmosphere. Rooms a spotless and very comfortably furnished, and meals are served on the attractive garden terrace. Good value, give the quality. Rs.2500, a/c Rs.4000

Randiya Muditha Mw, off Harischandra Mw ☏025 22 2868, ☼hotelrandiya.com; map p.326. Appealing mi range hotel with a new wing of smart, comfortable delux rooms. The standard rooms in the original building are le attractive but clean and functional. There's also an excelle in-house restaurant, a pool and a bar. B&B: standard $4 deluxe $55

★ **The Sanctuary at Tissawewa** Sacred Precinc near the Mirisavatiya dagoba ☏025 222 229 ☼tissawewa.com; map p.326. Anuradhapura's mo memorable place to stay, this famous old rest house is s in a rambling and gorgeously atmospheric nineteenth century mansion (built for a former British governor) the heart of the Sacred Precinct, with a decent restaura (see page 339) attached. The ground-floor deluxe roor are rather lacking in furniture; superior rooms upstairs a much more comfortable, and only slightly more expensiv Deluxe $137

Thilaka City Hotel 560/2 Godage Mw ☏025 223 587 ☼thilakacityhotel.com; map p.326. Twelve neat wh modern rooms with a/c and hot water – functional an totally lacking in atmosphere, but very comfortable a with world-class mattresses, all at a reasonable price. $3

AROUND ANURADHAPURA

★ **Palm Garden Village Hotel** Puttalam R Pandulagama, 6km west of town ☏025 222 396 ☼palmgardenvillage.com; map p.326. Idyllic countr resort-style hotel, occupying a scatter of elegant coloni style buildings set within extensive and beautiful tree studded gardens. Rooms are attractively kitted out wi teak and mahogany furnishings, and there's also goo food, a nice bar, huge pool and Ayurveda centre. $175

...agalla Resort Thirappane, 25km south
... Anuradhapura and about 2km east of the
...nuradhapura–Kandy road @ 025 567 1000,
...ugaescapes.com; map p.326. Stunning boutique
...sort set in almost sixty acres of beautiful gardens spread
...ound the immaculately restored 150-year-old *walauwe*
(manor) of a former local bigwig. Accommodation is in
twenty huge and very private chalets, stylishly designed
with wooden floors, huge windows, private decks and
plunge pools, while facilities include a sylvan spa and a
positive supermodel of a pool. **$475**

...ATING

...ere aren't many places to eat in Anuradhapura –
...though all the guesthouses and hotels above do food,
...d most people end up eating where they're staying.

...asserole Second floor, 279 Main St @ 025 222 4443;
...ap p.326. This cavernous modern restaurant makes a
...ange from yet more rice and curry, with a big menu of
...od-value Chinese meat, fish and veg standards spiced
... for its Sri Lankan clientele – far from authentic, but
...rprisingly tasty. Mains mostly Rs.450–600. Unlicensed.
...ily 11am–10pm.

...ilano Tourist Rest J.R. Jaya Mw @ 025 222 2364,
... milanotouristrest.com; map p.326. The well-run
...staurant at this excellent hotel (see page 338) is one
... the best in town, with cheery service and a usually
...nvivial atmosphere. The menu covers all bases, from
...e and curry through to seafood and assorted Chinese
...d Continental dishes – prices are slightly above average
...ost mains Rs.800–900) but generally worth it. Daily
...30am–11.30pm.

Rasa Gedara Main St; map p.326. Looking a tad
incongruous in Anuradhapura's busy main street, this faux-
village palm thatch-style construction serves up a decent
lunchtime rice and curry (veg Rs.350, chicken Rs.450) out
of traditional claypots, featuring around ten seasonally
changing dishes. Unlicensed. Daily 7am–5pm.

The Sanctuary at Tissawewa Sacred Precinct @ 025
222 2299; map p.326. This fine old colonial hotel (see
page 338) makes an excellent lunch stop while exploring
the Sacred Precinct, serving up assorted salads, sandwiches
and soups (Rs.300–850), plus more substantial Sri Lankan
mains (Rs.700–1400). Choose between the smart,
modern, colonial-style dining room inside or take a seat
on the terrace. No alcohol is served. Daily 7am–9.30pm.

Seedevi Family Restaurant Jayanthi Mw @ 025
222 5509; map p.326. Big modern "family" restaurant
(meaning no booze) offering a passable range of local and
international dishes, including Chinese, Thai and pasta
(mains Rs.400–900). Daily 6am–10.30pm.

...IRECTORY

...anks There are branches of all the major banks strung
...t along Main St, most with ATMs accepting foreign cards.
...ternet The Communications & Internet Centre next to
...e New Bus Station has a few machines.

Swimming Non-guests can use the pools at the Miridiya
Lake Resort (Rs.400) and at the *Rajarata* hotel just around
the corner (Rs.500); the pool at the latter is huge, and
given how moribund the hotel is, chances are you'll have
the entire thing to yourself.

...Mihintale

...IHINTALE, 12km east of Anuradhapura, is revered as the place where Buddhism
...as introduced to Sri Lanka. In 247 BC (the story goes) the king of Anuradhapura,
...evanampiya Tissa (r. 250–210 BC), was hunting in the hills of Mihintale. Pursuing a
...ag to the top of a hill, he found himself confronted by **Mahinda**, the son (or possibly
...other) of the great Buddhist emperor of India, Ashoka, who had been despatched
... convert the people of Sri Lanka to his chosen faith. Wishing first to test the king's
...telligence to judge his fitness to receive the Buddha's teaching, Mahinda proposed his
...lebrated **riddle of the mangoes:**

...hat name does this tree bear, O king?"
...his tree is called a mango."
...there yet another mango besides this?"
...here are many mango-trees."
...nd are there yet other trees besides this mango and the other mangoes?"
...here are many trees, sir; but those are trees that are not mangoes."
...nd are there, beside the other mangoes and those trees which are not mangoes, yet other trees?"
...here is this mango-tree, sir."

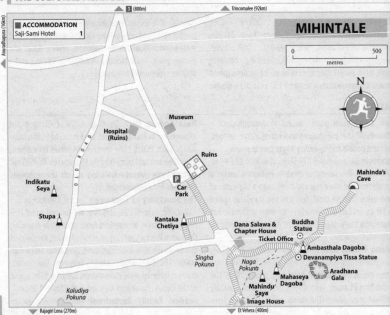

Having established the king's shrewdness through this laborious display of arboreal logic, Mahinda proceeded to expound the Buddha's teachings, promptly converting (according to the Mahavamsa) the king and his entire entourage of forty thousand attendants. The grateful king gave Mahinda and his followers a royal park in Anuradhapura, which became the core of the Mahavihara monastery, while Mihintale (the name is a contraction of *Mahinda tale*, or "Mahinda's hill") also developed into an important Buddhist centre. Although modern Mihintale is little more than a large village, it remains an important pilgrimage site, especially during **Poson Poya** (June), which commemorates the introduction of Buddhism to Sri Lanka by Mahinda, during which thousands of white-robed pilgrims descend on the place.

The ruins and dagobas at Mihintale are relatively ordinary compared to those at Anuradhapura, but the setting – with rocky hills linked by beautiful flights of stone steps shaded by frangipani trees – is gorgeous. Mihintale can be tiring, however: there are **1850 steps**, and if you want to see all the sights you'll have to climb almost every single one of them (although you can avoid the first flight by driving up the Old Road to the Dana Salawa level). It's a good idea to visit in the early morning or late afternoon to avoid having to tackle the steps in the heat of the day.

The site

Daily 24hr • Rs.500

At the bottom of the site, near the car park, lie the remains of a **hospital**, including fragments of treatment rooms and a large stone bath in which patients would have been washed in healing oils and herbs. Most of the island's larger religious complexes had similar infirmaries, where doctors used a highly developed system of Ayurvedic medicines and treatments that were perhaps not so far from those used in today's hotels and clinics. On the other side of the road stand the remains of a monastic structure, its buildings arranged in a characteristically Anuradhapuran quincunx pattern.

The Kantaka Chetiya

The broad first flight of steps heads up directly from the car park. At the first small terrace, steep steps lead off on the right to the remains of the **Kantaka Chetiya** dagoba. Not much remains of the body of this dagoba, which originally stood over 30m high, but the four Anuradhapura-style *vahalkadas*, decorated with elephants, dwarfs and other creatures, are extremely well preserved.

Just south of the dagoba, on a huge boulder perched precariously on its side, is an unusual **inscription** in a very early, proto-Brahmi script.

The Medamaluwa monastery

Returning to the main steps from the Kantaka Chetiya and continuing up brings you to a large terrace and the remains of the **Medamaluwa monastery**, the most important at Mihintale. The first building on your left is the **Dana Salawa** ("Alms Hall"), home to an enormous stone trough (plus a somewhat smaller one next to it at a right angle) that would have been filled with food for the monastery's monks by lay followers.

The terrace immediately above, built on enormous slabs of stone, was the site of the former **chapter house**, its doorway flanked with two large stone **tablets** in Sinhala. Erected during the tenth century, these stelae lay down the rules and responsibilities pertaining to the various monks and lay staff at the monastery – a kind of medieval Sinhalese job description. The brick bases of vanished dagobas lie all around, along with the remains of further monastic buildings, including the **Conversation Hall**, which preserves a few of its original 64 pillars.

On the opposite side of the terrace, near the top of Old Road, is the small **Singha Pokuna** ("Lion Pool"), named after the unusual, though very eroded, sculpture of a lion rampant, through whose mouth water was fed into a now vanished pool. The small frieze above is decorated with a well-preserved strip of carvings showing lions and dancers.

The upper terrace

To the right of the Conversation Hall, a long flight of steps leads up to the heart of Mihintale, the very spot (it's claimed) at which Devanampiya Tissa met Mahinda. You have to buy a **ticket** at the top of the stairs before entering the terrace, and take off your shoes.

At the centre of the terrace is the **Ambasthala dagoba**, a surprisingly small and simple structure for such an important site – the name means "Mango Tree Dagoba", referring to Mahinda's convoluted conundrum. The dagoba was subsequently roofed over, vatadage-style, as testified by the two rows of pillars around it. Immediately next to it is a single simple **sri pada**, surrounded by gold and silver railings, into which people throw coins for luck. Nearby is an extremely ancient **statue**, claimed to be of Devanampiya Tissa, though it might just be of a bodhisattva. Its arms have long since vanished, while its head has fallen off and now sits Yorick-like on a brick plinth in front. According to tradition, the Ambasthala dagoba covers the spot where Mahinda stood during the famous meeting, while the statue marks the position of Devanampiya Tissa, though given how far apart they are, this seems unlikely, unless their conversation – and the mango riddle – was conducted as a kind of shouting match.

Aradhana Gala

Various pathways lead from the upper terrace to a number of further sights. Close to the ancient statue, irregular rock-cut steps lead very steeply up the bare rock outcrop of **Aradhana Gala** ("Invitation Rock"), from which Mahinda preached his first sermon. On the other side, a shorter flight of steps leads up to a large, modern white **seated Buddha**, posed in an unusual composite posture: the left hand is in the meditation posture, while the right is in the "explanation" (*vitarka*) pose.

4

Mahinda's Cave

A long path from the upper terrace leads to **Mahinda's Cave** (Mahindu Guhawa), a bit of a hike down a rough woodland path (particularly challenging without shoes). The "cave" is actually an opening beneath a huge boulder poised precariously on the rim o the hillside at the edge of a large drop. On the floor is a simple rectangular outline cut out of the rock, popularly believed to be Mahinda's bed.

Mahaseya dagoba

Once you've seen all the sights around the upper terrace, collect your shoes (but don't put them on) and head up one final set of steps to the white **Mahaseya dagoba**, claimed to enshrine some ashes and a single hair of the Buddha. The dagoba (which can be seen quite clearly all the way from Anuradhapura) is the largest and the second highest at Mihintale, in a breezy hilltop location and with wonderful 360-degree view over the surrounding countryside – you can usually just make out the great dagobas o Anuradhapura in the distance. Immediately next to it are the substantial remains of th lower portion of a large brick dagoba, the **Mahindu Saya**, which is thought to enshrin relics associated with Mahinda.

Et Vehera

Walk past the Mahindu Saya (you can put your shoes on now) down a path cut into the rock to reach the ruins of an **image house** atop the usual stone base with flights of stairs and remains of pillars. From here, a tough ten-minute slog up steep steps (and lots of them) leads to **Et Vehera**, located at what is easily the highest point at Mihintale There's nothing much to see apart from the remains of a small brick dagoba – despite the great sense of altitude, the views aren't really any better than those from the Mahaseya dagoba.

Naga Pokuna

From Et Vehera you can retrace your steps to the image house and head back downhil via the **Naga Pokuna**, or "Snake Pool", a rock-cut pool guarded by a carving of a five-headed cobra (though it's sometimes submerged by water). Romantic legends associat this with the queen of Devanampiya Tissa, though the prosaic truth is that it was simply part of the monastery's water-supply system.

Outlying remains

West of the main site on the Old Road are the remains of another monastery and two dagobas, the larger known as **Indikatu Seya**. South of here lies the hill of **Rajagiri Lena** Brahmi inscriptions found here suggest that the caves on the hillside might have been home to Sri Lanka's first-ever Buddhist monks. The tranquil **Kaludiya Pokuna** pool nearby looks natural but is actually man-made. Beside it are the remains of a small tenth-century monastery, including a well-preserved cave building with windows and door – either a bathhouse or a monk's dwelling.

ARRIVAL AND DEPARTURE

By bus Buses leave for Mihintale from Anuradhapura's New Bus Station roughly every 15min.

By tuktuk A tuktuk from Anuradhapura costs arou Rs.3000 return including waiting time.

ACCOMMODATION

Saji-Sami Hotel Just west off the A9 Vavuniya Rd, about 800m north of Mihintale Junction ☎ 025 226 6864, ⊛ sajisamihotel.com; map p.340. Your best bet in the (unlikely) event that you want to stay the night in Mihintale; it has super-helpful owners and a peace location on the north side of town. Clean and comfy roo have a/c, hot water and satellite TV. There's also a nice p and bikes are free to rent. $50

Tantirimalai

On the boundary of Wilpattu National Park some 46km northwest of Anuradhapura, **Tantirimalai** (or Tantirimale) is one of the Cultural Triangle's most remote and least-visited destinations – which for many is a major part of its appeal. The ruins here, of the original **Tantirimalai Rajamaha Vihara** (royal temple), are said to date back to the third century BC, marking one of the places at which Princess Sangamitta (see page 428) rested while travelling to Anuradhapura to deliver a cutting from the legendary bo tree under which the Buddha gained enlightenment to the newly converted Devanampiya Tissa.

Tantirimalai Rajamaha Vihara

Daily 24hr; museum daily 8am–4.30pm • Free (although a donation may be requested)

The ruins of **Tantirimalai Rajamaha Vihara** are widely scattered over a strikingly lunar landscape of bare, undulating rock, dotted with the occasional stunted tree. On arrival, head for the small **museum**, where there's a map of the site in English (helpful, since most of the signage is in Sinhala) and you may also be able to find an English-speaking member of staff to give a you brief explanation of the site.

A modern dagoba marks the highest point of the site, while the nearby bo tree is said to have been grown from a cutting from the original one brought to the island by Sangamitta. Below this, a striking image of a meditating Buddha has been chiselled out of the side of a rock outcrop, while on the northern side of the dagoba is an even larger reclining Buddha, again hewn painstakingly from solid rock. Numerous other monastic ruins can be found dotted around the site, including the remains of the former monastic library, built into a cave, and a bathing pond that is said never to run dry.

ARRIVAL AND DEPARTURE

TANTIRIMALAI

By car The most direct approach is from Anuradhapura (about 1hr–1hr 30min each way; a car and driver will cost around Rs.4000–5000), heading northwest via Nikawewa village. There's an alternative approach via the A14 Mannar road, following the side track (unsurfaced) around 5km west of Neriyakulam on the main highway.

By bus Buses that pass through Tantirimalai depart from the bus stop on Bandaranaike Mawatha near the train line. The trip takes 45min–1hr (Rs.50). Check at the museum on arrival for the return bus times.

The east

KONESWARAM KOVIL

5 The east

Sri Lanka's east coast is a mirror image of its west. When it's monsoon season in the west, the sun is shining in the east; where the west coast is predominantly Sinhalese, the east is largely Tamil and Muslim; and where parts of the west coast are crowded with tourists and almost buried under a surfeit of hotels, the east remains much quieter – for the time being, at any rate.

Much of the east's beautifully pristine coastal scenery derives, ironically, from its tragic wartime past, during which time the region splintered into a fluid patchwork of territories controlled variously by government and LTTE forces. Two decades of fighting took a devastating toll on the east's already struggling economy: villages were abandoned, commerce collapsed and the coast's few hotels were simply blown up and allowed to fall into the sea. Meaningful reconstruction and economic development became possible only after the LTTE were finally driven out of the area in 2007, and although the lingering effects of war can still be seen in some places, the east's fortunes have now decisively turned: ambitious plans are being realized to tap into the coast's massive tourist potential, exemplified by the extraordinary glut of new resorts recently constructed around the formerly war-torn and deserted Passekudah Bay.

Most people here live in the long string of mainly Tamil and Muslim towns and villages that line the coast, backed by fine sandy beaches and labyrinthine lagoons; the vast swathes of predominantly Sinhalese country inland – whose arid climate has always discouraged settled agriculture – remain sparsely populated and largely undeveloped. Capital of the east is the vibrant town of **Trincomalee**, with its appealing blend of faded colonial charm, colourful Hindu temples and beautiful coastal scenery. Few tourists venture this way, however, except to press on to the extremely low-key beachside villages of **Uppuveli** and **Nilaveli**, just up the coast. South from here, the golden beaches at **Passekudah** are now home to the east's largest cluster of resort hotels, while continuing south brings you to the personable town of **Batticaloa**, strung out around its enormous lagoon. Further south, the laidback surfing hotspot of **Arugam Bay** is home to the east's most enjoyable beach and also provides the starting point for trips to the national parks of **Lahugala** and **Yala East**, and the remote forest hermitage at **Kudimbigala**.

The best **weather** and main tourist (and surfing) season is from April to September, although conditions are usually also pretty good in February and March, when hotel prices in places like Arugam Bay and Uppuveli are much cheaper and the area as a whole is less crowded.

Brief history

Although now something of a backwater, the east was for many centuries the most outward-looking and cosmopolitan part of the island, a fact borne out by its (for Sri Lanka) unusually heterogeneous **ethnic make-up** – with roughly equal numbers of Sinhalese, Tamils and Muslims, the region is the most culturally diverse in Sri Lanka. Much of the area's early history revolved around **Gokana** (modern Trincomalee), the island's principal trading port during the Anuradhapuran and Polonnaruwan eras, and the harbours of the east continued to serve as an important conduit for foreign influences in subsequent centuries. **Islam** spread widely along the coast thanks to visiting Arab, Malay and Indian traders, while the European powers also took a healthy interest in the region. The **Dutch** first established a secure presence on the island at the town of Batticaloa, while it was the lure of Trincomalee's superb deep-water harbour more than anything else that drew the **British** to the island.

With the rise of the new ports at Galle and later Colombo, the east gradually fell into decline, while its fortunes nose-dived during the **civil war**, which turned Tamils,

ARUGAM BAY

Highlights

❶ Trincomalee Founded around one of the world's finest deep-water harbours, bustling Trinco boasts a lovely coastal setting, a fine colonial fort and an absorbing mixture of Hindu, Muslim and Christian traditions. See page 349

❷ Batticaloa Wrapped in a labyrinth of maze-like waterways, historic Batticaloa is home to a venerable Dutch fort, time-warped colonial churches and deserted beaches. See page 360

❸ Arugam Bay The east coast's most appealing beach hangout, with quirky cabanas, mangrove-fringed lagoons and world-class surfing. See page 365

❹ Lahugala National Park Small but beautiful national park, home to the east's largest elephant population and conveniently close to Arugam Bay. See page 369

❺ Kudimbigala Remote forest hermitage, with shrines and stupas scattered amid dramatic, rock-strewn jungle. See page 370

❻ Maligawila This sleepy village is home to two superb large-scale Buddha statues, hidden away in an atmospheric forest setting. See page 372

HIGHLIGHTS ARE MARKED ON THE MAP ON PAGE 348

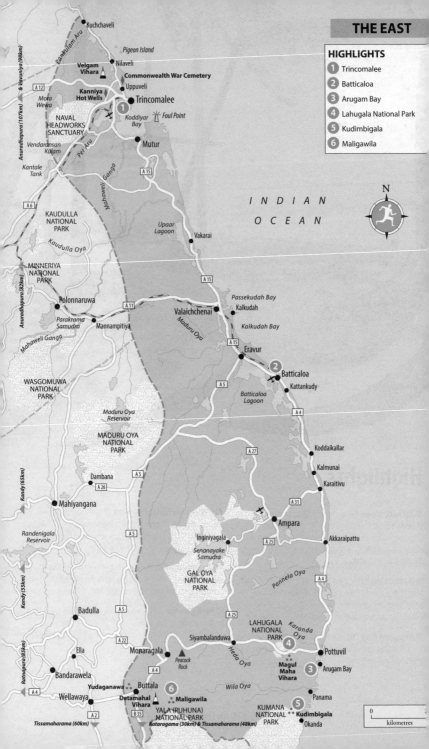

HIGHLIGHTS
1. Trincomalee
2. Batticaloa
3. Arugam Bay
4. Lahugala National Park
5. Kudimbigala
6. Maligawila

Kuchchaveli

Pigeon Island

Velgam
Vihara   Nilaveli

Rankulam Aru

Commonwealth War Cemetery

& Vavuniya (98km)

Uppuveli

Kanniya
Hot Wells   **Trincomalee**

Mora
Wewa

Anuradhapura (107km)

A 12

1

Foul Point

NAVAL
HEADWORKS
SANCTUARY

Koddiyar
Bay

Vendarasan
Kolam

Mutur

Kantale
Tank

A 6

A 15

Per Aru

Mahaweli Ganga

KAUDULLA
NATIONAL
PARK

Kaudulla Oya

Upaar
Lagoon

Vakarai

MINNERIYA
NATIONAL
PARK

Anuradhapura (82km)

A 15

I N D I A N

O C E A N

N

Polonnaruwa

A 11

Parakrama
Samudra   Mannampitiya

Maduru Oya

Passekudah Bay

Valaichchenai   Kalkudah

Kalkudah Bay

Mohaweli Ganga

A 15

Eravur

2   Batticaloa

WASGOMUWA
NATIONAL
PARK

A 5

Kattankudy

Batticaloa
Lagoon

A 4

Maduru Oya Reservoir

MADURU OYA
NATIONAL
PARK

Koddaikallar

A 27

Kalmunai

Dambana

A 26

A 5

Karaitivu

A 31

Kandy (65km)

Mahiyangana

Ampara

Akkaraipattu

Randenigala
Reservoir

Inginiyagala

A 25

Senanayake
Samudra

Pannela Oya

A 4

GAL OYA
NATIONAL
PARK

Kandy (55km)

A 5

Badulla

A 5

Ella

A 22

Ratnapura (85km)

Bandarawela

A 4

Wellawaya

A 2

Monaragala

A 4

Peacock
Rock

Siyambalanduwa

A 25

LAHUGALA
NATIONAL
PARK

Karanda
Oya

4

Pottuvil

3   Arugam Bay

Magul
Maha
Vihara

Heda Oya

Yudaganawa

Buttala   6

Maligawila

Detamahal
Vihara

YALA (RUHUNA)
NATIONAL PARK

Wila Oya

Panama

KUMANA
NATIONAL
PARK   5   **Kudimbigala**

B 35

Tissamaharama (60km)

Kataragama (30km) & Tissamaharama (48km)

Okanda

0   kilometres

Muslims and Sinhalese against one another in a frenzy of communal violence. LTTE attacks against unprotected Sinhalese and Muslim villagers were a recurring feature of the war years, including one particularly gruesome massacre of around 150 men and boys at Kattankudi mosque (just south of Batticaloa) in 1990. The LTTE also seized pockets of territory throughout the area (including, for a time, Batticaloa itself), and was only finally driven from its last eastern strongholds in 2007.

ARRIVAL AND GETTING AROUND THE EAST

By plane Getting to the east remains a bit of a slog unless you fly – currently Cinnamon Air (ⓦcinnamonair.com) flies from Colombo's international airport to Batticaloa (1 daily; 1hr 15min) and Trincomalee (1 daily; 1hr 15min). Helitours (ⓦhelitours.lk) offer services from Colombo's Ratmalana airport to Trincomalee (3 weekly; 45 min) and from Trincomalee to Palaly airport, near Jaffna (3 weekly; 30 min).

By road Major road upgrades have made getting around the east far quicker and more comfortable than was previously the case. The highway between Trincomalee and Batticaloa, formerly a pot-holed slog with three small ferry crossings en route, has now been rebuilt and equipped with new bridges, including the 396m Kinniya bridge outside Trinco, the longest in Sri Lanka. This now connects seamlessly with the A4, which continues on from Batticaloa to Pottuvil (for Arugam Bay) and Monaragala, and which is also in excellent condition.

By train There are stations at Trincomalee, Batticaloa and Valaichchenai (for Passekudah/Kalkudah), although the paucity and slowness of services means that they're not a huge amount of use.

Trincomalee

Eastern Sri Lanka's major town, **TRINCOMALEE** (or "Trinco") has been celebrated since antiquity for its superlative deep-water **harbour**, one of the finest in Asia – the legendary Panduvasudeva (see page 403) is said to have sailed into Trincomalee (or Gokana, as it was originally known) with his followers, while the town served as the major conduit for the island's seaborne trade during the Anuradhapuran and Polonnaruwan periods. The harbour was later fought over repeatedly during the colonial period and even attracted the hostile attentions of the Japanese air force during World War II.

Trincomalee suffered massively following the onset of the **civil war** in 1983. Although the town avoided the devastating bomb damage inflicted on Jaffna, its position close to the front line made it the island's major collecting point for war-displaced refugees, while tensions between its Tamil, Muslim and Sinhalese communities regularly erupted into communal rioting. Things have been a lot quieter since the expulsion of the LTTE from the east in 2007, and Trinco is now once again looking to the future with renewed optimism, with plans for an expressway link to Polonnaruwa and Jaffna in the works.

Although most visitors are drawn to this part of the island by the beaches at nearby Nilaveli and Uppuveli, a day in Trincomalee offers an interesting change of scenery. The setting is beautiful, straddling a narrow peninsula in the lee of the imposing **Swami Rock**, the dominant feature on the coast hereabouts, and the town itself possesses an understated but distinct charm all of its own, with a fascinating old **fort** and sleepy backstreets lined with pretty colonial villas and dotted with mosques, churches and dozens of colourful little **Hindu temples**. Catering to the predominantly Tamil local population, the temples give parts of Trinco a decidedly Indian flavour, especially at around 4pm when it fills with the ringing of bells and the sound of music for the late-afternoon puja.

Fort Frederick

Daily 24hr • Free

The centrepiece of Trincomalee is **Fort Frederick**, whose buildings sprawl across the narrow peninsula that juts out into the sea from the middle of town, dividing Back Bay from Dutch Bay. The fort was constructed by the Portuguese in 1623 and captured in

5

1639 by the Dutch. They held it until 1782, after which it was captured by the British and then the French, who ceded it back to the British, who returned it briefly to the Dutch before getting their hands on it for good in 1796. The British rechristened it Fort Frederick in 1803 after the then Duke of York and enjoyed undisputed possession of the place until independence, troubled only by a solitary Japanese air raid on April 9, 1942.

The fort is still in military use, although visitors are free to walk through along the road up to Swami Rock. Entrance is through the attractive **main gate**, its outer face carved with the date 1675 and a British coat of arms bearing the legend "Dieu et Mon Droit".

Wellesley Lodge

Inside the fort, the pleasantly shady grounds are dotted with fine old trees and home to a small population of wandering deer. A few colonial buildings survive, including one known variously as **Wellesley Lodge** or Wellington House, named after Arthur Wellesley, later the Duke of Wellington, who stayed here in 1800. A popular legend claims that the Iron Duke fell ill in Trincomalee and was thus unable to sail with his ship, which subsequently sank with the loss of all crew, although the story has got somewhat twisted in the telling. In fact, Wellesley made it as far as India before being struck down with a combination of fever and the "Malabar itch". A course of lard and sulphur failed to shift the infection, and the future prime minister was forced to stay behind in Bombay while the doomed ship sailed off without him.

Swami Rock

The main road through the fort leads up to **Swami Rock**, a towering clifftop vantage point offering sweeping views back to town, along the coast and down the sheer cliff face to the deep-blue waters way below – blue whales can occasionally be seen from here. At the highest point of Swami Rock sits the **Koneswaram Kovil** (see below), one of the five holiest Shaivite temples on the island, although there's not much visible evidence of its former glory.

Lover's Leap

Just outside Koneswaram Kovil, close to the highest point of Swami Rock, a tree clings precariously to the edge of the rock, its branches adorned with prayer flags that supplicants have somehow managed to attach. This spot is popularly known as **Lover's Leap**, in commemoration of a certain young Dutch woman, Francina van Rhede, who is said to have jumped from the cliff here in 1687. The details are confused: some

---

KONESWARAM ABOVE AND BELOW THE WAVES

There's thought to have been a shrine on the site of the **Koneswaram Kovil** for at least 2500 years. According to legend, Indra, king of the gods, worshipped here, while Rawana is said to have brought the temple's venerated *swayambhu* lingam here from Mount Kailash in the Himalayas. Rawana subsequently tried to make off with the entire temple but was stopped by Shiva; the cleft in Swami Rock is said to have been created when Shiva forced him to drop his sword.

The medieval temple was patronized by the great Chola, Pandyan and Pallava dynasties of southern India, developing into Sri Lanka's pre-eminent Hindu shrine – the "**Rome of the Orient**", as it was described – with three separate temples spread across the headland, soaring gopurams and a magnificent "thousand-columned" hall. Unfortunately, the splendour of the complex attracted the attentions of the Portuguese, who destroyed it in 1624 during one of their iconoclastic rampages. Some stones from the various temples were reused in the construction of the neighbouring fort, while the rest of the complex was simply shoved over the edge of the cliff into the waters below, where it remained largely forgotten for 350 years, before being rediscovered in the 1960s by author Arthur C. Clarke and photographer Mike Wilson. Wilson also recovered the famous *swayambhu* lingam, subsequently enshrined (along with other statues recovered from the waves) in the modest modern temple you see today.

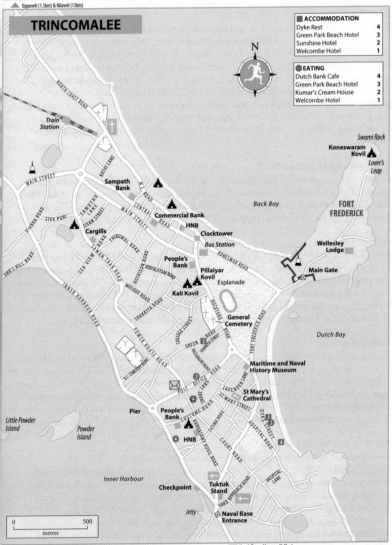

TRINCOMALEE

ACCOMMODATION	
Dyke Rest	4
Green Park Beach Hotel	3
Sunshine Hotel	2
Welcome Hotel	1

● EATING	
Dutch Bank Cafe	4
Green Park Beach Hotel	3
Kumar's Cream House	2
Welcombe Hotel	1

N

Swami Rock

Koneswaram Kovil

Lover's Leap

Back Bay

FORT FREDERICK

Train Station

NORTH COAST ROAD

MAIN STREET

ROTHI LANE

Sampath Bank

K.C. ROAD

CENTRAL ROAD

Commercial Bank

HNB

Clocktower

Bus Station

KONESWAR ROAD

Wellesley Lodge

Main Gate

SAMPTHE LANE

SIVAN STREET

MAIN STREET

THIRUMAL ROAD

HUSTISON ROAD

SIVA PURI

VIHARA ROAD

Cargills

DOW'S HILL ROAD

SEA VIEW ROAD

SAMAN THAR ROAD

MOSQUE ROAD

VIDYALAYAM ROAD

People's Bank

Pillaiyar Kovil

Esplanade

INNER HARBOUR ROAD

THAKKITA ROAD

Kali Kovil

COLLEGE STREET

POWER HOUSE ROAD

GREEN ROAD

DOCKYARD ROAD

General Cemetery

FANNA STREET

FORT FREDERICK ROAD

Dutch Bay

K.C. CHETTAR ROAD

POST OFFICE

Maritime and Naval History Museum

LAVENDER LANE

St Mary's Cathedral

@

DYKE'S LANE ROAD

ST MARY STREET

Little Powder Island

Powder Island

Pier

People's Bank

CUSTOMS ROAD

FATIMA ROAD

KANDASAMY KOVIL ROAD

COURT ROAD

HOSPITAL ROAD

DYKE STREET

HNB

Inner Harbour

Checkpoint

Tuktuk Stand

HOSPITAL LANE

Jetty

YARD APPROACH ROAD

Naval Base Entrance

0	500
metres	

say that the heartbroken van Rhede, who had been abandoned by her lover, leapt out survived the fall; others claim that she didn't even jump. Whatever the truth, government archives record her subsequent marriage eight years later, after which she (presumably) lived happily ever after.

The commercial centre

West of the fort, modern Trincomalee's **commercial centre** comprises an undistinguished and low-key trio of parallel streets lined by tiny one-storey shops and dotted with the occasional small mosque.

5

Back Bay

Bounding the northern side of the commercial centre, **Back Bay** is largely obscured by shops and houses, although it's possible to reach the waterfront by taking any of the various tiny side roads running north off N.C. Road (officially Ehamparam Road) to reach a narrow scrap of beach usually three-quarters buried beneath fishing boats and piles of nets. The area around five minutes' walk northwest down N.C. Road from the clocktower (go down the little side street opposite the Jewel One Shop) is particularly magical, with small pastel-painted Hindu temples on one side, boats drawn up at the water's edge on the other, and rabbit warrens of tiny shacks behind, their neat, brightly painted facades giving the beachfront a prettiness which belies the very basic conditions in which most of the people here live.

The Esplanade and around

At the southeastern end of the commercial centre lies the wide and grassy **Esplanade**. A couple of pretty Hindu temples enliven the western side of the green, the large **Kali Kovil** and the much smaller (though equally gaudy) **Pillaiyar Kovil**. Both burst into life with drumming, music and lines of supplicants during the late-afternoon puja (around 4–5pm).

General Cemetery

Just south of the Esplanade lies the decaying and neglected old **General Cemetery** (aka St Stephen's Cemetery), the final resting place of Trinco's Christian population, with a few picturesquely dilapidated colonial tombs dating back to the 1820s alongside more modern graves. Jane Austen's brother, Charles, is supposed to be buried here – but it's all but impossible to find him. The cemetery is usually kept locked, but it's easy enough to hop over the low wall (although slightly more difficult to climb out again).

Dutch Bay

The oceanfront Fort Frederick Road along **Dutch Bay** offers fine sea views, while the beach that edges the road is a popular spot around dusk, when half the town seems to congregate here to promenade along the seafront and loll around on the sands. Beyond here lie further understated but charming rows of colonial villas, most particularly along **Dyke Street**, lined with colourful facades. Nearby, it's also worth hunting out the colonial-era **St Mary's Cathedral**, an imposing blue structure buried amid lush gardens.

Maritime and Naval History Museum

Junction of Dockyard and Fort Frederick roads • Mon & Wed–Sun 8.30am–4.30pm • Free • ☎ 026 222 1530

Roughly halfway along the bay stands Trincomalee's imposing **Maritime and Naval History Museum**, opened in 2014 inside the elegant two-storey colonnaded building that served as the official residence of the Dutch Naval Commissioner from 1602 until 1795. exhibits include the inevitable models of ships, Chinese ceramics, coins and other objects recovered from the waves, an informative display on local ecosystems and an 8m-long artillery cannon unearthed in Colombo during the construction of the *Shangri-La* hotel. There are also some interesting fragments of old film include footage of the sinking of the British *HMS Hermes*, the world's first purpose-built aircraft carrier, off Batticaloa in 1942, while photos upstairs chart the restoration of the building itself from virtual ruins.

The Inner Harbour

A number of roads run southwest from the centre down towards the **Inner Harbour**. Much of this quarter of town retains a pleasantly old-fashioned feel, with numerous colonial villas, some of them embellished with quirky, slightly Art Deco-looking decorative motifs. The expansive harbour itself is an attractive and breezy spot, its choppy waters dotted with container ships and various port facilities, framed against a circle of rugged green hills that ring the bay – it's particularly lovely at night, when a thousand lights twinkle around its perimeter.

Hoods Tower Museum

Mon–Fri 2–5pm, Sat & Sun 9am–6pm • $10 • Since the museum is in a secure military area, to access it you need first to get permission to enter the naval base from the checkpoint around 100m northwest of the main gates (issued on the spot; bring your passport); next, hire a tuktuk (Rs.1000) from the stand opposite the main gate into the base (tuktuk drivers elsewhere in town will most likely never have heard of the place); it's a 2km drive through the naval base to the museum – you'll be accompanied back and forth by a naval officer

Keen students of maritime or colonial history might enjoy a tour of the little-visited **Hoods Tower Museum**, deep inside the town's Sri Lanka Navy base. The museum is located in Fort Ostenburg, which overlooks the entrance to the Inner Harbour. Built by the Dutch, the fort was subsequently strengthened by the British with a fearsome array of artillery in order to defend the large Royal Navy base within.

The museum itself is named after the **Hoods observation tower** – steps lead to the top, from where there are superb 360-degree harbour views. Items on show include a few of the fort's original colonial artillery pieces alongside modern exhibits including a captured LTTE Sea Tigers boat and a suicide launch – interesting enough, although hardly justifying the sky-high entrance price.

ARRIVAL AND DEPARTURE | TRINCOMALEE

By plane Cinnamon Air (⦿ cinnamonair.com) operates scheduled services from Colombo's international airport to Trincomalee via Sigiriya (daily; 1hr 15min). Tickets cost $262 one way. Less frequent but much cheaper flights are also operated by Helitours (⦿ helitours.lk) from Colombo's Ratmalana airport to Trinco (3 weekly); a return ticket costs Rs.18,500. The airport is at China Bay, a few kilometres out of town; a tuktuk to the centre costs around Rs. 350–400.
By bus Buses arrive at the bus station, right in the centre of Trinco at the bottom of Main St.

Destinations Anuradhapura (2 daily; 3hr); Batticaloa (every 30min; 3hr 30min); Colombo (every 30min; 7hr); Habarana (every 30min; 1hr 30min); Jaffna (8 daily; 6hr); Kandy (4 daily; 5hr); Polonnaruwa (3 daily; 2hr 30min).
By train The train station is at the northwest end of town. There's currently just one, slow, overnight direct service to Colombo (daily; 8hr 30min). Otherwise, there's a 7am service as far as Gal Oya junction, where it's possible to connect with the morning train from Batticaloa to Colombo Fort.

ACCOMMODATION

There's still not a great deal of choice of accommodation in Trinco, and costs are relatively high, though there's somewhere to stay in most price brackets.

★ **Dyke Rest** 228 Dyke St ☎ 026 222 5313, ⦿ dykerest.comuv.com; map p.351. Easily the nicest of the various small hotels along Dyke St, with five affordable but surprisingly stylish rooms of varying sizes, plus friendly service and good food. The upstairs rooms have excellent views and a/c. A back door gives direct access to a small sliver of beach with good snorkelling. **Rs.3000**, a/c **Rs.3500**
Green Park Beach Hotel 312 Dyke St ☎ 026 222 2369, ✉ greenparktco@live.com; map p.351. Well-run mid-range option in a picturesque setting on Dutch Bay. Rooms all with a/c, hot water, TV and fridge) are modern, tiled and clean, albeit relatively pricey, and there's also a decent in-house Indian restaurant (see page 353). **Rs.5740**

Sunshine Hotel 45 Green Rd ☎ 026 222 0288, ⦿ sunshinehotelhall.com; map p.351. Currently Trinco's best budget deal, this functional hotel-cum-wedding hall offers neat tiled rooms with fans at bargain rates, assuming you don't mind the wafer-thin mattresses and function room noise, while a/c doubles the price. **Rs.1500**, a/c **Rs.3500**
Welcombe Hotel 66 Lower Rd, Orr's Hill, 2km west of the centre ☎ 026 222 2373, ⦿ welcombehotel.com; map p.351. Trinco's priciest hotel, occupying a lovely position high above the Inner Harbour in a striking modern building topped with recycled railway sleepers (or copies thereof). Standard rooms (all with a/c, TV and fridge) are spacious but spartan; more expensive "luxury" rooms are decorated with colonial-style wooden furniture but are starting to look dated. There's also a large pool, musty bar and passable restaurant (see page 354). B&B **Rs.9500**

EATING

Dutch Bank Café 88 Inner Harbour Rd ☎ 077 269 3600, ⦿ facebook.com/dutchbankcafe; map p.351. Occupying a beautifully restored old Dutch colonial building, this chic new café looks like a little slice of Galle or Colombo improbably dropped into Trinco's old-fashioned waterfront. Food comprises a well-prepared and attractively presented mix of local and international dishes,

from *kottu rotty* to beef *frikandel* (mains Rs.880–1450), plus assorted snacks and coffee. Daily 8am–10pm.
Green Park Beach Hotel 312 Dyke St ☎ 026 222 2369; map p.351. Sedate hotel restaurant offering a huge menu of Indian food including meat, fish and veg standards – tandooris, kormas, *vadais*, *shorbas* and so on (mains Rs.450–550). Quality is average, but the setting

5

is nice, and portions are huge. It's also a good place for Western and Sri Lankan breakfasts (Rs.500). Unlicensed. Daily 7am–9.30pm.

Kumar's Cream House Post Office Rd; map p.351. Bright little modern bakery selling drinks, short eats (samosas, cutlets, *vadais*), plus Indian sweets, cakes and Elephant House ice cream. Daily 6.30am–1pm & 2.30–6.30pm.

Welcombe Hotel 66 Lower Rd, Orr's Hill ☎ 026 222 2373 map p.351. Decent hotel restaurant, with seating either on the beautiful outdoor terrace above the Inner Harbour (although you can't see much after dark, when the midges and mozzies come out in force) or in the glassed-in dining room within. Food (mains Rs.850–1200) comprises a mix of the usual Sri Lankan standards plus a few generic European offerings competently if unexceptionally prepared. Daily 6am–10pm.

DIRECTORY

Banks There are plenty of banks with ATMs that accept foreign cards scattered around town.

Internet Available at a couple of places on Power House Rd near the junction with Post Office Rd; try Google internet café (daily 9am–9pm; Rs.80/hr).

Swimming Non-guests can use the pool at the *Welcombe Hotel* for Rs.700.

North of Trincomalee

North of Trincomalee the coast is lined with a fine strand of wide golden beach, beginning at the village of **Uppuveli** and continuing through to **Nilaveli** and beyond. It's a superb stretch of coast whose enormous tourism potential is only slowly being developed – which is a large part of its appeal. The **Kuchchaveli** area, some 10km further north, has been earmarked as another major tourist zone along the lines of Passekudah with (if you believe it) three thousand new hotel rooms apparently planned, although all that's materialized so far is the halcyon *Jungle Beach*.

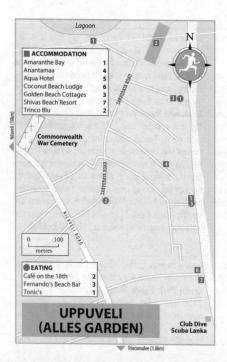

ACCOMMODATION
Amaranthe Bay	1
Anantamaa	4
Aqua Hotel	5
Coconut Beach Lodge	6
Golden Beach Cottages	3
Shivas Beach Resort	7
Trinco Blu	2

EATING
Café on the 18th	2
Fernando's Beach Bar	3
Tonic's	1

UPPUVELI (ALLES GARDEN)

Lagoon
Commonwealth War Cemetery
Nilaveli (10km)
Trincomalee (1.8km)
Club Dive Scuba Lanka

Uppuveli and around

Just a few kilometres north of Trinco, the low-key village of **UPPUVELI** is currently experiencing a moderate tourism boom, with an ever-increasing array of guesthouses, some larger resort hotels, a few fishing boats and a great many palm trees. The atmosphere remains pretty somnolent, especially out of season, when many places operate reduced hours or close entirely.

Commonwealth War Cemetery

On the main Nilaveli Rd, 200m north of *Chaaya Blu* • Daily 24hr • Free

The **Commonwealth War Cemetery** holds 362 graves, mainly of Allied and other servicemen who died in Sri Lanka during World War II. Military personnel of many nationalities are buried together here, including Indians, Italians, Australians, Canadians, Dutch, Burmese and, of course, numerous British fighters, including the air crews killed during the Japanese air raid of April 1942 and seamen who perished

WHALE-WATCHING AROUND TRINCOMALEE

Although not as developed as in Mirissa, the Trincomalee area is one of the best places in Sri Lanka for whale-watching tours. **Blue whales** in particular (plus smaller numbers of sperm whales) can regularly be seen around six to eight nautical miles east of Trincomalee (about 30min by boat), and can even occasionally be spotted from the land – Swami Rock (see page 350) offers the best vantage point. **Dolphins** (mainly Spinner) can also be seen regularly all year round. Most **sightings** occur between March/April and August/September, as whales continue their migrations around the island from the south coast (where they mainly congregate from December to April) – this means that Sri Lanka offers around ten months of continuous whale-watching annually at different points around the coast. **Tours** usually depart at around 6am, last three hours or so and cost around $30-40 per person (minimum two people, cheaper in larger groups). These can be arranged through many local hotels. In Uppuveli, try *Anantamaa*, *Coconut Beach Lodge* and *Trinco Blu* – although the last is usually a lot more expensive than other places. In Nilaveli, trips are laid on by the *Nilaveli Beach Hotel*.

aboard various Royal Navy vessels sunk by the Japanese in the Indian Ocean. In striking contrast to the General Cemetery in Trinco, the War Cemetery is beautifully looked after, and the long lines of graves and the ages recorded on the headstones (few of those interred here were older than 25) makes a visit a rather sombre experience.

Kanniya Hot Wells

Around 8km inland from Uppuveli, 1km south of the road to Anuradhapura • Wed-Sun 8.30am-4.30pm •Rs.50 (foreigners only)

Said to have been created by Vishnu himself, the **Kanniya Hot Wells** have long been a sacred bathing spot for locals, although a recent renovation has turned the area into a bit of a tourist trap, with dozens of vendors selling cheap souvenirs as you walk from the car park to the entrance. You can't actually submerge yourself in the waters here – the springs are collected in seven small tiled wells, and you use a bucket to pour the water over yourself – but they're fun for a quick splash.

Velgam Vihara

A few kilometres beyond Kanniyai Hot Wells towards Anuradhapura and 4km north of the main road • Donation requested

A trip to the Kanniyai Hot Wells can be combined with a visit to the remains of the Velgam Vihara. The temple is thought to date back to the era of King Devanampiya Tissa, who is said to have planted a bo tree here, and although it was subsequently abandoned to the jungle following the collapse of Polonnaruwa, extensive remains survive, including a stupa, image house and a well-preserved standing Buddha. It's a rather eerie place, with a small information centre displaying gruesome photos from the war years, run by the monks of the adjacent temple. A word of warning: keep an eye out for the monkeys, which can be aggressive.

ARRIVAL AND DEPARTURE   **UPPUVELI AND AROUND**

By bus or tuktuk Buses run from Trinco to Uppuveli every 20–30min, although they tend to get nightmarishly packed; it's well worth catching a tuktuk instead (Rs.400).

ACCOMMODATION

The area loosely known as Uppuveli sprawls along the coast north of Trincomalee for a considerable distance, although most accommodation is clustered within a fairly compact area known as **Alles Garden**, some 5km north of Trinco. Accommodation **prices** both here and in neighbouring Nilaveli have skyrocketed recently, and are now poor value during high season, although rates fall dramatically (usually by at least a third) at other times.

Amaranthe Bay 101/17 Alles Garden ☏ 026 205 0200, ⓦ amaranthebay.com; map p.354. Stylish and secluded resort hotel situated on a lagoon at the northern end of Uppuveli, with a special boat service three times a day taking guests to the beach. The standard rooms are quite spartan but the more expensive junior suites, with hot tubs, are very comfortable and have excellent views. Friendly peacocks roam the gardens and there's also a pool and spa. $150

5

DIVING AND WATERSPORTS AROUND UPPUVELI AND NILAVELI

There are around ten **dive schools** in the area, mainly offering PADI courses and trips around Pigeon Island and Swami Rock. All open during the season, from around April/May to September/October only. In Uppuveli there are dive schools at (among other places) *Trinco Blu*, *Shivas Beach Resort* (W uppuvelidiving.com) and *Aqua Hotel* and *Club Dive Paradise French Garden* – the latter also arranges watersports including banana-boating, tubing, wakeboarding and windsurfing (but no surfing or kiting). In Nilaveli there are dive schools at the *Nilaveli Beach Hotel* and at *High Park Hotel* (W nilavelidiving.com), just south of Coral Bay.

Anantamaa 7/42 Alles Garden ☎ 026 205 0250, W anantamaa.com; map p.354. Functional, modern mini-resort set back from the beach with red-tiled roofed buildings arranged around pleasant gardens and a pool. Rooms are stylish, albeit a bit lacking in furniture; all come with balcony or veranda, and a few also have beach views. $110

Aqua Hotel 12 Alles Garden ☎ 026 205 0202, W aquahotel-trincomalee.com; map p.354. Functional lodgings in a rather ugly three-storey concrete block painted in lurid shades of orange, green and blue. Rooms (some with a/c, plus hot water for an extra Rs.300/day) are a bit shabby and uninspiring but reasonable value by local standards, and there's a small pool and the enjoyable *Fernando's Beach Bar* at the bottom of the garden. If you're on a serious budget, check out the extraordinary hobbit-hole-style lodgings in the garden (Rs.1000) – basically just a mattress inside an industrial-sized pipe buried in the ground. Rs.3500, a/c Rs.5000

Coconut Beach Lodge 178/19 Alles Garden ☎ 026 222 4888, E coconutbeachlodge@gmail.com; map p.354. This lovely boutique guesthouse is arranged around gorgeous gardens and has a real home-from-home feel. "Luxury" rooms inside the main house (Rs.8000) are attractively kitted out with repro-colonial furniture, four-poster beds and quality artworks. Cheaper "semi-luxury" garden rooms are a mite less polished, but still very

comfortable, and have a lovely garden-facing veranda to laze upon. There's also an appealing terrace restaurant and cosy communal lounge. Rs.5000

★ **Golden Beach Cottages** 24 Alles Garden ☎ 026 493 2010, W goldenbeachcottages.com; map p.354. Cheerful British-run beachfront cottages, with spotless, comfortable and tastefully decorated rooms, all with a/c. The attached *Tonic's* restaurant (see below) serves meals and snacks throughout the day, making this a convenient place to relax and enjoy the beach. Rs.13500

Shivas Beach Resort 178 Alles Garden ☎ 026 320 4882, W trincomalee-guesthouse.com; map p.354. This long-running hotel has a rather bland exterior, but the comfortably furnished rooms are bright and spacious, plus there's an attractive little beach restaurant. Rs.3500, a/c Rs.4000

Trinco Blu 175 Alles Garden ☎ 026 222 1611 W cinnamonhotels.com; map p.354. This resort has been rebranded and refurbished, and though it's fairly pricey it has decent amenities, including a pool, and two restaurants. Rooms are brightly furnished, if on the small side, and there's also a nice dive school (see above) and whale-watching trips (see page 355), although published rates are a rip-off – look for discounts online or, even better, head to the *Nilaveli Beach Hotel* (see page 357) down the road. B&B $240

EATING

Uppuveli's food scene continues to grow and improve, with some excellent options along **Sarvodaya Road**, as well as on the beachfront. The larger hotels all have decent but much pricier restaurants.

Café on the 18th 18 Sarvodaya ☎ 077 765 8428, W facebook.com/cafeonthe18th; map p.354. One of the few places on the east coast with an espresso machine, this small café has both indoor and outdoor seating, and also serves excellent food, including an all-day breakfast menu (Rs.350), paninis (Rs.550–700) and grilled seafood (Rs.1450–1850). The homemade chocolate brownie (Rs.200) is excellent. Daily 9am–9pm.

Fernando's Beach Bar Aqua Hotel 12 Alles Garden ☎ 026 205 0202; map p.354. Long-running beachfront

bar with rustic wooden decor, a well-stocked bar and a music collection not entirely made up of bootleg Bob Marley CDs. They dish up a so-so range of pasta, pizza and burgers, although you're probably better off sticking to their seafood or Sri Lankan standards. Most mains around Rs.1000. Daily 8am–10pm.

Tonic's 24 Alles Garden ☎ 026 493 2010, W goldenbeachcottages.com; map p.354. Excellent beachside restaurant serving super-fresh seafood meals (Rs.1200–1500), as well as burgers, toasties, pasta and curries (Rs. 600–900). They also cater for vegetarians with tasty veggie platters and salads (Rs. 450–1200), and there's no better place on the beach for a refreshing G&T (Rs.600). Daily 7am–10pm.

Nilaveli and around

Some 10km north of Uppuveli is the straggling settlement of **NILAVELI**, home to another fine stretch of largely deserted beach. Guesthouses and hotels are sparsely scattered along the coast and the entire area retains a decidedly back-of-beyond atmosphere that makes even Uppuveli look like Ibiza. If you like very quiet days spent wave-gazing, beachcombing, snorkelling and hanging with the locals, Nilaveli is perfect.

ARRIVAL AND DEPARTURE
NILAVELI AND AROUND

By bus or tuktuk Buses run from Trinco to Nilaveli (every 20–30min; 30min), although they tend to get extremely crowded, and can be horrible if you've got luggage. In addition, the various hotels in Nilaveli are a further hike (up to 1km) from the main road. Instead, consider catching a tuktuk (around Rs.800–1000 depending on how far up the beach you go).

ACCOMMODATION

All the hotels listed here offer **food**, although only at the *Nilaveli Beach Hotel* and *Anilana* will you find anything more than simple tourist staples.

NILAVELI BEACH

Anilana 1508/4 Irakkakandi ☎ 011 203 0900, ⓦ anilana. com; map p.357. This swanky resort, with velvet sofas in the lobby, seems out of place in beachside Nilaveli. Rooms in the four-storey main building have balconies, and the slightly pricier ($263) pool chalets are placed on either side of a pair of adjacent pools at the end of the enormously long and thin sea-facing garden (Rs.1000 to non-guests). Chalets come with cool white decor, big French windows, bathrooms with open-air shower and garden verandas, while facilities include a spa. B&B $200

★ **Nilaveli Beach Hotel** 11th mile post ☎ 026 223 2295, ⓦ tangerinehotels.com; map p.357. Long-running resort (completely rebuilt after the tsunami) with attractive modern buildings set among idyllic tree-studded gardens running down to the beach, the whole place managing to feel pleasantly intimate despite its size. Rooms are comfortable enough, if rather austerely furnished, and there's also a big L-shaped pool (Rs.750 for non-guests) and two restaurants. B&B $150

Pigeon Island Beach Resort 11th mile post ☎ 026 738 8388, ⓦ pigeonislandresort.com; map p.357. Small resort hotel overlooking a long, thin garden running down to the sea. It looks dated from the outside, but its rooms have been recently and attractively renovated and upgraded, and facilities and activities include an Ayurveda spa, basic gym, medium-sized pool and cookery classes. B&B $145

Shahira Hotel 10th mile post ☎ 026 223 2323; map p.357. Old-style, small hotel very close to the beach, set around a nice garden courtyard and with basic restaurant attached. Rooms (fan only) are old but spacious and well looked after – good value by overpriced Nilaveli standards. $25

Surya Lagoon 18th mile post ☎ 071 272 8504, ⓦ suryalagoon-nilaveli.com; map p.357. Attractive guesthouse in a colonial-style villa, with four pleasant (if rather scanty) furnished rooms and extensive grounds running down to the adjacent lagoon. B&B $65

NORTH OF NILAVELI

★ **Amanta Beach Resort** 6km north of the NBH, Pulmoddai Rd, Kumpurupiddi ☎ 026 225 2220, ⓦ amantabeach.com; map p.357. Stylish eco-friendly resort with six very comfortable a/c en-suite rooms set around a courtyard swimming pool. *Amanta's* restaurant, with walls constructed with cinnamon sticks and a bar top made from an airplane wing, serves fabulous French–Sri Lankan fusion cuisine. The enormous garden, with some unusual sculptures, stretches down to the beach where there are a variety of cabanas and lounges. B&B $80

Kuchchaveli, **1** (5km) & **2** (17km)

IRRAKANDI

0   500
metres

Ticket Office

■ ACCOMMODATION

Amanta Beach Resort	1
Anilana	5
Jungle Beach	2
Nilaveli Beach Hotel	6
Pigeon Island Beach Resort	3
Shahira Hotel	7
Surya Lagood	4

Pigeon Island (3km)

PULMODDAI ROAD

NILAVELI

N

B424

NILAVELI

Uppuveli (9km) & Trincomalee (12.5km)

5

SNORKELLING AT PIGEON ISLAND AND SWAMI ROCK

About 1km offshore from Nilaveli, tiny **Pigeon Island** (now protected as a marine national park) is home to one of the east coast's finest patches of coral reef, although it's only open from April to October. The main reason to visit is to enjoy the island's excellent **snorkelling**. All the live coral lies on the sea-facing side of the island, some 40m off the beach in water around 1.5m deep. The coral on the beach-facing side is unfortunately dead, although the waters here compensate with a remarkable range of tropical fish – well over a hundred species have been recorded.

Tickets to visit Pigeon Island are sold at the tiny office (daily 8am–5pm) on the beach at the foot of the *Anilana* hotel grounds, not far from the NBH. Tickets currently cost $12 plus additional charges and taxes, which add around another $5 per boatload. **Boats** to reach the island can be hired on the beach next to the ticket office (Rs.2000/boat seating around eight people) or, for a surcharge, via the NBH or Pigeon Island Beach Resort in Nilaveli, or via Coconut Beach Lodge, Anantamaa or Trinco Blu in Uppuveli. Boatmen on the beach also have **snorkelling equipment** for rent (Rs.1000), or alternatively you might be able to pick this up this through the dive centre at the NBH.

A cheaper although slightly less memorable alternative to visiting Pigeon Island is to take a snorkelling trip from Uppuveli to **Swami Rock** (see page 350). There's not much coral here but you'll see plenty of tropical fish, and possibly turtles if you're lucky. Trips can be arranged through *Coconut Beach Lodge* and *Anantamaa* and cost around Rs.4000/per person (minimum two people).

Jungle Beach 9km north of the NBH, Pulmoddai Rd, Kuchchaveli ☎026 567 1000, ⓦugaescapes. com/junglebeach; map p.357. The Trinco area's most luxurious and private resort with a choice of beach- or lagoon-facing rooms, plus wilder lodgings surrounded by jungle. The gorgeous design is the acme of rustic chic, wit plenty of wood, bamboo and rock, and cool modern room artfully concealed under shaggy thatched roofs. There also a gorgeous little tree-shaded pool, spa and gym. B& **$250**

Passekudah and Kalkudah

Way back in the 1970s and early 1980s, the twin beaches of **Passekudah** and **Kalkudah** were the east coast's most developed tourist destinations, home to a modest cluster of resort hotels and drawing a steady string of European tourists to this far-flung corner of the island. All that ended following the outbreak of war. The hotels were first abandoned, and subsequently blown up by the LTTE to prevent them being used by the Sri Lankan Army – only their ghostly skeletons remained, standing sentry over the deserted beaches. Today, the area is in the middle of a second, and even more dramatic, coming.

Passekudah Bay

Earmarked as a special tourist development zone in the late noughties, the formerly deserted arc of **Passekudah Bay** is now ringed with more than a dozen big resort hotels which have transformed this previously sleepy backwater into the east coast's answer to Beruwala. Resorts apart there's not a lot to it, however, and the area has yet to develop any meaningful identity with very little in the way of cafés, shops or beach life along the rather subdued seafront. Most visitors simply stay in their hotels, although **watersports** can be arranged through the LSR centre (ⓦlsrhotels.com) at the *Marina Beach* hotel, close to the *Uga Bay* hotel (open in season only).

Kalkudah

In contrast to Passekudah, **KALKUDAH** village retains much of its original character, with a handful of quiet budget guesthouses strung out along the main street. Neighbouring **Kalkudah Bay** also remains mercifully unchanged, so far at least, with a superb sweep of powder-fine golden sand – blissfully deserted and unspoiled, although a couple of plots

f land have already been fenced off for future development, suggesting that Kalkudah's
lays as a sleepy backwater are also numbered. See it while you can.

ARRIVAL AND DEPARTURE

By bus Buses run regularly from Batticaloa to the town
of Valaichchenai, about 4km west of Kalkudah, and less
frequently from Polonnaruwa. There are currently only
three buses daily from Valaichchenai to Kalkudah village;
a tuktuk costs around Rs.300.

PASSEKUDAH AND KALKUDAH

By train It's easiest to make for Valaichchenai station,
which has connections with Colombo (2 daily; 8hr) and
Batticaloa (5 daily; 45min–1hr).

ACCOMMODATION

Rates at both **Passekudah**'s big resort hotels and
Kalkudah's low-key guesthouses are currently excellent
value, especially compared to prices at Uppuveli and
Arugam Bay further up and down the coast – and there
are often some serious bargains to be had online. There are
virtually no independent **restaurants** at present – most
visitors eat where they are staying.

PASSEKUDAH BAY

Amaya Beach Passekudah Rd ☎065 205 0200,
ⓦamayaresorts.com; map p.359. This attractive resort
has a smooth, minimalist design – all crisp whites and
ochre browns – and cooling water channels flowing around
and between the lovely open-air bar and restaurant, plus a
big pool. The stylishly furnished rooms come with either
garden or ocean view, attractive wood-panelled bathrooms
and big windows, and facilities include two restaurants,
spa and gym. $250

Maalu Maalu Coconut Board Rd ☎065 738 8388,
ⓦmaalumaalu.com; map p.359. Stylish boutique
beach resort, designed like a miniature (but very upmarket)
fishing village, with two wings of palm-thatched wooden
chalets framing views of a wonderful infinity pool and
beach and a carpet-smooth and very shallow stretch of
sea beyond, protected by a coral reef. Rooms are simply

furnished with fish-inspired decor but have lovely big
bathrooms. Facilities include Ayurveda spa, a jazz bar,
karaoke and nightclub, a small coral museum, plus a beach
bar in a salvaged boat. B&B $254

★ **Sunrise by Jetwing** Coconut Board Rd ☎065 205
8865, ⓦjetwinghotels.com; map p.359. A smart new
addition to Passekudah's resort line up, *Sunrise* has been
nicely designed to fit with the natural environment, uses
solar power and has a calm ambience. The 108-metre
pool (the longest on the east coast) snakes its way from
the restaurant towards the beach. The rooms are stylishly
decorated using colourful local fabrics and natural
materials, and have cosy balconies attached. There's also a
fitness centre, spa and open-air hot tub. $150

Uga Bay Coconut Board Rd ☎065 567 1000,
ⓦugaescapes.com; map p.359. The ritziest of
Passekudah resorts, arranged around a pair of fountains
and sweeping infinity pool laid end to end between
the cute hotel entrance and its fine stretch of beach.
Rooms are located in a contrastingly ordinary horseshoe
of two-storey brick-and-concrete chalets laid out
around the gardens and pool, although they're nicely
designed inside with wooden floors, funky fabrics and
sea views. Facilities include an appealing grotto-style
spa underneath the pool, an in-house mini-cinema

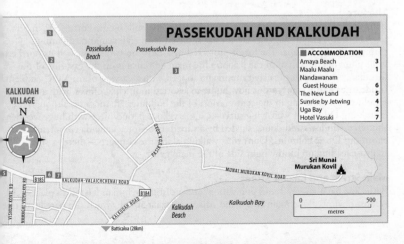

PASSEKUDAH AND KALKUDAH

Passekudah
Beach   Passekudah Bay

KALKUDAH
VILLAGE
N

PASSEKUDAH ROAD

■ **ACCOMMODATION**

Amaya Beach	3
Maalu Maalu	1
Nandawanam Guest House	6
The New Land	5
Sunrise by Jetwing	4
Uga Bay	2
Hotel Vasuki	7

B185   KALKUDAH-VALAICHCHENAI ROAD

B184

VISHUK KOVIL RD
MAMANGAI VIDYALAYA RD

KALKUDAH ROAD

Kalkudah
Beach

MUNAI MURUKAN KOVIL ROAD

Sri Munai
Murukan Kovil

Kalkudah Bay

0   500
metres

▼ Batticaloa (28km)

5

for rainy days, well-equipped gym and chic glassed-in restaurant, while barbecue dinners are served on the beach. Published rates are high, but often significantly discounted online. B&B $190

KALKUDAH VILLAGE

Nandawanam Guest House Main St ☎ 065 225 7258, ✉ nandawanam@live.com; map p.359. A spacious family house surrounded by attractive gardens, with twelve large and pleasingly furnished a/c rooms. The whole place is kept spotlessly clean and the evening meals of curry and rice are excellent. Rs.4500

The New Land Main St ☎ 065 568 0440; map p.359. Friendly, long-established place with a mix of four old but perfectly respectable fan rooms at super-cheap rates

plus four newer a/c rooms (cold water only). The ver helpful owner also has free bikes for guests and serves u inexpensive food. Rs.2000, a/c Rs.5000

Hotel Vasuki Main St ☎ 065 364 8809, ✉ hotelvasuki@ yahoo.com; map p.359. Welcoming little guesthous with neat and comfortable rooms with hot water, qualit mattresses and optional a/c (Rs.1000), plus a cute littl restaurant in what looks like an oversized wooden birdcage The helpful owner can arrange lagoon trips, snorkellin and other excursions, and guests get free tuktuk transfer to the beach. Rs2500

Victoria Guest House Main St ☎ 065 205 0205 ⓦ victoriaghouse.com; map p.359. Spacious an spotless modern tiled rooms, most with a/c and all wit hot water. Rs.2500, a/c Rs.3500

Batticaloa and around

The principal east-coast settlement south of Trincomalee, **BATTICALOA** (often shortened to "Batti") is one of Sri Lanka's most appealing but least-known larger towns. Historically, it's best known as the site of the first landing (in 1602) by the Dutch in Sri Lanka, and as the place where they established their first lasting foothold on the island by seizing the local fort from the resident Portuguese in 1638. More recently the town and surrounding area was a major LTTE stronghold throughout the **civil war**, with the army controlling the town and the Tigers running their own parallel administration – complete with courts, police force and tax collectors – from the village of Kokkadicholai, a short drive south. As Indian journalist Nirupama Subramanian put it in *Sri Lanka: Voices from a War Zone*: "Technically, Batticaloa town came under the government … That was by day. By night, the town took orders from the Tigers."

The LTTE are long gone, and the mercantile hustle and bustle of the main commercial areas suggests a town now increasingly on the mend, although intriguing reminders of Batti's long colonial history can still be seen. Moreover, the town's setting is magical, perched on a narrow sliver of land backed by the serpentine **Batticaloa Lagoon** and surrounded by water on three sides, with the constantly shifting views of land, lagoon and ocean lending it an interesting – if disorienting – character.

The fort

Batticaloa's solid-looking **fort** was one of the last to be built by the Portuguese in Sri Lanka (1628), and its rugged exterior has survived both civil war and tsunami in surprisingly good shape. The fort is protected by a moat on two sides, with its northern walls plunging directly into the lagoon. The main **entrance** is on the east side of the fort, flanked by a pair of rusty cannon and topped with a carving of the VOC emblem. Inside, the **central courtyard** is now home to assorted municipal offices, with a small Hindu shrine standing in the centre. Most of the buildings are modern, although the crumbling Dutch-era west wing survives, a marvellous period piece with huge wooden-shuttered windows and doors, shaded by a superb two-storey veranda complete with enormous Doric columns. Don't miss walking along the ramparts – there's a small staircase leading up on the right side of the main gate.

Main Street and Bazaar Street

Batticaloa has a largely Tamil population, and a distinctly Indian flavour in places. This is most obvious along **Main Street** and adjacent **Bazaar Street**, which run parallel to one

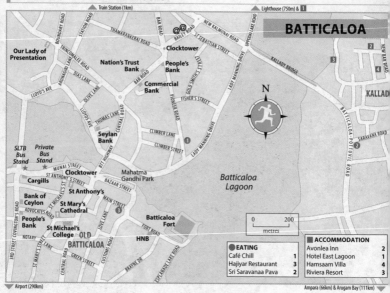

another along the south side of the central lagoon west of the fort, offering a colourful medley of jewellers, clothes shops and fancy goods emporia.

Old Batticaloa

Up the hill from Main Street, roads climb into the heart of **old Batticaloa**, an atmospheric tangle of streets lined with tree-swathed villas and dotted with a sequence of imposing colonial-era churches. Immediately behind Main Street lies **St Anthony's**, a lovely old cream-coloured structure, topped with an enormous expanse of red tiles and with a rustic, barn-like interior beneath a huge sloping wooden roof. Further up the hill sits the even larger **St Mary's Cathedral**, a sprawling, sky-blue Neoclassical edifice with soaring facade. Opposite is the venerable old **St Michael's College**, founded in 1872 and one of the largest and most prestigious schools in the east.

East to Kallady

North of the lagoon it's worth having a look at the landmark **Our Lady of Presentation**, a huge, bizarre-looking blue structure topped with a strange octagonal tower and glass cupola – like a miniature lighthouse plonked on top of a pagoda.

From here, it's a twenty-minute walk through the modern town centre along Trinco, Bar and Bailey roads to reach the new bridge over the lagoon and, next to it, the creaking old **Kallady Bridge**, dating from the 1930s (when it was known as Lady Manning Bridge) and formerly the longest in the country. Now closed to traffic, it offers fine views across the water, as well as (it's said) the best spot from which to hear Batti's famous **singing fish** (see page 363).

Kallady

Over Kallady Bridge lies the sleepy beachside suburb of **Kallady**, home to several of the town's better accommodation options and with a pleasantly village-like atmosphere – quite different from the bustle of central Batti just over the lagoon. The far side of the district is bounded by a long sweep of fine golden **beach**, usually lined with boats and busy with fishermen sorting the day's catch or mending nets.

THE SINGING FISH OF BATTICALOA

Batti is famous in Sri Lankan folklore for its **singing fish**. According to tradition, between April and September a strange noise – described variously as resembling a plucked guitar or violin string, or the sound produced by rubbing a wet finger around the rim of a glass – can be heard issuing from the depths of the lagoon. The "singing" is allegedly strongest on full moon nights, though no one knows exactly what causes it. The most popular explanation is that it's produced by some form of marine life – anything from catfish to mussels – while another theory states that it's made by water flowing between boulders on the lagoon floor. The best way to listen to the singing is apparently to dip one end of an oar in the water and hold the other end to your ear. The old Kallady Bridge is traditionally held to be a good place to tune in.

ARRIVAL AND DEPARTURE
BATTICALOA

By plane Cinnamon Air fly from Colombo's international airport to Batticaloa (daily; 1hr 30min). One-way tickets cost around $230. The airport is around 3km southwest of the centre; a tuktuk should cost around Rs.350–400.

By bus There are separate bus stands for SLTB and private buses, next to one another on the south side of the lagoon. Services to Colombo leave mainly either first thing in the morning or in the evening between 8pm and 10pm (with a couple more services in the afternoon). If you're heading down the coast to Arugam Bay, catch a bus to Pottuvil, then a tuktuk to Arugam Bay. If there's no Pottuvil bus available, catch a bus to Kalmunai and change onto a Pottuvil bus there.

Destinations Colombo (hourly; 8hr); Kalmunai (every 15min; 1hr); Kandy (2 daily; 6hr 30min); Karaitivu (for Ampara and Gal Oya; every 30min; 1hr 15min); Polonnaruwa (hourly; 2hr 30min); Pottuvil (hourly; 3hr); Trincomalee (every 30min; 3hr 30min); Valaichchenai (for Passekudah/Kalkudah; every 30min; 1hr).

By train The train station is on the north side of town, just over 1km from the centre.

Destinations Colombo (2 daily; 7–8hr); Polonnaruwa (5 daily; 2hr 30min); Valaichchenai (5 daily; 45min–1hr).

TOURS AND ACTIVITIES

Tours East N' West On Board (☎065 222 6079, ⌨eastnwestonboard.com) is a pioneering local travel agency now busily opening up all sorts of new destinations around Batti, with a wide selection of activities including city and country walks, cycling, boat trips, birdwatching and cooking classes. Their excellent website is full of information about little-known local attractions.

Boat trips Riviera Resort can arrange lagoon trips in their own little awning-covered boat to the nearby lighthouse and/or Batticaloa fort (Rs.750 per person for both). It's around 25min return to the fort, and 40min return to the lighthouse (which is up some way beyond East Lagoon Hotel). They also have kayaks for hire (one-person Rs.500, two-person Rs.800, including life jacket and buoyancy aid).

Diving Sri Lanka Diving Tours at the Deep Sea Resort offers PADI courses and dives to local sites (mid-March to Sept only), including the wreck of the famous HMS Hermes, sunk by the Japanese in 1942.

ACCOMMODATION

Accommodation in Batti is split mainly between the **town centre** and the quieter beachside suburb of **Kallady**, a Rs.300 tuktuk ride (or 20min walk) from the centre. East N' West on Board (see page 363) can organize homestays in Kallady and around Batti. Check the website (⌨eastnwestonboard.com) for details.

TOWN CENTRE AND AROUND

Hotel East Lagoon Munai Lane, Uppodai Lake Rd, 1km north of town ☎065 222 9222, ⌨hoteleastlagoon.lk; map p.362. Batticaloa's first large-scale hotel, this modern resort occupies a lovely location between two strips of lagoon. The hotel itself, in a trio of four-storey white buildings, has zero charm or atmosphere, but is comfy enough at a reasonable price, with huge (if uninspiring) rooms, plus a small pool and modest in-house restaurant. **$55**

KALLADY AND AROUND

Avonlea Inn 57a Nagathambiran Kovil Lane, New Dutch Bar Rd ☎065 222 8113; map p.362. Homely family guesthouse set around an intimate little garden. Rooms (including a couple with a/c) are simple but spacious and immaculately maintained, and the helpful owner offers various activities including boat rides to the lighthouse (see page 363), local excursions and tuktuk city tours. There are also bikes for hire (Rs.400/day) and all meals available. **Rs.2200**, a/c **Rs.3850**

Hamsaam Villa 35/1A New Dutch Bar Rd ☎077 580 3845, ⌨hamsaamvilla.com; map p.362. Cosy little family guesthouse with just three neat and spotless rooms (with hot water, plus optional a/c for Rs.1000). Breakfast and dinner are available if ordered in advance, and there's 24hr tea and coffee, bikes for hire (Rs.500) and tours. Good value. **Rs.2200**

5

Riviera Resort Off New Dutch Bar Rd ☎ 065 222 2164, ⓦ riviera-online.com; map p.362. Long-running and still deservedly popular place with accommodation in a scatter of buildings of various ages dotted around attractive lagoonside gardens, ranging from good-value fan rooms (including a couple of very cheap doubles with shared bathroom) through to smart and attractively furnished new rooms with a/c and hot water. There's also a nice garden restaurant (pre-order at least an hour in advance) and a big pool (guests pay a one-off Rs.250 charge) with hot tub and baby pool attached, and an Ayurvedic massage room (Rs.3000). Shared bathrooms __Rs.1500__, en suite __Rs.3300__, a/c __Rs.5700__

EATING

Café Chill Pioneer Rd ☎ 077 777 9598; map p.362. This funky little café, with some unusual cabana-style seating areas, is a great place for a cappuccino (Rs.300) or a fresh juice (from Rs.100). They also have hotdogs (from Rs.150) and chicken and veggie burger meals (from Rs.230). Daily 10am–8pm.

Hajiyar Restaurant East end of Main St ☎ 065 222 5639; map p.362. The smartest of the several food joints along this stretch of Main St. They serve a few basic rice-and-curry and buriani-style dishes during the day (virtually everything under Rs.300) and come alive at dusk with the clatter of machete-wielding *kottu rotty* makers Daily 8am–9.30pm.

Sri Saravanaa Pava Saravanan Street, Kallady ☎ 065 205 0301; map p.362. Excellent Indian vegetarian restaurant serving delicious rice and curry (Rs.150), plus dosas (Rs.150), *rotty* (from Rs.60) and quick eats (from Rs.40). Daily 6.30am–10pm

DIRECTORY

Banks There are banks all over town. The ATMs at the Commercial and Seylan banks on Bar Rd, and the HNB ATM on Fort Rd all accept foreign Visa and MasterCards.

Internet Wisdom internet café, 39/B Bailey Rd, or Ra Communications, further down the same road (both daily 8am–8pm; Rs.60/hr).

Swimming Non-guests can use the pool at the *Riviera Resort* for Rs.500.

South of Batticaloa

Beyond Batticaloa, the fine new coastal highway sweeps traffic effortlessly south – although disappointingly it runs out of sight of the sea except around the expansive **Koddaikallar lagoon**, a memorable maze of palm-fringed water. Much of the road is lined with an endless succession of mainly Tamil and Muslim settlements, surprisingly built up in places, particularly along the stretch of coast between the twin towns of **Kalmunai** and **Karaitivu** with their entertaining clutter of mosques, temples and makeshift shops, plus the occasional cow wandering across the road.

From Karaitivu, the A31 highway turns inland towards **Ampara**, offering a striking contrast between the bustling commercial towns of the Tamil–Muslim coast and the largely unpopulated and undeveloped rural hinterland, still predominantly Sinhalese, with little to interrupt the landscape apart from the occasional mud hut amid endless paddy fields.

Ampara

Set on the east side of the picturesque Ampara Tank, unassuming **AMPARA** is a typical one-horse rural Sri Lankan town that's rarely visited by foreign tourists. Its main draw is as a possible jumping-off point for the nearby **Gal Oya National Park** (see page 365), although there are also a couple of modest sights closer to hand.

Mandala Mahavihara

Follow the road running north of the main road near the Commercial Leasing office

In town, the **Mandala Mahavihara** temple is notable for its unusual dagoba. Sitting on a grass-covered terrace, this concrete structure looks perfectly ordinary from the outside. The real surprise lies within: a small door leads into the hollow interior, its ceiling painted to resemble the sky, supported on a single giant pillar and boasting as impressive an echo as you could hope to hear.

Japanese Peace Pagoda
4km west of town; head along Inginiyagala Road, then take the signed turn-off on the right just past the 3km post

The main local attraction hereabouts is the **Japanese Peace Pagoda** (Nipponzan Myohoji) of 1988, set in peaceful countryside west of Ampara. The florid dagoba itself, surrounded by a covered walkway, occupies a fine setting overlooking Ampara tank – wild elephants can often be seen marching past, particularly in the hours before dusk.

ARRIVAL AND DEPARTURE
AMPARA

By bus Regular buses connect Ampara and the coast; change at Karaitivu for Batticaloa (5 daily; 3hr), or head to Akkaraipattu

for Pottuvil and Arugam Bay (2 daily; 3hr). Frequent services also run to Siyambalanduwa and Monaragala.

ACCOMMODATION AND EATING

Monty Hotel First Ave (down the road past the Terrel Residencies) ☎063 222 2215, ⓦmontyhotel. com. This is a large and unexpectedly chic hotel for such a backwater town. There's a wide range of a/c rooms in various price categories ranging from standard through to fancy "luxury" rooms with hot water, TV and attractive furnishings (Rs.10,550). Facilities include a pool and neat little gardens. **Rs.5550**

Terrel Residencies Stores Rd, just off Main St down the side road diagonally opposite the Commercial Leasing office ☎063 222 2215. Rather gloomy-looking place offering a wide spread of accommodation ranging from simple but comfortable fan rooms through to smarter furnished deluxe rooms with a/c, TV and hot water (Rs.7000). The restaurant serves Western and Chinese-inspired dishes. **Rs.3500**

Gal Oya National Park
Around 20km west of Ampara; entrance at Inginiyagala • Daily 6am–6pm • $12 per person, plus the usual additional charges and taxes (see page 50) • Trips can be arranged through the *Monty Hotel* in Ampara (see page 365); boats can be hired at the entrance

The enormous **Gal Oya National Park** lies some 50km inland from the coast in a little-visited corner of the island. Like the nearby Maduru Oya (see page 238), it was closed for much of the civil war and remains poorly set up for visitors at present. The park's centrepiece is the vast **Senanayake Samudra**, one of the largest lakes in the country, and tours of the park are usually made – uniquely in Sri Lanka – by boat. As usual, elephants are the main draw, with herds of up to 150 visiting during their annual peregrinations. Elephant-spotting is best from March to July.

ACCOMMODATION
GAL OYA NATIONAL PARK

★ **Gal Oya Lodge** Bibile–Ampara road near the 30km post, on the northwestern edge of the park ☎076 842 1612, ⓦgaloyalodge.com. Idyllic wildlife lodge with nine eco-friendly rooms and a family villa constructed from local

materials spread over twenty acres of jungle – beautifully simple but unquestionably chic. Activities include boat and jeep safaris, walks and tours with local Veddhas, and there's also a pool, plus bar and restaurant. B&B **$195**

Arugam Bay and around

Easy-going **Arugam Bay** is by far the most engaging of the east coast's resorts. A-Bay, as it's often known, has long been popular with the **surfing** fraternity, who come here to ride what are generally acknowledged to be the best waves in Sri Lanka. It's also a good launching pad from which to explore the gorgeous surrounding countryside and its varied attractions, from the elephant-rich **Lahugala National Park** and the little-visited **Kumana National Park** to the atmospheric forest hermitage at **Kudimbigala**.

Arugam Bay

There's not much to **ARUGAM BAY** village itself: just a single main road running parallel to the beach that's dotted with guesthouses, cafés and shops, including various quirky, homespun architectural creations – rustic palm-thatch cabanas, teetering tree houses and other quaint structures. The **beach** is fairly clean, thanks to the efforts of locals,

5

although plastic waste washed up from the sea can be a problem. The southern end is where most local fishing boats moor up when not out at sea, while the northern end is generally emptier and quieter.

A-Bay also marks the rough border between the Sinhalese-majority areas to the south and the mainly Tamil and Muslim areas further up the coast, and boasts an unusually eclectic but harmonious mix of all three ethnic groups – as well as a growing number of Western expats. Persistent fears that the village's uniquely (for Sri Lanka) alternative and slightly off-the-wall character will be erased by larger and more mainstream tourism developments remain, although for the time being Arugam Bay preserves its own enjoyably eccentric charm.

ARRIVAL AND INFORMATION   ARUGAM BAY

By bus There are currently around ten buses heading west daily from Panama via Arugam Bay to Monaragala, a couple of which continue all the way to Colombo (at 6am and 8pm at the time of research). Heading north, there's one direct service to Batticaloa in the morning; alternatively, take one of the regular buses (every 30min) from Pottuvil

to Kalmunai, from where there are frequent onward connections. For Ampara, take a Kalmunai bus from Pottuvil and change at Akkaraipattu.

Tourist information ⓦ arugam.info is an excellent resource. The *Stardust* (ⓦ arugambay.com) and *Siam View* (ⓦ arugam.com) hotels also have useful websites.

ACCOMMODATION

Arugam Bay offers plenty of accommodation options, from budget to boutique, although prices are often surprisingly high and everything gets booked up quickly. A-Bay remains reasonably lively out of season, though rates at many places fall by at least a third.

CENTRAL ARUGAM BAY

★ **Bay Vista** Main St ☏ 063 224 8577, ⓦ bayvistahotel.com; map p.367. In a fantastic central location, this well-run and friendly hotel is great value. The rooms are clean, simple and comfortable, and the beach-facing ones all have balconies with superb views. The lobby area restaurant is excellent and in the busier months there's a health food café and yoga space on the roof. B&B **Rs.12,100**

The Danish Villa Main St ☏ 077 695 7936, ⓦ thedanishvilla.com; map p.367. One of the village's classier options, in a low-slung white villa set amid pretty gardens with six attractively furnished rooms of various sizes and prices, split between the main house and an attractive garden bungalow around the back, plus one simpler budget room ($30). Optional a/c costs around $11 extra. **$38**

Galaxy Lounge Galaxy Rd ☏ 063 224 8415, ⓦ galaxysrilanka.com; map p.367. A mix of stilted and budget palm-thatch cabanas plus two new a/c luxury rooms in a nice beachfront location, with a breezy open-air restaurant. **Rs.5000**

Hideaway Main St ☏ 063 224 8259, ⓦ hideawayarugambay.com; map p.367. Another A-Bay stalwart, hidden amid lush gardens on the landside of the main road, although it's getting cluttered with continual enlargements. The cheaper fan rooms in the attractive Bawa-esque main house are the best deal,

but there are also some bigger but rather humdrum and decidedly expensive hexagonal-shaped a/c cabanas ($175) and further rooms scattered around the spacious grounds. There's also a good restaurant and bar (see page 368), a roadside café, a Sunday market, new pool (Rs.750 for non-guests) and a yoga chalet. **$50**, a/c **$110**

Long Hostel Panama Rd ☏ 077 394 3199, ⓦ thelonghostel.com; map p.367. A-Bay's newest budget option with small but clean bunk-bed dorms (with fan or a/c) and a/c double rooms. There's also a coffee shop and restaurant serving breakfast (Rs.400). Dorms **Rs.1350** doubles **Rs.3800**

Nice Place Tsunami Hotel Rd ☏ 063 224 8193, ⓦ niceplaceguesthousesrilanka.weebly.com; map p.367. Intimate little guesthouse, not quite on the beach but very close. The spacious, high-ceilinged rooms come with thick mattresses and powerful fans, and there are wicker chairs on verandas around the pretty little garden. Fan rooms are decent value; the identical a/c a lot less so. **$35**, a/c **$45**

★ **Ranga's Beach Hut** Beach Hut Rd ☏ 077 16 6203, ⓦ arugambaybeachhut.com; map p.367. A quintessential slice of Arugam Bay, with a selection of rustic wooden cabanas in a quirky range of styles (including a couple on stilts, and a picturesque tree house). It's rustic and fairly basic (the cheapest cabanas come with shared bathroom), but excellent value, and has bags of laidback charm and character. Also a sociable choice for evening meals, with good, inexpensive Sri Lankan food served at a communal table (best to book in advance). **Rs.2500**

Roccos Main St ☏ 071 810 7777, ⓦ arugambayrocco. lk; map p.367. Rather bland new hotel with 22 white concrete cubes set around a pool (Rs.1500 for non-guest, including lunch), with the more expensive ones close to the

each. The cube rooms have simple pine furniture as well as ceiling fans and a/c. B&B $150

Sandy Beach Hotel Off Water Music Rd ☎063 224 8403, �🌐arugambay-hotel.com; map p.367. Modern white building in a gorgeous location right above the waves with four sea-facing rooms with a/c, hot water and balcony, two spacious villa rooms and a surfers cabana. Rs.6000, a/c Rs.12000

★ **Spice Trail** Main St ☎063 224 8403, �🌐thespicetrails.com; map p.367. Nestled amid a pleasant garden with a pool, the twelve charming and spacious boutique villas here come with king-size beds, large bathrooms and private courtyard gardens. The atmosphere is friendly and laid back, and the restaurant is excellent (see page 368). B&B $175

Stardust Beach Hotel Main St ☎063 224 8191, ⍟arugambay.com; map p.367. One of Arugam Bay's original hotels, with bright and stylish rooms (those upstairs have great ocean views from the sea-facing balconies) and a selection of reasonably priced wooden cabanas, plus some upmarket villa-style apartments with two double rooms and a kitchen. There's also a yoga pavilion (group and individual classes available), a canoe for lagoon trips and a good restaurant (see page 368). Cabanas $43 , doubles $70, apartments $180

★ **Surf N Sun** Main St ☎077 865 9656; map p.367. Popular surfers' hangout set in luxuriant, green gardens. Accommodation is in some of the village's most attractive cabanas – a mix of simpler wooden structures and larger concrete-walled affairs almost buried under vast palm-thatch roofs – plus a couple of more upmarket and very attractively designed villas (sleeping 2–5 people) further down the endless garden. At the time of research, two new units with kitchens were being built. There's also (in season) a lively restaurant and cocktail bar, yoga classes, surf shop and a good range of tours available. Cabanas $40, villas $100

NORTH OF ARUGAM BAY

★ **Jetwing Surf** 4km north of Arugam Bay, Kottukal Beach Road, Pottuvil ☎063 203 0300, ⍟jetwinghotels.com; map p.367. Newly opened, upmarket eco-resort on a quiet and pristine stretch of beach north of Arugam Bay. The twenty luxurious cabanas, all constructed and decorated with natural grasses, palm leaves, coir and local timbers, have indoor and outdoor showers and comfortable lounge seating. There's no a/c but it's possible to sleep under a mosquito net with the veranda doors open. There's also an in-pool bar and the in-house restaurant serves gourmet cuisine with some innovative twists on Sri Lankan standards. B&B $480

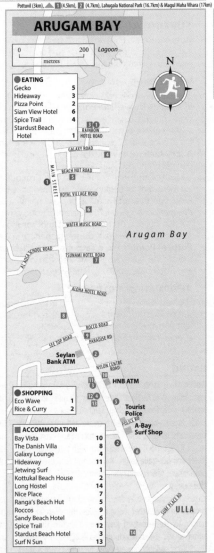

Pottuvil (3km), ⛰ 1 (4.5km), 2 (4.7km), Lahugala National Park (16.7km) & Magul Maha Vihara (17km)

ARUGAM BAY

0 ——— 200 metres — Lagoon

N

● EATING

Gecko	5
Hideaway	3
Pizza Point	2
Siam View Hotel	6
Spice Trail	4
Stardust Beach Hotel	1

RAINBOW HOTEL ROAD
GALAXY ROAD
MAIN STREET
BEACH HUT ROAD
ROYAL VILLAGE ROAD
WATER MUSIC ROAD

Arugam Bay

AL KASA SCHOOL ROAD
TSUNAMI HOTEL ROAD
ALOHA HOTEL ROAD
ROCCO ROAD
SEE TOP ROAD
PARADISE RD

Seylan Bank ATM
NYLON CENTRE ROAD
HNB ATM

● SHOPPING

| Eco Wave | 1 |
| Rice & Curry | 2 |

Tourist Police
POLICE RD
A-Bay Surf Shop

■ ACCOMMODATION

Bay Vista	10
The Danish Villa	8
Galaxy Lounge	4
Hideaway	11
Jetwing Surf	1
Kottukal Beach House	2
Long Hostel	14
Nice Place	7
Ranga's Beach Hut	5
Roccos	9
Sandy Beach Hotel	6
Spice Trail	12
Stardust Beach Hotel	3
Surf N Sun	13

SURF PLACE RD
ULLA

Panama (13km), Kudimbigala (25km), Kumana National Park (28km) & ⛴ Okanda (30km)

Kottukal Beach House 4km north of Arugam Bay, Kottukal Beach Road, Pottuvil ☎077 534 8807, ⍟jetwinghotels.com; map p.367. Chic two-storey luxury beach villa with four rooms and two chalets located near the southern end of the Pottuvil Point surfing break. The rooms have excellent ocean views, and the coconut tree garden provides shelter for lounging around the pool. B&B $320

5

5

SURFING AT ARUGAM BAY

With waves fresh from Antarctica crashing up onto the beach, Arugam Bay is sometimes claimed to be one of the top ten **surf** points in the world, and periodically plays host to international tournaments. The **best time** for surfing is between April and October/November.

WHERE TO GO

There are several breaks close to Arugam Bay, plus others further afield. The biggest waves in A-Bay itself are at **The Point** (at the southern end of the beach), a long right-hand break which has (on a good day) 2m waves and a 400m ride. Another good break can be found straight off the beach by the *Siam View Hotel*. **Baby Point** (between *Mambo's* and *Siam View Hotel*) is ideal for beginners, with smaller waves and a sandy bottom (unlike The Point, which is coral-bottomed), while the beach break in front of the *Stardust Beach Hotel* is also good for beginners and bodysurfing.

South of Arugam Bay, the break near **Crocodile Rock** (3km south of Arugam Bay) is an excellent spot for beginner and intermediate surfers if there's sufficient swell. Some 5km further on, **Peanut Farm** has two surf points: a perfect tube for expert surfers and a smaller ride ideal for beginners; there are also good waves further south at **Okanda**.

A number of spots **north of Pottuvil** are also becoming popular among more experienced surfers (and are generally quieter than those in A-Bay). About 9km north of Arugam Bay, **Pottuvil Point** breaks off a long and deserted sandy beach; the ride can be as long as 800m, though the waves are a bit smaller than in A-Bay. Other nearby breaks include Whiskey Point and Lighthouse Point (aka "The Green Room").

INFORMATION AND RENTAL

The best places for general surfing **info and equipment hire** are A-Bay Surf Shop and the surf shop at the *Surf N Sun* guesthouse. These places and some of the village's guesthouses rent bodyboards and surfboards (Rs.800/day for shortboards, Rs.1000 for longboards), as well as operating **surfing safaris** to various other spots along the coast.

EATING

Gecko Main St ☎ 063 224 8212, ⓦ geckoarugambay. net; map p.367. Neat little place serving up good, healthy café food including sandwiches (with home-made bread), home-made ice cream and cakes, all-day breakfasts, burgers, salads, pasta and rice and curry (most mains Rs.950–1595), washed down with tasty sugar-free juices and fair-trade coffee. You can also refill used water bottles here, saving money and plastic. Daily 8am–10pm.

Hideaway Main St ☎ 063 224 8259, ⓦ hideawayarugambay.com; map p.367. An enjoyable contrast to most other A-Bay eateries, this peaceful little garden-terrace restaurant feels more Colombo chic than surfer shack. Food (lunch mains Rs.800–1000, dinner Rs.2000) is stylishly prepared and presented with a short menu of upmarket, regularly changing international dishes. Also does a good breakfast selection. Daily 7am–9.30pm.

Pizza Point Main St ☎ 077 254 3043; map p.367. Friendly wood-fire pizza restaurant run by a gang of young lads and using homemade tomato sauce and locally produced basil and mozzarella for various combinations (Rs.1000-1800). Also serves a variety of pasta (from Rs.900) and salads (from Rs.800). Daily 11am–10pm.

★ **Siam View Hotel** Main St ☎ 077 320 0201, ⓦ arugam.com; map p.367. Usually one of the best places for a night out in the village, with a good cocktail list, smooth soundtrack and simultaneous movies, sport and music videos on their three screens. The restaurant occupies an open-sided first-floor wooden pavilion with menu focusing on reasonable Thai food (with perhaps some non-Thai dishes during season); mains around Rs.700–850. Reduced hours out of season. Daily 7am–3am.

★ **Spice Trail** Main St ☎ 063 224 8403, ⓦ thespicetrail. com; map p.367. This is fast becoming one of A-Bay's best restaurants and is the only place where you can get Japanese cuisine including sushi, ramen and okonomiyaki (Rs. 900–1200). The roasted pumpkin and wild rice and mango salads (Rs. 700-875) are also scrumptious. Their Bit Bake Bar is open during the busier months only and sells cakes and biscuits. Daily 7.30am–10pm.

Stardust Beach Hotel Main St ☎ 063 224 8191, ⓦ arugambay.com; map p.367. Attractive pavilion restaurant with an appetizing selection of snacks and well-prepared meals (most mains around Rs.1100–1500 including a good selection of breakfasts and sandwiches (with home-made bread) alongside international dishes ranging from pasta and goulash through to dosas and rice and curry. Don't miss the home-made ice cream. Daily 7.45am–10pm.

SHOPPING

Eco Wave Main St ☎ 063 373 0404, ⓦ ecowave.lk; map p.367. Fun little shop run by the local Eco Wave social enterprise and selling a range of ethically sourced produce and souvenirs – organic tea, spices and fruits, chemical-free rice, pressed-flower greeting cards, hats fashioned from woven palmyra leaves and so on. Profits support local community projects and they also arrange an excellent range of tours (see below). Reduced hours out of season. Daily 8am–8pm.

Rice & Carry Main St ⓦ riceandcarry.com; map p.367. The new flagship store of this excellent east coast-based social enterprise sells a variety of bags, pouches, totes and other useful items made by local women from recycled rice and spice sacks, plus wallets, key tags and surfboard wax combs made from discarded plastic shopping bags. Reduced hours out of season. Daily 9.30am–5.30pm.

DIRECTORY

Bank There are HNB and Seylan Bank ATMs in the middle of the village, both of which accept foreign Visa and MasterCards, plus several banks in nearby Pottuvil.

Lahugala National Park

Free • Guesthouses in Arugam Bay can arrange jeeps to Lahugala, though you can't drive these in the park; alternatively, catch a bus or tuktuk (around Rs.3500)

Some 15km inland from Arugam Bay, the main road west passes through the small but beautiful **Lahugala National Park**, comprising Lahugula Tank and a magnificent swathe of dry mixed evergreen forest, dotted with lofty rosewoods and satinwoods. The park is best known for its **elephants**: up to 150 congregate around the tank during July and August, when the rest of Lahugala's waters dry up, to drink and feed on the *beru* grass which grows prolifically on its shores. The tank area is also good for spotting a wide range of **birds**, including innumerable snowy white egrets that can often be seen hitching a ride on the backs of obliging elephants. When the rains come the elephants disperse, and large sections of the park turn a brilliant, post-monsoonal green.

Lahugala isn't officially open to the public, and no vehicles are allowed in, although you're free to walk into the park from the main Arugam Bay–Monaragala road, which runs right through it. Be aware, however, that walking through jungle with a large elephant population carries a degree of risk, so it's best to stick to one of the recognized **viewpoints** close to the road. The easiest (and safest) option is to head to **Lahugala**

TOURS FROM ARUGAM BAY

For a convenient whistle-stop tour of the area, the Ceylon Walking Tour (ⓦceylonwalkingtours.com) and the *Surf N Sun* guesthouse run useful **day-trips** by tuktuk (Rs.6000/vehicle) taking in most of the major local attractions, including Kudimbigala, Okanda, Magul Maha Vihara and Lahugala. The **Pottuvil Lagoon Tour** (2hr; Rs.6000/two-person boat; bookings and info on ☎075 824 1432) consists of a gentle canoe trip, during which a local fisherman will paddle you out into Pottuvil lagoon, 8km north of town, and through the beautiful mangrove swamps that fringe its shores, offering the chance to spot birds, monitor lizards and perhaps the occasional crocodile or elephant. It's also possible to arrange **sea safaris** with any of the companies listed above (2hr; Rs.6000) in engine-powered boats, with a good chance of seeing dolphins, flying fish and other marine life. **Surfing tours** (see page 368) are also popular, as are trips to (the edges of) Lahugala (see page 369) and Kumana (see page 371) **national parks**.

At the north end of the village, **Eco Wave** (see page 369) also run an interesting range of responsible tours and activities (all of which require a minimum of two people; per-person prices fall in larger groups). These include cookery classes with local women (Tues, Thurs and on request; 2–3hr; Rs.3000pp for minimum group of 2); tours to Kumana and Panama village (7hr; Rs.10,000pp including park entrance); Pottuvil lagoon tours (3–4hr; Rs.3300pp); and visits to Magul Maha Vihara and a local village (4hr; Rs.4,000pp).

5

Hospital (at the 306km post). Just west of here along the main road, several small paths run off to the right to the raised bund at the edge of Lahugala Tank, about 100m away, which offers a secure vantage point and good chances of spotting elephants.

Magul Maha Vihara

Just east of Lahugala (and signposted from the main road just west of the 307km post) • No set hours • Donation

According to tradition, the evocative remains of the **Magul Maha Vihara** temple mark the site of the wedding of Kavan Tissa and Viharamahadevi (see page 190), one of ancient Sri Lanka's most famous celebrity couples – you can still see the *poruwa*, a special wedding platform decorated with a lion frieze, which was erected for the event at the back of the enclosure on the right-hand side. Following the ceremony, the land was enclosed in an impressive circuit of walls and presented to the Sangha, who established a monastery here. The unexcavated remains of Kavan Tissa's palace lie in jungle to the south; it was here that the couple's son, the legendary Dutugemunu (see page 330), was born and lived until his teens, when he and his parents moved to Tissa.

Stone inscriptions found at the site record that the current temple buildings were erected by King Dhatusena during the mid-fifth century, and later restored in the mid-fourteenth century. The extensive remains include an image house, dagoba, *poyage* and well-preserved moonstones, as well as the finely carved *poruwa*, all lent an additional layer of mystery by the thick jungle that surrounds them on every side.

South of Arugam Bay

The countryside and coastline **south of Arugam Bay** is beautifully unspoiled. Buses run three times daily along the good tarmac road which rolls through rice paddies and scrub jungle as far as the dusty little village of **PANAMA**, 12km south of Arugam Bay. There are miles of superb deserted beach along this stretch, and a pair of huge rock outcrops popularly known as **Elephant Rock** and **Crocodile Rock** for their alleged resemblance to these creatures, though you'll need a tuktuk (or 4X4) to reach them. Elephants are sometimes seen wandering in the vicinity. Panama itself has a fine, dune-backed beach, 1km south of town; to reach it, pass through the village and follow the road round to the left.

The road **south of Panama** is currently unsurfaced, although the dirt track is kept in reasonable condition and is usually passable in a jeep (and tuktuks make the journey with ease). The countryside here is almost completely uninhabited, and very similar in appearance to that of Yala National Park, with extensive lagoons, scrub jungle and huge populations of birds, as well as occasional elephants and crocodiles.

Kudimbigala

Just beyond the 12km post on the road south of Panama, and 500m along a turning on the right (a 60min drive from Arugam Bay) • 6am-5pm

The hundreds of caves at the beautiful forest hermitage of **Kudimbigala** are thought to have been occupied by Buddhist monks as far back as the first century BC. From the car park, follow the path ahead of you (keeping the modern rock-top dagoba to your right) into the surrounding woodland, and keep to the track as it squeezes through the trees and between enormous rock outcrops. After about ten minutes you reach the **Sudasharna Cave**, a small white shrine half-covered by an overhanging rock outcrop bearing the faint remains of ancient Brahmi script next to an unusual little carving symbolizing the Triple Gem.

Following the path to the left of the cave leads after another ten minutes up to the **Madhya Mandalaya** ("Plain of Ruins"), with a small dagoba and other monastic remains scattered over a rocky hilltop. Alternatively, heading right from the cave brings you o the huge **Belumgala**, a towering rock outcrop topped by yet another small dagoba. Rock-cut steps lead to the top, a breathless ten-to-fifteen-minute climb, at the end of which you'll be rewarded by one of the finest views anywhere in the east: a vast swathe of jungle dotted with huge rock outcrops running down to the sea, and with scarcely a single sign of human habitation in sight.

Okanda

Beyond Kudimbigala, 30km south of Arugam Bay, the village of **OKANDA** has another popular surfing spot, and also boasts a major **Hindu temple**, marking the spot where Kataragama is said to have landed on the island; it is now an important staging point on the overland pilgrimage to Kataragama. The village is also the entrance point for Kumana National Park.

Kumana National Park

0km south of Arugam Bay • Daily 6am–6pm • $15 per person, plus the usual additional charges and taxes (see page 50) • Some guesthouses in Arugam Bay including *Sun N Surf* can arrange transport to and around the park by jeep (seating 4–6 people) for around s.10,000 (not including park entrance ticket); it might also be possible to include a visit to Kudimbigala in the same tour

Kumana National Park (still widely known by its old name of Yala East National Park) suffered major damage during the war years, when it served as an LTTE hideout, but it has now been largely rehabilitated. Wildlife is still less plentiful that in neighbouring Yala, but Kumana sees only a fraction of the number of visitors, meaning that you'll usually have the place pretty much to yourself. The main attraction is the **Kumana Bird Sanctuary**, incorporated within the park and comprising the Kumana Wewa tank and surrounding mangroves, one of the island's most important breeding and nesting grounds – over 250 species have been recorded here. Other wildlife includes leopard, some forty elephants, lots of crocodiles and a few extremely reclusive sloth bears.

Monaragala and around

Just beyond the easternmost fringes of the hill country east of Wellawaya, the small town of **MONARAGALA** sits at the foot of the huge **Peacock Rock**, whose sheer sides loom dramatically over the countryside hereabouts. The town itself is principally of interest as the gateway to Arugam Bay, and also provides a convenient base for visiting the remote and magical Buddhist statues of **Maligawila** and the huge ruined stupa of **Yudaganawa**. In addition, it serves as the gateway to a pair of fine eco-lodges in the surrounding countryside.

ARRIVAL AND DEPARTURE   MONARAGALA

By bus The bus station is bang in the centre of town. There are around ten buses daily from Monaragala to Arugam Bay (last bus currently at 5pm). Alternatively, take a bus to Pottuvil or catch a bus to Siyambalanduwa, from where there are more regular connections onto Pottuvil/Arugam Bay. If you're heading west, it's often easiest to catch a bus to Wellawaya or Badulla, from where there are plentiful onward connections.

Destinations Ampara (hourly; 3hr); Arugam Bay (10 daily; 2hr); Badulla (every 30min; 3hr); Buttala (every 30min; 45min); Wellawaya (every 15min; 1hr 15min).

ACCOMMODATION

Accommodation options in Monaragala are – not surprisingly – limited, although all the following are fine for a night, and do reasonable food as well.

★ **Kandaland** Araliya Uyana Rd ☏ 055 227 6925, ☏ raxawa.com; map p.372. This welcoming family guesthouse is easily Monaragala's most appealing place to stay, with exceptionally spacious and spotless rooms and home-cooked rice and curry on request. Excellent value, unless you opt for pricey optional a/c (Rs.2000 extra). The owners can also arrange trips (Rs.1000) by tuktuk and on foot to their rubber estate at Raxawa, set in beautiful countryside on a hill high above Monaragala. <u>Rs.2000</u>

Rest House Wellawaya Rd ☏ 055 227 6815; map p.372. Characterful old rest house set behind a spacious

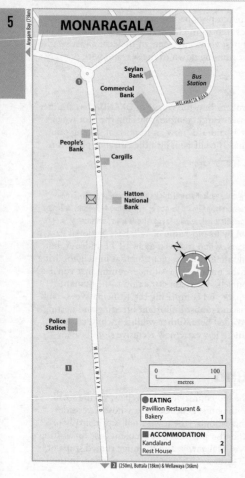

MONARAGALA

▲ Arugam Bay (73km)

Seylan Bank
Bus Station
Commercial Bank
WELAWATTA ROAD
People's Bank
Cargills
Hatton National Bank
N
Police Station
0   100
metres

● EATING
Pavillion Restaurant & Bakery   1

■ ACCOMMODATION
Kandaland   2
Rest House   1

▼ 2 (250m), Buttala (18km) & Wellawaya (36km)

garden and pleasant terrace restaurant. Rooms (a with hot water) are basic but good value, assumin you skip the pricey a/c and don't mind a bit c mustiness. **Rs.2750**, a/c **Rs.3500**

EATING

Pavillion Restaurant & Bakery Pottuvil Rd ☎ 05 227 6127; map p.372. A good place for grabbin some baked goods, if you're pushed for time. They als serve a delicious rice and curry buffet (from Rs.300) Daily 6am–9.30pm.

Maligawila and around

The remote village of **MALIGAWILA**, little more than a sandy clearing surrounded by a few makeshift shacks, is home to two giant standing seventh-century Buddhist **statues**, fashioned out of crystalline limestone, which are thought to have once formed part of an extensive monastic complex. The images, which had collapsed and fallen to bits, were restored in 1991, when the various pieces were rescued from the jungle floor and painstakingly reassembled – though the Maitreya statue still looks rather patched up. The statues are impressive in themselves, but are made additionally mysterious by their setting, hidden away in a stretch of pristine lowland jungle with an active monkey population.

From the car park, a path leads into the woods, reaching a T-junction after about 300m. Turn left to reach the first of the two statues, an 11m-high standing **Buddha** in the *abhaya mudra* ("Have No Fear") pose, freestanding apart from a discreet supporting brick arch at the back and recently covered with a metal shelter.

Return to the T-junction and follow the other path for 200m to reach the second statue, dating from the seventh century AD and thought to represent either the bodhisattvas **Maitreya** or **Avalokitesvara**. This is a more elaborate structure, with the remains of ornate entrance steps, a moonstone and two flanking guardstones, plus a pillar inscription in medieval Sinhala erected during the reign of Mahinda IV (956–972), recording acts performed by the king in support of the Buddhist order. The statue itself is set on a sequence of five raised plinths, like a ziggurat, and clothed in a richly ornamented dress; unfortunately, it's currently protected by an ugly concrete pavilion.

Detamahal Vihara

If you have your own transport, it's worth making the short detour about 6km west of Maligawila to the **Detamahal Vihara**, a pleasant temple with marvellous views over the paddy fields. Its origins date right back to the first or second century BC, and an ancient-looking, red-brick stupa survives, along with traces of Polonnaruwa-era

tonework in the main shrine, itself built on an even older stone base. Next to here
modern brick building, in a traditional style, houses a striking, blackened twelfth-
century Buddha image. Behind here is a partially excavated area scattered with the
foundations of vanished buildings, guardstones and other ruins.

ARRIVAL AND DEPARTURE	MALIGAWILA AND AROUND
By bus Buses from Monaragala to Maligawila leave roughly every 45min and take around 1hr, dropping you in the tiny village's dusty main square, from where it's a short walk to the statues.	**By taxi or tuktuk** A taxi from Monaragala will cost around Rs.4000, a tuktuk around Rs.3000.

Yudaganawa and around

km west of Buttala • Daily 24hr • Free

Just west of the small town of **BUTTALA** (and 20km southwest of Monaragala) lie the
remains of the huge **Yudaganawa dagoba**, one of the biggest in the east. The stupa is said
to mark the location of a battle between Dutugemunu (see page 330) and his younger
brother Saddhatissa. Dutugemunu was victorious, and Saddhatissa fled to the Detamahal
Vihara (see page 372), although the brothers were subsequently reconciled – the dagoba
was commissioned by Saddhatissa to commemorate the peace. Parakramabahu I (see page
14) is said to have subsequently enshrined the ashes of his mother here.

The dagoba

Of the original dagoba, only the huge, three-tiered **base** now survives (heavily restored),
although even this gives an impressive sense of the enormity of the original structure,
with a circumference of 310m, even bigger than the mighty Ruwanwelisaya dagoba in
Anuradhapura. A small Kandyan-era **shrine** stands in front of the stupa, richly decorated
inside with intricate, though faded, murals and a painted wooden ceiling – the pictures
flanking the door are particularly fine, showing a meditating Buddha shaded by a
grinning cobra on one side and an unusually slim, black-headed Ganesh on the other.
Note that you'll probably be asked for a small donation when entering the shrine,
although you don't need to give any money to see the dagoba itself.)

On the way out you'll pass the slight remains of the **Chulangani Vihara**, said to mark
the site of the first clash between Dutugemunu and Saddhatissa, although little now
remains of the original temple beyond a small mossy dagoba and fragments of two very
bashed-up Buddhas – only the torsos survive, plus a single pair of feet.

ARRIVAL AND DEPARTURE	YUDAGANAWA AND AROUND
By car To reach the stupa, head 1km west of Buttala along the Wellaway Road, then 1km down a side road signed on	the right. If you don't have your own transport you'll have to walk from Buttala or catch a tuktuk.

ACCOMMODATION

Well off the beaten track, the remote countryside around Buttala is an unlikely home to two of the island's most memorable – and idiosyncratic – **eco-retreats**.

Kumbuk River 9km east of Buttala ☎ 077 045 5494, ☜ kumbukriver.com. This unique riverside retreat offers you probably the only chance you'll ever get to sleep *in* an elephant – an extraordinary 12m-long, thatch-roofed beast constructed from local *kumbuk* wood. There's also an equally comfortable and spacious jungle cabin, a modern two-storey tree house and a boat house moored on the river. B&B: jungle cabin $140, elephant villa $160, tree house $180, boat house $120

★ **Tree Tops Jungle Lodge** 10km southeast of Buttala ☎ 077 703 6554, ☜ treetopsjunglelodge. com. Offering the chance to get right into the heart of Sri Lankan nature, this lodge is integrated with the jungle on the "wild" side of an electric fence designed to limit the wanderings of local elephants – it's a marvellous place to stay if you want a real lost-in-the-forest experience. Accommodation is in three en-suite tented rooms and there's a thatched mud-hut restaurant, and although there are no mod cons (and no electricity) it manages to be very comfortable even so. Advance booking required; two-night minimum stay. Full board $290

Jaffna and the north

NALLUR KANDASWAMY TEMPLE

Jaffna and the north

The north is a world away from the rest of Sri Lanka. Geographically closer to southern India than to Colombo, the region was settled early on by Tamil migrants from across the Palk Strait and has retained its own unique character and culture, one which owes as much to Hindu India as to Buddhist Sri Lanka. From 1983 to 2009 the entire region was engulfed in the civil war between the rebel guerrillas of the LTTE (Liberation Tigers of Tamil Eelam, or Tamil Tigers) and the Sri Lankan Army (SLA), the decades of fighting further reinforcing the two-thousand-year history of difference that separates the Tamil north from the Sinhalese south.

The apocalyptic conclusion to the civil war in 2009 left much of the region in physical tatters. Almost a decade on, the long process of postwar rehabilitation is drawing to a conclusion. Most of the region's shattered towns and villages have now been rebuilt, fields have been demined, refugees returned to their former homes, major highways repaired and upgraded and the previously defunct railway lines to Jaffna and Mannar reopened.

For the traveller, the north remains Sri Lanka's final frontier. The fascinating little city of **Jaffna** is the region's highlight, with its absorbing mixture of colonial charm and vibrant Tamil culture, while the **Jaffna Peninsula** and surrounding **islands** offer a string of remote temples, beaches and an eclectic medley of offbeat attractions. Further south the vast swathe of sparsely populated countryside known as the **Vanni** is little visited, even by Sri Lankans, although a trickle of adventurous travellers are now making it to the towns of **Kilinochchi** and **Mullaitivu**, scenes of the civil war's two major concluding battles.

Southeast from here, the remote church at **Madhu** draws a steady stream of pilgrims of all faiths, while arid and far-flung **Mannar Island** is also beginning to attract increasing numbers of intrepid kitesurfers, birdwatchers and those seeking a complete escape from the Sri Lankan mainstream.

GETTING AROUND

Transport The reopening of the railway lines to both Jaffna and Mannar means that both towns can now be reached in relatively speedy air-conditioned comfort (see page 391), while travelling by road is now almost equally swift following comprehensive upgrades to all the region's major highways. Note, however, that tourism remains nascent going on nonexistent in most parts of the north, meaning that if you want to hire a car and English-speaking driver to explore in more depth you'll probably find it easier to bring one with you from elsewhere in the island.

Safety There are currently no major safety concerns in the north bar the danger from uncleared landmines. In the unlikely event that you find yourself in areas of remote northern countryside or jungle, be sure to stick to roads or well-defined paths.

The Vanni

The huge area of northern Sri Lanka between **Vavuniya** and the Jaffna Peninsula – **the Vanni** – was always one of the island's least developed and most sparsely populated areas even before the civil war, which laid waste to most of the region's towns and villages. For many of the years between 1983 and 2009 the Vanni was controlled by the LTTE, who established their own de facto independent state stretching from just north

MANNAR DONKEYS

Highlights

❶ Mannar Wander with wild ponies, scout for rare Indian bird species and kitesurf amongst the islets of Adam's Bridge at this magical and little-visited island. See page 380

❷ Jaffna Quite unlike anywhere else on the island, the vibrant city of Jaffna offers a fascinating insight into Sri Lankan Tamil culture, as well as many reminders of its colonial and civil war history. See page 386

❸ Nallur Kandaswamy Temple and Festival Sri Lanka's finest Hindu temple, and home to the north's largest and longest festival – a 25-day extravaganza of colour, ceremony and spectacle. See page 391

❹ Jaffna Peninsula The fertile Jaffna peninsula is home to myriad contrasting sights, from desert dunes and sacred springs to ancient dagobas and war-torn temples. See page 393

❺ The islands Splintering off the tip of the Jaffna Peninsula, the starkly beautiful islands of Kayts, Karaitivu, Nainativu and Delft are home to remote Hindu temples, colonial forts and remote beaches. See page 397

HIGHLIGHTS ARE MARKED ON THE MAP ON PAGE 378

of Vavuniya through to Elephant Pass, with its "capital" at the modest provincial town of **Kilinochchi**. Kilinochchi apart, much of the Vanni remains eerily empty, still covered in places with swathes of the dense jungle in which the LTTE's guerrilla fighters hid themselves so successfully during the long years of conflict.

Vavuniya

Gateway to the Vanni is the town of **VAVUNIYA** (pronounced "Vowvneeya"), the largest between Anuradhapura and Jaffna. Vavuniya sits roughly at the border between Sinhalese and Tamil Sri Lanka and frequently found itself on or close to the front line of the fighting during the war years. There's a significant Tamil

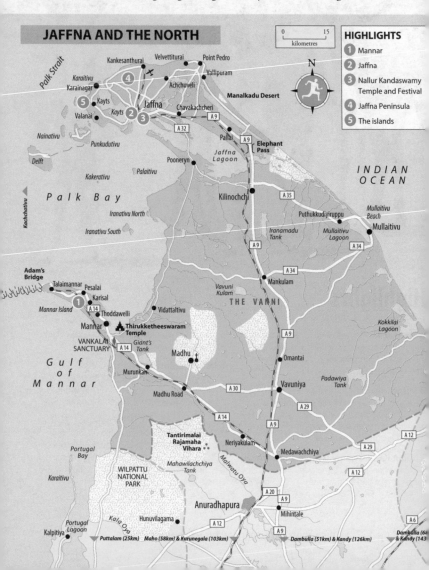

JAFFNA AND THE NORTH

HIGHLIGHTS

1. Mannar
2. Jaffna
3. Nallur Kandaswamy Temple and Festival
4. Jaffna Peninsula
5. The islands

NARROW ROADS TO THE DEEP NORTH

Looking at most road maps of Sri Lanka you'll most likely assume that in order to reach the north you'll have to first head inland and follow the A9 to Medawachchiya, north of Anuradhapura, where the main roads to Mannar and Jaffna split. Approaching from Colombo/Negombo, however, there's a much more direct, interesting and adventurous road straight up **the west coast**. You'll need first to follow the main highway to Puttalam, then the smaller road to the village of Eluvankulam, at the entrance to Wilpattu National Park. From here, a 40km gravel road heads north through the park (around a 90min–2hr drive), after which the tarmac resumes and you've a straightforward drive onto Mannar, and then north, via Pooneryn, to Jaffna. The track is driveable for most cars and vans (and tuktuks too, for that matter) except perhaps during Dec–Jan when mud from the monsoon rains can be a problem, although you might struggle to find a driver willing to take you, while larger cars with low clearance might struggle at any time of year. Buses also travel along this route between Kalpitiya/Puttalam and Mannar (around 5 daily), although services may be disrupted during Dec–Jan if there have been heavy rains. Your best source of information on the route is **Wilpattu House** (see page 111), which also makes a great place to break the journey up along of Sri Lanka's less-travelled byways.

Reaching Jaffna via the **east coast** is equally feasible nowadays thanks to highway improvements, with a sealed road heading north from Trincomalee and Uppuveli all the way up the coast to Mullaitivu (with a brief detour inland around the Kokkilai Lagoon).

population here, and if you've travelled up from Anuradhapura, you'll start to notice subtle cultural changes in language, food and attire compared with places further south.

Vavuniya's only attraction, the modest **Archeological Museum** has a small collection of fifth- to tenth-century Buddhist statues, although it is only erratically open.

ARRIVAL AND INFORMATION

VAVUNIYA

By bus Vavuniya is a major transport hub and the starting point for buses west to Mannar (although if approaching from the south it's quicker to catch a bus from Medawachchiya).

Destinations Anuradhapura (every 45min; 1hr 30min); Colombo (hourly; 7hr); Jaffna (hourly; 3hr); Kandy (hourly; 5hr); Madhu (every 2hr; 2hr); Mannar (hourly; 2hr); Trincomalee (5 daily; 2hr 30min).

By train The town is a major stop on the northern railway line, with regular connections north and south.

Destinations Anuradhapura (5–7 daily; 50min–1hr 10min); Colombo (5–7 daily; 4hr 30min–6hr 45min); Jaffna (5 daily; 1hr 45min–3hr).

ACCOMMODATION

Hotel Nelly Star 84, 2nd Cross St ☎ 024 222 4477, ⓦ nellystarhotel.com. Vavuniya's most upmarket option (not that that's saying much), efficiently run and with an a/c restaurant and bar plus decent-sized (although rather murky-looking) pool. To reach the hotel head south down the main road from the clocktower then left down Second Cross St; the hotel is about 300m down the road on your right. B&B Rs.2500, a/c Rs.3800

Madhu

Some 45km northwest of Vavuniya lies the remote village of **MADHU**, the most important place of Christian pilgrimage in Sri Lanka. The large, nineteenth-century Portuguese-style church here is home to the allegedly miraculous statue of **Our Lady of Madhu**. The image was brought to Madhu in 1670 by Catholics fleeing Dutch persecution in the Mannar area, and subsequently became revered for its magical qualities, particularly its supposed ability to protect devotees against snakebite. The shrine is revered by both Sinhalese and Tamil Catholics and, in characteristic Sri Lankan fashion, has also become popular among non-Christians. A **festival** in honour of the statue held here annually in August draws huge crowds – an estimated 500,000 pilgrims visited in 2011.

Giant's Tank and Vankalai Sanctuary

Flanking the main highway to Mannar, the impressive **Giant's Tank** (Yoda Wewa) is every bit as big as its name suggests. Built by King Dhatusena (see page 404), it's still one of the island's largest tanks, and home to prolific birdlife.

A little further north along the highway, alongside the causeway to Mannar Island, the **Vankalai Sanctuary** is one of northern Sri Lanka's finest birding sights, protecting a diverse mix of habitats including wetlands, sand dunes, tanks, mangroves, salt marshes and scrub. The sanctuary is home to numerous aquatic birds including a number of rare migrants, many of which travel south across India and make their first Sri Lankan landfall in the Mannar region – flamingos are a common sight.

Thirukketheeswaram Temple

Facing Mannar over the lagoon from the mainland, 9km from Mannar Town, the fine **Thirukketheeswaram** (aka Ketheeswaram) **Temple** marks one of Sri Lanka's *pancha iswarams*, the "Five Abodes of Shiva" (the others being at Naguleswaram near Jaffna, Koneswaram in Trincomalee, Munneswaram near Chilaw, and Tenavaram near Matara). The original temple was destroyed by the Portuguese in 1575 and not rebuilt until 1903, since when it's been gradually extended, with a huge *mandapa* currently under construction around the back.

Close by, on the main Jaffna road by the turn off to the temple, you can't help but notice the recently restored **Our Lady of Lourdes Church**, a deliciously eye-catching vanilla and baby-blue confection which looks positively edible.

Mannar Island

Connected to the mainland by a 2km bridge, **Mannar Island** pokes out into the sea, like a skinny finger pointing westwards towards India, around 30km distant over the Gulf of Mannar. The landscape here is quite unlike anything else in Sri Lanka thanks to the Mannar's geographical location and unusually arid climate, with dense green swathes of spiky palmyrah palms poking up out of the sandy soil and the blue waves of the Indian Ocean lapping beyond – an outlandishly beautiful contrast to the much more lush, coconut palm-fringed beaches of the south

For the time being, Mannar remains one of Sri Lanka's more authentically off-the-beaten-track experiences. The island is emerging as a major **kitesurfing** hotspot (best from around April/May through to Sept/Oct), with winds to rival the increasingly busy Kalpitiya down the coast. It's also a top **birdwatching** destination (best in December), being the first Sri Lankan stop on the routes of many migratory species heading south from India and offering the chance to spot Deccan species not easily seen further south.

Brief history

Mannar was long famous for its **pearl banks**, which were exploited from antiquity until the colonial period: as late as 1905 some five thousand divers recovered a staggering eighty million oysters here in a single season – they also provided the inspiration for Bizet's *The Pearl Fishers*, probably the only opera ever to be set in Sri Lanka. Arab traders also flocked to Mannar, introducing donkeys (an animal virtually unknown elsewhere in Sri Lanka), and planting the baobab trees that remain another of the island's distinctive features. Mannar suffered greatly during the war, when its position close to India made it a major conduit for refugees fleeing the country. The island's large Muslim population, a legacy of its years of Arab trade, was driven out by the LTTE in 1990, though the local population still includes many Catholics – some forty percent, the highest proportion of anywhere in Sri Lanka.

6

Mannar Town

The island's main settlement, **MANNAR TOWN**, makes a dramatic first impression when seen driving in over the long, low-slung bridge from the mainland, rising gradually above the waters like some kind of Sri Lankan Atlantis emerging from the waves. Second impressions reveal the town for the rather dusty, workaday sort of place it really is, although the water-ringed location is beautiful, while the innumerable wild donkeys which roam the town's streets (said to be the descendants of animals originally introduced by Arab sailors) give the place an entertainingly whimsical touch.

The main sight in the town centre is the crumbling **Portuguese fort** (later strengthened by the Dutch), perched right on the waterside near the bridge, with a cluster of old buildings nestling inside its well-preserved walls.

Around 1km north of town stands a famous **baobab** tree, thought to have been planted by Arab sailors in 1477 and now claimed to be the largest (or at least fattest) tree in Asia, standing just 7.5m tall but with a circumference of almost 20m.

Talaimannar

Buses run hourly between Mannar and Talaimannar (1hr)

At the far western end of the island, the small town of **TALAIMANNAR** was formerly the departure point for ferries to Rameshwaram in India, until all services were suspended in 1983 – you can still see the rusty and increasingly derelict pier poking out to sea, with a large white lighthouse beside and vast flocks of gulls and egrets wading the waters and swirling overhead.

Adam's Bridge

West of Talaimannar, a chain of islets and sandbanks known as **Adam's Bridge** stretch all the way to India, 30km distant. According to the Ramayana, these were the stepping stones used by the monkey god Hanuman to travel from India to Lanka, and also served as the causeway by which the earliest human settlers reached the island some 250,000 to 300,000 years ago. The sandbanks lie less than 2m under water in many places and (according to local temple records) may have been submerged following a cyclone as recently as 1480.

ARRIVAL AND DEPARTURE
MANNAR ISLAND

Most visitors approach Mannar either by train or via the main A14 highway from Medawachchiya (just north of Anuradhapura), although it's also possible to drive directly from the south along the old coastal road from Puttalam through Wilpattu National Park (see page 379). Heading north **to Jaffna**, a superb (and still little-used) road heads up along the coast to Jaffna over the bridge at Pooneryn.

By bus There are regular services to Vavuniya (for Jaffna and Trinco) and Anuradhapura (for everywhere else).

Destinations Anuradhapura (hourly; 3hr); Colombo (4 daily; 7–8hr); Jaffna (via Pooneryn 4 daily, 3hr; via Vavuniya 4 daily; 5hr); Vavuniya (hourly; 2hr).

By train The station is about 2km west of the town centre along South Bar Rd, while the train line extends to the far end of the island, at Talaimannar pier, with two intermediate stations (at Thoddawelli and Pesalai) en route. Destinations Anuradhapura (2 daily; 2hr 30min); Colombo (2 daily; 8hr); Madhu Rd (3 daily; 45min); Talaimannar (3 daily; 30min).

ACCOMMODATION

MANNAR TOWN

Hotel Agape 7 Seminary Rd ☎023 225 1678, ✉hotelagape.mannar@gmail.com. Easily the best place to stay in Mannar town, with friendly, efficient service and a range of comfortable, well-equipped a/c rooms, plus restaurant. Choose between the older downstairs rooms or the smart, sunlit new rooms above (Rs.1000 extra). B&B <u>Rs.5000</u>

Baobab Guest House 83 Field St ☎023 222 2306, ⓦbaobabguesthouse.com. The cheapest deal in town, with basic but acceptable fan rooms (optional ac for Rs.1000 extra) in a quiet side street north of the centre. Breakfast available, but no other meals. <u>Rs.2000</u>

Mannar Guest House 55/12 Uppukulam, ☎077 316 8202, ⓦmannarguesthouse.com. This conveniently central guesthouse, about 400m from the bus station, usually has space when other places are full, and is a good choice if you don't mind the slightly grubby fan rooms (optional a/c for Rs.500) and Fawlty Towers-style service. No meals apart from breakfast, which is best avoided. Bearable for a night. B&B Rs.2500

THE REST OF THE ISLAND

Four Tees Rest Inn Station Rd, Thoddawelli, 8km northwest of Mannar Town ☎ 023 323 0008, ✉ 4teesrestinn@gmail.com. The oldest guesthouse in Mannar, with friendly service, decent food and large, old-fashioned rooms (a couple with a/c). Close to Thoddawelli train station, one stop beyond Mannar Town, although rather a long way from anywhere else. Rs.3000, a/c Rs.4000

The Palmyrah House Talaimannar Rd, Karisal, 11km from Mannar Town (and 4km from Pesalai train station) ☎ 023 205 0910 or ☎ 077 772 3534, ✇ palmyrahhouse.com. Roughly halfway across Mannar Island, this upmarket

boutique guesthouse is a real get-away-from-it-all haven, and a great spot for birding too. Accommodation is in fourteen soothingly stylish rooms set amidst private grounds, while amenities include a well-equipped mini gym and a neat little pool. Full board $160

Shell Coast Resort Uvary, Pesalai, about 17km from Mannar Town ☎ 077 144 9062, ✇ shellcoastresort.com. Neat but pricey little a/c wooden cabanas on a remote stretch of beach on the southern side of Mannar Island, with attached restaurant and pool. $80

Vayu Western end of the island ☎ 077 368 6235, ✇ kitesurfingmannar.com. Remote retreat spectacularly located amidst coastal sandbanks at the far western end of Mannar Island, with gorgeous views over the first four islets of Adam's Bridge. Mainly aimed at kitesurfers coming to ride the crisp breezes blowing in steadily from the Gulf of Mannar, although it's great for birding too. Accomodation is in a mix of tents and rustic cabana-style "bungalows", and there are also yoga classes, motorbike hire and other activities available. Full board: tents €70, bungalows €100

Kilinochchi

The small town of **KILINOCHCHI**, about 80km north of Vavuniya, served as the headquarters of the LTTE administration – effectively the Tamil Tiger capital – for many years. It was finally recaptured in January 2009 after an intense three-month battle between government troops and rebel cadres, an event which effectively marked the beginning of the end for the Tigers.

The town – which was more or less obliterated in the course of the 2008–09 siege – has now risen energetically from the ashes. A rash of shiny new shops, offices and government buildings has sprung up along the main road and almost all the wartime devastation has been patched up, although a huge **water tower**, blown up by the LTTE during the final stages of fighting, has been left where it fell next to the road, serving as a powerful reminder of the appalling physical devastation wrought by the war. Slightly further down the road stands a striking **war memorial** – an enormous grey stone cube, pierced by an artillery shell and with a lotus blooming out of the top.

ARRIVAL AND DEPARTURE

By bus Virtually all buses between the Jaffna Peninsula and the rest of the island travel via Kilinochchi.
Destinations Jaffna (every 30min; 1hr 15min); Vavuniya (every 30min; 1hr 45min).

By train Kilinochchi's neat, modern station is right in the centre of town.
Destinations Jaffna (5 daily; 50min–1hr 30min); Vavuniya (5 daily; 1hr–1hr 25min).

East to Mullaitivu

Reopened to foreigners only in 2015, the area around the coastal town of **Mullaitivu** is one of Sri Lanka's most remote and sombre destinations, scene of the concluding battle of the civil war in 2009 during which thousands of helpless Tamil civilians were penned into a narrow strip of beach north of the town and then ruthlessly butchered by both the Sri Lankan Army and LTTE. Physical mementoes of the battle are now increasingly thin on the ground following extensive post-war reconstruction, although the entire area is rich in associations for anyone with an interest in the island's tragic recent past, providing a painful but necessary reminder of the many innocent lives pointlessly lost.

KILINOCHICHI TO MULLATIVU

By tour Regular buses run between Jaffna and Mullaitivu, although to really explore the area you'll need you own transport, most conveniently arranged through Sri Lanka Click in Jaffna (see page 392), who run extended day-tours of the area.

Puthukkudiyiruppu

Around 16km before Mullaitivu itself, the tongue-twisting town of **PUTHUKKUDIYIRUPPU** was largely destroyed during the final phase of the civil war but is now gradually reviving. Next to the main road around 3.5km east of the centre is another of those grandiose war memorials inflicted on a beleaguered Tamil populace by the victorious Sinahlese government, set in the middle of a lake and showing a soldier apparently buried from the waist down in a huge pile of rocks. A sign commemorates "the remarkable success and achievements" of those involved in what is laughably described as the "Wanni [Vanni] Humanitarian Operation" – a curious description of the Sri Lankan Army's massacre of thousands of defenceless and desperate Tamils. A small museum next to the lake shows photos of the conflict (explanations in Sinhala only), including images of the victorious army's heroic humanitarian efforts.

Around 7km north of the town, you may also be able to track down the bizarre **LTTE swimming pool** (geo-coordinates 9.362289, 80.687338), hidden amid the trees. The huge, steeply stepped pool is said to have been used as a training tool for the LTTE's Sea Tiger divers.

Mullaitivu Lagoon and beach

Stretching for around 10km north of Mullaitivu itself, **Mullaitivu lagoon** and **beach** are where the horrendous final act of the civil war was played out in 2009. Pursued by the Sri Lankan Army (SLA) following the fall of Kilinochchi, surviving LTTE forces fled east, followed by thousands of Tamil refugees, who were encouraged to take refuge in two "no fire zones" established by the army, hemmed in between the sea on one side and the SLA and the Mullaitivu Lagoon on the other. Having rounded up the fleeing refugees, the SLA began systematically shelling the alleged safe zones in which they had been told to assemble. Those who attempted to flee, it's said, were shot in the back by LTTE troops. Thousands died (the exact number will never be known) and, while allegations of widespread war crimes were levelled against both sides, not a single military commander has even been charged.

The area today is strangely – almost eerily – peaceful, with miles of largely deserted beach and a few dusty villages dozing beneath the palms. Most roads and houses have now been rebuilt, although the area remains one of the poorest and least developed in the country, with most of the population still scraping a meagre living from fishing and agriculture.

Farah III
Geo-coordinates 9.314141, 80.792373

Towards the southern end of the beach around 6km north of Mullaitivu are the scant remains of the **Farah III** Jordanian cargo ship, lying in shallow waters just off the beach - haunting images of the rusting mega-vessel's beached skeleton still provide one of the civil's war most striking visual images, although little now survives of the original ship. One of the stranger casualties of the civil war, the Farah III experienced engine troubles whilst passing Sri Lanka en route from India to South Africa in 2006 and dropped anchor off Mullaitivu, where it was promptly boarded by the Sea Tigers, the naval wing of LTTE, who cut the anchor, causing it to run aground on the coast. The crew were released unharmed but the vessel was appropriated, being used as an operational base for the Sea Tigers and gradually being stripped bare of all usable equipment, and much of its metal as well – the remains of an improvised armoured vehicle, perhaps constructed using iron salvaged from the boat, can still be seen on the beach nearby.

6

6

THE LIBERATION TIGERS OF TAMIL EELAM

Terrorists in the eyes of some, freedom fighters to others, the **Liberation Tigers of Tamil Eelam** (LTTE), popularly known as the **Tamil Tigers**, were until their final defeat in 2009 one of the world's most committed, effective and ruthless militant organizations. The LTTE was founded in the early 1970s, one of a string of paramilitary groups established by young Tamils in response to the decades of official discrimination meted out by the Sinhalese governments of Colombo to the Tamils of the north and east. The failure of the older Tamil leaders to secure political justice for Tamils and the heavy-handed behaviour of the Sinhalese-dominated Sri Lankan Army and police in Tamil areas drove many young Tamils to espouse violence. All these militant groups called for the establishment of an independent Tamil state in the north and east of the island, to be called **Eelam** ("Precious Land"), and a number received training from special Indian government forces who were initially sympathetic to their cause.

PRABHAKARAN: ELUSIVE LEADER

The LTTE gradually rose to pre-eminence thanks to its ruthless suppression of all competing political groups and the assassination of rival politicians, and by the beginning of the civil war in 1983 had become the leading player in Tamil affairs. At the heart of its mystique lay its founder and leader, the enigmatic **Velupillai Prabhakaran** (1954–2009). Legends about this reclusive figure abound. According to some, he was a shy and bookish student with a fascination for Napoleon and Alexander the Great, who turned militant when he saw an uncle burned alive by Sinhalese mobs, and who later trained himself to endure pain by lying in sacks of chillies. Known as *Thambi*, or "Little Brother", Prabhakaran was held in quasi-religious veneration by many of his recruits and proved both a consummate political survivor and a gifted military strategist, although reports suggest that many of the LTTE's earlier engagements were based on the study of *Rambo* and Arnold Schwarzenegger videos – a classic example of life imitating (bad) art.

GUERRILLA TACTICS

The LTTE began life as a classic **guerrilla operation**, harrying the (to begin with) far better equipped and numerically superior forces of the Sri Lankan Army and later the Indian Peacekeeping Force (see page 416) with hit-and-run attacks, before retreating back into the countryside and mixing with local populations. These guerrilla tactics were combined with gruesome, attention-grabbing attacks such as that at Anuradhapura in 1985, when dozens of civilians and pilgrims were gunned down by LTTE soldiers in the symbolic centre of Sinhalese culture. The LTTE also pioneered the practice of **suicide bombing** (whose technology they are believed to have exported to militant Palestinian organizations such as Hamas), with notable attacks in Colombo, at the international airport and in the Temple of the Tooth in Kandy, among many others. Suicide bombers were also used in a string of high-profile **political**

Mullaitivu

Now comprehensively rebuilt, **Mullaitivu** itself (approached via a pretty twisting causeway over the deadly Mullaitivu Lagoon) was largely obliterated during the SLA offensive of 2009, but now offers virtually no reminders of the war years. The main road, lined with shiny new banks, shops and offices, looks virtually indistinguishable from any other provincial town in Sri Lanka, running down to a wide and beautiful beach, dotted with fishing boats and a ramshackle fish market.

Elephant Pass

Some 15km north of Kilinochchi along the A9, the **Elephant Pass** is where a narrow causeway connects the Jaffna Peninsula with the rest of the island – a rather bleak and featureless stretch of land divided by a narrow strip of water. The pass was so named after the elephants that were once driven across to the peninsula here, though it's now best known as the location of two of the civil war's largest **battles**, fought here in 1991 and 2000; it was during the latter that the LTTE finally succeeded in dislodging the Sri Lankan Army from its heavily fortified position at the entrance to the Jaffna Peninsula

assassinations – victims included former Indian Prime Minister Rajiv Gandhi in 1991, and Sri Lankan Prime Minister Ranasinghe Premadasa in 1993, making the LTTE the only militant organization to have assassinated two world leaders. As the war progressed and the LTTE acquired better armaments and military know-how, they gradually began to function more as a conventional army – exemplified by their seizure of Elephant Pass, at the southern end of the Jaffna Peninsula, from the heavily entrenched forces of the SLA in 2000.

The LTTE's ability to take on and defeat the huge forces of the Indian and Sri Lankan armies reflected its legendary discipline and commitment to the cause, fostered by relentless **political indoctrination** and quasi-monastic **discipline**. In addition, hardly any LTTE fighters were ever captured alive, thanks to the phials of cyanide which all cadres wore around their necks. They also – by Asian standards at least – had impeccable **feminist** credentials. The shortage of men of fighting age led to many women – the so-called "Freedom Birds", memorably described by British writer William Dalrymple as "paramilitary feminist death squads" – being absorbed into the LTTE military apparatus and often pitched into its toughest fighting engagements.

DOWNFALL AND LEGACY

Attitudes towards the LTTE have always been sharply divided. In the early years of the civil war they were often seen as heroes who were prepared to lay down their lives in the fight against Sinhalese oppression. As the conflict dragged on, however, opinions changed thanks to the LTTE's systematic assassination of rival Tamil politicians; their massacres of innocent Sinhalese civilians, Muslims and suspected "collaborators"; their use of child soldiers and abduction of young Tamils to fight for the LTTE; the widespread extortion of money from Tamils at home and abroad; the ethnic cleansing of areas under their control; and their indiscriminate use of suicide bombers – all of which led to their being proscribed as a **terrorist organization** by over thirty governments worldwide. In addition, their apparent use of thousands of Tamil civilians as human shields during the concluding stages of the war would most likely have seen their leaders charged with war crimes, had any of them survived.

Virtually the entire leadership of the LTTE was killed by the end of the war (as well as a large proportion of its fighters), with Prabhakaran himself finally ambushed and killed by the SLA in May 2009. Rumours of surviving LTTE activists attempting to resurrect the organization regularly circulate, although it seems unlikely that the Tigers will rise again in any meaningful way, not least because their widespread **atrocities** against their own people effectively destroyed whatever popular support they once enjoyed. The fact that the LTTE are held responsible for the deaths of over eight thousand of their fellow Tamils proves that it was ultimately the Tigers, far more than any Sinhalese government, that ended up oppressing and brutalizing the very people they claimed to protect.

– a crucial moment in the progress of the war, though they narrowly failed to follow up this victory with the capture of the Jaffna Peninsula itself. The tables were turned in 2009 following the fall of Kilinochchi when the SLA returned, driving the remnants of the LTTE out of their long-held positions. A triumphalist **war memorial** now stands next to the main highway on the north side of the causeway, showing four hands holding up a map of Sri Lanka with a lotus blossoming from the Jaffna Peninsula.

Some 2.5km futher south, over the causeway on the west side of the highway, the scorched remains of an **armoured bulldozer** provide another – altogether more realistic – memorial of the conflict. The bulldozer was used as an improvised tank by the LTTE during their unsuccessful attempt to capture the Elephant Pass in 1991. Seeing the damage machine-gun fire from the vehicle was causing to government positions, young Sri Lankan Lance Corporal **Gamini Kularatne** jumped aboard the vehicle and detonated two grenades, instantly killing himself and everyone inside – an act of suicidal bravery for which he subsequently became the first recipient of the Parama Weera Vibhushanaya, Sri Lanka's highest military honour. A large memorial to Kularatne stands close by.

Jaffna

Far and away the largest town in northern Sri Lanka, **JAFFNA** has always been a place apart, closer to India than Colombo, and culturally more akin to the Indian state of Tamil Nadu just over the Palk Strait than to the Sinhalese south. Arriving in Jaffna can come as something of a culture shock if you've spent much time in the rest of the island. You can't fail to notice the profound **Indian influence** here, exemplified by the replacement of the Buddhist dagoba with the Hindu gopuram and by the switch from singsong cadences of Sinhala to the quickfire patter of Tamil – as well as myriad other details, like the sultry Indian pop music that blares out of shops and cafés, the quasi-subcontinental hordes of kamikaze cyclists who rattle around the congested streets, and the occasional free-range cow wandering placidly amid the busy traffic. Yet although there's a fair bit of India in Jaffna, the town has its own unique and complex identity shaped, in true Sri Lankan fashion, by a wide cross-section of influences, including Muslim, Portuguese, Dutch, British and Sinhalese. Although Hinduism remains the dominant religion, Christianity is also strong, and Jaffna presents an intriguing mixtur of Tamil and European elements, with colourful temples set next to huge churches, and streets of a beguiling, faded colonial charm dotted with old Dutch and British residences.

Brief history

The Jaffna Peninsula has always been a focus for **Tamil settlement** in Sri Lanka, thanks to its proximity to India's Tamil heartlands. The earliest settlers arrived as far back as the second or third century BC, and this population was constantly supplemented ove successive centuries by migrants, mercenaries and assorted adventurers. Interestingly, some of these early settlers may have been Buddhist rather than Hindu, as borne out b the enigmatic cluster of dagobas at Kantharodai (see page 395).

By the thirteenth century Jaffna had developed into the capital of a powerful Tamil kingdom known as **Jaffnapatnam**. In 1284, a Pandyan general, Arya Chakravati, seized control of the north. Over the next fifty years, his successors extended their power gradually southwards, gaining control of Mannar and its valuable pearl industry and continuing to push south. For a brief period in the mid-fourteenth century they gained control of the whole of the west coast, almost as far as Colombo – the greatest expansion of Tamil power in the history of Sri Lanka – before being pushed back.

Northern power suffered further blows following the arrival of the Portuguese, who seized Jaffna in 1621, destroying Hindu temples and building churches in their place. In 1658 the Portuguese were evicted from Jaffna by the **Dutch**, who gave the town an imposing fort before being succeeded in their turn by the **British**, who took over in 1796. Jaffna became something of a backwater during the later colonial era, although the railway arrived in 1905 and the Jaffna Tamils continued to thrive under the British administration.

Following **independence**, Jaffna found itself increasingly at the centre of the island's growing ethnic storm, with regular clashes between young Tamil militants and Sinhalese soldiers and police culminating in the infamous destruction of the Jaffna library by government thugs in 1981. The town was the focal point of many of the early **civil war**'s fiercest battles, suffering considerable physical damage, although having remained under government control since 1995 it at least avoided being caught up in the devastating fighting that enveloped the rest of northern Sri Lanka during 2008–09

Central Jaffna

Jaffna divides into the busy, modern **commercial district** centred on the Hospital Road and the area around the bus station, and the much more sedate colonial-era suburbs

6

JAFFNA

ACCOMMODATION

Aster Guest House	8
D'Villa Guest House	10
Green Grass Hotel	3
Jaffna Heritage Hotel	5
Jetwing Jaffna	11
Kais Guest House	4
Lux Etoiles	2
Morgan's Guest House	9
Old Park Villa	1
Theresa Inn	6
The Thinnai	7

● EATING

Cosy Restaurant	5
Jetwing Jaffna	7
Lingam Cream House	3
Malayan Café	4
Mangos	2
Rio's Ice Cream	1
Hotel Rolex	6

DRINKING

Green Grass Hotel	2
Jetwing Jaffna Rooftop Bar	1

east of the centre, with their enormous churches and atmospheric Dutch-era buildings. Hospital Road forms the spine of the commercial district, a vibrant mercantile thoroughfare lined with shops and banks. Traces of old Jaffna can still be seen here and there, particularly in the old-fashioned shops around the *Hotel Rolex* (opposite the large white central market building) with their colourful hand-painted signs, wooden counters and glass-fronted display cabinets stacked high with merchandise. You may also see a few of the lovingly preserved **vintage cars** – Morris Minors, Morris Oxfords, Austin Cambridges and the like – that were formerly a common sight in Jaffna, kept going through the long decades of the civil war when the import of new vehicles was banned.

North of Hospital Road

On the northwest side of the centre, up Kankesanthurai (KKS) Road, a tall grey-blue gopuram marks the **Vaitheeswara Temple**, the most interesting of central Jaffna's numerous Hindu temples, built during the Dutch era by an influential local merchant and dedicated to Shiva. At its centre lies a richly decorated stone shrine surrounded by a beautiful old wooden-roofed ambulatory, rather like a Dutch veranda, complete with Doric columns. As with all Jaffna's Hindu temples, the best time to visit is during the late afternoon puja (roughly 4–5pm) when the resident bare-chested Brahmin priests dash about the temple performing their devotions to the various gods amid great clouds of incense and the tremendous clanging of a remarkable little mechanical-bell contraption which sits just inside the main door.

A short walk east of the Vaitheeswara Temple is **Kasturiya Road**, the heart of Jaffna's jewellery industry, home to a long sequence of jewellers, mainly trading in gold. Continue east along Stanley Road and then turn north to reach the grand **Varatharaja Perumal Kovil**, with a flamboyant, polychromatic gopuram and brightly coloured buildings set in a large sandy compound.

Jaffna Fort

daily 8am–6pm • Free

The largest Dutch fortress in Asia, the huge **Jaffna Fort** was built on the site of the former Portuguese stronghold in the characteristic star shape favoured by the Dutch (the pointed bastions offering greater protection against cannon fire). The inner defences were completed in 1680 and the outer ring of bastions in 1792, with a moat separating the two, though just four years after it was completed the fort was surrendered to the British without a shot being fired. Having survived two hundred years without seeing action, the fort was finally pressed into military service during the civil war, when the outer defences were repeatedly bombarded by both sides and the old Dutch buildings inside tragically destroyed, including the beautiful **Groote Kerk** "Great Church" – also known as Kruys Kerk).

The fort's battered remains have now been comprehensively restored with Dutch government assistance, although the central courtyard is still largely empty save for huge quantities of rubble laid out in neat rows and piles. Entrance to the interior is via an archway emblazoned "Anno 1680" on the fort's east side, where you'll also find a small display on its history and the restoration of the fort. The huge and largely empty interior courtyard is dotted with the indecipherable ruins of vanished buildings, with steps leading up to the ramparts and offering fine views over town.

Chelvanayakum Monument

East of the fort, the enormous Hindu-style column at the south end of Esplanade Road is a monument to the famous local politician **S.J.V. Chelvanayakum** (1898–1977), founder and first leader of the Tamil United Liberation Front. A leading figure in post-

6

independence Sri Lanka, Chelvanayakum became increasingly frustrated with Sinhalese political oppression and was an early advocate of Tamil separatism, although his love of Gandhian-style *satyagraha* (non-violent protest) could hardly have been further removed from the tactics used by the rebels who subsequently adopted the cause of Tamil Eelam.

Jaffna Public Library

Esplanade Rd • Mon–Sat 4.30–6pm • Free

Immediately north of the Chelvanayakum Monument, an impressive Indo-Saracenic-style building is home to the **Jaffna Public Library**. The original library was torched by Sinhalese mobs during election riots in 1981, an act of vandalism which reduced one of South Asia's greatest public collections (including many irreplaceable works of Tamil literature) to ashes – a key event in the build-up to the civil war. In a symbolic gesture, this was the first major public building to be rebuilt following the temporary ceasefire of 2002.

Currently under construction on the north side of the library is the state-of-the-art **Jaffna Cultural Centre**, funded by the Indian Government and planned to house an impressive suite of new cultural amenities, including a theatre, library, museum and exhibition space.

The clocktower

Pointing skywards just northeast of the library is the town's unusually tall and slender **clocktower**, an endearing architectural mongrel mixing Islamic and Gothic styles. Built in 1875 to commemorate a visit by the Prince of Wales, the tower was designed by British architect J.G. Smither, who was also responsible for Colombo's Old Town Hall and National Museum.

East of the centre

East of the commercial centre, Jaffna assumes a residential and colonial character, with quiet, tree-shaded streets lined by sedate Dutch villas and a string of imposing churches. **Main Street** (rather sleepy, despite its name) is particularly atmospheric, lined with crumbling old colonial houses and assorted churches and other religious foundations. The first you come to is the **Rosarian Convent**, occupying a beautiful sequence of Dutch colonial buildings; the Rosarian Sisters are well known hereabouts for their home-made wine cordial and grape juice. A little further east along Main Street is the equally atmospheric **St Martin's Seminary**, an attractive Victorian neo-Gothic period piece dating from the 1880s, with verandaed buildings and a musty little chapel in the middle.

Just south of St Martin's Seminary stands the largest of Jaffna's outsize churches, the gigantic **St Mary's Cathedral**. It's quasi-Portuguese in style, although actually dates from the Dutch era, and is built on a positively industrial scale, with a pleasingly simple interior.

The Archeological Museum

Navalar Rd • Mon & Wed–Sun 8am–5pm • Donation

Jaffna's modest little **Archeological Museum** houses various Hindu artefacts from the surrounding area, including a number of small and beautiful wooden *vahanams* ("vehicles"), the various animals – horse, bull, elephant, lion – on which Hindu gods rode from place to place. Other curiosities include a pile of whale bones, a seven-mouthed musical pot and a fetching wooden model of Harischandra – the legendary Indian king who never told a lie – and his wives. Look out, too, for the much-abused portrait of the young Queen Victoria recovered from the Fort – the tears in the canvas are apparently bullet holes.

Nallur Kandaswamy Temple

Jaffna's most notable sight is the large **Nallur Kandaswamy Temple**, about 2km northeast of the town centre. Dedicated to Murugam (known to the Buddhist Sinhalese as Kataragama), this is the most impressive Hindu temple in Sri Lanka, and the only one on the island to rival the great shrines of India. The original temple is thought to date back to the mid-fifteenth century, though it was destroyed in 1620 by the Portuguese. The present structure was begun in 1807 and has now developed into an enormous religious complex, surrounded by red-and-white striped walls. There are numerous shrines inside, richly decorated corridors framed in rows of golden arches and a beautiful courtyard with a large tank. Men must remove their shirts before entering. There are no fewer than six **pujas** daily, with three between 4pm and 5pm, the best time to visit.

ARRIVAL AND DEPARTURE

JAFFNA

The once gruelling journey to Jaffna is now positively pleasurable following highway improvements and the reopening of the railway line.

By plane Helitours (268 Stanley Rd, ☎011 311 0472, ⦿www.helitours.lk) operate inexpensive flights (3 weekly; Rs.14,500 one way) via Trincomalee between Colombo's Ratmalana airport and Jaffna's Palaly airport, around 15km north of Jaffna town – although see page 31 for safety concerns.

By train Reopened in October 2014 after a gap of 24 years, the railway to Jaffna provides the fastest and most comfortable means of reaching the city. For timetables, see Basics (page 32). There are also services to Kankesanthurai, at the northern edge of the Jaffna Peninsula (5 daily; 20–35min).

Destinations Anuradhapura (5–6 daily; 2hr 40min–4hr); Colombo (5 daily; 6hr 15min–9hr); Kilinochchi (5 daily; 50min–1hr 30min); Vavuniya (5 daily; 1hr 50min–2hr 50min).

By bus From Colombo, Jaffna is served by SLTB services from the Central Bus Station and much more comfortable private buses run by various companies along Galle Rd around Wellawatta Market. Buses arrive right in the middle of Jaffna, either at the SLTB bus station on Hospital Rd or at the private bus stand close by. The large information office on the west side of the station can point you in the right direction if you get stuck. Bus tickets for Colombo can be bought directly from the various private bus company offices on Hospital Rd, diagonally opposite the south side of the SLTB bus station. Buses to and from the capital include a range of non-a/c and "luxury" a/c services (around Rs.1000/Rs.1300); most services either travel overnight (currently three departures at 8pm, 9pm & 10pm) or leave early in the morning (currently 7.30am & 8am). Arriving in Colombo, buses run across the city, dropping off passengers en route before terminating in Wellawatta. Heading south to Anuradhapura you'll need to change in Vavuniya.

Destinations Batticaloa (3 daily; 10hr); Colombo (14 daily; 10–12hr); Kandy (7 daily; 8–10hr); Mannar (via Pooneryn 4 daily, 3hr; via Vavuniya 4 daily; 5hr); Trincomalee (8 daily; 6hr); Vavuniya (every 30min; 3hr).

THE NALLUR FESTIVAL

Nallur Kandaswamy Temple is a fascinating place to visit at any time, but becomes unforgettable during the latter stages of the annual **Nallur Festival**, which runs for 25 days, finishing on the poya day in August. The crowds of festival-goers rival those at the far better-known Kandy Esala Perahera, and many Jaffna expatriates return for the celebrations. Men dress in fresh white sarongs, while women don their best saris, transforming the entire temple complex into a vast sea of intense blues, reds and greens. Held on the 24th of the 25 days, the **Ther** festival is the biggest night, when an enormous chariot is pulled around the town by huge crowds of sarong-clad men; on the following day, particularly enthusiastic devotees mortify themselves by driving skewers through their bodies in honour of the god as they make their way to the shrine accompanied by drumming and piping, stopping periodically to dance en route. Even more extraordinary are the devotees who, using skewers driven through their backs, suspend themselves from poles. These poles are then attached to the front of trucks and tractors, and the devotees are driven through town to the temple, dangling in front of their vehicle like bait on a fishing line. Supplicants who perform these self-mortifications believe that the god will protect them from any sense of pain. Many also carry a **kavadi**, the distinctive symbol of Murugam (or Kataragama), a semicircular yoke, placed across the shoulders, with peacock feathers at either end.

6

GETTING AROUND

By bike or motorbike These can be hired from Sri Lanka Click tours (see page 392) and from a number of guesthouses around town including *D'Villa* and *Morgans* for around Rs.500/day and Rs.1500/day respectively.

By tour Sri Lanka Click (447 Stanley Rd, ☎ 077 848 8800, ⊛ srilankaclick.com) offer a wide range of insightful tours led by local guide Mohan — easily the best way of exploring the tricky-to-reach sights around Jaffna and

beyond. Trips include half-day tours of Jaffna city (either by bike or vehicle) and a combined tour of Nainativu and Kayts islands, while full-day tours include jaunts around the eastern and western sides of the Jaffna peninsula, trips to Delft island, plus epic excursions to Mannar and Mullaitivu (the latter a 330km round trip usually done by car, although it's also possible to do it by motorbike). Tours start from around Rs.5000 for a half day.

ACCOMMODATION

Aster Guest House 744 Hospital Rd ☎ 021 221 9591; map p.388. Small guesthouse with a handful of clean, modern rooms at a very competitive price (although with hot water only in a couple of rooms). They also have bikes and scooters for hire, but no food available. **Rs.2000**, a/c **Rs.3000**

★ **D'Villa Guest House** 6 Pentecostal Lane (the small side road opposite the Ceylon Pentecostal Mission), off Kandy Rd ☎ 021 720 0444, ⊛ dvillajaffna.lk; map p.388. The best budget option in town, squirrelled away in a quiet residential side street with just five simple but very comfortable little a/c rooms with hot water and TV, plus bikes and scooters for hire and all the local advice you need from super-helpful owner Dilan. Brilliant value. There's also a second sister property, the *D'Villa Garden House*, close by, at similar rates. **Rs.2500**

Green Grass Hotel 33 Aseervatham Lane, off Hospital Rd ☎ 021 222 4385, ⊛ jaffnagreengrass.com; map p.388. Large hotel right next to the train station with boxy and rather battered a/c rooms — overpriced, although the in-house bar and a good-sized pool compensate if you don't mind a bit of noise from after-dark boozers. **Rs.4400**

Jaffna Heritage Hotel 195 Temple Rd ☎ 021 222 2424, ⊛ jaffnaheritage.com; map p.388. Smart, modern hotel given a modest "heritage" look thanks to a garnish of traditional wooden shutters, furniture and other decorative trimmings, plus a small pool and restaurant. Nice enough, although a bit pricey at current rates. B&B **$80**

★ **Jetwing Jaffna** 37 Mahathma Gandhi Rd ☎ 021 221 5571, ⊛ jetwinghotels.com; map p.388. A sign of the rapidly changing times in Jaffna, this upmarket new hotel by Sri Lanka's leading hotel group boasts stylish, modern rooms in a brilliantly central location (with great views from higher floors), plus an excellent restaurant (see page 393) and rooftop bar (page 393) — although no pool. Good value, given the quality. B&B **$115**

Kais Guest House 69 Colombogam Rd ☎ 021 222 7229, ⊛ kaisguesthouse.com; map p.388. Old-world

Jaffna style at a very affordable price, with just three neat rooms (optional a/c for Rs.500 extra) in a lovely old colonial villa. B&B **Rs.3000**

Lux Etoiles 34 Chetty Street Lane ☎ 021 222 3966, ⊛ luxetoiles.com; map p.388. Run-of-the-mill hotel with plain, poky and overpriced a/c rooms but above-average facilities including a passable restaurant, bar and a large (albeit rather drab) covered pool. **Rs.4700**

★ **Morgan's Guest House** 215 Temple Rd ☎ 021 222 3666 or ☎ 077 635 1719; map p.388. *Morgan's* is one of those places that seems to have been around forever, but just gets better and better with age. Set in a lovingly maintained colonial villa with bags of character, the four a/c rooms here are full of understated old-school charm, while the setting, almost in the shadow of the Nallur Temple, can hardly be beaten. The owner also has scooters for rent and can arrange tours of the city and peninsula in his own vehicle (Rs.6000/day). Not surprisingly rooms go fast, so book well in advance. **Rs.4500**

Old Park Villa 76 Kandy Rd ☎ 021 222 3790, ⊛ oldparkvillajaffna.com; map p.388. Spacious — if slightly bare — a/c rooms in a gracious old villa with big windows, high ceilings and thick mattresses, plus a simple in-house restaurant. That said, rates are on the high side and slight road noise (and a faint smell of mothballs) intrudes. **Rs.6600**

Theresa Inn 72 Racca Rd ☎ 071 222 8615, ⊛ theresainnjaffna.com; map p.388. Not the most inspiring place in town, but very competitively priced, with bright, modern tiled rooms and optional a/c for a modest Rs.750 extra. **Rs.2250**

The Thinnai 86 Palaly Rd ☎ 021 203 0400, ⊛ thethinnai.com; map p.388. On the northern edge of town around 3km from the centre, this cool resort offers relatively luxurious lodgings in a laid-back setting — although a bit of a way from most places of interest. Accommodation is in forty-odd brightly coloured suites and apartments arranged around neat courtyard gardens — more expensive ones come with their own kitchen, lounge and even plunge pool. Facilities include a decent-sized pool plus buffet and à la carte restaurants. **$120**

ATING

here aren't many culinary frills in Jaffna – although the pening of the new *Jetwing Jaffna* hotel has finally given the wn centre one decent upscale restaurant at least. It's also e only one of the places listed below which serves alcohol, though *Cosy* are happy for you to bring your own.

osy Restaurant Stanley Rd ⊙021 222 7100; map 388. Huge array of competently prepared North Indian eat and veg dishes (most mains around Rs.400–450), lus assorted Chinese offerings and a few local Jaffna-style ains. Tandoori meat dishes and breads are the speciality venings from 6pm only), prepared in the restaurant's ndoor oven. Unlicensed, although you can bring your wn booze (no corkage). Daily 11am–11pm.

★ **Jetwing Jaffna** 37 Mahathma Gandhi Rd ⊙021 21 5571; map p.388. The beautiful restaurant at this ave new hotel (see page 392) brings a welcome dash of ulinary class to Jaffna's threadbare dining options, served p in a beautiful room stuffed full with traditional wooden rniture. Food includes a good selection of North Indian eat and veg classics alongside richly spiced Jaffna-style ups and curries and assorted Western dishes plus – a real rprise this – a dedicated vegan menu. Mains Rs.1000–500. Daily noon to 2.30pm & 7–10.30pm.

ingam Cream House 119 Kasturiya Rd, lingamcoolbar.com; map p.388. An enjoyable town-entre rival to the better-known *Rio's*, dishing up assorted uorescent flavours of local ice cream in colourful pea-reen premises. Daily 8.30am–8.30pm.

Malayan Café 36–38 Grand Bazaar, Bazaar North Rd; map p.388. Time-warped slice of traditional Jaffna, with a lovely old wood-panelled dining room constantly busy with locals filling up on bargain rice and curry served up on glossy banana leaves (deposit your leaf in the "Used Banana Leaf" chute by the washbasins once finished). Daily 7am–8pm.

★ **Mangos** 359 Temple Road ⊙021 222 8294; map p.388. Just north of the Nallur Kandaswamy Temple, this big, barn-like vegetarian restaurant has functional furnishings but first-rate food including a big selection of north Indian mains (Rs.500–800) alongside inexpensive South Indian dosas (Rs.300-400) and Sri Lankan *kottu rotty* in the evenings, plus juices, shakes and ice creams. Big portions and plenty of flavour. Daily 8–10.30am, 11am–3.30pm & 5.30–10.30pm.

Rio's Ice Cream Behind the Nallur Temple; map p.388. One of a number of colourful ice-cream parlours around the back of the Nallur Temple, this perenially popular Jaffna institution serves up big helpings of ice cream (around Rs.80) in unusual flavours. Daily 8am–10pm.

Hotel Rolex 340 Hospital Rd ⊙021 222 2808; map p.388. Cheery little café near the bus station offering a range of food including rice and curry, burianis and devilled chicken and fish (mains around Rs.300) served up from the buffet counter at the front. Daily 6.30am–10pm.

RINKING

ffna is one of the dryest towns in Sri Lanka. Apart from the aces listed below, options are limited to the nondescript ars at the *Lux Etoiles* and *Tilko Jaffna City Hotel*.

reen Grass Hotel 33 Aseervatham Lane, off Hospital d ⊙021 222 4385; map p.388. Away from the centre, is shady garden restaurant-cum-bar is the nicest place r a drink on the east side of the centre, although the food nothing to write home about. Daily 11am–11pm.

etwing Jaffna Rooftop Bar 37 Mahathma Gandhi d ⊙021 221 5571; map p.388. The bar that Jaffna

has been crying out for all these years. The view alone is worth the price of a tipple, stretching lagoonwards on one side past the clocktower and library and inland on the other, with much of the town below almost invisible beneath a blanket of palm trees save for assorted temple towers rising out of a sea of green. Good drinks list, too, and given the setting prices are refreshingly reasonable, especially during the 4–8pm happy hour, with draught beer at just Rs.200 a pull. Daily 11.30am–10pm.

The Jaffna Peninsula

he agricultural hinterland of Jaffna town – and the source of much of its former rosperity – is the **Jaffna Peninsula**, a fertile arc of land crisscrossed with a lattice of mall country roads and lined with endless walled gardens and smallholdings in which he peninsula's famed mangos are grown, along with a wide variety of other crops ncluding chillies, onions, bananas, jackfruit and grapes. Physically the peninsula is irtually an island, and culturally it feels almost completely detached from the rest of he country – and, indeed, the rest of the north – having always been far more densely opulated than the more arid lands of the Vanni further south.

6

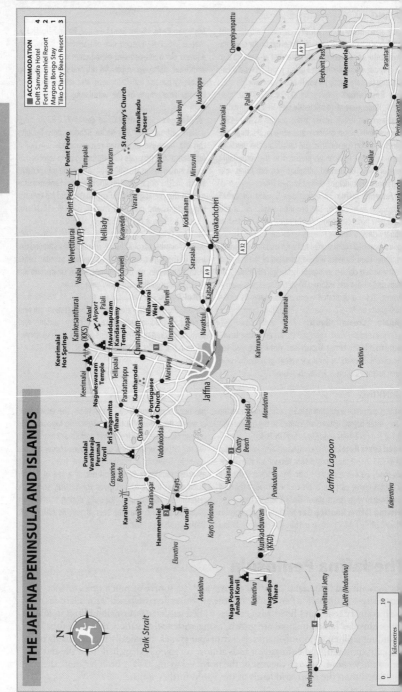

THE JAFFNA PENINSULA AND ISLANDS

ACCOMMODATION
Delft Samudra Hotel — 4
Fort Hammenhiel Resort — 2
Margosa Bongo Stay — 1
Tilko Charty Beach Resort — 3

Palk Strait

Casuarina Beach

Keerimalai Hot Springs
Keerimalai
Naguleswaram Temple
Punmalai Varatharaja Perumal Kovil
Sri Sangamitta Vihara
Kankesanthurai (KKS)
Palali Airport
Maviddapuram Kandaswamy Temple
Chunnakam
Pandattaripu
Tellipalai
Kantharodai
Portuguese Church
Chankanai
Vaddukoddai
Manipay
Jaffna

Point Pedro
Point Pedro (PPD)
Tumpalai
St Anthony's Church
Manalkadu Desert
Puloli
Valalai
Velvettiturai (VVT)
Nelliady
Karaveddi
Atchuveli
Puttur
Nilavarai Well
Nirveli
Urumpirai
Kopai
Navatkuli
Valliupuram
Varani
Kodikamam
Sarasalai
Kaitadi
A9
A32
Chavakachcheri

Chempiyanpattu
War Memorial
Elephant Pass
A9
Parantan
Periyamaranan
Nallur
Chemmankundu
Pooneryn

Kudarappu
Nakarkoyil
Mukamalai
Miirusuvil
Ampani
Palali

Kalmunai
Kavutarimunai
Palaitivu
Jaffna Lagoon
Kakeraitivu
Mandaitivu
Allaippiddi
Chatty Beach
Velanai
Pungudutivu
Kayts (Velanai)
Kayts
Karainagar
Karaitivu
Eluvaitivu
Analaitivu
Ninaitivu
Naga Pooshani Ambal Kovil
Nagadipa Vihara
Kurikadduwan (KKD)
Hammenhiel
Urundi
Punmalai

Mavelitturai Jetty
Delft (Neduntivu)
Periyanthurai

N

0   kilometres   10

Kadikattu (15km)

North to Keerimalai

The 20km journey **north of Jaffna** across the peninsula to the opposite coast at Keerimalai offers a good taste of the peninsula's rural scenery and combines a number of attractions en route, including the fine temples of **Maviddapuram** and **Naguleswaram**, the enigmatic dagobas of **Kantharodai** and the **hot springs** at Keerimalai itself.

Kantharodai

Daily 24hr • Free

About 10km north of Jaffna, and 2km west of the village of Chunnakam on the main road to Kankesanthurai (KKS), lies the curious archeological site of **Kantharodai** – an unusual huddle of around twenty miniature dagobas, ranging in height from one to three metres and crammed together in a small plot along with the unexcavated bases of many other dagobas. The site is quite unlike anything else in Sri Lanka, and is of great antiquity, dating back at least two thousand years, though no one can quite agree on its exact purpose – a popular theory is that the dagobas enshrine the remains of Buddhist monks; others claim that they are "votive" dagobas erected in fulfilment of answered prayers.

Maviddapuram Kandaswamy Temple

Around 20km north of Jaffna, next to the turn-off to Keerimalai, stands the imposing **Maviddapuram Kandaswamy Temple**. It is said to have been commissioned by a grateful Pandyan princess, a certain Maruthapura Veeravalli, whose face is supposed to have borne an unfortunate resemblance to a horse until a dip in the nearby Keerimalai hot springs (see below) restored the lady to her true beauty.

Naguleswaram Temple

naguleswaram.org

Right on the coast some 2km north of Maviddapuram Kandaswamy Temple, and next to the Keerimalai hot springs, is the grand **Naguleswaram Temple**, one of Sri Lanka's five holiest Shiva temples, the *pancha iswaram*. The original temple was destroyed by the Portuguese in 1620, rebuilt in the late nineteenth century, and then largely destroyed again by Sri Lankan Army shells in 1990. Reconstruction work continues apace.

Keerimalai hot springs

A few metres beyond the Naguleswaram Temple on the peninsula's northern shore are the **Keerimalai hot springs**, whose therapeutic powers have been recognized since the time of the Mahabharata: Pandyan princess Maruthapura Veeravalli (see page 395) and a local Indian holy man, Nagula Muni – whose austerities had given his features the appearance of a mongoose (*keeri*) – both found cures here. Locals flock here to bathe, following in their footsteps, in the neat little concrete pool overlooking the ocean in which the springs have been captured, while fine beaches stretch away on either side.

Sri Sangamitta Vihara

From Keerimalai a syvlan country road hugs the northern coast of the peninsula, running west to Karaitivu. About 8km west of Keerimalai a rare (for Jaffna) Buddhist temple, the **Sri Sangamitta Vihara**, marks the spot where, according to legend, Sangamitta (see page 402), daughter of the great Indian emperor Asoka, landed in around 246 BC. A stylized miniature boat floating in the middle of a small pond and a statue of the princess commemorate the historic event.

Point Pedro and around

Arrowing northeast across the peninsula, the congested AB20 highway connects Jaffna with the peninsula's second-largest town, Point Pedro. About 8km from Jaffna, right next to the highway, is the **Nilavarai Well**. Despite its unexciting appearance, the well is traditionally believed to have been the work of Rama himself, who created it by sticking an arrow into the ground to assuage his thirst. Its waters are said to be bottomless and appear to be somehow connected directly to the sea: the water is fresh near the top, but becomes increasingly salty the deeper you go.

From here it's another twenty-odd kilometres to the bustling little town of **POINT PEDRO** (PPD), at the extreme northeastern tip of the Jaffna Peninsula. There's not much to see here – the town's only real sight (and not a very exciting one at that) is the **Theru Moodi Madam**, a traditional travellers' rest house comprising a roofed stone archway, with pillared shelters to either side, built across a road on the east side of town.

Just east of here **Point Pedro Lighthouse** (no photography) marks the most northerly point in Sri Lanka.

Velvettiturai

Due west of Point Pedro, the fishing village of **VELVETTITURAI** (widely abbreviated to VVT) is best known as the birthplace of the former leader of the LTTE, Velupillai Prabhakaran, although the house in which he was born (see page 384) has now been demolished.

On the east side of the village lies a large **Amman Temple**, whose festival in April draws enormous crowds. Immediately behind this is a second large temple, dedicated to Shiva, which was formerly owned by Prabakharan's family and which the rebel leader often visited as a child.

Vallipuram

Around 5km south of Point Pedro, the village of **VALLIPURAM** was formerly one of the peninsula's principal towns, and is still home to its second largest **temple**: a sprawling, rustic complex which is thought to date back to the first century AD. It's also one of the very few in Sri Lanka dedicated to Vishnu, who according to legend appeared here in the form of a fish.

Manalkadu Desert

To the southeast of Vallipuram is the so-called **Manalkadu Desert**, a rather far-fetched name for a small range of coastal sand dunes. You may be able to find the remains of **St Anthony's Church**, built around 1900 and now picturesquely half-buried in the sand. From the church there's a clear view of the strange and melancholy seafront **cemetery** nearby, with dozens of crosses stuck into the top of the dunes marking the graves of locals, most of whom perished in the tsunami; the fateful date 2004.12.26 is written on cross after cross.

GETTING AROUND | **THE JAFFNA PENINSULA**

There are regular **buses** between Jaffna and Point Pedro (every 30min; 1hr), as well as other towns around the peninsula, plus a few **trains** between Jaffna, Chunnakam and Kankesanthurai (KKS). To get to most of these places, however, you'll really need your own transport. *Morgan's* *Guest House* (see page 392) is a good place to arrange a **car**, and most places can also be easily (if less comfortably) reached by **tuktuk**. Easiest of all is to take a **tour** with Sri Lanka Click (see page 392), who offer two in-depth full-day tours of the eastern and western sides of the peninsula.

ACCOMMODATION

There's very little accommodation around the Jaffna peninsula, although a new guesthouse in Kankesanthurai (KKS), the *D'Villa Beach House*, (launched by the owner of the excellent *D'Villa Guest House* in Jaffna), should have opened by the time you read this. Avoid the army-owned and operated *Thalsevana Holiday Resort*, also near KKS allegedly built on land stolen by the military – and also a truly awful hotel.

Margosa Bongo Stay Putur Rd, Chunnakam, around 10km north of Jaffna ☎021 224 0242; map p.394.

Smooth boutique guesthouse out in the countryside roughly halfway between Jaffna and the north coast of the peninsula, offering tranquil rural lodgings in a stylishly updated colonial villa. $100

The islands

West of Jaffna, a string of **islands** drift out into the waters of the Palk Strait towards India. Two of them – **Kayts** and **Karaitivu** – virtually join up with the mainland, to which they're connected by causeways, while Kayts itself is connected to **Punkudutivu**, further west. Punkudutivu is the starting point for ferries to **Nainativu**, home to two important religious shrines, and the remote island of **Delft** – it's possible to visit both in a single, albeit long, day.

Specific sights are relatively few and far between on the islands. The real point and pleasure of a trip here is in the journey itself, and in the subtle but memorable land- and seascapes, with the flat and largely uninhabited islands merging almost imperceptibly with the shallow blue waters of the Jaffna lagoon and Palk Strait.

Kayts

Kayts (pronounced "Kites"; also known locally as **Velanai** and occasionally by its old Dutch name of Leiden) is the largest of the islands and the closest to Jaffna – its eastern tip lies just over the lagoon from Jaffna town and is reached via a causeway through very shallow water. Like the other islands, Kayts is only lightly populated and largely devoid of buildings – a pancake-flat expanse studded with innumerable palmyra palms and a succession of imposing Hindu temples standing in proud isolation in the middle of empty countryside. There's also a modest sliver of sand at **Chatty** (aka Charty) **Beach**, close to **Velanai** town on the southern side of the island.

Kayts town and around

At the far (western) end of the island is **KAYTS** town (actually little more than a sleepy village), where you'll find the beautiful nineteenth-century **St James Church** – the facade bears the date 1716, but the building actually dates from 1815. Roofless for many years, the church was beautifully restored in 2015 and now looks as good as new.

Just beyond the village lie the scant remains of **Urundi Fort**, also known as Fort Eyrie, although the ruins lie within the grounds of a naval base and are now off limits to visitors. Urundi and Hammenhiel (see page 398) forts were originally built by the Portuguese to control this entrance to the Jaffna lagoon, though the Dutch neglected Urundi, concentrating their defences in Hammenhiel – of which there's a beautiful view from here.

Karaitivu and around

The most northerly of the islands, **Karaitivu** is reached by road some 12km north of Jaffna. En route to the island, 10km from Jaffna at the village of **Vaddukoddai**, you'll pass the barn-like **Portuguese church**, in whose churchyard are 27 tombstones, moved here for safekeeping from the Groote Kerk in Jaffna fort. Most are Dutch colonial; the oldest dates back to 1666. Around 5km further down the road, just before the causeway to Karaitivu, is the **Punnalai Varatharaja Perumal Kovil**, dedicated to Vishnu and one of the peninsula's two oldest temples. The shrine holds an ancient stone tortoise which was apparently fished ashore here.

Casuarina Beach

Catch a bus from Jaffna to Karainagar (every 30min; 1hr) and alight at the junction with Sivan Kovil Rd about 500m before you reach Karainagar, from where you can catch a tuktuk for the final 2km to the beach itself

On the north coast of Karaitivu itself is **Casuarina Beach**, the peninsula's best and most popular patch of sand – although it's not particularly clean. Swimming is safe (though the water is shallow), and facilities include a couple of cafés, toilets and plenty of sunshades and benches under the eponymous Casuarina trees which dot the shore.

Hammenhiel Fort

Just off the southern tip of the island, appearing to float magically in the waters of the lagoon between Karaitivu and Kayts, is **Hammenhiel Fort**, now converted into an upmarket hotel (see page 398). Its name, literally "Heel of Ham", refers to the prosaic old Dutch belief that Sri Lanka resembled a leg of ham.

ARRIVAL AND DEPARTURE

KAYTS AND KARAITIVU

By bus Buses leave Jaffna's bus station roughly every 30min to Kayts and Karainagar, the main village on Karaitivu, from Jaffna's bus station; the journey to either takes around 1hr.

By ferry An antiquated chain ferry (foot passengers and bikes/motorbikes only) runs between Kayts town and Karaitivu (12 daily 6.20am–6.15pm; 10min).

ACCOMMODATION

Fort Hammenhiel Resort ☎ 011 381 8215, ⓦ forthammenhielresort.lk; map p.394. Owned and operated by the Sri Lankan Navy, this historic fort (see page 398) is one of the island's more unusual places to stay, with four neatly modernized a/c rooms. Access is by boat only, taking a few minutes to cross the water from the jetty on Karaitivu, where you'll also find a shiny, modern restaurant and bar. Non-guests can visit for a meal, although the boat trip alone costs a rather pricey Rs.3000. $110
Tilko Charty Beach Resort Charty Beach, Velanai ☎ 077 343 8373; map p.394. Functional resort, with big bare a/c rooms in a cluster of cabanas set among pleasant gardens, right next to Chatty Beach. Rs.5500

Punkudutivu

The island of **Punkudutivu** lies southwest of Kayts, to which it's connected by a 4km causeway through very shallow water – looking out of the windows of your vehicle while crossing will give you the bizarre illusion that you're driving across the top of the sea. The road across the island reveals constantly shifting vistas of sea and land, passing tiny country hamlets and a succession of large Hindu temples, often the only buildings to be seen in this very rural landscape – as throughout the Jaffna region, the number and size of these shrines seems completely out of proportion with the island's very modest number of inhabitants. At the end of the road, a tiny jetty on the island's western side at the village of **Kurikadduwan** is the departure point for boats to Nainativu and Delft.

Nainativu

A couple of kilometres west of Punkudutivu is the small island of **Nainativu**, just 4km from top to bottom and barely more than a kilometre wide. Immediately in front of the ferry jetty is the ornate **Naga Pooshani Ambal Kovil**, a Hindu temple sacred to the goddess Ambal; newborn babies are brought here to receive the goddess's blessings. The original temple was, as usual, destroyed by the Portuguese, and the large and impressive complex you see today dates from 1788; the gopuram was added in 1935. Thousands of people attend a major festival here in June/July.

A ten-minute walk south of here leads to the **Nagadipa Vihara**, a rare place of Buddhist worship in the Hindu north. This marks the spot of the Buddha's second legendary visit to Sri Lanka, when he is said to have achieved the reconciliation of two warring *naga* kings. A rather modest little temple marks the spot; the building next to it houses a superb golden Buddha from Thailand. The temple sits within an area used by the Sri Lankan Navy, so you'll have to talk your way through a checkpoint to visit.

ARRIVAL AND DEPARTURE	PUNKUDITIVU AND NAINATIVU
By bus Buses run daily roughly every hour from Jaffna to Kurikadduwan (KKD) village on Punkudutivu, taking around 1hr 30min.	**By ferry** Ferries run from KKD to Nainativu every 30min or so from 7.30am until 5.30pm, taking around 15min to make the crossing.

Delft (Neduntivu) and around

By the time you reach the island of **DELFT**, some 20km southwest of Punkudutivu, you'll begin to feel you're a very long way from the rest of Sri Lanka – from the western tip of the island on a clear day, you can occasionally see the communications mast in Rameswaram, 40km distant over the water in India. Named after the famous Dutch town (although better known locally by its Tamil name of **Neduntivu**), the island was occupied, despite its remoteness, by all three colonial powers. It's a place of bleak, minimalist beauty, crisscrossed with coral-rock walls and boasting an unusual population of **wild ponies**, the descendants of animals first introduced by the Portuguese – they're found mainly in the southern centre of the island.

Pick up a tuktuk at the ferry dock for a tour of Delft's eclectic smattering of sights (around Rs.1500 for 2hr). A short distance west of the ferry dock, behind the island's hospital, lie the remains of an old Dutch **fort** and **hospital** and, nearby, a quaint little dovecote-like "**pigeon tower**". South of the ferry dock is a rare African **baobab tree**, thought to have been planted by Arab seamen. You'll probably also be shown the island's famous **growing stone** on the eastern side of the island, currently standing at a little over 1m tall and said to be steadily increasing in size. There's also a nice **beach** just east of the fort.

Some 30km southwest of Delft lies the tiny island of **Kachchativu**, used as a base by passing Sri Lankan and Indian fishermen but otherwise uninhabited, inaccessible and boasting just a single man-made structure, the church of **St Anthony** – Sri Lanka's most isolated building and almost as close to India as to Jaffna.

ARRIVAL AND DEPARTURE	DELFT (NEDUNTIVU) AND AROUND
By bus and ferry Buses leave Jaffna every 30min for the 1hr 30min journey to Kurikadduwan (KKD) village on Punkudutivu, from where the ferry departs for Delft. There are usually three boats daily, leaving KKD at 8am, 9.30am and 1.30pm, and returning from Delft at 11am, 2.30pm and 4.30pm at the time of writing (although timings change regularly – check latest times locally before	setting out). The crossing costs Rs.100 and takes around 1hr – seas can be rough and the ferry hot (there's no cover) and overcrowded. The ferry docks in the island's northeast corner. **By tour** Sri Lanka Click (see page 392) offer useful full-day tours to Delft, taking the headache out of getting there and around.

ACCOMMODATION

Delft Samudra Hotel Maveli Periyathurai Rd ☎021 221 5282; map p.394. If you want to spend a night in Sri Lanka's remotest hotel, this is your place, with a neat circle of simple but spotless modern rooms arranged around an incongruously fancy fountain. **$50**

TEMPLE OF THE TOOTH, KANDY

Contexts

History

Sri Lanka's past is sunk in an inextricable mixture of the historical and the mythological, exemplified by the curious story of Prince Vijaya (see page 403), from whom the Sinhalese people claim descent. Early hominids (Homo erectus) are thought to have reached the island by around 500,000 BC (perhaps much earlier), crossing the land bridge that formerly connected India and Sri Lanka until as recently as 5000 BC, while vestiges of prehistoric settlements dating back to around 125,000 BC have been discovered – evidence of a Sri Lankan branch of Homo sapiens popularly known as "Balangoda Man" after archeological discoveries made in the vicinity of modern Balangoda, in the southern hill country. The only modern survivors of these prehistoric peoples are the Veddhas (see page 239), probably related to the aborigines of Australia, the Nicobar Islands and Malaysia. The Veddhas initially lived by hunting and gathering, and later developed knowledge of iron and agriculture, while quartz tools have been discovered at Bandarawela and simple pottery at Balangoda.

Most of the history of Sri Lanka, however, is concerned with two immigrant, rather than indigenous, peoples: the North Indian-descended **Sinhalese**, who form the majority of modern Sri Lanka's population; and the minority, South Indian-descended **Tamils**, found mainly in the north and east of the island – relations between these two ethnic groups have shaped much of the country's history, and continue to do so. Early Sri Lankan history thus remains a controversial subject, as both Sinhalese and Tamils continue to argue about who arrived first, their respective rights to the island, and exactly what it means to be Sri Lankan.

The argument continues to this day, given the lack of firm historical evidence. The early Sinhalese conveniently equipped themselves with a legendary historical pedigree, as recounted in the Mahavamsa and encapsulated in the legend of Prince Vijaya. The history of Tamil settlement in the island remains an altogether cloudier affair. According to the Sinhalese version of events there was no substantial Tamil presence in the island until the Chola invasions of the tenth century AD, although archeological discoveries, the fact that Tamil kings were ruling at Anuradhapura from as early as the second century BC, and plain common sense, given the island's proximity to the Tamil areas of South India, suggest that Tamil settlement of some kind dates back far earlier, whatever modern Sinhalese historians and politicians might claim.

The arrival of the Sinhalese

From around the fifth century BC, waves of Indo-Aryan immigrants began to arrive in Sri Lanka from northern India. Their exact origins remain obscure, though it's thought that the first settlers came from present-day Gujarat, followed by second waves

125,000 BC	c.500 BC	377 BC	246 BC	161 BC
Early homo sapiens – aka "Balangoda Man" – living in Sri Lanka.	First Sinhalese immigrants arrive in Sri Lanka.	Founding of Anuradhapura.	Arrival of Buddhism.	Dutugemunu defeats Elara at Anuradhapura and takes control of island.

THE MAHAVAMSA AND CULAVAMSA

Much of our knowledge of early Sri Lankan history is owed to the **Mahavamsa** ("Great Chronicle") and its continuation, the **Culavamsa** ("Little Chronicle"). The Mahavamsa was compiled by Buddhist monks during the sixth century (the Culavamsa dates from the thirteenth century) and was intended to commemorate and legitimize the Sinhalese royal lineage and the island's impeccable Buddhist credentials. Their narration of actual historical events is therefore at best questionably biased, and at worst totally imaginary – a fact illustrated by the Mahavamsa's meticulous descriptions of the three visits that the Buddha himself is claimed to have made to the island.

For more information on both books, visit ⓦ mahavamsa.org.

of colonists from Orissa and Bengal. These people, the ancestors of the present-day **Sinhalese**, first arrived on the western coast of the island. At first they were limited to river valleys, these being the only areas in which they were able to cultivate rice, but as their expertise in irrigation increased, they were able to strike inland towards the island's dry northern plains – during which expansion the indigenous Veddhas were either absorbed by intermarriage with the new arrivals or driven east and south.

The Anuradhapura period

The first major Sinhalese kingdom developed around the city of **Anuradhapura**, in the island's dry northern plains. The city's origins are shrouded in the semi-legendary depths of early Sinhalese history, though archeological evidence suggests that the city has been occupied for at least three thousand years. The first documented history comes from the Mahavamsa, which states that Anuradhapura was founded in 377 BC by the third king of the Vijaya dynasty, Pandukabhaya (reigned 380–367 BC), a rebellious noble of the Vijaya clan, who built a new capital on the site of the palace of his great-uncle, a certain Anuradha, after whom the new city was named.

The arrival of Buddhism

The fledgling city initially enjoyed only limited power over the surrounding region, though its status rose significantly during the reign of **Devanampiya Tissa** (c.300–260 BC), who oversaw the arrival of Buddhism in the island and established the city as a major centre of Buddhist pilgrimage and learning. According to the Mahavamsa, **Mahinda**, son of the great Indian Buddhist emperor Ashoka, arrived in Sri Lanka in 246 BC with a retinue of monks to proselytize on behalf of Buddhism, quickl y converting the king of Anuradhapura, Devanampiya Tissa. Mahinda was soon followed by his sister, **Sangamitta**, who arrived with a valuable collection of relics including the Buddha's begging bowl, collarbone and a cutting from the sacred bo tree under which the Buddha attained enlightenment in Bodhgaya – the tree subsequently grown from this cutting still flourishes today.

Buddhism found a ready audience in Sri Lanka, and within half a century the island's Sinhalese had all converted to the new faith. Buddhism gave the Sinhalese a new-found sense of national identity and inspired the development of a distinctively Sri Lankan culture, exemplified by the religious architecture of Anuradhapura, whose

89 BC	67 AD	114–136	274–301
Vattagamini Abhaya expels Tamils and seizes throne.	Lambakanna dynasty begins.	Reign of Gajabahu; military campaigns against Cholas of South India.	Reign of Mahasena; construction of numerous major tanks and the Jetavana monastery in Anuradhapura.

PRINCE VIJAYA

According to Sinhalese tradition, recorded in the *Mahavamsa*, the Sinhalese people trace their origins back to the union between a lion ("sinha", hence Sinhalese) and a rather disreputable North Indian princess ("Very fair she was and very amorous, and for shame the king and queen could not suffer her"). The princess is said to have been travelling in a caravan when the lion attacked. The princess's companions fled, but, as the Mahavamsa touchingly relates:

… the lion beheld her [the princess] from afar. Love laid hold on him, and he came towards her with waving tail and ears laid back. Seeing him…without fear she caressed him, stroking his limbs. The lion, roused to fiercest passion by her touch, took her upon his back and bore her with all speed to his cave, and there he was united with her.

In due course the princess gave birth to twins, a boy and a girl, who subsequently married one another. The fruit of this incestuous union was sixteen sons, the eldest of whom was **Prince Vijaya**. Growing to manhood, Vijaya made such a nuisance of himself that there were calls for him and seven hundred of his male companions to be put to death. Instead, the king packed them all into a boat and sent them off into exile. Vijaya and his friends arrived on Sri Lanka sometime in the sixth century BC.

Landing on the island's west coast, they were confronted by a *yaksa*, or devil, who appeared to them in the form of a dog. Following the dog, they found another *yaksa*, this one in the shape of a woman hermit named **Kuveni**, who proceeded to magically ensnare all Vijaya's friends until the prince, protected by a magic thread conferred by the god Vishnu himself, seized her and threatened to cut off her head. Kuveni released the men, agreed to hand over the kingdom to Vijaya and, transforming herself into a young and desirable woman, retired with Vijaya to a splendidly appointed bed. They subsequently married and had two children, though Vijaya eventually came to feel the need for a more reputable consort, and drove Kuveni back into the forest. Their children escaped and married one another; it was their descendants who became, according to tradition, the **Veddhas**.

The lack of women on the island was finally relieved when Vijaya sent to the Pandyan court in India for wives for himself and his followers. Vijaya himself married a Pandyan princess, but failed to produce an heir, and towards the end of his reign sent for his younger brother to come and take his place as ruler. The brother, unwilling to leave his native land, instead sent his youngest son, **Panduvasudeva**. Having landed with 32 followers on the east coast at Gokana (present-day Trincomalee), Panduvasudeva was duly enthroned and continued the Vijaya dynasty.

To what extent these mythological events reflect actual history is a matter of considerable speculation. Vijaya himself was perhaps a symbolic rather than an actual historical figure – his name means "victory", perhaps representing the triumph of the North Indian immigrants over the native Veddhas. Equally, Vijaya's union with Kuveni would seem to commemorate the intermingling of the Sinhalese immigrants with the Veddhas, while his subsequent marriage to a Pandyan princess again probably has its roots in actual historic links between the early Sinhalese and the Tamils of South India – even Panduvasudeva may simply be another symbolic figure representing the second wave of settlement. The essentially symbolic nature of the tale is supported by fact that the Sinhalese themselves – and indeed the staunchly Buddhist writers of the Mahavamsa – feel no compunction in tracing their ancestry to a violent outcast whose immediate ancestry included both bestial and incestuous relations.

normous stupas were among early Asia's greatest monuments. Sri Lanka's proximity to outh India made it a constant target of invasions, however, while the reliance of the

73	491	853	993
hatusena murdered by 's son Kassapa, who stablishes new capital at igiriya.	Mogallana defeats Kassapa at Sigiriya and returns capital to Anuradhapura.	Anuradhapura sacked by South Indian Pandyans.	Final destruction of Anuradhapura by Chola king, Rajaraja, who establishes new capital at Polonnaruwa.

Sinhalese on Tamil mercenaries (given the traditional Buddhist regard for the sanctity of life, the Sinhalese have always had difficulties raising an effective army – at least until the past few decades) left them at the mercy of their own fighting forces. Tamils had already begun migrating to the island from the third century BC, and shortly after Devanampiya's death, two Tamil captains in the Anuradhapuran army – Sena and Guttika – staged a coup and ruled over the city for two decades. Following their murder, another Tamil soldier, **Elara**, seized power around 205 BC and ruled the city for a further 44 years. Elara's reign was finally ended in 161 BC by **Dutugemunu** (see page 330), the legendary Buddhist warrior-king who eventually defeated the old Tamil general after a protracted conflict and succeeded in uniting Sri Lanka under Sinhalese rule for the first time.

Dutugemunu's heady combination of military heroics and unimpeachable Buddhist piety proved an inspiration for all who followed him, even if none of the other 113 kings (and two queens) of Anuradhapura was able to emulate his achievements. Of the kings who followed, fifteen ruled for under a year, 22 were murdered, four committed suicide, thirteen were killed in battle and eleven were dethroned.

Soon after Dutugemunu's death, Anuradhapura was once again the target of South Indian attacks, and this constant external pressure, combined with incessant internal feuding, regularly succeeded in reducing the city to chaos. Tamil invaders seized Anuradhapura again in 103 BC, and despite being swiftly evicted by Vattagamini Abhaya (r. 89–77 BC), founder of the Abhayagiri monastery and the cave temples at Dambulla, the kingdom soon descended once again into a period of chaos, exemplified by the reign of the notorious queen Anula (r. 48–44 BC) who in five years is said to have married and then murdered 32 husbands.

The great tank builders

In 67 AD, the accession to the throne of Vasabha (r. 67–111), the first of the **Lambakanna** dynasty, inaugurated Anuradhapura's greatest era of peace and prosperity. Vasabha initiated the first of the massive irrigation works that transformed the arid plains of the northern part of the island into fecund agricultural land capable of supporting a dense population and a highly developed civilization. Despite further struggles with invading Tamil forces – encapsulated in the legendary exploits of **Gajabahu**, who reigned from 114–136 (see page 210) – the following four centuries of Lambakanna rule were largely peaceful. Later kings contributed further to the city's magnificent Buddhist heritage and the northern island's irrigation system, most notably **Mahasena** (r. 274–301), who is said to have constructed no fewer than sixteen major reservoirs, including the Minneriya and Kaudulla tanks, as well as the Jetavana, the last of the city's three great monasteries.

A new period of uncertainty began in 429 with yet another invasion from South India and the rule of seven Tamil generals who reigned in succession until being evicted by **Dhatusena** (r. 455–473), who celebrated in the by now customary fashion by constructing (according to the Mahavamsa) no fewer than eighteen new temples and the enormous Kalawewa reservoir, near Aukana. Dhatusena met an unholy end at the hands of his own son, **Kassapa** (see page 300), who temporarily removed the capital to Sigiriya, before another of Dhatusena's sons, Mogallana, succeeded in wresting back control, albeit again with South Indian assistance.

1070	1153–86	1186–96
Vijayabahu drives Cholas from island and re-establishes Sinhalese rule.	Reign of Parakramabahu the Great; golden age of Polonnaruwa.	Reign of Nissankamalla.

This event signalled a renewal of Tamil influence: the island's kings again sought Tamil support in their own disputes, and South Indian mercenaries became both an important and unpredictable faction in the Sinhalese state and a powerful influence at court. **Tamil** influence in Sri Lankan affairs continued to grow during the fifth century AD, following the resurgence of Hinduism in southern India and the rise of three powerful new Tamil kingdoms there: the Cholas (based in Thanjavur), the Pandyas (Madurai) and the Pallavas (Kanchipuram), all of whom would at various times become entangled in Sri Lankan affairs.

Decline and fall

A final interlude of peace was enjoyed during the reigns of Aggabodhi I (r. 571–604) and Aggabodhi II (r. 604–14), who between them restored many of Anuradhapura's religious edifices and carried out further irrigation projects. The latter's death ushered in the most chaotic period in the history of the Anuradhapura kingdom, with incessant civil wars and the growing influence of South Indian mercenaries, who were recruited by disaffected Sinhalese nobles or rival claimants to the throne and frequently paid for by wealth plundered from Buddhist monasteries.

By the end of the seventh century, power had effectively passed to these Tamil mercenaries, who acted as kingmakers until the last of the great Anuradhapuran kings, **Manavamma** (r. 684–718), was placed on the throne with the support of the Pallavas, establishing a second Lambakanna dynasty. Manavamma's reign ushered in a final century of relative peace before Anuradhapura's destruction. In 853, an invading Pandyan army sacked Anuradhapura before being bought off at great cost. Despite the best efforts of Sri Lankan diplomacy, the ever-present threat of South Indian invasion continued to hang over the kingdom, fuelled by the religious animosity that the Hindu kingdoms of South India bore towards their Buddhist neighbour. In 946–947, the Cholas sacked Anuradhapura, and the city's soldiers were obliged to flee to Ruhunu until the Cholas had returned home. By 992, the last king of Anuradhapura, Mahinda V (r. 983–993), found he had no funds to pay the wages of his mercenaries and was forced to flee to Ruhunu. Anuradhapura and the northern areas of the island fell into chaos, with bands of soldiers pillaging at will. Attracted by the disorder, the Chola king Rajaraja despatched an army that sacked Anuradhapura for the very last time in the fateful year of **993**, reducing the once great city to ruins – the single greatest watershed in Sri Lankan history.

The Polonnaruwa period

Having destroyed Anuradhapura, the Cholas established themselves in the city of **Polonnaruwa**, from where they ruled for the next 75 years until **Vijayabahu I** ejected them from the island in 1070 AD. Although Vijayabahu had himself crowned for symbolic reasons amid the ruins of Anuradhapura, he decided to move the capital to Polonnaruwa, which was further removed from India and situated in more easily defensible territory.

The relocation ushered in the beginning of a final Sinhalese golden age. Vijayabahu's successor **Parakramabahu I** (see page 314), who reigned from 1153–86, reformed the island's economy, transformed Polonnaruwa into one of the great cities of South Asia

215	1232
South Indian mercenary Magha seizes control of Polonnaruwa; widespread disorder and collapse of Sinhalese civilization in Rajarata; Arya Chakaravarti founds new Tamil kingdom, Jaffnapatnam, in north.	Vijayabahu III establishes new capital at Dambadeniya.

and even launched raids against the Pandyas and a naval expedition against Burma. After Parakramabahu, the throne passed to his Tamil brother-in-law, **Nissankamalla** (see page 317), who reigned from 1186–96, and the influence of South India increased once again. Nissankamalla was the last effective ruler of Polonnaruwa, though his zeal for lavish new building projects came close to bankrupting the state, which had already been labouring under the expense of Parakramabahu's wars overseas.

Nissankamalla's death without a designated heir resulted in the usual disorder. A series of weaker rulers followed until, in 1212, a new wave of Tamil invaders, the Pandyans, arrived in the island and seized power, only to be displaced three years later by another South Indian adventurer, the despotic **Magha** (r. 1215–55), who instituted a chaotic reign of terror during which the kingdom's complex irrigation systems gradually fell into disrepair, and the population began to abandon Polonnaruwa and move steadily southwards.

The Sinhalese move south

The following period of Sri Lankan history presents a complex and disordered picture, as various Sinhalese and South Indian factions jockeyed for position amid an increasingly politically fragmented island. As Polonnaruwa fell into chaos under Magha, so the Sinhalese aristocracy began to establish rival centres of power located in inaccessible terrain beyond his reach. Initially, the Sinhalese established a new capital at **Dambadeniya**, about seventy miles southwest of Polonnaruwa, under Vijayabahu III (r. 1232–36). Vijayabahu III's successor, **Parakramabahu II** (r. 1236–70), succeeded in expelling Magha with Pandyan help, though further political instability soon followed. Under Bhuvanekabahu I (r. 1272–84) the Sinhalese capital was moved briefly northwards to the isolated rock fortress of **Yapahuwa**. After further skirmishes, Bhuvanekabahu II (r. 1293–1302) moved the capital south again, to **Kurunegala**, although increasing political fragmentation meant that none of these kings enjoyed much real power. By around 1340, the monarchy itself had split, with rival Sinhalese kings established at **Gampola** and **Dedigama**.

The southwards drift of Sinhalese power had dramatic social and economic consequences. As the island's population moved quickly from one town to another, so the complex **irrigation systems** that had supported the advanced civilization of the dry zone fell into further disrepair. The carefully oiled machinery of Sinhalese society wound down: the great tanks and canals of the northern plains dried up, reducing the area of cultivable land (with a consequent decline in population and revenue), while a losing battle was fought against the encroaching jungle, which began to reclaim the abandoned cities and villages. The Sinhalese increasingly found themselves driven south into the central highlands. Capital cities were now selected mainly for their defensibility, and became military strongholds rather than economic centres, situated in difficult terrain and away from populous areas. As irrigation systems and large-scale agriculture broke down, so fewer taxes were paid to the state, further weakening centralized control.

These economic changes also had implications for the island's cherished Buddhist faith. As revenues – literally – dried up, so the funds available to the Buddhist establishment declined. Kings continued as patrons of Buddhism, but their own

1272	1293	c.1340	c.1350 onward
Bhuvanekabahu I moves capital to Yapahuwa.	Bhuvanekabahu II moves capital to Kurunegala.	Rival Sinhalese kings ruling from Gampola and Dedigama.	Rise of Kotte kingdom near modern Colombo

reduced circumstances meant that Buddhist institutions no longer enjoyed the wealth they once had. The great monasteries of Anuradhapura and Polonnaruwa were disbanded, while indiscipline and theological schisms spread throughout the **Buddhist Sangha** (clergy). The influence of Hinduism once again rose, with Hindu gods assuming increasingly important roles in the island's Buddhist temples and festivals.

The Jaffna kingdom

The erosion of Sinhalese authority left a power vacuum in the north of the island. Following the invasion of Magha in 1215 a South Indian general, **Arya Chakaravarti**, seized power in the north, founding a Tamil kingdom, **Jaffnapatnam**, with its capital at Nallur in the Jaffna Peninsula. This kingdom soon expanded southwards, coming into conflict with the centres of Sinhalese power, until by the mid-fourteenth century the Tamil kingdom even attacked and defeated the rulers of Gampola (near present-day Colombo), establishing its own tax collectors in the kingdom.

As the Sinhalese migrated steadily south and the Tamils established an independent kingdom in the north, so the island became increasingly divided into two along the linguistic, cultural and religious lines that survive to this day. Previously, Tamil settlements had been interspersed among the Sinhalese. Now, for the first time, the island's northern and eastern areas became predominantly Tamil (compounded by fresh migrations from South India following the collapse of the Pandyan kingdom in the fourteenth century). Jaffna became a major seat of Tamil culture, its society organized along similar lines to the Tamil regions of South India, while the Tamil language became entrenched in the island, developing a literary culture that was nurtured by the kings of Jaffna and enriched by contact with South India.

The rise of Kotte

The Jaffna kingdom's mid-fourteenth-century attack against Gampola marked its high-water point. In the second half of the fourteenth century a new Sinhalese dynasty, the **Alagakkonaras** (or Alakesvaras) rose to power in Gampola. Establishing a fort at **Kotte**, near Colombo, they expelled the Tamil tax collectors and re-established their independence, though internal feuding fatally weakened them. In 1405, a Ming Chinese fleet under the legendary general **Cheng Ho** arrived in Sri Lanka on a mission to gain possession of the **Tooth Relic**. The Alagakkonaras, not surprisingly, refused to hand it over. A few years later, Cheng Ho returned and carried off the last of the Alagakkonara rulers, Vira Alekesvara, to China for five years in retaliation.

Vira Alekesvara was eventually returned unharmed to Sri Lanka, only to find that during his absence a minor member of the Gampola nobility had seized power and had himself crowned as **Parakramabahu VI** of Kotte (r. 1412–67). The last of the great Sinhalese unifiers, Parakramabahu first subdued the independent kingdom of the highlands, then saw off an invasion of the Vijayanagarans (the dominant power in South India at that time), and finally, in 1450, succeeded in taking possession of the Jaffna kingdom and uniting the entire island, for the final time, under Sinhalese rule. As on so many previous occasions, however, the unity achieved by one strong ruler failed to survive his death, and within a few years the kingdoms of Jaffna, Rajarata

1405	1412–67	1497	1505
Chinese admiral Cheng Ho visits Sri Lanka.	Reign of Parakramabahu VI of Kotte; island reunited under Sinhalese rule for final time.	Vasco da Gama discovers sea route to India.	Portuguese fleet arrives in Sri Lanka.

and the central highlands had once more asserted their independence, so that the subsequent rulers of Kotte, although they continued to claim sovereignty over the whole of Sri Lanka, increasingly found themselves hemmed into a small area in the island's southwestern corner.

The Portuguese

As agricultural revenues declined following the collapse of irrigation systems and the loss of territory, so **trade** became increasingly important. Spices were the most important exports: cinnamon, found in the southwestern forests, was first exported in the fourteenth century, and was soon followed by pepper and other spices – all of them subject to royal monopolies. Colombo, Galle and other coastal settlements in the island's southwest developed into important **ports**, attracting foreign merchants and establishing wide-ranging commercial contacts – as early as 1283 Bhuvanekabahu I had despatched a trade mission to the Mamluk sultan of Egypt. The most important of these traders were the **Arabs**, who began visiting Sri Lanka from around the tenth century and who established settlements around the coast – including the small town of Kolamba, the forerunner of modern Colombo. They also brought Islam to the island, while exporting cinnamon and other spices that had begun to fetch premium prices in Western markets.

The island's trading possibilities soon began to attract attention from even further afield. In 1497, the **Portuguese** navigator Vasco da Gama pioneered the sea route to India around the southern tip of Africa, opening the Indian Ocean to European mariners. In 1505, a Portuguese fleet, prospecting for spices, was blown off course into the mouth of the Kelani Ganga, near Colombo. The Portuguese received a friendly audience from the king of Kotte, Vira Parakramabahu, who was understandably fascinated by these exotic, armour-clad foreigners, described by one of the king's scouts as "a race of men, exceeding white and beautiful. They wear boots and hats of iron, and they are always in motion. They eat white stones [bread] and they drink blood [wine]."

Kotte and Sitawake

The Portuguese had noted the island's commercial and strategic value – in particular its vast supply of cinnamon – and soon returned, being granted trading concessions and permission to build a fort at Colombo. They found themselves rapidly overtaken by the imbroglio of Sri Lankan politics, however, and spent the next seventy years fighting to retain a foothold on the island. In 1521 three sons of the then king of Kotte, Vijayabahu, put their father to death and divided the kingdom between themselves. The oldest of the brothers, **Bhuvanekabahu**, ruled at Kotte, while the two others set up independent kingdoms at Sitawake and Rayigama. The ambitious king of Sitawake, **Mayadunne**, soon began the attempt to seize control of his brother's kingdom at Kotte; Bhuvanekabahu, in turn, sought Portuguese assistance, becoming increasingly reliant on their military support.

Mayadunne gradually succeeded in capturing a large part of the Kotte kingdom, and following his death, his son **Rajasinha** continued to prosecute the war against the Portuguese successfully on land, though he had no way of combating Portuguese sea power. Following Rajasinha's death in 1593, however, the Portuguese were able to take

1518	1521	1593–1638
Portuguese build fort in Colombo.	Kingdom of Kotte splits into kingdoms of Kotte, Sitawake and Rayigama. Mayadunne, ruler of Sitawake, begins to launch attacks against Portuguese.	Portuguese seize control of coastal areas as far as Jaffna, and launch unsuccessful attacks against Kingdom of Kandy.

TAKING THE PORTUGUESE TO KOTTE

When the first Portuguese arrived on the coast of Sri Lanka, they were invited to present themselves to the king of Kotte, who was understandably intrigued by these strange foreigners. A delegation was prepared and dispatched to meet the king. However, before they could do so, the king's messengers, in order to disguise the smallness of their kingdom and the fact that the royal capital lay a mere 13km inland, led the Portuguese on a convoluted three-day march around the coastal regions in a vain attempt to delude them into believing the kingdom of Kotte a much grander affair than it actually was. Sadly, the Portuguese saw straight through this attempted subterfuge, but despite the failure of the attempt, the expression "**Taking the Portuguese to Kotte**" remains to this day a Sri Lankan euphemism for double-dealing of all kinds.

---

control of much of Kotte, while a series of northwards expeditions were also launched, culminating in the conquest of the kingdom of Jaffna in 1619. The Portuguese continued to expand their control, annexing the lower reaches of the central highlands, the east-coast ports of Trincomalee and Batticaloa, and eventually gaining control over the entire island except for the kingdom of Kandy in the central highlands.

Portuguese rule largely retained the traditional Sinhalese systems of caste and tribute, using local officials from the Sinhalese nobility who were loyal to the incomers; however, all tribute that had been due to the Sinhalese kings was now taken by the Portuguese, including a monopoly in elephants and cinnamon, and control of the lucrative trade in pepper and betel nuts. Even so, the burdens they placed upon the island's inhabitants led to hardship and popular hostility.

Portuguese rule was also marked by intense Roman Catholic **missionary activity**. Missionary orders were lavishly endowed, often using funds appropriated from Buddhist and Hindu temples, while members of the landed aristocracy embraced Christianity and took Portuguese surnames – the ancestors of the thousands of de Silvas, de Zoysas, Fernandos and Pereiras who still fill the telephone directories of modern Sri Lanka. Many coastal communities underwent mass conversion, particularly around Jaffna, Mannar and along the coast north of Colombo. Surnames and religion apart, hardly any physical evidence remains of Portuguese rule – virtually all their modest houses, churches and forts were subsequently rebuilt or knocked down by the Dutch or the British.

The Kandyan kingdom and the arrival of the Dutch

The origins of the Kingdom of **Kandy**, situated in the remote and rugged hill country at the heart of the island, date back to the fourteenth century (see page 207). By the time the Portuguese arrived, it had developed into one of the island's three main kingdoms, along with Kotte and Jaffna. The Portuguese first turned their attention to Kandy in 1591, though their attempt to place a puppet ruler on the throne was thwarted by an ambitious Sinhalese nobleman sent to accompany the Portuguese nominee, who enthroned himself instead, proclaiming independence from the Portuguese and taking the name of **Vimala Dharma Suriya**. Using guerrilla tactics, Vimala Dharma Suriya routed a Portuguese attack in 1594, as well as subsequent attacks in 1611, 1629 and 1638.

1602	1630	1638–40	1652
First Dutch emissaries arrive in island, meeting with king of Kandy.	Kandyans attack Colombo and Galle but are eventually driven off.	Dutch begin attacking and driving Portuguese out of their coastal strongholds.	Dutch resume attacks against Portuguese in alliance with Kandyans.

Realizing he couldn't drive the Portuguese out of Sri Lanka without sea power, Dharma Suriya saw the arrival of the **Dutch**, who had had their eyes on the island for a number of years, as an opportunity to gain naval support against his adversaries. Dutch envoys met Dharma Suriya in 1602 and determined upon a joint attack against the Portuguese. At least that was the plan. The Dutch leader, Admiral Sebald de Weert, invited the king to come back to the coast and inspect his ships. Dharma Suriya demurred, replying that he was reluctant to leave his queen, Dona Caterina, alone. De Weert, who appears to have been somewhat the worse for drink, replied that from what he had heard the queen was unlikely to be alone for long, whereupon he and his companions were, perhaps not surprisingly, hacked to death.

Despite this unfortunate turn of events, Dharma Suriya's successor, **Senarat**, continued to seek Dutch support. The Dutch again promised military help, though in the event they were unable to provide it and the king turned instead to the Danes, who dispatched an expedition, though by the time it arrived Senarat had concluded a peace agreement with the Portuguese (the tardy Danes instead founded a colony on the Coromandel coast of India). The truce was short-lived, however, and in 1630 the Kandyans invaded Portuguese territory, laying siege to Colombo and Galle, though again their lack of sea power prevented them from dislodging the Portuguese permanently.

The Dutch seize control

In 1635, Senarat was succeeded by his son **Rajasinha II**. The new king once again sent emissaries to the Dutch, who arrived in Sri Lanka with a fleet of ships and began attacking Portuguese positions. Between 1638 and 1640 they drove the Portuguese out of a number of important coastal towns, but refused to hand over their conquests to Rajasinha, saying they had not been paid their expenses. The king of Kandy was still waiting when, in 1640, the offensive against the Portuguese was temporarily halted by a truce declared in Europe between the United Provinces of the Netherlands and Spain, which at that time ruled Portugal and its overseas possessions.

Fighting eventually resumed in 1652. The Kandyans launched attacks on Portuguese positions in the interior, pushing them back to their coastal strongholds despite fierce resistance. The Dutch, meanwhile, laid siege to Colombo by sea and land, and in May 1656 the Portuguese finally surrendered the city to the Dutch, who promptly shut the Kandyans out of its gates. Faced with this duplicity, Rajasinha torched the lands around Colombo and then withdrew back to the hills. Despite this loss of local support, the Dutch continued to drive the Portuguese from the island, attacking Portuguese strongholds in northern Sri Lanka until, with the conquest of Jaffna in 1658, they had replaced the Portuguese as masters of coastal Sri Lanka.

Compared with the Portuguese, the Dutch were less interested in saving souls than in making money. Even so, the early years of **Dutch rule** did see an enthusiastic effort to spread the Reformed Calvinist faith in Sri Lanka. Roman Catholicism was declared illegal, and its priests banned from the country; Catholic churches were given to the Reformed faith, and many Sinhalese and Tamil Catholics nominally embraced Protestantism. Meanwhile, the Dutch tried to promote trade with neighbouring countries, though these efforts were stifled by the strict monopolies that they maintained in the lucrative export markets of cinnamon, elephants, pearls and betel nuts.

1656	1658	1794
Dutch capture Colombo from Portuguese. Beginning of Dutch rule.	Dutch take Jaffna from Portuguese and consolidate hold over much of island.	British East India Company forces occupy Dutch territory following fall of Netherlands to the French in Europe.

Their most lasting contributions to Sri Lanka, however, can be seen in the nation's cuisine, culture and architecture. The Dutch are credited with the invention of the popular dish of *lamprais* (see page 39), while the classic Sri Lankan rice and curry spread may also have been inspired by the *rijsttafel* (literally "rice table"), an elaborate type of meal created by the Dutch in Indonesia and comprising numerous contrasting dishes accompanied by rice. They also brought several classic Southeast Asian fruits such as durian, mangosteen and rambutan from their colonies in the Dutch East Indies (modern-day Indonesia), from where they also imported the stitched sarong and the art of batik-making. In architecture they established the style of colonial villa – with shady interior courtyards and huge, pillared verandas – which is still widely employed to this day, and which can be seen at its finest in the magnificent old fort at **Galle**, the Sri Lankan Dutch colonial town par excellence. Dutch settlers stayed in Sri Lanka even after they had lost control of the island to the British (see below), and their descendants – the so-called **Burghers** (see box, page 144) – remain a small but significant element in the nation's life right up to the present day.

The arrival of the British

The French Revolution initiated a major shake-up in relations between the leading European powers. When the Netherlands fell to the French in 1794, the **British East India Company**'s forces occupied Sri Lanka, having already for some time coveted the magnificent natural harbour at Trincomalee. In theory, the British were meant to be protecting Dutch territory against the French, though the forgivably suspicious Dutch mounted a half-hearted resistance before surrendering the island to their British "protectors" in 1796. Despite the supposedly temporary nature of the British administration, the new colonists soon began to appreciate Sri Lanka's strategic and commercial value, and quickly moved to make their hold on the island permanent, and, in 1802, Sri Lanka was ceded to Britain under the Treaty of Amiens with France.

One of the priorities of the new colonizers was to subdue the Kandyan kingdom and finally unify the island under a single rule. The British launched a disastrous expedition against the kingdom in 1803, but it wasn't until 1815 that they finally achieved their end, when the Kandyans – enraged by the megalomaniac behaviour of their king, Sri Wickrama Rajasinha – simply stood to one side and allowed British soldiers to march in and occupy the city. After two centuries of spirited resistance, the last bastion of Sri Lankan independence had finally been extinguished.

Though reluctant to upset traditional Sinhalese institutions, the British abolished slavery, relieved native officials of judicial authority and relaxed the system of compulsory-service tenure. Agriculture was encouraged, and production of cinnamon, pepper, sugar cane, cotton and coffee flourished. Internal communications were extended, Christian missions dispatched and restrictions on European ownership of land lifted. English became the official language of government and the medium of instruction in schools. In addition, the British quickly opened up the island's economy, abolishing all state monopolies. Crown land was sold off cheaply to encourage the establishment of new plantations, and capital flowed in. The most notable result of these changes was the spectacular growth in the island's **coffee** production from around 1830 to 1870. As the area under cultivation for coffee expanded, so new roads, rail

1802	1815	1820s
Sri Lanka ceded to British under Treaty of Amiens.	Fall of Kandy, the last independent Sinhalese kingdom; British rule extended across entire island.	Construction of first road linking Kandy to the coast

lines and port facilities were constructed to service the industry, while indentured labourers from southern India begin arriving in large numbers to make good the island's labour shortage – almost a million arrived between 1843 and 1859. In the 1870s, however, the island's coffee production was destroyed by a leaf disease. The void was soon filled by the introduction of **tea** (see page 445), with plantations quickly spreading around the slopes of the central highlands, while rubber and coconuts also acquired increasing importance.

The rise of nationalism

Sri Lanka's traumatic encounters with European colonial powers led to a major re-evaluation of its own traditional culture. In the nineteenth century, revivalist Buddhist and Hindu movements sprang up, with the aim both of modernizing native institutions in the face of the Western onslaught, and of defending the island's traditional culture against missionary Christianity. The major figure in this movement was the charismatic David Hewavitharane (1864–1933), who subsequently adopted the name **Anagarika Dharmapala** ("Protector of the Dharma") upon committing himself to a life of Buddhist activism – almost every town in Sri Lanka now has a road named after him. Dharmapala campaigned tirelessly for Buddhist rights and recognition, receiving unexpected support from the maverick American theosophist **Henry Steel Olcott** (see page 73). Gradually, this burgeoning **nationalist consciousness** acquired a political dimension. Grass-roots organizations began to demand greater Sri Lankan participation in government, though the uncoordinated nature of these protests meant they were easily ignored by the government – even so, **constitutional reforms** passed in 1910 made the small concession of allowing a limited number of "educated" Sri Lankans to elect one member to the government's Legislative Council.

During World War I, the forces of nationalism gathered momentum. British arrests of prominent Sinhalese leaders after minor civil disturbances in 1915 provoked widespread opposition, leading in 1919 to the foundation of the **Ceylon National Congress**, which united both Sinhalese and Tamil organizations and drafted proposals for constitutional reforms. Concessions slowly followed, and in 1931 a new constitution gave the island's leaders the chance to exercise political power and gain legislative experience, with a view towards eventual self-government. In addition, the new constitution granted universal franchise, bringing all Sri Lankans into the political process for the first time, and making the country the first Asian colony to achieve universal suffrage.

During **World War II**, Sri Lankan nationalist leaders supported the British war effort while continuing to lobby for full independence. When Singapore, Indonesia and Burma fell to the Japanese, Sri Lanka suddenly found itself close to the front line of the war in the east, a fact brought home by Japanese bombing raids against Colombo and Trincomalee (during which a number of British warships were sunk). By the end of 1942, Sri Lanka had become the major base of British operations in Asia. Lord Mountbatten established his South East Asia Command headquarters at Kandy, while Trincomalee hosted a wing of the Special Operations Executive, which launched saboteurs and resistance coordinators behind Japanese lines.

1870s	1880	1910
Collapse of coffee industry and beginning of tea production; thousands of Tamil immigrants arrive to work on the new plantations.	Arrival of Henry Steel Olcott and Madame Blavatsky, who champion Buddhist causes as part of islandwide Buddhist revival.	Constitutional reforms allow election of one Sri Lankan member to government's Legislative Council.

Independence

Sri Lanka's long-awaited **independence** finally came on February 4, 1948, with power passing from the British to the **United National Party** (**UNP**), under the leadership of D.S. Senanayake. The essentially conservative UNP was dominated by the English-educated leaders of the colonial era, though it did include people from all the country's ethno-linguistic groups.

The first years of independence were kind to Sri Lanka: exports were doing well in world markets, there was a sizeable sterling balance earned during the war, while the island even came close to eradicating malaria. There were, however, some basic weaknesses. The ruling parties largely represented the views of the island's English-educated, Westernized elite – an ideology that most of the population found incomprehensible or irrelevant. In addition, **economic difficulties** began gradually to emerge. Falling rubber and tea prices on the world markets, rises in the cost of imported food and a rapidly increasing population ate quickly into the country's foreign exchange, while the expanded school system produced large numbers of educated persons unable to find suitable employment. Meanwhile, Tamil plantation workers found themselves suddenly disenfranchised by the UNP (conveniently so, given that they largely voted for their own, sectarian, Tamil parties). The Senanayake government insisted on classifying the **Plantation Tamils** as "foreigners", even if they had been living on the island for generations, and attempted to repatriate them to India, an episode that tarnished relations between the two countries for years.

In 1952, D.S. Senanayake died after being thrown from his horse on Galle Face Green in Colombo and was briefly succeeded by his son, Dudley Senanayake, though he was forced to resign following disastrous attempts to cut rice subsidies, an act that provoked widespread strikes and rioting. In 1953, he was succeeded by his uncle, **John Kotelawala**, a bout of nepotism that earned the UNP the name of the "Uncle Nephew Party".

The Bandaranaikes

As the 1950s progressed, the UNP's Westernized and elitist political leaders proved increasingly out of touch with the views and aspirations of the majority of the island's population. In the elections of 1956, the UNP lost to the socialist-nationalist **Sri Lanka Freedom Party** (**SLFP**) under the leadership of the charismatic **S.W.R.D. Bandaranaike**, ushering in an extraordinary dynastic sequence in which power alternated between various members of the Senanayake clan (through the guise of the UNP), and assorted Bandaranaikes (through various incarnations of the SLFP).

The new government immediately set about changing the country's political landscape, instigating a huge programme of nationalization, making Sinhala the sole official language and instigating state support for the Buddhist faith and Sinhalese culture, largely in reaction to the Anglo-Christian values foisted upon the land by the British. Bandaranaike's new policies had the unfortunate side effect of stoking the fires of ethnic and religious tension. His language policy alienated the Tamils, his educational policies outraged the small but influential Christian community, while even factions among the Sinhalese communities were disturbed by his cultural and religious reforms. As passions grew, the island experienced its first major **ethnic riots**, in May 1958. Tamils were driven from Colombo and other

1919	1931	1942
First national political party, the Ceylon National Congress, founded.	New constitution devolves limited political power to local leaders and grants universal suffrage to all Sri Lankans.	Sri Lanka becomes major base of operations for British war effort in Southern Asia; Japanese air force attacks Trincomalee.

places where they had traditionally lived alongside the Sinhalese, while Sinhalese in turn fled from Tamil areas in the north and east. In September 1959, Bandaranaike opened **talks with the Tamils** in an attempt to calm the situation, and was promptly assassinated by a militant Buddhist monk – not the first or last time the island's Buddhist clergy would play a role in stoking up religious intolerance on the island.

Bandaranaike was succeeded by his widow, Sirimavo – or **Mrs Bandaranaike**, as she is usually known – who thus became the world's first-ever female prime minister. Mrs Bandaranaike's government continued to implement the policies of Sinhalese nationalism: all private schools were nationalized in an attempt to neutralize the influence of Christian missions in the educational system, while important national industries were also taken over by the state; in addition, she had half a million Plantation Tamils deported to India. Despite her symbolic importance for women worldwide, Mrs Bandaranaike was less appreciated at home, and had to survive an attempted coup before being finally trounced at the polls in 1965 by the UNP, who returned to power under **Dudley Senanayake**, with the emphasis once again on private enterprise and economic stability.

The JVP and the road to civil war

The Sri Lankan electorate's habit of kicking out whichever party happened to be in power repeated itself in the **1970 elections**, when the UNP were defeated and the irrepressible Mrs Bandaranaike once again became prime minister at the head of a new SLFP-led coalition, the **United Front**. The interminable yo-yoing between parties and policies thus continued, with Mrs Bandaranaike reversing the policies of the UNP and resuming her old aims of restricting private enterprise and increasing nationalization of key industries, while introducing policies aimed at reducing social inequality via an ambitious programme of land reform. Her government also ditched a further memento of the island's colonial past by changing its **name** from Ceylon to Sri Lanka (see page 416).

Though these measures appeased the island's underprivileged, they did nothing to address basic economic problems such as the mounting trade deficit. The country's youth, impatient for radical change, expressed their discontent through the extreme left-wing and anti-Tamil **JVP** (Janatha Vimukthi Peramuna, or People's Liberation Front). In 1971, the JVP launched an armed rebellion with the aim of overthrowing the government, but despite brief successes, the insurrection was easily and ruthlessly suppressed by the army, with thousands of the poorly organized rebels (mainly students) losing their lives. Meanwhile, Sri Lanka's **economic decline** continued, and the immense power held by the state provided the party in power with the opportunity for patronage, nepotism and corruption. Mrs Bandaranaike continued her nationalization programme, seizing hold of tea estates and private agricultural lands, two of the few areas of the economy that were still functioning successfully. By 1977, unemployment had risen to about fifteen percent.

The LTTE and civil war

In June 1977, the United Front was defeated by a reinvigorated UNP under the leadership of **J.R. Jayawardene**, who became the first non-Senanayake to control the

1948	1952	1953
Sri Lanka attains independence; D.S. Senanayake becomes prime minister at head of United National Party (UNP).	D.S. Senanayake dies following riding accident and is succeeded by his son, Dudley Senanayake.	S.W.R.D. Bandaranaike becomes prime minister at head of new Sri Lanka Freedom Party.

UNP. Jayawardene immediately began to tamper with the democratic process, however, writing yet another new constitution in 1978 that gave the country's president (previously an essentially ceremonial role) new powers. In the same year, Jayawardene resigned as prime minister and was promptly elected the country's first president (and re-elected in 1982, after further tinkering with the constitution).

The Jayawardene government again tried to revitalize the private sector and attract back some of the foreign capital driven away by Mrs Bandaranaike. These policies enjoyed some success: by 1983, unemployment had been halved, while the island became self-sufficient in rice by 1985. Meanwhile tourism and expatriate Sri Lankans working in the Middle East brought in valuable foreign currency, though these gains were undercut by rampant inflation, unstable tea and rubber prices and, most seriously, by the country's descent into **civil war**.

The origins of this latest Sinhalese–Tamil conflict had first been sparked in the early 1970s via new legislation designed to cut the number of Tamil places at the country's universities, while the new constitution of 1972 further aggravated Tamil sensibilities by declaring Buddhism to hold the "foremost place" among the island's religions. These measures provoked growing unrest amongst Sri Lanka's Tamils, culminating in a **state of emergency** that was imposed on northern areas of the island for several years from 1971. Since the police and army who enforced this state of emergency included few Tamils (one result of the constitution's insistence that only Sinhala speakers be allowed to occupy official posts), and were often undisciplined and heavy-handed, they were increasingly seen by the Tamils as an occupying force.

The rise of the Tigers

By the mid-1970s some young Tamils had begun to resort to violence, calling for an independent Tamil state, **Eelam** ("Precious Land"). Tamil bases were established in jungle areas of northern and eastern Sri Lanka, as well as in the southern districts of the Indian state of Tamil Nadu, where Tamil groups received considerable support. A number of militant groups emerged, most notably the **LTTE**, or Liberation Tigers of Tamil Eelam, popularly known as the **Tamil Tigers** (see page 384). Founded in 1976, the LTTE rapidly established a reputation for violence and ruthlessness under their elusive leader, **Velupillai Prabhakaran**, consolidating themselves as the leaders of the resistance struggle thanks to their repeated attacks against Sinhalese government forces and also to their murderous suppression of rival Tamil groups.

Despite limited **reforms** – such as the promotion of Tamil to the status of a "national language" to be used in official business in Tamil areas – violence continued to escalate in the north. The point of no return arrived in 1983, following the ambush and massacre of an army patrol by a group of Tamil Tiger guerrillas near Jaffna. For several weeks afterwards – a period subsequently christened "**Black July**" – Sinhalese mobs rampaged across the south, indiscriminately killing Tamils and looting and destroying their shops and houses. As many as two thousand Tamils were murdered during these weeks, while some Tamil-majority areas, notably Colombo's Pettah district, were reduced to rubble.

The government, police and army, meanwhile, showed themselves singularly unable – or unwilling – to stop the violence. Tens of thousands of Tamils fled to the north of the island, while many others left the country altogether. Equally, Sinhalese started to

1958	1959	1965
Anti-Tamil riots convulse island.	S.W.R.D. Bandaranaike is assassinated by a Buddhist monk; his widow, Sirimavo Bandaranaike, succeeds him, becoming the world's first female prime minister.	UNP returns to power under Dudley Senanayake.

SRI LANKA OR CEYLON?

The origins of Sri Lanka's colonial name, **Ceylon**, stretch back to the island's ancient Sanskrit name of Sinhaladvipa, meaning the land (*dvipa*) of the Sinhala tribe. In the classical Buddhist language of Pali, Sinhala is Sihalam, pronounced "Silam", which mutated over the centuries into the Portuguese Ceilão, and thence into the Dutch Zeylan and the British Ceylon. Arab traders, meanwhile, transformed Sihalam into Serendib (or Serendip), the root of the English word "serendipity" (or the making of fortuitous discoveries by accident), coined in the eighteenth century by the English man of letters Horace Walpole, inspired by a Persian fairy tale, "The Three Princes of Serendip".

Not that this was the only name by which the island was known overseas. The Greeks and Romans had previously called the island **Taprobane**, derived from another ancient Sanskrit name for the island, Tambapanni, after the copper-coloured beach on which Prince Vijaya and his followers (see page 403) are claimed to have first landed. The island's own inhabitants, however, have always known the island by a different name entirely: in Sinhalese, **Lanka**, and in Tamil as **Ilankai**. The reversion from the British colonial Ceylon to the indigenous **Sri Lanka** (or, to be precise, the Democratic Socialist Republic of Sri Lanka) was finally made in 1972 – the additional "Sri" is Sinhalese for "auspicious" or "resplendent".

move out of Jaffna and other Tamil areas. In the following years, violence continued to escalate, with several massacres, including a notorious attack at Anuradhapura in May 1985, when 150 mainly Sinhalese victims were gunned down by the LTTE at one of the symbolic centres of the island's Buddhist culture. Both sides were routinely accused of torture, intimidation and disappearances.

The government's offer, in the mid-1980s, of **limited Tamil self-government** proved to be too little and too late. By the end of 1985, fighting between Sri Lankan government forces and the LTTE had spread across the north and down the east coast, while fighting between Tamils and the east coast's large Muslim population also flared up. War had a devastating effect on the economy. Tourism slumped, military spending rose and aid donors threatened to cut money as a result of human rights abuses. And, to add to the country's woes, tea prices collapsed.

The Indian Peace Keeping Force

In 1987, government forces succeeded in pushing the LTTE back to Jaffna, prompting a further exodus of Tamil refugees to India. The Indian government (for whom the fate of the Sri Lankan Tamils has always been a sensitive issue, given the massive number of Tamils in its own country) began supplying food by air and sea to the beleaguered Tamils, leading to clashes between the Indian and Sri Lankan navies. In the same year, President Jayawardene came to an arrangement with India whereby the government pledged that the Sri Lankan Army would hand its positions over to an **Indian Peace Keeping Force**, or **IPKF**, whose aim would be to disarm the Tamil rebels and maintain peace in the north and east.

The deal attracted opposition from all quarters, including Muslims and the LTTE, and provoked riots in Colombo among Sinhalese, who saw the Indian presence in the north as a threat to national sovereignty and a latter-day re-enactment of previous

1970	1971	1972
Sirimavo Bandaranaike returns to power.	JVP insurrection, ruthlessly surpressed by government forces. State of emergency declared in Tamil areas in the north.	Name of country changed from Ceylon to Sri Lanka.

ndian invasions. In the event, the Indian army's hopes of simply keeping the peace roved to be purest fantasy. No sooner had they arrived than they became embroiled n clashes with the LTTE, which soon escalated into full-scale war, culminating in the loody siege and capture of Jaffna itself.

Then, in 1987–88, a second **JVP rebellion** broke out in the south of the island, aunching a series of strikes and political assassinations which terrorized the inhabitants f the highlands and crippled the economy. At the end of 1988, President Jayawardene etired, and the new UNP leader, **Ranasinghe Premadasa**, defeated the indefatigable Mrs Bandaranaike in new presidential elections. Premadasa was a new thing in ri Lankan politics: a low-caste boy made good, who had grown up in a shack in Colombo and who introduced a blast of fresh air into the insular world of island olitics. Premadasa promised to end the fighting against both the JVP and the LTTE nd succeeded at least in the first pledge. When the JVP refused to lay down its rms, Premadasa sent out paramilitary death squads, which went about the country ssassinating suspected JVP activists. By the end of 1989, most JVP leaders were dead r in prison, while thousands of their sympathizers disappeared amid an international uman rights outcry. Some estimates put the number of those killed in the insurrection s high as seventeen thousand.

The IPKF, meanwhile, remained in an impossible position. Despite the Indians' aving managed to contain the LTTE, Sinhalese nationalists were vociferous in emanding that the IPKF leave the country. The LTTE themselves, who had suffered o greatly at their hands, agreed a ceasefire in the hope of seeing the back of them, and he IPKF finally pulled out in March 1990. At their height they had numbered some ighty thousand soldiers, a thousand of whom had died in the fighting.

The 1990s

he fact that a home-grown guerrilla organization like the LTTE had been able to urvive a massive offensive by the world's second-largest army enormously enhanced its wn sense of power and self-confidence, and no sooner had the IPKF withdrawn than resumed hostilities against the Sri Lankan government – a new phase of the conflict ften referred to as "**Eelam War II**". By the end of 1990, the LTTE had recaptured nuch of the north, though the east was back under government control. This new war eached a peak in mid-1991 with a series of battles around Jaffna, while the LTTE's nfluence also reached into India itself, where they assassinated India's former prime ninister, Rajiv Gandhi, using a new and deadly weapon – the **suicide bomber**. In nid-1992, a major new assault against the LTTE was launched by the Sri Lankan Army, coupled with a long-overdue attempt to rebuild relations with terrorized Tamil ivilians. By this time, tens of thousands had died in the conflict, while 700,000 people ad been displaced, including 200,000 Sri Lankan Tamils who had fled to Tamil Nadu n India, about half of whom were living in refugee camps.

In 1993, President Premadasa became the first Sri Lankan head of state to be ssassinated, blown up by another suicide bomber – the LTTE, though suspected, ever claimed responsibility. At around the same time, **Chandrika Bandaranaike umaratunga**, the daughter of S.W.R.D. and Sirimavo Bandaranaike, gained leadership f the SLFP (it was around this time that people began referring to the SLFP as the

975 onwards	1977	1978
mergence of Tamil militant roups in the north, most otably the LTTE (Tamil gers).	UNP returns to power under leadership of J.R. Jayawardene who rewrites constitution to enhance presidential powers.	J.R. Jayawardene elected president.

"Sri Lanka Family Party"). Following her election victory in 1994 at the head of the SLFP-dominated **People's Alliance (PA)** coalition, Kumaratunga became Sri Lanka's first female president. One of her first acts was to appoint her mother prime minister, thus continuing the clannishness that had marked the country's politics since the early days of independence.

The new PA was largely unrecognizable from the old SLFP, having abandoned Sinhalese nationalism and pseudo-socialism in favour of national reconciliation and free-market economics. The PA's principal pledge was to end the civil war, but Kumaratunga's attempts to negotiate with the LTTE in 1995 soon broke down, leading to a new round of fighting – "**Eelam War III**" – involving renewed attacks against LTTE positions followed by retaliatory LTTE **bomb attacks**, most notably the devastating strikes against the Central Bank in Colombo in 1996 and the Temple of the Tooth in Kandy in 1998. Thousands of troops were dispatched to the Jaffna Peninsula, while Jaffna itself was taken by the Sri Lankan Army in December 1995; further major offensives against the LTTE followed in 1997 and 1998. In December 1999, shortly before new presidential elections, Kumaratunga survived an assassination attempt, though she was blinded in one eye. A few days later, she was re-elected president for a second term.

Despite her electoral success, Kumaratunga was unable to make any steps towards a lasting peace. In addition, her policy of trying to negotiate from a position of military strength received a huge blow in April 2000 when the LTTE captured the strategic **Elephant Pass** – perhaps their greatest military success of the entire conflict. A year later, in July 2001, LTTE suicide bombers led a daring raid against the **international airport**, destroying half of SriLankan Airlines' fleet. The pictures of bombed-out planes and eyewitness accounts by hapless holiday-makers caught in the crossfire made headline news around the globe, and had a predictably disastrous effect on the country's already fragile tourist industry.

The ceasefire

In October 2001, Kumaratunga dissolved parliament just before a no-confidence vote which her PA coalition looked likely to lose. In the ensuing **elections of December 2001**, the UNP won a narrow victory under the leadership of **Ranil Wickremasinghe**, meaning that for the first time Sri Lanka's prime minister and president came from different parties. Wickremasinghe had made an end to the civil war central to his candidacy, and he quickly moved to open **negotiations with the LTTE**, mediated by diplomats from Norway – who had previously played a key role in securing the famous peace deal between Israel and the Palestinians in 1993. The timing for talks seemed propitious. Both the Tamil and Sinhalese people had become intensely war-weary, while Wickremasinghe's conciliatory approach was also an important factor. In addition, events of September 11 and the subsequent US-led "War on Terror" threatened to cut off international funding for the LTTE, who had recently been proscribed as a terrorist organization by many countries, including the US and UK.

In December 2001, the LTTE declared a temporary **ceasefire**, which was made permanent in February 2002. Events thereafter moved with unexpected swiftness: decommissioning of weapons began; the road connecting Jaffna to the rest of the island

1983	1985	1987
Black July, during which thousands of Tamil civilians massacred and Tamil communities devastated in the south by Sinhalese mobs.	LTTE massacre of 150 civilians at Anuradhapura; fighting between government forces and LTTE spreads across north and east.	Arrival of Indian Peace Keeping Force in the north amid widespread opposition; Jaffna captured after intense fighting.

was reopened; and in September 2002 the government lifted its ban on the LTTE. The initial stages of the peace process proved hugely positive, but despite early successes, the inevitable **problems** began to emerge during the latter part of 2002 and 2003. President Kumaratunga became an increasingly vociferous critic of the peace process, claiming that the government was making too many concessions to the Tamils and accusing the Norwegian mediators of bias – including one famous outburst during which she labelled them "salmon-eating busy-bodies". Sporadic clashes between the LTTE and the Sri Lankan Army, as well as serious civilian conflicts between Tamils and Muslims in the east of the country, were seen by Kumaratunga and her allies as evidence that the LTTE was simply using the peace process as a cover under which to regroup and rearm. In April 2003, against a background of increasing political uncertainty and arguments over the implementation of the peace process, the LTTE pulled out of talks. Meanwhile the government itself was in increasing disarray thanks to growing conflict between president Kumaratunga and prime minster Wickremasinghe, culminating in Kumaratunga declaring a state of emergency in late 2003.

With the peace process paralysed and the government in limbo, fresh **parliamentary elections** were called for April 2004, won by the SLFP-led **United People's Freedom Alliance (UPFA)**, partnered with the newly respectable JVP (Kumaratunga thus found herself sharing power with the people who had assassinated her husband, the popular actor-turned-politician Vijaya Kumaratunga, in 1988). The populist southern politician **Mahinda Rajapakse** was appointed prime minister.

Despite the change of government, the peace process, which had already stumbled under Wickremasinghe, became completely stalled under Rajapakse. Although both sides paid lip service to the agreement, growing violence in the east between the Sri Lankan military, the LTTE and the remains of Colonel Karuna's forces suggested that a return to all-out war was simply a matter of time.

The tsunami

The country's deteriorating political situation, however, was suddenly and dramatically overshadowed by a far more immediate and tragic natural disaster. Early on the morning of December 26, 2004, a sub-oceanic earthquake off the coast of Indonesia generated a massive **tsunami** which, radiating outwards in all directions, caused havoc along the coastlines of countries around the Indian Ocean as far apart as Malaysia and Tanzania, and which wrought particular devastation in Sri Lanka, with three-quarters of the island's coastline reduced to a rubble of collapsed houses, smashed boats and wrecked vehicles. Over forty thousand people were killed and a million displaced from their homes, while thousands of buildings were destroyed, along with at least half the island's fishing boats and significant sections of road and rail line – the total damage was estimated at well over a billion dollars. The only good news was that, mercifully, Colombo itself was largely untouched.

The scale of the devastation was astonishing, although the massive **international response** to the event was heartening. Sadly, the Sri Lankan government itself appeared to contribute very little to the frantic global relief effort. Few Sri Lankans received anything more than token insurance payouts, while even fewer received direct government aid, despite the millions of dollars pouring into the country.

987–89	1988	1990
Second JVP insurrection brings chaos to the south; thousands die during ensuing fighting.	Ranasinghe Premadasa of UNP elected president.	Indian Peace Keeping Force withdraws from Sri Lanka. LTTE retake Jaffna.

Post-tsunami reconstruction efforts were also considerably hindered by **worsening violence** in the east and north of the country. Periodic clashes between the Sri Lankan military and the LTTE continued throughout 2005, while August saw the assassinatio by the LTTE of one of the country's most respected politicians, Foreign Minister **Lakshman Kadirgamar**, another Tamil who had consistently fought against the LTTE.

The presidency of **Chandrika Kumaratunga**, the woman who had dominated Sri Lankan politics for a decade, thus stumbled towards a messy and unsatisfactory conclusion. In July 2005, incumbent prime minister Mahinda Rajapakse was chosen as the SLFP's presidential candidate and successor to Kumaratunga in the forthcoming elections.

The Rajapakse era

The **presidential elections of November 2005** were widely seen as one of the most important in Sri Lankan history: effectively a head-to-head between the former prime minister **Ranil Wickremasinghe**, the business-minded and peace-oriented UNP leader who had brokered the original ceasefire in 2002 and the populist, nationalist SLFP prime minister **Mahinda Rajapakse**. The choice appeared clear: between a Westernized liberal candidate committed to the ongoing peace process, and a populist Sinhalese demagogue who was likely to tip the island back into civil war. Shortly before the election, Rajapakse signed a controversial agreement with the JVP. In return for their backing, Rajapakse agreed to refuse the LTTE the right to share aid and promised to remove the Norwegians from their role as mediators in the peace process. He also committed himself to reviewing (and potentially revoking) the ceasefire agreement and perhaps most importantly, to denying the possibility of self-rule under a federal system for the north and east – a stridently confrontational, anti-Tamil agenda that drew howls of protest even from members of his own party, including outgoing president Chandrika Kumaratunga.

In the event, Rajapakse triumphed over Wickremasinghe by the narrowest of margin assisted by an **LTTE-imposed boycott** that ensured that none of the Tamils living in LTTE-controlled areas or the Jaffna Peninsula was able to vote (the only person who did his hand cut off). The loss of these votes – which would traditionally have gon to Wickremasinghe – almost certainly cost him the presidency, although the reasons for the LTTE boycott remain unclear. One theory is that they wished completely to dissociate themselves from the Sinhalese electoral process; another, and more sinister, explanation is that in helping Rajapakse to power, they increased the possibility of an early return to hostilities, which many people believe was their objective all along.

Rajapakse's election was followed, unsurprisingly, by a massive **upsurge in violence** in the north and east, with a spate of landmine and bomb attacks, mainly aimed at SLA personnel. Violence continued apace against both military and civilian targets, with massacres of non-combatants on both sides of the ethnic divide and repeated bomb attacks against buses, markets and other unprotected targets claiming hundreds of live By early 2006, the general consensus was that although the ceasefire might still exist on paper, in reality, the north and east of the country had returned to a state of undeclare civil war.

1991	1993	1994
Continued fighting between government forces and LTTE; LTTE suicide bomber assassinates former Indian premier Rajiv Gandhi in Tamil Nadu.	President Premadasa assassinated by LTTE suicide bomber in Colombo.	Chandrika Bandaranaike Kumaratunga elected Sri Lanka's fir female president at head of SLFP-le People's Alliance coalition.

ighting in the east...

he two sides were finally tipped back into full-scale war in July 2006, when the
igers closed the sluice gates of the **Mavil Oya reservoir**, in LTTE territory south
f Trincomalee, cutting off the water supply to thousands of villages further down
he river in government-held areas. Heavy fighting ensued, as government forces
rst captured the reservoir itself, and then beat off large-scale LTTE assaults around
rincomalee, Mutur and the Jaffna Peninsula.

These sudden attacks heightened SLA fears about the vulnerability of Trincomalee
arbour to attack from nearby LTTE posts, and SLA forces set about driving the Tigers
om the town of **Sampur**, near Mutur. The LTTE launched inevitable retaliatory
ttacks, including a strike against Galle harbour, the furthest point south they had ever
entured. They also staged a notable coup in March 2007 when they launched their
rst-ever **air attack**, targeting the military airport adjoining the international airport
t Katunayake, apparently using small Czech-made light aircraft which had been
nuggled into the country piece by piece and then reassembled and fitted with home-
1ade bomb racks.

Following the capture of Sampur, the government began to talk openly about its
lan to drive the LTTE from the few remaining pockets of territory that they still held
1 the east. The SLA's next target was the town of **Vakarai**, about halfway between
atticaloa and Trincomalee – and the Tigers' last piece of eastern territory with direct
ccess to the sea. Heavy fighting and the displacement of thousands of civilians, many
f whom died in the clashes, ensued before the town was finally captured in January
007. The SLA followed this up with successful attacks against LTTE-held areas first
1 Ampara district and finally in Thoppigala region, northwest of Batticaloa. By July
007, the whole of eastern Sri Lanka was under government control for the first time
1 twenty years.

..and the north

ack **in the north**, clashes between the SLA and LTTE along the front lines dividing
heir respective territories had become an almost daily fact of life, with the SLA making
ome territorial gains during the later part of 2007.

The year **2008** began in ominous fashion: on January 2, the government officially
ulled out of the by-now derisory official ceasefire as if symbolically to clear the
ecks for a final assault on the LTTE. The SLA was now larger, more disciplined and
etter equipped and financed than perhaps at any time in its previous history, as well
s being backed by the implacable political will of Rajapakse and his hard-line allies
1 Colombo. At the same time, the LTTE's international reputation was becoming
1creasingly tarnished, while its sources of foreign funding and supply lines through
1dia and eastern Sri Lanka were being increasingly squeezed, or cut off entirely.

Despite setbacks, during the first half of 2008 the SLA began to advance slowly
ut steadily northwards into LTTE territory. By the middle of the year the army had
ecaptured the whole of the Mannar area. By October they had fought their way to
rithin two kilometres of the hugely symbolic town of Kilinochchi, the de facto capital
f the Tigers' independent northern regime. By November, a further wing of the
LA had succeeded in pushing up to Pooneryn, clearing the entire western coast of

995	**2000**
overnment–LTTE talks break down; renewed fighting north leads to capture of Jaffna by Sri Lankan Army; umaratunga re-elected president after narrowly urviving attempted assassination.	LTTE forces drive Sri Lankan Army out of strategic Elephant Pass.

LTTE fighters and reopening a land route between the Jaffna Peninsula and the rest of government-controlled Sri Lanka for the first time in decades.

The long-awaited **fall of Kilinochchi**, after months of intense fighting, finally occurred on January 2, 2009. Within a week the SLA had captured the strategically and symbolically important Elephant Pass, and by the end of the month had taken the east coast town of Mullaitivu, the last significant LTTE stronghold.

Meanwhile, tens of thousands of refugees had fled ahead of the advancing army, eventually reaching the sea near Mullaitivu, where they sought refuge inside a government-designated **no-fire zone**, encompassing an area of coast stretching for around 20km north of the town. Here they were soon joined by the LTTE's few surviving fighters, who also set up within the no-fire zone in preparation for a last stand against the SLA. The SLA, meanwhile, commenced shelling the area relentlessly, launching twenty to thirty major artillery attacks daily and indiscriminately killing thousands of the trapped and utterly defenceless civilians within. Those non-combatants who attempted to escape were either (according to different sources) shot down in cold blood by LTTE fighters defending the zone or killed (whether unintentionally or not) in crossfire between the warring parties. The end result was one of the most appalling civilian bloodbaths of modern history – estimates of the number killed are hotly contested but are likely to have been at least 30,000, possibly much higher.

This last enclave of LTTE territory finally fell in late May 2009, at which point Rajapakse triumphantly announced victory for the SLA and an end to all hostilities, capped off with news of the **death of Prabhakaran**, shot dead while attempting to escape from advancing government forces – finally putting an end to the famously elusive rebel leader who had almost single-handedly driven the LTTE through its three decades of bloody resistance.

After the war: Rajapakse vs Fonseka

Not surprisingly, the enormous human and financial cost of bringing the civil war to a close was felt in virtually every corner of Sri Lankan society, and despite the general mood of triumphalism, serious questions remained to be answered. Foremost among these were widespread allegations of **war crimes** by both LTTE and SLA forces during the conflict's closing stages. Serious concerns were raised by a range of governmental departments and NGOs, focusing particularly on the SLA's alleged shelling of the no-fire zone and the summary execution of surrendering LTTE cadres, as well as other civilians suspected of LTTE involvement. The Sri Lankan government staunchly rejected all such accusations, promising a full enquiry, although the committee it set up to investigate the allegations – the **Lessons Learnt and Reconciliation Commission** (LLRC) – was widely seen as a whitewash.

Allegations of war crimes aside, Rajapakse's first serious postwar challenge came from an entirely unexpected source. The **presidential elections of 2010** might have been considered a formality, given the recent successful conclusion of hostilities. Instead, Rajapakse found himself facing an unlikely opponent in the form of **General Sarath Fonseka**, the former supreme commander of the Sri Lankan Army – a national military hero who had played a crucial role in defeating the LTTE, and who had

2001	2002
LTTE suicide bombers destroy half the SriLankan Airlines fleet during attack on international airport. UNP win parliamentary elections, and Ranil Wickremasinghe becomes prime minister. LTTE declare ceasefire.	LTTE ceasefire declared permanent; beginnings of Norwegian-sponsored peace process. Road to Jaffna reopened.

previously enjoyed a close relationship with the president. In the event, Rajapakse won comfortably, with 57 percent of the vote versus 40 percent for Fonseka, although the victory was tainted by serious allegations of electoral malpractice, while the immediate post-election arrest and imprisonment of Fonseka himself for alleged "military offences" added further to the sense of disquiet.

A fresh round of **parliamentary elections**, held in April 2010, led to further government gains and a consolidation of Rajapakse's position against an opposition once again led by the increasingly toothless Ranil Wickremasinghe. Further constitutional amendments followed soon afterwards, allowing the country's president (previously restricted to two terms in office) to serve for an unlimited period – thus opening the possibility of Rajapakse becoming Sri Lanka's supreme ruler in perpetuity.

Peace and prejudice

Even before the war was concluded, Rajapakse had launched into a major bout of development aimed at transforming the island's infrastructure and economy. Foremost among these new projects was the construction of a **new international airport** (see page 25) and Chinese-sponsored **deep-water port** at Rajapakse's home town of Hambantota, as well as the controversial **Colombo Port City** (see page 77). The island's creaking infrastructure also enjoyed a long-overdue upgrade, headlined by the Southern Expressway motorway from Colombo to Galle and by the reopening of the railway lines to Jaffna and Mannar.

At the same time Rajapakse further extended his increasingly vice-like grip on national politics. Threats and violence against any journalists who dared speak out against the regime became routine (the January 2009 murder of the hugely respected *Sunday Leader* editor Lasantha Wickramatunga being the most flagrant example), while relations between the government and the Tamil community continued to be deeply strained. The government also turned a blind eye to (or possibly even sponsored) other expressions of rising **communal tension**. Churches in Hikkaduwa were attacked by a mob (allegedly including eight monks) in early 2014, while full-scale rioting erupted in mid-2014 after Buddhist hooligans attacked Muslims in Aluthgama and Beruwala, leaving several dead

Meanwhile, Rajapakse family members continued to monopolize positions of political and economic power, most notably Mahinda's brothers **Basil Rajapakse**, widely regarded as the Machiavellian power behind the throne (popularly known as "Mr Ten Percent" on account of the cut he allegedly took from every business deal passing across his desk), and **Gotabhaya Rajapakse**, a former army lieutenant-colonel turned Defense Secretary. Many other Rajapakse family members also held influential posts, including Speaker of Parliament, Chief Minister of Uva Province, Director and Chairman of SriLankan Airlines, and ambassadors to the USA and Russia.

Rajapakse vs Sirisena

Having rewritten the constitution to allow him to stand for a third presidential term, Mahinda Rajapakse – perhaps fearing his support was sliding away – called for surprise presidential elections in January 2015, nearly two years ahead of schedule. Despite his

2003	2004	2005
Increasing setbacks to peace process; LTTE pull out of talks, while Colonel Karuna leads breakaway faction of eastern LTTE forces.	Asian tsunami devastates island's coast.	Worsening violence in north and east; Mahinda Rajapakse elected president.

falling ratings it was assumed that his total control of the government, press, TV and army would provide him with a way of winning by whatever means, especially given that the opposition was struggling even to identify a credible presidential candidate.

The candidate finally surfaced in November 2014 in the unexpected shape of Health Minister **Maithripala Sirisena**, a leading government figure who split, virtually overnight, from long-time ally Rajapakse, declaring that Sri Lanka was heading toward a dictatorship which he had no alternative but to fight. The many disjointed opposition factions immediately threw their weight behind Sirisena, backed by an unlikely cross-section of political heavyweights including arch-liberal Ranil Wickremasinghe, the recently released General Fonseka and even former president Chandrika Kumaratunga.

Elections passed relatively calmly, despite widespread attempts at intimation by Rajapakse supporters. In the early hours of January 9 it was announced, to widespread shock, that Sirisena had scored 51 percent of the votes. Shortly afterwards, Mahinda Rajapakse **conceded defeat** with unexpected placidity, ending a decade in power – although it was subsequently alleged that he and Gotabhaya had attempted to get the army out to overturn the result in an impromptu coup before realizing the futility of their position.

A new era

The arrival of the pope on an official visit to Sri Lanka just a few days after Sirisena's election was widely seen as a sign of better – and more honest – times to come. Meanwhile Sirisena threw himself into making good on his many election promises, with Ranil Wickremasinghe as his new prime minister. Press censorship was lifted and work temporarily suspended on the controversial Colombo Port City and other Rajapakse-sponsored projects. Promises to reduce presidential powers and limit future incumbents to a maximum of two terms in office were also kept, with various powers being given back to parliament and the judiciary. Ordinary voters saw an immediate return thanks to wage increases and sizeable cuts in fuel and electricity prices. Numerous Rajapakse cronies were dismissed and a string of high-profile corruption charges launched.

Reforms, however, soon became increasingly bogged down by the island's still deeply confused political landscape. Pro-Rajapakse members of parliament had decamped to the opposition following Sirisena's victory, leaving his parliamentary deputy Wickremasinghe with a minority, and increasingly unable to push through legislation. Hoping to resolve the situation, **parliamentary elections** were called ten months ahead of schedule in August 2015. Wickremasinghe's UNP-led coalition made decisive gains – still short of an overall majority, although at least enough to avert the prospect of a rapid and unlikely return to politics for Mahinda Rajapakse, who had been widely touted as the new prime minister in the event of a victory for the SLFP-led opposition (still going under the name of the United People's Freedom Alliance, or UPFA). Wickremasinghe and Sirisena, meanwhile, agreed to continue working together for two years.

Sri Lanka was therefore left with a government lacking an overall majority and a president and prime minister from opposite sides of the political spectrum. Not surprisingly, relations between Sirisena and Wickremasinghe slowly become fatally

2006	2007	2008
Resumption of full-scale fighting between LTTE and Sri Lankan Army.	LTTE defeated in the east.	Final Sri Lankan Army offensive against LTTE in the north.

uptured. Their formal partnership, agreed after the 2015 parliamentary elections, expired in mid-2017 and was not renewed, while Wickremasinghe himself became increasingly caught up in a major bonds scandal which severely compromised his reputation for good, corruption-free governance.

Rajapakse returns?

Despite the struggles of the ruling coalition, few anticipated the results of the nationwide **local elections** held in February 2018, which saw Mahinda Rajapakse re-enter the political fray at the head of the new Sri Lanka Podujana Peramuna (SLPP) party. In an outcome almost as unexpected as Sirisena's own electoral victory of three years previously, the SLPP won 231 out of 340 seats with over forty percent of the votes, reducing the share of Sirisena's UPFA to a humiliating twelve percent. Sirisena refused calls to resign, vowing to see out his final two years in office, although many saw his position as fatally compromised.

Worse was to follow however, at the end of February, when a series of anti-Muslim riots broke out in Ampara, after a group of Sinhalese thugs attacked a Muslim restaurant owner who they claimed had been putting "sterilization pills" in their food. Rioting later spread to the Kandy area, sparked by the beating of a Sinhalese truck driver by four Muslim youths. Over a period of two weeks numerous mosques, Muslims and Muslim-owned properties were attacked, with a ten-day state of emergency imposed (the first since the civil war) and many social media channels blocked.

The future

At a superficial level, Sri Lanka still looks like a country on a steeply upward trajectory. Landmark new infrastructure projects (Colombo's Lotus Tower, the Kataragama railway extension, the Central Expressway – not to mention the vast new Colombo Port City) continue to be unveiled on an almost annual basis, while parts of the capital are rapidly transforming into a kind of South Asian Singapore. Many problems remain, however. Economic growth has stagnated since 2015, while huge levels of foreign debt and dwindling overseas investment (particularly following the ongoing bonds scandal) are increasingly strangling public finances, leading in turn to rising costs and increasing hardship amongst the island's poor. In extreme cases financial difficulties have even led to an abrogation of the island's sovereignty. In late 2017, finding itself unable to service debts to China for their construction of Hambantota port, the government was forced to lease the port and a large surrounding area to the Chinese for 99 years. The subsequent raising of a Chinese flag over the port was widely resented, but provided an apt symbol of the way Sri Lanka had dramatically sold out during Chinese interests during the Rajapakse years, and the problems he has left behind.

Political and ethnic tensions persist as well. Not a single soldier has been brought to trial for war crimes – which has surprised no one – nor a single leading member of the Rajapakse clan prosecuted for corruption (or even, in the case of his son Yoshitha, for suspected murder). And although the north is now peaceful and largely rebuilt, the military still controls large swathes of appropriated land, while many educated **Tamils**

2009	2010	2011
Fall of Kilinochchi and final defeat of LTTE accompanied by mass civilian casualties; Prabhakaran killed.	Mahinda Rajapakse re-elected president.	Opening of Sri Lanka's first motorway, the E01 Expressway from Colombo to Galle.

continue to move abroad rather than stay in a country in which they fear they will forever be seen as second-class citizens. Torture (according to the findings of the UN) is still being routinely used against those suspected of former LTTE involvement – even while prosecutions against Sinhalese military suspected of war crimes have ground to a halt. One judge reported that in 2017 he was forced to exclude ninety percent of confessions in cases brought in under the Prevention of Terrorism Act due to his belief that they had been extracted under duress.

Meanwhile, the paranoid delusions of Sri Lanka's ultra-nationalistic Sinhalese fringe are now increasingly focused on the island's **Muslims**, who thanks to changing demographics may overtake Sri Lanka's Tamils as the island's largest minority in the foreseeable future. The island has already experienced two major waves of anti-Muslim rioting in the past five years, and Islamophobic invective has become increasingly prevalent now that the perceived Tamil threat to Sri Lanka's Buddhist hegemony has passed. And meanwhile, the lurking shadow of a return to power for Mahinda Rajapakse himself (who will be 74 by the time of the next presidential elections in 2020) continues to cloud the political landscape. So far, so good. But what comes next is anyone's guess.

2015	2018
Maithripala Sirisena elected present	Mahinda Rajapakse-led Sri Lanka Podujana Peramuna party scores unexpected triumph in local elections. Anti-Muslim riots subsequently convulse Kandy and other parts of the country. Opening of the Lotus Tower in Colombo, South Asia's tallest building.

Sri Lankan Buddhism

Buddhism runs deep in Sri Lankan life. The island was one of the first places to convert to the religion, in 247 BC, and has remained unswervingly faithful in the two thousand years since. As such, Sri Lanka is often claimed to be the world's oldest Buddhist country, and the religion's trappings are apparent everywhere, most obviously in the island's myriad temples, as well as in its vibrant festivals and large and highly visible population of monks.

The life of the Buddha

Siddhartha Gautama, the Buddha-to-be, was (according to tradition) born the son of the king in the small kingdom of Lumbini in what is now southern Nepal during the fourth or fifth century BC – 563 BC is often suggested as a possible date, though modern scholars have suggested that it might have been as much as a century later. Auspicious symbols accompanied the prince's conception and birth: his mother dreamt that a white elephant had entered her womb, and according to legend Siddhartha emerged from beneath his mother's right arm and immediately talked and walked, a lotus flower blossoming beneath his foot after each of his first seven steps.

Astrologers predicted that the young prince would become either a great king or a great ascetic. His father, keen to prevent the latter outcome, determined to protect his son from all knowledge of worldly suffering, ensuring that Siddhartha knew only the pampered upbringing of a closeted prince. Not until the age of 29 did he even venture out of his palace to ride through the city. Despite his father's attempts to clear all elderly, ugly and sick people from the streets, a frail elderly man wandered into the path of Siddhartha's chariot. The young prince, who had never seen an old person before, was, not surprisingly, deeply troubled by the sight, having previously been spared all knowledge of the inevitability of human mortality and physical decay.

On subsequent occasions the prince travelled from his palace three more times, seeing first a sick person, then a corpse, and finally an ascetic sitting meditating beneath a tree – an emblematic representation of the inevitability of age, sickness and death, and of the possibility of searching for a state that transcended such suffering. Determined to discover the path that led to this state, Siddhartha slipped away from the palace during the night, leaving his wife and young son asleep, exchanging his royal robes for the clothes of his servant, and set out to follow the life of an ascetic.

For six years Siddhartha wandered the countryside, studying with sages who taught him to achieve deep meditative trances. Siddhartha quickly equalled the attainments of his teachers, but soon realized that these accomplishments failed to release him from the root causes of human suffering. He then met up with five other ascetics who had dedicated themselves to the most extreme austerities. Siddhartha joined them and followed their lifestyle, living on a single grain of rice and a drop of water each day until he had wasted away virtually to nothing. At which point Siddhartha suddenly realized that practising pointless austerities was equally unhelpful in his spiritual quest. He therefore determined to follow the so-called **middle way**, a route that involved neither extreme austerities nor excessive self-indulgence.

Enlightenment

His five companions having contemptuously abandoned him on account of his apparent lack of willpower, Siddhartha sat down beneath a bo tree and vowed to remain there until he had found an answer to the riddle of existence and suffering. Siddhartha plunged himself into profound meditation. Mara, the god of desire, seeing that the prince was attempting to free himself from craving – and therefore from Mara's control – attempted to distract him with storms of rocks, coals, mud and darkness. When this failed, he sent his three beautiful daughters to tempt Siddhartha, but this attempt to distract the prince also proved fruitless. Finally, Mara attempted to dislodge the prince from the ground he was sitting on, shaking the very earth beneath him. Siddhartha extended his right hand and touched the earth, calling it to witness his unshakeable concentration, after which Mara withdrew.

Having conquered temptation, Siddhartha continued to meditate. As the night progressed he had a vision of all his millions of previous lives and gained an understanding of the workings of karma and of the way in which good and bad actions and desires bear fruit in subsequent lives, creating a potentially infinite and inescapable sequence of rebirths. During the final phase of his great meditation, Siddhartha realized that it was possible to pass beyond this cycle of karma and to reach a spiritual state – which he called **nirvana** – where desire, suffering and causality finally end. At this point he attained **enlightenment** and ceased being Prince Siddhartha Gautama, instead becoming **the Buddha**, "the Enlightened One".

Following his enlightenment, the Buddha at first felt reluctant to talk to others of his experience, doubting that it would be understood. According to tradition, it was only at the intervention of the god Brahma himself that the Buddha agreed to attempt to communicate his unique revelation and help others towards enlightenment. He preached his **first sermon** to his former ascetic companions, whom he found in the Deer Park in Sarnath, near present-day Varanasi in north India. In this sermon he outlined the **Four Noble Truths** (see page 429). The five companions quickly understood the Buddha's message and themselves became enlightened.

After this, the Buddha's teaching spread with remarkable rapidity. An order of monks, the **Sangha**, was established (as well as an order of nuns, or *bhikkuni*) and the Buddha appears to have travelled tirelessly around northeast India preaching. He continued to travel and teach right up until his death – or, to be precise, his passing into nirvana – at the age of around eighty at the town of Kusinagara.

The history of Buddhism in Sri Lanka

Over the centuries following the Buddha's death, Buddhism rapidly established itself across much of India, becoming the state religion under the great Indian emperor **Ashoka**. Ashoka despatched various Buddhist missions to neighbouring countries, one of which, under the leadership of his son Mahinda, arrived in Sri Lanka in 247 BC (see page 339). Mahinda's mission was spectacularly successful and Buddhism quickly became the dominant faith on the island, the religion giving the Sinhalese people a new-found sense of identity. Buddhism and Sinhalese nationalism have remained closely connected ever since, linked to a view of Sri Lanka as the chosen land of the faith – a kind of Buddhist Israel.

Buddhism gradually withered away in India over the following centuries, but continued to flourish in Sri Lanka despite repeated Tamil invasions and the attendant influx of Hindu ideas. It was the chaos caused by these invasions, and the fear that the principal Buddhist teachings, the so-called **Tripitaka** (which had hitherto been passed orally from generation to generation), would be lost that prompted King Vattagamini Abhaya to have them transcribed in the first century BC in the monastery at Aluvihara – the first time that the key Buddhist texts were committed to writing.

Although Buddhism in India had fallen into terminal decline by the fourth century AD, it continued to spread to new countries. From India it travelled north into Nepal, Tibet and China, developing in the process a new type of Buddhism – **Mahayana** (see page 431). Sri Lanka, by contrast, preserved the **Theravada** tradition (see page 430), which it subsequently exported to Burma and Thailand, from where it spread to neighbouring countries – Buddhists in Southeast Asia still regard Sri Lanka as the guardian of the original Theravada tradition.

Buddhism continued to flourish throughout the Anuradhapuran and Polonnaruwan eras. For much of this period Sri Lanka was virtually a theocracy: huge monasteries were established and much of the island's agricultural surplus went to supporting a vast population of monks. The resources devoted to maintaining the clergy meant that the practice of begging for alms largely disappeared in Sri Lanka from an early date, while the Buddha's traditional requirement that monks lead a wandering life in order to spread the religion was similarly ignored.

Not until the abandonment of Polonnaruwa in the face of further Tamil assaults in the thirteenth century did Sri Lankan Buddhism begin to face serious difficulties. As Sinhalese power and civilization fragmented, so Buddhism lost its central role in the state. Monasteries were abandoned and the population of monks declined. Hinduism became entrenched in the north, where a new Tamil kingdom had been established in the Jaffna Peninsula, while further religious competition was provided by the traders who began to arrive from Arabia from around the eighth century, and who established sizeable Muslim enclaves around parts of the coast.

The colonial era

Buddhism reached its lowest point in Sri Lanka during the seventeenth and eighteenth centuries as the coast fell to Portuguese (and later Dutch) colonists. Portuguese missionaries set about winning over the natives for the Roman Catholic faith with a will, ordering the destruction of innumerable temples and converting considerable sections of the population. Meanwhile, the throne of the Kingdom of Kandy, the island's last independent region, passed into Tamil hands, and Hindu influence gradually spread.

By 1753, the situation had become so bad that there were not enough monks left to ordain any further Buddhist clergy. The king of Kandy, Kirti Sri Rajasinha, sent out for monks from Thailand, who performed the required ordination services, thus re-establishing the Sangha in the island and founding the so-called **Siyam Nikaya**, or "Siam Order". The revived order flourished, although it became increasingly exclusive, allowing only those belonging to the land-owning Goyigama caste to be ordained (a very un-Buddhist practice). A second sect, the **Amarapura Nikaya**, was established, again with Thai monks providing the initial ordinations. Further disputes over points of doctrine led to the foundation of the **Ramanna Nikaya** in the late nineteenth century. These three *nikayas* remain the principal orders right up to the present day, with each sect preserving its own ordination tradition.

Sri Lankan Buddhism was also threatened by Victorian missionary Christianity – and the influence of Western ideas generally – for much of the British colonial period. Faced with the Western onslaught, many local Buddhists reaffirmed their traditional beliefs and the later part of the nineteenth century saw something of a **Buddhist revival**. This was stimulated by the arrival of Madame Blavatsky and Colonel Olcott (see page 73), the founders of Theosophy, who arrived in Sri Lanka in 1880 and declared themselves to be Buddhists. Olcott returned many times to the island, playing a major role in the revival and establishing hundreds of Buddhist schools islandwide to counterbalance the influence of the increasingly dominant British Anglican educational system. One of Blavatsky and Olcott's young assistants, **Angarika Dharmapala** (1864–1933) subsequently became the movement's leading figure, travelling the world in order to promote the Buddhist cause – and also sparking a modest Buddhist revival in India in the process. He remains a revered figure in Sri Lanka to this day, with many streets renamed in his honour.

The Buddhist belief system

The Buddha's teachings, collectively known as the **dharma**, were codified after his death and passed on orally for several centuries until finally being written down at Aluvihara in Sri Lanka in the first century BC. The essence of Buddhist belief is encapsulated in the **Four Noble Truths**. Simply put, these are (1) life is suffering; (2) suffering is the result of craving; (3) there can be an end to suffering; and (4) that there is a path that leads to the end of suffering, encapsulated in the so-called **Noble Eightfold Path**, a set of simple rules to encourage good behaviour and morals.

All beings, Buddhism asserts, will experience a potentially infinite sequence of rebirths in various different forms: as a human, an animal, ghost or god, either on earth or in one of various heavens or hells. The engine that drives this permanent sequence of reincarnations is **karma**. Meritorious actions produce good karma, which enables creatures to be reborn higher up the spiritual chain; bad actions have the opposite result. In this classically elegant system, good deeds really are their own reward. No amount of good karma, however, will allow one to escape the sequence of infinite rebirths – good behaviour and the acquiring of merit is simply a stage on the route to enlightenment and the achievement of nirvana. Every desire and action plants seeds of karma that create the impetus for further lives, and further actions and desires – and so on. Some schools of ancient Indian philosophy took this idea to its logical conclusion – the Jains, for example, decided that the best thing to do in life was nothing at all, and more extreme proponents of that religion still occasionally sit down and starve themselves to death in order to avoid involvement in worldly actions, for good or bad.

The exact route to enlightenment and nirvana is long and difficult – at least according to the older schools of Buddhism – requiring millions of lifetimes. Exactly what **nirvana** is meant to be remains famously vague. The Buddha himself was notoriously elusive on the subject. He compared a person entering nirvana to a flame being extinguished – the flame doesn't go anywhere, but the process of combustion ceases.

Theravada and Mahayana

Theravada Buddhism (the "Law of the Elders") is the dominant form of the religion in Sri Lanka, as well as in Southeast Asia. It is the older of the two main schools of Buddhism and claims to embody the Buddha's teachings in their original form. These teachings emphasize that all individuals are responsible for their own spiritual welfare, and that any person who wishes to achieve enlightenment must pursue the same path trodden by the Buddha himself, giving up worldly concerns and developing spiritual attainments through meditation and self-sacrifice. This path of renunciation is, of course, impossible for most members of the Theravada community to follow, which explains the importance of **monks** in Sri Lanka (and in other Theravada countries), since only members of the Sangha are considered fully committed to the Theravada path, and thus capable of achieving enlightenment – and even then only in rare instances. Lay worshippers do have a (limited) role in the Theravada tradition, though this is mainly to earn merit by offering material support to monks. Otherwise they can hope for little except to lead a moral life and to be reborn as a monk themselves at some point in the future.

THE BUDDHIST FLAG

One of Sri Lanka's most instantly recognizable Buddhist symbols is the multicoloured **Buddhist Flag**, which can be seen flying from temples and bo trees across the island, and many other places besides. The flag was designed in 1885 by a panel of local notables and first raised on Vesak Poya day, April 28, 1885, the first time Vesak had been celebrated as a public holiday under British rule. The flag was subsequently adopted by Buddhist countries around the world (sometimes with minor variations in colour), serving as an international symbol of the religion.

The flag consists of six vertical strips, representing the six colours of the aura that is said to have shone out of the body of the Buddha following his enlightenment. The colours are: **blue** (*nila*; symbolizing universal compassion); **yellow** (*pita*; The Middle Way); **red** (*lohita*; the blessings arising from the practice of Buddhism); **white** (*odata*; the purity of the Buddha's teachings and the liberation they bring); and **orange** (*manjesta*; the Buddha's teachings – wisdom). The wider sixth strip shows all five colours superimposed, symbolizing the compound hue said to be formed by their combination, known as *pabbhassara*, or "essence of light".

The rather elitist aspect of Theravada doctrine led to it being dubbed **Hinayana Buddhism**, or "Lesser Vehicle", a slightly pejorative term which compares it unfavourably with the **Mahayana**, or "Greater Vehicle", sect. Mahayana Buddhism developed as an offshoot of Theravada Buddhism, eventually becoming the dominant form of the religion in China, Tibet and Japan, although it has had only a slight influence on Sri Lankan Buddhism. As Theravada Buddhism developed, it came to be believed that the Buddha himself was only the latest of a series of Buddhas – Sri Lankan tradition claims that there have been either sixteen or 24 previous Buddhas, and holds that another Buddha, Maitreya, will appear at some point in the remote future when all the last Buddha's teachings have been forgotten. The Mahayana tradition expanded this aspect of Buddhist cosmology to create a grand array of supplementary deities, including various additional Buddhas and **bodhisattvas** – a Buddha-to-be who has chosen to defer entering nirvana in order to remain on earth (or in one of the various Buddhist heavens) to help others towards enlightenment. Instead of trying to emulate the Buddha, devotees simply worship one or more of the Mahayana deities and reap the spiritual rewards. Not surprisingly, this much more populist – and much less demanding – form of the religion became widely established in place of the Theravada tradition. Compared with the countless lifetimes of spiritual self-improvement that Theravada Buddhism requires its followers to endure, some schools of Mahayana claim that even a single prayer to the relevant bodhisattva can cause one to be reborn in one of the Buddhist heavens – hence its description of itself as the "Greater Vehicle", a form of the religion capable of carrying far greater numbers of devotees to enlightenment.

The Buddhist pantheon in Sri Lanka

While it's true that Buddhism in Sri Lanka hasn't experienced the byzantine transformations it has undergone in, say, China, Tibet or Japan, the religion in Sri Lanka has acquired its own particular flavour and local characteristics – mainly the result of the strong influence of Hinduism over many centuries. Buddhism evolved from the same roots as **Hinduism** and makes many of the same assumptions about the universe, so the inclusion of many Hindu deities within the Sri Lankan Buddhist pantheon isn't as inconsistent as it might initially appear. (The Buddha himself never denied the existence or powers of the myriad gods of ancient Indian cosmology, simply arguing that they were subject to the same laws of karma and rebirth as any other creature – indeed according to tradition, the Buddha ascended to the various heavens to preach to the gods on several occasions.) Thus, although other gods may be unable to assist in helping one towards the ultimate goal of attaining nirvana, they still have power to assist in less exulted aims – the success of a new business, the birth of a child, the abundance of a harvest – and are therefore to be worshipped alongside the Buddha.

Various Hindu gods have been appropriated by Sri Lankan Buddhism over the centuries, going in and out of fashion according to the prevailing religious or political climate. There are countless shrines across the island dedicated to these subsidiary gods, either as lesser shrines within Buddhist temples or as separate, self-contained temples – these shrines or temples are known as **devales** to differentiate them from purely Buddhist temples (viharas) and Hindu temples (kovils). Thus, the supreme Hindu deity, **Vishnu** (often known locally as **Upulvan**), is regarded in Sri Lanka as a protector of Buddhism and is worshipped by Buddhists, as is the god **Kataragama** (see page 192), another deity of mixed Hindu–Buddhist descent. Other popular gods in the Buddhist pantheon include **Saman** (see page 53) and **Pattini** (see page 220), while the elephant-headed Hindu god **Ganesh** is also widely worshipped.

Daily Buddhist ritual and belief

Despite the Buddha's emphasis on the search for enlightenment and nirvana, for most Sri Lankans, daily religious life is focused on more modest goals. Theravada Buddhism traditionally states that only monks can achieve enlightenment, and even then only on very rare occasions: Sri Lanka's last *arhat* (enlightened monk) is supposed to have died in the first century BC. Thus, rather than trying to emulate the Buddha's own spiritual odyssey and attempt the near-impossible task of achieving enlightenment, the average Sri Lankan Buddhist will concentrate on leading a moral life and on acquiring religious merit in the hope of ensuring rebirth higher up the spiritual ladder.

To become a Buddhist, one simply announces the fact that one is "taking refuge" in the **Three Jewels**: the Buddha, the Dharma and the Sangha. There is no form of organized or congregational worship in Buddhism, as there is in Christianity or Islam – instead, devotees visit their local temple when they please, saying prayers at the dagoba or Buddha shrine (or that of another god), perhaps offering flowers, lighting a candle or reciting (or having monks recite) Buddhist scriptures, an act known as **pirith**. Although Theravada holds that the Buddha himself should not be worshipped, many Sinhalese effectively do so.

Buddhist places of pilgrimage and festivals play a vital role in sustaining the faith. The island's major **places of pilgrimage** – the Temple of the Tooth at Kandy, the revered "footprint" of the Buddha at Adam's Peak, and the Sri Maha Bodhi at Anuradhapura – attract thousands of pilgrims year-round. The timing of pilgrimages is often linked to significant dates in the Buddhist calendar, which is punctuated by a further round of Buddhist holidays and festivals. Full-moon – or **poya** – days are considered particularly important, particularly **Vesak Poya**, the day on which the Buddha is said to have been born, achieved enlightenment and passed into nirvana. Buddhist devotees traditionally visit their local temple on poya days to spend time in prayer or meditation; they might also practise certain abstinences, such as fasting or refraining from alcohol and sex. Some poya days are also celebrated with elaborate **festivals**, often taking the form of enormous **processions** (peraheras), when locals parade along the streets, sometimes accompanied by elaborately costumed elephants. Nowhere are these processions more extravagant than during the magnificent **Esala Perahera** in Kandy (see page 210), one of Sri Lanka's – indeed Asia's – most visually spectacular pageants.

The Sangha

Even if you don't go near a temple, you won't travel far in Sri Lanka without seeing a shaven-headed Buddhist monk clad in striking orange or red robes. Collectively known as **the Sangha**, the island's fifteen thousand or so monks form one of the most visible and distinctive sections of Sri Lankan society, and serve as living proof of the island's commitment to the Buddhist cause. The monastic tradition is deeply embedded in the national culture, and the importance of the Buddhist clergy can be seen in myriad ways, from the monks who sit in the nation's parliament to the seats in every bus that are reserved for their use. The Sinhala language, meanwhile, features special forms of address only used when talking to a monk, even including a different word for "yes".

Young boys are traditionally chosen to be monks if they show a particular religious bent, or if their horoscope appears favourable – although many are given to the Sangha by poor Sinhalese families in order to provide them with a decent standard of living and an education. Boy monks are first initiated into the Sangha as novices around their tenth birthday, going to live and study in a monastery and largely severing their ties with home (there is no minimum age at which boys can be ordained – according to tradition, a boy can become a novice when he's old enough to chase away crows). Higher ordination occurs at the age of 20. At this point the monk becomes a full member of the **Sangha**. Monks are supposed to commit themselves to the Sangha for life – the custom, popular in Thailand and Myanmar (Burma), of laymen becoming monks for a short period then returning to normal life is not considered acceptable in Sri Lanka – although in practice significant numbers of monks fail to last the course and return to secular society, often once they've secured an education.

On entering the Sangha the new monk shaves his head and dons the characteristic robes of a Buddhist cleric (usually saffron, sometimes red or yellow – the precise colour has no significance, and monks wear whatever is given to them, apart from forest-dwelling monks, who tend to wear brown robes). He also takes a new name: the honorific *thero* or *thera* is often added after it, along with the name of the town or village in which the monk was born, while "The Venerable" (or "Ven.") is frequently added as a prefix. Monks commit themselves to a code of conduct that entails various prohibitions. These traditionally include: not to kill; not to steal; not to have sex; not to lie about spiritual attainments; not to drink alcohol; not to handle money; not to eat after midday; and not to own more than a bare minimum of personal possessions.

The great monastic foundations of ancient Sri Lanka have largely vanished, and most monks now live in local village temples. These temples are intimately connected to the life of the village they serve, which usually provides the resident monks with their only source of material support via regular offerings, in return for which the monks act as teachers and spiritual mentors to the local population. The actual functions required of a Buddhist monk are few. The only ceremonies they preside at are funerals, although they are sometimes asked to recite Buddhist scriptures (*pirith*). Monks traditionally act as spiritual advisers; some monks also gain reputations as healers or astrologers.

A less savoury aspect of the Sri Lankan Buddhist clergy has been their involvement in **ultra-nationalistic politics** – the view that many monks hold of Sri Lanka as the "chosen land" of Buddhism has disturbing parallels with hard-line Jewish attitudes towards Israel. In 1959, Prime Minister S.W.R.D Bandaranaike was shot dead by a Buddhist monk, and the clergy have constantly involved themselves in politics ever since; some of the more right-wing monks reputedly formed a clandestine ultra-nationalist group called the Circle of Sinhalese Force, whose members used Nazi salutes and spouted wild propaganda about the perceived threat to their land, race and religion – a mixture of Mahavamsa and *Mein Kampf*.

In earlier decades, monks had contented themselves with influencing politicians, though since the turn of the century they have started entering politics on their own account, representing the monk-led **Jathika Hela Urumaya** party (National Heritage Party; JHU). A Buddhist monk was first elected to parliament in 2001, and they also formed a small but significant fraction of Mahinda's Rajapakse's ruling coalition, although subsequently sided with Sirisena in the 2015 presidential election.

Recent years have also seen the emergence of the even more rabidly xenophobic **Bodu Bala Sena**, founded in 2012 by a splinter group of the JHU which was widely suspected (possibly with government encouragement) of being behind the anti-Muslim riots of 2014 (see page 423) and also of sponsoring attacks on Muslim-owned businesses – although it appears more likely to have been involved in the 2018 riots. Throughout the later war years, leading monks consistently denounced any attempts by the government to cede autonomy to the Tamils of the north and campaigned vigorously for a military rather than a negotiated solution to the conflict, led by the vociferous former JHU leader Athurliye Rathana, dubbed the "War Monk" by the Sri Lankan press. Even following the end of the conflict certain monks appear determined to continue stoking up sectarian tensions. In late 2011, cleric Amatha Dhamma led a group of other monks and lay followers in destroying a Muslim shrine in Anuradhapura – a confrontational and inflammatory act with disturbing parallels to the notorious destruction of the Babri Mosque in India in 1992. Unfortunately, some at least of Sri Lanka's Sangha apparently see no contradiction between the Buddhist ideals in which they profess to believe and their frequently xenophobic, intolerant and rampantly sectarian rhetoric – all the more unfortunate, given that they continue to command widespread popular support and respect.

Sri Lankan Buddhist art and architecture

Sri Lanka's art and architecture – ranging from Dravidian temples to Portuguese Baroque churches – offer a fascinating visual legacy of the varied influences that have shaped the island's eclectic culture. Despite the number of races and religions that have contributed to the artistic melting pot, however, the influence of Buddhism remains central to the nation's cultural fabric, and it is in Buddhist art and architecture that Sri Lanka's greatest artistic achievements can be found.

Although the **Mahayana** doctrines (see page 431) that transformed Buddhist art in many other parts of Asia largely bypassed Sri Lanka, the island's religious art was significantly enriched from around the tenth century by the influence of **Hinduism**, introduced by the numerous Tamil dynasties that periodically overran parts of the north. This influence first showed itself in the art of **Polonnaruwa**, and later blended with Sinhalese traditions to create the uniquely syncretized style of **Kandyan** temple architecture, which reached its apogee during the fifteenth to eighteenth centuries.

Buddha images

Early Buddhist art was symbolic rather than figurative. The Buddha himself (according to some traditions) asked that no images be made of him after his death, and for the first few centuries he was represented symbolically by objects such as dagobas, bo trees, thrones, wheels, pillars, trees, animals or footprints.

Exactly why the first **Buddha images** were made remains unclear, though they seem initially to have appeared in India in around the first century BC. Buddha images are traditionally highly stylized: the intention of Buddhist art has always been to represent the Buddha's transcendental, superhuman nature rather than to describe a personality (unlike, say, Western representations of Jesus). The vast majority of Buddha figures are shown in one of the canonical poses, or **mudras** (see page 435).

Many sculptural details of Buddha figures are enshrined in tradition and preserved in the *Sariputra*, a Sinhalese treatise in verse for the makers of Buddha images. Some of the most important features of traditional Buddha images include the **ushnisha**, the small protuberance on the top of the head, denoting superior mental powers; the **siraspata**, or flame of wisdom (the Buddhist equivalent of the Christian halo), growing out of the *ushnisha*; the elongated **earlobes**, denoting renunciation (the holes in the lobes would have contained jewels that the Buddha gave up when he abandoned his royal position); the shape of the **eyes**, modelled after the form of lotus petals; the **eyebrows**, whose curves are meant to resemble two bows; the **mouth**, usually closed and wearing the hint of a smile; and the **feet**, which traditionally bear 32 different auspicious markings.

The one area in which Mahayana Buddhism has had a lasting impact on Sri Lankan religious art is in the **gigantic Buddha statues**, some standing up to 30m high, which can be found all over the island, dating from both ancient (Aukana, Sasseruwa, Maligawila, Polonnaruwa) and modern (Dambulla, Weherehena, Wewurukannala, Aluthgama) times. Such larger-than-life depictions reflect the change from Theravada's emphasis on the historical, human Buddha to Mahayana's view of the Buddha as a cosmic being who could only be truly represented in figures of superhuman dimensions.

Dagobas (stupas)

The stupa, or **dagoba**, as they're known in Sri Lanka, is the world's most universal Buddhist architectural symbol, ranging from the classically simple hemispherical forms found in Sri Lanka and Nepal to the spire-like stupas of Thailand and Burma and the pagodas of China and Japan (the Sinhalese "dagoba" has even been mooted as one possible source for the word "pagoda"). Dagobas originally developed from the Indian burial mounds that were raised to mark the graves of important personages, although popular legend traces their distinctive form back to the Buddha himself. Upon being asked by his followers what shape a memorial to him should take, the Buddha is said to have folded his robe into a square and placed his upturned begging bowl and umbrella on top of it, thus outlining the dagoba's basic form.

As Buddhist theology developed, so the elements of the dagoba acquired more elaborate symbolic meanings. At its simplest level, the dagoba's role as an enormous burial mound serves to recall the memory of the Buddha's passing into nirvana. A more elaborate explanation describes the dagoba in cosmological terms: the main dome (*anda*), built in the shape of a hill, is said to represent Mount Meru, the sacred peak that lies at the centre of the Buddhist universe, while the spire (*chattravali*) symbolizes the *axis mundi*, or cosmic pillar, connecting earth and heaven and leading upwards out of the world towards nirvana.

The earliest dagobas were built to enshrine important **relics** of the Buddha himself or of other revered religious figures (the Buddha's own ashes were, according to tradition, divided into forty thousand parts, providing the impetus for a huge spate of dagoba building, while many notable monks were also interred in dagobas). These relics were

---

BUDDHIST MUDRAS AND THEIR MEANINGS

The following are the *mudras* most commonly encountered in Sri Lankan art, though others are occasionally encountered, such as the *varada mudra* ("Gesture of Gift Giving"), and the *asisa mudra* ("Gesture of Blessing", a variant form of the *abhaya mudra*), employed in the famous Aukana Buddha.

Abhaya mudra The "Have No Fear" pose shows the Buddha standing with his right hand raised with the palm facing the viewer.

Dhyani or **samadhi mudra** Shows the Buddha in meditation, seated in the lotus or half-lotus position, with his hands placed together in his lap.

Bhumisparsha mudra The "Earth-Witness" pose shows the Buddha touching the ground with the tips of the fingers of his left hand, commemorating the moment in his enlightenment when the demon Mara, in attempting to break his concentration, caused the earth to shake beneath him, and the Buddha stilled the ground by touching it.

Vitarka mudra and **dharmachakra mudra** In both positions ("Gesture of Explanation" and "Gesture of the Turning of the Wheel of the Law" respectively) the Buddha forms a circle with his thumb and one finger, representing the wheel of dharma. Used in both standing and sitting poses.

Reclining poses In Asian Buddhist art, the reclining pose is traditionally considered to represent the Buddha at the moment of his death and entrance into nirvana – the so-called Parinirvana pose. Reclining poses are particularly common in Sri Lanka, although the island's sculptors make a subtle distinction between two types of reclining image: the sleeping pose, and the true *parinirvana* pose. Sleeping and *parinirvana* Buddhas are distinguished by six marks (although the distinctions between the two are often quite subtle). In the sleeping pose: the eyes are open; the right hand is at least partially beneath the head; the stomach is a normal size; the robe is smooth beneath the left hand; the bottom of the hem of the robe is level; and the toes of the two feet are in a straight line. In the *parinirvana* pose, the hand is away from the head; the eyes are partially closed; the stomach is shrunken; the robe is bunched up under the left hand (the clenched hand and crumpled robe indicating the pain of the Buddha's final illness); the hem at the bottom of the robe is uneven; and the left knee is slightly flexed, so that the toes of the two feet are not in a straight line.

traditionally placed in or just below the *harmika*, the square relic chamber at the top of the dome. As Buddhism spread, the building of dagobas became seen as an act of religious merit, resulting in the construction of innumerable smaller, or "votive", dagobas, some no larger than a few feet high.

Dagobas still serve as important objects of pilgrimage and religious devotion: as in other Buddhist countries, devotees typically make clockwise circumambulations of the dagoba – an act known as *pradakshina* – which is meant to focus the mind in meditation, although this practice is less widespread in Sri Lanka than in other countries (similarly, the prohibition against walking around dagobas in an anticlockwise direction, which is frowned upon in some other countries, isn't much observed).

Structure and shape

It was in the great dagobas of Anuradhapura and Polonnaruwa, however, that early Sri Lankan architecture reached its highest point, both figuratively and literally. These massive construction feats were Asia's nearest equivalent to the Egyptian pyramids. The foundations were trampled down by elephants, then the main body of the dagobas filled with rubble and vast numbers of bricks (it's been estimated that the Jetavana dagoba at Anuradhapura uses almost one hundred million), after which the entire structures were plastered and painted with a coat of lime-wash.

Dagobas consist of four principal sections. The whole structure usually sits on a square terrace whose four sides are oriented towards the cardinal points. Many larger stupas have four small shrines, called **vahalkadas** (or *adimukas*), arranged around the base of the dagoba at the cardinal points – a uniquely Sri Lankan architectural element. The main hemispherical body of the stupa is known as the **anda**, and is surmounted by

A BUDDHIST BESTIARY

Animals, both real and imaginary, form an important element in Buddhist iconography. The following are some of the most common.

Makaras The *makara* is a mythical beast of Indian origin, formed from parts of various different animals: the body of a fish; the foot of a lion; the eye of a monkey; the trunk and tusk of an elephant; the tail of a peacock; the ear of a pig; and the mouth of a crocodile. One of the most ubiquitous features of Sri Lankan Buddhist architecture is the *makara torana*, or "dragon arch", made up of two *makaras* connected to a dragon's mouth, which is designed to ward off evil spirits and used to frame entrances and Buddha images in virtually every temple in the island.

Nagarajas *Nagarajas* (snake kings) are represented as human figures canopied by cobra hoods. They apparently derive from pre-Hindu Indian beliefs and are regarded as symbols of fertility and masters of the underground world. Despite their apparently pagan origins, they derive some Buddhist legitimacy from the fact that the *nagaraja* Muchalinda is said to have sheltered the meditating Buddha as he achieved enlightenment – as a result of which cobras are held sacred. *Nagarajas* (plus attendant dwarfs) are often pictured on the guardstones that flank the entrances to many ancient Sri Lanka buildings, and were intended, like *makara toranas*, to prevent evil influences from entering the building.

Dwarfs *Nagarajas* are often shown with dwarfs (*gana*), who can also often be seen supporting the base of steps or temple walls – these jolly-looking pot-bellied creatures are associated with Kubera, the god of wealth, though their exact significance and origins remain obscure.

Elephants Carved in low relief, elephants commonly adorn the walls enclosing religious complexes, their massive presence symbolically supporting the temple buildings.

Lions Though they possess no definite religious significance except to suggest the Buddha's royal origins, lions are also common features of Buddhist architecture. The animal is also an emblem of the Sinhalese people, who trace their ancestry back to – and indeed owe their name to – a lion.

Geese Considered a symbol of spiritual knowledge and purity, geese (*hamsa*) are often found on moonstones, and used decoratively elsewhere in temples.

MOONSTONES

Originally from India, the **moonstone** developed in Sri Lanka from a plain slab to the elaborate semicircular stones, carved in polished granite, which are found at Anuradhapura, Polonnaruwa and many other places across the island. Moonstones are placed at the entrances to shrines to concentrate the mind of the worshipper upon entering. Carved in concentric half-circles, they represent the spiritual journey from samsara, the endless succession of deaths and rebirth, to nirvana and the escape from endless reincarnations.

CLASSIC DESIGN ELEMENTS

The exact design of moonstones varies; not all contain every one of the following elements, and the different animals are sometimes combined in the same ring.

Flames Flames (often in the outermost ring) represent the flames of desire – though they also purify those who step across them.

The four Buddhist animals Representing the inevitability of birth, death and suffering, are the elephant (symbolizing birth), the horse (old age), the lion (illness) and the bull (death and decay) – the way in which the images in each ring chase one another around the moonstone symbolizes samsara's endless cycle of deaths and rebirths. The animals are sometimes shown in separate rings, but more usually combined into a single one.

Vines Vines (or, according to the interpretations of some art historians, snakes), represent desire and attachment to life.

Geese Purity (the goose is a Hindu symbol: as Hamsa it is the vehicle of Brahma, and a sign of wisdom).

Lotus At the centre of the design, the lotus is the symbol of the Buddha and nirvana, and of escape from the cycle of reincarnation.

EVOLVING DESIGN

The classic moonstone pattern as outlined above experienced two important modifications during the **Polonnaruwa period**. To begin with, the bull was omitted: as an important Hindu image (the bull Nandi is the vehicle, or chariot, of Shiva), this particular animal had become too sacred to be trodden on in the increasingly Hinduized city. In addition, the lion was also usually absent (although one can be seen in the moonstone at the Hatadage) due to its significance as a royal and national symbol of the Sinhalese.

Moonstone design continued to evolve right up until the **Kandyan period**, by which time it had mutated into the almost triangular designs found at the Temple of the Tooth and many other shrines in the central highlands. During this evolution, the moonstone also lost virtually all its symbolic meaning; the floral designs found on Kandyan-era moonstones are of purely decorative import, although the lotus survives at the heart.

cube-like structure, the **harmika** (relic chamber), from which rises the **chattravali**. In the earliest Indian stupas this was originally a pillar on which a series of umbrella-like structures were threaded, though in Sri Lankan-style dagobas the umbrellas have fused into a kind of spire. The interior of almost all dagobas consists of completely solid brick, although a few hollow dagobas can also be found, including those at Kalutara, Ampara and the Sambodhi Chaitya in Colombo's Fort district.

Sri Lankan dagobas preserve the classic older **form and shape** of the stupa, following the pattern of the great stupa at Sanchi in central India erected in the third century BC by the emperor Ashoka – although constant repairs (and the fact that new outer shells were often constructed around old stupas) means that it's often difficult to determine the exact origins or original shape of some of the island's most famous dagobas. Despite the superficial similarities shared by all Sri Lankan dagobas, there are subtle variations, with six different basic shapes being recognized, ranging from the perfectly hemispherical "bubble-shape" favoured by the builders of ancient Anuradhapura and Polonnaruwa through to the narrower and more elongated "bell-shape" that became fashionable during the nineteenth century, as well as innumerable other small nuances in design.

Buddhist temples

Sri Lankan **Buddhist temples** (viharas or viharayas) come in a bewildering array of shapes and sizes, ranging from the intimate cave temples of Dambulla and Mulkirigala to the enormous monastic foundations of Anuradhapura and Polonnaruwa. As well as purely Buddhist temples, there are also numerous **devales**, independent shrines dedicated to other gods such as Vishnu, Kataragama, Pattini or Saman – nominally Buddhist, though often showing a strong dash of Hindu influence. These shouldn't be confused with **kovils**, however, which are purely Hindu temples, and have no connection with Buddhism at all.

Despite their enormous variety, most of the island's Buddhist temples comprise three basic elements: an image house, a dagoba (see above), and a bo tree enclosure. The **image house** (*pilimage* or *patimaghara*) houses the temple's Buddha image (or images) along with statues and/or paintings of other gods and attendants; it may be preceded by an antechamber or surrounded by an ambulatory, although there are countless variations in the exact form these shrines take and in the particular gods found inside them. Larger temples may have **additional shrines** to other gods considered important by Sri Lankan Buddhists – Vishnu (considered a protector of Buddhism in Sri Lanka) is the most frequently encountered, although other deities from the Hindu pantheon such as Ganesh and Pattini can also sometimes be seen, while the eternally popular Kataragama (see page 192) is also well represented.

During the late Polonnaruwan and early Kandyan period, image houses developed into the **gedige**, a type of Buddha shrine strongly influenced by South Indian Hindu temple architecture, being constructed entirely out of stone on a rectangular plan, with enormously thick walls and corbelled roofs. Important examples can be found at Polonnaruwa, Nalanda and at the Natha Devale in Kandy. Other variations on the standard image house include the **tampita**, a small shrine raised on pillars, and the distinctive **vatadage**, or circular image house. These have a small dagoba at their centre usually flanked by four Buddha images at the cardinal points and surrounded by concentric rows of pillars that would originally have supported a wooden roof. There are notable examples at Medirigiya, at the Thuparama in Anuradhapura and in the Quadrangle at Polonnaruwa.

The **bo tree enclosure** (*bodhighara*) is a uniquely Sri Lankan feature. The Buddha achieved enlightenment while meditating beneath a bo (or bodhi) tree, and these trees serve as symbols of, and a living link with, that moment – many of the island's specimens have been grown from cuttings taken from the great tree at Anuradhapura, which is itself believed to have been grown from a cutting taken from the very tree (long since vanished) under which the Buddha meditated in India. More important bo trees are often surrounded by gold railings, with tables set around them on which devotees place flower offerings; the trees themselves or the surrounding railings are often draped in colourful strings of prayer flags. Older and larger bo trees are sometimes enclosed by retaining brick terraces with conduits at each corner into which devotees pour water to feed the tree's hidden roots; these are gradually built up around the trunk as it grows, and can sometimes reach a surprising size and height, as at the massive Wel-Bodhiya in the Pattini Devale in Kandy.

Many temples old and new are also attached to monasteries boasting living quarters and refectories, as well as a **poyage** ("House of the Full Moon") in which monks assemble to recite Buddhist scriptures and confess breaches of the monastic code on poya (full-moon) days. Temples in the Kandy area also sometimes have a **digge**, or drummer's hall, usually an open-sided columned pavilion, where drummers and dancers would have performed during temple ceremonies – there's a good example at the Vishnu Devale in Kandy.

Buddhist temple iconography

Sri Lankan temples typically sport a wealth of symbolic decorative detail. The bases of stairways and other entrances into temples are often flanked by **guardstones** (*doratupalas* or *dvarapalas*), showing low-relief carvings of protective **nagarajas**, or snake kings (see page 436), who are believed to ward off malign influences. Another notable feature of Sri Lankan art found at the entrances to temples is the **moonstone** (see page 437).

Many details of Buddhist iconography depict real or imaginary animals (see page 436). Another standard decorative element is the **lotus**, the sacred flower of Buddhism, often painted decoratively on ceilings and walls or carved at the bases of columns. The fact that these pure white flowers blossom directly out of muddy waters is considered symbolic of the potential for Buddhahood that everyone is believed to carry within them – seated Buddha figures are often shown sitting on lotus thrones. Other common symbolic devices include the **chakra**, or Buddhist wheel, symbolizing the Buddha's teaching – the eight spokes represent the Eightfold Path (see page 430). A common detail in the doors of Kandyan temples is the **sun and moon** motif, originally a symbol of the Buddha during the Anuradhapura period, though later appropriated by the kings of Kandy as a royal insignia.

Temples are often decorated with **murals** of varying degrees of sophistication, ranging from primitive daubs to the great narrative sequences found in the cave temples at Dambulla. Perhaps the most popular subject for murals, especially in the south of the island, are tales from the **Jatakas**, the moral fables describing the Buddha's 547 previous lives, while pictures of **pilgrimage sites** around the island are another common theme.

Sri Lankan wildlife

Sri Lanka boasts a variety of wildlife quite out of proportion to its modest size, including a large elephant population alongside an array of other fauna ranging from leopards, sloth bears and giant squirrels through to huge monitor lizards and crocodiles – not to mention a fascinating collection of endemic birdlife. This richness is partly a result of Sri Lanka's complex climate and topography, ranging from the denuded savannas of the dry zone to the lush montane forests of the hill country, and partly due to its geographical position, which makes it a favoured wintering spot for numerous birds, as well as a nesting site for five of the world's species of marine turtles.

Elephants

No animal is as closely identified with Sri Lanka as the elephant – and few other countries offer such a wide range of opportunities to see them both in captivity and in the wild. The kings of Anuradhapura used them to pound down the foundations of their city's huge religious monuments, while the rulers of Kandy employed them to execute prisoners by trampling them to death. During the Dutch era they helped tow barges and move heavy artillery, and under the British they were set to clearing land for tea plantations – even today, trained elephants are used to move heavy objects in places inaccessible to machinery.

The Sri Lankan elephant (*Elephas maximus maximus*) is a subspecies of the Asian elephant (*Elephas maximus*), which is lighter and has smaller ears than the African elephant (*Loxodonta africana*), and also differs from its African cousins in that fewer than one in ten males – so-called **tuskers** – have tusks. This at least had the benefit of discouraging ivory poachers, although it failed to deter British colonial hunters, who saw the elephant as the ultimate big-game target – the notorious Major Rogers is said to have dispatched well over a thousand of the unfortunate creatures during a twelve-year stint around Badulla, before his murderous career was terminated by a well-aimed blast of lightning. By the beginning of the twentieth century there were only around twelve thousand elephants left in the wild in Sri Lanka, while towards the end of the civil war in 2007 that figure had fallen as low as an estimated three thousand, although numbers have now recovered to around 4000 – far and away the highest number of pachyderms per square kilometre in Asia. Efforts to reduce the number of domesticated elephants mean that there are now just 235 in captivity in the whole island (including eighty at Pinnewala).

Following the end of the civil war, the principal pressure on elephants nowadays is **habitat loss**, as more and more of the island's undeveloped areas are cleared for agriculture. This has led to conflicts between villagers and roaming elephants, with frequently tragic consequences – 88 Sri Lankans were killed in 2016 by wild elephants, for example, with 279 elephants killed in retaliation or self-defence. Elephant herds still migrate across the island for considerable distances, sometimes gathering in large herds during the dry season around the shores of receding lakes and other water sources, most spectacularly at Minneriya National Park. Large sections of these well-established migratory routes – popularly known as "**elephant corridors**" – now fall within areas protected by various national parks, but despite this, there are still frequent conflicts between farmers and wandering herds, which trample crops and raid sugar plantations (elephants have a very sweet tooth). Herds are periodically rounded up and chased back to the national parks, though these so-called "elephant drives" have frequently become a source of friction between locals and conservationists.

Elephants can live for up to 70 years, and their gestation period averages 22 months. **Wild elephants** usually live in close-knit family groupings of around fifteen under the leadership of an elderly female; each herd needs a large area of around five square kilometres per adult to survive, not surprising given that a grown elephant drinks 150 litres of water and eats up to 200kg of vegetation daily. **Captive elephants** work under the guidance of skilled **mahouts**, who manipulate their charges using a system of 72 pressure points, plus various verbal commands – a measure of the animal's intelligence is given by the fact that elephants trained to recognize instructions in one language have been successfully re-educated to follow commands in a different one. The life of a trained elephant can be demanding, and it's likely that not all are treated as well as they should be – mahouts are occasionally injured or even killed by their disgruntled charges, proving the truth of the old adage about elephants never forgetting (one particular elephant who had killed two of his mahouts was even put on trial in a court of law – and subsequently acquitted after evidence was presented that he had been mistreated by his handlers). That said, elephants can also become objects of remarkable veneration, most famously in the case of the venerable Maligawa Tusker Raja (see page 217), whose death in 1998 prompted the government to declare a day of national mourning.

Leopards

The Sri Lankan **leopard** (*Panthera pardus*) is the island's most striking – and one of its most elusive – residents. These magnificent animals, which can grow to over 2m in length, are now endangered in Sri Lanka due to habitat destruction, although the island still has more of the creatures per square kilometre than anywhere else in the world. It's thought that there are around five hundred in the whole of the country. Each hunts within a set territory, preying on smaller or less mobile mammals, most commonly deer; most hunting is done at dawn or dusk, which is generally the best time to spot them. Although leopards have a diverse diet, some develop a taste for certain types of meat – the notorious man-eating leopard of Punanai, whose story is recounted in Christopher Ondaatje's *The Man-Eater of Punanai* (see page 449), is said to have acquired a particular fondness for human flesh. They are also expert climbers, and can sometimes be seen sitting in trees, where they often store the remains of their kills; they are also commonly spotted basking in the sun on rocky outcrops.

Leopards can be found in various parts of the island, including many national parks. Easily the best place to spot one (if you're prepared to put up with the increasingly horrendous crowds) is **Yala National Park**, where it's estimated some two hundred are concentrated, and there are also significant numbers in Wilpattu National Park, although you'll have to be amazingly lucky to come across one anywhere else. Block 1 of Yala (the area that is open to the public) is thought to have a leopard density of as high as one animal per square kilometre, probably the highest in the world – although exact numbers are extraordinarily difficult to verify. Leopards here, particularly young males, have become remarkably habituated to human visitors, and often stroll fearlessly along the tracks through the park.

Monkeys

Three species of **monkey** are native to Sri Lanka. The most distinctive and widely encountered is the graceful **grey langur** (*Semnopithecus priam thersites*; also known as the common or Hanuman langur), a beautiful and delicate long-limbed creature with silver-grey hair, a small black face and an enormous tail. Also relatively common, though rather less attractive, is the endemic **toque macaque** (*Macaca sinica*; also known as the red-faced macaque), a medium-sized, reddish-brown creature with a rather baboon-like narrow pink face topped by a distinctive circular tuft of hair. Macaques are much bolder (and noisier) than langurs, and sometimes behave aggressively toward humans when searching for food.

The third native species, also endemic to Sri Lanka, is the **purple-faced leaf monkey** (*Trachypithecus vitulus*; also known as the purple-faced langur). This is similar in build to the grey langur, with long, slender limbs, but with a blackish coat and a white rump and tail. They're found along the west coast, while a more shaggy-coated subspecies, known as the **bear monkey**, is found in the hill country, particularly in the area around Horton Plains.

Other mammals

Sri Lanka's most endearing mammal is the rare **sloth bear** (*Melursus ursinus*), an engagingly shaggy, shambling creature, about 1m in length, which is occasionally spotted in Yala and other national parks. You're far more likely to see the island's various types of **deer** – species include the spotted, sambar and muntjac (or "barking") deer. Wild **buffalo** are also common. Sri Lanka boasts several species of **squirrel**, ranging from the beautifully delicate little palm squirrels, instantly recognizable by their striped bodies and found everywhere (even on the beach), to the rare giant squirrels that can occasionally be seen in montane forests. **Flying foxes** – large, fruit-eating bats that can reach up to 1m in length – are a common sight islandwide, while **mongooses** are also often encountered in the national parks, as are **rabbits**. Less frequently seen is the **wild boar**, similar to the wild boars of Europe, and equally ugly. A number of local mammals are largely nocturnal, including the **porcupine** and **pangolin**, as well as the rare **fishing cat**, a large, greyish-brown creature that can grow up to almost 1m in length. They usually live near water, scooping prey out with their paws – hence the name.

Birds

Sri Lanka is a rewarding and well-established destination for dedicated birders: the island's range of habitats – from coastal wetlands to tropical rainforest and high-altitude cloudforest – supports a huge variety of birdlife, which is further enriched by migrants from the Indian subcontinent and further afield. The island boasts 233 **resident species**, including 34 **endemics**, while another two hundred-odd **migratory species** have been recorded here. Most of the latter visit the island during the northern hemisphere's winter, holidaying in Sri Lanka from around August through to April. In addition, some pelagic birds visit Sri Lanka during the southern hemisphere's winter.

Some species are confined to particular **habitats**, and most of the island's endemics are found in the wet zone that covers the southwestern quarter of the country. For casual bird-spotters, any of Sri Lanka's national parks should yield a large range of species – Bundala, Yala and Uda Walawe are all excellent destinations, and a day's birdwatching in any of these could easily turn up as many as a hundred species. Dedicated birders generally head to specialist sites such as Sinharaja, which is home to no fewer than seventeen endemics (although they can be difficult to see), and Horton Plains and Hakgala Botanical Gardens in the hill country, both excellent for spotting montane species. With careful planning, dedicated birders might succeed in seeing all the island's endemics in a week or two.

Sri Lanka's **endemic birds** range from the spectacular, multicoloured Sri Lanka blue magpie to relatively dowdy species such as the tiny and elusive Legge's flowerpecker and the Sri Lanka jungle fowl, the island's national bird, which can often be seen rootling around the ground in the island's forests. **Common species** include bee-eaters, scarlet minivets, orioles, parakeets, Indian rollers, Indian pittas, hoopoes, sunbirds and the arious species of kingfisher – which are a frequent sight around water (or perched on cables) throughout the island.

The rich population of resident and migrant **water birds** includes various species of grebe, cormorant, pelican, bittern, heron, egret, stork, ibis, plover, lapwing, sandpiper, tern and stilt. Look out particularly for the colourful painted stork, the magnificent Indian darter and the huge (and impressively ugly) lesser adjutant, while Bundala National Park attracts huge flocks of migrant flamingos. **Birds of prey** include the common Brahminy kite (frequently spotted even in the middle of Colombo), the majestic sea eagle and the huge black eagle and grey-headed fish eagle. The island's fine range of **owls** includes the extraordinary-looking spot-bellied eagle owl, oriental scops owl and the difficult-to-spot frogmouth.

Finally, one bird you can't avoid in Sri Lanka is the **crow** – indeed the rasping and cawing of flocks of the creatures is one of the distinctive sounds of the island. Burgeoning numbers of these avian pests can be found wherever there are heaps of rubbish, and infestations are now common not only in towns but also in formerly unspoilt areas such as Horton Plains National Park, where they have been responsible for eating many of the beautiful lizards that formerly lived there.

Reptiles

Sri Lanka boasts two species of **crocodile: mugger** (also known as marsh or swamp) crocodile (*Crocodilus palustris*), and the **saltwater** (or estuarine) crocodile (*Crocodilus porosus*); both species live in burrows and feed on fish, birds and small mammals, killing their prey by drowning. Muggers can grow up to 4m in length and tend to frequent shallow freshwater areas around rivers, lakes and marshes; the larger and more aggressive saltwater crocs can reach lengths of up to 7m and prefer the brackish waters of river estuaries and lagoons near the sea. Crocodiles are commonly seen in Bundala and Yala. Despite their fearsome appearance they aren't usually considered dangerous unless provoked, although attacks are not unknown (including, most recently, British journalist Paul McClean, killed by a crocodile while washing his hands in a lagoon at Arugam Bay in 2017).

Sri Lankan crocodiles are occasionally confused with **water monitors**, or *kabaragoya* (*Varanus bengalensis*), though these grow up to only 2m in length and have a quite different – and much more lizard-like – appearance, with a narrower, blue-black head and yellow markings on their back. Water monitors are just one of numerous impressive monitor species found here, including the similar land monitor, or *talagoya* (*Varanus salvator*). The island also boasts a wide and colourful range of smaller lizards, which can be seen islandwide, from coastal beaches to the high-altitude moorlands of Horton Plains National Park.

Sri Lanka is home to eighty-odd species of **snake**, including five poisonous varieties, all relatively common (especially in northern dry zones) and including the cobra and the extremely dangerous Russell's viper. The island has the dubious distinction of having one of the highest number of **snakebite** fatalities, per capita, of any country in the world.

Turtles

Five of the world's seven species of **marine turtle** visit Sri Lanka's beaches to nest, a rare ecological blessing that could potentially make the island one of the world's leading turtle-watching destinations. Official support for conservation efforts remains lukewarm, however, despite the number of privately run turtle hatcheries along the west coast.

Turtles are among the oldest reptiles on earth, and offer a living link with the dinosaur age, having first evolved around two hundred million years ago; they also have a longer lifespan than most creatures, with some of them living for more than

100 years. All five of the species that visit Sri Lanka are now highly endangered, thanks to marine hazards such as fishing nets and rubbish thrown into the sea, as well as widespread poaching of eggs, hunting for meat and shells, and the disturbance or destruction of nesting sites.

The most widespread marine turtle – and the one most commonly sighted in Sri Lanka – is the **green turtle** (*Chelonia mydas*), named for its greenish fat; green turtles are actually brown in colour, albeit with a greenish tinge. They grow to up to 1m in length and 140kg in weight and are found in warm coastal waters worldwide, feeding mainly on marine grasses. The females are the most prolific egg-producers of any sea turtle, laying six or seven hundred eggs every two weeks.

The largest and more remarkable sea turtle is the **leatherback** (*Dermochelys coriacea*), which commonly grows to over 2m in length (indeed unconfirmed sightings of 3m-long specimens have been reported) and weighs up to 800kg. One of the planet's greatest swimmers, the leatherback can be found in oceans worldwide, ranging from tropical waters almost to the Arctic Circle. They can also dive to depths of up to a kilometre and hold their breath for half an hour.

The reddish-brown **loggerhead** (*Caretta caretta*) is another immense creature, reaching lengths of up to 2m; it's similar in appearance to the green turtle, but with a relatively larger head. The **hawksbill** (*Eretmochelys imbricata*) is one of the smaller sea turtles, reaching a length of around 0.5m and a weight of 40kg – it's so called because of its unusually hooked jaws, which give its head a rather birdlike appearance. Lastly, there's the **olive ridley** (*Lepidochelys olivacea*) – named for its greenish colour – which has a wide, rounded shell and reaches sizes of up to 1m.

Whales and dolphins

Sri Lanka has developed into a major whale-watching destination over the past decade and is one of the best places in the world for seeing blue whales, with sperm whales and other species also being frequently spotted. **Blue whales** are the most commonly seen cetacean off the Sri Lankan coast. Believed to be the largest animal ever to have lived on the planet, they reach over 30m in length and weigh almost two hundred tons. If you're lucky, you may also catch sight of a **sperm whale** (named for the milky-white "spermaceti" oil found in tubes in the front of their heads), slightly smaller than the blue whale, though with the largest brain of any creature on the planet. The easiest way to distinguish between the two while at sea is usually by comparing their "blows": that of the blue whale is tall (typically around 10m) and upright, while that of the sperm whale is smaller and more "bushy", and also typically slanted forwards and to the left. **Humpback** and **Bryde's whales** are also occasionally spotted.

In addition to whales, numerous pods of **spinner dolphins** can be found around the island, extrovert creatures named after their acrobatic spins out of the water. In parts of the island, as many as two thousand spinner dolphins have been sighted at one time, most notably off the coast around Kalpitiya. **Risso's and bottlenose dolphins** are other species known to inhabit Sri Lanka's waters.

Ceylon tea

In the minds of many outsiders, Sri Lanka remains synonymous with one thing: tea. Tea cultivation underpinned much of the island's prosperity during the British colonial period, and also had major cultural and environmental side effects, leading to the clearance of almost all the highland jungles and the arrival of large numbers of Tamil labourers, drafted in to work the plantations. The industry remains crucial to Sri Lanka's economy, and tea estates still dominate the hill country, with endless miles of neatly trimmed bushes carpeting the rolling uplands.

The first use of the leaves of the **tea** plant as a beverage is generally credited to the Chinese emperor Sheng-Nung, who – in truly serendipitous manner – discovered the plant's notable qualities around 2700 BC when a few leaves chanced to fall off a wild tea bush into a pot of boiling water. Tea developed into a staple drink of the Chinese, and later the Japanese, though it wasn't until the nineteenth century that it began to find a market outside Asia. The British began commercial production in India in the 1830s, establishing tea plantations in Assam and, later, Darjeeling, where it continues to flourish.

The success of Ceylon tea (as it's still usually described, rather than "Sri Lankan") was built on the collapse of the island's coffee trade. Throughout the early British colonial period, coffee was the principal plantation crop in the highlands, until the insidious leaf virus *hemileia vastatrix* – popularly know as "Devastating Emily" – laid waste to the industry during the 1870s. Tea bushes had been grown in Sri Lanka in Peradeniya Botanical Gardens as far back as 1824, but it wasn't until 1867 that the island's first commercial tea plantation was established by the Scottish planter **James Taylor**, a modest nineteen-acre affair at Loolecondera, southeast of Kandy. When the coffee industry finally collapsed, a decade later, interest in tea really took off. Bankrupt coffee estates were snapped up for a song and converted to tea production, while rapid fortunes were made from what soon became known as Sri Lanka's "green gold". Hundreds of colonial planters and speculators began descending on the island to clear new land and establish estates of their own, clearing vast swathes of hill-country jungle to make way for new tea gardens in the process.

The introduction of tea also had a significant social by-product. The coffee estates had already employed large numbers of migrant Tamil labourers, brought to Sri Lanka from south India due to a chronic shortage of local manpower in the hills. Work on the coffee plantations was seasonal, meaning that these labourers returned to South India for six months of the year. By contrast, tea production continued year-round, which led to the permanent settlement of thousands of expatriate labourers, Sri Lanka's so-called **"Plantation" Tamils**, whose descendants still work the island's tea gardens today, although they remain one of the island's poorest and most marginalized communities.

Tea remains vital to the **economy** of modern Sri Lanka – so much so that the entire industry was nationalized, with disastrous consequences, in 1975. The government's inept management of the estates over the following decade led to plummeting standards that came close to crippling the entire industry, after which estates were gradually restored to private ownership, where they remain to this day. Sri Lanka is currently one of the world's top three exporters, along with India and Kenya, and tea still makes up around a quarter of the country's export earnings. Almost half these exports now go to Middle Eastern countries, however, which has made the industry vulnerable to the effects of warfare and sanctions in that region, although significant quantities of low-grade tea particles find their way into the tea-bags of major international brands such as Tetley and Lipton's.

Tea production

The tea "bush" is actually an evergreen tree, *Camellia sinensis*, which grows to around ten metres in height in the wild. Cultivated tea bushes are constantly pruned, producing a repeated growth of fresh young buds and leaves throughout the year. Ceylon tea is divided into three types, depending on the altitude at which it is grown. The best-quality tea, so-called **high-grown**, only flourishes above 1200m in a warm climate and on sloping terrain, for which Sri Lanka's hill country provides the perfect location. Bushes at higher altitude grow more slowly but produce a more delicate flavour – among connoisseurs, premium high-grown Ceylon teas are rated as second only to the finest Indian Darjeelings in terms of subtlety. **Low-grown tea** (cultivated below 600m) is stronger and less subtle in taste; **mid-grown tea** is somewhere between the two – in practice, blends of the various types are usually mixed to produce the required flavour and colour.

The island's finest teas are grown in Uva province and around Nuwara Eliya, Dimbula and Dickoya; the flavours from these different regions are quite distinct, showing (at least to trained palates) how sensitive tea is to subtle variations in soil and climate. Low-grown teas are mainly produced in the Galle, Matara and Ratnapura regions. Most Ceylon tea is black (fermented), though a few estates have diversified into producing fine green (unfermented) and oolong (partially fermented) teas, the staple form of the drink in China and Japan.

Tea production remains a labour-intensive, resolutely low-tech industry, and the manufacturing process – indeed often the machinery itself – has remained pretty much unchanged since Victorian times. The entire tea production process, from plucking to packing, takes around 24 hours. The first stage – **plucking** the leaves – is still extremely labour-intensive, providing work for some 300,000 estate workers across the island (mainly but not exclusively female). Tea pickers select the youngest two leaves and bud from the end of every branch – bushes are plucked every seven days in the dry season, twice as often in the wet. Following plucking, leaves are **dried** (or "withered") by being spread out in huge troughs while hot air is blown through them to remove moisture, after which they are **crushed** for around thirty minutes, an action that releases juices and enzymes and triggers fermentation – the conditions and length of time under which the leaves ferment is one of the crucial elements in determining the quality of the tea. Once sufficient fermentation has taken place, the tea is **fired** in an oven, preventing further fermentation and producing the black tea that is the staple form of the drink consumed worldwide.

Types of tea

The resultant "bulk" tea is then filtered into different-sized particles and **graded**. Like wine, tea comes in an endless variety of forms and flavours, and a complex and colourful vocabulary has grown up over the centuries to describe the various styles and standards available. The finest teas – also described as "leaf" teas, since they consist of relatively large pieces of unbroken leaf – are known as **Orange Pekoe** (OP), signifying a tea made with young, whole leaves, and the slightly lower-quality **Broken Orange Pekoe** (BOP), which uses broken pieces of the same leaves. Finer grades of OP and BOP come with the added designations "Flowery", "Golden" or "Tippy", signifying teas which also include varying quantities and types of young buds mixed in with the leaves to give the tea a distinctively delicate flavour, such as the prized FTGFOP, or (to give it its full name) Finest Tippy Golden Flowery Orange Pekoe – also known among aficionados as Far Too Good For Ordinary People.

Lower grades are designated as "**fannings**" (BOPF) or as an even finer residue, unappetizingly described as "**dust**" (D). Despite the unprepossessing names, these grades are perhaps the two most important, since their tiny particles produce a rich, strong, instant brew that is perfect for the tea bags favoured in many parts of the world – Ceylon tea, blended with leaves from other countries, is used in many major

SIR THOMAS LIPTON AND THE RISE OF CEYLON TEA

For all the pioneering efforts of Sir James Taylor, the father of Sri Lanka's tea industry, it was another Scot, **Sir Thomas Lipton**, who almost single-handedly put Ceylon tea on the global map. Born in 1850 in Glasgow, Lipton displayed his appetite for adventure young, stowing away at the age of 14 on a ship to the US, where he worked for five years as a farm labourer and grocery clerk. Returning to Glasgow, Lipton opened his first grocery store in 1871, using the sort of eye-catching **publicity stunts** he had seen employed to tremendous effect in America, including leading a parade of well-fed pigs through the streets of Glasgow, their backs hung with placards declaring "I'm going to Lipton's, the best shop in town for Irish bacon!" By 1880 he had twenty shops; by 1890, three hundred.

In 1889, Lipton moved into **tea** retailing, announcing his new wares with a parade of brass bands and bagpipers; by undercutting the then going price by two-thirds, he succeeded in selling ten million pounds of tea in just two years. The real birth of the Lipton's tea dynasty, however, began in 1890. En route to Australia, Lipton stopped off in Ceylon and – true to his "cut out the middleman" motto – bought up five bankrupt tea estates, including what would become his favourite, at Dambatenne, near Haputale. Trumpeting his new acquisitions with relentless advertising and a new slogan ("Direct from the Tea Gardens to the Teapot"), Lipton put Ceylon tea firmly on the world map and massively stimulated demand for it back in Britain. His was also the first company to sell tea in pre-packaged cartons, thus guaranteeing quantity and quality to hard-pressed housewives – while ensuring that the Lipton's brand received the widest possible exposure.

As a commercial expression of the might of the British Empire, Lipton's tea was **unparalleled**. Lipton succeeded not only in establishing his brand as the number one tea at home and throughout the colonies, but also largely killed off demand for the traditional and more delicate but unpredictable China teas that had previously formed the mainstay of the trade, fostering a taste for the black, full-bodied and reliably strong blends that remain the norm in the UK right up to the present day. The Lipton's tea phenomenon in turn paved the way for the commercial success of other brands established in the late nineteenth century, such as Typhoo (despite the compellingly oriental-sounding name, the tea itself was, again, sourced entirely from Sri Lanka) and Brooke Bond's PG Tips.

The fortunes of Lipton's own brand were mixed, however. It continued to be a major player in British markets well into the twentieth century, but gradually lost out to **Brooke Bond**, Typhoo and others, largely due to the fact that it was sold only through Lipton's own shops. With the rise of supermarkets such as Tesco (which itself had its roots in the tea trade – the name is an amalgam of the surname of another entrepreneurial grocer, Jack Cohen, with that of his tea dealer, T.E. Stockwell), sales slowly decreased and the Lipton's brand largely disappeared from Britain, leading to the final irony whereby Lipton's, which is still synonymous with tea throughout Asia and in many other parts of the world, is now largely unknown in the land of its founder's birth.

international tea brands, including Lipton's and Tetley. The larger OP and BOP grades, which yield a much paler and more delicate liquor, are traditionally favoured in the Middle East.

Following production, tea is **sampled** by tea tasters – a highly specialist profession, as esteemed in Sri Lanka as wine tasting is in France – before being sent for auction, mostly in Colombo. The vast majority of Sri Lanka's tea is exported, although there's an increasingly good range of home-grown teas available in local shops and supermarkets (especially Cargills) including various blends by major Sri Lankan tea retailers Dilmah and Tea Tang, while unblended, single-origin estate teas are also increasingly available – Ceylon tea at its purest. When buying, look out for the Ceylon Tea Board lion logo, which guarantees that the stuff you're buying comprises only pure Ceylon tea.

Books

Contemporary Sri Lanka has a rich literary tradition, and the island has produced a string of fine novelists in recent years, including Booker Prize-winner Michael Ondaatje. Although virtually all of them now live abroad, the island, its culture and twentieth-century history continue to loom large in their work – all the novels of Shyam Selvadurai and Romesh Gunesekera, for instance, deal with Sri Lankan themes, even though Gunesekera now lives in London and Selvadurai in Canada.

In the selection of books below, only small-press publishers outside the US or UK are named. The ★ symbol marks titles that are particularly recommended.

FICTION

Ashok Ferrey *Colpetty People*. Whimsical, crisply written and enjoyably wry collection of short stories by one of modern Sri Lanka's most entertaining writers. His other books, including *The Good Little Ceylonese Girl* and *Love in the Tsunami*, cover similar ground, offering a satirical, enjoyably subversive look at the social quirks and absurdities of Sri Lankan life.

★ **Romesh Gunesekera** *Reef*, a deceptively simple but haunting story about a house boy, his master and their twin obsessions – cooking and marine science – beautifully captures the flavour of the island, as well as plumbing some surprising depths. The same author's *Noontide Toll* is also worth a read for its understated portrait of the island in the aftermath of the civil war.

★ **Shehan Karunatilaka** *Chinaman*. Possibly the best novel ever to come out of Sri Lanka, Karunatilaka's 2012 debut follows an alcoholic sportswriter's attempts to hunt down the mysterious spin bowler Pradeep S. Mathew via a gloriously madcap narrative replete with googlies, arrack, corrupt officials, match-fixers, a six-fingered coach and enough cricketing lore to fill a small encyclopedia – at once a wildly entertaining black comedy, a memorable snapshot of Colombo in the raw and a strangely moving portrait of failed ambition and wrecked talent.

★ **Michelle de Kretser** *The Hamilton Case*. Set in the years just before and after independence, this beautifully written and cunningly plotted novel – part period piece, part elegant whodunnit – chronicles the career of lawyer Sam Obeysekere, a loyal subject of the Empire, whose life and loyalties are blighted by his chance involvement in the mysterious murder of a British tea planter.

Carl Muller The prolific novelist and journalist Muller is something of a cultural institution in Sri Lanka. His most famous work, *The Jam Fruit Tree* trilogy (*The Jam Fruit Tree*, *Yakada Yaka* and *Once Upon a Tender Time*), is an intermittently entertaining account of the lives, loves and interminable misadventures of the von Bloss clan, a family of ruffianly, party-loving and permanently inebriated Burghers. Other books include the comic short stories of *A Funny Thing Happened on the Way to the Cemetery*; the chunky historical epics *The Children of the Lion* (based on the mythological history of early Sri Lanka) and *Colombo*; and a collection of essays, *Firing At Random*.

Shyam Selvadurai *Funny Boy* and *Cinnamon Gardens*. *Funny Boy* presents a moving and disquieting picture of Sri Lanka seen through the eyes of a gay Tamil boy growing up in Colombo in the years leading up to the civil war. *Cinnamon Gardens* offers a similarly simple but eloquent account of those trapped by dint of their sex or sexuality in the stiflingly conservative society of 1930s Colombo.

Shyam Selvadurai (editor). *Many Roads Through Paradise: An Anthology of Sri Lankan Literature*. Absorbing anthology of Sri Lankan writers, featuring prose and poetry from both Sinhalese and Tamil writers from the 1950s through to the present day.

A. Sivanandan *When Memory Dies*. Weighty historical epic describing the travails of three generations of a Sri Lankan family living through the end of the colonial period and the island's descent into civil war. The same author's *Where The Dance Is* comprises a sequence of inventive and keenly observed short stories set in Sri Lanka, India and England.

★ **Leonard Woolf** *The Village in the Jungle*. Future luminary of the Bloomsbury set, Leonard Woolf served for several years as a colonial administrator in the backwaters of Hambantota. First published in 1913, this gloomy little masterpiece tells a starkly depressing tale of love and murder in an isolated Sri Lankan village, stifled by the encroaching jungle and by its own poverty and backwardness.

RAVELOGUES AND MEMOIR

uliet Coombe and Daisy Perry Around the Fort in) Lives (Sri Serendipity Publishing, Sri Lanka). Warm, vocative and beautifully illustrated portrait of today's alle Fort, told in a series of affectionate sketches of s diverse cast of idiosyncratic characters, from street eddlers to millionaire expats.

★ **Sonali Deraniyagala** Wave: A Memoir of Life After e Tsunami. Written by a tsunami survivor who lost her usband, parents and two children in the disaster, this urageously understated and brutally honest memoir is robably the nearest any of us will get to understanding e unimaginable grief of those who lost their entire milies to the wave. Harrowing but essential reading.

hristopher Ondaatje The Man-Eater of Punanai. mous Sri Lankan expatriate Christopher Ondaatje returns the island of his birth to search for leopards in the war-rn east, and for memories of his own youth – including e spectre of his maverick father, who also appears as one f the stars of Running in the Family (see p.448).

★ **John Gimlette** Elephant Complex. An outstanding cent addition to the tiny number of really good Sri Lankan

travel books, featuring encounters with an eclectic cast of characters ranging from Veddahs and farmers through to test cricketers and a former president, all illuminated by Gimlette's laser-sharp perceptions and consummate mastery of recondite facts.

★ **William McGowan** Only Man Is Vile. Written in the late 1980s, this classic account of the civil war and JVP insurrection combines war reportage, travelogue and social commentary to produce a stark, compelling and extremely depressing insight into the darker aspects of the Sinhalese psyche.

★ **Michael Ondaatje** Running in the Family. Perhaps the best book ever written about the island, this marvellous memoir of Ondaatje's Burgher family and his variously dipsomaniac and wildly eccentric relations is at once magically atmospheric and wonderfully comic. Ondaatje's other Sri Lankan book, the altogether more sombre Anil's Ghost, offers a very lightly fictionalized account of the civil war and JVP insurrection seen through the eyes of a young forensic pathologist attempting to expose government-sponsored killings.

ISTORY AND RELIGION

asmine and Brendan Gooneratne This Inscrutable nglishman: Sir John D'Oyly (1774–1824). Detailed ography of the brilliant English diplomat who brokered e surrender of the Kandyan kingdom to the British in \|15 – the sheer drama of the events described makes an interesting read, despite the authors' laboriously ademic tone.

★ **John Clifford Holt (ed)** The Sri Lanka Reader: story, Culture, Politics. This weighty but fascinating lume offers an absorbing overview of the island's story and culture, anthologizing a vast selection of xts ranging from the Mahavamsa and Sigiriya graffiti rough to colonial-era documents and contemporary ewspaper articles (including the moving "And Then ey Came for Me" by murdered journalist Lasantha ckrematunga) – all threaded together by the editor.

A.J. Hulugalle Ceylon of the Early Travellers (Arjuna llugalle, Sri Lanka). This tiny book offers a series entertaining snapshots of Sri Lankan history seen rough the eyes of foreign travellers, traders and ldiers, including accounts of some of the more bizarre cidents in the island's past, such as the British plan to pture Colombo using a giant cheese.

bert Knox An Historical Relation of Ceylon (Tisara akasakayo, Sri Lanka). Knox's account of his near venty-year captivity in the Kandyan kingdom ee p.219) is an interesting read, especially the tobiographical section, which deals with his own Job-e trials and tribulations and culminates in the nail-ing story of his carefully planned escape.

Dennis B. McGilvray Crucible of Conflict, Tamil and Muslim Society on the East Coast of Sri Lanka. Detailed ethnographic study – academic, but absorbing – of eastern Sri Lanka, centred on the town of Akkaraipattu and offering unrivalled insights into the region's cultural and religious complexities.

Roy Moxham Tea: Addiction, Exploitation and Empire. This detailed and readable account of the development of the tea industry in the British colonies paints a compelling portrait of Victorian enterprise and greed – and of the terrible human price paid by Indian plantation workers. Includes extensive coverage of Sri Lanka.

K.M. de Silva A History of Sri Lanka (Vikas, India). The definitive history of the island, offering a considered and intelligent overview of events from prehistory to the late twentieth century.

Nath Yogasundram A Comprehensive History of Sri Lanka: From Prehistory to Tsunami (Vijitha Yapa, Sri Lanka). Less scholarly than de Silva's History (see above), though intelligently written, and also more up to date, with coverage up to 2006.

Nira Wickramasinghe Sri Lanka in the Modern Age: A History. Styling itself as a history of the people rather than a history of the state, politics and power, Wickramasinghe's books travels from colonial times through the modern postwar era, with many interesting and entertainingly quirky insights en route. It's also the most up-to-date history currently available, covering events right up to 2013.

THE CIVIL WAR

Ajith Boyagoda and Sunila Galappatti *A Long Watch: War, Captivity and Return in Sri Lanka*. Eloquent account by former naval office Ajith Boyagoda of his eight years as a captive of the LTTE – and one which bravely challenges many Sinhalese prejudices and preconceptions about the hated Tigers.

Frances Harrison *Still Counting the Dead: Survivors of Sri Lanka's Hidden War*. Written by a former BBC Sri Lanka correspondent, *Still Counting the Dead* recounts the horrific stories of those caught up in the brutal final months of the civil war, including first-hand accounts of life – or, more usually, death – inside the infamous "no-fire" zone. A damning record of the many brutal atrocities committed by the Sri Lankan government under Mahinda Rajapakse – and for which it has still to be brought to account.

M.R. Narayan Swamy *Inside An Elusive Mind: Prabhakaran* (Vijitha Yapa, Sri Lanka). Detailed account of the career of the LTTE supremo, covering events up until the turn of the millennium, although many of the LTTE's less savoury activities – such as their numerous massacres of civilians, political assassinations, the use of child soldiers and the widespread terrorizing of their own people – are conveniently ignored or whitewashed. The same author's *Tigers of Lanka* covers very similar ground (although again only up to the turn of the millennium) while the more recent *The Tiger Vanquished: LTTE's Story* completes the story.

Anita Pratap *Island of Blood: Frontline Reports from Sri Lanka, Afghanistan and other South Asian Flashpoints* (Vijitha Yapa, Sri Lanka). Vivid, if sometimes irritating self-congratulatory, eyewitness accounts of various Asia flashpoints by a well-known Indian journalist, includin extended coverage of the Sri Lankan civil war.

K.M. de Silva *Reaping the Whirlwind: Ethnic Conflic Ethnic Politics in Sri Lanka*. Definitive exploration of th social and political roots of the island's Tamil–Sinhales conflict. Excellent on the decades preceding the wa although with relatively little coverage of the war itself.

★ **Nirupama Subramanian** *Sri Lanka: Voices from War Zone* (Vijitha Yapa, Sri Lanka). Published in 2005, th eloquent collection of essays by an Indian Tamil journalis gives a powerful account of the later stages of the civil wa combining military and political analysis of the confli with the personal stories of those affected by the fightir on both sides of the ethnic divide.

★ **Gordon Weiss** *The Cage: the Fight for Sri Lanka an the Last Days of the Tamil Tigers*. Written by a former U staffer in Colombo, this searing book offers a meticulous documented account of the last months of the civil w and its aftermath, serving up a grim indictment of bo government and LTTE military as well as a scorchir critique of Rajapakse family rule. The preliminary histo expertly unravels the origins of the conflict, while th eyewitness accounts and reconstructions of battlefie events – and the horrific sufferings of Tamil civilia trapped in the fighting – are unlikely to be bettered.

ART, ARCHITECTURE AND CULTURE

Emma Boyle *Culture Smart! Sri Lanka: A Quick Guide to Customs and Culture*. Insightful look at Sri Lankan society, customs and cultural quirks by a seasoned UK expat.

★ **Ronald Lewcock, Barbara Sansoni and Laki Senanayake** *The Architecture of an Island: the Living Heritage of Sri Lanka*. This gorgeous book, a work of art in itself, offers revealing insights into the jumble of influences that have gone into creating Sri Lanka's distinctive architectural style. The text discusses 95 examples of traditional island architecture – from palm shacks and

hen coops to Kandyan temples and colonial cathedra all beautifully illustrated with line drawings by Barba Sansoni.

★ **David Robson** *Geoffrey Bawa: The Complete Work* Written by a long-term Bawa associate, this comprehensi volume offers the definitive overview of the work Sri Lanka's outstanding modern architect, with copic beautiful photographs and fascinating text on Bawa's l and creations, plus many revealing insights into Sri Lank culture and art.

FLORA AND FAUNA

Indraneil Das and Anslem de Silva *Snakes and Other Reptiles of Sri Lanka*. Excellent photographic pocket guide to Sri Lanka's fascinating but little-known population of lizards, snakes and other slithery creatures.

John Harrison and Tim Worfolk *A Field Guide to the Birds of Sri Lanka*. The definitive guide to Sri Lanka's avifauna.

★ **Gehan de Silva Wijeyeratne** *Naturalist's Guide the Birds of Sri Lanka*. Invaluable, lightweight starter guid with excellent photos and clear descriptions of all specie **Gehan de Silva Wijeyeratne** *Sri Lankan Wildlife: Visitor's Guide*. Excellent introductory primer covering t full range of island wildlife, from elephants, leopards a birds through to dragonflies, lizards and whales.

Language

Sri Lanka is a trilingual nation. The main language, Sinhala, is spoken by around 75 percent of the population; Tamil is spoken by around 25 percent (including not only the Tamils themselves, but many of the island's Muslims). English is also widely used by Westernized and urban sections of the population, and is the first language of most Sri Lankan Burghers – many people speak it more or less fluently, and even native Sinhala speakers (especially in Colombo) often employ English in conversation alongside their native tongue, switching between languages as the mood takes them. English sometimes serves as a link language between the island's communities, too – relatively few northern Tamils speak Sinhala, and even fewer Sinhalese speak Tamil.

Language is an emotive issue in Sri Lanka – the notorious "Sinhala Only" legislation of 1956, which downgraded Tamil from the status of an official language and effectively barred Tamils from most forms of government employment, was one of the most significant root causes behind the subsequent civil war, and although Tamil was restored to the status of an official language in 1988, the subject is still politically sensitive. All official signs, banknotes, government publications and the like are printed in all three languages, and (except in the north, where Sinhala is rarely seen or heard) many businesses and shops follow suit.

Sinhala

Sinhala (or Singhala; also referred to as Sinhalese/Singhalese, although properly speaking this is the name of the people themselves, rather than their language) is an Indo-Aryan language, related to other North Indian languages such as Hindi and Bengali, as well as to Sanskrit, the classic ancient language of the Indian subcontinent, and Pali, the sacred language of Buddhism. The language was first brought to Sri Lanka by the original Sinhalese settlers from North India around the fifth century BC, though it has developed since then in complete geographical isolation from other North Indian Indo-Aryan languages, being heavily influenced by Tamil, as well as acquiring numerous words from Dutch, Portuguese, Malay and English. Sinhala is found only in Sri Lanka; its closest relative is Dhivehi, spoken in the Maldives.

Sinhala **pronunciation** is relatively straightforward – most Sinhala words, despite their sometimes fearsome length, are generally built up out of chains of simple vowel sounds, typically a vowel plus a consonant, as in the expression for "please", *karuna karala*. There are a few awkward consonant clusters, but these are relatively uncommon. Written Sinhala uses a beautifully elegant and highly distinctive system of 47 curvilinear characters. Most characters represent a consonant plus a vowel sound that is indicated by a subtle addition to the basic character (see box opposite).

There's little **printed material** available on Sinhala. The best resource is Lonely Planet's *Sinhala Phrasebook* by Swarna Pragnaratne. *Say it in Sinhala* by J.B. Dissanayake and the *Sri Lanka Words and Phrases* phrasebook published by Arjuna Hulugalle are both useful.

Tamil

Tamil is one of the most important of the various Dravidian languages of South India, and is spoken by almost sixty million people in the southern Indian state of Tamil

THE SINHALA ALPHABET

ඇ ah	ඔ o	ඨ tah	භ bhah
ඈ aah	ඕ oh	ඩ dah	ම mah
ඇ a	ඖ au	ණ nah	ය yah
ඇෑ aa	ක kah	ත tah	ර rah
ඇං ahng	ඛ khah	ථ thah	ල lah
ඉ i	ග gah	ද dhah	ව vah
ඊ ee	ඝ ghah	ධ dhah	ශ shah
උ u	ච cha	න nah	ෂ shah
ඌ oo	ඡ chah	ප pah	ස sah
එ e	ජ jah	ඵ phah	හ hah
ඒ eh	ට tah	බ bah	ළ lah

Some vowel sounds are represented using the characters shown above. Others are shown by modifying a basic consonant character, either by adding small additional strokes to it or by placing vowel symbols on one or both sides of the basic character. Most characters follow the same basic pattern:

ප pah (basic character)	පූ poo	පි pi
පු pu	පා paah	පො po
ප් p (consonant only)	පෙ pe	පී pee

Nadu, as well as by Tamils in Sri Lanka, Singapore, Malaysia and elsewhere around the world. The language in Sri Lanka has developed in isolation from the Tamil spoken in South India, acquiring its own accent and vocabulary – the relationship between Indian and Sri Lankan Tamil is roughly similar to that between British and North American English.

Tamil has a long and distinguished history, and a literary tradition stretching back to the third century BC – surpassed among Indian languages only by Sanskrit. It's also a famously difficult language to master, thanks to its complex grammar, extended alphabet and repertoire of distinctive sounds (the so-called "reflexive consonants", common to all Dravidian languages, pronounced with the tongue curled against the back of the teeth) – these also make the language virtually impossible to transliterate into Roman script. The language is written in the beautiful **Vattelluttu** ("round script") a combination of rectangular shapes and elegant curvilinear flourishes.

Sri Lankan English

As with Indian English, the version of the language spoken in Sri Lanka, sometimes referred to as "**Sringlish**" (not to be confused with "Singlish", or Singaporean English) is not without its own charming idiosyncrasies of grammar, spelling and punctuation, along with a few colourful local expressions. A "bake house" is of course a bakery, though you might not realize that a "cool spot" is a small café, or that a "colour house" is a paint shop. Remember too that "taxis" are most often just everyday tuktuks, while a "hotel" is frequently a cheap eating establishment rather than a place to stay. And if someone at your (real) hotel starts talking about their "backside", don't worry – they're referring to the rear of the building, not a part of their anatomy. You might also come across classic old-time Sri Lankan idioms such as "men" (which can be used to refer to anyone listening, men and women); the monosyllabic "Is it?" (meaning anything from "I'm sorry, I don't quite understand" to "Go jump off a cliff"); or the quintessentially Sri Lankan "What to do?" – a kind of verbal shrug of the shoulders, which can mean virtually anything from "What shall we do?" to "The situation's completely hopeless" o "Let's have another beer."

For more on the idiosyncrasies of Sringlish, get hold of a copy of Michael Meyler's comprehensive and entertaining *A Dictionary of Sri Lankan English*.

Useful Sinhala and Tamil words and expressions

BASICS

ENGLISH SINHALA *TAMIL*

hello/welcome hello/ayubowan *vanakkam*

goodbye ayubowan *varavaanga*

yes oh-ooh *aam*

no nay *illai*

please karuna karala *thayavu seithu*

thank you es-toothee *nandri*

OK hari (or hari-hari) *sari (or sari-sari)*

excuse me sama venna *enga*

sorry kana gartui *mannikkavum*

do you speak English? Oh-ya Inghirisee kata karenavada? *ningal angilam paysu virhala?*

I don't understand matah obahvah thehrum *enakku puriyavillaiye gahna baha*

what is your name? nama mokada? *ungaludaya peyr enna?*

my name is… mahgay nama… *ennudaya peyr…*

how are you? kohomada? *ningal eppadi irukkirigal?*

well, thanks hondeen innava *romba nallayirukkudhu*

not very well vadiya honda nay *paruvayillai*

this mayka *ithu*

that ahraka *athu*

when? kawathatha? *eppa?*

where? kohedah? *enge?*

when does it open/close? ehika kiyatada ahrinnay/ vahhannee *e thirakkiruthu/moodukiradu*

I want mata onay *enakku venam*

is there any…? …-da? *vere ethavathu irikkirutha*

how much? ahhekka keeyada? *ahdu evvalah-vur?*

can you give me a discount? karuna karala gana? *ithil ethavathu salugai adukaranna irikkirutha?*

big loku *pareya (perisu)*

small podi *sarreya*

excellent hari hondai *miga nallathu*

hot (weather) rasnai *ushnamana*

open erala *thira*

closed vahala *moodu*

shop kaday *kadi (kadai)*

post office teppa kantorua *anja lagam*

bank bankua *vangi*

toilet vesikili *kahlippadem*

police polisiya *kavalar*

pharmacy farmisiya/bayhet sapua *marunthu kadai*

doctor dostara *maruthuvar (vaidyar)*

hospital rohala *aspathri*

ill asaneepai *viyathi*

GETTING AROUND

ENGLISH SINHALA *TAMIL*

boat bohtua *padadur*

bus bus ekka *bas*

bus station bus stand *baas nilayem*

train kohchiya *rayil*

train station dumriya pala *rayil nilayem*

car car *car*

bicycle bicycle *saikal*

road para *pathai*

left vama *idathu*

right dakuna *valathu*

straight on kelin yanna *naerakapogavum*

near langa *arukkil*

far athah *turam*

station is-stashama *nilayam*

ticket tiket ekkah *anumati situ*

ACCOMMODATION

ENGLISH SINHALA *TAMIL*

hotel hotelaya *hotel*

guesthouse guesthouse ekka *virun-dhinnar vidhudheh*

bathroom nahnah kamarayak *kulikkum arai*

clean suda *suththam*

cold seethai *kulir*

dirty apirisidui *alukku (azhukku)*

room kamaraya *arai*

do you have a room? kamara teeyenavada? *arekil kidehkkumah?*

may I see the room? kamaraya karuna karala? *koncham kanpikkireengala penvanna?*

is there an a/c room? a/c kamaraya teeyenavada? *kulir seithu arayai park mudiyama?*

is there hot water? unuvatura teeyenavada? *sudu thanir irukkuma?*

please give me the bill karuna karala bila ganna *bill tharavum*

SINHALA PLACE NAMES

Aluthgama	අළුත්ගම	Kataragama	කතරගම
Ambalangoda	අම්බලන්ගොඩ	Kitulgala	කිතුල්ගල
Anuradhapura	අනුරාධපුර	Kurunegala	කුරුණෑගල
Arugam Bay	ආරුගම්බේ	Matara	මාතර
Badulla	බදුල්ල	Mihintale	මිහින්තලේ
Bandarawela	බන්ඩාරවෙල	Mirissa	මිරිස්ස
Batticaloa	මඩකලපුව	Monaragala	මොණරාගල
Bentota	බෙන්තොට	Negombo	මීගමුව
Beruwala	බේරුවෙල	Nilaveli	නිලාවෙලි
Colombo	කොළඹ	Nuwara Eliya	නුවර එළිය
Dambulla	දඹුල්ල	Polonnaruwa	පොළොන්නරුව
Ella	ඇල්ල	Ratnapura	රත්නපුර
Galle	ගාල්ල	Sigiriya	සිගිරිය
Giritale	ගිරිතලේ	Tangalla	තංගල්ල
Habarana	හබරණ	Tissamaharama	තිස්සමහාරාමය
Hambantota	හම්බන්තොට	Trincomalee	ත්‍රිකුණාමලය
Haputale	හපුතලේ	Unawatuna	උණවටුන
Hikkaduwa	හික්කඩුව	Uppuveli	උප්පුවේලි
Jaffna	යාපනය	Weligama	වැලිගම
Kalutara	කළුතර	Wellawaya	වැල්ලවාය
Kandy	මහනුවර		

NUMBERS

ENGLISH SINHALA *TAMIL*

1 ekka *ontru*
2 dekka *erantru*
3 toona *moontru*
4 hatara *nangu*
5 paha *ainthu*
6 hiya *aru*
7 hata *aelu*
8 ahta *ettu*
9 navighya *onpathu*

10 dahhighya *pattu*
20 vissai *erpathu*
30 teehai *mupathu*
40 hatalihai *natpathu*
50 panahai *ompathu*
100 seeya *nooru*
200 dayseeya *irunooru*
1000 daha *aiyuram*
2000 daidaha *iranda iuram*
100,000 lakshaya *latcham*

TIME

ENGLISH SINHALA *TAMIL*

today ada *indru*
tomorrow heta *naalay*
yesterday eeyai *neh-truh*
morning udai *kaalai*

afternoon havasa *matiyam*
day davasa *pakal*
night reh *eravu*
last/next week giya/ilanga sahtiya *pona/adutha vaaram*

FOOD AND DRINK

USEFUL PHRASES
ENGLISH SINHALA *TAMIL*

restaurant aapana salawa *unavu aalayam*
the menu, please menu eka penvanna *thayavu seithu thinpandangal patti tharavum*
I'm vegetarian mama elavalu vitaray *naan oru saivam kannay*
please give me the bill karuna karala bila ganna *bill tharavum*

BASICS
ENGLISH SINHALA *TAMIL*

bread paan *rotti/paan*
egg bittaraya *muttai*
ice ay-is *ice*
rice (cooked) baht *arisi*
water wathurah *thannir*
mineral water (bottle) wathurah botalayak genna *oru pottal soda panam*
tea tay *teyneer*

offee kopi *kapi*
ilk kiri *paal*
gar seeni *seeni*
utter bahta *butter/vennai*
ggery hakuru *seeni/vellam*

RUIT AND VEGETABLES
NGLISH SINHALA *TAMIL*
uit palaturu *palam*
anana keselkan *valaipalam*
oconut pol *thengali*
ango amba *mangai*
apaya papol *pappa palam*
ineapple annasi *annasi*
egetables elavelu *kai kari vagaigal*

MEAT AND FISH
ENGLISH SINHALA *TAMIL*
meat harak mas *mamism*
chicken kukulmas *koli (kozhi)*
pork uroomas *pantri*
beef harak mas *maattu mamism*
lamb batalu mas *aattu mamism*
crab kakuluvo *nandu*
prawns isso *iraal*
lobster pokirissa *periya iraal*
fish malu *min*

Glossary

bhaya mudra "Have No Fear" pose in traditional Buddhist iconography

dimuka Alternative name for a *vahalkada* (the small shrines placed at the four cardinal points of a stupa)

mbalama Traditional pilgrim's rest house

nda The main, hemispherical section of a dagoba

psara Heavenly nymph

rhat Enlightened monk

valokitesvara Mahayana Bodhisattva who is worshipped as the lord of infinite compassion, able to save all beings from suffering

yurveda Ancient Indian system of holistic healthcare

arama or **-rama** park, garden or monastic residence

etel Popular and mildly narcotic snack, combining leaves from the betel tree with flakes of areca nut, a pinch of lime and sometimes a piece of tobacco; produces the characteristic red spittle whose stains can be seen on pavements throughout the country

hikku Buddhist monk

o tree (*Ficus religiosa*; also known as the bodhi tree) Species of tree held sacred by Buddhism, since the Buddha is believed to have achieved enlightenment while meditating beneath one

odhigara Bo tree enclosure

odhisattva A Buddha-to-be who, rather than passing into nirvana, has chosen to stay in the world to improve the spiritual welfare of other, unenlightened beings

und Bank of a reservoir or tank

urghers Sri Lankans of European (usually Dutch) descent

etiya/chaitya Alternative Sinhalese word for a stupa

hattravali Spire-like pinnacle at the top of a stupa

hena Slash-and-burn farming

holas (or **Colas**) The dominant power in South India from the tenth to the twelfth centuries, with their capital at Thanjavur in Tamil Nadu; overran Sri Lanka in the late tenth century, sacking Anuradhapura in 993, after which they established a new capital at Polonnaruwa

coir Fibre made out of coconut husks

Culavamsa The "Lesser Chronicle" and continuation of the Mahavamsa

dagoba Stupa, a type of hemispherical monument found throughout the Buddhist world, traditionally enshrining religious relics and symbolizing both the person of the Buddha himself and the route to enlightenment

devale Shrine or temple to a deity, either freestanding or part of a Buddhist temple; nominally Buddhist, but often showing strong Hindu influence

dhyani mudra Meditation pose

digge Drummers' hall; often a pillared hall or pavilion in a temple where drummers and dancers rehearse

Durga The most terrifying of female Hindu deities, the demon-slaying Durga is considered an aspect of Shiva's consort, Parvati

duwa Small island

dwarfs Attendants of Kubera, the god of wealth, and thus symbols of prosperity

-ela Stream

-gaha Tree

-gala Rock

-gama Village

Ganesh Popular elephant-headed Hindu god, the son of Shiva, remover of obstacles and bringer of success and prosperity

ganga River

-ge Hall or house

gedige South Indian-style shrine, rectangular in shape and built entirely of stone or brick

-giri Rock

gopuram Tower of a Hindu temple, usually richly decorated with multicoloured statues

guardstone Carved figure placed at the entrance to a temple to protect against malign influences; often shows a figure of a *nagaraja*

Hanuman Monkey god who assisted Rama in recovering Sita from the demon Rawana, as related in the Ramayana

harmika The box-shaped section of a dagoba that sits on top of the dome (*anda*) and supports the *chattravali*

Hinayana Alternative and pejorative name for Theravada Buddhism

hypostyle Building constructed using many columns

image house (pilimage) Building in a Buddhist temple housing a statue of the Buddha

Jatakas Stories describing the 547 previous lives of the Buddha

JHU Jathika Hela Urumaya, or National Heritage Party, led by Buddhist monks; promotes a broadly right-wing, nationalist and anti-Tamil agenda

JVP Janatha Vimukthi Peramuna, or People's Liberation Front. Marxist party with an extreme nationalist, anti-Tamil agenda. Originally made up largely of rural poor and students, the JVP launched armed insurrections against the government in 1971 and 1987–89, both put down with considerable loss of life. Since the second insurrection, it has transformed itself into an important mainstream political party with a strong parliamentary presence

-kanda or -kande Hill/mountain

Kataragama One of the principal Sri Lankan deities, believed to reside in the town of Kataragama

kavadi The "peacock dance" performed by devotees of the god Kataragama

kolam Masked dance-drama

kovil Hindu temple

-kulam Tank, lake

Lakshmi Hindu goddess of wealth, Vishnu's consort

lingam Phallic symbol representing Shiva; often placed within a *yoni*, representing female sexuality

LTTE Liberation Tigers of Tamil Eelam, popularly known as the Tamil Tigers

maha Great

Mahavamsa The "Great Chronicle", the semi-mythical account of early Sri Lankan history as narrated by the island's Sinhalese Buddhist clergy

Mahayana Buddhism One of the two major schools of Buddhism, and the dominant form of the religion in China, Japan and Tibet, though it has had only superficial influence on Sri Lankan Buddhism

mahout Elephant handler

Maitreya The next Buddha. Mahayana Buddhists believe Maitreya will reintroduce Buddhism to the world when all knowledge of the religion has been lost

makara Imaginary composite animal derived from Indian bestiary

makara torana Arch formed from two linked *makaras*

mandapa Pillared hall or pavilion

mawatha (abbreviated to "Mw") Street

moonstone Carved semicircular stone placed in front of entrance to shrine. Also a type of gemstone mined in the island

Moors Sri Lankans of Arab or Indian-Arab descent

mudra Traditional pose in Buddhist iconography

naga stone Stone decorated with the image of a hooded cobra

nagaraja Serpent king

nikaya Order of Buddhist monks

nuwara Town

ola/ola leaf Parchment made from the talipot palm; used as a writing material in Sri Lanka up to the nineteenth century

oya or stream Small river

Pali The sacred language of Theravada Buddhism. This early Indo-European language, related to Sanskrit, is close to the language spoken by the Buddha himself. The scriptures of Theravada Buddhism were originally written in Pali and are still recited in this language in Buddhist ceremonies

Pallavas South Indian Tamil dynasty (fifth to ninth centuries), based in Kanchipuram, who, along with the Pandyans and Cholas, periodically interfered in Sri Lankan affairs

Pandyans Major Tamil dynasty (sixth to fourteenth centuries), based in Madurai, who vied for control of South India with the Cholas and Pallavas from the ninth to thirteenth centuries and periodically involved themselves in Sri Lankan affairs. Sacked Anuradhapura in the ninth century

parinirvana mudra Reclining pose showing the Buddha on the point of entering into nirvana. One of the most common *mudras* in Sri Lankan art

pasada/prasada Palace

Pattini Hindu goddess worshipped as paragon of marital fidelity

perahera Procession

Pillaiyar Ganesh (Tamil)

pirith Ceremonial chanting of Buddhist scriptures

-pitiya Field or park

poya Full-moon day

poyage Building in a monastery used for ceremonial gatherings of monks on poya days (hence the name); sometimes translated as "chapter house"

puja Hindu or Buddhist religious offering or ceremony

-pura/-puram Town

Rajarata Literally "The King's Land" – the traditional name for the area now more generally known as the Cultural Triangle

Rama The seventh incarnation of Vishnu and hero of the Ramayana

Rawana (or **Ravana**) Demon-king and arch villain of the Ramayana; responsible for kidnapping Rama's wife Sita and holding her captive in Sri Lanka

Ruhunu (or **Rohana**) Traditional name for southern Sri Lanka

samadhi (dhyani) mudra Pose showing Buddha in state of meditation, seated in the lotus or half-lotus position

Saman The god of Adam's Peak

samudra Large tank

Sangha The worldwide community of Buddhist monks

Shiva One of the two principal Hindu gods, worshipped in many forms, both creative and destructive

Shiva Nataraj Classic subject of Hindu sculpture, showing a four-armed dancing Shiva enclosed by a circle of fire

sinha Lion

skanda Son of Shiva (also known as Murugam and Subramanian). His identity in Sri Lanka has merged with that of Kataragama

SLA Sri Lankan Army

SLFP One of the two main Sri Lankan political parties, led successively by S.W.R.D. Bandaranaike, his wife and his daughter. Policies have tended to be the opposite of the pro-Western, free-market UNP, leaning instead towards a brand of populist nationalism (often with an anti-Tamil bias) featuring extensive state control of the economy

sri pada Holy footprint

thampita A small shrine raised on pillars

tank Large man-made lake constructed for irrigation – almost always much larger than the English word suggests

-tara/-tota Port

Theravada Buddhism The older of the two main schools of Buddhism, and the dominant form of the religion in Sri Lanka

tuktuk Motorized rickshaw; also known as a three-wheeler, trishaw or taxi

UNP United National Party; one of Sri Lanka's two main political parties and the first ruling party of independent Sri Lanka. Policies have traditionally tended to be pro-Western and free-market

Upulvan Sri Lankan name for Vishnu

vahalkadas Shrines placed at the four cardinal points of a stupa

vatadage Characteristic Sri Lankan style of building formed by adding a roof and ambulatory to a dagoba

Veddha Sri Lanka's original inhabitants (see page 239)

ves Style of traditional costume and dancing employed by Kandyan dancers

Vibhishana The youngest brother of Rawana. Despite his demonic nature, Vibhishana is revered in Sri Lanka, since he pleaded the captive Sita's cause with Rawana and later fought with Rama against his brother, suggesting the potential for right action in even the lowest creature

vidiya Street (in Kandy)

vidyalaya School

vihara (sometimes spelt *vehera* or *wehera*) Buddhist temple or monastery

vimana Palace of a god or celestial being

Vishnu One of the two principal Hindu gods, considered a protector of Buddhism in Sri Lanka

VOC Vereenigde Oost-Indische Compagnie (Dutch East India Company)

walauuwa or **walauuwe** Traditional country manor of local village headman

-watte Garden

-wewa (pronounced "-vava") Man-made reservoir (tank)

-wila Pond

Small print and index

A ROUGH GUIDE TO ROUGH GUIDES

Published in 1982, the first Rough Guide – to Greece – was a student scheme that became a publishing phenomenon. Mark Ellingham, a recent graduate in English from Bristol University, had been travelling in Greece the previous summer and couldn't find the right guidebook. With a small group of friends he wrote his own guide, combining a contemporary, journalistic style with a thoroughly practical approach to travellers' needs.

The immediate success of the book spawned a series that rapidly covered dozens of destinations. And, in addition to impecunious backpackers, Rough Guides soon acquired a much broader readership that relished the guides' wit and inquisitiveness as much as their enthusiastic, critical approach and value-for-money ethos. These days, Rough Guides include recommendations from budget to luxury and cover more than 120 destinations around the globe, from Amsterdam to Zanzibar, all regularly updated by our team of roaming writers.

Browse all our latest guides, read inspirational features and book your trip at **roughguides.com**.

Rough Guide credits

Editor: Georgia Stephens
Cartography: Carte; Katie Bennett
Managing editor: Rachel Lawrence
Picture editor: Aude Vauconsant

Cover photo research: Aude Vauconsant
Senior DTP coordinator: Dan May
Head of DTP and Pre-Press: Rebeka Davies

Publishing information

Sixth edition 2018
Distribution
UK, Ireland and Europe
Apa Publications (UK) Ltd; sales@roughguides.com
United States and Canada
Ingram Publisher Services; ips@ingramcontent.com
Australia and New Zealand
Woodslane; info@woodslane.com.au
Southeast Asia
Apa Publications (SN) Pte; sales@roughguides.com
Worldwide
Apa Publications (UK) Ltd; sales@roughguides.com
Special Sales, Content Licensing and CoPublishing
Rough Guides can be purchased in bulk quantities
at discounted prices. We can create special editions,
personalised jackets and corporate imprints tailored to
our needs. sales@roughguides.com.
roughguides.com

Printed in China by CTPS
All rights reserved
© Gavin Thomas, 2018
Maps © 2018 Apa Digital (CH) AG
License edition © Apa Publications Ltd UK All rights
reserved. No part of this publication may be reproduced,
stored in or introduced into a retrieval system, or
transmitted in any form, or by any means (electronic,
mechanical, photocopying, recording or otherwise) without
the prior written permission of the copyright owner.
A catalogue record for this book is available from the
British Library
The publishers and authors have done their best to ensure
the accuracy and currency of all the information in **The
Rough Guide to Sri Lanka**, however, they can accept
no responsibility for any loss, injury, or inconvenience
sustained by any traveller as a result of information or
advice contained in the guide.

Help us update

We've gone to a lot of effort to ensure that the edition of
the Rough Guide to Sri Lanka is accurate and up-to-date.
However, things change – places get "discovered", opening
hours are notoriously fickle, restaurants and rooms raise
prices or lower standards. If you feel we've got it wrong
or left something out, we'd like to know, and if you can
remember the address, the price, the hours, the phone
number, so much the better.

Please send your comments with the subject
line "**Rough Guide Sri Lanka Update**" to mail@
uk.roughguides.com. We'll credit all contributions and
send a copy of the next edition (or any other Rough Guide
if you prefer) for the very best emails.

ABOUT THE AUTHORS

Gavin Thomas has spent much of his life trying to be somewhere else. He first visited Sri
Lanka in 2001 and has been returning regularly ever since, as well as visiting some fifty other
countries around the world, from Argentina to New Zealand, en route. He now works as a full-
time travel writer, his enthusiasm for abroad undimmed despite various life-threatening on-
the-road encounters which have so far included being chased by wild elephants, being shot
by Mexican bandits and being forced to eat dangerously large quantities of airline catering.
He is also the author of the Rough Guides to Dubai and Oman, and co-author of the Rough
Guides to Myanmar, Cambodia, and Rajasthan, Delhi & Agra.

Sally McLaren first visited Sri Lanka in 2008 and in recent years was based in Colombo
working on documentary films, studying Sinhala and learning how to cook spicy curries. A big
fan of Sri Lankan art, design and architecture, she enjoys rambling around the island on local
transport and exploring little-known places with fascinating histories. Sally is currently a Kyoto-
based writer and researcher, and also a co-author of the Rough Guide to Japan.

Reader's update

Thanks to all the readers who have taken the time to write in with comments and suggestions (and apologies if we've inadvertently omitted or misspelt anyone's name):

Pippa Behr, Emma Boyle, Clive Collins, Christopher Craig, Meera Dattani, Jacob Devriese, Jane Ellis, Nathan Fieldsend, John Garratt, Teresa & Martin González, Gavin Goy, Kay & Fraser Hunter, Kaye Kent, Marc & Charlotte Lybol, Monica Mackaness, Tom Neill, Kennedy Newton, Andy Pearce, Peter Phillips, John Scott, Jax Tan, Frances Thompson, Clint Westwood, Lilamani Woolrych.

Acknowledgements

Gavin Thomas In Sri Lanka, I owe a massive debt of thanks as ever to Nimal de Silva (Ⓦ dsltours.com), who once again drove me all over the island with unfailing skill, patience, perseverance and good humour – the best companion any travel writer could hope for, and without whom this book would be infinitely poorer. Big thanks also to Mark Thamel, Tim Beltman, Henry Fitch, Nadeem Rajabdeen, Iran Karannagoda, Volker Bethke, Ashan Senaratne, Faiesz & Sue Samad, Sumane & Kanthi Bandara, Nilu Crowe, Nisa Pallegedara, Pasanna Welangoda, and Mohan in Jaffna. A big bouquet too for Emma Boyle for introductions in Colombo and an endless supply of information, ideas and inspiration.

At Rough Guides, a big shout out to my exemplary editor Georgia Stephens for keeping an entire cupboard's worth of plates spinning effortlessly under the most trying circumstances; to Sally McLaren for gallantly stepping into the breach a such short notice; and to Ed Aves for all his work on previous editions of the book and long-term moral support – things won't be the same without you. Also to Gehan de Silva Wijeyeratne, and to Mark Ellingham, without whom none of this would exist. And finally a huge hug for my long-suffering family, who once again kept the home fires burning during my absence: Allison, with whom I first discovered Sri Lanka; and Laura and Jamie, who I hope will one day discover it for themselves. This book is for you, with love.

Sally McLaren I firstly want to thank my many wonderful friends in Colombo, especially Chandani, Nishelli, Jennifer & Madhura, and Nalin, for their kindness and support. Much gratitude also to Emma Boyle for her generous insights and updates. I am forever grateful to the many kind and big-hearted Sri Lankans who went out of their way to help me, in particular, Upali in Polonnaruwa, Ajith and his crew in Tissa, Ruwan in Arugam Bay, Sandrine in Batti, Tharuka in Nilaveli, Ranjan in Anuradhapura and Rasi in Galle. Thanks to fellow Sri Lanka enthusiast Gavin and editor Georgia at Rough Guides. Many thanks to Yakko for accompanying me to the outer edges of the Cultural Triangle, and to Albie for continual love, support and good humour.

Photo credits

ndex

Map symbols

The symbols below are used on maps throughout the book

Expressway	@	Internet access	☾	Sand dunes		Dagoba/Buddhist temple
Pedestrianized road	(i)	Tourist office		Cave		Hindu temple
Steps	⊠	Post office		National park		Church (regional maps)
Unpaved road	⊞	Hospital		Spring/spa		Church (town maps)
Railway	⊙	Statue		Marsh		Market
Path		Gardens		Waterfall		Stadium
Wall		Golf course		Tree		Building
Ferry route		Fortress		Zoo		Park/jungle/forest
International airport	⊠	Gate/entrance		Bird sanctuary		Beach
Domestic airport	▲	Peak		Viewpoint		Christian cemetery
Transport stop		Rock		Lighthouse		Muslim cemetery
P Parking		Reef		Ruins		

Listings key

■	Accommodation
●	Eating
▤	Drinking/nightlife
●	Shopping

EXPLORE THE WILD SIDE OF SRI LANKA

Travel near and far to where the wild things are. From the best eco luxury resort in the island that's home to exotic guests like the endangered grey slender loris to witnessing over 300 wild elephants converging for the famous gathering. From following the trail of leopards roaming wild and free to getting up close and personal to the wonders of the ocean. Jetwing welcomes you to the home of the wild.

Jetwing Yala • Jetwing Lake • Jetwing Vil Uyana • Jetwing Lighthouse

For reservations, call +94 114709400 or
email: reservations@jetwinghotels.com #jetwinghotels

JETWING, THE HOME OF SRI LANKAN HOSPITALITY.   www.jetwinghotels.com